THE INTERSECTIONS COLLECTION

PEARSON CUSTOM SOCIOLOGY

Formerly published as Intersections, Crossroads & Inequalities

EDITORS

KATHLEEN A. TIEMANN
University of North Dakota
Introduction to Sociology, Social Problems & Issues, Inequalities & Div

RALPH B. MCNEAL, JR.
University of Connecticut
Introduction to Sociology

BETSY LUCAL
Indiana University South Bend
Inequalities & Diversity

MORTEN G. ENDER
United States Military Academy, West Point
Inequalities & Diversity

COMPILED BY:
LA 102
Introduction to Sociology
Monroe College

Pearson Learning Solutions

New York Boston San Francisco
London Toronto Sydney Tokyo Singapore Madrid
Mexico City Munich Paris Cape Town Hong Kong Montreal

Senior Vice President, Editorial and Marketing: Patrick F. Boles
Associate Editor: Ana Díaz-Caneja
Development Editor: Abbey Lee Briggs
Marketing Manager: Jack Cooney
Operations Manager: Eric M. Kenney
Production Manager: Jennifer Berry
Rights Manager: Jillian Santos
Art Director: Renée Sartell
Cover Designer: Renée Sartell

Cover Art: "Figures," courtesy of Eugenie Lewalski Berg; "Abstract Crowd," courtesy of Diana Ong/Superstock; "R&B Figures," courtesy of Diana Ong/Superstock; "Bramante's Staircase," courtesy of Veer/Photodisc Photography; "Hand Prints," courtesy of Veer/Photodisc Photography; "People Running-Falling," courtesy of Veer/Campbell Laird; "Sunbathers on Beach," courtesy of Veer/Scott Barrow.

Printed in the United States of America.

Please visit our website at *www.pearsoncustom.com.*

Attention bookstores: For permission to return any unsold stock, contact us at *pe-uscustomreturns@pearson.com*.

Pearson Learning Solutions, 501 Boylston Street, Suite 900, Boston, MA 02116
A Pearson Education Company
www.pearsoned.com

ISBN 10: 0-558-73044-2
ISBN 13: 978-0-558-73044-4

The Intersections Collection includes chapters from the following Pearson textbooks:

Marriages and Families: Changes, Choices and Constraints, Sixth Edition
Nijole V. Benokraitis

Think Sociology, First Edition
John Carl

Social Problems, Tenth Edition
James William Coleman and Harold R. Kerbo

Social Problems, Eleventh Edition
D. Stanley Eizen, Maxine Baca Zinn, and Kely Eitzen Smith

Sociology: A Down-to-Earth Approach, Ninth Edition
James M. Henslin

Essentials of Sociology: A Down-to-Earth Approach, Eighth Edition
James M. Henslin

Social Problems in a Diverse Society, Fifth Edition
Diana Kendall

Sociology Now, First Edition
Michael Kimmel and Amy Aronson

Sociology Now, The Essentials, First Edition
Michael S. Kimmel and Amy Aronson

Sociology, Twelfth Edition
John J. Macionis

Society: The Basics, Tenth Edition
John J. Macionis

Strangers to These Shores: Race and Ethnic Relations in the United States, Ninth Edition
Vincent N. Parrillo

Women, Men, and Society, Fifth Edition
Claire M. Renzetti and Daniel J. Curran

Racial and Ethnic Groups, Eleventh Edition
Richard T. Schaefer

Racial and Ethnic Groups, Twelfth Edition
Richard T. Schaefer

Marriages and Families: Diversity and Change, Sixth Edition
Mary Ann Schwartz and BarBara Maleine Scott

Global Problems: The Search for Equity, Peace, and Sustainability, Second Edition
Scott R. Sernau

Marriages, Families, and Intimate Relationships: A Practical Introduction, Second Edition
Brian K. Williams, Stacey C. Sawyer and Carl M. Wahlstrom

The Intersections Collection offers suggested readings to use with the following textbooks:

Think Sociology, First Edition
John Carl
TOC recommended by John Carl

Sociology, A Brief Introduction, Seventh Edition
Alex Thio
TOC recommended by Alex Thio

Strangers to These Shores, Ninth Edition
Vincent N. Parrillo
TOC recommended by Vincent N. Parrillo

Women, Men, and Society, Fifth Edition
Claire M. Renzetti and Daniel J. Curran
TOC recommended by Claire M. Renzetti

Marriages, Families, and Intimate Relationships: A Practical Introduction, Second Edition
Brian K. Williams, Stacey C. Sawyer, and Carl M. Wahlstrom
TOC recommended by Carl M. Wahlstrom

Sociology Now, First Edition
Michael S. Kimmel and Amy Aronson
TOC recommended by Michael S. Kimmel

THE INTERSECTIONS COLLECTION

Dear Student,

On behalf of Pearson Custom Library, thank you for purchasing this book for your sociology course. You might not realize this, but your instructor made a thoughtful decision when building, reviewing, and ultimately adopting this book, choosing to bypass standard—and often more costly—textbooks and using our Pearson Custom Library program to pull together material that is customized to your course syllabus and learning objectives.

This innovative program enables instructors to create what we believe is the best possible instructional material delivered at superior value to you and your classmates.

Your instructor takes your education seriously and so do we, which is why we are interested in your feedback on this custom book. How well did it support you during the semester? Please visit us on **Facebook**, keyword search "Intersections Collection," and click on **Become a Fan** to post a comment on our wall.

Sincerely,

Pearson Custom Library

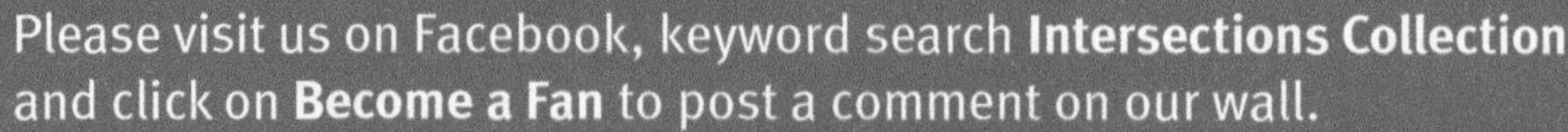

Contents

The Sociological Perspective

Images, Inc. – Blend Images/Jon Feingers

The sociological perspective shows us that the society around us influences how we act and even what we think and how we feel. Learning to see the world sociologically is useful in many ways—and it is also fun!

Corbis RF/Smart Creatives

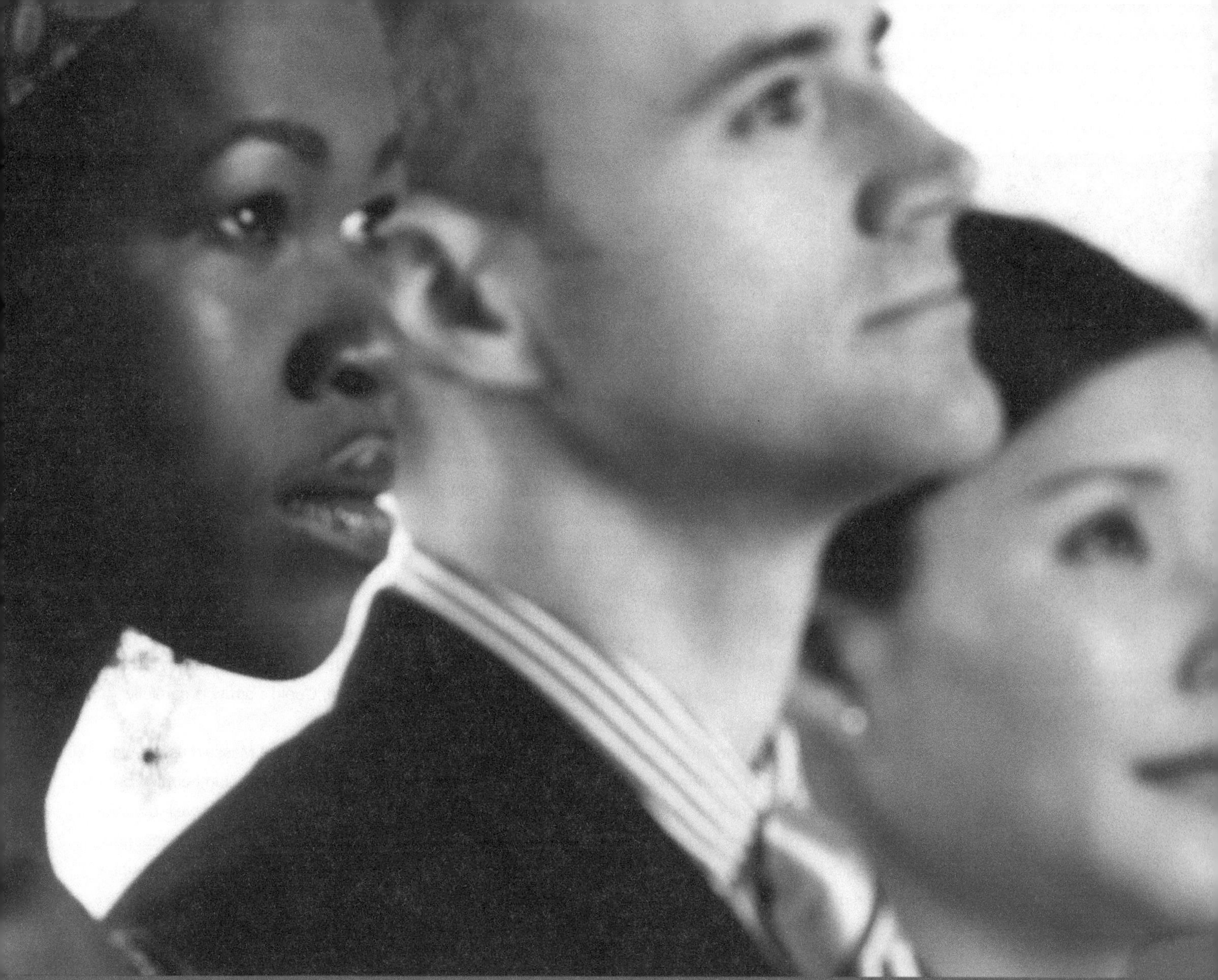

The Sociological Perspective

Corbis RF/Simon Jarratt

Corbis – NY/© Robert Wallis/Corbis, All Rights Reserved

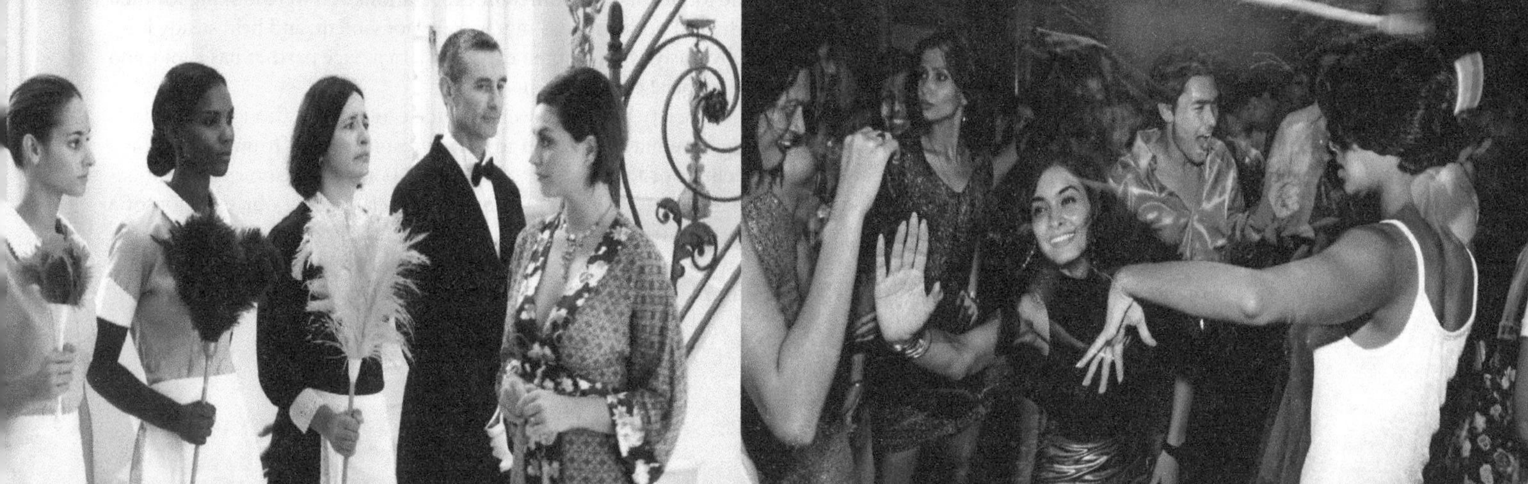

CHAPTER OVERVIEW

This chapter introduces the discipline of sociology. The most important skill to gain from this course is the ability to use what we call the *sociological perspective*. This chapter also introduces *sociological theory*, which helps us build understanding from what we see using the sociological perspective.

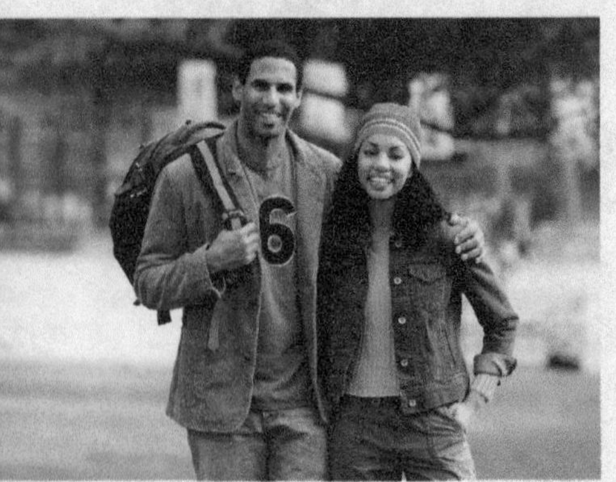

Getty Images – Entertainment/Mark Scott

From the moment he first saw Gina step off the subway train, Marco knew she was "the one." As the two walked up the stairs to the street and entered the building where they were both taking classes, Marco tried to get Gina to stop and talk. At first, she ignored him. But after class, they met again, and she agreed to join him for coffee. That was three months ago. Today, they are engaged to be married.

If you were to ask people in the United States, "Why do couples like Gina and Marco marry?" it is a safe bet that almost everyone would reply, "People marry because they fall in love." Most of us find it hard to imagine a happy marriage without love; for the same reason, when people fall in love, we expect them to think about getting married.

But is the decision about whom to marry really just a matter of personal feelings? There is plenty of evidence to show that if love is the key to marriage, Cupid's arrow is carefully aimed by the society around us.

Society has many "rules" about whom we should and should not marry. In all states but Massachusetts, Vermont, Maine, New Hampshire, Connecticut, and Iowa the law rules out half the population, banning people from marrying someone of the same sex, even if the couple is deeply in love. But there are other rules as well. Sociologists have found that people, especially when they are young, are very likely to marry someone close in age, and people of all ages typically marry others in the same racial category, of similar social class background, of much the same level of education, and with a similar degree of physical attractiveness (Schwartz & Mare, 2005; Schoen & Cheng, 2006; Feng Hou & Myles, 2008). People end up making choices about whom to marry, but society narrows the field long before they do.

When it comes to love, the decisions people make do not simply result from the process philosophers call "free will." Sociology teaches us that the social world guides all our life choices in much the same way that the seasons influence our choice of clothing.

The Sociological Perspective

Sociology is *the systematic study of human society*. At the heart of sociology is a special point of view called the *sociological perspective.*

Seeing the General in the Particular

Years ago, Peter Berger (1963) described the **sociological perspective** as *seeing the general in the particular*. By this he meant that sociologists look for general patterns in the behavior of particular people. Although every individual is unique, a society shapes the lives of people in various categories (such as children and adults, women and men, the rich and the poor) very differently. We begin to see the world sociologically by realizing how the general categories into which we fall shape our particular life experiences.

For example, does social class position affect what women look for in a spouse? In a classic study of women's hopes for their marriages, Lillian Rubin (1976) found that higher-income women typically expected the men they married to be sensitive to others, to talk readily, and to share feelings and experiences. Lower-income women, she found, had very different expectations and were looking for men who did not drink too much, were not violent, and held steady jobs. Obviously, what women expect in a marriage partner has a lot to do with social class position.

Society has the power to guide our actions, thoughts, and feelings. We may think that marriage results simply from the personal feelings of love. Yet the sociological perspective shows us that factors such as age, sex, race, and social class guide our selection of a partner. It might be more accurate to think of love as a feeling we have for others who match up with what society teaches us to want in a mate.

sociology the systematic study of human society

sociological perspective the special point of view of sociology that sees general patterns of society in the lives of particular people

SEEING SOCIOLOGY in Everyday Life

What effect did your social class background have on your decision to go to college? How do you think your background shapes the kind of job you expect to have after you graduate?

Corbis – NY/Caroline Penn

Minh-Thu Pham

Paul W. Liebhardt

Paul W. Liebhardt

Robert Harding World Imagery/Alan Evrard

Paul W. Liebhardt

We can easily see the power of society over the individual by imagining how different our lives would be had we been born in place of any of these children from, respectively, Bolivia, Ethiopia, Thailand, Mali, South Korea, and India.

Seeing the Strange in the Familiar

At first, using the sociological perspective may seem like *seeing the strange in the familiar.* Consider how you might react if someone were to say to you, "You fit all the right categories, which means you would make a wonderful spouse!" We are used to thinking that people fall in love and decide to marry based on personal feelings. But the sociological perspective reveals the initially strange idea that society shapes what we think and do.

Because we live in an individualistic society, learning to see how society affects us may take a bit of practice. If someone asked you why you "chose" to enroll at your particular college, you might offer one of the following reasons:

> "I wanted to stay close to home."
>
> "I got a basketball scholarship."
>
> "With a journalism degree from this university, I can get a good job."
>
> "My girlfriend goes to school here."
>
> "I didn't get into the school I *really* wanted to attend."

Any of these responses may well be true. But do they tell the whole story?

Thinking sociologically about going to college, it's important to realize that only about 5 out of every 100 people in the world earn a college degree, with the enrollment rate much higher in high-income nations than in poor countries (Organization for Economic Cooperation and Development, 2008; World Bank, 2008). Even in the United States a century ago, going to college was not an option for most people. Today, going to college is within the reach of far more people. But a look around the classroom shows that social forces still have much to do with who goes to college. For instance, most U.S. college students are young, generally between eighteen and about thirty. Why? Because in our society, attending college is linked to this period of life. But more than age is involved, because fewer than half of all young men and women actually end up on campus.

Another factor is cost. Because higher education is so expensive, college students tend to come from families with above-average incomes. If you are lucky enough to belong to a family earning more than $75,000 a year, you are almost three times as likely to go to college as someone whose family earns less than $20,000. Is it reasonable, in light of these facts, to say that attending college is simply a matter of personal choice?

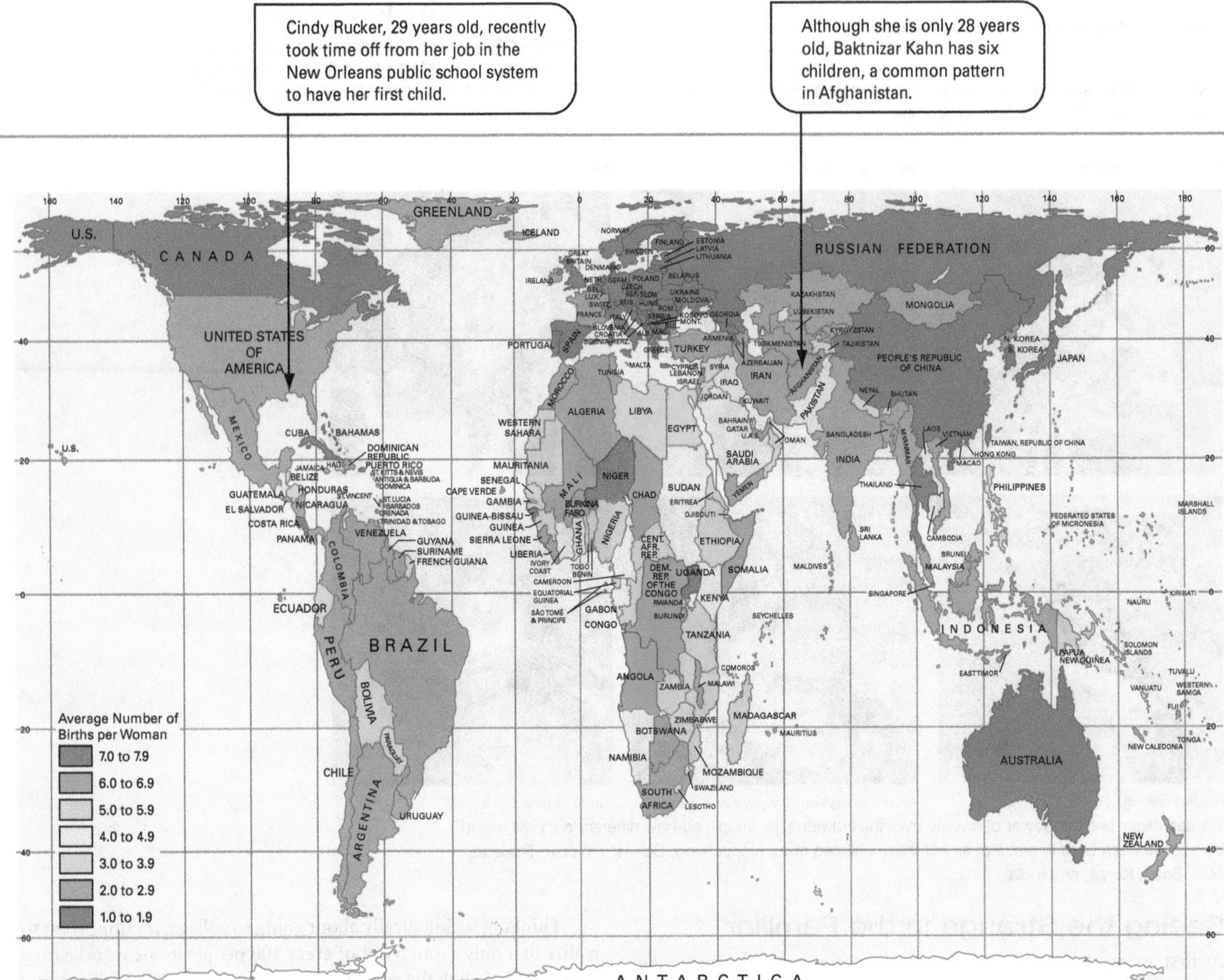

Window on the World

GLOBAL MAP 1 **Women's Childbearing in Global Perspective**

Is childbearing simply a matter of personal choice? A look around the world shows that it is not. In general, women living in poor countries have many more children than women in rich nations. Can you point to some of the reasons for this global disparity? In simple terms, such differences mean that if you had been born into another society (whether you are female or male), your life might be quite different from what it is now.

Sources: Data from Martin et al. (2007), Population Reference Bureau (2007), United Nations Development Programme (2007), and Central Intelligence Agency (2008). Map projection from *Peters Atlas of the World* (1990).

Seeing Society in Our Everyday Lives

To see how society shapes personal choices, consider the number of children women have. As shown in Global Map 1, the average woman in the United States has about two children during her lifetime. In India, however, the average is about three; in Guatemala, about four; in Ethiopia, about five; in Yemen, about six; and in Niger, the average woman has seven children (United Nations Development Programme, 2007).

What accounts for these striking differences? Because poor countries provide women with less schooling and fewer economic opportunities, women's lives are centered in the home, and they are less

SEEING SOCIOLOGY in Everyday Life

Single people are at higher risk of suicide than married people. Can you explain why?

likely to use contraception. Clearly, society has much to do with the decisions women and men make about childbearing.

Another illustration of the power of society to shape even our most private choices comes from the study of suicide. What could be a more personal choice than the decision to end your own life? But Emile Durkheim (1858–1917), one of sociology's pioneers, showed that even here, social forces are at work.

Examining official records in France, his own country, Durkheim found that some categories of people were more likely than others to take their own lives. Men, Protestants, wealthy people, and the unmarried had much higher suicide rates than women, Catholics and Jews, the poor, and married people. Durkheim explained the differences in terms of *social integration:* Categories of people with strong social ties had low suicide rates, and more individualistic categories of people had high suicide rates.

In Durkheim's time, men had much more freedom than women. But despite its advantages, freedom weakens social ties and thus increases the risk of suicide. Likewise, more individualistic Protestants were more likely to commit suicide than more tradition-bound Catholics and Jews, whose rituals encourage stronger social ties. The wealthy have much more freedom than the poor, but once again, at the cost of a higher suicide rate.

A century later, Durkheim's analysis still holds true. Figure 1 shows suicide rates for various categories of people in the United States. Keep in mind that suicide is very rare—a rate of 10 suicides for every 100,000 people is about the same as 6 inches in a mile. Even so, we can see some interesting patterns. In 2005, there were 12.3 recorded suicides for every 100,000 white people, more than twice the rate for African Americans (5.1). For both races, suicide was more common among men than among women. White men (19.7) were more than four times as likely as white women (5.0) to take their own lives. Among African Americans, the rate for men (8.7) was about five times higher than for women (1.8) (Kung et al., 2008). Applying Durkheim's logic, the higher suicide rate among white people and men reflects their greater wealth and freedom, just as the lower rate among women and African Americans reflects their limited social choices. As Durkheim did a century ago, we can see general patterns in the personal actions of particular individuals.

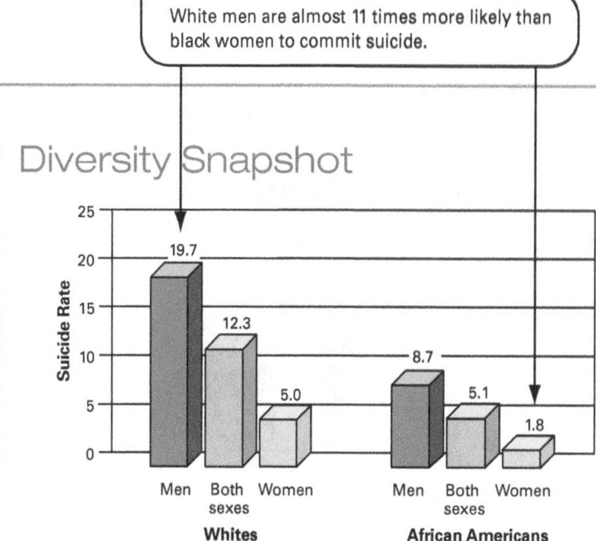

FIGURE 1 Rate of Death by Suicide, by Race and Sex, for the United States

Suicide rates are higher for white people than for black people and higher for men than for women. Rates indicate the number of deaths by suicide for every 100,000 people in each category for 2005.

Source: Kung et al. (2008).

Seeing Sociologically: Marginality and Crisis

Anyone can learn to see the world using the sociological perspective. But two situations help people see clearly how society shapes individual lives: living on the margins of society and living through a social crisis.

From time to time, everyone feels like an outsider. For some categories of people, however, being an outsider—not part of the dominant group—is an everyday experience. The greater people's social marginality, the better they are able to use the sociological perspective.

For example, no African American grows up in the United States without understanding the importance of race in shaping people's lives. Rap lyrics by groups such as Three 6 Mafia, who say that they "Done seen people killed, done seen people deal, done seen people live in poverty with no meals," show that some people of color—especially African Americans living in the inner city—feel like their hopes and dreams are crushed by society. But white people, as the dominant majority, think less often about race and the privileges it provides, believing that race affects only people of color and not themselves as well. People at the margins of social life, including women, gay people, people with disabilities, and the very old, are aware of social patterns that others rarely think about. To become better at using the sociological perspective, we must step back from our familiar routines and look at our lives with a new curiosity.

Periods of change or crisis make everyone feel a little off balance, encouraging us to use the sociological perspective. The sociologist C. Wright Mills (1959) illustrated this idea using the Great Depression of the 1930s. As the unemployment rate soared to 25 percent, people who were out of work could not help but see general social forces at work in their particular lives. Rather than saying,

global perspective the study of the larger world and our society's place in it

high-income countries the nations with the highest overall standards of living

middle-income countries nations with a standard of living about average for the world as a whole

low-income countries nations with a low standard of living in which most people are poor

People with the greatest privileges tend to see individuals as responsible for their own lives. Those at the margins of society, by contrast, are quick to see how race, class, and gender can create disadvantages. The rap artist Kanye West has given voice to the frustration felt by many African Americans living in this country's inner cities.

"Something must be wrong with me; I can't find a job," they took a sociological approach and realized, "The economy has collapsed; there are no jobs to be found!" Mills believed that using what he called the "sociological imagination" in this way helps people understand not only their society but also their own lives, because the two are closely related. The Seeing Sociology in Everyday Life box takes a closer look.

Just as social change encourages sociological thinking, sociological thinking can bring about social change. The more we learn about how "the system" operates, the more we may want to change it in some way. Becoming aware of the power of gender, for example, has caused many women and men to try to reduce gender inequality in our society.

The Importance of a Global Perspective

December 10, Fez, Morocco. This medieval city—a web of narrow streets and alleyways—is alive with the laughter of playing children, the silence of veiled women, and the steady gaze of men leading donkeys loaded with goods. Fez seems to have changed little over the centuries. Here, in northwestern Africa, we are just a few hundred miles from the more familiar rhythms of Europe. Yet this place seems a thousand years away. Never have we had such an adventure! Never have we thought so much about home!

As new information technology draws even the farthest reaches of the planet closer together, many academic disciplines are taking a **global perspective,** *the study of the larger world and our society's place in it.* What is the importance of a global perspective for sociology?

First, global awareness is a logical extension of the sociological perspective. Sociology shows us that our place in society shapes our life experiences. It stands to reason, then, that the position of our society in the larger world system affects everyone in the United States. The Thinking Globally box later in this chapter describes a "global village" to show the social shape of the world and the place of the United States within it.

The world's 194 nations can be divided into three broad categories according to their level of economic development. **High-income countries** are the *nations with the highest overall standards of living.* The sixty-six countries in this category include the United States and Canada, Argentina, the nations of Western Europe, South Africa, Israel, Saudi Arabia, Japan, and Australia. Taken together, these nations produce most of the world's goods and services, and the people who live there own most of the planet's wealth. Economically speaking, people in these countries are very well off, not because they are smarter or work harder than anyone else but because they were lucky enough to be born in a rich region of the world.

A second category is **middle-income countries,** *nations with a standard of living about average for the world as a whole.* People in any of these seventy-two nations—many of the countries of Eastern Europe, some of Africa, and almost all of Latin America and Asia—are as likely to live in rural villages as in cities and to walk or ride tractors, scooters, bicycles, or animals as to drive automobiles. On average, they receive eight to ten years of schooling. Most middle-income countries also have considerable social inequality within their own borders, so that some people are extremely rich (members of the business elite in nations across North Africa, for example), but many more lack safe housing and adequate nutrition (people living in the shanty settlements that surround Lima, Peru, or Mumbai, India).

MAKING THE GRADE

Mills used the term "sociological imagination" to mean the same thing as the term "sociological perspective" used by Peter Berger and others.

MAKING THE GRADE

The box below suggests that C. Wright Mills hoped the sociological imagination would spark social change toward a more equal society.

SEEING SOCIOLOGY IN EVERYDAY LIFE

The Sociological Imagination: Turning Personal Problems into Public Issues

As Mike opened the envelope, he felt the tightness in his chest. The letter he dreaded was in his hands—his job was finished at the end of the day. After eleven years! Years in which he had worked hard, sure that he would move up in the company. All those hopes and dreams were now suddenly gone. Mike felt like a failure. Anger at himself—for not having worked even harder, for having wasted eleven years of his life in what had turned out to be a dead-end job—grew inside him.

But as he returned to his work station to pack his things, Mike soon realized that he was not alone. Almost all his colleagues in the tech support group had received the same letter. Their jobs were moving to India, where the company was able to provide telephone tech support for less than half the cost of keeping workers in California.

By the end of the weekend, Mike was sitting in the living room with a dozen other ex-employees. Comparing notes and sharing ideas, they now realized that they were simply a few of the victims of a massive outsourcing of jobs that is part of what analysts call the "globalization of the economy."

In good times and bad, the power of the sociological perspective lies in making sense of our individual lives. We see that many of our particular problems (and our successes, as well) are not unique to us, but are the result of larger social trends. Half a century ago, sociologist C. Wright Mills pointed to the power of what he called the sociological imagination to help us understand everyday events. As he saw it, society—not people's personal failings—is the main cause of poverty and other social problems. By turning *personal problems* into *public issues*, the sociological imagination also is the key to bringing people together to create needed change.

In this excerpt, Mills (1959:3–5) explains the need for a sociological imagination:*

> When society becomes industrialized, a peasant becomes a worker; a feudal lord is liquidated or becomes a businessman. When classes rise or fall, a man is employed or unemployed; when the rate of investment goes up or down, a man takes new heart or goes broke. When wars happen, an insurance salesman becomes a rocket launcher; a store clerk, a radar man; a wife lives alone; a child grows up without a father. Neither the life of an individual nor the history of a society can be understood without understanding both.
>
> Yet men do not usually define the troubles they endure in terms of historical change. . . . The well-being they enjoy, they do not usually impute to the big ups and downs of the society in which they live. Seldom aware of the intricate connection between the patterns of their own lives and the course of world history, ordinary men do not usually know what this connection means for the kind of men they are becoming and for the kinds of history-making in which they might take part. They do not possess the quality of mind essential to grasp the interplay of men and society, of biography and history, of self and world. . . .
>
> What they need . . . is a quality of mind that will help them [see] what is going on in the world and . . . what may be happening within themselves. It is this quality . . . [that] may be called the sociological imagination.

*In this excerpt, Mills uses "man" and male pronouns to apply to all people. As far as gender was concerned, even this outspoken critic of society reflected the conventional writing practices of his time.

WHAT DO YOU THINK?

1. As Mills sees it, how are personal troubles different from public issues? Explain this difference in terms of what happened to Mike in the story above.
2. Living in the United States, why do we often blame ourselves for the personal problems we face?
3. By using the sociological imagination, how do we gain the power to change the world?

The remaining fifty-six nations of the world are **low-income countries,** *nations with a low standard of living in which most people are poor.* Most of the poorest countries in the world are in Africa, and a few are in Asia. Here again, a few people are very rich, but the majority struggle to get by with poor housing, unsafe water, too little food, and perhaps most serious of all, little chance to improve their lives.

It is crucial to comparisons between the United States and other nations for four reasons:

1. **Where we live shapes the lives we lead.** As we saw in Global Map 1, women living in rich and poor countries have very different lives, as suggested by the number of children they have. To understand ourselves and appreciate how others live, we must understand something about how countries differ.
2. **Societies throughout the world are increasingly interconnected.** Historically, people in the United States took only passing note of the countries beyond our own borders. In recent decades, however, the United States and the rest of the world have become linked as never before. Electronic technology now transmits sounds, pictures, and written documents around the globe in seconds.

MAKING THE GRADE

Think of the global perspective as an extension of the sociological perspective. Here at home, where we are "placed" within society affects how we act, think, and feel. Expanding our vision shows that our nation's place in the world affects the lives of all who live in this country.

SEEING SOCIOLOGY in Everyday Life

How would your life be different if you had been born into a family in a poor farming village in Asia? What might you be doing right now instead of reading this textbook?

THINKING GLOBALLY

The Global Village: A Social Snapshot of Our World

Earth is currently home to 6.7 billion people who live in the cities and villages of 194 nations. To grasp the social shape of the world on a smaller scale, imagine shrinking the planet's population to a "global village" of just 1,000 people. In this village, more than half (604) of the inhabitants would be Asian, including 198 citizens of the People's Republic of China. Next, in terms of numbers, we would find 145 Africans, 109 Europeans, 86 people from Latin America and the Caribbean, 5 people from Australia and the South Pacific, and just 50 North Americans, including 45 people from the United States.

A close look at this settlement would reveal some startling facts: The village is a rich place, with a spectacular range of goods and services for sale. Yet most of the villagers can only dream about such treasures, because they are so poor: 75 percent of the village's total income is earned by just 200 people.

For most, the greatest problem is getting enough food. Every year, village workers produce more than enough to feed everyone; even so, about 150 people in the village do not get enough to eat, and many go to sleep hungry every night. These 150 residents (who together have less money than the single richest person in the village) lack both clean drinking water and safe shelter. Weak and often unable to work, they are at risk of contracting deadly diseases and dying.

The village has many schools, including a fine university. About 50 inhabitants have completed a college degree, but about one-fifth of the village's adults are not even able to read or write.

We in the United States, on average, would be among the village's richest people. Although we may like to think that our comfortable lives are the result of our individual talent and hard work, the sociological perspective reminds us that our achievements also result from our nation's privileged position in the worldwide social system.

WHAT DO YOU THINK?

1. Do any of the statistics presented in this box surprise you? Which ones? Why?
2. How do you think the lives of poor people in a lower-income country differ from those typical of people in the United States?
3. Is your "choice" to attend college affected by the country in which you live? How?

Sources: Calculations by the author based on international data from the United Nations Development Programme (2007) and the U.S. Census Bureau (2008).

One effect of new technology is that people the world over now share many tastes in food, clothing, and music. Rich countries such as the United States influence other nations, whose people are ever more likely to gobble up our Big Macs and Whoppers, dance to the latest hip-hop music, and speak English.

But the larger world also has an impact on us. We all know the contributions of famous immigrants such as Arnold Schwarzenegger (who came to the United States from Austria) and Gloria Estefan (who came from Cuba). About 1.5 million immigrants enter the United States each year, bringing their skills and talents, along with their fashions and foods, greatly increasing the racial and cultural diversity of this country (U.S. Department of Homeland Security, 2008b).

Trade across national boundaries has also created a global economy. Large corporations make and market goods worldwide. Stock traders in New York pay close attention to the financial markets in Tokyo and Hong Kong even as wheat farmers in Kansas watch the price of grain in the former Soviet republic of Georgia. Because most new U.S. jobs involve international trade, global understanding has never been more important.

3. **Many social problems that we face in the United States are far more serious elsewhere.** Poverty is a serious problem in the United States, but poverty in Latin America, Africa, and Asia is both more common and more serious. In the same way, although women have lower social standing than men in the United States, gender inequality is even greater in the world's poor countries.
4. **Thinking globally helps us learn more about ourselves.** We cannot walk the streets of a distant city without thinking about what it means to live in the United States. Comparing life in various settings also leads to unexpected lessons. For instance, a squatter settlement in Chennai, India, despite desperate poverty, people thrive in the love and support of family members. Why, then, are so many poor people in our own country angry and alone? Are material things—so central to our definition of a "rich" life—the best way to measure human well-being?

In sum, in an increasingly interconnected world, we can understand ourselves only to the extent that we understand others. Sociology is an invitation to learn a new way of looking at the world around us. But is this invitation worth accepting? What are the benefits of applying the sociological perspective?

SEEING SOCIOLOGY in Everyday Life

This discussion shows you that using the sociological perspective is valuable for changing society by shaping public policy, for your personal enrichment, and for advancing your career.

Applying the Sociological Perspective

Applying the sociological perspective is useful in many ways. First, sociology is at work guiding many of the laws and policies that shape our lives. Second, on an individual level, making use of the sociological perspective leads to important personal growth and expanded awareness. Third, studying sociology is excellent preparation for the world of work.

Sociology and Public Policy

Sociologists have helped shape public policy—the laws and regulations that guide how people in communities live and work—in countless ways, from racial desegregation and school busing to laws regulating divorce. For example, in her study of how divorce affects people's income, the sociologist Lenore Weitzman (1985, 1996) discovered that women who leave marriages typically experience a dramatic loss of income. Recognizing this fact, many states passed laws that have increased women's claims to marital property and enforced fathers' obligations to provide support for women raising their children.

Sociology and Personal Growth

By applying the sociological perspective, we are likely to become more active and aware and to think more critically in our daily lives. Using sociology benefits us in four ways:

1. **The sociological perspective helps us assess the truth of "common sense."** We all take many things for granted, but that does not make them true. One good example is the idea that we are free individuals who are personally responsible for our own lives. If we think we decide our own fate, we may be quick to praise very successful people as superior and consider others with fewer achievements personally deficient. A sociological approach, by contrast, encourages us to ask whether such common beliefs are actually true and, to the extent that they are not, why they are so widely held. The Seeing Sociology in Everyday Life box later in this chapter gives an example of how the sociological perspective sometimes makes us rethink commonsense ideas about other people.
2. **The sociological perspective helps us see the opportunities and constraints in our lives.** Sociological thinking leads us to see that in the game of life, we have a say in how to play our cards, but it is society that deals us the hand. The more we understand the game, the better players we will be. Sociology helps us learn more about the world so that we can pursue our goals more effectively.
3. **The sociological perspective empowers us to be active participants in our society.** The more we understand how society works, the more active citizens we become. As C. Wright Mills (1959) explained, it is the sociological perspective that turns a personal problem (such as being out of work) into a public issue (a lack of good jobs). As we come to see how society affects us, we may support society as it is, or we may set out with others to change it.
4. **The sociological perspective helps us live in a diverse world.** North Americans represent just 5 percent of the world's people, and many of the other 95 percent live very differently than we do. Still, like people everywhere, we tend to define our own way of life as "right," "natural," and "better." The sociological perspective encourages us to think critically about the relative strengths and weaknesses of all ways of life, including our own.

Careers: The "Sociology Advantage"

Most students at colleges and universities today are very interested in getting a good job. A background in sociology is excellent preparation for the working world. Of course, completing a bachelor's degree in sociology is the right choice for people who decide they would like to go

Getty Images/Time Life Pictures/Steve Liss

Just about every job in today's economy involves working with people. For this reason, studying sociology is good preparation for your future career. In what ways does having "people skills" help police officers perform their job?

SEEING SOCIOLOGY in Everyday Life

Write down five jobs that appeal to you. Then identify ways in which sociological thinking would increase your chances for success in each one.

SEEING SOCIOLOGY IN EVERYDAY LIFE

Nickel and Dimed: On (Not) Getting By in America

All of us know people who work at low-wage jobs as waitresses at diners, clerks at drive-throughs, or sales associates at discount stores such as Wal-Mart. We see such people just about every day. Many of us actually *are* such people. In the United States, "common sense" tells us that the jobs people have and the amount of money they make reflect their personal abilities as well as their willingness to work hard.

Barbara Ehrenreich (2001) had her doubts. To find out what the world of low-wage work is really like, the successful journalist and author decided to leave her comfortable middle-class life to live and work in the world of low-wage jobs. She began in Key West, Florida, taking a job as a waitress for $2.43 an hour plus tips. Right away, she found out that she had to work much harder than she ever imagined. By the end of a shift, she was exhausted, but after sharing tips with the kitchen staff, she averaged less than $6.00 an hour. This was barely above the minimum wage at the time and provided just enough income to pay the rent on her tiny apartment, buy food, and cover other basic expenses. She had to hope that she didn't get sick, because the job did not provide health insurance and she couldn't afford to pay for a visit to a doctor's office.

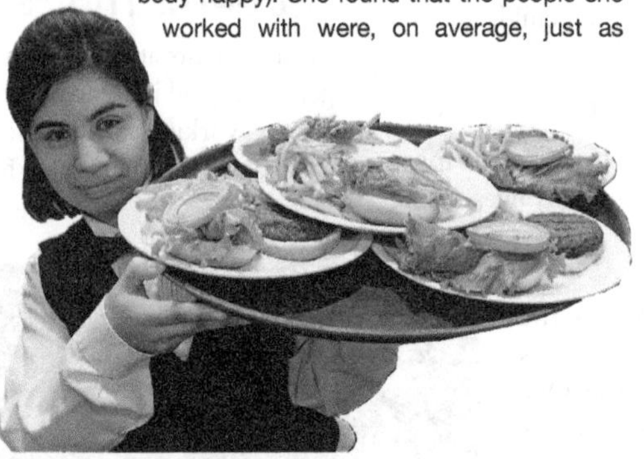

PhotoEdit Inc./Jeff Greenberg

After working for more than a year at a number of other low-wage jobs, including cleaning motels in Maine and working on the floor of a Walmart in Minnesota, she had rejected quite a bit of "common sense." First, she now knew that tens of millions of people with low-wage jobs work very hard every day. If you don't think so, Ehrenreich says, try one of these jobs yourself. Second, these jobs require not just hard work (imagine thoroughly cleaning three motel rooms per hour all day long) but also special skills and real intelligence (try waiting on ten tables in a restaurant at the same time and keeping everybody happy). She found that the people she worked with were, on average, just as smart, clever, and funny as those she knew who wrote books for a living or taught at a college.

Why, then, do we think of low-wage workers as lazy or as having less ability? It surprised Ehrenreich to learn that many low-wage workers felt this way about themselves. In a society that teaches us to believe personal ability is everything, we learn to size people up by their jobs. Subject to the constant supervision, random drug tests, and other rigid rules that usually come along with low-wage jobs, Ehrenreich imagined that many people end up feeling unworthy, even to the point of not trying for anything better. Such beliefs, she concludes, help support a society of extreme inequality in which some people live very well thanks to the low wages paid to the rest.

WHAT DO YOU THINK?

1. Have you ever held a low-wage job? If so, would you say you worked hard? What was your pay? Were there any benefits?
2. Ehrenreich claims that most well-off people in the United States are dependent on low-wage workers. What do you think she means by this?
3. Do you think most people with jobs at Wendy's or Wal-Mart have a real chance to enroll in college and to work toward a different career? Why or why not?

on to graduate work and eventually become a professor or researcher in this field. Throughout the United States, tens of thousands of men and women teach sociology in universities, colleges, and high schools. But just as many professional sociologists work as researchers for government agencies or private foundations and businesses, gathering important information on social behavior and carrying out evaluation research. In today's cost-conscious world, agencies and companies want to be sure that the programs and policies they set in place get the job done at the lowest cost. Sociologists, especially those with advanced research skills, are in high demand for this kind of work (Deutscher, 1999).

In addition, a smaller but increasing number of professional sociologists work as clinical sociologists. These women and men work, much as clinical psychologists do, with the goal of improving the lives of troubled clients. A basic difference is that sociologists focus on difficulties not in the personality but in the individual's web of social relationships.

But sociology is not just for people who want to be sociologists. People who work in criminal justice—in police departments, probation offices, and corrections facilities—gain the "sociology advantage" by learning which categories of people are most at risk of becoming criminals as well as victims, how effective various policies and programs are at preventing crime, and why people turn to crime in the first place. Similarly, people who work in health care—including doctors, nurses, and technicans—also gain a sociology advantage by learning about patterns of health and illness within the population, as well as how factors such as race, gender, and social class affect human health.

The American Sociological Association (2002) reports that sociology is also excellent preparation for jobs in dozens of additional fields,

MAKING THE GRADE

Sociology developed when and where social change was greatest.

Comte's Three Stages of Society

Theological Stage	Metaphysical Stage	Scientific Stage
(the Church in the Middle Ages)	(the Enlightenment and the ideas of Hobbes, Locke, and Rousseau)	(physics, chemistry, sociology)

positivism a scientific approach to knowledge based on "positive" facts as opposed to mere speculation

including advertising, banking, business, education, government, journalism, law, public relations, and social work. In almost any type of work, success depends on understanding how various categories of people differ in beliefs, family patterns, and other ways of life. Unless you plan to have a job that never involves dealing with people, you should consider the workplace benefits of learning more about sociology.

Photo Researchers, Inc./Frank Zullo

What we see depends on our point of view. When gazing at the stars, lovers see romance, but scientists see thermal reactions.

The Origins of Sociology

Like the "choices" made by individuals, major historical events rarely just happen. The birth of sociology was itself the result of powerful social forces.

Social Change and Sociology

Striking changes took place in Europe during the eighteenth and nineteenth centuries. Three kinds of change were especially important in the development of sociology: the rise of a factory-based industrial economy, the explosive growth of cities, and new ideas about democracy and political rights.

A New Industrial Economy

During the Middle Ages in Europe, most people plowed fields near their homes or worked in small-scale *manufacturing* (a term derived from Latin words meaning "to make by hand"). By the end of the eighteenth century, inventors used new sources of energy—the power of moving water and then steam—to operate large machines in mills and factories. Instead of laboring at home or in small groups, workers became part of a large and anonymous labor force, under the control of strangers who owned the factories. This change in the system of production took people out of their homes, weakening the traditions that had guided community life for centuries.

The Growth of Cities

Across Europe, landowners took part in what historians call the *enclosure movement*—they fenced off more and more farmland to create grazing areas for sheep, the source of wool for the thriving textile mills. Without land, countless tenant farmers had little choice but to head to the cities in search of work in the new factories.

As cities grew larger, these urban migrants faced many social problems, including pollution, crime, and homelessness. Moving through streets crowded with strangers, they faced a new and impersonal social world.

Political Change

Europeans in the Middle Ages viewed society as an expression of God's will: From the royalty to the serfs, each person up and down the social ladder played a part in the holy plan. This theological view of society is captured in lines from the old Anglican hymn "All Things Bright and Beautiful":

> The rich man in his castle,
> The poor man at his gate,
> God made them high and lowly
> And ordered their estate.

But as cities grew, tradition came under attack. In the writings of Thomas Hobbes (1588–1679), John Locke (1632–1704), and Adam Smith (1723–1790), we see a shift in focus from a moral obligation to God and king to the pursuit of self-interest. In the new political climate, philosophers spoke of *personal liberty* and *individual rights.* Echoing these sentiments, our own Declaration of Independence states that every person has "certain unalienable rights," including "life, liberty, and the pursuit of happiness."

The French Revolution, which began in 1789, was an even greater break with political and social tradition. The French social analyst Alexis de Tocqueville (1805–1859) thought the changes in society brought about by the French Revolution were so great that they amounted to "nothing short of the regeneration of the whole human race" (1955:13, orig. 1856).

A New Awareness of Society

Huge factories, exploding cities, a new spirit of individualism—these changes combined to make people more aware of their surroundings. The new discipline of sociology was born in England, France, and Germany—precisely where the changes were greatest.

Seeing SOCIOLOGY in the 

Rocky Mountain News

Interest in Military on the Rise

By DAVID MONTERO
February 2, 2009

Across the street from the U.S. Navy recruiting station in Aurora [Colorado] is a restaurant that has gone out of business. Less than a mile away, bankrupt Circuit City is unloading its merchandise at deep discounts.

Inside the narrow office, four recruiters and two freshly minted recruits are talking about what seems like the topic on most Americans' minds: jobs and the economy.

Troy Torreyson, wearing a blue Navy hat and a white T-shirt that reads, "Property of the U.S. Navy," can't wait to start basic training in May. The 30-year-old is scheduled to go to the Great Lakes naval facility in Illinois for nine weeks and after that will train to be a Navy corpsman.

He wants to be in nursing care, but the economy sidelined those plans for awhile.

"It's a huge issue," he said. "I have a culinary arts degree and I work at Burger King right now. I can't find a job."

Chief Petty Officer Mario Laracuente has heard similar tales before. He's been hearing it for months actually, ever since the economy went south. People getting laid off. People having trouble finding work and making ends meet. People looking for a [bit] of stability.

Laracuente believes the military is well-positioned in this environment to meet and exceed recruiting goals—even as the United States continues to fight in Iraq and Afghanistan.

"You can sense that as the economy appears more unstable, people are looking at the military more," Laracuente said. . . .

Stable jobs attractive

All branches of the military are showing strong recruiting numbers with the flagging economy.

The last reporting period for December showed the Army and Marine Corps exceeding recruitment goals, reaching 115 percent and 113 percent of their goals, respectively.

The Air Force and Navy met their targets as well.

Those results came as private employers made sweeping rounds of layoffs. In December, the U.S. Department of Labor reported that unemployment rates increased from 6.8 percent to 7.2 percent. . . .

Finding refuge in the military during tough economic times isn't unusual. Safe harbors can often be found in government and the military, which accounts for about a fifth of the nation's budget and is set at $515 billion for fiscal year 2009.

Gordon Von Stroh, professor of management at the University of Denver, said the lure of incentive-laden deals offered by the military coupled with staggering job losses make for plum pickings among military recruiters.

"They get a larger pool of people and can be more selective," he said. "For the applicants, they see an opportunity to train in some fairly advanced fields while having the job stability provided by the military."

Job dries up

Mark Sabatino got laid off last week from his job as a commercial sign installer. . . . The 22-year-old from Arvada had thought about the

Science and Sociology

And so it was that the French social thinker Auguste Comte (1798–1857) coined the term *sociology* in 1838 to describe a new way of looking at society. This makes sociology one of the youngest academic disciplines—far newer than history, physics, or economics, for example.

Of course, Comte was not the first person to think about the nature of society. Such questions fascinated many of the brilliant thinkers of ancient civilizations, including the Chinese philosopher K'ung Fu-tzu, or Confucius (551–479 B.C.E.), and the Greek philosophers Plato (c. 427–347 B.C.E.) and Aristotle (384–322 B.C.E.).[1] Over the next several centuries, the Roman emperor Marcus Aurelius (121–180), the medieval thinkers Saint Thomas Aquinas (c. 1225–1274) and Christine de Pisan (c. 1363–1431), and the English playwright William Shakespeare (1564–1616) wrote about the workings of society.

Yet these thinkers were more interested in imagining the ideal society than in studying society as it really was. Comte and other pioneers of sociology all cared about how society could be improved, but their major objective was to understand how society actually operates.

Comte (1975, orig. 1851–54) saw sociology as the product of a three-stage historical development. During the earliest, the *theological stage,* from the beginning of human history to the end of the European Middle Ages about 1350 C.E., people took a religious view that society expressed God's will.

With the dawn of the Renaissance in the fifteenth century, the theological approach gave way to a *metaphysical stage* of history in which people saw society as a natural rather than a supernatural system. Thomas Hobbes (1588–1679), for example, suggested that society reflected not the perfection of God so much as the failings of a selfish human nature.

What Comte called the *scientific stage* of history began with the work of early scientists such as the Polish astronomer Copernicus (1473–1543), the Italian astronomer and physicist Galileo (1564–1642), and the English physicist and mathematician Isaac Newton (1642–1727). Comte's contribution came in applying the scientific approach—first used to study the physical world—to the study of society.[2]

[1]The abbreviation B.C.E. means "before the common era." We use this throughout the text instead of the traditional B.C. ("before Christ") to reflect the religious diversity of our society. Similarly, in place of the traditional A.D. (*anno Domini*, or "in the year of our Lord"), we use the abbreviation C.E. ("common era").

[2]Illustrating Comte's stages, the ancient Greeks and Romans viewed the planets as gods; Renaissance metaphysical thinkers saw them as astral influences (giving rise to astrology); by the time of Galileo, scientists understood planets as natural objects moving according to natural laws.

military before, but decided after high school to see if he could make a go of it in the private sector first.

Things went pretty well. The work was steady, the money was good and Sabatino figured his ambitions of working with airplanes could wait awhile.

Then it all slowed down.

He said when things were going well, he'd have five jobs a week installing signs on businesses as well as doing some side jobs with smaller signs. But as businesses constricted, the jobs dried up to about one per week.

It wasn't enough.

"I had bills," he said. "They weren't going away."

So on Thursday, Sabatino found himself sitting in an overheated U.S. Marine Corps recruiting station in Thornton answering questions about his education and job history and explaining why he wanted to join.

Staff Sgt. Chris Tari dutifully filled out the paperwork, told Sabatino that he'd have to pass some tests and that, if all went according to plan, he could ship out to recruit training as early as August—though September was more likely.

In the meantime, his plan is to learn aviation electronics and eventually cycle back into the private sector and work with planes.

"I'll probably get out when the going is good again," he said.

For love of country

Sgt. 1st Class Brett Scarcelli is pure U.S. Army. Standing in the recruiting station at Metropolitan State College in Denver, he clutches a tennis ball in one hand and never lowers his gaze when talking to someone. For him, the Army is about service to country. Period.

But that approach doesn't necessarily work on potential recruits. So, Scarcelli is armed with the things that might matter to college students wandering around the Tivoli Student Union on the Auraria campus. There are increasing tuition costs, budget cuts at state universities, and difficulties in getting hired right now straight out of college, for instance.

The message seems to work.

"I talked to a guy who just got his degree and has six months before he has to start paying. And he can't find a job," Scarcelli said. "The Army is willing to pay off the loans, and he can wait four years to see what the economy does."

WHAT DO YOU THINK?

1. How does the surge in military recruiting reflect not just personal choices by individuals but also larger changes in society?
2. Can you point to other personal choices people are making that may be linked to the weaker economy? What are they?
3. Did the weakening economy affect your life in terms of work? What about your decision to attend college? Explain.

Comte's approach is called **positivism,** *a way of understanding based on science.* As a positivist, Comte believed that society operates according to its own laws, much as the physical world operates according to gravity and other laws of nature.

By the beginning of the twentieth century, sociology had spread to the United States and showed the influence of Comte's ideas. Today, most sociologists still consider science a crucial part of sociology. But we now realize that human behavior is far more complex than the movement of planets or even the actions of other living things. We are creatures of imagination and spontaneity, so human behavior can never be fully explained by any rigid "laws of society." In addition, early sociologists such as Karl Marx (1818–1883) were troubled by the striking inequalities of industrial society. They hoped that the new discipline of sociology would not just help us understand society but also lead to change toward greater social justice.

Sociological Theory

The desire to translate observations into understanding brings us to the important aspect of sociology known as *theory*. A **theory** is *a statement of how and why specific facts are related.* The job of sociological theory is to explain social behavior in the real world. For example, recall Emile Durkheim's theory that categories of people with low social integration (men, Protestants, the wealthy, and the unmarried) are at higher risk of suicide. Seeing Sociology in the News explains one consequence of the recent economic recession.

Sociologists test their theories by gathering evidence using various research methods. Durkheim did exactly this, finding out which categories of people were more likely to commit suicide and which were less likely and then devising a theory that best squared with all available evidence. National Map 1 displays the suicide rate for each of the fifty states.

In building theory, sociologists face two basic questions: What issues should we study? And how should we connect the facts? In the process of answering these questions, sociologists look to one or more theoretical approaches as "road maps." Think of a **theoretical approach** as *a basic image of society that guides thinking and research.* Sociologists make use of three major theoretical approaches: the structural-functional approach, the social-conflict approach, and the symbolic-interaction approach.

The Structural-Functional Approach

The **structural-functional approach** is *a framework for building theory that sees society as a complex system whose parts work together to promote solidarity and stability.* As its name suggests, this approach points to **social structure,** *any relatively stable pattern of*

theory a statement of how and why specific facts are related

theoretical approach a basic image of society that guides thinking and research

structural-functional approach a framework for building theory that sees society as a complex system whose parts work together to promote solidarity and stability

social structure any relatively stable pattern of social behavior

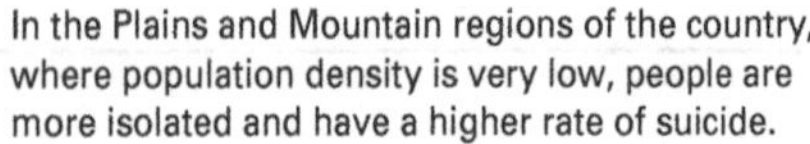

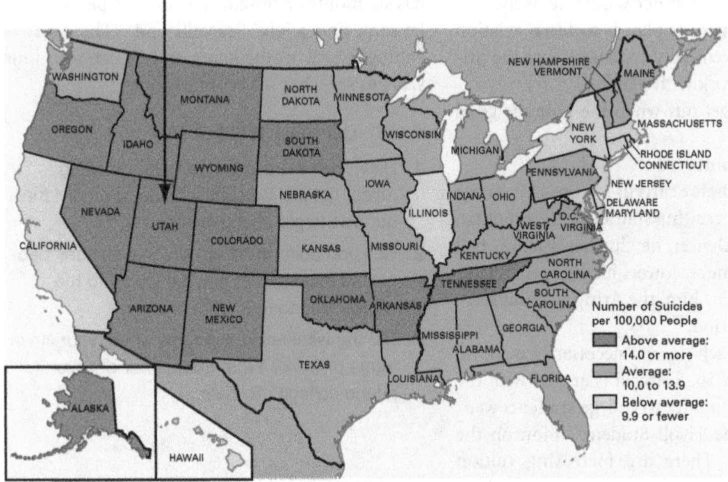

Seeing Ourselves

NATIONAL MAP 1

Suicide Rates across the United States

This map shows which states have high, average, and low suicide rates. Look for patterns. By and large, high suicide rates occur where people live far apart from one another. More densely populated states have low suicide rates. Do these data support or contradict Durkheim's theory of suicide? Why?

Source: Kung et al. (2008).

social behavior. Social structure gives our lives shape—in families, the workplace, the classroom, and the community. This approach also looks for a structure's **social functions,** *the consequences of any social pattern for the operation of society as a whole.* All social structures, from a simple handshake to complex religious rituals, function to keep society going, at least in its present form.

The structural-functional approach owes much to Auguste Comte, who pointed out the need to keep society unified at a time when many traditions were breaking down. Emile Durkheim, who helped establish the study of sociology in French universities, also based his work on this approach. A third structural-functional pioneer was the English sociologist Herbert Spencer (1820–1903). Spencer compared society to the human body. Just as the structural parts of the human body—the skeleton, muscles, and various internal organs—function interdependently to help the entire organism survive, social structures work together to preserve society. The structural-functional approach, then, leads sociologists to identify various structures of society and investigate their functions.

Robert K. Merton (1910–2003) expanded our understanding of the concept of social function by pointing out that any social structure probably has many functions, some more obvious than others. He distinguished between **manifest functions,** *the recognized and intended consequences of any social pattern,* and **latent functions,** *the unrecognized and unintended consequences of any social pattern.* For example, the manifest function of the U.S. system of higher education is to provide young people with the information and skills they need to perform jobs after graduation. Perhaps just as important, although less often acknowledged, is college's latent function as a "marriage broker," bringing together young people of similar social backgrounds. Another latent function of higher education is to limit unemployment by keeping millions of young people out of the labor market, where many of them might not easily find jobs.

But Merton also recognized that not all the effects of social structure are good. Thus a **social dysfunction** is *any social pattern that may disrupt the operation of society.* People often disagree about what is helpful and what is harmful to society as a whole. In addition, what is functional for one category of people (say, high profits for Wall Street bank executives) may well be dysfunctional for other categories of people (workers who lose pension funds invested in banks that fail, people who cannot pay their mortgages and end up losing their homes).

CRITICAL REVIEW The main idea of the structural-functional approach is its vision of society as stable and orderly. The main goal of the sociologists who use this approach, then, is to figure out "what makes society tick."

In the mid-1900s, most sociologists favored the structural-functional approach. In recent decades, however, its influence has declined. By focusing on social stability and unity, critics point out, structural-functionalism ignores inequalities of social class, race, and gender, which cause tension and conflict. In general, its focus on stability at the expense of conflict makes this approach somewhat conservative. As a critical response, sociologists developed the social-conflict approach.

CHECK YOUR LEARNING How do manifest functions differ from latent functions? Give an example of a manifest function and a latent function of automobiles in the United States.

social functions the consequences of a social pattern for the operation of society as a whole

manifest functions the recognized and intended consequences of any social pattern

latent functions the unrecognized and unintended consequences of any social pattern

social dysfunction any social pattern that may disrupt the operation of society

social-conflict approach a framework for building theory that sees society as an arena of inequality that generates conflict and change

gender-conflict approach a point of view that focuses on inequality and conflict between women and men

feminism support of social equality for women and men

race-conflict approach a point of view that focuses on inequality and conflict between people of different racial and ethnic categories

The Social-Conflict Approach

The **social-conflict approach** is *a framework for building theory that sees society as an arena of inequality that generates conflict and change.* Unlike the structural-functional emphasis on solidarity and stability, this approach highlights inequality and change. Guided by this approach, which includes the gender-conflict and race-conflict approaches, sociologists investigate how factors such as social class, race, ethnicity, gender, sexual orientation, and age are linked to a society's unequal distribution of money, power, education, and social prestige. A conflict analysis rejects the idea that social structure promotes the operation of society as a whole, focusing instead on how social patterns benefit some people while harming others.

Sociologists using the social-conflict approach look at ongoing conflict between dominant and disadvantaged categories of people—the rich in relation to the poor, white people in relation to people of color, and men in relation to women. Typically, people on top try to protect their privileges while the disadvantaged try to gain more for themselves.

A conflict analysis of our educational system shows how schooling carries class inequality from one generation to the next. For example, secondary schools assign students to either college preparatory or vocational training programs. From a structural-functional point of view, such "tracking" benefits everyone by providing schooling that fits students' abilities. But conflict analysis argues that tracking often has less to do with talent than with social background, with the result that well-to-do students are placed in higher tracks while poor children end up in the lower tracks.

Thus young people from privileged families get the best schooling, which leads them to college and later to high-income careers. The children of poor families, by contrast, are not prepared for college and, like their parents before them, typically get stuck in low-paying jobs. In both cases, the social standing of one generation is passed on to the next, with schools justifying the practice in terms of individual merit (Bowles & Gintis, 1976; Oakes, 1982, 1985).

Many sociologists use the social-conflict approach not just to understand society but also to bring about societal change that would reduce inequality. Karl Marx championed the cause of the workers in what he saw as their battle against factory owners. In a well-known statement (inscribed on his monument in London's Highgate Cemetery), Marx asserted, "The philosophers have only interpreted the world, in various ways; the point, however, is to change it."

Everett Collection/Giovanni Rufino/The CW

The social-conflict approach points out patterns of inequality in everyday life. In the TV show *Gossip Girl*, Jenny Humphrey, a girl from a modest background, often feels awkward in the presence of her more affluent classmates. Do you see similar patterns of social inequality on your campus?

Feminism and the Gender-Conflict Approach

One important type of social-conflict analysis is the **gender-conflict approach,** *a point of view that focuses on inequality and conflict between women and men.* The gender-conflict approach is closely linked to **feminism,** *support of social equality for women and men.*

The importance of the gender-conflict approach lies in making us aware of the many ways in which our way of life places men in positions of power over women: in the home (where men are usually considered "head of the household"), in the workplace (where men earn more income and hold most positions of power), and in the mass media (how many hip-hop stars are women?).

Another contribution of the gender-conflict approach is making us aware of the importance of women to the development of sociology. Harriet Martineau (1802–1876) is regarded as the first woman sociologist. Born to a wealthy English family, Martineau made her mark in 1853 by translating the writings of Auguste Comte from French into English. In her own published writings, she documented the evils of slavery and argued for laws to protect factory workers, defending workers' right to unionize. She was particularly concerned

MAKING THE GRADE

The feminist and gender-conflict approaches and the race-conflict approach are all examples of social-conflict theory.

We can use the sociological perspective to look at sociology itself. All of the most widely recognized pioneers of the discipline were men. This is because in the nineteenth century, it was all but unheard of for women to be college professors, and few women took a central role in public life. But Jane Addams was an early sociologist in the United States, who founded Hull House, a Chicago settlement house where she spent many hours helping young people.

about the position of women in society and fought for changes in education policy so that women could have more options in life than marriage and raising children.

In the United States, Jane Addams (1860–1935) was a sociological pioneer whose contributions began in 1889 when she helped found Hull House, a Chicago settlement house that provided assistance to immigrant families. Although widely published (she wrote eleven books and hundreds of articles), Addams chose the life of a public activist over that of a university sociologist, speaking out on issues involving immigration and the pursuit of peace. Despite the controversy caused by her pacifism during World War I, she was awarded the Nobel Peace Prize in 1931.

The Race-Conflict Approach

Another important type of social-conflict analysis is the **race-conflict approach,** *a point of view that focuses on inequality and conflict between people of different racial and ethnic categories.* Just as men have power over women, white people have numerous social advantages over people of color, including, on average, higher incomes, more schooling, better health, and longer life expectancy.

The race-conflict approach also points out the contributions made by people of color to the development of sociology. Ida Wells Barnett (1862–1931) was born to slave parents but rose to become a teacher and then a journalist and newspaper publisher. She campaigned tirelessly for racial equality and, especially, to put an end to the lynching of black people. She wrote and lectured about racial inequality throughout her life (Lengerman & Niebrugge-Brantley, 1998).

An important contribution to understanding race in the United States was made by William Edward Burghardt Du Bois (1868–1963). Born to a poor Massachusetts family, Du Bois (pronounced doo-boyss) enrolled at Fisk University in Nashville, Tennessee, and then at Harvard University, where he earned the first doctorate awarded by that university to a person of color. Like most people who follow the social-conflict approach (whether focusing on class, gender, or race), Du Bois believed that sociologists should try to solve society's problems. He therefore studied the black community (1967, orig. 1899), spoke out against racial inequality, and served as a founding member of the National Association for the Advancement of Colored People (NAACP). The Thinking About Diversity box takes a closer look at the ideas of W. E. B. Du Bois.

CRITICAL REVIEW The various social-conflict approaches have gained a large following in recent decades, but like other approaches, they have met with criticism. Because any conflict analysis focuses on inequality, it largely ignores how shared values and interdependence unify members of a society. In addition, say critics, to the extent that the conflict approaches pursue political goals, they cannot claim scientific objectivity. Supporters of social-conflict approaches respond that *all* theoretical approaches have political consequences.

A final criticism of both the structural-functional and the social-conflict approaches is that they paint society in broad strokes—in terms of "family," "social class," "race," and so on. A third type of theoretical analysis—the symbolic-interaction approach—views society less in general terms and more as the everyday experiences of individual people.

CHECK YOUR LEARNING Why do you think sociologists characterize the social-conflict approach as "activist"? What is it actively trying to achieve?

macro-level orientation a broad focus on social structures that shape society as a whole

structural-functional approach
social-conflict approach

micro-level orientation a close-up focus on social interaction in specific situations

symbolic-interaction approach a framework for building theory that sees society as the product of the everyday interactions of individuals

THINKING ABOUT DIVERSITY: RACE, CLASS, & GENDER

An Important Pioneer: W. E. B. Du Bois on Race

One of sociology's pioneers in the United States, William Edward Burghardt Du Bois saw sociology as the key to solving society's problems, especially racial inequality.

Du Bois spoke out against racial separation and was a founding member of the National Association for the Advancement of Colored People (NAACP). He made his colleagues in sociology—and people everywhere—aware of the deep racial divisions in the United States. White people can simply be "Americans," Du Bois pointed out; African Americans, however, have a "double consciousness," reflecting their status as people who are never able to escape identification based on the color of their skin.

In his sociological classic *The Philadelphia Negro: A Social Study* (1899), Du Bois explored Philadelphia's African American community, identifying both the strengths and the weaknesses of people who were dealing with overwhelming social problems on a day-to-day basis. He challenged the belief—widespread at that time—that blacks were inferior to whites, and he blamed white prejudice for creating the problems that African Americans faced. He also criticized successful people of color for being so eager to win white acceptance that they gave up all ties with the black community, which needed their help.

Du Bois described race as the major problem facing the United States in the twentieth century. Early in his career, he was hopeful about overcoming racial divisions. By the end of his life, however, he had grown bitter, believing that little had changed. At the age of ninety-three, Du Bois left the United States for Ghana, where he died two years later.

Art Resource/Schomburg Center for Research in Black Culture

WHAT DO YOU THINK?

1. If he were alive today, what do you think Du Bois would say about racial inequality in the twenty-first century?
2. How much do you think African Americans today experience a "double consciousness"?
3. In what ways can sociology help us understand and reduce racial conflict?

Sources: Based in part on Baltzell (1967) and Du Bois (1967, orig. 1899).

The Symbolic-Interaction Approach

The structural-functional and social-conflict approaches share a **macro-level orientation,** *a broad focus on social structures that shape society as a whole.* Macro-level sociology takes in the big picture, rather like observing a city from high above in a helicopter and seeing how highways help people move from place to place or how housing differs from rich to poor neighborhoods. Sociology also uses a **micro-level orientation,** *a close-up focus on social interaction in specific situations.* Exploring urban life in this way occurs at street level, where you might watch how children invent games on a school playground or how pedestrians respond to homeless people they pass on the street. The **symbolic-interaction approach,** then, is *a framework for building theory that sees society as the product of the everyday interactions of individuals.*

How does "society" result from the ongoing experiences of tens of millions of people? One answer is that society is nothing more than the shared reality that people construct as they interact. Human beings live in a world of symbols, attaching *meaning* to virtually everything, from the words on this page to the wink of an eye. "Reality," therefore, is simply how we define our surroundings, our obligations toward others, and even our own identities.

The symbolic-interaction approach has roots in the thinking of Max Weber (1864–1920), a German sociologist who emphasized the need to understand a setting from the point of view of the people in it.

Since Weber's time, sociologists have taken micro-level sociology in a number of directions. George Herbert Mead (1863–1931)

MAKING THE GRADE

The Applying Theory table summarizes the three major theoretical approaches in sociology. Study the table to be sure you understand each one.

APPLYING THEORY

Major Theoretical Approaches

	Structural-Functional Approach	Social-Conflict Approach	Symbolic-Interaction Approach
What is the level of analysis?	Macro-level	Macro-level	Micro-level
What image of society does the approach have?	Society is a system of interrelated parts that is relatively stable. Each part works to keep society operating in an orderly way. Members generally agree about what is morally right and morally wrong.	Society is a system of social inequalities based on class (Marx), gender (feminism and gender-conflict approach), and race (race-conflict approach). Society operates to benefit some categories of people and harm others. Social inequality causes conflict that leads to social change.	Society is an ongoing process. People interact in countless settings using symbolic communications. The reality people experience is variable and changing.
What core questions does the approach ask?	How is society held together? What are the major parts of society? How are these parts linked? What does each part do to help society work?	How does society divide a population? How do advantaged people protect their privileges? How do disadvantaged people challenge the system seeking change?	How do people experience society? How do people shape the reality they experience? How do behavior and meaning change from person to person and from one situation to another?

explored how our personalities develop as a result of social experience. Erving Goffman's (1922–1982) *dramaturgical analysis* describes how we resemble actors on a stage as we play our various roles. Other contemporary sociologists, including George Homans and Peter Blau, have developed *social-exchange analysis.* In their view, social interaction is guided by what each person stands to gain or lose from the interaction. In the ritual of courtship, for example, people seek mates who offer at least as much—in terms of physical attractiveness, intelligence, and wealth—as they offer in return.

CRITICAL REVIEW Without denying the existence of macro-level social structures such as the family and social class, the symbolic-interaction approach reminds us that society basically amounts to *people interacting*. That is, micro-level sociology tries to show how individuals actually experience society. But on the other side of the coin, by focusing on what is unique in each social scene, this approach risks overlooking the widespread influence of culture, as well as factors such as class, gender, and race.

CHECK YOUR LEARNING How does a micro-level analysis differ from a macro-level analysis? Provide an illustration of a micro-level social pattern and another of a social pattern that operates at a macro level.

The Applying Theory table summarizes the main characteristics of sociology's three major theoretical approaches: the structural-functional approaches, the social-conflict approach, and the symbolic-interaction approach. Each of these approaches is helpful in answering particular kinds of questions about society. However, the fullest understanding of our social world comes from using all three, as you can see in the following analysis of sports in the United States.

SEEING SOCIOLOGY in Everyday Life

Apply the three theoretical approaches to the issues that opened this chapter—love and marriage. Consider questions such as these: What categories of people are you most likely to date? Why? Why are today's younger college students likely to wait many more years to marry than students did fifty years ago?

Applying the Approaches: The Sociology of Sports

Who among us doesn't enjoy sports? Children as young as six or seven take part in organized sports, and many teens become skilled at three or more. Weekend television is filled with sporting events for viewers of all ages, and whole sections of our newspapers are devoted to teams, players, and scores. In the United States, top players such as Mark McGwire (baseball), Tiger Woods (golf), and Serena Williams (tennis) are among our most famous celebrities. Sports in the United States are also a multibillion-dollar industry. What can we learn by applying sociology's three theoretical approaches to this familiar part of everyday life?

The Functions of Sports

A structural-functional approach directs our attention to the ways in which sports help society operate. The manifest functions of sports include providing recreation as well as offering a means of getting in physical shape and a relatively harmless way to let off steam. Sports have important latent functions as well, from building social relationships to creating tens of thousands of jobs across the country. Sports encourage competition and the pursuit of success, both of which are values that are central to our society's way of life.

Sports also have dysfunctional consequences. For example, colleges and universities that try to field winning teams sometimes recruit students for their athletic skill rather than their academic ability. This practice not only lowers the academic standards of a school but also shortchanges athletes, who spend little time doing the academic work that will prepare them for later careers (Upthegrove, Roscigno, & Charles, 1999).

Sports and Conflict

A social-conflict analysis of sports points out that the games people play reflect their social standing. Some sports—including tennis, swimming, golf, sailing, and skiing—are expensive, so taking part is largely limited to the well-to-do. Football, baseball, and basketball, however, are accessible to people at almost all income levels.

Throughout history, sports have been oriented mostly toward males. For example, the first modern Olympic Games, held in 1896, barred women from competition; in the United States, Little League teams in most parts of the country have only recently let girls play. Traditional ideas that girls and women lack the strength to play sports have now been widely rejected. But our society still encourages men to become athletes while expecting women to be attentive observers and cheerleaders. At the college level, men's athletics attracts a greater amount of attention and resources compared to women's athletics, and men greatly outnumber women as coaches, even in women's sports (Welch & Sigelman, 2007). At the professional level, women also take a back seat to men, particularly in the sports with the most earnings and social prestige.

For decades, big league sports excluded people of color, who were forced to form leagues of their own. Only in 1947 did Major League Baseball admit the first African American player when Jackie Robinson joined the Brooklyn Dodgers. More than fifty years later, professional baseball honored Robinson's amazing career by retiring his number 42 on *all* of the teams in the league. In 2007, African Americans (13 percent of the U.S. population) accounted for 8 percent of Major League Baseball players, 66 percent of National Football League (NFL) players, and 76 percent of National Basketball Association (NBA) players (Lapchick, 2008).

One reason for the high number of African Americans in many professional sports is that athletic performance—in terms of batting average or number of points scored per game—can be precisely measured and is not influenced by racial prejudice. It is also

Photofest/NBC

As the television show *Friday Night Lights* makes clear, sports are an important element of social life in countless communities across the United States. Sociology's three theoretical approaches all contribute to our understanding of the role of sports in society.

MAKING THE GRADE

Figures are useful because they contain a lot of information in a small space. In Figure 2, look first at the title to see what the figure shows. Then read the caption, which should summarize a pattern. Then look at the art to see the pattern for yourself.

76% of quarterbacks but only 2% of cornerbacks are white.

Diversity Snapshot

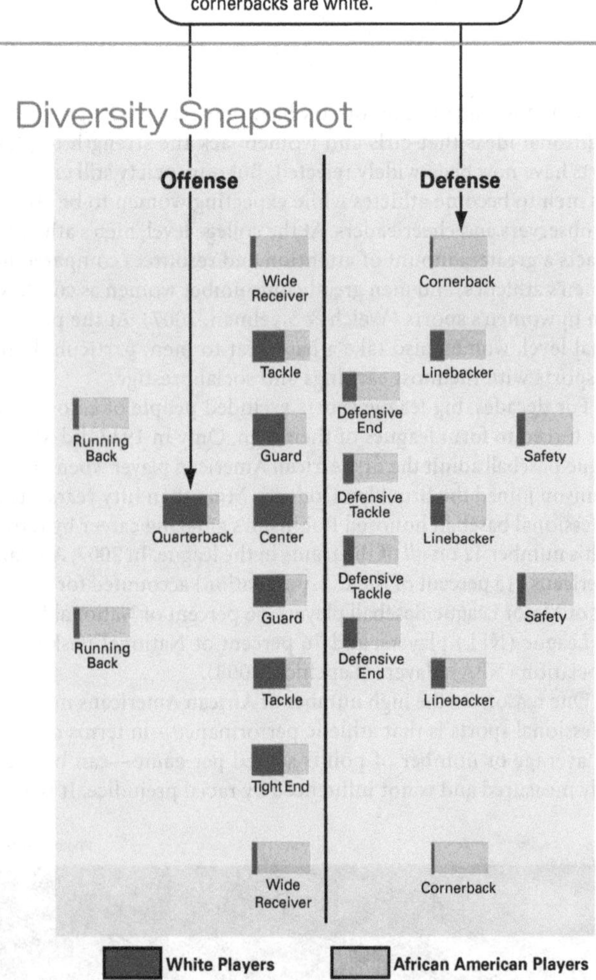

FIGURE 2 "Stacking" in Professional Football

Does race play a part in professional sports? Looking at the various positions in professional football, we see that white players are more likely to play the central and offensive positions. What do you make of this pattern?

Source: Lapchick (2008).

true that some people of color make a particular effort to excel in athletics, where they see greater opportunity than in other careers (S. Steele, 1990; Edwards, 2000; Harrison, 2000). In recent years, in fact, African American athletes have earned higher salaries, on average, than white players.

But racial discrimination still exists in professional sports. For one thing, race is linked to the *positions* athletes play on the field, in a pattern called "stacking." Figure 2 shows the results of a study of race in football. Notice that white athletes are much more likely than African American athletes to play offense and to take the central positions on both sides of the line. More broadly, African Americans have a large share of players in only five sports: baseball, basketball, football, boxing, and track. In all professional sports, the vast majority of managers, head coaches, and owners of sports teams are white (Lapchick, 2008).

Although many individual players get supersized salaries and millions of fans enjoy following their teams, sports are a big business that provides big profits for a small number of people (predominantly white men). In sum, sports in the United States are bound up with inequalities based on gender, race, and economic power.

Sports as Interaction

At the micro-level, a sporting event is a complex, face-to-face interaction. In part, play is guided by the players' assigned positions and the rules of the game. But players are also spontaneous and unpredictable. Following the symbolic-interaction approach, we see sports less as a system than as an ongoing process.

From this point of view, too, we expect each player to understand the game a little differently. Some players enjoy a setting of stiff competition; for others, love of the game may be greater than the need to win.

In addition, the behavior of any single player may change over time. A rookie in professional baseball, for example, may feel self-conscious during the first few games in the big leagues but go on to develop a comfortable sense of fitting in with the team. Coming to feel at home on the field was slow and painful for Jackie Robinson, who knew that many white players, and millions of white fans, resented his presence. In time, however, his outstanding ability and his confident and cooperative manner won him the respect of the entire nation.

The three theoretical approaches—the structural-functional approach, the social-conflict approach, and the symbolic-interaction approach—provide different insights into sports, and none is more correct than the others. Applied to any issue, each approach generates its own interpretations. To appreciate fully the power of the sociological perspective, you should become familiar with all three.

The Controversy & Debate box discusses the use of the sociological perspective and reviews many of the ideas presented in this chapter. This box raises a number of questions that will help you understand how sociological generalizations differ from the common stereotypes we encounter every day.

SEEING SOCIOLOGY in Everyday Life

Can you recall hearing someone use a stereotype about some category of students on your campus? How valid do you think the stereotype is?

stereotype a simplified description applied to every person in some category

CONTROVERSY & DEBATE

Is Sociology Nothing More than Stereotypes?

Jena: (*raising her eyes from her notebook*) Today in sociology class, we talked about stereotypes.

Marcia: (*trying to focus on her science lab*) OK, here's one: Roommates don't like to be disturbed when they're studying.

Jena: Seriously, my studious friend, we all have stereotypes, even professors.

Marcia: (*becoming faintly interested*) Like what?

Jena: Professor Chandler said today in class that if you're a Protestant, you're likely to kill yourself. And then Yannina—this girl from, I think, Ecuador—says something like, "You Americans are rich, you marry, and you love to divorce!"

Marcia: My brother said to me last week that "everybody knows you have to be black to play professional basketball." Now there's a stereotype!

College students, like everyone else, are quick to make generalizations about people. And as this chapter has explained, sociologists, too, love to generalize by looking for social patterns. However, beginning students of sociology may wonder if generalizations aren't really the same thing as stereotypes. For example, are the statements reported by Jena and Marcia true generalizations or false stereotypes?

Let's first be clear that a **stereotype** is *a simplified description applied to every person in some category*. Each of the statements made at the beginning of this box is a stereotype that is false for three reasons. First, rather than describing averages, each statement describes every person in some category in exactly the same way; second, even though many stereotypes often contain an element of truth, each statement ignores facts and distorts reality; and third, each statement seems to be motivated by bias, sounding more like a "put-down" than a fair-minded observation.

What about sociology? If our discipline looks for social patterns and makes generalizations, does it express stereotypes? The answer is no, for three reasons. First, *sociologists do not carelessly apply any generalization to everyone in a category.* Second, *sociologists make sure that a generalization squares with the available facts.* And third, *sociologists offer generalizations fair-mindedly, with an interest in getting at the truth.*

Jena remembered her professor saying (although not in quite the same words) that the suicide rate among Protestants is higher than among Catholics or Jews. Based on information presented earlier in this chapter, that is a true statement. However, the way Jena incorrectly reported the classroom remark—"If you're a Protestant, you're likely to kill yourself"—is not good sociology. It is not a true generalization because the vast majority of Protestants do no such thing. It would be just as wrong to jump to the conclusion that a particular friend, because he is a Protestant male, is about to end his own life. (Imagine refusing to lend money to a roommate who happens to be a Baptist, explaining, "Well, given the way people like you commit suicide, I might never get paid back!")

Second, sociologists shape their generalizations to the available facts. A more factual version of the statement Yannina made in class is that on average, the U.S. population does have a high standard of living, almost everyone in our society does marry at some point in life, and although few people take pleasure in divorcing, our divorce rate is also among the world's highest.

Third, sociologists try to be fair-minded and want to get at the truth. The statement made by Marcia's brother, about African Americans and basketball, is an unfair stereotype rather than good sociology for two reasons. First, it is simply not true, and second, it seems motivated by bias rather than truth-seeking.

The bottom line is that good sociological generalizations are *not* the same as harmful stereotyping. A college sociology course is an excellent setting for getting at the truth behind common stereotypes. The classroom encourages discussion and offers the factual information you need to decide whether a particular statement is a valid sociological generalization or just a stereotype.

Photodisc/Getty Images

A sociology classroom is a good place to get at the truth behind common stereotypes.

WHAT DO YOU THINK?

1. Can you think of a common stereotype of sociologists? What is it? After reading this box, do you still think it is valid?
2. Do you think taking a sociology course can help correct people's stereotypes? Why or why not?
3. Can you think of a stereotype of your own that might be challenged by sociological analysis?

Seeing Sociology in Everyday Life

The Sociological Perspective

"Why do couples marry?"

We asked this question at the beginning of this chapter. The commonsense answer is that people marry because they are in love. But as this chapter has explained, society guides our everyday lives, affecting what we do, think, and feel. Look at the three photographs, each showing a couple who, we can assume, is "in love." In each case, can you provide some of the rest of the story? By looking at the categories that the people involved represent, explain how society is at work in bringing the two people together.

HINT Society is at work on many levels. Consider (1) rules about same-sex and other-sex marriage, (2) laws defining the number of people who may marry, (3) the importance of race and ethnicity, (4) the importance of social class, (5) the importance of age, and (6) the importance of social exchange (what each partner offers the other). All societies enforce various rules that state who should or should not marry whom.

Jada Pinkett met Will Smith in 1995 when she auditioned for a part on his hit show, *The Fresh Prince of Bel Air*. Two years later, they married. What social patterns do you see?

Getty Images Inc. – Hulton Archive Photos/Victor Malafront

Mark Savage/Corbis Entertainment/Corbis, All Rights Reserved

AP Wide World Photos/Paul Skipper

In 1997, during the fourth season of her hit TV show, *Ellen*, Ellen DeGeneres "came out" as a lesbian, which put her on the cover of *Time* magazine. Since then, she has been an activist on behalf of gay and lesbian issues. Following California's brief legalization of same-sex marriage in 2008, she married her longtime girlfriend, Australian actress Portia de Rossi.

In 2000, at the age of fifty-six, Michael Douglas ended a twenty-three-year marriage in order to marry actress Catherine Zeta-Jones, who was then thirty-one. How likely is it that a fifty-six-year-old woman would marry a thirty-one-year-old man?

Applying SOCIOLOGY in Everyday Life

1. Analyze the marriages of your parents, other family members, and friends in terms of class, race, age, and other factors. What evidence can you find that society guides the feeling we call "love"?
2. The U.S. divorce rate has risen and fallen several times over the past century. Using the sociological perspective, try to identify societal factors that caused the divorce rate to rise or fall.
3. Explore your local area, and draw a sociological map of the community. Include the types of buildings (for example, "big, single-family homes," "rundown business district," "new office buildings," "student apartments") found in various places, and guess at the categories of people who live or work there. What patterns do you see?

MAKING THE GRADE

The Sociological Perspective

What Is the Sociological Perspective?

The **SOCIOLOGICAL PERSPECTIVE** reveals the power of society to shape individual lives.

- What we commonly think of as personal choice—whether or not to go to college, how many children we will have, even the decision to end our own life—is affected by social forces.
- Peter Berger described the sociological perspective as "seeing the general in the particular."
- C. Wright Mills called this point of view the "sociological imagination," claiming it transforms personal troubles into public issues.
- The experience of being an outsider or of living through a social crisis can encourage people to use the sociological perspective.

sociology the systematic study of human society

sociological perspective the special point of view of sociology that sees general patterns of society in the lives of particular people

The Importance of a Global Perspective

Where we live—in a **high-income country** like the United States, a **middle-income country** such as Brazil, or a **low-income country** such as Mali—shapes the lives we lead.

Many social problems that we face in the United States are far more serious in other countries.

Learning about life in other societies helps us learn more about ourselves.

Societies throughout the world are increasingly interconnected.

- New technology allows people around the world to share popular trends.
- Immigration from around the world increases the racial and ethnic diversity of the United States.
- Trade across national boundaries has created a global economy.

global perspective the study of the larger world and our society's place in it

high-income countries nations with the highest overall standards of living

middle-income countries nations with a standard of living about average for the world as a whole

low-income countries nations with a low standard of living in which most people are poor

Applying the Sociological Perspective

Research by sociologists plays an important role in shaping **public policy**.

A background in sociology is excellent preparation for success in many different **careers**.

On a **personal level**, using the sociological perspective helps us see the opportunities and limits in our lives and empowers us to be active citizens.

Origins of Sociology

RAPID SOCIAL CHANGE in the eighteenth and nineteenth centuries made people more aware of their surroundings and helped trigger the development of sociology:

- The **rise of an industrial economy** moved work from homes to factories, weakening the traditions that had guided community life for centuries.
- The **explosive growth of cities** created many social problems, such as crime and homelessness.
- **Political change** based on ideas of individual liberty and individual rights encouraged people to question the structure of society.

AUGUSTE COMTE named sociology in 1838 to describe a new way of looking at society.

- Early philosophers had tried to describe the ideal society.
- Comte wanted to understand society as it really is by using **positivism**, a way of understanding based on science.
- Karl Marx and many later sociologists used sociology to try to make society better.

positivism a way of understanding based on science

✓ *The countries that experienced the most rapid social change were those in which sociology developed first.*

Sociological Theory

A **THEORY** states how facts are related, weaving observations into insight and understanding. Sociologists use three major **THEORETICAL APPROACHES** to describe the operation of society.

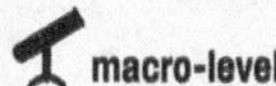

The **STRUCTURAL-FUNCTIONAL APPROACH** explores how **social structures**—patterns of behavior, such as religious rituals or family life—work together to help society operate.

- Auguste Comte, Emile Durkheim, and Herbert Spencer helped develop the structural-functional approach.
- Thomas Merton pointed out that social structures have both **manifest functions** and **latent functions**; he also identified **social dysfunctions** as patterns that may disrupt the operation of society.

The **SOCIAL-CONFLICT APPROACH** shows how inequality creates conflict and causes change.

- Karl Marx helped develop the social-conflict approach.
- The **gender-conflict approach**, linked to **feminism**, focuses on ways in which society places men in positions of power over women. Harriet Martineau is regarded as the first woman sociologist.
- The **race-conflict approach** focuses on the advantages—including higher income, more schooling, and better health—that society gives to white people over people of color.
- W. E. B. Du Bois identified the "double consciousness" of African Americans.

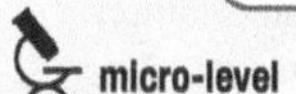

The **SYMBOLIC-INTERACTION APPROACH** studies how people, in everyday interaction, construct reality.

- Max Weber's claim that people's beliefs and values shape society is the basis of the social-interaction approach.
- Social-exchange analysis states that social life is guided by what each person stands to gain or lose from the interaction.

See the Applying Theory table in this chapter.

✓ *To get the full benefit of the sociological perspective, apply all three approaches.*

theory a statement of how and why specific facts are related

theoretical approach a basic image of society that guides thinking and research

structural-functional approach a framework for building theory that sees society as a complex system whose parts work together to promote solidarity and stability

social structure any relatively stable pattern of social behavior

social functions the consequences of any social pattern for the operation of society as a whole

manifest functions the recognized and intended consequences of any social pattern

latent functions the unrecognized and unintended consequences of any social pattern

social dysfunction any social pattern that may disrupt the operation of society

social-conflict approach a framework for building theory that sees society as an arena of inequality that generates conflict and change

gender-conflict approach a point of view that focuses on inequality and conflict between women and men

feminism support of social equality for women and men

race-conflict approach a point of view that focuses on inequality and conflict between people of different racial and ethnic categories

macro-level orientation a broad focus on social structures that shape society as a whole

micro-level orientation a close-up focus on social interaction in specific situations

symbolic-interaction approach a framework for building theory that sees society as the product of the everyday interactions of individuals

Applying the Approaches: The Sociology of Sports

The Functions of Sports

The structural-functional approach looks at how sports help society function smoothly.

- Manifest functions of sports include providing recreation, a means of getting in physical shape, and a relatively harmless way to let off steam.
- Latent functions of sports include building social relationships and creating thousands of jobs.

stereotype a simplified description applied to every person in some category

Sports and Conflict

The social-conflict approach looks at the links between sports and social inequality.

- Historically, sports have benefited men more than women.
- Some sports are accessible mainly to affluent people.
- Racial discrimination exists in professional sports.

Sports as Interaction

The social-interaction approach looks at the different meanings and understandings people have of sports.

- Within a team, players affect each other's understanding of the sport.
- The reaction of the public can affect how players perceive their sport.

✓ *Sociology helps us understand the difference between well-grounded generalizations and unfair stereotypes.*

MAKING THE GRADE

Sample Test Questions

Multiple-Choice Questions

1. **What does the sociological perspective tell us about whom any individual chooses to marry?**
   a. There is no explaining personal feelings like love.
   b. People's actions reflect human free will.
   c. The operation of society guides many of our personal choices.
   d. In the case of love, opposites attract.

2. **Which early sociologist studied patterns of suicide?**
   a. Peter Berger
   b. Emile Durkheim
   c. Auguste Comte
   d. Karl Marx

3. **The personal value of studying sociology includes**
   a. seeing the opportunities and constraints in our lives.
   b. the fact that it is good preparation for a number of jobs.
   c. being more active participants in society.
   d. All of the above are correct.

4. **The discipline of sociology first developed in**
   a. countries experiencing rapid social change.
   b. countries with little social change.
   c. countries with a history of warfare.
   d. the world's poorest countries.

5. **Which early sociologist coined the term *sociology* in 1838?**
   a. Karl Marx
   b. Herbert Spencer
   c. Adam Smith
   d. Auguste Comte

6. **Which theoretical approach is closest to that taken by early sociologists Auguste Comte and Emile Durkheim?**
   a. the symbolic-interaction approach
   b. the structural-functional approach
   c. the social-conflict approach
   d. None of the above is correct.

7. **Which term refers to the recognized and intended consequences of a social pattern?**
   a. manifest functions
   b. latent functions
   c. eufunctions
   d. dysfunctions

8. **Sociology's social-conflict approach draws attention to**
   a. how structure contributes to the overall operation of society.
   b. how people construct meaning through interaction.
   c. patterns of social inequality.
   d. the stable aspects of society.

9. **Which woman, among the first sociologists, studied the evils of slavery and also translated the writings of Auguste Comte?**
   a. Elizabeth Cady Stanton
   b. Jane Addams
   c. Harriet Martineau
   d. Margaret Mead

10. **Which of the following illustrates a micro-level focus?**
    a. analyzing the operation of the U.S. political system
    b. studying patterns of global terrorism
    c. describing class inequality in the armed forces
    d. observing two new dormitory roommates getting to know one another

ANSWERS: 1 (c); 2 (b); 3 (d); 4 (a); 5 (d); 6 (b); 7 (a); 8 (c); 9 (c); 10 (d).

Essay Questions

1. Explain why applying the sociological perspective can make us seem less in control of our lives. In what ways does it actually give us greater power over our lives?
2. Guided by the discipline's three major theoretical approaches, come up with sociological questions about (a) television, (b) war, and (c) colleges and universities.

Sociological Investigation

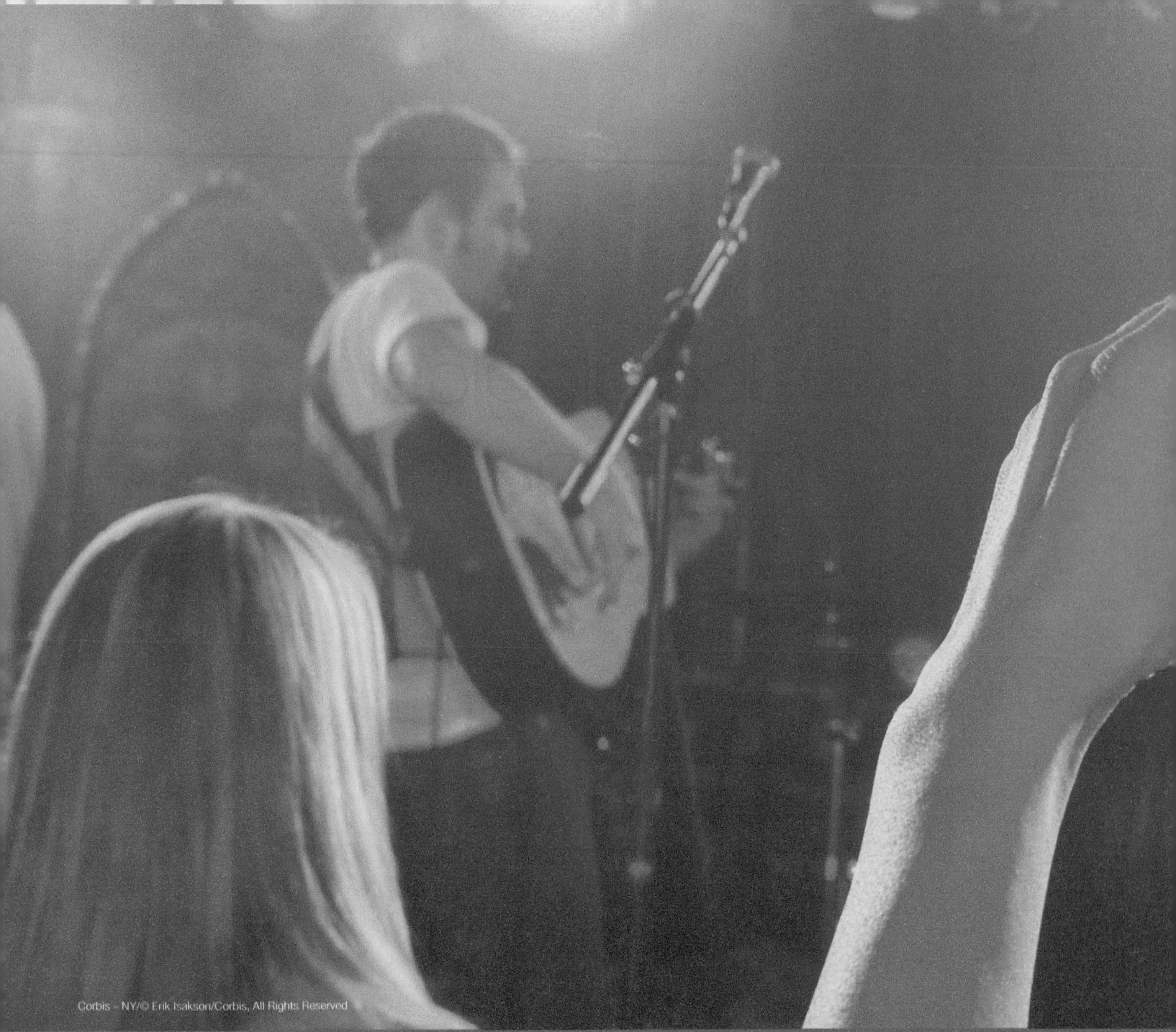

Corbis - NY/© Erik Isakson/Corbis, All Rights Reserved

Sociology isn't just a way of looking at our surroundings; it is also a system for learning about how society operates and finding out how people experience their world.

Ken Karp/Pearson Education/PH College

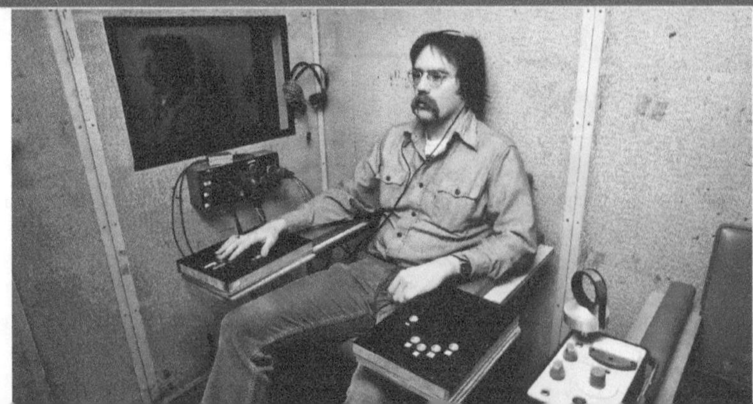

Sociological Investigation

Anthro-Photo File/Irven De Vore

Doranne Jacobson International Images

CHAPTER OVERVIEW

This chapter explains how sociologists "do" sociology. First, it looks at science as a way of knowing and then discusses two limitations to scientific sociology that are addressed by two other approaches to knowing—interpretive sociology and critical sociology. Finally, it explains four methods of data collection.

Lois Benjamin /Reuben Burrell/Hampton University

While on a visit to Atlanta during the winter holiday season, the sociologist Lois Benjamin (1991) called up the mother of an old college friend. Benjamin was eager to learn about Sheba; both women had dreamed about earning a graduate degree, landing a teaching job, and writing books. Now a successful university professor, Benjamin had seen her dream come true. But as she soon found out, this was not the case with Sheba.

Benjamin recalled early signs of trouble. After college, Sheba had begun graduate work at a Canadian university. But in letters to Benjamin, Sheba became more and more critical of the world and seemed to be cutting herself off from others. Some classmates wondered if she was suffering from a personality disorder. But as Sheba saw it, the problem was racism. As an African American woman, she felt she was the target of racial hostility. Before long, she flunked out of school, blaming the failure on her white professors. At this point, she left North America, earning a Ph.D. in England and then settling in Nigeria. Benjamin had not heard from her friend in the years since.

Benjamin was happy to hear that Sheba had returned to Atlanta. But her delight dissolved into shock when she saw Sheba and realized that her friend had suffered a mental breakdown and was barely responsive to anyone.

For months, Sheba's emotional collapse troubled Benjamin. Obviously, Sheba was suffering from serious psychological problems. Having felt the sting of racism herself, Benjamin wondered if this might have played a part in Sheba's story. Partly as a tribute to her old friend, Benjamin set out to explore the effects of race in the lives of bright, well-educated African Americans in the United States.

Benjamin knew she was calling into question the common belief that race is less of a barrier than it used to be, especially to talented African Americans (W. J. Wilson, 1978). But her own experiences—and Sheba's too, she believed—seemed to contradict such thinking.

To test her ideas, Benjamin spent the next two years asking 100 successful African Americans across the country how race affected their lives. In the words of these "Talented One Hundred"[1] men and women, she found evidence that even among privileged African Americans, racism remains a heavy burden.

Later in this chapter, we will take a closer look at Lois Benjamin's research. For now, notice how the sociological perspective helped her spot broad social patterns in the lives of individuals. Just as important, Benjamin's work shows us the *doing* of sociology, the process of *sociological investigation.*

Many people think that scientists work only in laboratories, carefully taking measurements using complex equipment. But as this chapter explains, although some sociologists do conduct scientific research in laboratories, most work on neighborhood streets, in homes and workplaces, in schools and hospitals, in bars and prisons—in short, wherever people can be found.

This chapter examines the methods that sociologists use to conduct research. Along the way, we shall see that research involves not just ways of gathering information but controversies about values: Should researchers strive to be objective? Or should they point to the need for change? Certainly Lois Benjamin did not begin her study just to show that racism exists; she wanted to bring racism out in the open as a way to challenge it. We shall tackle questions of values after presenting the basics of sociological investigation.

[1] W. E. B. Du Bois used "The Talented Tenth" to refer to African American leaders.

science a logical system that develops knowledge from direct, systematic observation

empirical evidence information we can verify with our senses

Basics of Sociological Investigation

Sociological investigation starts with two simple requirements. The first, *Apply the sociological perspective.* This point of view reveals curious patterns of behavior all around us that call for further study. It was Lois Benjamin's sociological imagination that prompted her to wonder how race affects the lives of talented African Americans.

This brings us to the second requirement: *Be curious and ask questions.* Benjamin wanted to learn more about how race affects people who are high achievers. She began by asking questions: Who are the leaders of this nation's black community? What effect does being part of a racial minority have on their view of themselves? On the way white people perceive them and their work?

Seeing the world sociologically and asking questions are basic to sociological investigation. As we look for answers, we need to realize that there are various kinds of "truth."

Science as One Form of Truth

Saying that we "know" something can mean many things. Most people in the United States, for instance, say they believe in God. Few claim to have direct contact with God, but they say they believe all the same. We call this kind of knowing "belief" or "faith."

A second kind of truth comes from recognized experts. Students with a health problem, for example, may consult a campus physician or search the Internet for articles written by experts in the field.

A third type of truth is based on simple agreement among ordinary people. Most of us in the United States would probably say we "know" that sexual intercourse among ten-year-old children is wrong. But why? Mostly because just about everyone says it is.

People's "truths" differ the world over, and we often encounter "facts" at odds with our own. Imagine yourself a Peace Corps volunteer just arrived in a small, traditional village in Latin America. Your job is to help local people grow more crops. On your first day in the fields, you observe a strange practice: After planting seeds, the farmers lay a dead fish on top of the soil. When you ask about this, they explain that the fish is a gift to the god of the harvest. A village elder adds sternly that the harvest was poor one year when no fish were offered.

From that society's point of view, using fish as gifts to the harvest god makes sense. The people believe in it, their experts endorse it, and everyone seems to agree that the system works. But with scientific training in agriculture, you have to shake your head and wonder. The scientific "truth" in this situation is something entirely different: The decomposing fish fertilize the ground, producing a better crop.

Science represents a fourth way of knowing. **Science** is *a logical system that bases knowledge on direct, systematic observation*. Standing apart from faith, the wisdom of "experts," and general agreement, scientific knowledge rests on **empirical evidence,** that is, *information we can verify with our senses.*

AP Wide World Photos/Rick Rycroft

In a complex and ever-changing world, there are many different "truths." This Peace Corps volunteer on a small island in the South Pacific learned a crucial lesson—that other people often see things in a different way. There is great value in our own scientific approach to truth, but there are also important truths in the ancient traditions of people living around the world.

Our Peace Corps example does not mean that people in traditional villages ignore what their senses tell them or that members of technologically advanced societies use only science to know things. A medical researcher using science to develop a new drug for treating cancer, for example, may still practice her religion as a matter of faith, turn to financial experts when making decisions about money, and pay attention to the political opinions of her family and friends. In short, we all hold various kinds of truths at the same time.

Common Sense versus Scientific Evidence

Like the sociological perspective, scientific evidence sometimes challenges our common sense. Here are six statements that many North Americans assume are true:

1. **"Poor people are far more likely than rich people to break the law."** Not true. If you regularly watch television shows like *COPS,* you might think that police arrest only people from "bad" neighborhoods. Poor people do stand out in the official arrest statistics. But research also shows that police and prosecutors are more likely to treat well-to-do people more leniently, as when a Hollywood celebrity is accused of shoplifting or drunk driving. Some laws

SEEING SOCIOLOGY IN EVERYDAY LIFE

Is What We Read in the Popular Press True? The Case of Extramarital Sex

Every day, we see stories in newspapers and magazines that tell us what people think and how they behave. But a lot of what we read turns out to be misleading or even untrue.

Take the issue of extramarital sex, which refers to a married person having sex with someone other than his or her spouse. A look at the cover of many of the so-called women's magazines you find in the checkout aisle at the supermarket or a quick reading of the advice column in your local newspaper might lead you to think that extramarital sex is a major issue facing married couples. The popular media seem full of stories about how to keep your spouse from "cheating" or pointing out clues to tip you off that your spouse is having an affair. Most of the studies reported in the popular press and on Internet Web sites suggest that more than half of married people—women as well as men—cheat on their spouses.

But is extramarital sex really that widespread? No. Researchers who conduct sound sociological investigation have found that in a given year, only about 3 or 4 percent of married people have an extramarital relationship and no more than 15 to 20 percent of married people have *ever* done so. Why, then, do surveys in the popular media report rates of extramarital sex that are so much higher? We can answer this question by taking a look at who fills out "pop" surveys.

First, it is people with a personal interest in some topic who are most likely to respond to an offer to complete a survey on that topic. For this reason, people who have had personal experience with extramarital sex (either their own behavior or their partner's) are more likely to show up in these studies. In contrast, studies correctly done by skilled researchers involve carefully selected subjects so that the results are representative of the entire population.

Second, because the readership of the magazines and online sources that conduct these surveys is, on average, young, their surveys end up attracting a high proportion of young respondents. And one thing we know about young people—married or unmarried—is that they are more likely to have sex. For example, the typical married person who is thirty years of age is more than twice as likely to have had an extramarital relationship than the typical married person over age sixty.

Third, women are much more likely than men to read the popular magazines that feature sex surveys. Therefore, women are more likely to fill out the surveys. In recent decades, the share of women (especially younger women) who have had extramarital sex has gone up. Why are today's younger women more likely than women a generation or two earlier to have had extramarital sex? Probably because women today are working outside of the home and many are traveling as part of their job. This lifestyle gives today's women a wider social network that brings them into contact with more men.

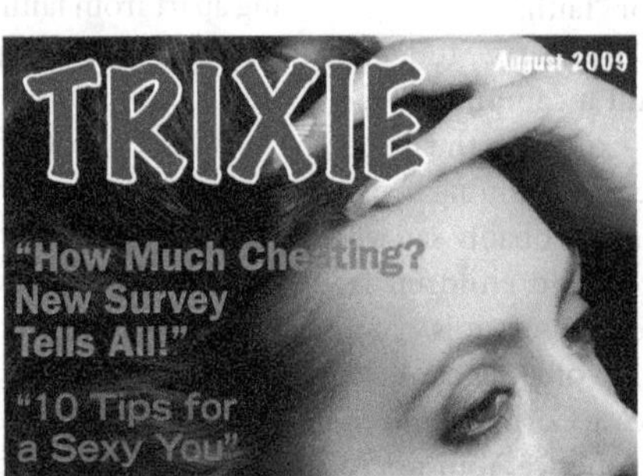

PhotoEdit Inc./Vic Bider.

Remember that a lot of what you read in the popular media and online may not be as true as some people think.

WHAT DO YOU THINK?

1. Can you think of other issues in which pop media surveys may give misleading information? What are they?
2. Explain why we should have more trust in the results of sound research carried out by skilled sociologists than in the surveys conducted by the popular media.
3. Do you think companies are likely to sell more magazines or newspapers if they publish "research" results that distort the truth? Explain.

Sources: T. W. Smith (2006), Black (2007), and Parker-Pope (2008).

are even written in a way that criminalizes poor people more and affluent people less.

2. **"The United States is a middle-class society in which most people are more or less equal."** False. Data show that the richest 5 percent of U.S. families control 60 percent of the nation's total wealth, but almost half of all families have scarcely any wealth at all (Mishel, Bernstein, & Allegretto, 2009).
3. **"Most poor people don't want to work."** Wrong. Research indicates that this statement is true of some but not most poor people. In fact, about half of poor individuals in the United States are children and elderly people who are not expected to work.
4. **"Differences in the behavior of females and males are just 'human nature.'"** Wrong again. Much of what we call "human nature" is constructed by the society in which we live. Further, some societies define "feminine" and "masculine" very differently from the way we do.
5. **"People change as they grow old, losing many interests as they focus on their health."** Not really. Aging changes our personalities very little. Problems of health increase in old age,

positivist sociology the study of society based on scientific observation of social behavior

concept a mental construct that represents some aspect of the world in a simplified form

variable a concept whose value changes from case to case

but by and large, elderly people keep the distinctive personalities they have had throughout their adult lives.

6. **"Most people marry because they are in love."** Not always. To members of our society, few statements are so obvious. Surprisingly, however, in many societies, marriage has little to do with love.

These examples confirm the old saying that "it's not what we *don't* know that gets us into trouble as much as the things we *do* know that *just aren't so.*" The Seeing Sociology in Everyday Life box explains why we also need to think critically about "facts" we find in the popular media and on the Internet.

We have all been brought up hearing many widely accepted truths, being bombarded by "expert" advice in the popular media, and feeling pressure to accept the opinions of people around us. As adults, we need to evaluate more critically what we see, read, and hear. Sociology can help us do that.

Three Ways to Do Sociology

"Doing" sociology means learning more about the social world. There is more than one way to do this. Just as sociologists can use one or more theoretical approaches, they may also use different research orientations. The following sections describe three ways to do research: positivist sociology, interpretive sociology, and critical sociology.

Positivist Sociology

Early sociologists such as Auguste Comte and Emile Durkheim applied science to the study of society just as natural scientists investigate the physical world. **Positivist sociology,** then, is *the study of society based on systematic observation of social behavior.* A positivist approach to the world assumes that an objective reality exists "out there." The job of the scientist is to discover this reality by gathering empirical evidence, facts we can verify with our senses, say, by seeing, hearing, or touching.

Concepts, Variables, and Measurement

Let's take a closer look at how science works. A basic element of science is the **concept,** *a mental construct that represents some part of the world in a simplified form.* Sociologists use concepts to label aspects of social life, including "the family" and "the economy," and to categorize people in terms of their "gender" or "social class."

A **variable** is *a concept whose value changes from case to case.* The familiar variable "price," for example, has a value that changes from item to item in a supermarket. Similarly, we use the concept "social class" to describe people's social standing as "upper-class," "middle-class," "working-class," or "lower-class."

© Doranne Jacobson International Images

One principle of scientific research is that sociologists and other investigators should try to be objective in their work, so that their personal values and beliefs do not distort their findings. But such a detached attitude may discourage the connection needed for people to open up and share information. Thus sociologists have to decide how much to pursue objectivity and how much to show their own feelings.

The use of variables depends on **measurement,** *a procedure for determining the value of a variable in a specific case.* Some variables are easy to measure, as when you step on a scale to see how much you weigh. But measuring sociological variables can be far more difficult. For example, how would you measure a person's social class? You might start by evaluating the person's clothing, patterns of speech, or home and neighborhood. Or trying to be more precise, you might seek details about the person's income, occupation, and education.

Because most variables can be measured in more than one way, sociologists often have to decide which factors to consider. For example, having a very high income might qualify a person as "upper-class." But what if the income comes from selling automobiles, an

measurement a procedure for determining the value of a variable in a specific case

operationalize a variable specifying exactly what is to be measured before assigning a value to a variable

reliability consistency in measurement

validity actually measuring exactly what you intend to measure

SEEING SOCIOLOGY in Everyday Life

Write three questions you might ask to measure people's social class. Why would you have to ask more than one question?

SEEING SOCIOLOGY IN EVERYDAY LIFE

Three Useful (and Simple) Descriptive Statistics

The admissions office at your school is preparing a new brochure, and as part of your work-study job in that office, your supervisor asks you to determine the average salary received by last year's graduating class. To keep matters simple, assume that you talk to only seven members of the class (a real study would require contacting many more) and gather the following data on their present incomes:

$30,000	$42,000	$22,000
$165,000	$22,000	$35,000
$34,000		

Sociologists use three different descriptive statistics to report averages. The simplest statistic is the *mode,* the value that occurs *most often* in a series of numbers. In this example, the mode is $22,000, since that value occurs two times and each of the others occurs only once. If all the values were to occur only once, there would be no mode; if two different values each occurred two or three times, there would be two modes. Although it is easy to identify, sociologists rarely use the mode because it reflects only some of the numbers and is therefore a crude measure of the "average."

A more common statistic, the *mean,* refers to the *arithmetic average* of a series of numbers, calculated by adding all the values together and dividing by the number of cases. The sum of the seven incomes is $350,000. Dividing by 7 yields a mean income of $50,000. But notice that the mean in this case is not a very good "average" because it is higher than six of the seven incomes and is not particularly close to any of the actual numbers. Because the mean is "pulled" up or down by an especially high or low value (in this case, the $165,000 paid to one graduate, an athlete who signed as a rookie with the Cincinnati Reds farm team), it can give a distorted picture of data that include one or more extreme scores.

The *median* is the *middle case,* the value that occurs midway in a series of numbers arranged from lowest to highest. Here the median income for the seven graduates is $34,000, because when the numbers are placed in order from lowest to highest, this value occurs exactly in the middle, with three incomes higher and three lower. (With an even number of cases, the median is halfway between the two middle cases.) The median (unlike the mean) is not affected by any extreme scores. In such cases, the median gives a better picture of what is "average" than the mean.

WHAT DO YOU THINK?

1. Your grade point average (GPA) is an example of an average. Is it a mode, a median, or a mean? Explain.
2. Sociologists generally use the median instead of the mean when they study people's incomes. Can you see why?
3. Do a quick calculation of the mean, median, and mode for these simple numbers: 1, 2, 5, 6, 6.

Answers: mode = 6, median = 5, mean = 4.

occupation most people think of as "middle-class"? Would having only an eighth-grade education make the person "lower-class"? In a case like this, sociologists usually combine these three measures—income, occupation, and education—to determine social class.

Sociologists also face the problem of dealing with huge numbers of people. For example, how do you report income for thousands or even millions of U.S. families? Listing streams of numbers would carry little meaning and tells us nothing about the people as a whole. To solve this problem, sociologists use *descriptive statistics* to state what is "average" for a large number of people. The Seeing Sociology in Everyday Life box explains how.

Defining Concepts Measurement is always somewhat arbitrary because the value of any variable in part depends on how it is defined. In addition, it is easy to see that there is more than one way to measure abstract concepts such as "love," "family," or "intelligence."

Good research therefore requires that sociologists **operationalize a variable** by *specifying exactly what is to be measured before assigning a value to a variable.* Before measuring the concept of "social class," for example, you would have to decide exactly what you were going to measure—say, income level, years of schooling, or occupational prestige. Sometimes sociologists measure several of these things; in such cases, they need to specify exactly how they plan to combine these variables into one overall score. The next time you read the results of a study, notice the way the researchers operationalize each variable. How they define terms can greatly affect the results.

When deciding how to operationalize variables, sociologists often take into account the opinions of the people they study. Starting in 1977, for example, researchers at the U.S. Census Bureau defined race and ethnicity in terms of making a choice from this list: white, black, Hispanic, Asian or Pacific Islander, and American Indian or Alaska Native. One problem with this system is that someone can be both Hispanic *and* white or black; similarly, people of Arab ancestry might not identify with any of these choices. Just as important, an increasing number of people in the United States are *multiracial.* Because of the changing face of the U.S. population, the 2000 census was the first one to allow people to describe their race and ethnicity by selecting more than one category and almost 7 million people did

cause and effect a relationship in which change in one variable (the independent variable) causes change in another (the dependent variable)

independent variable the variable that causes the change

dependent variable the variable that changes

so. The multiracial option has resulted in a more accurate description of the true diversity of the population.

Reliability and Validity For a measurement to be useful, it must be both reliable and valid. **Reliability** refers to *consistency in measurement.* A measurement is reliable if repeated measurements give the same result time after time. But consistency does not guarantee **validity,** which means *actually measuring exactly what you intend to measure.*

Getting a valid measurement is sometimes tricky. Say you want to know just how religious the students at your college are. You might ask students how often they attend religious services. But is going to a church, temple, or mosque really the same thing as being religious? People may attend religious services because of deep personal beliefs, but they may also do so out of habit or because others pressure them to go. And what about spiritual people who avoid organized religion altogether? Even when a measurement yields consistent results (making it reliable), it may not measure what we want it to (and therefore lack validity). Measuring religiosity should take account of not only participation in prayer services but also a person's beliefs and the degree to which a person lives by religious convictions. Good sociological research depends on careful measurement, which is always a challenge to researchers.

Relationships among Variables Once measurements are made, investigators can pursue the real payoff: seeing how variables are related. The scientific ideal is **cause and effect,** *a relationship in which change in one variable causes change in another.* Cause-and-effect relationships occur around us every day, as when studying hard for an exam results in a high grade. *The variable that causes the change* (in this case, how much you study) is called the **independent variable.** *The variable that changes* (the exam grade) is called the **dependent variable.** The value of one variable depends on the value of another. Linking variables in terms of cause and effect is important because it allows us to *predict* the outcome of future events—if we know one thing, we can accurately predict another. For example, knowing that studying hard results in a better exam grade, we can predict with confidence that if you do study hard for the next exam, you will receive a higher grade, and if you do not study hard, your grade will suffer.

But just because two variables change together does not mean that they are linked by a cause-and-effect relationship. For example, sociologists have long recognized that juvenile delinquency is more common among young people who live in crowded housing. Say we operationalize the variable "juvenile delinquency" as the number of times a person under the age of eighteen has been arrested, and we define "crowded housing" by a home's number of square feet of living space per person. It turns out that these variables are related: Delinquency rates are high in densely populated neighborhoods. But should we conclude that crowding in the home (in this case, the independent variable) is what causes delinquency (the dependent variable)?

FIGURE 1 **Correlation and Cause: An Example**

Correlation is not the same as cause. Here's why.

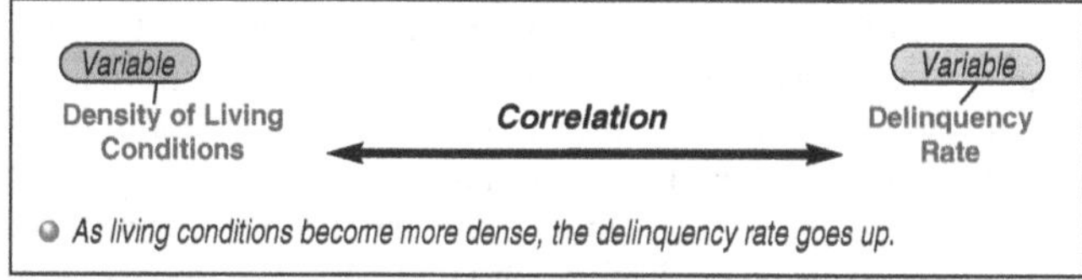

(a) If two variables increase and decrease together, they display correlation.

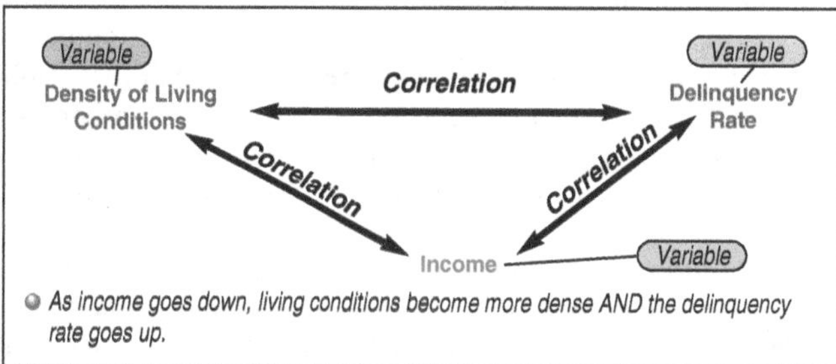

(b) Here we consider the effect of a third variable: income. Low income may cause *both* high-density living conditions *and* a high delinquency rate.

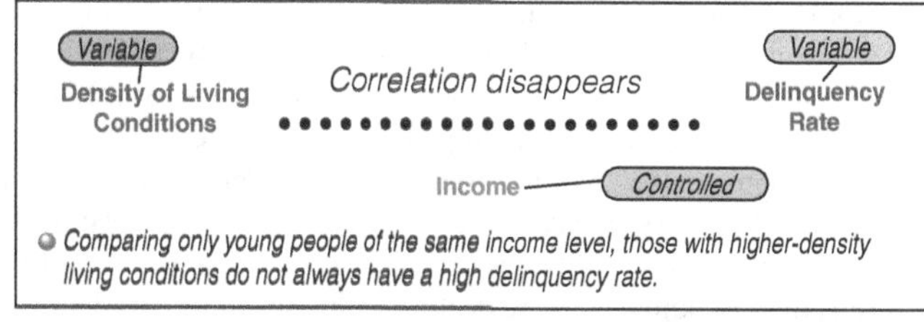

(c) When we control for income—that is, examine only young people of the same income level—we find that density of living conditions and delinquency rate no longer increase and decrease together.

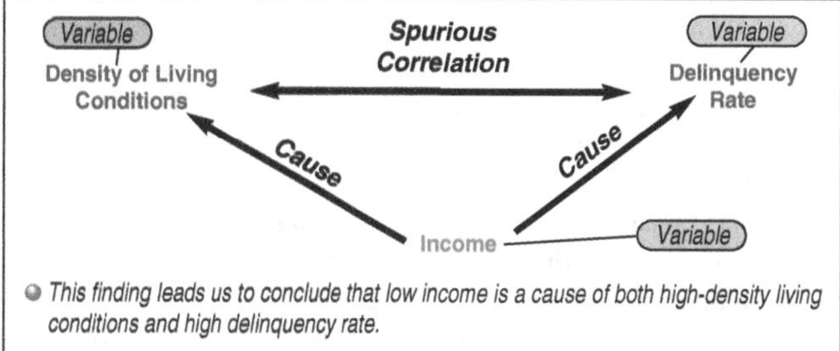

(d) Density of living conditions and delinquency rate are correlated, but their correlation is *spurious* because neither one causes the other.

correlation a relationship in which two (or more) variables change together

spurious correlation an apparent but false relationship between two (or more) variables that is caused by some other variable

control holding constant all variables except one in order to see clearly the effects of that variable

Not necessarily. **Correlation** is *a relationship in which two (or more) variables change together.* We know that density and delinquency are correlated because they change together, as shown in part (a) of Figure 1. This relationship *may* mean that crowding causes more arrests, but it could also mean that some third factor is causing change in *both* of the variables under observation. To identify a third variable, think what kinds of people live in crowded housing: people with less money and few choices—the poor. Poor children are also more likely to end up with police records. In reality, crowded housing and juvenile delinquency are found together because *both* are caused by a third factor—poverty—as shown in part (b) of Figure 1. In short, the apparent connection between crowding and delinquency is "explained away" by a third variable—low income—that causes them both to change. So our original connection turns out to be a **spurious correlation,** *an apparent but false relationship between two (or more) variables that is caused by some other variable.*

Exposing a correlation as spurious requires a bit of detective work, assisted by a technique called **control,** *holding constant all variables except one in order to see clearly the effect of that variable.* In our example, we suspect that income level may be causing a spurious link between housing density and delinquency. To check whether the correlation between delinquency and crowding is spurious, we control for income—that is, we hold income constant by looking at only young people of one income level. If the correlation between density and delinquency remains, that is, if young people of the same income level living in more crowded housing show higher rates of arrest than young people in less crowded housing, we have more reason to think that crowding does, in fact, cause delinquency. But if the relationship disappears when we control for income, as shown in part (c) of Figure 1, then we know we were dealing with a spurious correlation. In fact, research shows that the correlation between crowding and delinquency just about disappears if income is controlled (Fischer, 1984). So we have now sorted out the relationship among the three variables, as illustrated in part (d) of the figure. Housing density and juvenile delinquency have a spurious correlation; evidence shows that both variables rise or fall according to income.

To sum up, correlation means only that two (or more) variables change together. To establish cause and effect, three requirements must be met: (1) a demonstrated correlation, (2) an independent (causal) variable that occurs before the dependent variable, and (3) no evidence that a third variable could be causing a spurious correlation between the two.

Natural scientists usually have an easier time than social scientists in identifying cause-and-effect relationships because most natural scientists work in laboratories, where they can control other variables. Carrying out research in a workplace or on the streets, however, makes control very difficult, so sociologists often have to settle for demonstrating only correlation. Also, human behavior is highly complex, involving dozens of causal variables at any one time, so establishing all the cause-and-effect relationships in any situation is extremely difficult.

The Ideal of Objectivity

Ten students are sitting around a dorm lounge discussing the dream vacation spot for the upcoming spring break. Do you think one place will end up being everyone's clear favorite? That hardly seems likely.

In scientific terms, each of the ten people probably operationalizes the concept "dream vacation" differently. For one, it might be a deserted, sunny beach in Mexico; for another, the choice might be New Orleans, a lively city with a very active social scene; for still another, hiking the Rocky Mountains below snow-capped peaks may be the choice. Like so many other "bests" in life, the best vacations turn out to be mostly a matter of individual taste.

Personal values are fine when it comes to choosing travel destinations, but they pose a challenge to scientific research. Remember, science assumes that reality is "out there." Scientists need to study this reality without changing it in any way, and so they strive for **objectivity,** *personal neutrality in conducting research.* Objectivity means that researchers carefully hold to scientific procedures and do not let their own attitudes and beliefs influence the results.

Scientific objectivity is an ideal rather than a reality, of course, because no one can be completely neutral. Even the topic someone chooses to study reflects a personal interest of one sort or another, as Lois Benjamin showed us in the reasons for her decision to investigate race. But the scientific ideal is to keep a professional distance or sense of detachment from the results, however they turn out. With this ideal in mind, you should do your best when conducting research to see that conscious or unconscious biases do not distort your findings. As an extra precaution, many researchers openly state their personal leanings in their research reports so that readers can interpret the conclusions with those considerations in mind.

The German sociologist Max Weber expected that people would select their research topics according to their personal beliefs and interests. Why else, after all, would one person study world hunger, another investigate the effects of racism, and still another examine how children manage in one-parent families? Knowing that people select topics that are *value-relevant,* Weber urged researchers to be *value-free* in their investigations. Only by controlling their personal feelings and opinions (as we expect any professionals to do) can researchers study the world *as it is* rather than tell us *how they think it should be.* This detachment, for Weber, is a crucial element of science that sets it apart from politics. Politicians are committed to particular outcomes; scientists try to maintain an open mind about the results of their investigations, whatever they may turn out to be.

SEEING SOCIOLOGY in Everyday Life

Why do you think many doctors, teachers, and police officers avoid working professionally with their own children?

objectivity personal neutrality in conducting research

replication repetition of research by other researchers

Magnum Photos, Inc./Steve McCurry

PhotoEdit Inc./Michael Newman

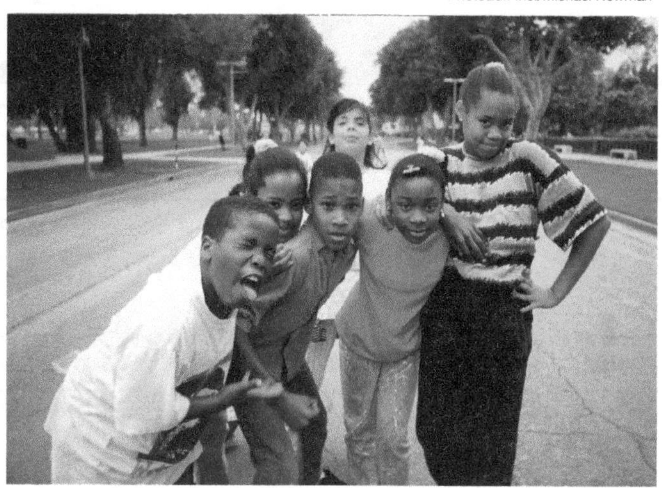

A basic lesson of social research is that being observed affects how people behave. Researchers can never be certain precisely how this will occur; some people resent public attention, but others become highly animated when they think they have an audience.

Weber's argument still carries much weight, although most sociologists admit that we can never be completely value-free or even aware of all our biases. Keep in mind, however, that sociologists are not "average" people: Most are white, highly educated, and more politically liberal than the population as a whole (Klein & Stern, 2004). Remember that sociologists, like everyone else, are influenced by their social backgrounds.

One way to limit distortion caused by personal values is **replication,** *repetition of research by other investigators.* If other researchers repeat a study using the same procedures and obtain the same results, we gain confidence that the results are accurate (both reliable and valid). The need for replication in scientific investigation probably explains why the search for knowledge is called "*re*-search" in the first place.

Keep in mind that the logic of science does not guarantee objective, absolute truth. What science offers is an approach to knowledge that is *self-correcting* so that in the long run, researchers stand a good chance of limiting their biases. Objectivity and truth lie, then, not in any one study but in the scientific process itself as it continues over time.

Some Limitations of Scientific Sociology

Science is one important way of knowing. Yet, applied to social life, science has several important limitations.

1. **Human behavior is too complex for sociologists to predict any individual's actions precisely.** Astronomers calculate the movement of objects in the skies with remarkable precision, but comets and planets are unthinking objects. Humans, by contrast, have minds of their own, so no two people react to any event (whether it be a sports victory or a natural disaster) in exactly the same way. Sociologists must therefore be satisfied with showing that *categories* of people *typically* act in one way or another. This is not a failing of sociology. It simply reflects the fact that we study creative, spontaneous people.
2. **Because humans respond to their surroundings, the presence of a researcher may affect the behavior being studied.** An astronomer's gaze has no effect on a distant comet. But most people react to being observed. Try staring at someone for a few minutes and see for yourself. People being watched may become anxious, angry, or defensive; others may be especially friendly or helpful. The act of studying people can cause their behavior to change.
3. **Social patterns vary; what is true in one time or place may not hold true in another.** The same laws of physics will apply tomorrow as today, and they hold true all around the world. But human behavior is so variable that there are no universal sociological laws.
4. **Because sociologists are part of the social world they study, they can never be 100 percent value-free when conducting social research.** Barring a laboratory mishap, chemists are rarely personally affected by what goes on in their test tubes. But sociologists live in their "test tube," the society they study. Therefore, social scientists may find it difficult to control—or even to recognize—personal values that may distort their work.

research orientations

positivist sociology the study of society based on systematic observation of social behavior

interpretive sociology the study of society that focuses on discovering the meanings people attach to their social world

critical sociology the study of society that focuses on the need for social change

SUMMING UP

Three Research Orientations in Sociology

	Positivist Sociology	Interpretive Sociology	Critical Sociology
What is reality?	Society is an orderly system. There is an objective reality "out there."	Society is ongoing interaction. People construct reality as they attach meanings to their behavior.	Society is patterns of inequality. Reality is that some categories of people dominate others.
How do we conduct research?	Using a scientific orientation, the researcher carefully observes behavior, gathering empirical, ideally quantitative, data. Researcher tries to be a neutral observer.	Seeking to look "deeper" than outward behavior, the researcher focuses on subjective meaning. The researcher gathers qualitative data, discovering the subjective sense people make of their world. Researcher is a participant.	Seeking to go beyond positivism's focus on studying the world as it is, the researcher is guided by politics and uses research as a strategy to bring about desired social change. Researcher is an activist.
Corresponding theoretical approach	Structural-functional approach	Symbolic-interaction approach	Social-conflict approach

Interpretive Sociology

Not all sociologists agree that science is the only way—or even the best way—to study human society. This is because, unlike planets or other elements of the natural world, humans do not simply move around as objects in ways that can be measured. Even more important, people are active creatures who attach meaning to their behavior, meaning that cannot be directly observed.

Therefore, sociologists have developed a second research orientation, known as **interpretive sociology,** *the study of society that focuses on the meanings people attach to their social world.* Max Weber, the pioneer of this framework, argued that the proper focus of sociology is *interpretation,* or understanding the meaning that people create in their everyday lives.

The Importance of Meaning

Interpretive sociology does not reject science completely, but it does change the focus of research. Interpretive sociology differs from positivist sociology in four ways. First, positivist sociology focuses on actions—on what people do—because that is what we can observe directly. Interpretive sociology, by contrast, focuses on people's understanding of their actions and their surroundings. Second, positivist sociology claims that objective reality exists "out there," but interpretive sociology counters that reality is subjective, constructed by people in the course of their everyday lives. Third, positivist sociology tends to favor *quantitative* data—numerical measurements of people's behavior—while interpretive sociology favors *qualitative* data, or researchers' perceptions of how people understand their world. Fourth, the positivist orientation is best suited to research in a laboratory, where investigators stand back and take careful measurements. On the other hand, the interpretive orientation claims that we learn more by interacting with people, focusing on subjective meaning, and learning how they make sense of their everyday lives. This type of research is best carried out in a natural or everyday setting.

Weber's Concept of *Verstehen*

Max Weber believed the key to interpretive sociology lay in *Verstehen* (pronounced "fair-SHTAY-in"), the German word for "understanding." The interpretive sociologist does not just observe *what* people do but also tries to understand *why* they do it. The thoughts and feelings of subjects, which scientists tend to dismiss because they are difficult to measure, are the focus of the interpretive sociologist's attention.

Critical Sociology

Like the interpretive orientation, critical sociology developed in reaction to the limitations of positivist sociology. In this case, however, the problem involves the central principle of scientific research: objectivity.

Positivist sociology holds that reality is "out there" and the researcher's task is to study and document how society works. But Karl Marx, who founded the critical orientation, rejected the idea that society exists as a "natural" system with a fixed order. To assume that society is somehow "fixed," he claimed, is the same as saying that society cannot be changed. Positivist sociology, from this point of view, ends up supporting the status quo. **Critical sociology,** by contrast, is *the study of society that focuses on the need for social change.*

Imagine that you are a positivist sociologist. How might you criticize critical sociology? Now imagine that you are a critical sociologist. How might you criticize positivist sociology?

gender the personal traits and social positions that members of a society attach to being female or male

The Importance of Change

Rather than asking the scientific question "How does society work?" critical sociologists ask moral and political questions, such as "Should society exist in its present form?" Their answer to this question, typically, is that it should not. Critical sociology does not reject science completely—Marx (like critical sociologists today) used scientific method to learn about inequality. But critical sociology does reject the positivist claim that researchers should try to be "objective" and limit their work to studying the status quo.

One recent account of this orientation, echoing Marx, claims that the point of sociology is "not just to research the social world but to change it in the direction of democracy and social justice" (Feagin & Hernán, 2001:1). In making value judgments about how society should be improved, critical sociology rejects Weber's goal that researchers be value-free and emphasizes instead that they should be social activists in pursuit of greater social equality.

Sociologists using the critical orientation seek to change not just society but the character of research itself. They often identify personally with their research subjects and encourage them to help decide what to study and how to do the work. Typically, researchers and subjects use their findings to provide a voice for less powerful people and to advance the political goal of a more equal society (Hess, 1999; Feagin & Hernán, 2001; Perrucci, 2001).

Sociology as Politics

Positivist sociologists object to taking sides in this way, charging that critical sociology (whether feminist, Marxist, or of some other critical orientation) becomes political, lacks objectivity, and cannot correct for its own biases. Critical sociologists reply that *all* research is political or biased—either it calls for change or it does not; sociologists thus have no choice about their work being political, but they can choose *which* positions to support.

Critical sociology is an activist approach that ties knowledge to action and seeks not just to understand the world as it exists but also to improve it. Generally speaking, positivist sociology appeals to researchers with nonpolitical or more conservative political views; critical sociology appeals to those whose politics range from liberal to radical left.

If you ask only male subjects about their attitudes or actions, you may be able to support conclusions about "men" but not more generally about "people." What would a researcher have to do to ensure that research data support conclusions about all of society?

Research Orientations and Theory

Is there a link between research orientations and sociological theory? There is no precise connection, but each of the three research orientations—positivist, interpretive. and critical—does stand closer to one of the theoretical approaches. The positivist orientation is linked to the structural-functional approach (because both are concerned with understanding society as it is), interpretive sociology to the symbolic-interaction approach (because both focus on the meanings people attach to their social world), and critical sociology to the social-conflict approach (because both seek to reduce social inequality). The Summing Up table provides a quick review of the differences among the three research orientations. Many sociologists favor one orientation over another; however, because each provides useful insights, it is a good idea to become familiar with all three (Gamson, 1999).

Gender and Research

Sociologists also know that research is affected by **gender,** *the personal traits and social positions that members of a society attach to being female or male.* Margrit Eichler (1988) identifies five ways in which gender can shape research:

1. **Androcentricity.** Androcentricity (literally, "focus on the male") refers to approaching an issue from a male perspective.

SEEING SOCIOLOGY in Everyday Life

Think of three research topics about U.S. society that might be affected by the gender of the researcher. In each case, explain why.

research method a systematic plan for doing research

experiment a research method for investigating cause and effect under highly controlled conditions

Sometimes researchers act as if only men's activities are important, ignoring what women do. For years, researchers studying occupations focused on the paid work of men and overlooked the housework and child care traditionally performed by women. Research that seeks to understand human behavior cannot ignore half of humanity.

Gynocentricity—seeing the world from a female perspective—can also limit good sociological investigation. However, in our male-dominated society, this problem arises less often.

2. **Overgeneralizing.** This problem occurs when researchers use data drawn from people of only one sex to support conclusions about "humanity" or "society." Gathering information by talking to only male students and then drawing conclusions about an entire campus would be an example of overgeneralizing.
3. **Gender blindness.** Failing to consider gender at all is known as gender blindness. As is evident throughout this book, the lives of men and women differ in countless ways. A study of growing old in the United States might suffer from gender blindness if it overlooked the fact that most elderly men live with their wives but elderly women typically live alone.
4. **Double standards.** Researchers must be careful not to distort what they study by judging men and women differently. For example, a family researcher who labels a couple as "man and wife" may define the man as the "head of the household" and treat him as important while assuming that the woman simply plays a supporting role.
5. **Interference.** Another way gender can distort a study is if a subject reacts to the sex of the researcher, interfering with the research operation. While studying a small community in Sicily, for instance, Maureen Giovannini (1992) found that many men treated her as a woman rather than as a researcher. Some thought it was wrong for an unmarried woman to speak privately with a man. Others denied Giovannini access to places they considered off-limits to women.

There is nothing wrong with focusing research on people of one sex or the other. But all sociologists, as well as people who read their work, should be mindful of how gender can affect an investigation.

Research Ethics

Like all researchers, sociologists must be aware that research can harm as well as help subjects or communities. For this reason, the American Sociological Association (ASA)—the major professional association of sociologists in North America—has established formal guidelines for conducting research (1997).

Sociologists must try to be skillful and fair-minded in their work. They must disclose all research findings without omitting significant data. They should make their results available to other sociologists who may want to conduct a similar study.

Sociologists must also make sure that the subjects taking part in a research project are not harmed, and they must stop their work right away if they suspect that any subject is at risk of harm. Researchers are also required to protect the privacy of anyone involved in a research project, even if they come under pressure from authorities, such as the police or the courts, to release confidential information. Researchers must also get the *informed consent* of participants, which means that the subjects must understand the responsibilities and risks that the research involves before agreeing to take part.

Another guideline concerns funding. Sociologists must reveal in their published results the sources of all financial support. They must avoid accepting money from a source if there is any possibility of a conflict of interest. For example, researchers must never accept funding from any organization that seeks to influence the research results for its own purposes.

The federal government also plays a part in research ethics. Colleges and universities that seek federal funding for research involving human subjects must have an *institutional review board* (IRB) to review grant applications and ensure that research will not violate ethical standards.

Finally, there are global dimensions to research ethics. Before beginning research in another country, an investigator must become familiar enough with that society to understand what people *there* are likely to regard as a violation of privacy or a source of personal danger. In a diverse society such as the United States, the same rule applies to studying people whose cultural background differs from your own. The Thinking About Diversity box offers some tips on the sensitivity outsiders should apply when studying Hispanic communities.

Methods of Sociological Research

A **research method** is *a systematic plan for doing research.* Four commonly used methods of sociological investigation are experiments, surveys, participant observation, and the use of existing data. None is better or worse than any other. Rather, just as a carpenter selects a particular tool for a specific task, researchers select a method—or mix several methods—according to whom they want to study and what they wish to learn.

Testing a Hypothesis: The Experiment

The **experiment** is *a research method for investigating cause and effect under highly controlled conditions.* Experiments closely follow the logic of science, and experimental research is typically *explanatory,* asking not just what happens but also why. In most cases, researchers create

hypothesis a statement of possible relationship between two (or more) variables

THINKING ABOUT DIVERSITY: RACE, CLASS, & GENDER

Studying the Lives of Hispanics

JORGE: If you are going to include Latinos in your research, you need to learn a little about their culture.

MARK: I'm interviewing lots of different families. What's special about interviewing Latinos?

JORGE: Sit down and I'll tell you a few things. . . .

Because U.S. society is racially, ethnically, and religiously diverse, all of us have to work with people who differ from ourselves. The same is true of sociologists. Learning, in advance, the ways of life of any category of people can ease the research process and ensure that there will be no hard feelings when the work is finished.

Gerardo Marín and Barbara Van Oss Marín (1991) have identified five areas of concern in conducting research with Hispanic people:

1. **Be careful with terms.** The Maríns point out that the term "Hispanic" is a label of convenience used by the U.S. Census Bureau. Few people of Spanish descent think of themselves as "Hispanic" or "Latino"; most identify with a particular country (generally, with a Latin American nation, such as Mexico or Argentina, or with Spain).
2. **Be aware of cultural differences.** By and large, the United States is individualistic and competitive. Many Hispanics, by contrast, place more value on cooperation and community. An outsider may judge the behavior of a Hispanic subject as conformist or overly trusting when in fact the person is simply trying to be helpful. Researchers should also realize that Hispanic respondents might agree with a particular statement merely out of politeness.
3. **Anticipate family dynamics.** Generally speaking, Hispanic cultures have strong family loyalties. Asking subjects to reveal information about another family member may make them uncomfortable or even angry. The Maríns add that in the home, a researcher's request to speak privately with a Hispanic woman may provoke suspicion or outright disapproval from her husband or father.
4. **Take your time.** Spanish cultures, the Maríns explain, tend to place the quality of relationships above simply getting a job done. A non-Hispanic researcher who tries to hurry an interview with a Hispanic family out of a desire not to delay the family's dinner may be considered rude for not proceeding at a more sociable and relaxed pace.
5. **Think about personal space.** Finally, Hispanics typically maintain closer physical contact than many non-Hispanics. Thus researchers who seat themselves across the room from their subjects may seem standoffish. Researchers might also wrongly label Hispanics as "pushy" if they move closer than non-Hispanic people find comfortable.

Of course, Hispanics differ among themselves just as people in any category do, and these generalizations apply to some more than to others. But investigators should be aware of cultural dynamics when carrying out any research, especially in the United States, where hundreds of distinctive categories of people make up our multicultural society.

PhotoEdit Inc./Tony Freeman

WHAT DO YOU THINK?

1. Give a specific example of damage to a study that might take place if researchers are not sensitive to the culture of their subjects.
2. What do researchers need to do to avoid the kinds of problems noted in this box?
3. Discuss the research process with classmates from various cultural backgrounds. In what ways are the concerns raised by people of different cultural backgrounds similar? In what ways do they differ?

an experiment to test a **hypothesis,** *a statement of a possible relationship between two (or more) variables.* A hypothesis typically takes the form of an *if-then* statement: *If* this particular thing were to happen, *then* that particular thing will result.

An experiment gathers the evidence needed to reject or not to reject the hypothesis in four steps: (1) State which variable is the *independent variable* (the "cause" of the change) and which is the *dependent variable* (the "effect," the thing that is changed). (2) Measure the initial value of the dependent variable. (3) Expose the dependent variable to the independent variable (the "cause" or "treatment"). (4) Measure the dependent variable again to see what change, if any, took place. If the expected change took place, the experiment supports the hypothesis; if not, the hypothesis must be modified.

But a change in the dependent variable could be due to something other than the supposed cause. (Think back to our discussion of spurious correlations.) To be certain that they identify the correct

Hawthorne effect a change in a subject's behavior caused simply by the awareness of being studied

SEEING SOCIOLOGY in Everyday Life

How might Zimbardo's findings help explain the abuse of Iraqi prisoners by U.S. soldiers in the Abu Ghraib prison?

cause, researchers carefully control other factors that might affect the outcome of the experiment. Such control is easiest in a laboratory, a setting specially constructed to neutralize outside influences.

Another strategy to gain control is dividing subjects into an *experimental group* and a *control group.* Early in the study, the researcher measures the dependent variable for subjects in both groups but later exposes only the experimental group to the independent variable or treatment. (The control group typically gets a *placebo,* a treatment that the members of the group think is the same but really has no effect on the experiment.) Then the investigator measures the subjects in both groups again. Any factor occurring during the course of the research that influences people in the experimental group (say, a news event) would do the same to those in the control group, thus controlling or "washing out" the factor. By comparing the before and after measurements of the two groups, a researcher can learn how much of the change is due to the independent variable.

The Hawthorne Effect

Researchers need to be aware that subjects' behavior may change simply because they are getting special attention, as one classic experiment revealed. In the late 1930s, the Western Electric Company hired researchers to investigate worker productivity in its Hawthorne factory near Chicago (Roethlisberger & Dickson, 1939). One experiment tested the hypothesis that increasing the available lighting would raise worker output. First, researchers measured worker productivity or output (the dependent variable). Then they increased the lighting (the independent variable) and measured output a second time. Productivity had gone up, a result that supported the hypothesis. But when the research team later turned the lighting back down, productivity increased again. What was going on? In time, the researchers realized that the employees were working harder (even if they could not see as well) simply because people were paying attention to them and measuring their output. From this research, social scientists coined the term **Hawthorne effect** to refer to *a change in a subject's behavior caused simply by the awareness of being studied.*

Illustration of an Experiment: The "Stanford County Prison"

Prisons can be violent settings, but is this due simply to the "bad" people who end up there? Or as Philip Zimbardo suspected, does the prison itself somehow generate violent behavior? This question led Zimbardo to devise a fascinating experiment, which he called the "Stanford County Prison" (Zimbardo, 1972; Haney, Banks, & Zimbardo, 1973).

Zimbardo thought that once inside a prison, even emotionally healthy people are likely to engage in violence. Thus Zimbardo treated the *prison setting* as the independent variable capable of causing *violence,* the dependent variable.

To test this hypothesis, Zimbardo's research team constructed a realistic-looking "prison" in the basement of the psychology building on the campus of California's Stanford University. Then they placed an ad in the local newspaper, offering to pay young men to help with a two-week research project. To each of the seventy who responded they administered a series of physical and psychological tests and then selected the healthiest twenty-four.

The next step was to randomly assign half the men to be "prisoners" and half to be "guards." The plan called for the guards and prisoners to spend the next two weeks in the mock prison. The prisoners began their part of the experiment soon afterward when the city police "arrested" them at their homes. After searching and handcuffing the men, the police drove them to the local police station, where they were fingerprinted. Then police transported their captives to the Stanford prison, where the guards locked them up. Zimbardo started his video camera rolling and watched to see what would happen next.

The experiment turned into more than anyone had bargained for. Both guards and prisoners soon became embittered and hostile toward one another. Guards humiliated the prisoners by assigning them tasks such as cleaning out toilets with their bare hands. The prisoners resisted and insulted the guards. Within four days, the researchers removed five prisoners who displayed "extreme emotional depression, crying, rage and acute anxiety" (Haney, Banks, & Zimbardo, 1973:81). Before the end of the first week, the situation had become so bad that the researchers had to cancel the experiment. Zimbardo explains:

> The ugliest, most base, pathological side of human nature surfaced. We were horrified because we saw some boys (guards) treat others as if they were despicable animals, taking pleasure in cruelty, while other boys (prisoners) became servile, dehumanized robots who thought only of escape, of their own individual survival and of their mounting hatred for the guards. (Zimbardo, 1972:4)

The events that unfolded at the "Stanford County Prison" supported Zimbardo's hypothesis that prison violence is rooted in the social character of jails themselves, not in the personalities of guards and prisoners. This finding raises questions about our society's prisons, suggesting the need for basic reform. Notice, too, that this experiment shows the potential of research to threaten the physical and mental well-being of subjects. Such dangers are not always as obvious as they were in this case. Therefore, researchers must carefully consider the potential harm to subjects at all stages of their work and halt any study, as Zimbardo did, if subjects suffer harm of any kind.

CRITICAL REVIEW In carrying out the "Stanford County Prison" study, the researchers chose to do an experiment because they were interested in testing a hypothesis. In this case, Zimbardo and his colleagues wanted to find out if the prison setting itself (rather than the personalities of individual guards and

population the people who are the focus of research

sample a part of a population that represents the whole

SEEING SOCIOLOGY in Everyday Life

Suggest a research topic that might lead a researcher to use a questionnaire. What about a topic that would call for interviews?

prisoners) is the cause of prison violence. The fact that the "prison" erupted in violence—even using "healthy" people—supports their hypothesis.

CHECK YOUR LEARNING What was Zimbardo's conclusion? How might Zimbardo's findings help explain the abuse of Iraqi prisoners by U.S. soliders in the Abu Ghraib prison in Iraq?

Asking Questions: Survey Research

A **survey** is *a research method in which subjects respond to a series of statements or questions on a questionnaire or in an interview.* The most widely used of all research methods, surveys are especially good for studying what cannot be observed directly, such as political attitudes or religious beliefs. Sometimes surveys provide clues about cause and effect, but typically they yield *descriptive* findings, painting a picture of people's views on some issue.

Population and Sample

A survey targets some **population,** *the people who are the focus of research.* Lois Benjamin, in her study of racism described at the beginning of this chapter, studied a select population—talented African Americans. Other surveys, such as political polls that predict election results, treat every adult in the country as the population.

Obviously, contacting millions of people is impossible for even the best-funded and most patient researcher. Fortunately, there is an easier way that yields accurate results: Researchers collect data from a **sample,** *a part of a population that represents the whole.* Benjamin chose 100 talented African Americans as her sample. National political polls typically survey a sample of about 1,000 people.

Everyone uses the logic of sampling all the time. If you look at students sitting near you and notice five or six heads nodding off, you might conclude that the class finds the day's lecture dull. In reaching this conclusion, you are making a judgment about *all* the people in the class (the population) from observing *some* of your classmates (the sample).

But how can researchers be sure that a sample really represents the entire population? One way is through *random sampling,* in which researchers draw a sample from the population at random so that every person in the population has an equal chance of being selected. The mathematical laws of probability dictate that a random sample is likely to represent the population as a whole. Selecting a random sample usually involves listing everyone in the population and using a computer to make random selections to make up the sample.

Beginning researchers sometimes make the mistake of assuming that "randomly" walking up to people on the street or in a mall produces a sample that is representative of the entire city. But this technique does *not* produce a random sample because it does not give every person an equal chance to be included in the study. For one thing, any street or mall, whether in a rich neighborhood or near a college campus, contains more of some kinds of people than others. The fact that some people are more approachable than others is another source of bias.

Although constructing a good sample is no simple task, it offers a considerable savings in time and expense. We are spared the tedious work of contacting everyone in a population, yet we can obtain essentially the same results.

Using Questionnaires

Selecting subjects is just the first step in carrying out a survey. Also needed is a plan for asking questions and recording answers. Most surveys use a questionnaire for this purpose.

A **questionnaire** is *a series of written questions a researcher presents to subjects.* One type of questionnaire provides not only the questions but also a selection of fixed responses (similar to a multiple-choice examination). This *closed-ended format* makes it fairly easy to analyze the results, but by narrowing the range of responses, it can also distort the findings. For example, Frederick Lorenz and Brent Bruton (1996) found that the number of hours per week students say they study for a college course depends on the options offered to them on

Philip G. Zimbardo, Inc./Philip G. Zimbardo, Inc.

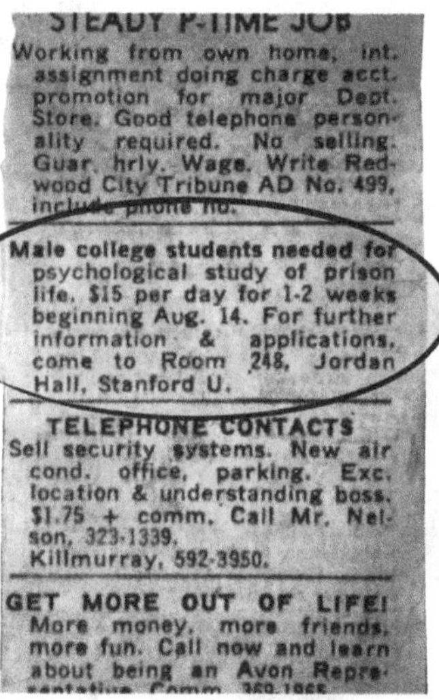

STEADY P-TIME JOB
Working from own home, int. assignment doing charge acct. promotion for major Dept. Store. Good telephone personality required. No selling. Guar. hrly. Wage. Write Redwood City Tribune AD No. 499, include phone no.

Male college students needed for psychological study of prison life. $15 per day for 1-2 weeks beginning Aug. 14. For further information & applications, come to Room 248, Jordan Hall, Stanford U.

TELEPHONE CONTACTS
Sell security systems. New air cond. office, parking. Exc. location & understanding boss. $1.75 + comm. Call Mr. Nelson, 323-1339. Killmurray, 592-3950.

GET MORE OUT OF LIFE!
More money, more friends, more fun. Call now and learn about being an Avon Representative.

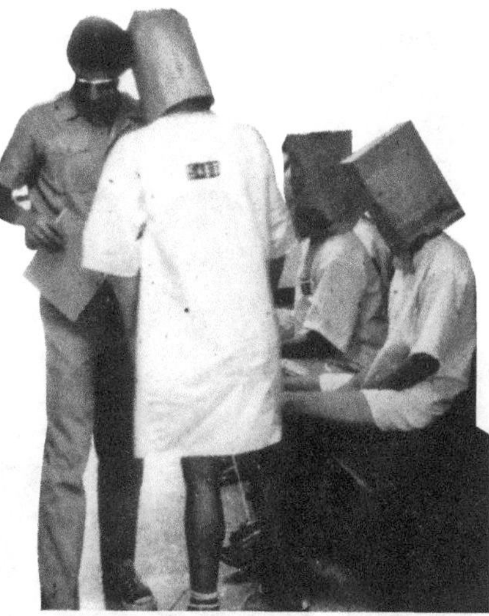

Philip Zimbardo's research helps explain why violence is a common element in our society's prisons. At the same time, his work demonstrates the dangers that sociological investigation poses for subjects and the need for investigators to observe ethical standards that protect the welfare of people who participate in research.

MAKING THE GRADE

A *population* is all the people we want to learn about; you can collect data from an entire population if it is small enough (say, campus sociology majors). If the population is too large, select a *sample*, which will give good results as long as it is representative of the entire population.

survey a research method in which subjects respond to a series of statements or questions on a questionnaire or in an interview

questionnaire a series of written questions a researcher presents to her subjects

interview a series of questions a researcher asks respondents in person

the questionnaire. When the researchers presented students with options ranging from one hour or less to nine hours or more, 75 percent said that they studied four hours or less per week. But when subjects in a comparable group were given choices ranging from four hours or less to twelve hours or longer (a higher figure that suggests students should study more), they suddenly became more studious; only 34 percent reported that they studied four hours or less each week.

A second type of questionnaire, using an *open-ended format,* allows subjects to respond freely, expressing various shades of opinion. The drawback of this approach is that the researcher has to make sense out of what can be a very wide range of answers.

The researcher must also decide how to present questions to subjects. Most often, researchers use a *self-administered survey,* mailing or e-mailing questionnaires to respondents and asking them to complete the form and send it back. Since no researcher is present when subjects read the questionnaire, it must be both inviting and clearly written. *Pretesting* a self-administered questionnaire with a small number of people before sending it to the entire sample can prevent the costly problem of finding out—too late—that instructions or questions were confusing.

Using the mail or e-mail allows a researcher to contact a large number of people over a wide geographic area at minimal expense. But many people treat such questionnaires as junk mail, so typically no more than half are completed and returned (in 2000, just two-thirds of people returned U.S. Census Bureau forms). Researchers must send follow-up mailings (or, as the Census Bureau does, visit people's homes) to urge reluctant subjects to respond.

Alamy Images Royalty Free/Jupiter Images/Polka Dot

Focus groups are a type of survey in which a small number of people representing a target population are asked for their opinions about some issue or product. Here a sociology professor asks students to evaluate textbooks for use in her introductory class.

Finally, keep in mind that many people are not capable of completing a questionnaire on their own. Young children obviously cannot, nor can many hospital patients or a surprising number of adults who simply lack the required reading and writing skills.

Conducting Interviews

An **interview** is *a series of questions a researcher asks respondents in person.* In a closed-format design, researchers read a question or statement and then ask the subject to select a response from several that are presented. More commonly, however, interviews are open-ended so that subjects can respond as they choose and researchers can probe with follow-up questions. In either case, the researcher must guard against influencing a subject, which can be as easy as raising an eyebrow when a person begins to answer.

Although subjects are more likely to complete a survey if contacted personally by the researcher, interviews have some disadvantages: Tracking people down is costly and takes time, especially if subjects do not live in the same area. Telephone interviews allow far greater "reach," but the impersonality of cold calls by telephone (and reaching answering machines) can lower the response rate.

In both questionnaires and interviews, how a question is worded greatly affects how people answer. For example, when asked during the last presidential campaign if Barack Obama's race would make them less likely to vote for him, only 3 or 4 percent of people said yes. Yet if the question was changed to ask if the United States is ready to elect a black president, then almost 20 percent expressed some doubt. Similarly, if researchers asked U.S. adults if they support our military, a large majority of people said yes. Yet when researchers asked people if they supported what the military was trying to do in Iraq, most said no.

When it comes to survey questions, the exact wording will always affect responses. This is especially true if emotionally loaded language is used. Any words that trigger an emotional response in subjects will sway the results. For instance, using the expression "welfare mothers" rather than "women who receive public assistance" adds an emotional element to a question that encourages people to express a negative attitude.

Another problem is that researchers may confuse respondents by asking a double question, such as "Do you think that the government should reduce the deficit by cutting spending and raising taxes?" The issue here is that a subject could very well agree with one part of the question but not the other, so that forcing a subject to say yes or no distorts the opinion the researcher is trying to measure.

Conducting a good interview means standardizing the technique—treating all subjects in the same way. But this, too, can be problematic. Drawing people out requires establishing rapport, which in turn depends on responding naturally to the particular person

MAKING THE GRADE

In general, questionnaires allow a researcher to collect lots of easily reported information—age, sex, voter participation—from lots of people. Interviews allow researchers to explore in-depth attitudes on a particular topic from a few people.

being interviewed, as you would in a normal conversation. In the end, researchers have to decide where to strike the balance between uniformity and rapport (Lavin & Maynard, 2001).

Illustration of Survey Research: Studying the African American Elite

This chapter began by explaining how Lois Benjamin came to investigate the effects of racism on talented African American men and women. Benjamin suspected that personal achievement did not prevent hostility based on skin color. She believed this because of her own experiences after becoming the first black professor at the University of Tampa. But was she the exception or the rule? To answer this question, Benjamin set out to discover whether—and if so, how—racism affected other successful African Americans.

Benjamin decided to interview subjects rather than distribute a questionnaire because she wanted to talk with her subjects, ask follow-up questions, and pursue topics that she could not anticipate. A second reason Benjamin favored interviews over questionnaires is that racism is a sensitive topic. A supportive investigator can make it easier for subjects to respond to painful questions more freely (Bergen, 1993).

Choosing to conduct interviews made it necessary to limit the number of people in the study. Benjamin settled for a sample of 100 men and women. Even this small number kept Benjamin busy for more than two years as she scheduled interviews, traveled all over the country, and met with her respondents. She spent two more years analyzing the tapes of her interviews, deciding what the hours of talk told her about racism, and writing up her results.

In selecting her sample, Benjamin first considered using all the people listed in *Who's Who in Black America*. But she rejected this idea in favor of starting out with people she knew and asking them to suggest others. This strategy is called *snowball sampling* because the number of individuals included grows rapidly over time.

Snowball sampling is an easy way to do research—we begin with familiar people who introduce us to their friends and colleagues. But snowball sampling rarely produces a sample that is representative of the larger population. Benjamin's sample probably contained many like-minded individuals, and it was certainly biased toward people willing to talk openly about race and prejudice. She understood these problems, and she did what she could to make her sample diverse in terms of sex, age, and region of the country. The Thinking About Diversity box presents a statistical profile of Benjamin's respondents and some tips on how to read tables.

Benjamin based all her interviews on a series of questions with an open-ended format so that her subjects could say whatever they wished. As usually happens, the interviews took place in a wide range of settings. She met subjects in offices (hers or theirs), in hotel rooms, and in cars. In each case, Benjamin tape-recorded the conversation, which lasted from two-and-one-half to three hours, so that she would not be distracted by taking notes.

As research ethics demand, Benjamin offered full anonymity to participants. Even so, many—including notables such as Vernon E. Jordan Jr. (former president of the National Urban League) and Yvonne Walker-Taylor (first woman president of Wilberforce University)—were used to being in the public eye and allowed Benjamin to use their names.

What surprised Benjamin most about her research was how eager many people were to be interviewed. These normally busy men and women seemed to go out of their way to contribute to her project. Benjamin reports, too, that once the interviews were under way, many became very emotional—at some point in the conversation, about 40 of her 100 subjects cried. For them, apparently, the research provided a chance to release feelings long kept inside. How did Benjamin respond? She reports that she cried right along with them.

Of the research orientations described earlier in the chapter, you will see that Benjamin's study fits best under interpretive sociology (she explored what race meant to her subjects) and critical sociology (she undertook the study partly to document that racial prejudice still exists). Many of her subjects reported fearing that race might someday undermine their success, and others spoke of a race-based "glass ceiling" preventing them from reaching the highest positions in our society. Benjamin concluded that despite the improving social standing of African Americans, black people in the United States still feel the sting of racial hostility.

CRITICAL REVIEW Professor Benjamin chose the survey as her method because she wanted to ask a lot of questions and gather information from her subjects. Certainly, some of the information she collected could have been done using a questionnaire. But she decided to carry out interviews because she was dealing with a complex and sensitive topic. Interacting with her subjects, one on one, for several hours, she could put them at ease, discuss personal matters, and ask them follow-up questions.

CHECK YOUR LEARNING Do you think this research could have been carried out by a white or Asian American sociologist? Why or why not?

In the Field: Participant Observation

Lois Benjamin's research demonstrates that sociological investigation takes place not only in laboratories but also "in the field," that is, where people carry on their everyday lives. The most widely used strategy for field study is **participant observation,** *a research method in which*

MAKING THE GRADE

In her study of the African American elite, Lois Benjamin made great effort to explain who her subjects were. Always consider this question when reading anyone's research results.

THINKING ABOUT DIVERSITY: RACE, CLASS, & GENDER

Using Tables in Research: Analyzing Benjamin's African American Elite

Say you want to present a lot of information about a diverse population. How do you do it quickly and easily? The answer is by using a *table*. A table provides a lot of information in a small amount of space, so learning to read tables can increase your reading efficiency. When you spot a table, look first at the title to see what information it contains. The title of the table presented here provides a profile of the 100 subjects participating in Lois Benjamin's research. Across the top of the table, you will see eight variables that describe these men and women. Reading down each column, note the categories within each variable; the percentages in each column add up to 100.

Starting at the top left, we see that Benjamin's sample was mostly men (63 percent, versus 37 percent women). In terms of age, most of the respondents (68 percent) were in the middle stage of life, and most grew up in a predominantly black community in the South or in the North or Midwest region of the United States.

These individuals are indeed a professional elite. Notice that half have earned either a doctorate (32 percent) or a medical or law degree (17 percent). Given their extensive education (and Benjamin's own position as a professor), we should not be surprised that the largest share (35 percent) work in academic institutions. In terms of income, these are wealthy individuals, with most (64 percent) earning more than $50,000 annually back in 1990 (a salary that only 37 percent of full-time workers make even today).

Finally, we see that these 100 individuals are generally left-of-center in their political views. In part, this reflects their extensive schooling (which encourages progressive thinking) and the tendency of academics to fall on the liberal side of the political spectrum.

WHAT DO YOU THINK?

1. Why are statistical data, such as those in this table, an efficient way to convey a lot of information?
2. Looking at the table, can you determine how long it took most people to become part of this elite? Explain your answer.
3. Do you see any ways in which this African American elite might differ from a comparable white elite? If so, what are they?

The Talented One Hundred: Lois Benjamin's African American Elite

Sex	Age	Childhood Racial Setting	Childhood Region	Highest Educational Degree	Job Sector	Income	Political Orientation
Male 63%	35 or younger 6%	Mostly black 71%	West 6%	Doctorate 32%	College or university 35%	More than $50,000 64%	Radical left 13%
Female 37%	36 to 54 68%	Mostly white 15%	North or Midwest 32%	Medical or law 17%	Private, for-profit 17%	$35,000 to $50,000 18%	Liberal 38%
	55 or older 26%	Racially mixed 14%	South 38%	Master's 27%	Private, nonprofit 9%	$20,000 to $34,999 12%	Moderate 28%
			Northeast 12%	Bachelor's 13%	Government 22%	Less than $20,000 6%	Conservative 5%
			Other 12%	Less 11%	Self-employed 14%		Depends on issue 14%
					Retired 3%		Unknown 2%
100%	100%	100%	100%	100%	100%	100%	100%

Source: Adapted from Lois Benjamin, *The Black Elite: Facing the Color Line in the Twilight of the Twentieth Century* (Chicago: Nelson-Hall, 1991), p. 276.

investigators systematically observe people while joining them in their routine activities.

This method allows researchers an inside look at social life in any natural setting, from a nightclub to a religious seminary. Sociologists call their account of social life in some setting a *case study*. Cultural anthropologists use participant observation to study other societies, calling this method *fieldwork* and their research results an *ethnography*.

research method a systematic plan for doing research

experiment
a research method for investigating cause and effect under highly controlled conditions

survey
a research method in which subjects respond to a series of statements or questions on a questionnaire or in an interview

participant observation
a research method in which investigators systematically observe people while joining them in their routine activities

use of existing sources

At the beginning of a field study, most investigators do not have a specific hypothesis in mind. In fact, they may not yet realize what the important questions will turn out to be. Thus most field research is *exploratory* and *descriptive.*

As its name suggests, participant observation has two sides. On one hand, getting an insider's look depends on becoming a participant in the setting—"hanging out" with the research subjects and trying to act, think, and even feel the way they do. Compared to experiments and survey research, participant observation has fewer hard-and-fast rules. But it is precisely this flexibility that allows investigators to explore the unfamiliar and adapt to the unexpected.

Unlike other research methods, participant observation may require that the researcher enter the setting not just for a week or two but for months or even years. At the same time, however, the researcher must maintain some distance as an observer, mentally stepping back to record field notes and later to interpret them. Because the investigator must both "play the participant" to win acceptance and gain access to people's lives and "play the observer" to maintain the distance needed for thoughtful analysis, there is an inherent tension in this method. Carrying out the twin roles of insider participant and outsider observer often comes down to a series of careful compromises.

Most sociologists perform participant observation alone, so they—and readers, too—must remember that the results depend on the work of a single person. Participant observation usually falls within interpretive sociology, yielding mostly qualitative data—the researcher's accounts of people's lives and what they think of themselves and the world around them—although researchers sometimes collect some quantitative (numerical) data. From a scientific point of view, participant observation is a "soft" method that relies heavily on personal judgment and lacks scientific rigor. Yet its personal approach is also a strength: Where a high-profile team of sociologists administering formal surveys might disrupt many social settings, a sensitive participant observer can often gain important insight into people's behavior.

The Seeing Sociology in the News article later in this chapter provides a recent example of a sociologist using participant observation to study gang behavior in one of Chicago's toughest housing projects. Next we turn to a classic sociological study using participant observation that took place in Boston many decades earlier.

Illustration of Participant Observation: *Street Corner Society*

Did you ever wonder what everyday life was like in an unfamiliar neighborhood? In the late 1930s, a young graduate student at Harvard University named William Foote Whyte (1914–2000) was fascinated by the lively street life of a nearby, rather rundown section of Boston. His curiosity led him to carry out four years of participant observation in this neighborhood, which he called "Cornerville," and in the process to produce a sociological classic.

At the time, Cornerville was home to first- and second-generation Italian immigrants. Many were poor, and many people living in the rest of Boston considered Cornerville a place to avoid: a poor slum that was home to racketeers. Unwilling to accept easy stereotypes, Whyte set out to discover for himself exactly what kind of life went on in this community. His celebrated book, *Street Corner Society* (1981, orig. 1943), describes Cornerville as a complex community with its own code of values, complex social patterns, and particular social conflicts.

In beginning his investigation, Whyte considered a range of research methods. Should he take questionnaires to one of Cornerville's community centers and ask local people to fill them out? Should he invite members of the community to come to his Harvard office for interviews? It is easy to see that such a formal approach would have gained little cooperation from the local people. Whyte decided, therefore, to set out on his own, working his way into Cornerville life in the hope of coming to understand this rather mysterious place.

Right away, Whyte discovered the challenges of even getting started in field research. After all, an upper-middle-class WASP graduate student from Harvard did not exactly fit into Cornerville life. Even a friendly overture from an outsider could seem pushy and

The Image Works/Michael Doolittle

Participant observation is a method of sociological research that allows a researcher to investigate people as they go about their everyday lives in some "natural" setting. At its best, participant observation makes you a star in your own reality show; but living in what may be a strange setting far from home for months at a time is always challenging.

Seeing SOCIOLOGY in the 

The New York Times

If You Want to Observe 'Em, Join 'Em

By WILLIAM GRIMES
January 16, 2008

On a hot summer day in 1989, Sudhir Venkatesh, a callow sociology student with a ponytail and tie-dyed T-shirt, walked into one of Chicago's toughest housing projects, clipboard in hand, ready to ask residents about their lives. Sample question: "How does it feel to be black and poor?" Suggested answers: "very bad, somewhat bad, neither bad nor good, somewhat good, very good." Actual answers: unprintable.

Mr. Venkatesh got rid of the clipboard and the questionnaire, but not his fascination with life in the Chicago housing projects. He stuck around, befriended a gang leader and for the next decade lived a curious insider-outsider life at the notorious Robert Taylor Homes on the city's South Side, an eye-opening experience he documented in the high-octane *Gang Leader for a Day*. In a bit of bravado Mr. Venkatesh, who now teaches at Columbia, styles himself a "rogue sociologist." Dissatisfied with opinion surveys and statistical analysis as ways to describe the life of the poor, he reverted to the methods of his predecessors at the University of Chicago, who took an ethnographic approach to the study of hobos, hustlers and politicians. Much like a journalist, he observed, asked questions and drew conclusions as he accumulated raw data. . . .

Mr. Venkatesh, reared in the comfortable suburbs of Southern California by Indian parents, crossed the line from observer to participant on more than one occasion as he penetrated deeper into the life of the Black Kings and its local captain, the ruthless, charismatic J. T.

When a rival gang swept by, guns blazing, he dodged bullets and helped drag a gang lieutenant to safety. When local squatters meted out street justice to a crackhead who had beaten a woman in the projects, he got a boot in.

One glorious day J. T. let Mr. Venkatesh get a taste of power and the problems that come with it. He allowed him to make the daily rounds of the platoons under his command—six-man crews that deal in crack cocaine—and try to sort out the petty squabbles and mistakes endemic in a criminal enterprise comprising 250 underpaid, uneducated and violent soldiers.

All this is much better than toting a clipboard. "It was pretty thrilling to have a gang boss calling me up to go hang out with him," wrote Mr. Venkatesh, who ridiculed his own naïveté. . . .

Without question, Mr. Venkatesh was dazzled by J. T. and seduced by the gang life. He maintained enough distance, however, to appraise the information he was given and to build up, through careful observation, a detailed picture of life at the project. He writes what might be called tabloid sociology, but it rests on a solid foundation of data, like records of the gang's finances turned over to him by T-Bone, its treasurer. . . .

The Black Kings, which Mr. Venkatesh observed throughout the 1990s, operated a hugely

---

rude. One night, Whyte dropped in at a local bar, hoping to buy a woman a drink and encourage her to talk about Cornerville. Looking around the room, he could find no woman alone. But then he saw a man sitting down with two women. He walked up to them and asked, "Pardon me. Would you mind if I joined you?" Instantly, he realized his mistake:

> There was a moment of silence while the man stared at me. Then he offered to throw me down the stairs. I assured him that this would not be necessary, and demonstrated as much by walking right out of there without any assistance. (1981:289)

As this incident suggests, gaining entry to a community is the difficult (and sometimes hazardous) first step in field research. "Breaking in" requires patience, quick thinking, and a little luck. Whyte's big break came when he met a young man named "Doc" at a local social service agency. Whyte explained to Doc how hard it was to make friends in Cornerville. Doc responded by taking Whyte under his wing and introducing him to others in the community. With Doc's help, Whyte soon became a neighborhood regular.

Whyte's friendship with Doc illustrates the importance of a *key informant* in field research. Such people not only introduce a researcher to a community but often remain a source of information and help. But using a key informant also has its risks. Because any person has a particular circle of friends, a key informant's guidance is certain to "spin" or bias the study in one way or another. In addition, in the eyes of others, the reputation of the key informant, good or bad, usually rubs off on the investigator. So although a key informant is helpful early on, a participant observer must soon seek a broader range of contacts.

Having entered the Cornerville world, Whyte quickly learned another lesson: A field researcher needs to know when to speak up and when to shut up. One evening, he joined a group discussing neighborhood gambling. Wanting to get the facts straight, Whyte asked innocently, "I suppose the cops were all paid off?"

> The gambler's jaw dropped. He glared at me. Then he denied vehemently that any policeman had been paid off and immediately switched the conversation to another subject. For the rest of that evening I felt very uncomfortable.

The next day, Doc offered some sound advice:

> "Go easy on that 'who,' 'what,' 'why,' 'when,' 'where' stuff, Bill. You ask those questions and people will clam up on you. If people accept you, you can just hang around, and you'll learn the answers in the long run without even having to ask the questions." (1981:303)

In the months and years that followed, Whyte became familiar with life in Cornerville and even married a local woman with whom he would spend the rest of his life. In the process, he learned that the common stereotypes were wrong. In Cornerville, most people worked hard, many were quite successful, and some even boasted of sending children to college. Even today, Whyte's book is a fascinating story of the deeds, dreams, and disappointments of immigrants and their children living in one ethnic community, and it contains the rich detail that can come only from years of participant observation.

profitable drug ring, often selling crack in building lobbies, and extorted protection money from every project resident engaged in economic activity, no matter how trivial: prostitutes, street-corner car mechanics, squatters, home beauticians and even old women selling candy from their apartments to earn an extra $20 a week.

Mr. Venkatesh failed to gauge the feelings of project residents about the Black Kings, probably because he was perceived as part of them and therefore someone to steer clear of. Most residents avoided him . . . or limited their conversation to "a quick hello." . . .

On the other hand, Mr. Venkatesh, through sheer persistence, unraveled a complex, intertwined system of political and economic relationships that made the housing project run in the near-total absence of city services. The police and ambulance crews, in particular, regarded Robert Taylor as a no-go area. . . . Local warlords like J. T. and quasi-political figures like the fearsome Ms. Bailey, a building president who manipulated her connections to the Chicago Housing Authority, held sway. They exacted tribute and dispensed favors. . . .

No one got rich. Mr. Venkatesh was shocked to discover that foot soldiers in the drug operation barely made minimum wage. . . .

Violent, paranoid and manipulative, [J. T.] offered a fascinating study in leadership, and Mr. Venkatesh made the most of his opportunity, trying desperately to maintain some saving skepticism. Smitten, he never quite got over his initial attraction, even when J. T. double-crossed him, ingeniously, by encouraging him to carry out a detailed study of the housing project's economy, whose results he used to tighten his hold on the residents.

Overnight Mr. Venkatesh became a pariah. A sympathetic prostitute told him . . ., "Just don't take the stairs when you leave, 'cause if you get caught there, they may never find your body." . . .

. . . The City of Chicago began demolishing the Robert Taylor Homes soon after [Mr. Venkatesh] completed his research.

WHAT DO YOU THINK?

1. Why do you think Sudhir Venkatesh chose to use participant observation to do this research? What advantages and disadvantages can you see in his choice?
2. What special dangers did this research pose to the researcher?
3. From this article, did you learn anything about gang life that surprised you? If so, what?

CRITICAL REVIEW To study the community he called "Cornerville," William Whyte chose participant observation. This was a good choice because he did not have a specific hypothesis to test, nor did he know at the outset exactly what the questions were. By moving into this community and living there for several years, Whyte was able to come to know the place and to paint a complex picture of social life there.

CHECK YOUR LEARNING Give an example of a topic for sociological research that would be best studied using (1) an experiment, (2) a survey, and (3) participant observation.

Using Available Data: Existing Sources

Not all research requires investigators to collect their own data. Sometimes sociologists analyze existing sources, data already collected by others.

The most widely used statistics in social science are gathered by government agencies. The U.S. Census Bureau continuously updates a wide range of data about the U.S. population. Comparable data on Canada are available from Statistics Canada, a branch of that nation's government. For international data, there are various publications of the United Nations and the World Bank. In short, data about the whole world are as close as your library or the Internet.

Using available data, whether government statistics or the findings of individual researchers, saves time and money. This approach has special appeal to sociologists with low budgets. For anyone, however, government data are generally more extensive and more accurate than what most researchers could obtain on their own.

But using existing data has problems of its own. For one thing, available data may not exist in the exact form needed. For example, you may be able to find the average salary paid to professors at your school but not separate figures for the amounts paid to women and to men. Further, there are always questions about the meaning and accuracy of work done by others. For example, in his classic study of suicide, Emile Durkheim soon discovered that there was no way to know whether a death classified as a suicide was really an accident or vice versa. In addition, various agencies use different procedures and categories in collecting data, so comparisons may be difficult. In the end, then, using existing data is a little like shopping for a used car: There are plenty of bargains out there, but you have to shop carefully.

Illustration of the Use of Existing Sources: A Tale of Two Cities

Why might one city have been home to many famous people and another's history show hardly any famous people at all? To those of us living in the present, historical data offer a key to unlocking secrets of the past. The award-winning study *Puritan Boston and Quaker Philadelphia*, by E. Digby Baltzell (1979), is a good example of how a researcher can use available data to do historical research.

This story begins with Baltzell making a chance visit to Bowdoin College in Maine. As he walked into the college library, he saw up

MAKING THE GRADE

Using existing sources—especially in clever and creative ways, as Baltzell did—is the key to conducting historical research in sociology.

on the wall three large portraits—of the celebrated author Nathaniel Hawthorne, the famous poet Henry Wadsworth Longfellow, and Franklin Pierce, the fourteenth president of the United States. He soon learned that all three men were members of the same class at Bowdoin, graduating in 1825. How could it be, Baltzell wondered, that this small college had graduated more famous people in a single year than his own, much bigger University of Pennsylvania had graduated in its entire history? To answer this question, Baltzell was soon paging through historical documents to see whether New England had really produced more famous people than his native Pennsylvania.

What were Baltzell's data? He turned to the *Dictionary of American Biography,* twenty volumes profiling more than 13,000 outstanding men and women in fields such as politics, law, and the arts. The dictionary told Baltzell *who* was great, and he realized that the longer the biography, the more important the person is thought to be.

By the time Baltzell had identified the seventy-five individuals with the longest biographies, he saw a striking pattern. Massachusetts had the most by far, with twenty-one of the seventy-five top achievers. The New England states, combined, claimed thirty-one of the entries. By contrast, Pennsylvania could boast of only two, and all the states in the Middle Atlantic region had just twelve. Looking more closely, Baltzell discovered that most of New England's great achievers had grown up in and around the city of Boston. Again, in stark contrast, almost no one of comparable standing came from his own Philadelphia, a city with many more people than Boston.

What could explain this remarkable pattern? Baltzell drew inspiration from the German sociologist Max Weber (1958, orig. 1904–05), who argued that a region's record of achievement was influenced by its major religious beliefs. In the religious differences between Boston and Philadelphia, Baltzell found the answer to his puzzle. Boston was originally a Puritan settlement, founded by people who highly valued the pursuit of excellence and public achievement. Philadelphia, by contrast, was settled by Quakers, who believed in equality and avoided public notice.

Both the Puritans and the Quakers were fleeing religious persecution in England, but the two religions produced quite different cultural patterns. Boston's Puritans saw humans as innately sinful, so they built a rigid society in which family, church, and school regulated people's behavior. The Puritans celebrated hard work as a means of glorifying God and viewed public success as a reassuring sign of God's blessing. In short, Puritanism fostered a disciplined life in which people both sought and respected achievement.

Philadelphia's Quakers, by contrast, built their way of life on the belief that all human beings are basically good. They saw little need for strong social institutions to "save" people from sinfulness. They believed in equality, so that even those who became rich considered themselves no better than anyone else. Thus rich and poor alike lived modestly and discouraged one another from standing out by seeking fame or running for public office.

In Baltzell's sociological imagination, Boston and Philadelphia took the form of two social "test tubes": Puritanism was poured into one, Quakerism into the other. Centuries later, we can see that different "chemical reactions" occurred in each case. The two belief systems led to different attitudes toward personal achievement, which in turn shaped the history of each region. Today, we can see that Boston's Kennedys (despite being Catholic) are only one of that city's many families who exemplify the Puritan pursuit of recognition and leadership. By contrast, there has never been even one family with such public stature in the entire history of Philadelphia.

Baltzell's study uses scientific logic, but it also illustrates the interpretive approach by showing how people understood their world. His research reminds us that sociological investigation often involves mixing research orientations to fit a particular problem.

CRITICAL REVIEW The main reason Baltzell chose to use existing sources is that this is a good way to learn about history. The *Dictionary of American Biography* offers a great deal of information about people who lived long ago and obviously are not available for an interview. At the same time, existing sources were not created with the purpose of answering a modern-day sociologist's questions. For this reason, using such documents requires a critical eye and a good deal of creative thinking.

CHECK YOUR LEARNING What other questions about life in the past might you wish to answer using existing sources? What sources might you use to find the answers?

The Summing Up table provides a quick review of the four major methods of sociological investigation. We now turn to our final consideration: the link between research results and sociological theory.

The Interplay of Theory and Method

No matter how sociologists collect their data, they have to turn facts into meaning by building theory. They do this in two ways: inductive logical thought and deductive logical thought.

Inductive logical thought is *reasoning that transforms specific observations into general theory.* In this mode, a researcher's thinking runs from the specific to the general and goes something like this: "I have some interesting data here; I wonder what they mean." Baltzell's research illustrates the inductive logical model. His data

inductive logical thought reasoning that transforms specific observations into general theory

deductive logical thought reasoning that transforms general theory into specific hypotheses suitable for testing

SUMMING UP

Four Research Methods

	Experiment	Survey	Participant Observation	Existing Sources
Application	For explanatory research that specifies relationships between variables Generates quantitative data	For gathering information about issues that cannot be directly observed, such as attitudes and values Useful for descriptive and explanatory research Generates quantitative or qualitative data	For exploratory and descriptive study of people in a "natural" setting Generates qualitative data	For exploratory, descriptive, or explanatory research whenever suitable data are available
Advantages	Provides the greatest opportunity to specify cause-and-effect relationships Replication of research is relatively easy	Sampling, using questionnaires, allows surveys of large populations Interviews provide in-depth responses	Allows study of "natural" behavior Usually inexpensive	Saves time and expense of data collection Makes historical research possible
Limitations	Laboratory settings have an artificial quality Unless the research environment is carefully controlled, results may be biased	Questionnaires must be carefully prepared and may yield a low return rate Interviews are expensive and time-consuming	Time-consuming Replication of research is difficult Researcher must balance roles of participant and observer	Researcher has no control over possible biases in data Data may only partially fit current research needs

showed that one region of the country (the Boston area) had produced many more high achievers than another (the Philadelphia region). He worked "upward" from ground-level observations to the high-flying theory that religious values were a key factor in shaping people's attitudes toward achievement.

A second type of logical thought moves "downward," in the opposite direction: **Deductive logical thought** is *reasoning that transforms general theory into specific hypotheses suitable for testing.* The researcher's thinking runs from the general to the specific: "I have this hunch about human behavior; let's collect some data and put it to the test." Working deductively, the researcher first states the theory in the form of a hypothesis and then selects a method by which to test it. To the extent that the data support the hypothesis, a researcher concludes that the theory is correct; on the other hand, data that refute the hypothesis suggest that the theory needs to be revised or perhaps rejected entirely.

Philip Zimbardo's "Stanford County Prison" experiment illustrates deductive logic. Zimbardo began with the general theory that a social environment can change human behavior. He then developed a specific, testable hypothesis: Placed in a prison setting, even emotionally well-balanced young men will behave violently. The violence that erupted soon after his experiment began supported Zimbardo's hypothesis. Had his experiment produced friendly behavior between prisoners and guards, his hypothesis clearly would have been wrong.

Just as researchers often employ several methods over the course of one study, they typically use *both* kinds of logical thought. Figure 2 illustrates both types of reasoning: inductively building theory from observations and deductively making observations to test a theory.

Finally, turning facts into meaning usually involves organizing and presenting statistical data. Precisely how sociologists arrange their numbers affects the conclusions they reach. In short, preparing your results amounts to spinning reality in one way or another.

Often we conclude that an argument must be true simply because there are statistics to back it up. However, we must look at statistics with a cautious eye. After all, researchers choose what data to present, they interpret their statistics, and they may use tables and

MAKING THE GRADE

The ten steps listed below are a summary of what is needed to conduct good sociological research.

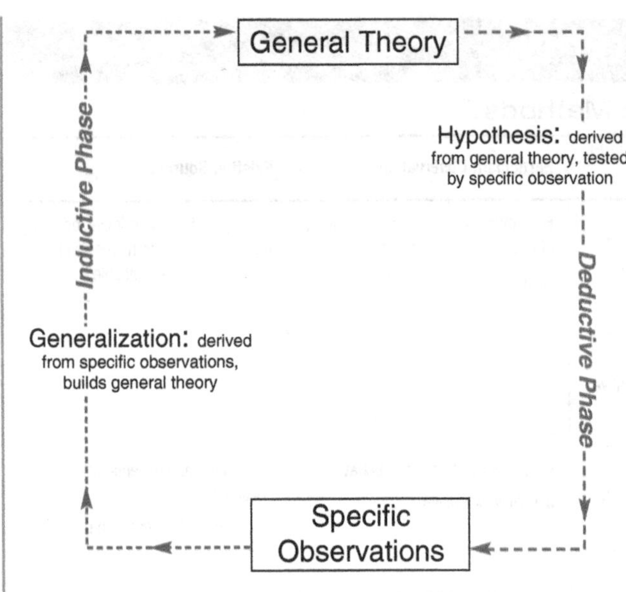

FIGURE 2 **Deductive and Inductive Logical Thought**

Sociologists link theory and method through both inductive and deductive logic.

graphs to steer readers toward particular conclusions. The Controversy & Debate box takes a closer look at this important issue.

Putting It All Together: Ten Steps in Sociological Investigation

We can summarize this chapter by outlining ten steps in the process of carrying out sociological investigation. Each step takes the form of an important question.

1. **What is your topic?** Being curious and applying the sociological perspective can generate ideas for social research at any time and in any place. Pick a topic that you find interesting and important to study.
2. **What have others already learned?** You are probably not the first person with an interest in the issue you have selected. Visit the library to see what theories and methods other researchers have applied to your topic. In reviewing the existing research, note problems that have come up to avoid repeating past mistakes.
3. **What, exactly, are your questions?** Are you seeking to explore an unfamiliar social setting? To describe some category of people? To investigate cause and effect among variables? If your study is exploratory or descriptive, identify *whom* you wish to study, *where* the research will take place, and *what* kinds of issues you want to explore. If it is explanatory, you must also formulate the hypothesis to be tested and operationalize each variable.
4. **What will you need to carry out research?** How much time and money are available to you? Is special equipment or training necessary? Will you be able to complete the work yourself? You should answer all these questions as you plan the research project.
5. **Are there ethical concerns?** Not all research raises serious ethical questions, but you must be sensitive to this possibility. Can the research cause harm or threaten anyone's privacy? How might you design the study to minimize the chances for injury? Will you promise anonymity to the subjects? If so, how will you ensure that anonymity will be maintained?
6. **What method will you use?** Consider all major research strategies, as well as combinations of approaches. Keep in mind that the best method depends on the kinds of questions you are asking as well as the resources available to you.
7. **How will you record the data?** Your research method is a plan for data collection. Record all information accurately and in a way that will make sense later (it may be some time before you actually write up the results of your work). Watch out for any bias that may creep into the research.
8. **What do the data tell you?** Study the data in terms of your initial questions, and decide how to interpret the data you have collected. If your study involves a specific hypothesis, you must decide whether to confirm, reject, or modify the hypothesis. Keep in mind that there may be several ways to look at your data, depending on which theoretical approach you use, and you should consider them all.
9. **What are your conclusions?** Prepare a final report stating your conclusions. How does your work advance sociological theory? Does it suggest ways to improve research methods? Does your study have policy implications? What would the general public find interesting in your work? Finally, evaluate your own work. What problems arose during the research process? What questions were left unanswered?
10. **How can you share what you've learned?** Consider sending your research paper to a campus newspaper or magazine or making a presentation to a class, a campus gathering, or perhaps a meeting of professional sociologists. The point is to share what you have learned with others and to let them respond to your work.

CONTROVERSY & DEBATE

Can People Lie with Statistics?

Josh: (*discussing job prospects after graduation*) Well, you know, college students today just aren't as smart as they were fifty years ago.

Sam: Come on, that's not true at all.

Josh: (*smugly*) Sorry, pal. I happen to have the data to prove it.

We have all been in arguments when someone has presented us with "data" as if that were "proof." But are numbers the same as "truth"? It is worth remembering the words of the nineteenth-century English politician Benjamin Disraeli, who once remarked, "There are three kinds of lies: lies, damned lies, and statistics!"

In a world that bombards us with numbers—often described as "scientific data" or "official figures"—it is important to realize that "statistical evidence" is not necessarily the same as truth. For one thing, any researcher can make mistakes. More important, because data do not speak for themselves, someone has to decide what they mean. Sometimes people (even sociologists) "dress up" their data almost the way politicians deliver campaign speeches—with an eye more to winning you over than to getting at the truth.

The best way to avoid being fooled is to understand how people can mislead with statistics.

1. **People select their data.** Many times, the data presented are not wrong, but they do not tell the whole story. Let's say someone who thinks that television is ruining our way of life presents statistics indicating that we watch more TV today than people did a generation ago. It also turns out that during the same period, SAT scores have fallen. Both sets of data may be correct, but the suggestion that there is a cause-and-effect link here—that television viewing is lowering test scores—is not proved. A person more favorable to television might counter with the additional "fact" that the U.S. population spends much more money buying books today than it did a generation ago, suggesting that television creates new intellectual interests. It is possible to find statistics that seem to support just about any argument.

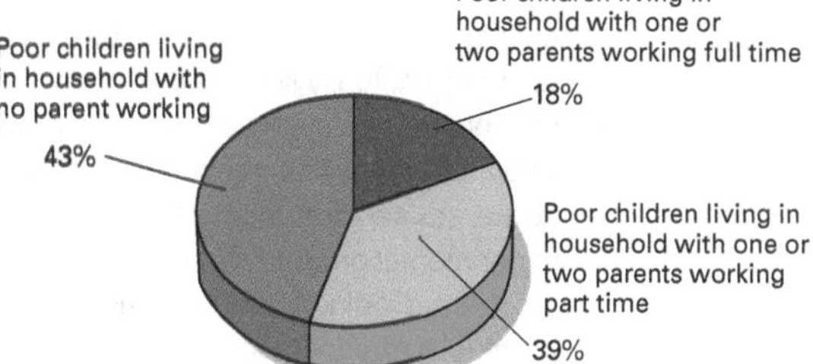

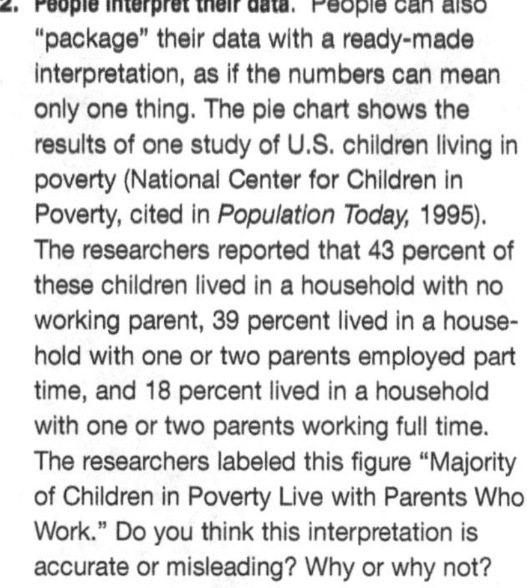

2. **People interpret their data.** People can also "package" their data with a ready-made interpretation, as if the numbers can mean only one thing. The pie chart shows the results of one study of U.S. children living in poverty (National Center for Children in Poverty, cited in *Population Today*, 1995). The researchers reported that 43 percent of these children lived in a household with no working parent, 39 percent lived in a household with one or two parents employed part time, and 18 percent lived in a household with one or two parents working full time. The researchers labeled this figure "Majority of Children in Poverty Live with Parents Who Work." Do you think this interpretation is accurate or misleading? Why or why not?

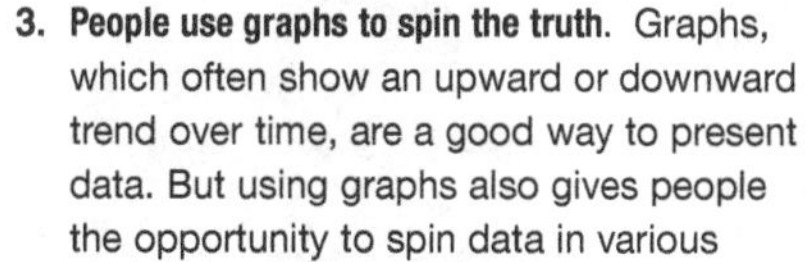

3. **People use graphs to spin the truth.** Graphs, which often show an upward or downward trend over time, are a good way to present data. But using graphs also gives people the opportunity to spin data in various ways. The trend depends in part on the time frame used. During the past ten years, for instance, the U.S. crime rate has fallen. But if we were to look at the past fifty years, we would see an opposite trend: The crime rate rose sharply.

The scale used to draw a graph is also important because it lets a researcher "inflate" or "deflate" a trend. Both graphs shown here present identical data for SAT critical reading scores between 1967 and 2008. But the left-hand graph stretches the scale to show a downward trend; the right-hand graph compresses the scale, making the trend seem steady. So understanding what statistics mean—or don't mean—depends on being a careful reader!

WHAT DO YOU THINK?

1. Why do you think people are so quick to accept "statistics" as true?
2. From a scientific point of view, is spinning the truth acceptable? Is this practice OK from a critical approach, in which someone is trying to advance social change?
3. Find a news story on some social issue that you think presents biased data or conclusions. What are the biases?

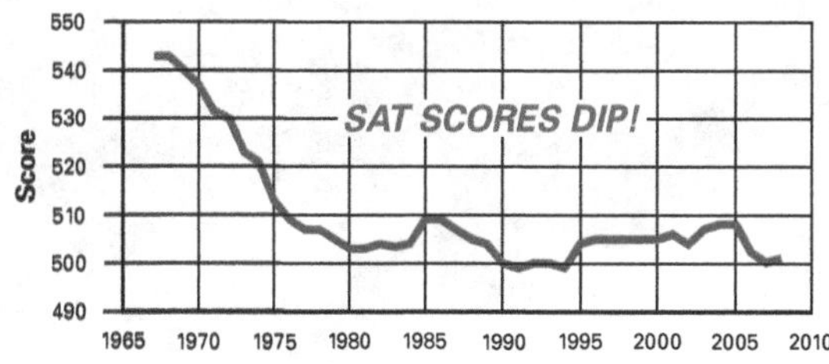

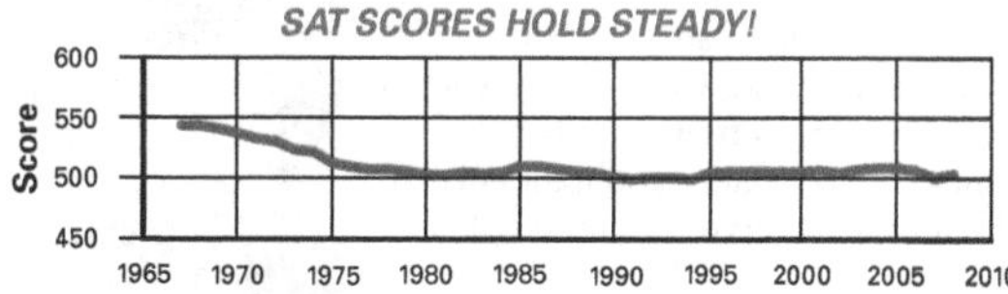

Seeing Sociology in Everyday Life

Sociological Investigation

What are friends for?

Sociological research is the key to a deeper understanding of our everyday social world and also to knowing more about ourselves. Take friendship, for example. Everyone knows that it is fun to be surrounded by friends. But did you know that friendship has real benefits for human health? What do you think these benefits might be? Take a look at the photos below and learn more about what research has taught us about the positive effects of having friends.

HINT In the first case, researchers defined having friends as the independent variable, and they defined longevity and health as the dependent variables. On average, those with friends (the experimental group) actually lived longer and were healthier than those without friends (the control group). In the second case, researchers found that women with many friends were several times more likely to survive their illness than those without friends. The third case reminds us that correlation does not demonstrate cause and effect. This study looked at more than 700 men, some with many friends (the experimental group) and also other men of comparable health (the control group) and few friends, over six years. Finding those with friends had better heart health tells us that friendship is the independent variable. In the fourth case, researchers did indeed find that the longer the people had been friends, the more positive the subject's attitude about making the climb turned out to be. Long live friendship!

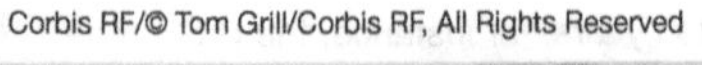

One ten-year study of older people found that those women and men who had many friends were significantly less likely to die over the course of the research than those with few or no friends. Other long-term research confirms that people with friends not only live longer but live healthier lives than those without friends. In basic terms, how would such a study be conducted?

Another study looked at 3,000 women diagnosed with breast cancer and compared the rate of survival for women with many friends with that for women with few or no friends. What do you think they concluded about the effect of friendship on surviving a serious illness?

Perhaps the reason that friendship improves health is that friends raise our spirits and give us a more positive attitude about our lives. A final study placed young college students carrying heavy backpacks at the base of a steep hill and asked them how tough it would be to climb to the top. Subjects in the company of a friend were much more optimistic that they could make the climb than those standing there alone. Would you expect that the better the friend, the more positive the person's attitude?

Corbis RF/Olivier Cadeaux

The "friendship effect" improves the health of men, too. A study of older men found that those with many friends had lower rates of heart disease than those without friends. How would you be sure of the causal direction linking these variables? That is, how can we be sure that friendship is improving health rather than good health encouraging friendship?

Getty Images/Stephen Derr

Applying SOCIOLOGY in Everyday Life

1. The research studies discussed above demonstrate that friendship means more to people than we might think. Recall Emile Durkheim's study of suicide. How did he use sociological research to uncover more about the importance of relationships?
2. Observe your instructor in class one day to grade his or her teaching skills. Operationalize the concept "good teaching" in terms of specific traits you can measure. How easy is it to measure "good teaching"?
3. Visit three sociology instructors (or other social science instructors) during their office hours. Ask each whether they think sociology is an objective science. Do they agree? Why or why not?

VISUAL SUMMARY

MAKING THE GRADE

Sociological Investigation

Basics of Sociological Investigation

Two basic requirements for **SOCIOLOGICAL INVESTIGATION** are

- Know how to apply the sociological perspective.
- Be curious and ready to ask questions about the world around you.

What people accept as "truth" differs around the world.

- **SCIENCE**—a logical system that bases knowledge on direct, systematic observation—is one form of truth.
- Scientific evidence gained from sociological research often challenges common sense.

science a logical system that bases knowledge on direct, systematic observation

empirical evidence information we can verify with our senses

positivist sociology the study of society based on systematic observation of social behavior

concept a mental construct that represents some part of the world in a simplified form

variable a concept whose value changes from case to case

measurement a procedure for determining the value of a variable in a specific case

operationalize a variable specifying exactly what is to be measured before assigning a value to a variable

reliability consistency in measurement

validity actually measuring exactly what you intend to measure

cause and effect a relationship in which change in one variable causes change in another

independent variable the variable that causes the change

dependent variable the variable that changes

correlation a relationship in which two (or more) variables change together

spurious correlation an apparent but false relationship between two (or more) variables that is caused by some other variable

control holding constant all variables except one in order to see clearly the effect of that variable

objectivity personal neutrality in conducting research

replication repetition of research by other investigators

Research Orientations: Three Ways to Do Sociology

POSITIVIST SOCIOLOGY studies society by systematically observing social behavior.
Positivist sociology

- requires carefully operationalizing variables and ensuring that measurement is both reliable and valid
- observes how variables are related and tries to establish cause and effect
- sees an objective reality "out there"
- favors quantitative data
- is well suited to research in a laboratory
- demands that researchers be objective and suspend their personal values and biases as they conduct research

✓ *Positivist sociology is also called* scientific sociology.

INTERPRETIVE SOCIOLOGY focuses on the meanings that people attach to behavior.
Interpretive sociology

- sees reality as constructed by people in the course of their everyday lives
- favors qualitative data
- is well suited to research in a natural setting

✓ *Weber's concept of* Verstehen *refers to learning how people understand their world.*

CRITICAL SOCIOLOGY uses research to bring about social change.
Critical sociology

- asks moral and political questions
- focuses on inequality
- rejects the principle of objectivity, claiming that all research is political

✓ *Marx, who founded the critical orientation, criticized scientific sociology as supporting the status quo.*

interpretive sociology the study of society that focuses on the meanings people attach to their social world

critical sociology the study of society that focuses on the need for social change

Research Orientations and Theory

- Positivist sociology is loosely linked to the structural-functional approach.
- Interpretive sociology is related to the symbolic-interaction approach.
- Critical sociology corresponds to the social-conflict approach.

See the Summing Up table, "Three Research Orientations in Sociology."

Gender and Research

Gender, involving both researcher and subjects, can affect research in five ways:
- androcentricity
- overgeneralizing
- gender blindness
- double standards
- interference

Research Ethics

Researchers must
- protect the privacy of subjects
- obtain the informed consent of subjects
- indicate all sources of funding
- submit research to an institutional review board (IRB) to ensure it doesn't violate ethical standards

Methods: Strategies for Doing Research

The **EXPERIMENT** allows researchers to study cause and effect between two or more variables in a controlled setting.
- Researchers conduct an experiment to test a **hypothesis**, a statement of a possible relationship between two (or more) variables.

✓ *Example of an experiment: Zimbardo's "Stanford County Prison"*

SURVEY research uses questionnaires or interviews to gather subjects' responses to a series of questions.
- Surveys typically yield descriptive findings, painting a picture of people's views on some issue.

✓ *Example of a survey: Benjamin's "Talented One Hundred"*

Through **PARTICIPANT OBSERVATION**, researchers join with people in a social setting for an extended period of time.
- Participant observation, also called *fieldwork*, allows researchers an "inside look" at a social setting. Because researchers are not attempting to test a specific hypothesis, their research is exploratory and descriptive.

✓ *Example of participant observation:* Whyte's *Street Corner Society*

Sometimes researchers analyze **EXISTING SOURCES**, data collected by others.
- Using existing sources, especially the widely available data collected by government agencies, can save researchers time and money.
- Existing sources are the basis of historical research.

✓ *Example of using existing sources:* Baltzell's *Puritan Boston and Quaker Philadelphia*

See the Summing Up table, "Four Research Methods."

✓ *Researchers combine these methods, depending on the specific goals of their study.*

✓ *Which method the researcher uses depends on the question being asked.*

gender the personal traits and social positions that members of a society attach to being female or male

research method a systematic plan for doing research

experiment a research method for investigating cause and effect under highly controlled conditions

hypothesis a statement of a possible relationship between two (or more) variables

Hawthorne effect a change in a subject's behavior caused simply by the awareness of being studied

survey a research method in which subjects respond to a series of statements or questions on a questionnaire or in an interview

population the people who are the focus of research

sample a part of a population that represents the whole

questionnaire a series of written questions a researcher presents to subjects

interview a series of questions a researcher asks respondents in person

participant observation a research method in which investigators systematically observe people while joining them in their routine activities

inductive logical thought reasoning that transforms specific observations into general theory

deductive logical thought reasoning that transforms general theory into specific hypotheses suitable for testing

MAKING THE GRADE

Sample Test Questions

Multiple-Choice Questions

1. ***Science* is defined as**
   a. a logical system that bases knowledge on direct, systematic observation.
   b. belief based on faith in some ultimate truth.
   c. knowledge based on a society's traditions.
   d. information that comes from recognized "experts."

2. ***Empirical evidence* refers to**
   a. quantitative rather than qualitative data.
   b. what people consider "common sense."
   c. information people can verify with their senses.
   d. patterns found in every known society.

3. **When trying to measure people's "social class," you would have to keep in mind that**
   a. your measurement can never be both reliable and valid.
   b. there are many ways to operationalize this variable.
   c. there is no way to measure "social class."
   d. in the United States, everyone agrees on what "social class" means.

4. **What is the term for the value that occurs most often in a series of numbers?**
   a. the mode
   b. the median
   c. the mean
   d. All of the above are correct.

5. **When measuring any variable, *reliability* refers to**
   a. whether you are really measuring what you want to measure.
   b. how dependable the researcher is.
   c. results that everyone would agree with.
   d. whether repeating the measurement yields consistent results.

6. **We can correctly say that two variables are *correlated* if**
   a. change in one causes no change in the other.
   b. one occurs before the other.
   c. their values vary together.
   d. both measure the same thing.

7. **Which of the following is *not* a defining trait of a cause-and-effect relationship?**
   a. The independent variable must happen before the dependent variable.
   b. Each variable must be shown to be independent of the other.
   c. The two variables must display correlation.
   d. There must be no evidence that the correlation is spurious.

8. **Interpretive sociology is a research orientation that**
   a. focuses on action.
   b. sees an objective reality "out there."
   c. focuses on the meanings people attach to behavior.
   d. seeks to increase social justice.

9. **To study the effects on test performance of playing soft music during an exam, a researcher conducts an experiment in which one test-taking class hears music and another does not. According to the chapter discussion of the experiment, the class hearing the music is called**
   a. the placebo.
   b. the control group.
   c. the dependent variable.
   d. the experimental group.

10. **In participant observation, the problem of "breaking in" to a setting is often solved with the help of a**
    a. key informant.
    b. research assistant.
    c. bigger budget.
    d. All of the above are correct.

ANSWERS: 1 (a); 2 (c); 3 (b); 4 (a); 5 (d); 6 (c); 7 (b); 8 (c); 9 (d); 10 (a).

Essay Questions

1. Explain the idea that there are various types of truth. What are the advantages and limitations of science as a way of discovering truth?
2. Compare and contrast scientific sociology, interpretive sociology, and critical sociology. Which of these approaches best describes the work of Durkheim, Weber, and Marx?

Culture

Getty Images Inc. - PhotoDisc/Jack Hollinsworth/Photodisc/Getty Images

Culture refers to a way of life, which includes what people do (such as forms of dance) and what people have (such as clothing). But culture is not only about what we see on the outside; it also includes what's inside—our thoughts and feelings.

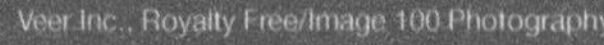

Veer Inc., Royalty Free/Image 100 Photography

Culture

John Macionis

Shutterstock/Lucien Coman

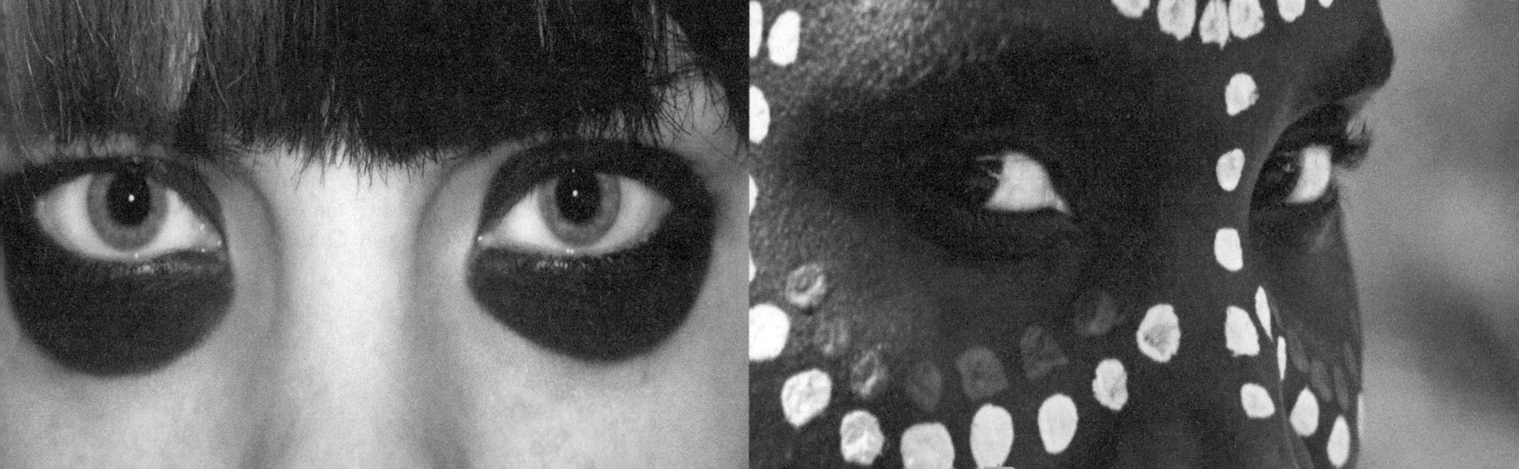

CHAPTER OVERVIEW

This chapter focuses on the concept of "culture," which refers to a society's entire way of life. Notice that the root of the word "culture" is the same as that of the word "cultivate," suggesting that people living together actually "grow" their way of life over time.

It's late on a Tuesday night, but Fang Lin gazes intently at her computer screen. Dong Wang, her husband, walks up behind the chair.

"I'm trying to finish organizing our investments," Fang explains, speaking in Chinese.

"I didn't realize that we could do that online in our own language," Dong says, reading the screen. "I like that a lot."

Fang and Dong are not alone in feeling this way. Back in 1990, executives of Charles Schwab & Co., a large investment brokerage corporation, gathered in a conference room at the company's headquarters in San Francisco to discuss ways they could expand their business. They came up with the idea that the company would profit by giving greater attention to the increasing cultural diversity of the United States. Pointing to data collected by researchers at the U.S. Census Bureau, they saw that the number of Asian Americans was rising rapidly, not just in San Francisco but all over the country. The data also showed that Asian Americans, on average, are doing pretty well, with more than half of households earning more than $75,000 a year (U.S. Census Bureau, 2008).

This meeting led Schwab to launch a diversity initiative, assigning three executives to work on building awareness of the company among Asian Americans. The program has taken off, and Schwab now employs more than 300 people who speak Chinese, Japanese, Korean, Vietnamese, or some other Asian language. Having account executives who speak languages other than English is smart because research shows that most immigrants who come to the United States prefer to communicate in their first language, especially when dealing with important matters such as investing their money. In addition, the company has launched Web sites using Chinese, Korean, and other Asian languages. Fang Lin and Dong Wang are just two of the millions of people who have opened accounts with companies that reach out to them in a language other than English.

Schwab now manages a significant share of the investments made by Asian Americans, who are expected to spend more than $500 billion a year by 2009. So any company would do well to follow the lead Schwab has taken. Other ethnic and racial categories that represent even larger markets in the United States are Hispanics and African Americans (each spending some $700 billion) (Fattah, 2002; Karrfalt, 2003; U.S. Department of Labor, 2007).

Businesses like Schwab are taking note of the fact that the United States is the most *multicultural* of all the world's nations. This cultural diversity reflects the country's long history of receiving immigrants from all over the world. The ways of life found around the world differ, not only in language and forms of dress but also in preferred foods, musical tastes, family patterns, and beliefs about right and wrong. Some of the world's people have many children, while others have few; some honor the elderly, while others seem to glorify youth. Some societies are peaceful, while others are warlike; and societies around the world embrace a thousand different religious beliefs as well as particular ideas about what is polite and rude, beautiful and ugly, pleasant and repulsive. This amazing human capacity for so many different ways of life is a matter of human culture.

What Is Culture?

Culture is *the ways of thinking, the ways of acting, and the material objects that together form a people's way of life.* Culture includes what we think, how we act, and what we own. Culture is both our link to the past and our guide to the future.

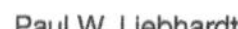

culture the ways of thinking, the ways of acting, and the material objects that together from a people's way of life

nonmaterial culture the ideas created by members of a society

material culture the physical things created by members of a society

Paul W. Liebhardt

Paul W. Liebhardt

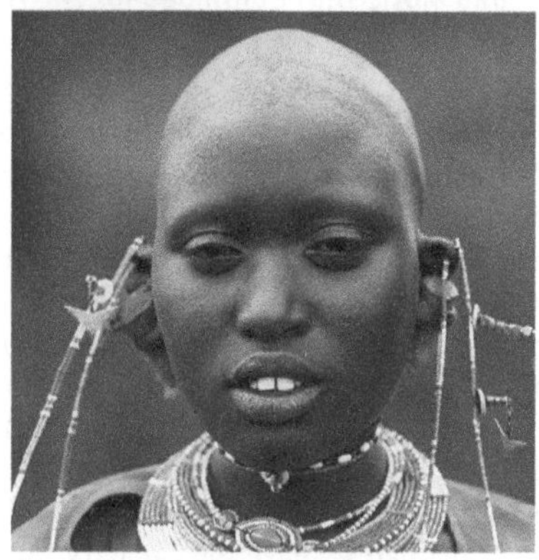

© Doranne Jacobson/International Images

Contact Press Images Inc.

Stock Boston/David Austen

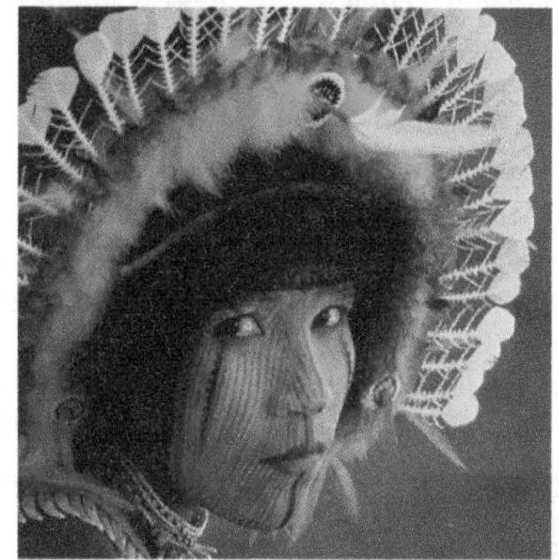

Getty Images Inc. – Stone Allstock/Art Wolfe

© Doranne Jacobson/International Images

Photo Researchers, Inc./Hubertus Kanus

Getty Images, Inc. – Stockbyte Royalty Free

Human beings around the globe create diverse ways of life. Such differences begin with outward appearance: Contrast the women shown here from Brazil, Kenya, New Guinea, South Yemen, and the United States and the men from Taiwan (Republic of China), India, Canada, and New Guinea. Less obvious but of even greater importance are internal differences, since culture also shapes our goals in life, our sense of justice, and even our innermost personal feelings.

culture shock personal disorientation when experiencing an unfamiliar way of life

SEEING SOCIOLOGY in Everyday Life

Can you describe specific practices or patterns familiar to us in the United States that would shock people living in some other part of the world? Explain your response.

To understand all that culture is, we must consider both thoughts and things. **Nonmaterial culture** is *the ideas created by members of a society,* ideas that range from art to Zen. **Material culture,** by contrast, is *the physical things created by members of a society,* everything from armchairs to zippers.

Culture shapes not only what we do but also what we think and how we feel—elements of what we commonly, but wrongly, describe as "human nature." The warlike Yąnomamö of the Brazilian rain forest think aggression is natural, but halfway around the world, the Semai of Malaysia live quite peacefully. The cultures of the United States and Japan both stress achievement and hard work, but members of our society value individualism more than the Japanese, who value collective harmony.

Given the extent of cultural differences in the world and people's tendency to view their own way of life as "natural," it is no wonder that travelers often find themselves feeling uneasy as they enter an unfamiliar culture. This uneasiness is **culture shock,** *personal disorientation when experiencing an unfamiliar way of life.* People can experience culture shock right here in the United States when, say, African Americans explore an Iranian neighborhood in Los Angeles, college students venture into the Amish countryside in Ohio, or New Yorkers travel through small towns in the Deep South. But culture shock is most intense when we travel abroad: The Thinking Globally box tells the story of a researcher from the United States making his first visit to the home of the Yąnomamö living in the Amazon region of South America.

January 2, high in the Andes Mountains of Peru. In the rural highlands, people are poor and depend on one another. The culture is built on cooperation among family members and neighbors who have lived nearby for generations. Today, we spent an hour watching a new house being built. A young couple had invited their families and friends, who arrived at about 6:30 in the morning, and right away they began building. By midafternoon, most of the work was finished, and the couple then provided a large meal, drinks, and music that continued for the rest of the day.

No way of life is "natural" to humanity, even though most people around the world view their own behavior that way. The cooperative spirit that comes naturally to people in the Andes Mountains of Peru is very different from the competitive living that comes naturally to many people in, say, Chicago or New York City. Such variations come from the fact that as human beings, we join together to create our own way of life. Every other animal, from ants to zebras, behaves very much the same all around the world because behavior is guided by *instincts,* biological programming over which the species has no control. A few animals—notably chimpanzees and related primates—have the capacity for limited culture, as researchers have noted by observing them using tools and teaching simple skills to their offspring. But the creative power of humans is far greater than that of any other form of life and has resulted in countless ways of "being human." In short, *only humans rely on culture rather than instinct to create a way of life and ensure our survival* (Harris, 1987; Morell, 2008). To understand how human culture came to be, we need to look back at the history of our species.

Redux Pictures/Hazel Thompson/*The New York Times*

All societies contain cultural differences that can provoke a mild case of culture shock. This woman traveling on a British subway is not sure what to make of the woman sitting next to her, who is wearing the Muslim full-face veil known as the *niqab*.

Culture and Human Intelligence

Scientists tell us that our planet is 4.5 billion years old (see the timeline inside the front cover of this text). Life appeared about 1 billion years later. Fast-forward another 2 to 3 billion years, and we find dinosaurs ruling Earth. It was after these giant creatures disappeared, some 65 million years ago, that our history took a crucial turn with the appearance of the animals we call primates.

The importance of primates is that they have the largest brains relative to body size of all living creatures. About 12 million years ago, primates began to evolve along two different

MAKING THE GRADE

Humans are not the only creatures who have culture, but we are the only creatures who *depend on* culture to survive.

THINKING GLOBALLY 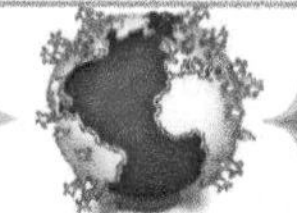

Confronting the Yąnomamö: The Experience of Culture Shock

A small aluminum motorboat chugged steadily along the muddy Orinoco River, deep within South America's vast tropical rain forest. The anthropologist Napoleon Chagnon was nearing the end of a three-day journey to the home territory of the Yąnomamö, one of the most technologically simple societies on Earth.

Some 12,000 Yąnomamö live in villages scattered along the border of Venezuela and Brazil. Their way of life could not be more different from our own. The Yąnomamö wear little clothing and live without electricity, automobiles, or other familiar conveniences. Their traditional weapon, used for hunting and warfare, is the bow and arrow. Most of the Yąnomamö knew little about the outside world, so Chagnon would be as strange to them as they would be to him.

By 2:00 in the afternoon, Chagnon had almost reached his destination. The heat and humidity were almost unbearable. He was soaked with perspiration, and his face and hands swelled from the bites of gnats swarming around him. But he hardly noticed, so excited was he that in just a few moments, he would be face to face with people unlike any he had ever known.

Chagnon's heart pounded as the boat slid onto the riverbank. He and his guide climbed from the boat and headed toward the sounds of a nearby village, pushing their way through the dense undergrowth. Chagnon describes what happened next:

> I looked up and gasped when I saw a dozen burly, naked, sweaty, hideous men staring at us down the shafts of their drawn arrows! Immense wads of green tobacco were stuck between their lower teeth and lips, making them look even more hideous, and strands of dark green slime dripped or hung from their nostrils—strands so long that they clung to their [chests] or drizzled down their chins.
>
> My next discovery was that there were a dozen or so vicious, underfed dogs snapping at my legs, circling me as if I were to be their next meal. I just stood there holding my notebook, helpless and pathetic. Then the stench of the decaying vegetation and filth hit me and I almost got sick. I was horrified. What kind of welcome was this for the person who came here to live with you and learn your way of life, to become friends with you? (1992:11–12)

Fortunately for Chagnon, the Yąnomamö villagers recognized his guide and lowered their weapons. Though reassured that he would survive the afternoon, Chagnon was still shaken by his inability to make any sense of the people surrounding him. And this was going to be his home for the next year and a half! He wondered why he had given up physics to study human culture in the first place.

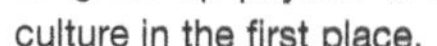

Corbis – NY/Herve Collart

WHAT DO YOU THINK?

1. As they came to know Chagnon, might the Yąnomamö, too, have experienced culture shock? Why?
2. Can you think of an experience you had that is similar to the one described here?
3. How can studying sociology help reduce the experience of culture shock?

lines, setting humans apart from the great apes, our closest relatives. Some 3 million years ago, our distant human ancestors climbed down from the trees of Central Africa to move about in the tall grasses. There, walking upright, they learned the advantages of hunting in groups and made use of fire, tools, and weapons; built simple shelters; and fashioned basic clothing. These Stone Age achievements may seem modest, but they mark the point at which our ancestors set off on a distinct evolutionary course, making culture their primary strategy for survival. By about 250,000 years ago, our own species, *Homo sapiens* (Latin for "intelligent person"), finally emerged. Humans continued to evolve so that by about 40,000 years ago, people who looked more or less like ourselves roamed the planet. With larger brains, these "modern" *Homo sapiens* developed culture rapidly, as the wide range of tools and cave art from this period suggests.

About 12,000 years ago, the founding of permanent settlements and the creation of specialized occupations in the Middle East (today's Iraq and Egypt) marked the "birth of civilization." About this point, the biological forces we call instincts had mostly disappeared, replaced by a more efficient survival scheme: *fashioning the natural environment for ourselves.* Ever since, humans have made and

MAKING THE GRADE

The United States is culturally diverse, reflecting our historically high level of immigration.

symbol anything that carries a particular meaning recognized by people who share a culture

remade their world in countless ways, resulting in today's fascinating cultural diversity.

Culture, Nation, and Society

The term "culture" calls to mind other similar terms, such as "nation" and "society," although each has a slightly different meaning. *Culture* refers to a shared way of life. A *nation* is a political entity, a territory with designated borders, such as the United States, Canada, Peru, or Zimbabwe. *Society* is the organized interaction of people who typically live in a nation or some other specific territory.

The United States, then, is both a nation and a society. But many nations, including the United States, are *multicultural;* that is, their people follow various ways of life that blend (and sometimes clash).

How Many Cultures?

In the United States, how many cultures are there? One indicator of culture is language; the Census Bureau lists more than 300 languages spoken in this country—about half of them are native languages, and half were brought by immigrants from nations around the world (NVTC, 2007).

Globally, experts document almost 7,000 languages, suggesting the existence of as many distinct cultures. Yet the number of languages spoken around the world is declining, and roughly half now are spoken by fewer than 10,000 people (Gordon, 2005). Experts expect that the coming decades may see the disappearance of hundreds of these languages, from Gullah, Pennsylvania German, and Pawnee (all spoken in the United States) to Han (spoken in northwestern Canada), Oro (spoken in the Amazon region of Brazil), Sardinian (spoken on the European island of Sardinia), Aramaic (the language of Jesus of Nazareth, still spoken in the Middle East), Nu Shu (a language spoken in southern China that is the only one known to be used exclusively by women), and Wakka Wakka and several other Aboriginal tongues spoken in Australia. What accounts for the decline? Likely causes include high-technology communication, increasing international migration, and an expanding global economy (UNESCO, 2001; Barovick, 2002; Hayden, 2003).

Getty Images Inc. – Stone Allstock/Margo Silver/Stone/Getty Images

People throughout the world communicate not just with spoken words but also with bodily gestures. Because gestures vary from culture to culture, they can occasionally be the cause of misunderstandings. For instance, the commonplace "thumbs up" gesture we use to express "Good job!" can get a person from the United States into trouble in Greece, Iran, and a number of other countries, where people take it to mean "Up yours!"

The Elements of Culture

Although cultures vary greatly, they all have common elements, including symbols, language, values, and norms. We begin our discussion with the one that is the basis for all the others: symbols.

Symbols

Like all creatures, humans use their senses to experience the surrounding world, but unlike others, we also try to give the world *meaning.* Humans transform elements of the world into *symbols.* A **symbol** is *anything that carries a particular meaning recognized by people who share a culture.* A word, a whistle, a wall covered with graffiti, a flashing red light, a raised fist—all serve as symbols. We can see the human capacity to create and manipulate symbols reflected in the very different meanings associated with the simple act of winking an eye, which can convey interest, understanding, or insult.

Societies create new symbols all the time. The Seeing Sociology in Everyday Life box describes some of the "cyber-symbols" that have developed along with our increasing use of computers for communication.

We are so dependent on our culture's symbols that we take them for granted. However, we become keenly aware of the importance of a symbol when someone uses it in an unconventional way, as when a person burns a U.S. flag during a political demonstration. Entering an unfamiliar culture also reminds us of the power of symbols; culture shock is really the inability to "read" meaning in strange surroundings. Not understanding the symbols of a culture leaves a person feeling lost and isolated, unsure of how to act, and sometimes frightened.

Culture shock is a two-way process. On one hand, travelers *experience* culture shock when encountering people whose way of life is

MAKING THE GRADE

Anything can serve as a symbol; what makes something a symbol is simply that humans attach meaning to it.

SEEING SOCIOLOGY IN EVERYDAY LIFE

New Symbols in the World of Instant Messaging

Molly: gr8 to c u!

Greg: u 2

Molly: jw about next time

Greg: idk, lotta work!

Molly: no prb, xoxoxo

Greg: thanx, bcnu

The world of symbols changes all the time. One reason that people create new symbols is that we develop new ways to communicate. Today, almost 100 million people in the United States (most of them young and many of them students) communicate using an instant messaging (IM) program. All you need to have is a computer connected to the Internet or a cell phone. The exchange featured above shows how everyday social interaction can take place quickly and easily using IM symbols. The symbols people use change all the time, so the IM language used a year from now will differ, just as IM symbols differ from place to place. Here are some common IM symbols:

b be
bc because
b4 before
b4n 'bye for now
bbl be back later
bcnu be seeing you
brb be right back
cu see you
def definitely
g2g got to go
gal get a life
gmta great minds think alike
gr8 great
hagn have a good night
h&k hugs and kisses
idc I don't care
Idt I don't think
idk I don't know
imbl it must be love
jk just kidding
jw just wondering
j4f just for fun
kc keep cool
l8r later
lmao laugh my ass off
ltnc long time no see
myob mind your own business
no prb no problem
omg oh my gosh
pcm please call me
plz please
prbly probably
qpsa ¿Que pasa?
rt right
thanx thanks
u you
ur you are
w/ with
w/e whatever
w/o without
wan2 want to
wtf what the freak
y why
2l8 too late
? question
2 to, two
4 for, four

Corbis RF/Fancy/Veer

WHAT DO YOU THINK?

1. What does the creation of symbols such as these suggest about culture?
2. Do you think that using such symbols is a good way to communicate? Does it lead to confusion or misunderstanding? Why or why not?
3. What other kinds of symbols can you think of that are new to your generation?

Sources: J. Rubin (2003) and Berteau (2005); updated by Megan Bacher, 2009.

different. For example, North Americans who consider dogs beloved household pets might be put off by the Masai of eastern Africa, who ignore dogs and never feed them. The same travelers might be horrified to find that in parts of Indonesia and the People's Republic of China, people roast dogs for dinner.

On the other hand, a traveler may *inflict* culture shock on local people by acting in ways that offend them. A North American who asks for a steak in an Indian restaurant may unknowingly offend Hindus, who consider cows sacred and never to be eaten. Global travel provides almost endless opportunities for this kind of misunderstanding.

Symbolic meanings also vary within a single society. To some people in the United States, a fur coat represents a prized symbol of success, but to others, it represents the inhumane treatment of animals. In the debate about flying the Confederate flag over the South Carolina statehouse a few years ago, some people saw the flag as a symbol of regional pride, but others saw it as a symbol of racial oppression.

language a system of symbols that allows people to communicate with one another

cultural transmission the process by which one generation passes culture to the next

Sapir-Whorf thesis the idea that people see and understand the world through the cultural lens of language

Language

An illness in infancy left Helen Keller (1880–1968) blind and deaf. Without these two senses, she was cut off from the symbolic world, and her social development was greatly limited. Only when her teacher, Anne Mansfield Sullivan, broke through Keller's isolation using sign language did Helen Keller begin to realize her human potential. This remarkable woman, who later became a famous educator herself, recalls the moment she first understood the concept of language:

> We walked down the path to the well-house, attracted by the smell of honeysuckle with which it was covered. Someone was drawing water, and my teacher placed my hand under the spout. As the cool stream gushed over one hand, she spelled into the other the word *water,* first slowly, then rapidly. I stood still, my whole attention fixed upon the motions of her fingers. Suddenly I felt a misty consciousness as of something forgotten—a thrill of returning thought; and somehow the mystery of language was revealed to me. I knew then that "w-a-t-e-r" meant the wonderful cool something that was flowing over my hand. That living word awakened my soul; gave it light, hope, joy, set it free! (1903:24)

Language, the key to the world of culture, is *a system of symbols that allows people to communicate with one another.* Humans have created many alphabets to express the hundreds of languages we speak. Several examples are shown in Figure 1. Even rules for writing differ: Most people in Western societies write from left to right, but people in northern Africa and western Asia write from right to left, and people in eastern Asia write from top to bottom. Global Map 1 shows where we find the three most widely spoken languages, English, Chinese, and Spanish.

إقرأوا Arabic	Read English	독서 Korean
կարդա Armenian	διαβαζω Greek	بخوانيد. Farsi
អាន Cambodian	קְרָא Hebrew	читать Russian
閱讀 Chinese	पढ़ना Hindi	¡Ven a leer! Spanish

FIGURE 1 Human Languages: A Variety of Symbols
Here the English word "read" is written in twelve of the hundreds of languages humans use to communicate with one another.

Language not only allows communication but is also the key to **cultural transmission,** *the process by which one generation passes culture to the next.* Just as our bodies contain the genes of our ancestors, our culture contains countless symbols of those who came before us. Language is the key that unlocks centuries of accumulated wisdom.

Throughout human history, every society has transmitted culture using speech, a process sociologists call the "oral cultural tradition." Some 5,000 years ago, humans invented writing, although at that time only a privileged few learned to read and write. Not until the twentieth century did high-income nations boast of nearly universal literacy. Still, at least 10 percent of U.S. adults (more than 30 million people) are functionally illiterate, unable to read and write in a society that increasingly demands such skills. In low-income countries of the world, 15 percent of men and 24 percent of women are illiterate (U.S. Department of Education, 2008; Population Reference Bureau, 2009).

Language skills may link us with the past, but they also spark the human imagination to connect symbols in new ways, creating an almost limitless range of future possibilities. Language sets humans apart as the only creatures who are self-conscious, aware of our limitations and ultimate mortality, yet able to dream and to hope for a future better than the present.

Does Language Shape Reality?

Does someone who speaks Cherokee, an American Indian language, experience the world differently from other North Americans who think in, say, English or Spanish? Edward Sapir and Benjamin Whorf claimed that the answer is yes, since each language has its own distinctive symbols that serve as the building blocks of reality (Sapir, 1929, 1949; Whorf, 1956, orig. 1941). Further, they noted that each language has words or expressions not found in any other symbolic system. Finally, all languages fuse symbols with distinctive emotions so that, as multilingual people know, a single idea may "feel" different when spoken in Spanish rather than in English or Chinese.

Formally, the **Sapir-Whorf thesis** states that *people see and understand the world through the cultural lens of language.* In the decades since Sapir and Whorf published their work, however, scholars have taken issue with this thesis. Current thinking is that although we do fashion reality from our symbols, evidence does not support the notion that language *determines* reality the way Sapir and Whorf claimed. For example, we know that children understand the idea of "family" long before they learn that word; similarly, adults can imagine new ideas or things before inventing a name for them (Kay & Kempton, 1984; Pinker, 1994).

Values and Beliefs

What accounts for the popularity of Hollywood film characters such as James Bond, Neo, Erin Brockovich, Lara Croft, and Rocky Balboa? Each is ruggedly individualistic, going it alone and relying on personal skill and savvy to challenge "the system." We are led to admire

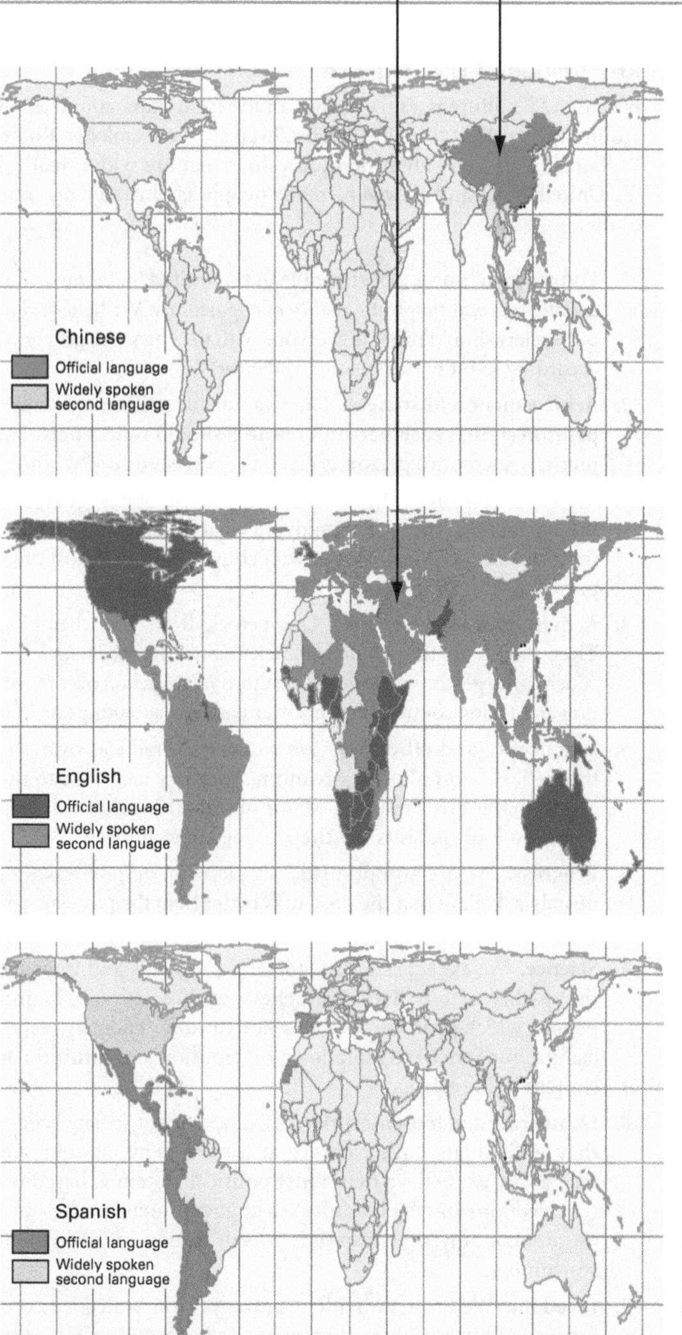

Window on the World

GLOBAL MAP 1 Language in Global Perspective

Chinese (including Mandarin, Cantonese, and dozens of other dialects) is the native tongue of one-fifth of the world's people, almost all of whom live in Asia. Although all Chinese people read and write with the same characters, they use several dozen dialects. The "official" dialect, taught in schools throughout the People's Republic of China and the Republic of Taiwan, is Mandarin (the dialect of Beijing, China's capital). Cantonese, the language of Canton, is the second most common Chinese dialect; it differs in sound from Mandarin roughly the way French differs from Spanish.

English is the native tongue or official language in several world regions (spoken by one-tenth of humanity) and has become the preferred second language in most of the world.

The largest concentration of Spanish speakers is in Latin America and, of course, Spain. Spanish is also the second most widely spoken language in the United States.

Sources: R.G. Gordon (2005) and National Virtual Translation Center (2007).

values culturally defined standards that people use to decide what is desirable, good, and beautiful and that serve as broad guidelines for social living

beliefs specific ideas that people hold to be true

SEEING SOCIOLOGY in Everyday Life

Think about the games you played when you were growing up, like Tag or Capture the Flag, or board games, like Monopoly or Chutes and Ladders. What cultural values do they teach? What about video games like Grand Theft Auto, God of War, or Rainbow Six Vegas?

Penguin Group USA, Inc.

The Australian artist and feminist Sally Swain alters famous artists' paintings to make fun of our culture's tendency to ignore the everyday lives of women. This spoof is titled *Mrs. Warhol Is of Two Minds About What to Cook for Dinner.*

Mrs. Warhol Is of Two Minds About What to Cook for Dinner, from *Great Housewives of Art* by Sally Swain, copyright © 1988, 1989 by Sally Swain. Used by permission of Viking Penguin, a division of Penguin Group (USA) Inc.

such characters by certain **values,** *culturally defined standards that people use to decide what is desirable, good, and beautiful and that serve as broad guidelines for social living.* Values are what people who share a culture use to make choices about how to live.

Values are broad principles that support **beliefs,** *specific thoughts or ideas that people hold to be true.* In other words, values are abstract standards of goodness, and beliefs are particular matters that individuals consider true or false. For example, because most U.S. adults share the *value* of providing equal opportunities for all, they believe that a qualified woman could serve as president of the United States, as the 2008 campaign of Hillary Clinton demonstrated (NORC, 2008:285).

Key Values of U.S. Culture

Because U.S. culture is a mix of ways of life from other countries all around the world, it is highly diverse. Even so, the sociologist Robin Williams (1970) has identified ten values that are widespread in the United States and viewed by many people as central to our way of life:

1. **Equal opportunity.** Most people in the United States favor not *equality of condition* but *equality of opportunity.* We believe that our society should provide everyone with the chance to get ahead according to individual talents and efforts.
2. **Achievement and success.** Our way of life encourages competition so that each person's rewards should reflect personal merit. A successful person is given the respect due a "winner."
3. **Material comfort.** Success in the United States generally means making money and enjoying what it will buy. Although we sometimes say that "money won't buy happiness," most of us pursue wealth all the same.
4. **Activity and work.** Popular U.S. heroes, from golf champion Tiger Woods to the winners of television's *American Idol,* are "doers" who get the job done. Our culture values action over reflection and taking control of events over passively accepting fate.
5. **Practicality and efficiency.** We value the practical over the theoretical, "doing" over "dreaming." Activity has value to the extent that it earns money. "Major in something that will help you get a job!" parents tell their college-age children.
6. **Progress.** We are an optimistic people who, despite waves of nostalgia, believe that the present is better than the past. We celebrate progress, viewing the "very latest" as the "very best."
7. **Science.** We expect scientists to solve problems and improve the quality of our lives. We believe we are rational, logical people, which probably explains our cultural tendency (especially among men) to look down on emotion and intuition as sources of knowledge.
8. **Democracy and free enterprise.** Members of our society believe that individuals have rights that governments should not take away. We believe that a just political system is based on free elections in which adults select government leaders and on an economy that responds to the choices of individual consumers.
9. **Freedom.** We favor individual initiative over collective conformity. While we know that everyone has responsibilities to others, we believe that people should be free to pursue their personal goals.
10. **Racism and group superiority.** Despite strong ideas about equal opportunity and freedom, most people in the United States judge

SEEING SOCIOLOGY in Everyday Life

Would you say that physical fitness is an emerging cultural value? Why or why not?

social control attempts by society to regulate people's thoughts and behavior

norms rules and expectations by which a society guides the behavior of its members

mores norms that are widely observed and have great moral significance

folkways norms for routine or casual interaction

individuals according to gender, race, ethnicity, and social class. In general, U.S. culture values males above females, whites above people of color, rich above poor, and people with northwestern European backgrounds above those whose ancestors came from other parts of the world. Although we like to describe ourselves as a nation of equals, there is little doubt that some of us are "more equal" than others.

Getty Images/M. Becker/American Idol 2009

How does the popularity of the television show *American Idol* illustrate many of the key values of U.S. culture listed here?

Values: Often in Harmony, Sometimes in Conflict

In many ways, cultural values go together. Williams's list includes examples of *value clusters* that are part of our way of life. For instance, we value activity and hard work because we expect effort to lead to achievement and success and result in greater material comfort.

Sometimes, however, one key cultural value contradicts another. Take the first and last items on Williams's list, for example: People in the United States believe in equality of opportunity, yet they may also look down on others because of their sex or race. Value conflict causes strain and often leads to awkward balancing acts in our beliefs. Sometimes people might say they support equal opportunity while at the same time opposing the acceptance of homosexual people in the U.S. military. In such cases, people simply learn to live with the contradictions.

Emerging Values

Like all elements of culture, values change over time. People in the United States have always valued hard work. In recent decades, however, we have placed increasing importance on leisure—having time off from work to do things such as reading, travel, or community service that provide enjoyment and satisfaction. Similarly, although the importance of material comfort remains strong, more people are seeking personal growth through meditation and other spiritual activity.

Values: A Global Perspective

Values vary from culture to culture around the world. In general, the values that are important in higher-income countries differ somewhat from those common in lower-income countries.

Lower-income nations develop cultures that value survival. This means that people place a great deal of importance on physical safety and economic security. They worry about having enough to eat and a safe place to sleep at night. In addition, lower-income nations tend to be traditional, with values that celebrate the past and emphasize the importance of family and religious beliefs. These nations, in which men have most of the power, typically discourage or forbid practices such as divorce and abortion.

People in higher-income countries develop cultures that value individualism and self-expression. These countries are rich enough that most of their people take survival for granted, focusing their attention instead on which "lifestyle" they prefer and how to achieve the greatest personal happiness. In addition, these countries tend to be secular-rational, placing less emphasis on family ties and religious beliefs and more on people thinking for themselves and being tolerant of others who differ from them. In higher-income countries, women have social standing more equal to men, and there is widespread support for practices such as divorce and abortion (World Values Survey, 2008). Figure 2 shows how selected countries of the world compare in terms of their cultural values.

Norms

Most people in the United States are eager to gossip about "who's hot" and "who's not." Members of American Indian societies, however, typically condemn such behavior as rude and divisive. Both patterns illustrate the operation of **norms**, *rules and expectations by which a society guides the behavior of its members.* In everyday life, people respond to each other with *sanctions,* rewards or punishments that encourage conformity to cultural norms.

SEEING SOCIOLOGY in Everyday Life

Figure 2 shows that as a rich nation, the United States ranks high in terms of self-expression but is more traditional than many other high-income nations, such as those in Europe. Can you point to specific beliefs or practices that set us apart from Europeans as more traditional?

SEEING SOCIOLOGY in Everyday Life

Give two examples of campus folkways and two examples of campus mores. What are the likely consequences of violating each type of norm?

Global Snapshot

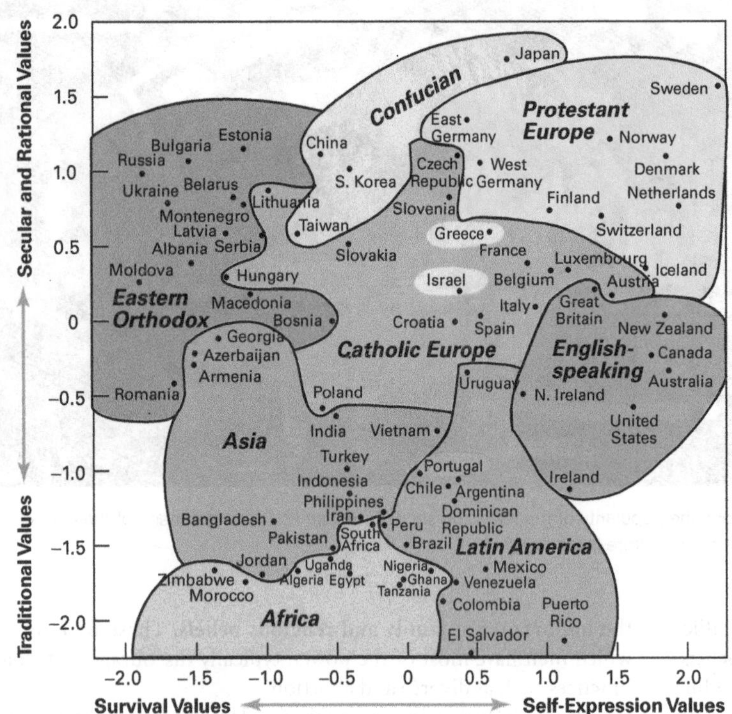

FIGURE 2 Cultural Values of Selected Countries

A general global pattern is that higher-income countries tend to be secular and rational and favor self-expression. By contrast, the cultures of lower-income countries tend to be more traditional and concerned with economic survival. Each region of the world, however, has distinctive cultural patterns, including religious traditions, that affect values. Looking at the figure, what patterns can you see?

Sources: Inglehart and Weizel (2005) and Inglehart (2009).

Mores and Folkways

William Graham Sumner (1959, orig. 1906), an early U.S. sociologist, recognized that some norms are more important to our lives than others. Sumner coined the term **mores** (pronounced "more-ayz") to refer to *norms that are widely observed and have great moral significance.* Mores, or *taboos,* include our society's insistence that adults not engage in sexual relations with children.

People are more flexible about **folkways,** *norms for routine or casual interaction.* Examples include ideas about appropriate greetings and proper dress. In short, mores distinguish between right and wrong, and folkways draw a line between right and *rude.* A man who does not wear a tie to a formal dinner party may raise eyebrows for violating folkways. If, however, he were to arrive at the party wearing *only* a tie, he would violate cultural mores and invite a more serious response.

Social Control

Mores and folkways are the basic rules of everyday life. Although we sometimes resist pressure to conform, we can see that norms make our dealings with others more orderly and predictable. Observing or breaking the rules of social life prompts a response from others, in the form of either reward or punishment. Sanctions—whether an approving smile or a raised eyebrow—operate as a system of **social control,** *attempts by society to regulate people's thoughts and behavior.*

As we learn cultural norms, we gain the capacity to evaluate our own behavior. Doing wrong (say, downloading a term paper from the Internet) can cause both *shame* (the painful sense that others disapprove of our actions) and *guilt* (a negative judgment we make of ourselves). Of all living things, only cultural creatures can experience shame and guilt. This is probably what Mark Twain had in mind when he remarked that people "are the only animals that blush—or need to."

Ideal and Real Culture

Values and norms do not describe actual behavior so much as they suggest how we *should* behave. We must remember that *ideal* culture always differs from *real* culture, which is what actually occurs in everyday life. For example, most women and men agree on the importance of sexual faithfulness in marriage, and most say they live up to that standard. Even so, about 20 percent of married people report having been sexually unfaithful to their spouses at some point in their marriage (NORC, 2008:1877). But a culture's moral standards are important even if they are sometimes broken, calling to mind the old saying "Do as I say, not as I do."

Material Culture and Technology

In addition to symbolic elements such as values and norms, every culture includes a wide range of physical human creations called *artifacts.* The Chinese eat with chopsticks rather than forks, the Japanese put mats rather than rugs on the floor, and many men and women in India prefer flowing robes to the close-fitting clothing common in

technology knowledge that people use to make a way of life in their surroundings

SEEING SOCIOLOGY in Everyday Life

If archaeologists dig up our civilization 50,000 years from now, based on the artifacts they find, what kind of people will they think we were? Point to specific artifacts (such as SUVs, cell phones, and credit cards) and what they say about us.

the United States. The material culture of a people may seem as strange to outsiders as their language, values, and norms.

A society's artifacts partly reflect underlying cultural values. The warlike Yąnomamö carefully craft their weapons and prize the poison tips on their arrows. By contrast, our society's emphasis on individualism and independence goes a long way toward explaining our high regard for the automobile: We own almost 250 million motor vehicles—more than one for every licensed driver—indicating the importance we place both on material things and the ability to move about independently.

In addition to reflecting values, material culture also reflects a society's **technology,** *knowledge that people use to make a way of life in their surroundings.* The more complex a society's technology is, the more its members are able (for better or worse) to shape the world for themselves. Advancements in technology have allowed us to crisscross the country with superhighways and to fill them with automobiles. At the same time, the internal-combustion engines in those cars release carbon dioxide into the atmosphere, which contributes to air pollution and global warming.

Danita Delimont Photography/Claudia Adams/DanitaDelimont.com

Standards of beauty—including the color and design of everyday surroundings—vary significantly from one culture to another. These two Ndebele women in South Africa dress in the same bright colors with which they decorate their homes. Members of North American and European societies, by contrast, make far less use of bright colors and intricate detail, so their housing appears much more subdued.

Because we attach great importance to science and praise sophisticated technology, people in our society tend to judge cultures with simpler technology as less advanced than our own. Some facts support such an assessment. For example, life expectancy for children born in the United States is more than seventy-seven years; the life span of the Yąnomamö is only about forty years.

However, we must be careful not to make self-serving judgments about other cultures. Although many Yąnomamö are eager to acquire modern technology (such as steel tools and shotguns), they are generally well fed by world standards, and most are very satisfied with their lives (Chagnon, 1992). Remember too that while our powerful and complex technology has produced work-reducing devices and seemingly miraculous medical treatments, it has also contributed to unhealthy levels of stress in the population and created weapons capable of destroying in a blinding flash everything that humankind has achieved.

Finally, technology is not equally distributed within our population. Although many of us cannot imagine life without a personal computer, television, and iPhone, many members of U.S. society cannot afford these luxuries. Others reject them on principle. The Amish, who live in small farming communities in Pennsylvania, Ohio, and Indiana, reject most modern conveniences on religious grounds. With their traditional black clothing and horse-drawn buggies, the Amish may seem like a curious relic of the past. Yet their communities flourish, grounded in strong families that give everyone a sense of identity and purpose. Some researchers who have studied the Amish have concluded that these communities are "islands of sanity in a culture gripped by commercialism and technology run wild" (Hostetler, 1980:4; Kraybill, 1994).

New Information Technology and Culture

Many rich nations, including the United States, have entered a postindustrial phase based on computers and new information technology. Industrial production is centered on factories and machinery that generate material goods. By contrast, postindustrial production is based on computers and other electronic devices that create, process, store, and apply information.

In this new information economy, workers need symbolic skills in place of the mechanical skills of the industrial age. Symbolic skills include the ability to speak, write, compute, design, and create images in fields such as art, advertising, and entertainment. In today's computer-based economy, people with creative jobs are generating new cultural ideas, images, and products all the time.

high culture cultural patterns that distinguish a society's elite

popular culture cultural pattens that are widespread among a society's population

subculture cultural patterns that set apart some segment of a society's population

counterculture cultural patterns that strongly oppose those widely accepted within a society

Cultural Diversity: Many Ways of Life in One World

In the United States, we are aware of our cultural diversity when we hear the distinctive accents of people from New England, the Midwest, or the Deep South. Ours is also a nation of religious pluralism, a land of class differences, and a home to individualists who try to be like no one else. Compared to a country like Japan, whose historic isolation has made it the most *monocultural* of all high-income nations, centuries of immigration have made the United States the most *multicultural* of all high-income countries.

Between 1820 (when the government began keeping track of immigration) and 2008, more than 75 million people came to our shores. Our cultural mix continues to increase as more than 1 million people arrive each year. A century ago, almost all immigrants came from Europe; today, most newcomers arrive from Latin America and Asia (U.S. Department of Homeland Security, 2008). To understand the reality of life in the United States, we must move beyond broad cultural patterns and shared values to consider cultural diversity.

High Culture and Popular Culture

Cultural diversity involves not just immigration but also social class. In fact, in everyday talk, we usually use the term "culture" to mean art forms such as classical literature, music, dance, and painting. We describe people who regularly go to the opera or the theater as "cultured," because we think they appreciate the "finer things in life."

We speak less kindly of ordinary people, assuming that everyday culture is somehow less worthy. We are tempted to judge the music of Haydn as "more cultured" than hip-hop, couscous as better than cornbread, and polo as more polished than Ping-Pong.

These differences arise because many cultural patterns are readily available to only some members of a society. Sociologists use the term **high culture** to refer to *cultural patterns that distinguish a society's elite* and **popular culture** to designate *cultural patterns that are widespread among a society's population.*

Common sense may suggest that high culture is superior to popular culture, but sociologists are uneasy with such judgments, for two reasons. First, neither elites nor ordinary people share all the same tastes and interests; people in both categories differ in many ways. Second, do we praise high culture because it is inherently better than popular culture or simply because its supporters have more money, power, and prestige? For example, there is no difference between a violin and a fiddle; however, we name the instrument a violin when it is used to produce classical music typically enjoyed by a person of higher position and a fiddle when the musician plays country tunes appreciated by people with lower social standing.

Sometimes the distinction between high culture and popular is not so clear. Bonham's Auction House in England recently featured spray-painted works by the graffiti artist Banksy. This particular one was expected to be sold for more than $250,000.

Subculture

The term **subculture** refers to *cultural patterns that set apart some segment of a society's population.* People who ride "chopper" motorcycles, traditional Korean Americans, New England "Yankees," Ohio State football fans, the southern California "beach crowd," Elvis impersonators, and wilderness campers all display subcultural patterns.

It is easy but often inaccurate to place people in some subcultural category because almost everyone participates in many subcultures without necessarily having much commitment to any of them. In some cases, however, cultural differences can set people apart from one another with tragic results. Consider the former nation of Yugoslavia in southeastern Europe. The 1990s' civil war there was fueled by extreme cultural diversity. This *one* small country used *two* alphabets, embraced *three* religions, spoke *four* languages, was home to *five* major nationalities, was divided into *six* political republics, and absorbed the cultural influences of *seven* surrounding countries. The cultural conflict that plunged this nation into civil war shows that subcultures are a source not only of pleasing variety but also of tension and even violence.

Many people view the United States as a "melting pot" where many nationalities blend into a single "American" cul-

multiculturalism a perspective recognizing the cultural diversity of the United States and promoting equal standing for all cultural traditions

Eurocentrism the dominance of European (especially English) cultural patterns

Afrocentrism emphasizing and promoting African cultural patterns

Getty Images/Michael Buckner/Discovery Channel

A generation ago, most people regarded tattoos as a mark of low social status. Today, this cultural pattern is gaining popularity among people at all social class levels. Kat Von D is a tattoo artist on the nationwide television show *L.A. Ink.*

ture (Gardyn, 2002). But given so much cultural diversity, how accurate is the "melting pot" image? For one thing, subcultures involve not just *difference* but also *hierarchy.* Too often what we view as "dominant" or "mainstream" culture are patterns favored by powerful segments of the population, and we view the lives of disadvantaged people as "subculture." But are the cultural patterns of rich skiers in Aspen, Colorado, any less a subculture than the cultural patterns of skateboarders in Los Angeles? Some sociologists therefore prefer to level the playing field of society by emphasizing multiculturalism.

Multiculturalism

Multiculturalism is *a perspective recognizing the cultural diversity of the United States and promoting equal standing for all cultural traditions.* Multiculturalism represents a sharp change from the past, when our society downplayed cultural diversity and defined itself primarily in terms of well-off European and especially English immigrants. Today there is a spirited debate about whether we should continue to focus on historical traditions or highlight contemporary diversity.

E pluribus unum, the Latin phrase that appears on all U.S. coins, means "out of many, one." This motto symbolizes not only our national political union but also the idea that immigrants from around the world have come together to form a new way of life.

But from the outset, the many cultures did not melt together as much as harden into a hierarchy. At the top were the English, who formed a majority early in U.S. history and established English as the nation's dominant language. Further down, people of other backgrounds were advised to model themselves after "their betters." In practice, then, "melting" was really a process of Anglicization—adoption of English ways. As multiculturalists see it, early in our history, this society set up the English way of life as an ideal that everyone else should imitate and by which everyone should be judged.

Ever since, historians have reported events from the point of view of the English and other people of European ancestry, paying little attention to the perspectives and accomplishments of Native Americans and people of African and Asian descent. Multiculturalists criticize this as **Eurocentrism,** *the dominance of European (especially English) cultural patterns.* Molefi Kete Asante, a supporter of multiculturalism, argues that "like the fifteenth-century Europeans who could not cease believing that the Earth was the center of the universe, many today find it difficult to cease viewing European culture as the center of the social universe" (1988:7).

One controversial issue involves language. Some people believe that English should be the official language of the United States; by 2009, legislatures in thirty states had enacted laws making it the official language (ProEnglish, 2009). But some 55 million men and women—nearly one in five—speak a language other than English at home. Spanish is the second most commonly spoken language, and across the country we hear several hundred other tongues, including Italian, German, French, Filipino, Japanese, Korean, and Vietnamese, as well as many Native American languages. National Map 1 shows where in the United States large numbers of people speak a language other than English at home.

Supporters of multiculturalism say it is a way of coming to terms with our country's increasing social diversity. With the Asian and Hispanic populations of this country increasing rapidly, some analysts predict that today's children will live to see people of African, Asian, and Hispanic ancestry become a *majority* of this country's population.

Supporters also claim that multiculturalism is a good way to strengthen the academic achievement of African American children. To counter Eurocentrism, some multicultural educators call for **Afrocentrism,** *emphasizing and promoting African cultural patterns,* which they see as necessary after centuries of minimizing or ignoring the cultural achievements of African societies and African Americans.

Although multiculturalism has found favor in recent years, it has drawn its share of criticism as well. Opponents say it encourages divisiveness rather than unity because it urges people to identify with their own category rather than with the nation as a whole. Instead of recognizing any common standards of truth, say critics, multiculturalism maintains that we should evaluate ideas according to the race (and sex) of those who present them. Our common humanity thus breaks down into an "African experience," an "Asian experience," and so on. In addition, critics say, multiculturalism actually harms minorities themselves. Multicultural policies (from African American studies to all-black dorms) seem to support the same racial segregation that our nation has struggled so long to overcome. Furthermore,

Elvira Martinez lives in Zapata County, Texas, where about three-quarters of the people in her community speak Spanish at home.

Jeffrey Steen lives in Adams County, Ohio, where almost none of his neighbors speaks a language other than English.

cultural integration the close relationships among various elements of a cultural system

cultural lag the fact that some cultural elements change more quickly than others, disrupting a cultural system

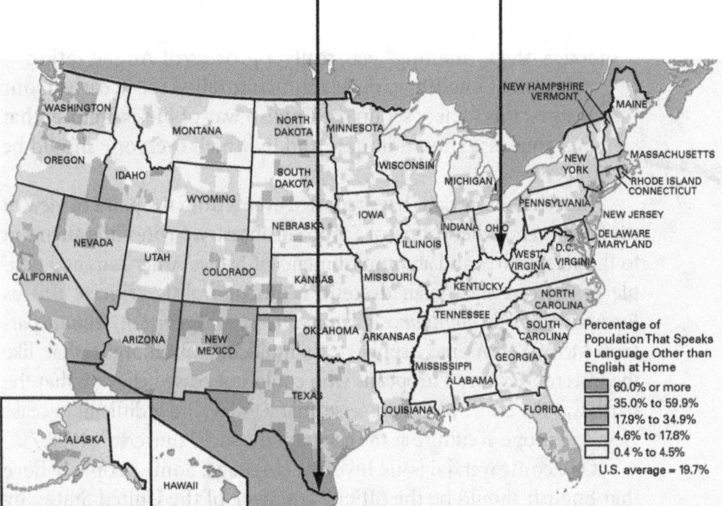

Seeing Ourselves

NATIONAL MAP 1

Language Diversity across the United States

Of more than 281 million people age five or older in the United States, the Census Bureau reports that more than 55 million (20 percent) speak a language other than English at home. Of these, 62 percent speak Spanish and 15 percent use an Asian language (the Census Bureau lists a total of 39 languages and language categories, each of which is favored by more than 100,000 people). The map shows that non-English speakers are concentrated in certain regions of the country. Which ones? What do you think accounts for this pattern?

Sources: U.S. Census Bureau (2008).

in the early grades, an Afrocentric curriculum may deny children a wide range of important knowledge and skills by forcing them to study only certain topics from a single point of view.

Finally, the global war on terror has drawn the issue of multiculturalism into the spotlight. In 2005, British Prime Minister Tony Blair responded to a terrorist attack in London, stating, "It is important that the terrorists realize [that] our determination to defend our values and our way of life is greater than their determination to . . . impose their extremism on the world." He went on to warn that the British government would expel Muslim clerics who encouraged hatred and terrorism (Barone, 2005; Carle, 2008). In a world of cultural difference and conflict, we have much to learn about tolerance and peacemaking.

Counterculture

Cultural diversity also includes outright rejection of conventional ideas or behavior. **Counterculture** refers to *cultural patterns that strongly oppose those widely accepted within a society.*

During the 1960s, for example, a youth-oriented counterculture rejected mainstream culture as overly competitive, self-centered, and materialistic. Instead, hippies and other counterculturalists favored a cooperative lifestyle in which "being" was more important than "doing" and the capacity for personal growth—or "expanded consciousness"—was prized over material possessions like homes and cars. Such differences led some people to "drop out" of the larger society.

Countercultures are still flourishing. At the extreme, small militaristic communities (made up of people born in this country) or bands of religious militants (from other countries) exist in the United States, some of them engaging in violence intended to threaten our way of life.

Cultural Change

Perhaps the most basic human truth of this world is that "all things shall pass." Even the dinosaurs, which thrived on this planet for 160 million years, exist today only as fossils. Will humanity survive for millions of years to come? All we can say with certainty is that given our reliance on culture, for as long as we survive, the human record will show continuous change.

Figure 3 shows changes in attitudes among first-year college students between 1969 (the height of the 1960s' counterculture) and 2008. Some attitudes have changed only slightly: Today, as a generation ago, most men and women look forward to raising a family. But today's students are less concerned with developing a philosophy of life and much more interested in making money.

Change in one part of a culture usually sparks changes in others. For example, today's college women are much more interested in making money because women are now far more likely to be in the labor force than their mothers or grandmothers were. Working for income may not change their interest in raising a family, but it does increase both the age at first marriage and the divorce rate. Such connections illustrate the principle of **cultural integration,** *the close relationships among various elements of a cultural system.*

Cultural Lag

Some elements of culture change faster than others. William Ogburn (1964) observed that technology moves quickly, generating new elements of material culture (things) faster than nonmaterial culture (ideas) can keep up with them. Ogburn called this inconsistency **cultural lag,** *the fact that some cultural elements change more quickly*

MAKING THE GRADE

Three sources of social change are mentioned here. ***Invention*** refers to creating new cultural elements, ***discovery*** refers to recognizing existing cultural elements, and ***diffusion*** is the spread of cultural elements from one place to another.

than others, disrupting a cultural system. For example, in a world in which a woman can give birth to a child by using another woman's egg, which has been fertilized in a laboratory with the sperm of a total stranger, how are we to apply traditional ideas about motherhood and fatherhood?

Causes of Cultural Change

Cultural changes are set in motion in three ways. The first is *invention,* the process of creating new cultural elements. Invention has given us the telephone (1876), the airplane (1903), and the computer (late 1940s); each of these elements of material culture has had a tremendous impact on our way of life. The same is true of the minimum wage (1938), school desegregation (1954), and women's shelters (1975), each an important element of nonmaterial culture. The process of invention goes on constantly. The timeline on the inside cover of this text shows other inventions that have helped change our way of life.

Discovery, a second cause of cultural change, involves recognizing and understanding more fully something already in existence—perhaps a distant star or the foods of another culture or women's political leadership skills. Some discoveries result from painstaking scientific research, and some result from political struggle. Some even result from luck, as in 1898, when Marie Curie left a rock on a piece of photographic paper, noticed that emissions from the rock had exposed the paper, and thus discovered radium.

The third cause of cultural change is *diffusion,* the spread of cultural traits from one society to another. Because new information technology sends information around the globe in seconds, cultural diffusion has never been greater than it is today.

Certainly our own society has contributed many significant cultural elements to the world, ranging from computers to jazz. Of course, diffusion works the other way, too, so that much of what we assume to be "American" actually comes from elsewhere. Most of the clothing we wear and the furniture we use, as well as the watch we carry and the money we spend, all had their origin in other cultures (Linton, 1937a).

It is certainly correct to talk about "American culture," especially when we are comparing our way of life to the culture of some other society. But this discussion of cultural change shows us that culture is always complex and always changing. The Thinking About Diversity box offers a good example of the diverse and dynamic character of culture with a brief look at the history of rock-and-roll music.

Ethnocentrism and Cultural Relativism

December 10, a small village in Morocco. *Watching many of our fellow travelers browsing through a tiny ceramics factory, we have little doubt that North*

Compared to college students 40 years ago, today's students are less interested in developing a philosophy of life and more interested in making money.

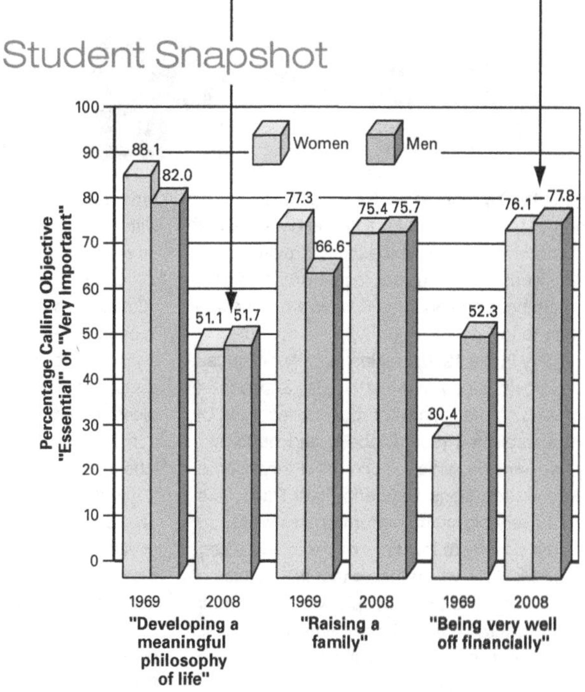

FIGURE 3 Life Objectives of First-Year College Students, 1969 and 2008

Researchers have surveyed first-year college students every year since 1969. While attitudes about some things such as the importance of family have stayed about the same, attitudes about other life goals have changed dramatically.

Sources: Astin et al. (2002) and Pryor et al. (2008).

Americans are among the world's greatest shoppers. We delight in surveying hand-woven carpets in China or India, inspecting finely crafted metals in Turkey, or collecting the beautifully colored porcelain tiles we find here in Morocco. Of course, all these items are wonderful bargains. But one major reason for the low prices is unsettling: Many products from the world's low- and middle-income countries are produced by children—some as young as five or six—who work long days for pennies per hour.

We think of childhood as a time of innocence and freedom from adult burdens like regular work. In poor countries throughout the world, however, families depend on income earned by children. So what people in one society think of as right and natural, people elsewhere find puzzling and even immoral. Perhaps the Chinese philosopher

MAKING THE GRADE

Youth cultures tend to develop as societies industrialize because young people gain more independence from parents and have more money to spend on their own interests.

ethnocentrism the practice of judging another culture by the standards of one's own culture

cultural relativism the practice of judging a culture by its own standards

THINKING ABOUT DIVERSITY: RACE, CLASS, & GENDER

Early Rock-and-Roll: Race, Class, and Cultural Change

In the 1950s, rock-and-roll emerged as a major part of U.S. popular culture. In the decades that followed, rock grew to become a cultural tide that swept away musical tastes and traditions and changed the country in ways we still experience today.

Early in the 1950s, mainstream "pop" music was largely aimed at white adults. Songs were written by professional composers, recorded by long-established record labels, and performed by well-known artists such as Perry Como, Eddie Fisher, Doris Day, and Patti Page. Just about every big-name performer was white.

The country at that time was also rigidly segregated racially, which meant that the cultures of white people and black people were different. In the subcultural world of African Americans, music had different sounds and rhythms, reflecting jazz, gospel singing, and rhythm and blues. All of these musical styles were the creations of African American composers and performers working with black-owned record companies broadcast on radio to an almost entirely black audience.

Class, too, divided the musical world of the 1950s, even among whites. A second musical subculture was country and western, a musical style popular among poorer whites, especially people living in the South. Like rhythm and blues, country and western music had its own composers and performers, its own record labels, and its own radio stations.

In the early 1950s, there were separate musical worlds in U.S. society, separated by the walls of race and class. "Crossover" music was rare, meaning that very few performers or songs moved from one world to gain popularity in another.

This musical segregation began to break down about 1955 with the birth of rock-and-roll. Rock was a new mix of many existing musical patterns, drawing on mainstream pop but including country and western and, especially, rhythm and blues.

The new rock-and-roll music drew together musical traditions, but it soon divided society in a new way—by age. Rock-and-roll was the first music clearly linked to the emergence of a youth culture—rock was all the rage among teenagers but was little appreciated or even understood by their parents. One reason for this age split was that in the prosperous 1950s, young people had more money to spend, and record companies quickly realized that they could make a fortune selling products to the new "youth market." Young performers and groups began springing up in suburban garages and on inner-city street corners, and many were signed by new record labels and their music played on new teen-targeted radio stations.

The new youth culture gave birth to musical stars who looked and acted nothing like their parents. The rock-and-roll performers were men

AP Wide World Photos/Carlos Rene Perez

Corbis – NY/© Bettmann/Corbis

Getty Images, Inc. – Getty News/Michael Ochs Archive

Elvis Presley (*center*) drew together the music of rhythm and blues singers, such as Big Mama Thornton (*left*), and country and western stars, including Carl Perkins (*right*). The development of rock-and-roll illustrates the ever-changing character of U.S. culture.

Confucius had it right when he noted that "all people are the same; it's only their habits that are different."

Just about every imaginable idea or behavior is commonplace somewhere in the world, and this cultural variation causes travelers both excitement and distress. The Australians flip light switches down to turn them on; North Americans flip them up. The Japanese name city blocks; North Americans name streets. Egyptians stand very close to others in conversation; North Americans are used to maintaining several feet of "personal space." Bathrooms lack toilet paper in much of rural Morocco, causing considerable discomfort for North Americans, who recoil at the thought of using the left hand for bathroom hygiene, as the locals do.

Given that a particular culture is the basis for each person's reality, it is no wonder that people everywhere exhibit **ethnocentrism,** *the practice of judging another culture by the standards of one's own culture.* Some degree of ethnocentrism is necessary for people to be

MAKING THE GRADE

During the 1950s, rock-and-roll helped bring together black and white musical styles, but because this music was popular among the young, it also divided people by age.

SEEING SOCIOLOGY in Everyday Life

Just for fun, go to http://www.TheSociologyPage. com, where you can hear one of the author's "cover" performances of oldies rock-and-roll.

(and a few women) who took a rebellious stand against "adult" culture. The typical rocker was a young man who looked like what parents might have called a "juvenile delinquent" and who claimed to be "cool," an idea that most parents did not even understand.

The first band to make it big in rock-and-roll was Bill Haley and His Comets. These men (Haley lowered his stated age to gain greater acceptance) came out of the country and western tradition. Haley's first hits in 1954—"Shake, Rattle, and Roll" and "Rock around the Clock"—were recordings of earlier rhythm and blues songs.

Very quickly, however, young people began to lose interest in older performers such as Bill Haley and turned their attention to younger performers who had a stronger juvenile delinquent image—musicians sporting sideburns, turned-up collars, and black leather jackets. By the end of 1955, the unquestioned star of rock-and-roll was a poor white southern boy from Tupelo, Mississippi, named Elvis Aron Presley. From his rural roots, Elvis Presley knew country and western music, and after he moved to his adopted hometown of Memphis, Tennessee, he learned all about black gospel and rhythm and blues.

Before the 1950s ended, Presley had become the first superstar of rock-and-roll—not only because he had talent but also because he had great crossover power. With early hits including "Hound Dog" (a rhythm and blues song originally recorded by Big Mama Thornton) and "Blue Suede Shoes" (written by country and western star Carl Perkins), Presley broke down many of the walls of race and class in the music of the United States.

Elvis went on to a twenty-year career as "the King." But during that time, illustrating the expanding and dynamic character of culture, popular music developed in many new and different directions. By the end of the 1950s, popular musical styles included soft rock (Ricky Nelson, Pat Boone), rockabilly (Johnny Cash), and dozens of doo-wop groups, both black and white (often named for birds—the Falcons, the Penguins, the Flamingos—or cars—the Imperials, the Impalas, the Fleetwoods).

During the 1960s, the diversity of rock music was even greater, including folk music (the Kingston Trio; Peter, Paul, and Mary; Bob Dylan), surf music (the Beach Boys, Jan and Dean), and the "British invasion" led by the Beatles.

The Beatles were at first very close to the clean-cut, pop side of rock, but they soon shared the spotlight with another British band who was proud of its "delinquent" clothing and street fighter looks—the Rolling Stones. During the 1960s, music became a huge business, including not just the hard rock of the Beatles and Stones but softer "folk rock" performed by the Byrds, the Mamas and the Papas, Simon and Garfunkel, and Crosby, Stills, and Nash. Mainstream rock continued with bands like the Who, but rhythm and blues gave birth to "Motown" (named after the "motor city," Detroit, the automobile-building capital of the United States at the time), and "soul" music, launching the careers of dozens of African American stars, including James Brown, Aretha Franklin, the Four Tops, the Temptations, and Diana Ross and the Supremes.

On the West Coast, San Francisco developed a more political rock music performed by Jefferson Airplane, the Grateful Dead, and Janis Joplin. West Coast spin-off musical styles included "acid rock," influenced by drug use, performed by the Doors and Jimi Hendrix. The jazz influence also returned to the world of rock, creating such "jazz rock" groups as Chicago and Blood, Sweat, and Tears.

What does this brief look at the early decades of rock-and-roll tell us about culture? It shows the power of race and class to divide and separate people, shaping different subcultural patterns. It also shows us that the production of culture—in terms of music as well as movies and music videos—has become a megabusiness. Most of all, it shows us that culture is not a rigid system that stands still but rather a living process, changing, adapting, and reinventing itself over time.

WHAT DO YOU THINK?

1. Many dimensions of our way of life shaped rock-and-roll. In what ways do you think the emergence of rock-and-roll changed U.S. culture?
2. Throughout this period of musical change, most musical performers were men. What does this tell us about our way of life? Do you think today's popular music is still dominated by men?
3. Can you carry on the story of musical change in the United States to the present? (Think of disco, heavy metal, punk rock, rap, and hip-hop.)

Source: Based on Stuessy & Lipscomb (2008).

emotionally attached to their way of life. But ethnocentrism also generates misunderstanding and sometimes conflict.

Even language is culturally biased. Centuries ago, people in Europe and North America referred to China as the "Far East." But this term, unknown to the Chinese, is an ethnocentric expression for a region that is far to the east *of us.* The Chinese name for their country translates as "Central Kingdom," suggesting that they, like us, see their own society as the center of the world.

The logical alternative to ethnocentrism is **cultural relativism,** *the practice of judging a culture by its own standards.* Cultural relativism can be difficult for travelers to adopt: It requires not only openness to unfamiliar values and norms but also the ability to put aside cultural standards we have known all our lives. Even so, as people of the world come into increasing contact with one another, the importance of understanding other cultures becomes ever greater.

MAKING THE GRADE

One good piece of evidence supporting the claim that a global culture is emerging is the widespread use of English as a second language almost everywhere in the world (see Global Map 3).

Photo Researchers, Inc./Alison Wright

In the world's low-income countries, most children must work to provide their families with needed income. This seven-year-old boy in eastern Ilam, Nepal, works long hours in a tea field. Is it ethnocentric for people living in high-income nations to condemn the practice of child labor because we think youngsters belong in school? Why or why not?

As the opening to this chapter explained, businesses in the United States are learning the value of marketing to a culturally diverse population. Similarly, businesses are learning that success in the global economy depends on awareness of cultural patterns around the world. IBM, for example, now provides technical support for its products using Web sites in more than thirty languages (IBM, 2008).

This trend is a change from the past, when many corporations used marketing strategies that lacked sensitivity to cultural diversity. Coors's phrase "Turn It Loose" startled Spanish-speaking customers by proclaiming that the beer would cause diarrhea. Braniff Airlines translated its slogan "Fly in Leather" so carelessly into Spanish that it read "Fly Naked." Similarly, Eastern Airlines' slogan "We Earn Our Wings Every Day" became "We Fly Daily to Heaven." Even poultry giant Frank Perdue fell victim to poor marketing when his pitch "It Takes a Tough Man to Make a Tender Chicken" was transformed into the Spanish words reading "A Sexually Excited Man Will Make a Chicken Affectionate" (Helin, 1992).

But cultural relativism introduces problems of its own. If almost any kind of behavior is the norm *somewhere* in the world, does that mean everything is equally right? Does the fact that some Indian and Moroccan families benefit from having their children work long hours justify child labor? Since we are all members of a single species, surely there must be some universal standards of proper conduct. But what are they? And in trying to develop them, how can we avoid imposing our own standards on others? There are no simple answers. But when confronting an unfamiliar cultural practice, it is best to resist making judgments before grasping what people in that culture think of the issue. Remember also to think about your own way of life as others might see it. After all, what we gain most from studying others is better insight into ourselves.

A Global Culture?

Today more than ever, we can observe many of the same cultural practices the world over. Walking the streets of Seoul, South Korea; Kuala Lumpur, Malaysia; Chennai, India; Cairo, Egypt; or Casablanca, Morocco, we see people wearing jeans, hear familiar music, and read ads for many of the same products we use at home. Seeing Sociology in the News takes a look at how U.S. rap music is taking root in China. Recall, too, from Global Map 1 that English is rapidly emerging as the preferred second language around the world. Are we witnessing the birth of a single global culture?

Societies now have more contact with one another than ever before, thanks to the flow of goods, information, and people:

1. **The global economy: The flow of goods.** International trade has never been greater. The global economy has spread many of the same consumer goods—from cars and TV shows to music and fashions—throughout the world.
2. **Global communications: The flow of information.** The Internet and satellite-assisted communications enable people to experience the sights and sounds of events taking place thousands of miles away, often as they happen. In addition, because most of the world's Web pages are written in English, the spread of computer technology has helped spread the English language around the world. Recall from Global Map 1 that English is now the preferred second language in most parts of the world.
3. **Global migration: The flow of people.** Knowing about the rest of the world motivates people to move to where they imagine life will be better. In addition, today's transportation technology, especially air travel, makes relocating easier than ever before. As a result, in most countries, significant numbers of people were born elsewhere, including some 38 million people in the United States, which is 13 percent of the total population (U.S. Census Bureau, 2008).

MAKING THE GRADE

The concept "cultural universal" is an older concept linked to the structural-functional approach. It is based on the idea that if some cultural trait is found everywhere, it must be very useful for society.

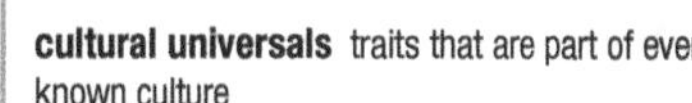

cultural universals traits that are part of every known culture

sociobiology a theoretical approach that explores ways in which human biology affects how we create culture

These global links help make the cultures of the world more similar. Even so, there are three important limitations to the global culture thesis. First, the global flow of goods, information, and people is uneven in different parts of the world. Generally speaking, urban areas (centers of commerce, communication, and people) have stronger ties to one another, while many rural villages remain isolated. In addition, the greater economic and military power of North America and Western Europe means that these regions influence the rest of the world more than the rest of the world influences them.

Second, the global culture thesis assumes that people everywhere are able to *afford* various new goods and services. Desperate poverty in much of the world deprives people of even the basic necessities of a safe and secure life.

Third, although many cultural practices are now found in countries throughout the world, people everywhere do not attach the same meanings to them. Do children in Tokyo draw the same lessons from reading the Harry Potter books as their counterparts in New York or London? Similarly, we enjoy foods from around the world while knowing little about the lives of the people who created them. In short, people everywhere still see the world through their own cultural lenses.

Theoretical Analysis of Culture

Sociologists have the special task of understanding how culture helps us make sense of ourselves and the surrounding world. Here we will examine several macro-level theoretical approaches to understanding culture.

The Functions of Culture: Structural-Functional Analysis

The structural-functional approach explains culture as a complex strategy for meeting human needs. Borrowing from the philosophical doctrine of *idealism,* this approach considers values the core of a culture (Parsons, 1966; R. M. Williams, 1970). In other words, cultural values direct our lives, give meaning to what we do, and bind people together. Countless other cultural traits have various functions that support the operation of society.

Thinking functionally helps us understand an unfamiliar way of life. Consider the Amish farmer plowing hundreds of acres on an Ohio farm with a team of horses. His farming methods may violate our cultural value of efficiency, but from the Amish point of view, hard work functions to develop the discipline necessary for a highly religious way of life. Long days of working together not only make the Amish self-sufficient but also strengthen family ties and unify local communities.

Of course, Amish practices have dysfunctions as well. The hard work and strict religious discipline are too demanding for some, who end up leaving the community. Then, too, strong religious beliefs sometimes prevent compromise; slight differences in religious practices have caused the Amish to divide into different communities (Kraybill, 1989; Kraybill & Olshan, 1994).

If cultures are strategies for meeting human needs, we would expect to find many common patterns around the world. **Cultural universals** are *traits that are part of every known culture.* Comparing hundreds of cultures, George Murdock (1945) identified dozens of cultural universals. One common element is the family, which functions everywhere to control sexual reproduction and to oversee the care of children. Funeral rites, too, are found everywhere, because all human communities cope with the reality of death. Jokes are another cultural universal, serving as a safe means of releasing social tensions.

CRITICAL REVIEW The strength of the structural-functional approach is that it shows how culture operates to meet human needs. Yet by emphasizing a society's dominant cultural patterns, this approach largely ignores the cultural diversity that exists in many societies, including our own. Also, because this approach emphasizes cultural stability, it downplays the importance of change. In short, cultural systems are not as stable or a matter of as much agreement as structural functionalism leads us to believe.

CHECK YOUR LEARNING In the United States, what are some of the functions of sports, July Fourth celebrations, and Black History Month?

Inequality and Culture: Social-Conflict Analysis

The social-conflict approach stresses the link between culture and inequality. Any cultural trait, from this point of view, benefits some members of society at the expense of others.

Why do certain values dominate a society in the first place? Many conflict theorists, especially Marxists, argue that culture is shaped by a society's system of economic production. "It is not the consciousness of men that determines their being," Karl Marx proclaimed; "it is their social being that determines their consciousness" (Marx & Engels, 1978:4, orig. 1859). Social-conflict theory, then, is rooted in the philosophical doctrine of *materialism,* which holds that a society's system of material production (such as our own capitalist economy) has a

Seeing SOCIOLOGY in the 

The New York Times

Now Hip-Hop, Too, Is Made in China

By JIMMY WANG
January 24, 2009

BEIJING—A week before Americans tune in to the Super Bowl, another televised mega-event will kick off on the other side of the globe. On Sunday more than half a billion people here are expected to watch the annual Chinese Lunar New Year gala. Organized by the state-owned China Central Television, the marathon event showcases the country's musical diversity with an extensive lineup of Chinese pop stars performing hit songs. But one genre audiences are unlikely to see is Chinese hip-hop, despite its growing popularity among the country's urban youth.

Over the last decade many students and working-class Chinese have been writing rap as a form of self-expression. Rougher and more rebellious than the well-scrubbed pop that floods the airwaves here, this kind of hip-hop is not sanctioned by broadcast media producers or state censors but has managed to attract a grass-roots fan base.

"Hip-hop is free, like rock 'n' roll—we can talk about our lives, what we're thinking about, what we feel," said Wang Liang, 25, a popular hip-hop D.J. known as Wordy. "The Chinese education system doesn't encourage you to express your own character. They feed you stale rules developed from books passed down over thousands of years. There's not much opportunity for personal expression or thought; difference is discouraged."

While American rappers like Eminem and Q-Tip have been popular in China since the 1990s, home-grown rap didn't start gaining momentum until a decade later. The group Yin Ts'ang (its name means "hidden"), one of the pioneers of Chinese rap, is made up of global nomads: a Beijinger, a Chinese-Canadian and two Americans.

"The big change was when rappers started writing verse in Chinese, so people could understand," said Zhong Cheng, 27, a member of the group who was raised in Canada but born in Beijing, where he returned in 1997. "Before that, kids listened to hip-hop in English but maybe less than 1 percent could actually understand."

Yin Ts'ang's first hit was "In Beijing," from the band's 2003 debut album, "Serve the People" (Scream Records); the title is a twist on an old political slogan. It sets a melody played on a thousand-year-old Chinese fiddle called the Erhu against a hip-hop beat that brings Run D.M.C. to mind. The song, an insider's look at Beijing's sights and sounds, took the underground music scene by storm, finding its way into karaoke parlors, the Internet and even the playlist of a radio station in Beijing. . . .

Since "In Beijing," the Chinese hip-hop scene has quickly grown. Hiphop.cn, a Web site listing events and links to songs, started with just a few hundred members in 2007; in 2008 it received millions of views, according to one of the site's directors.

Dozens of hip-hop clubs have opened up in cities across the country, and thousands of raps and music videos by Chinese M.C.'s are spreading over the Internet. But making Chinese hip-hop is

powerful effect on the rest of a culture. This materialist approach contrasts with the idealist leanings of structural functionalism.

Social-conflict analysis ties our cultural values of competitiveness and material success to our country's capitalist economy, which serves the interests of the nation's wealthy elite. The culture of capitalism further teaches us to think that rich and powerful people work harder or longer than others and therefore deserve their wealth and privileges. It also encourages us to view capitalism as somehow "natural," discouraging us from trying to reduce economic inequality.

Eventually, however, the strains of inequality erupt into movements for social change. Two examples in the United States are the civil rights movement and the women's movement. Both have sought greater equality, and both have encountered opposition from defenders of the status quo.

CRITICAL REVIEW The social-conflict approach suggests that cultural systems do not address human needs equally, allowing some people to dominate others. This inequity in turn generates pressure toward change. Yet by stressing the divisiveness of culture, this approach understates the ways that cultural patterns integrate members of society. We should therefore consider both social-conflict and structural-functional insights for a fuller understanding of culture.

CHECK YOUR LEARNING How might a social-conflict analysis of college fraternities and sororities differ from a structural-functional analysis?

Evolution and Culture: Sociobiology

We know that culture is a human creation, but does human biology influence how this process unfolds? A third theoretical approach, standing with one leg in biology and one in sociology, is **sociobiology,** *a theoretical approach that explores ways in which human biology affects how we create culture.*

Sociobiology rests on the theory of evolution proposed by Charles Darwin in *On the Origin of Species* (1859). Darwin asserted that living organisms change over long periods of time as a result of *natural selection,* a matter of four simple principles. First, all living things live to reproduce themselves. Second, the blueprint for reproduction is in the genes, the basic units of life that carry traits of one generation into the next. Third, some random variation in genes allows a species to "try out" new life patterns in a particular environment. This variation allows some organisms to survive better than others and pass on their advantageous genes to their offspring. Fourth and finally, over thousands of generations, the genetic patterns that promote reproduction survive and become dominant. In this way, as biologists say, a species *adapts* to its environment, and dominant traits emerge as the "nature" of the organism.

Sociobiologists claim that the large number of cultural universals reflects the fact that all humans are members of a single biological species. It is our common biology that underlies, for example, the apparently universal "double standard" of sexual behavior. As the sex researcher Alfred Kinsey put it, "Among all people everywhere in the world, the male is more likely than the still a relatively profitless—and often subversive—activity. Some Chinese rappers address what they see as the country's most glaring injustices. As Wang Li, a 24-year-old from Dongbei, says in one of his freestyle raps:

If you don't have a nice car or cash
You won't get no honeys
Don't you know China is only a heaven for rich old men
You know this world is full of corruption
Babies die from drinking milk.

. . . Mr. Wang, who became interested in hip-hop when he heard Public Enemy in the mid-'90s. [He] said rapping helps him deal with bitterness that comes with realizing he is one of the millions left out of China's economic boom.

"All people care about is money," he said. "If you don't have money, you're treated like garbage." . . .

In the recent hit "Hello Teacher," Yin Tsar, one of the hip-hop scene's biggest acts (its name means "The Three Shadows"), rails against the authority of unfair teachers: "You're supposed to be a role model, but I've seen you spit in public." . . .

While Beijing's underground music scene is generally under the authorities' radar—hip-hop, indie rock and reggae groups perform regularly at nightclubs here—the producers representing broadcast media in China avoid musicians perceived as threatening.

"There are pockets of freedom here," said Wang Miao, 24, the director of Acupuncture Records. . . . "Anyone can play what they want in clubs, and as long as you aren't insulting the party, generally you'll be left alone. But if you want to take the next step to becoming mainstream, you hit a wall. If you aren't singing their type of stuff or aren't incredibly rich, they won't sign you." . . .

After seven years together, Mr. Zhong and Mr. Johnston of Yin Ts'ang still struggle to pay the bills, but they haven't stopped making hip-hop. . . .

In a nondescript apartment on the west side of Beijing, Mr. Johnston nodded his head to a song playing on his computer while Mr. Zhong explained how the group started:

"When I got here and met Jeremy, we were both so inspired by these people, we were like, 'Let's drop some Chinese rhymes for the locals,' and our Chinese friends were like, 'There are no Chinese rhymes!,' and we were like, 'That's crazy!' From that day, we haven't stopped rhyming."

WHAT DO YOU THINK?

1. Explain how and why hip-hop in China is an example of cultural diffusion.
2. Do you think rap music is encouraging the development of counterculture in China? Why or why not?
3. Can you think of Chinese cultural patterns that have changed U.S. society? If so, give examples.

female to desire sex with a variety of partners" (quoted in Barash, 1981:49). Why is this so?

We all know that children result from joining a woman's egg with a man's sperm. But the biological importance of a single sperm and of a single egg is quite different. For healthy men, sperm represent a "renewable resource" produced by the testes throughout most of the life course. A man releases hundreds of millions of sperm in a single ejaculation—technically, enough to fertilize every woman in North America (Barash, 1981:47). A newborn female's ovaries, however, contain her entire lifetime supply of eggs. A woman generally releases a single egg cell from her ovaries each month. So although a man is biologically capable of fathering thousands of offspring, a woman is able to bear only a relatively small number of children.

Given this biological difference, men reproduce their genes most efficiently by being promiscuous—readily engaging in sex with any willing partner. This scheme, however, opposes the reproductive interests of women. Each of a woman's relatively few pregnancies demands that she carry the child for nine months, give birth, and provide care for years afterward. Thus efficient reproduction on the part of the woman depends on carefully selecting a mate whose qualities (beginning with the likelihood that he will simply stay around) will contribute to her child's survival and, later, successful reproduction.

The double standard certainly involves more than biology and is tangled up with the historical domination of women by men. But sociobiology suggests that this cultural pattern, like many others, has an underlying "bio-logic." Simply put, the double standard exists around the world because biological differences lead women and men everywhere to favor distinctive reproductive strategies.

CRITICAL REVIEW Sociobiology has generated intriguing theories about the biological roots of some cultural patterns. But the approach remains controversial for two main reasons.

First, some critics fear that sociobiology may revive biological arguments, from over a century ago, that claimed the superiority of one race or sex. But defenders counter that sociobiology rejects the past pseudoscience of racial and gender superiority. In fact, they say, sociobiology unites all of humanity because all people share a single evolutionary history. Sociobiology does assert that men and women differ biologically in some ways that culture cannot easily overcome. But far from claiming that males are somehow more important than females, sociobiology emphasizes that both sexes are vital to human reproduction and survival.

Second, say the critics, sociobiologists have little evidence to support their theories. Research to date suggests that biological forces do not *determine* human behavior in any rigid sense. Rather, humans *learn* behavior within a cultural system. The contribution of sociobiology, then, lies in explaining why some cultural patterns seem easier to learn than others (Barash, 1981).

MAKING THE GRADE

Because multiculturalism supports greater social equality for people of various cultural backgrounds, this theory falls within sociology's social-conflict approach.

MAKING THE GRADE

Theories dealing with how biology affects human behavior do not have wide support in sociology. Sociobiology is a theory—supported by some sociologists, not by others—that has one foot in biology and the other in sociology.

APPLYING THEORY

Culture

	Structural-Functional Approach	Social-Conflict Approach	Sociobiology Approach
What is the level of analysis?	Macro-level	Macro-level	Macro-level
What is culture?	Culture is a system of behavior by which members of societies cooperate to meet their needs.	Culture is a system that benefits some people and disadvantages others.	Culture is a system of behavior that is partly shaped by human biology.
What is the foundation of culture?	Cultural patterns are rooted in a society's core values and beliefs.	Cultural patterns are rooted in a society's system of economic production.	Cultural patterns are rooted in humanity's biological evolution.
What core questions does the approach ask?	How does a cultural pattern help society operate? What cultural patterns are found in all societies?	How does a cultural pattern benefit some people and harm others? How does a cultural pattern support social inequality?	How does a cultural pattern help a species adapt to its environment?

CHECK YOUR LEARNING Using the sociobiology approach, explain why some cultural patterns such as sibling rivalry are widespread.

Because any analysis of culture requires a broad focus on the workings of society, the three approaches discussed in this chapter, and summarized in the Applying Theory table, are all macro-level in scope.

Culture and Human Freedom

This chapter leads us to ask an important question: To what extent are human beings, as cultural creatures, free? Does culture bind us to each other and to the past? Or does culture enhance our capacity for individual thought and independent choice?

Culture as Constraint

As symbolic creatures, humans cannot live without culture. But the capacity for culture does have some drawbacks. We may be the only animal to name ourselves, but living in a symbolic world means that we are also the only creature that experiences alienation. In addition, culture is largely a matter of habit, which limits our choices and drives us to repeat troubling patterns, such as racial prejudice and sex discrimination, in each new generation.

Our society's emphasis on competitive achievement urges us toward excellence, yet this same pattern also isolates us from one another. Material things comfort us in some ways but divert us from the security and satisfaction that come from close relationships and spiritual strength.

Culture as Freedom

For better or worse, human beings are cultural creatures, just as ants and bees are prisoners of their biology. But there is a crucial difference. Biological instincts create a ready-made world; culture forces us to choose as we make and remake a world for ourselves. No better evidence of this freedom exists than the cultural diversity of our own society and the even greater human diversity around the world.

Learning more about this cultural diversity is one goal shared by sociologists. The Thinking Globally box offers some contrasts between the cultures of the United States and Canada. Wherever we may live, the better we understand the workings of the surrounding culture, the better prepared we are to use the freedom it offers us.

SEEING SOCIOLOGY in Everyday Life

Our tendency to pay little attention to countries with which we share borders is one example of ethnocentrism.

THINKING GLOBALLY

The United States and Canada: Two National Cultures or One?

The United States and Canada are two of the largest high-income countries in the world, and they share a common border of about 4,000 miles. But do the United States and Canada share the same culture?

One important point to make right away is that both nations are *multicultural.* Not only do the two countries have hundreds of Native American societies, but immigration has brought people from all over the world to both the United States and Canada. Most early immigrants to both countries came from Europe, but in recent decades, most have come from Asia and Latin America. The Canadian city of Vancouver, for example, has a Chinese community of about the same size as the Latino community in Los Angeles.

Canada and the United States differ in one important respect: Historically, Canada has had *two* dominant cultures: French (about 25 percent of the population) and British (roughly 40 percent). People of French ancestry are a large majority in the province of Quebec (where French is the official language) and represent almost half of the population of New Brunswick (which is officially bilingual).

Are the dominant values of Canada much the same as those we have described for the United States? Seymour Martin Lipset (1985) finds that they differ to some degree. The United States declared its independence from Great Britain in 1776, but Canada did not formally separate from Great Britain until 1982, and the British monarch is still Canada's official head of state. Thus, Lipset continues, the dominant culture of Canada lies somewhere between the culture of the United States and that of Great Britain.

The culture of the United States is more individualistic, and Canada's is more collective. In the United States, individualism is seen in the historical importance of the cowboy, a self-sufficient loner, and even outlaws such as Jesse James and Billy the Kid are regarded as heroes because they challenged authority. In Canada, by contrast, it is the Mountie—Canada's well-known police officer on horseback—who is looked on with great respect. Canada's greater emphasis on collective life is also evident in stronger unions: Canadian workers are three times more likely to be members of a union as workers in the United States (Steyn, 2008).

Politically, people in the United States tend to think individuals ought to do things for themselves. In Canada, however, much as in Great Britain, there is a strong sense that government should look after the interests of everyone. The U.S. Constitution emphasizes the importance of "life, liberty, and the pursuit of happiness" (words that place importance on the individual), while Canadian society is based on "peace, order, and good government" (words that place importance on the government) (Steyn, 2008). One clear result of this difference is that Canada has a much broader social welfare system (including universal health care) than the United States (the only high-income nation without such a program). It also helps explain the fact that about one-third of all U.S. households own a gun, and the idea that individuals are entitled to own a gun, although controversial, is widespread. In Canada, by contrast, the government restricts gun ownership, as in Great Britain.

WHAT DO YOU THINK?

1. Why do you think some Canadians feel that their way of life is overshadowed by that of the United States?
2. Ask your friends to name the capital city of Canada. (The correct answer is Ottawa, in the province of Ontario.) Are you surprised by how many know the answer? Why or why not?
3. Why do many people in the United States not know very much about either Canada or Mexico, countries with which we share long borders?

Corbis - NY/© Bettmann/Corbis

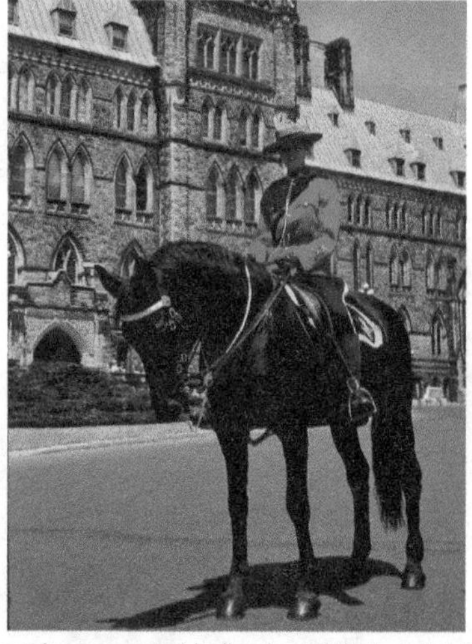

Canadian Government Travel Bureau

The individuals that a society celebrates as heroic are a good indication of that society's cultural values. In the United States, outlaws such as Jesse James (and later, Bonnie and Clyde) were regarded as heroes because they represented the individual standing strong against authority. In Canada, by contrast, people have always looked up to the Mountie, who symbolizes society's authority over the individual.

Seeing Sociology in Everyday Life

Culture

What clues do we have to a society's cultural values?

The values of any society—that is, what that society thinks is important—are reflected in various aspects of everyday life, including the things people have and the ways they behave. An interesting way to "read" our own culture's values is to look at the "superheroes" that we celebrate. Take a look at the characters in the three photos shown here and, in each case, describe what makes the character special and what each character represents in cultural terms.

Superman first appeared in an *Action Comic* book in 1938, as the United States struggled to climb out of economic depression and faced the rising danger of war. Since then, Superman has been featured in a television show as well as in a string of Hollywood films. One trait of most superheroes is that they have a secret identity; in this case, Superman's everyday identity is "mild-mannered news reporter" Clark Kent.

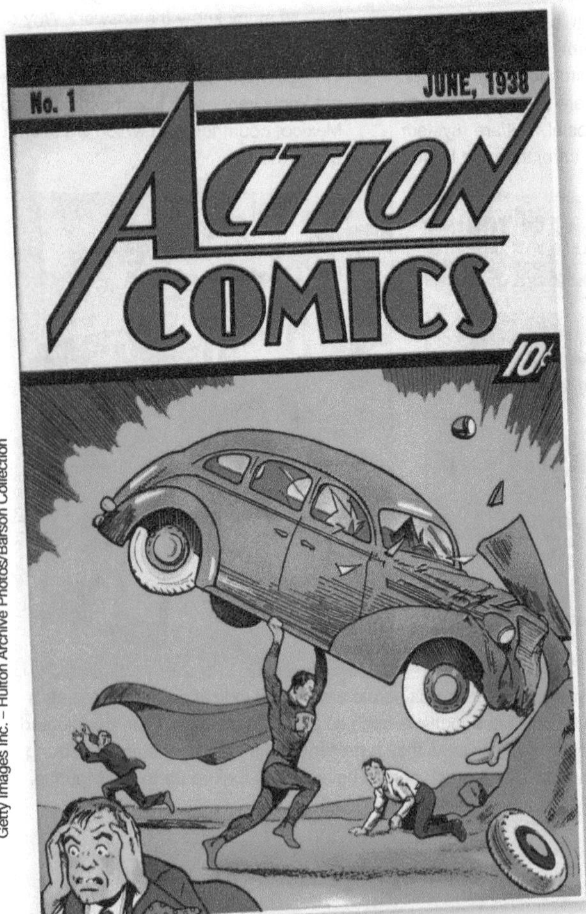

Getty Images Inc. – Hulton Archive Photos/Barson Collection

Buffy the Vampire Slayer, a more recent star of television, film, comic books, and video games, is a rare example of a woman playing a superhero character.

Picture Desk, Inc./Kobal Collection/20th Century Fox Television

HINT Superman (as well as Spiderman and Buffy) defines our society as good; after all, Superman fights for "truth, justice, and the American way." Many superheroes have stories that draw on great people in our cultural history, including religious figures such as Moses and Jesus: They have mysterious origins (we never really know their true families), they are "tested" through great moral challenges, and they finally succeed in overcoming all obstacles. (Today's superheroes, however, are likely to win the day using force and often violence.) Having a "secret identity" means superheroes can lead ordinary lives (and means we ordinary people can imagine being superheroes). But to keep their focus on fighting evil, superheroes must place their work ahead of any romantic interests ("Work comes first!"). Buffy also illustrates the special challenge to "do it all" faced by women in our society: Constantly called on to fight evil, she still must make time for her studies as well as her friends.

Another longtime superhero important to our culture is Spiderman. In all three *Spiderman* movies, Peter Parker (who transforms into Spiderman when he confronts evil) is secretly in love with Mary Jane Watson, but—in true superhero style—he does not allow himself to follow his heart.

Picture Desk, Inc./Kobal Collection/Marvel/Sony Pictures

Applying SOCIOLOGY in Everyday Life

1. What traits define popular culture "heroes" such as Clint Eastwood's film character "Dirty Harry," Sylvester Stallone's film characters "Rocky" as well as "Rambo," and Arnold Schwarzenegger's character "the Terminator"?

2. Find someone on campus who has lived in another country, and ask how the culture of that society differs from the way of life here. Look for ways in which the other person sees U.S. culture differently from people who have lived here all their lives.

3. Watch an animated Disney film such as *Finding Nemo, The Lion King, The Little Mermaid, Aladdin,* or *Pocahontas*. One reason for the popularity of these films is that they all share cultural themes. Using the list of key values of U.S. culture as a guide, what makes the film you selected especially "American"?

MAKING THE GRADE

VISUAL SUMMARY

Culture

What Is Culture?

Culture is a **WAY OF LIFE**.
- Culture is shared by members of a society.
- Culture shapes how we act, think, and feel.

Culture is a **HUMAN TRAIT**.
- Although several species display a limited capacity for culture, only human beings rely on culture for survival.

Culture is a **PRODUCT OF EVOLUTION**.
- As the human brain evolved, culture replaced biological instincts as our species' primary strategy for survival.

- We experience **CULTURE SHOCK** when we enter an unfamiliar culture and are not able to "read" meaning in our new surroundings.
- We create culture shock for others when we act in ways they do not understand.

✓ *Approximately 300 different cultures exist in the United States. Worldwide, there are roughly 7,000 different cultures .*

culture the ways of thinking, the ways of acting, and the material objects that together form a people's way of life

nonmaterial culture the ideas created by members of a society

material culture the physical things created by members of a society

culture shock personal disorientation when experiencing an unfamiliar way of life

The Elements of Culture

Culture relies on **SYMBOLS** in the form of words, gestures, and actions to express meaning.
- The fact that different meanings can come to be associated with the same symbol (for example, a wink of an eye) shows the human capacity to create and manipulate symbols.
- Societies create new symbols all the time (for example, new computer technology has sparked the creation of new cyber-symbols).

LANGUAGE is the symbolic system by which people in a culture communicate with one another.
- People use language—both spoken and written—to transmit culture from one generation to the next.
- Because every culture is different, each language has words or expressions not found in any other language.

VALUES are abstract standards of what *ought to be* (for example, equality of opportunity).
- Values can sometimes be in conflict with one another.
- Lower-income countries have cultures that value survival; higher-income countries have cultures that value individualism and self-expression.

BELIEFS are specific statements that people who share a culture hold to be true (for example, "A qualified woman could be elected president").

NORMS, rules that guide human behavior, are of two types:
- **mores** (for example, sexual taboos), which have great moral significance
- **folkways** (for example, greetings or dining etiquette), which are matters of everyday politeness

✓ *Values and norms (standards for how we should behave) reflect **ideal culture**, which differs from **real culture** (what actually occurs in everyday life).*

 See earlier in this chapter for ten key values of U.S. culture.

symbol anything that carries a particular meaning recognized by people who share a culture

language a system of symbols that allows people to communicate with one another

cultural transmission the process by which one generation passes culture to the next

Sapir-Whorf thesis the idea that people see and understand the world through the cultural lens of language

values culturally defined standards that people use to decide what is desirable, good, and beautiful and that serve as broad guidelines for social living

beliefs specific thoughts or ideas that people hold to be true

norms rules and expectations by which a society guides the behavior of its members

mores norms that are widely observed and have great moral significance

folkways norms for routine or casual interaction

social control attempts by society to regulate people's thoughts and behavior

technology knowledge that people use to make a way of life in their surroundings

Technology and Culture

- A society's **artifacts**—the wide range of physical human creations that together make up a society's material culture—reflect underlying cultural values and technology.
- The more complex a society's technology, the more its members are able to shape the world as they wish.

✓ *Members of societies that possess sophisticated technology should be careful not to judge cultures with simpler technology as inferior.*

Cultural Diversity

We live in a **CULTURALLY DIVERSE SOCIETY**.
- This diversity is due to our country's history of immigration.
- Diversity reflects regional differences.
- Diversity reflects differences in social class that set off **high culture** (available only to elites) from **popular culture** (available to average people).

A number of values are central to our way of life. But **CULTURAL PATTERNS** are not the same throughout our society.
Subculture is based on differences in interests and life experiences.
- Hip-hop fans and jocks are two examples of youth subcultures in the United States.

Multiculturalism is an effort to enhance appreciation of cultural diversity.
- Multiculturalism developed as a reaction to the earlier "melting pot" idea, which was thought to result in minorities' losing their identity as they adopted mainstream cultural patterns.

Counterculture is strongly at odds with conventional ways of life.
- Militant religious fundamentalist groups in the United States who plot to destroy Western society are examples of a counterculture.

CULTURAL CHANGE results from
- **invention** (examples include the telephone and the computer)
- **discovery** (for example, the recognition that women are capable of political leadership)
- **diffusion** (for example, the growing popularity of various ethnic foods and musical styles).

CULTURAL LAG results when some parts of a cultural system change faster than others.

How do we understand cultural differences?
- **ETHNOCENTRISM** links people to their society but can cause misunderstanding and conflict between societies.
- **CULTURAL RELATIVISM** is increasingly important as people of the world come into more and more contact with each other.

✓ *Global cultural patterns result from the worldwide flow of goods, information, and people.*

high culture cultural patterns that distinguish a society's elite

popular culture cultural patterns that are widespread among a society's population

subculture cultural patterns that set apart some segment of a society's population

multiculturalism a perspective recognizing the cultural diversity of the United States and promoting equal standing for all cultural traditions

Eurocentrism the dominance of European (especially English) cultural patterns

Afrocentrism emphasizing and promoting African cultural patterns

counterculture cultural patterns that strongly oppose those widely accepted within a society

cultural integration the close relationships among various elements of a cultural system

cultural lag the fact that some cultural elements change more quickly than others, disrupting a cultural system

ethnocentrism the practice of judging another culture by the standards of one's own culture

cultural relativism the practice of judging a culture by its own standards

Theoretical Analysis of Culture

The **STRUCTURAL-FUNCTIONAL APPROACH** views culture as a relatively stable system built on core values. All cultural patterns play some part in the ongoing operation of society.

The **SOCIAL-CONFLICT APPROACH** sees culture as a dynamic arena of inequality and conflict. Cultural patterns benefit some categories of people more than others.

SOCIOBIOLOGY explores how the long history of evolution has shaped patterns of culture in today's world.

See the Applying Theory.

cultural universals traits that are part of every known culture

sociobiology a theoretical approach that explores ways in which human biology affects how we create culture

Culture and Human Freedom

- Culture can limit the choices we make.
- As cultural creatures, we have the capacity to shape and reshape our world to meet our needs and pursue our dreams.

MAKING THE GRADE

Sample Test Questions

Multiple-Choice Questions

1. **Of all the world's countries, the United States is the most**
   a. multicultural.
   b. culturally uniform.
   c. slowly changing.
   d. resistant to cultural diversity.

2. **Ideas created by members of a society are part of**
   a. high culture.
   b. material culture.
   c. norms.
   d. nonmaterial culture.

3. **Sociologists define a symbol as**
   a. any gesture that insults others.
   b. any element of material culture.
   c. anything that has meaning to people who share a culture.
   d. any pattern that causes culture shock.

4. **U.S. culture holds a strong belief in**
   a. the traditions of the past.
   b. individuality.
   c. equality of condition for all.
   d. All of the above are correct.

5. **Cheating on a final examination is an example of violating campus**
   a. folkways.
   b. symbols.
   c. mores.
   d. high culture.

6. ***Subculture* refers to**
   a. a part of the population lacking culture.
   b. elements of popular culture.
   c. people who embrace high culture.
   d. cultural patterns that set apart a segment of a society's population.

7. **Which region of the United States has the largest share of people who speak a language other than English at home?**
   a. the Southwest
   b. the Northeast
   c. the Northwest
   d. the South

8. **Sociologists use the term "cultural lag" to refer to**
   a. the slowing of cultural change in the United States.
   b. the fact that some societies change faster than others do.
   c. that fact that some elements of culture change faster than others.
   d. people who are less cultured than others.

9. **Which of the following is a description of ethnocentrism?**
   a. taking pride in your ethnicity
   b. judging another culture using the standards of your own culture
   c. seeing another culture as better than your own
   d. judging another culture by its own standards

10. **Which theoretical approach focuses on the link between culture and social inequality?**
    a. the structural-functional approach
    b. the social-conflict approach
    c. the symbolic-interaction approach
    d. the sociobiology approach

ANSWERS: 1 (a); 2 (d); 3 (c); 4 (b); 5 (c); 6 (d); 7 (a); 8 (c); 9 (b); 10 (b).

Essay Questions

1. In the United States, hot dogs, hamburgers, French fries, and ice cream have long been considered national favorites. What cultural patterns help explain the love of these kinds of foods?
2. From what you have learned in this chapter, do you think that a global culture is emerging? Do you regard the prospect of a global culture as positive or negative? Why?

Society

All human beings live in societies. But societies around the world differ from one another in many ways, just as each society changes over time. This chapter presents classic theories that explain what "society" is all about.

Society

Photolibrary.com/Paul Nevin

Corbis – NY/Eligio Paoni/Contrasto

CHAPTER OVERVIEW

This chapter examines the concept of "society" through the work of one of today's leading sociologists, Gerhard Lenski, and three of sociology's founders, Karl Marx, Max Weber, and Emile Durkheim.

Washington Post Writers Group/©1996, *The Washington Post*. Photo by Carol Guzy. Reprinted with permission

Sididi Ag Inaka has never used instant messaging, logged on to the Internet, or spoken on a cell phone. Does such a person really exist in today's high-technology world? Well, how about this: Neither Inaka nor anyone in his family has ever been to a movie, watched television, or even read a newspaper.

Are these people visitors from another planet? Prisoners on some remote island? Not at all. They are Tuareg nomads who wander over the vast Sahara in the western African nations of Mali and Niger. Known as the "blue men of the desert" for the flowing blue robes worn by both men and women, the Tuareg herd camels, goats, and sheep and live in camps where the sand blows and the daytime temperature often reaches 120 degrees Fahrenheit. Life is hard, but most Tuareg try to hold on to traditional ways. With a stern look, Inaka says, "My father was a nomad. His father was a nomad. I am a nomad. My children will be nomads."

The Tuareg are among the world's poorest people. When the rains fail to come, they and their animals are at risk of losing their lives. Some are hopeful that the Tuareg people can gain some of the wealth that comes from mining uranium below the desert across which they have traveled for centuries. But whatever their economic fate, Inaka and his people are a society set apart, with little knowledge of the larger world and none of its advanced technology. But Inaka does not complain: "This is the life of my ancestors. This is the life that we know" (Buckley, 1996; Matloff, 1997; Lovgren, 1998; McConnell, 2007).

Society refers to *people who interact in a defined territory and share a culture.* In this chapter, you will learn more about human societies with the help of four important sociologists. We begin with the approach of **Gerhard Lenski,** who describes how societies have changed over the past 10,000 years. Lenski points to the importance of *technology* in shaping any society. Then we turn to three of sociology's founders. **Karl Marx,** like Lenski, took a long historical view of societies. But Marx's story of society is all about *social conflict* that arises as people work within an economic system to produce material goods. **Max Weber** tells a different tale, showing that the power of *ideas* shapes society. Weber contrasted the traditional thinking of simple societies with the rational thought that dominates complex societies today. Finally, **Emile Durkheim** helps us see the different ways that traditional and modern societies hang together.

All four visions of society answer a number of important questions: What makes the way of life of people such as the Tuareg of the Sahara so different from your life as a college student in the United States? How and why do all societies change? What forces divide a society? What forces hold a society together? This chapter will provide answers to all of these questions as we look at the work of important sociologists.

Gerhard Lenski: Society and Technology

Members of our society, who take instant messaging and television, as well as schools and hospitals, for granted, must wonder at the nomads of the Sahara, who live the same simple life their ancestors did centuries ago. The work of Gerhard Lenski (Nolan & Lenski, 2007) helps us understand the great differences among societies that have existed throughout human history.

Lenski uses the term **sociocultural evolution** to mean *changes that occur as a society gains new technology.* With only simple technology, societies such as the Tuareg have little control over nature, so they can support just a small number of people. Societies with complex technology such as cars and cell phones, while not necessarily "better," support hundreds of millions of people in far more affluent ways of life.

Inventing or adopting new technology sends ripples of change throughout a society. When our ancestors first discovered how to make a sail so that wind power could move a boat, they created a new form of transportation that would take them to new lands, greatly expand their economy, and increase their military power. In addition,

society people who interact in a defined territory and share a culture

Gerhard Lenski (society is defined by level of technology)

Karl Marx (society is defined by type of social conflict)

Max Weber (society is defined by ideas/mode of thinking)

Emile Durkheim (society is defined by its type of solidarity)

the more technology a society has, the faster it changes. Technologically simple societies change very slowly; Sididi Ag Inaka says he lives "the life of my ancestors." How many people in U.S. society can say that they live the way their grandparents or great-grandparents did? Modern, high-technology societies such as our own change so fast that people usually experience major social changes during a single lifetime. Imagine how surprised your great-grandmother would be to hear about "Googling" and instant messaging, artificial intelligence and iPods, replacement hearts and test-tube babies, space shuttles and screamo music.

Drawing on Lenski's work, we will examine five types of societies, defined by their technology: hunting and gathering societies, horticultural and pastoral societies, agrarian societies, industrial societies, and postindustrial societies.

After a nearby forest was burned, these Aboriginal women in Australia spent the day collecting roots, which they will use to make dye for their clothing. Members of such societies live closely linked to nature.

Hunting and Gathering Societies

In the simplest of all societies, people live by **hunting and gathering,** *making use of simple tools to hunt animals and gather vegetation for food.* From the time that our species appeared 3 million years ago until about 12,000 years ago, *all* humans were hunters and gatherers. Even in 1800, many hunting and gathering societies could be found around the world. But today just a few remain, including the Aka and Pygmies of Central Africa, the Bushmen of southwestern Africa, the Aborigines of Australia, the Kaska Indians of northwestern Canada, and the Batek and Semai of Malaysia.

With little ability to control their environment, hunters and gatherers spend most of their time looking for game and collecting plants to eat. Only in lush areas with lots of food do hunters and gatherers have much chance for leisure. Because it takes a large amount of land to support even a few people, hunting and gathering societies have just a few dozen members. They must also be nomadic, moving on to find new sources of vegetation or to follow migrating animals. Although they may return to favored sites, they rarely form permanent settlements.

Hunting and gathering societies depend on the family to do many things. The family must get and distribute food, protect its members, and teach the children. Everyone's life is much the same; people spend most of their time getting their next meal. Age and gender have some effect on what individuals do. Healthy adults do most of the work, leaving the very young and the very old to help out as they can. Women gather vegetation—which provides most of the food—while men take on the less certain job of hunting. Although men and women perform different tasks, most hunters and gatherers probably see the sexes as having about the same social importance (Leacock, 1978).

Hunting and gathering societies usually have a *shaman,* or spiritual leader, who enjoys high prestige but has to work to find food like everyone else. In short, people in hunting and gathering societies come close to being socially equal.

Hunters and gatherers use simple weapons—the spear, bow and arrow, and stone knife—but rarely to wage war. Their real enemy is the forces of nature: Storms and droughts can kill off their food supply, and there is little they can do for someone who has a serious accident or illness. Being at risk in this way encourages people to cooperate and share, a strategy that raises everyone's chances of survival. But the truth is that many die in childhood, and no more than half reach the age of twenty (Lenski, Nolan, & Lenski, 1995).

During the past century, societies with more powerful technology have closed in on the few remaining hunters and gatherers, reducing their food supply. As a result, hunting and gathering societies are disappearing. Fortunately, study of this way of life has given us valuable information about human history and our basic ties to the natural world.

Horticultural and Pastoral Societies

Some 10,000 to 12,000 years ago, as the timeline inside the back cover shows, a new technology began to change the lives of human beings. People developed **horticulture,** *the use of hand tools to raise crops.* Using a hoe to work the soil and a digging stick to punch holes in the

Seeing SOCIOLOGY in the 

Nomadic Herders Go High-Tech

By MARSHA WALTON
December 4, 2006

Satellites, cell phones and spectrometers: Probably not the first things you think of when you picture sheep and goat herders in Afghanistan. But those modern tools may soon make the lives of nomadic families a little more stable.

Afghanistan is the latest location for projects coordinated by the University of California-Davis and Texas A&M University, to provide early warning systems about animal health and to help pinpoint the location of the healthiest grazing areas.

A $4.4 million grant from the U.S. Agency for International Development's Mission to Afghanistan will fund the effort for four years.

"Agriculture is so fundamental to helping people become economically self-sufficient," said Elsa Murano, dean of Agriculture and Life Sciences at Texas A&M University in College Station, Texas.

"And the economic stability that comes from being able to sell your goods, produce your goods, and get an income from that is a stabilizing force like no other," she said.

Texas A&M research scientist Jay Angerer, who worked with herders in Mongolia, says there is a mixed reaction when he first explains the tools and how they might help.

"I think that they're welcoming in the sense that they're glad that someone is concerned about their issues and problems, and I think they're very curious and interested," said Angerer.

But he says it is also important to respect the understanding they have gained from generations of tending sheep, goats, cattle, and horses. In addition to the natural disasters of drought and dust storms, herding families in east Africa and Afghanistan have also had to survive civil wars and unstable governments.

"I always tell people that I train that this shouldn't be the only tool that you use to make a decision. There's lots of information out there," said Angerer.

The U.S. researchers are often joined by scientists and college students from the region to collect and analyze plant samples. That data about forage is added to information about climate and precipitation, some from satellite information, and some from ground reporting stations.

Computer models then predict how those plants will grow, based on soil conditions and rainfall. The researchers can then forecast where the richest vegetation will be, especially if drought or other crisis conditions exist.

"By giving that information you could provide the herder the information to know whether they need to sell animals, buy supplements or to make a decision that, 'I'm going to cope with this drought by hanging on just a little bit longer,'" said Angerer.

The livestock experts also gain important clues about animal health from the herds' manure.

"We're using a very convenient product, manure, to determine what the animals were consuming, what their diet was, which tells us, are they healthy? Are they going to gain weight? Are they going to meet their reproductive demands?"

ground to plant seeds may not seem like something that would change the world, but these inventions allowed people to give up gathering in favor of growing their own food. The first humans to plant gardens lived in fertile regions of the Middle East. Cultural diffusion spread this knowledge to Latin America and Asia and eventually all over the world.

Not all societies were quick to give up hunting and gathering for horticulture. Hunters and gatherers living where food was plentiful probably saw little reason to change their ways. People living in dry regions (such as the deserts of Africa or the Middle East) or mountainous areas found little use for horticulture because they could not grow much anyway. Such people (including the Tuareg) were more likely to adopt **pastoralism,** *the domestication of animals.* Today, societies that mix horticulture and pastoralism can be found throughout South America, Africa, and Asia. Seeing Sociology in the News describes how some nomadic herders in Afghanistan are benefiting from high technology supplied by scientists in the United States.

Growing plants and raising animals greatly increased food production, so populations expanded from dozens to hundreds of people. Pastoralists remained nomadic, leading their herds to fresh grazing lands. But horticulturalists formed settlements, moving only when the soil gave out. Joined by trade, these settlements formed societies with populations reaching into the thousands.

Once a society is capable of producing a *material surplus*—more resources than are needed to support the population—not everyone has to work at providing food. Greater specialization results: Some make crafts, while others engage in trade, cut hair, apply tattoos, or serve as priests. Compared to hunting and gathering societies, horticultural and pastoral societies are more socially diverse.

But being more productive does not make a society "better" in every sense. As some families produce more than others, they become richer and more powerful. Horticultural and pastoral societies have greater inequality, with elites using government power—and military force—to serve their own interests. But leaders do not have the ability to communicate or to travel over large distances, so they can control only a small number of people, rather than vast empires.

Religion also differs among types of societies. Hunters and gatherers believe that many spirits inhabit the world. Horticulturalists, however, are more likely to think of one God as the creator of the world. Pastoral societies carry this belief further, seeing God as directly involved in the well-being of the entire world. The pastoral roots of Judaism and Christianity are evident in the term "pastor" and the common view of God as a shepherd ("The Lord is my shepherd," says Psalm 23) who stands watch over us all.

Agrarian Societies

About 5,000 years ago, another revolution in technology was taking place in the Middle East, one that would end up changing life on Earth. This was the emergence of **agriculture,** *large-scale cultivation using plows harnessed to animals or more powerful energy sources.* So important was the invention of the animal-drawn plow, along with other breakthroughs of the period—including irrigation, the wheel, said Kris Banik, lab manager at the Grazingland Animal Nutrition Lab at Texas A&M.

At that Texas lab, samples from farms and ranches are carefully dried and pulverized before they are analyzed with a Near Infrared Reflectance Spectroscopy machine, or NIRS. The device provides a biochemical snapshot of the organic material, indicating how much protein and other digestible organic matter the animals have consumed.

But shepherds and herders, often on the move in mountains or deserts, do not have the luxury of a nearby lab. So researchers developed a tool to take to their turf.

A portable spectroscopy unit can accomplish the same thing, with almost instant results that can provide early warning to herders of their animals' health.

"If we can go out in the pasture in real time and be able to take a scan of that sample, and then be able to give an answer right then, we'll cut five days off that decision-making process," said Doug Tolleson, director of the Grazingland Animal Nutrition Lab. "If you had a rapid onset of a drought, that could make a lot of difference." . . .

[Professor Robert Kaitho, an animal nutritionist] says technology now goes beyond just keeping animals healthier. It can help families get a better price for their animals, through a cell phone, or any Internet connection. Sending a text message to a cell phone number will get within a couple of minutes the current market prices for livestock.

"They are able to get information otherwise that was only limited to middlemen, and those who had connections in the cities," he said. "Now, the common people have access to that same information." . . .

So how do the herders feel about scientists from other countries bringing in their new tools to a very established lifestyle?

Michael J. Jacobs . . . visited Policharkhe, an area where Kuchi tribespeople spend a few months between their summer and winter grazing lands.

Through a translator, Jacobs talked to one sheep and goat herder. At one point the translator started to chuckle. Jacobs asked him what the herder had said.

The translator said: "He is asking what took you so long to help them."

WHAT DO YOU THINK?

1. What specific benefits can nomadic herders in Afghanistan gain from cooperation with scientists using high technology?
2. What unexpected and possibly undesirable consequences might develop from this cooperation?
3. Do you think there are lessons high-technology societies can learn from these nomadic herders in Afghanistan? If so, what are they?

writing, numbers, and the use of various metals—that this moment in history is often called the "dawn of civilization."

Using animal-drawn plows, farmers could cultivate fields far bigger than the garden-sized plots planted by horticulturalists. Plows have the added advantage of turning and aerating the soil, making it more fertile. As a result, farmers could work the same land for generations, encouraging the development of permanent settlements. With the ability to grow a surplus of food and to transport goods using animal-powered wagons, agrarian societies greatly expanded in size and population. About 100 C.E., for example, the agrarian Roman Empire contained some 70 million people spread over 2 million square miles (Nolan & Lenski, 2007).

Greater production meant even more specialization. Now there were dozens of distinct occupations, from farmers to builders to metalworkers. With so many people producing so many different things, people invented money as a common standard of exchange, and the old barter system—in which people traded one thing for another—was abandoned.

Agrarian societies have extreme social inequality, typically more than modern societies such as our own. In most cases, a large number of the people are peasants or slaves, who do most of the work. Elites therefore have time for more "refined" activities, including the study of philosophy, art, and literature. This explains the historical link between "high culture" and social privilege.

Among hunters and gatherers and also among horticulturalists, women provide most of the food, which gives them social importance. Agriculture, however, raises men to a position of social dominance. Using heavy metal plows pulled by large animals, men take charge of food production in agrarian societies. Women are left with the support tasks, such as weeding and carrying water to the fields (Boulding, 1976; Fisher, 1979).

In agrarian societies, religion reinforces the power of elites by defining both loyalty and hard work as moral obligations. Many of the "Wonders of the Ancient World," such as the Great Wall of China and the Great Pyramids of Egypt, were possible only because emperors and pharaohs had almost absolute power and were able to control a large political system and order their people to work for a lifetime without pay.

Of the societies described so far, agrarian societies have the most social inequality. Agrarian technology also gives people a greater range of life choices, which is the reason that agrarian societies differ more from one another than horticultural and pastoral societies do.

Industrial Societies

Industrialism, which first took hold in the rich nations of today's world, is *the production of goods using advanced sources of energy to drive large machinery.* Until the industrial era began, the major source of energy had been the muscles of humans and the animals they tended. Around the year 1750, people turned to water power and then steam boilers to operate mills and factories filled with larger and larger machines.

sociocultural evolution changes that occur as a society gains new technology

hunting and gathering the use of simple tools to hunt animals and gather vegetation for food → **horticulture** the use of hand tools to raise crops

pastoralism the domestication of animals

→ **agriculture** large scale cultivation using plows harnessed to animals or more powerful energy sources → **industialism** the production of goods using advanced sources of energy to drive large machinery → **postindustrialism** the production of information using computer technology

Industrial technology gave people such power to alter their environment that change took place faster than ever before. It is probably correct to say that the new industrial societies changed more in one century than they had over the course of the previous thousand years. Change was so rapid that it sparked the birth of sociology itself. By 1900, railroads crossed the land, steamships traveled the seas, and steel-framed skyscrapers reached far higher than any of the old cathedrals that symbolized the agrarian age.

But that was only the beginning. Soon automobiles allowed people to move quickly almost anywhere, and electricity powered homes full of modern "conveniences" such as refrigerators, washing machines, air conditioners, and entertainment centers. Electronic communication, beginning with the telegraph and the telephone and followed by radio, television, and computers, gave people the ability to reach others instantly, all over the world.

Work also changed. In agrarian communities, most men and women worked in the home or in the fields nearby. Industrialization drew people away from home to factories situated near energy sources (such as coalfields) that powered their machinery. The result was a weakening of close working relationships, strong family ties, and many of the traditional values, beliefs, and customs that guide agrarian life.

Getty Images/Monty Brinton/CBS

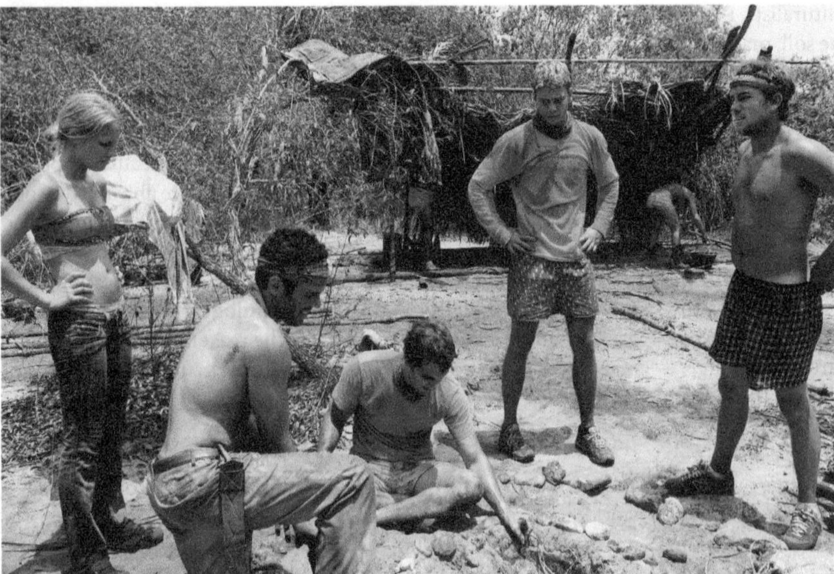

What would it be like to live in a society with simple technology? That's the premise of the television show *Survivor*. What advantages do societies with simple technology afford their members? What disadvantages do you see?

December 28, Moray, in the Andes highlands of Peru. *We are high in the mountains in a small community of several dozen families, miles from the nearest electric line or paved road. At about 12,000 feet, breathing is hard for people not used to the thin air, so we walk slowly. But hard work is no problem for the man and his son tilling a field near their home with a horse and plow. Too poor to buy a tractor, these people till the land in the same way that their ancestors did 500 years ago.*

With industrialization, occupational specialization became greater than ever. Today, the kind of work you do has a lot to do with your standard of living, so people now often size up one another in terms of their jobs rather than according to their family ties, as agrarian people do. Rapid change and people's tendency to move from place to place also make social life more anonymous, increase cultural diversity, and promote subcultures and countercultures.

Industrial technology changes the family, too, reducing its traditional importance as the center of social life. No longer does the family serve as the main setting for work, learning, and religious worship. Technological change also plays a part in making families more diverse, with a greater share of single people, divorced people, single-parent families, and stepfamilies.

Perhaps the greatest effect of industrialization has been to raise living standards, which increased fivefold in the United States over the past century. Although at first it only benefits the elite few, industrial technology is so productive that incomes rise over time and people have longer and more comfortable lives. Even social inequality decreases slightly, because industrial societies provide extended schooling and greater political rights. Around the world, industrialization has had the effect of increasing the demand for a greater political voice, a pattern evident in South Korea, Taiwan, the People's Republic of China, and the nations of Eastern Europe and the former Soviet Union.

Postindustrial Societies

Many industrial societies, including the United States, have now entered a new phase of technological development, and we can extend Lenski's analysis to take account of recent trends.

MAKING THE GRADE

The beginning of "modernity" is linked to the development of industrial production, first in Europe and soon after in the United States. The industrial era also sparked the development of sociology.

SEEING SOCIOLOGY in Everyday Life

How do the *Jurassic Park* movies portray the advantages and disadvantages of modern technology?

Getty Images Inc. – Hulton Archive Photos

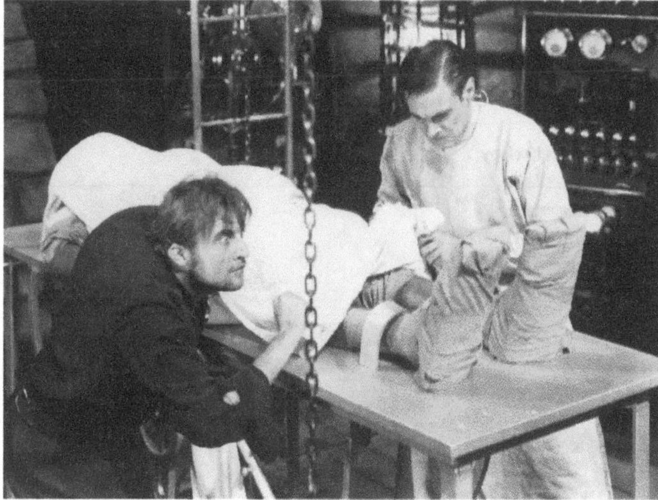

Everett Collection/Warner Bros.

Does advancing technology make society better? In some ways, perhaps. However, many films—as far back as *Frankenstein* (left) in 1931 and as recently as the 2009 film *Terminator Salvation* (right)—have expressed the concern that new technology not only solves old problems but also creates new ones. All the sociological theorists discussed in this chapter shared this ambivalent view of the modern world.

A generation ago, the sociologist Daniel Bell (1973) coined the term **postindustrialism** to refer to *the production of information using computer technology.* Production in industrial societies centers on factories and machinery generating material goods; postindustrial production relies on computers and other electronic devices that create, process, store, and apply information. Just as people in industrial societies learn mechanical skills, people in postindustrial societies such as ours develop information-based skills and carry out their work using computers and other forms of high-technology communication.

A postindustrial society uses less and less of its labor force for industrial production. At the same time, more jobs become available for clerical workers, teachers, writers, sales managers, and marketing representatives, all of whom process information.

The Information Revolution, which is at the heart of postindustrial society, is most evident in rich nations, yet new information technology affects people in all countires around the world. A worldwide flow of products, people, and information now links societies and has advanced a global culture. In this sense, the postindustrial society is at the heart of globalization.

The Summing Up table provides a review of how technology shapes life in societies at different stages of sociocultural evolution.

The Limits of Technology

More complex technology has made life better by raising productivity, reducing infectious disease, and sometimes just relieving boredom. But technology provides no quick fix for social problems. Poverty, for example, remains a reality for some 38 million women and men in the United States and 1.4 billion people worldwide (U.S. Census Bureau, 2008).

Technology also creates new problems that our ancestors (and people like Sididi Ag Inaka today) could hardly imagine. Industrial and postindustrial societies give us more personal freedom, but they often lack the sense of community that was part of preindustrial life. Most seriously, an increasing number of the world's nations with nuclear technology have stockpiles of weapons that could send the world back to the Stone Age—if we survive at all.

Advancing technology has also threatened the physical environment. Each stage in sociocultural evolution has introduced more powerful sources of energy and increased our appetite for Earth's resources. Ask yourself whether we can continue to pursue material prosperity without permanently damaging our planet.

Technological advances have improved life and brought the world's people closer. But establishing peace, ensuring justice, and protecting the environment are problems that technology alone cannot solve.

social conflict the stuggle between segments of society over valued resources

capitalists people who own and operate factories and other businesses in pursuit of profits

proletarians people who sell their labor for wages

SEEING SOCIOLOGY in Everyday Life

How might Marx view the advertising of products that promise to make our lives more meaningful as an example of false consciousness in a capitalist society?

SUMMING UP

Sociocultural Evolution

Type of Society	Historical Period	Productive Technology	Population Size
Hunting and Gathering Societies	Only type of society until about 12,000 years ago; still common several centuries ago; the few examples remaining today are threatened with extinction	Primitive weapons	25–40 people
Horticultural and Pastoral Societies	From about 12,000 years ago, with decreasing numbers after about 3000 B.C.E.	Horticultural societies use hand tools for cultivating plants; pastoral societies are based on the domestication of animals	Settlements of several hundred people, connected through trading ties to form societies of several thousand people
Agrarian Societies	From about 5,000 years ago, with large but decreasing numbers today	Animal-drawn plow	Millions of people
Industrial Societies	From about 1750 to the present	Advanced sources of energy; mechanized production	Millions of people
Postindustrial Societies	Emerging in recent decades	Computers that support an information-based economy	Millions of people

Karl Marx: Society and Conflict

The first of our classic visions of society comes from Karl Marx (1818–1883), an early giant in the field of sociology whose influence continues today. Keenly aware of how the Industrial Revolution had changed Europe, Marx spent most of his adult life in London, the capital of what was then the vast British Empire. He was awed by the size and productive power of the new factories going up all over Britain. Along with other industrial nations, Britain was producing more goods than ever before, drawing resources from around the world and churning out products at a dizzying rate.

What astounded Marx even more was that the riches produced by this new technology ended up in the hands of only a few people. As he walked around the city of London, he could see for himself that a handful of aristocrats and industrialists lived in fabulous mansions staffed by servants, where they enjoyed both luxury and privilege. At the same time, most people labored long hours for low wages and lived in slums. Some even slept in the streets, where they were likely to die young from diseases brought on by cold and poor nutrition.

Marx saw his society in terms of a basic contradiction: In a country so rich, how could so many people be so poor? Just as important, he asked, how can this situation be changed? Many people think Marx set out to tear societies apart. But he was motivated by compassion and wanted to help a badly divided society create a new and more just social order.

At the heart of Marx's thinking is the idea of **social conflict,** *the struggle between segments of society over valued resources.* Social conflict can, of course, take many forms: Individuals quarrel, colleges have longstanding sports rivalries, and nations go to war. For Marx, however, the most important type of social conflict was *class conflict* arising from the way a society produces material goods.

Society and Production

Living in the nineteenth century, Marx observed the early decades of industrial capitalism in Europe. This economic system, Marx explained, turned a small part of the population into **capitalists,** *people who own and operate factories and other businesses in pursuit of profits.* A capitalist tries to make a profit by selling a product for more

social institutions the major spheres of social life, or societal subsystems, organized to meet human needs

false consciousness explaining social problems as the shortcomings of individuals rather than as the flaws of society

MAKING THE GRADE

Marx's analysis of society uses the social-conflict approach. In his eyes, class conflict (rather than gender conflict or racial conflict) is most important.

Settlement Pattern	Social Organization	Examples
Nomadic	Family-centered; specialization limited to age and sex; little social inequality	Pygmies of Central Africa, Bushmen of southwestern Africa, Aborigines of Australia, Semai of Malaysia, Kaska Indians of Canada
Horticulturalists form small permanent settlements; pastoralists are nomadic	Family-centered; religious system begins to develop; moderate specialization; increased social inequality	Middle Eastern societies about 5000 B.C.E., various societies today in New Guinea and other Pacific islands, Yąnomamö today in South America
Cities become common, but they generally contain only a small proportion of the population	Family loses significance as distinct religious, political, and economic systems emerge; extensive specialization; increased social inequality	Egypt during construction of the Great Pyramids, medieval Europe, numerous predominantly agrarian societies of the world today
Cities contain most of the population	Distinct religious, political, economic, educational, and family systems; highly specialized; marked social inequality persists, lessening somewhat over time	Most societies today in Europe and North America, Australia, and Japan, which generate most of the world's industrial production
Population remains concentrated in cities	Similar to industrial societies, with information processing and other service work gradually replacing industrial production	Industrial societies are now entering the postindustrial stage

than it costs to produce. Capitalism turns most of the population into industrial workers, whom Marx called **proletarians,** *people who sell their labor for wages.* To Marx, a system of capitalist production always ends up creating conflict between capitalists and workers. To keep profits high, capitalists keep wages low. But workers want higher wages. Since profits and wages come from the same pool of funds, the result is conflict. As Marx saw it, this conflict could end only with the end of capitalism itself.

All societies are composed of **social institutions,** *the major spheres of social life, or societal subsystems, organized to meet human needs.* Examples of social institutions include the economy, the political system, the family, religion, and education. In his analysis of society, Marx argued that one institution—the economy—dominates all the others and defines the true nature of a society. Drawing on the philosophical approach called *materialism,* which says that how humans produce material goods shapes their experiences, Marx believed that the other social institutions all operate in a way that supports a society's economy. Lenski focused on how technology molds a society, but Marx argued that the economy is a society's "real foundation" (1959:43, orig. 1859).

Marx viewed the economic system as society's *infrastructure* (*infra* is Latin, meaning "below"). Other social institutions, including the family, the political system, and religion, are built on this foundation; they form society's *superstructure* and support the economy. Marx's theory is illustrated in Figure 1. For example, under capitalism, the legal system protects capitalists' wealth, and the family allows capitalists to pass their property from one generation to the next.

Marx was well aware that most people living in industrial-capitalist societies do not recognize how capitalism shapes the entire operation of their society. Most people, in fact, regard the right to own private property or pass it on to their children as "natural." In the same way, many of us tend to see rich people as having "earned" their money through long years of schooling and hard work; we see the poor, on the other hand, as lacking skills and the personal drive to make more of themselves. Marx rejected this type of thinking, calling it **false consciousness,** *explaining social problems as the shortcomings of individuals rather than as the flaws of society.* Marx was saying, in effect, that it is not "people" who make society so unequal but rather the system of capitalist production. False consciousness, he believed, hurts people by hiding the real cause of their problems.

MAKING THE GRADE

Take a careful look at Figure 1, which shows Marx's belief that the economy is the foundation of society (the "infrastructure") that affects the operation of the other social institutions as well as cultural ideas and values (the "superstructure"). This approach is called *materialism* because how a society produces material goods is seen as defining the whole social system.

class conflict conflict between entire classes over the distribution of a society's wealth and power

class consciousness workers' recognition of themselves as a class unified in opposition to capitalists and ultimately to capitalism itself

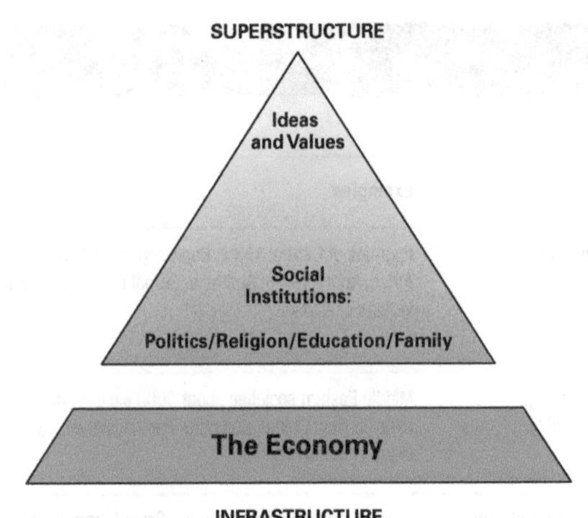

FIGURE 1 **Karl Marx's Model of Society**

This diagram illustrates Marx's materialist view that the system of economic production shapes the entire society. Economic production involves both technology (industry, in the case of capitalism) and social relationships (for capitalism, the relationship between the capitalists, who own the factories and businesses, and the workers). On this infrastructure, or foundation, rests society's superstructure, which includes its major social institutions as well as core cultural values and ideas. Marx maintained that every part of a society supports the economic system.

Conflict and History

For Marx, conflict is the engine that drives social change. Sometimes societies change at a slow, *evolutionary* rate. But they may erupt in rapid, *revolutionary* change.

To Marx, early hunters and gatherers formed primitive communist societies. *Communism* is a system in which people commonly own and equally share the food and other things they produce. People in hunting and gathering societies do not have much, but they share what they have. In addition, because everyone does the same kind of work, there is little chance of social conflict.

With technological advance comes social inequality. Among horticultural, pastoral, and early agrarian societies—which Marx lumped together as the "ancient world"—warfare was frequent, and the victors made their captives slaves.

Agriculture brings still more wealth to a society's elite but does little for most other people, who labor as serfs and are barely better off than slaves. As Marx saw it, the state supported the feudal system (in which the elite or nobility had all the power), assisted by the church, which claimed that this arrangement was God's will. This is why Marx thought that feudalism was simply "exploitation, veiled by religious and political illusions" (Marx & Engels, 1972:337, orig. 1848).

Gradually, new productive forces started to break down the feudal order. As trade steadily increased, cities grew, and merchants and skilled craftsworkers formed the new capitalist class or *bourgeoisie* (a French word meaning "people of the town"). After 1800, the bourgeoisie also controlled factories, becoming richer and richer so that they soon rivaled the ancient landowning nobility. For their part, the nobles looked down their noses at this upstart "commercial" class, but in time, these capitalists took control of European societies. To Marx's way of thinking, then, new technology was only part of the Industrial Revolution; it also served as a class revolution in which capitalists overthrew the old agrarian elite.

Industrialization also led to the growth of the proletariat. English landowners converted fields once plowed by serfs into grazing land for sheep to produce wool for the textile mills. Forced from the land, millions of people migrated to cities to work in factories. Marx envisioned these workers one day joining together to form a revolutionary class that would overthrow the capitalist system.

Capitalism and Class Conflict

"The history of all hitherto existing society is the history of class struggles." With these words, Marx and his collaborator, Friedrich Engels, began their best-known statement, the *Manifesto of the Communist Party* (1972:335, orig. 1848). Industrial capitalism, like earlier types of society, contains two major social classes: the ruling class, whose members (capitalists or bourgeoisie) own productive property, and the oppressed (proletarians), who sell their labor, reflecting the two basic positions in the productive system. Like masters and slaves in the ancient world and like nobles and serfs in feudal systems, capitalists and proletarians are engaged in class conflict today. Currently, as in the past, one class controls the other as productive property. Marx used the term **class conflict** (and sometimes *class struggle*) to refer to *conflict between entire classes over the distribution of a society's wealth and power.*

Class conflict is nothing new. What distinguishes the conflict in capitalist society, Marx pointed out, is how out in the open it is. Agrarian nobles and serfs, for all their differences, were bound together by traditions and mutual obligations. Industrial capitalism dissolved those ties so that loyalty and honor were replaced by "naked self-interest." Because the proletarians had no personal ties to the capitalists, Marx saw no reason for them to put up with their oppression.

Marx knew that revolution would not come easily. First, workers must *become aware* of their oppression and see capitalism as its true cause. Second, they must *organize and act* to address their problems. This means that false consciousness must be replaced with **class consciousness,** *workers' recognition of themselves as a class unified in opposition to capitalists and ultimately to capitalism itself.* Because the inhumanity of early capitalism was plain for him to see, Marx

alienation the experience of isolation and misery resulting from powerlessness

MAKING THE GRADE

Pay attention to Marx's concept of alienation, one of his most important contributions to sociology. Later on, we will discuss Max Weber's view of alienation, which has a somewhat different meaning, so try to keep the two clear.

concluded that industrial workers would soon rise up to destroy this economic system.

How would the capitalists react? Their wealth made them strong. But Marx saw a weakness in the capitalist armor. Motivated by a desire for personal gain, capitalists feared competition with other capitalists. Marx predicted, therefore, that capitalists would be slow to band together despite their common interests. In addition, he reasoned, capitalists kept employees' wages low in order to maximize profits, which made the workers' misery ever greater. In the long run, Marx believed, capitalists would bring about their own undoing.

Capitalism and Alienation

Marx also condemned capitalist society for producing **alienation,** *the experience of isolation and misery resulting from powerlessness.* To the capitalists, workers are nothing more than a source of labor, to be hired and fired at will. Dehumanized by their jobs (repetitive factory work in the past and processing orders on a computer today), workers find little satisfaction and feel unable to improve their situation. Here we see another contradiction of capitalist society: As people develop technology to gain power over the world, the capitalist economy gains more control over people.

Marx noted four ways in which capitalism alienates workers:

1. **Alienation from the act of working.** Ideally, people work to meet their needs and to develop their personal potential. Capitalism, however, denies workers a say in what they make or how they make it. Further, much of the work is a repetition of routine tasks. The fact that today we replace workers with machines whenever possible would not have surprised Marx. As far as he was concerned, capitalism had turned human beings into machines long ago.
2. **Alienation from the products of work.** The product of work belongs not to workers but to capitalists, who sell it for profit. Thus, Marx reasoned, the more of themselves workers invest in their work, the more they lose.
3. **Alienation from other workers.** Through work, Marx claimed, people build bonds of community. Industrial capitalism, however, makes work competitive rather than cooperative, setting each person apart from everyone else and offering little chance for companionship.
4. **Alienation from human potential.** Industrial capitalism alienates workers from their human potential. Marx argued that a worker "does not fulfill himself in his work but denies himself, has a feeling of misery rather than well-being, does not freely develop his physical and mental energies, but is physically exhausted and mentally debased. The worker, therefore, feels himself to be at home only during his leisure time, whereas at work he feels homeless" (1964:124–25, orig. 1848). In short, industrial capitalism turns an activity that should express the best qualities in human beings into a dull and dehumanizing experience.

Marx viewed alienation, in its various forms, as a barrier to social change. But he hoped that industrial workers would overcome their alienation by uniting into a true social class, aware of the cause of their problems and ready to change society.

Revolution

The only way out of the trap of capitalism, Marx argued, is to remake society. He imagined a system of production that could provide for the social needs of all. He called this system *socialism.* Although Marx knew that such a dramatic change would not come easily, he must have been disappointed that he did not live to see workers in England rise up. Still, convinced that capitalism was a social evil, he believed that in time the working majority would realize they held the key to a better future. This change would certainly be revolutionary and perhaps even violent. Marx believed that a socialist society would bring class conflict to an end.

Changes in industrial-capitalist societies since Marx's time help to explain why the revolution he wanted never took place. In addition, Marx failed to foresee that the revolution he imagined could take the

Photofest

A common fear among thinkers in the early industrial era was that people, now slaves to the new machines, would be stripped of their humanity. No one captured this idea better than the comic actor Charlie Chaplin, who wrote and starred in the 1936 film *Modern Times*.

rationalization of society the historical change from tradition to rationality as the main type of human thought

tradition values and beliefs passed from generation to generation

rationality a way of thinking that emphasizes deliberate, matter-of-fact calculation of the most efficient way to accomplish a particular task

ideal type an abstract statement of the essential characteristics of any social phenomenon

form of repressive regimes, such as Stalin's government in the Soviet Union, that would end up killing tens of millions of people (R. F. Hamilton, 2001). But in his own time, Marx looked toward the future with hope: "The proletarians have nothing to lose but their chains. They have a world to win" (Marx & Engels, 1972:362, orig. 1848).

Max Weber: The Rationalization of Society

With a wide knowledge of law, economics, religion, and history, Max Weber (1864–1920) produced what many experts regard as the greatest individual contribution to sociology. This scholar, born to a prosperous family in Germany, had much to say about how modern society differs from earlier types of social organization.

Weber understood the power of technology, and he shared many of Marx's ideas about social conflict. But he disagreed with Marx's philosophy of materialism. Weber's philosophical approach, called *idealism,* emphasized how human ideas—especially beliefs and values—shape society. He argued that societies differ not in terms of how people produce things but in how people think about the world. In Weber's view, modern society was the product of a new way of thinking.

Weber compared societies in different times and places. To make the comparisons, he relied on the **ideal type,** *an abstract statement of the essential characteristics of any social phenomenon.* Following Weber's approach, for example, we might speak of "preindustrial" and "industrial" societies as ideal types. The use of the word "ideal" does not mean that one or the other is "good" or "best." Nor does an ideal type refer to any actual society. Rather, think of an ideal type as a way of defining a type of society in its pure form. We have already used ideal types in comparing "hunting and gathering societies" with "industrial societies" and "capitalism" with "socialism."

Everett Collection/IFC Films

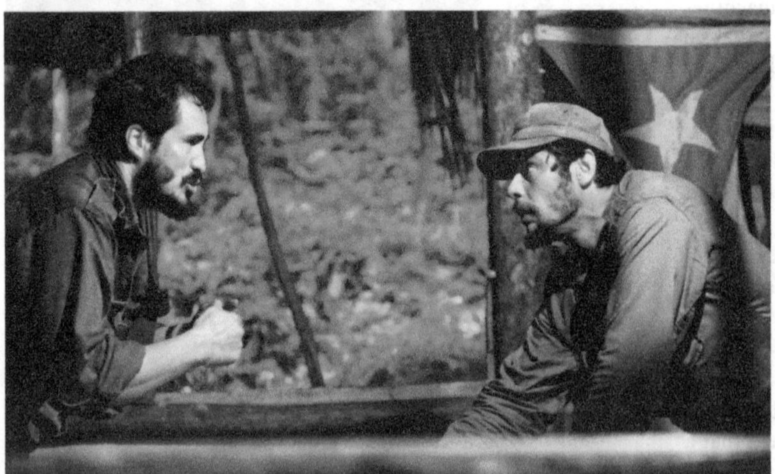

The 2008 film *Che* tells the story of Ernesto "Che" Guevara, who put Marxist theory into action by encouraging revolutionary movements throughout Latin America. Che played an important role as an advisor to Fidel Castro during the Cuban revolution, after which he went on to organize an unsuccessful revolution in Bolivia.

Two Worldviews: Tradition and Rationality

Rather than categorizing societies according to their technology or productive systems, Weber focused on ways people think about their world. Members of preindustrial societies are bound by *tradition,* and people in industrial-capitalist societies are guided by *rationality.*

By **tradition,** Weber meant *values and beliefs passed from generation to generation.* In other words, traditional people are guided by the past. They consider particular actions right and proper mostly because they have been accepted for so long.

People in modern societies, however, favor **rationality,** *a way of thinking that emphasizes deliberate, matter-of-fact calculation of the most efficient way to accomplish a particular task.* Sentimental ties to the past have no place in a rational worldview, and tradition becomes simply one kind of information. Typically, modern people think and act on the basis of what they see as the present and future consequences of their choices. They evaluate jobs, schooling, and even relationships in terms of what they put into them and what they expect to receive in return.

Weber viewed both the Industrial Revolution and the development of capitalism as evidence of modern rationality. Such changes are all part of the **rationalization of society,** *the historical change from tradition to rationality as the main type of human thought.* Weber went on to describe modern society as "disenchanted" because scientific thinking has swept away most of people's sentimental ties to the past.

The willingness to adopt the latest technology is one strong indicator of how rationalized a society is. To illustrate the global pattern of rationalization, Global Map 1 shows where in the world personal computers are found. In general, the high-income countries of North America and Europe use personal computers the most, but they are rare in low-income nations.

Why are some societies more eager than others to adopt new technology? Those with a more rational worldview might consider new computer or medical technology a breakthrough, but those with a very traditional

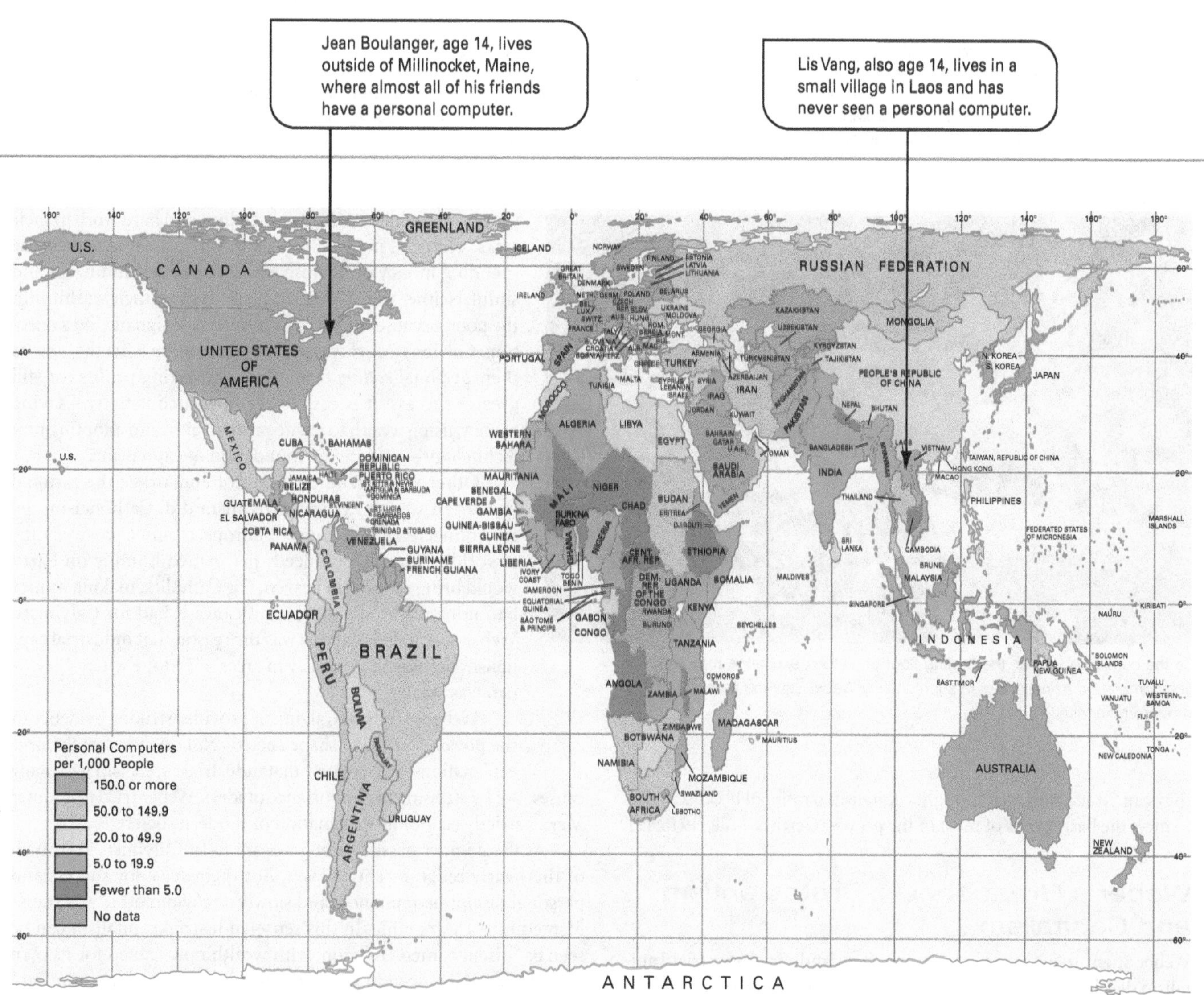

Window on the World

GLOBAL MAP 1 **High Technology in Global Perspective**

Countries with traditional cultures cannot afford, choose to ignore, or even intentionally resist new technology that nations with highly rationalized ways of life quickly embrace. Personal computers, central to today's high technology, are commonplace in high-income countries such as the United States. In low-income nations, by contrast, they are unknown to most people.

Source: International Telecommunication Union (2006, 2007).

culture might reject such devices as a threat to their way of life. The Tuareg nomads of northern Mali, described at the beginning of this chapter, shrug off the idea of using telephones: Why would anyone in the desert want a cell phone? Similarly, in the United States, the Amish refuse to have telephones in their homes because it is not part of their traditional way of life.

In Weber's view, the amount of technological innovation depends on how a society's people understand their world. Many people throughout history have had the opportunity to adopt new technology, but only in the rational cultural climate of Western Europe did people exploit scientific discoveries to spark the Industrial Revolution (Weber, 1958, orig. 1904–05).

Is Capitalism Rational?

Is industrial capitalism a rational economic system? Here again, Weber and Marx were on different sides. Weber considered industrial capitalism highly rational because capitalists try to make money in any way

MAKING THE GRADE

Weber's approach, *idealism*, is opposite to Marx's materialism. Weber tries to show that the way people think about their world affects all of society, including production. Weber agreed with Marx that economic production can shape ideas, but he claimed that the process also works the other way around.

MAKING THE GRADE

It is probably fair to say that Weber viewed modern capitalism as Calvinism minus Christianity: a *religious* ethic evolving into a *work* ethic.

Getty Images, Inc. – Liaison/ Tim Boyle

To the outside observer, the trading floor of a stock exchange may look like complete craziness. But in such activity Weber saw the essence of modern rationality.

they can. Marx, however, thought capitalism irrational because it fails to meet the basic needs of most of the people (Gerth & Mills, 1946:49).

Weber's Great Thesis: Protestantism and Capitalism

Weber spent many years considering how and why industrial capitalism developed in the first place. Why did it emerge in parts of Western Europe during the eighteenth and nineteenth centuries?

Weber claimed that the key to the birth of industrial capitalism lay in the Protestant Reformation. Specifically, he saw industrial capitalism as the major outcome of Calvinism, a Christian religious movement founded by John Calvin (1509–1564). Calvinists approached life in a highly disciplined and rational way. One of Calvin's most important ideas was *predestination,* the belief that an all-knowing and all-powerful God had predestined some people for salvation and others for damnation. Believing that everyone's fate was set before birth, early Calvinists thought that people did not know what their destiny was and could do nothing to change it. So Calvinists swung between hopeful visions of spiritual salvation and anxious fears of eternal damnation.

Frustrated at not knowing their fate, Calvinists gradually came to a resolution of sorts. Wouldn't those chosen for glory in the next world, they reasoned, see signs of divine favor in *this* world? In this way, Calvinists came to see worldly prosperity as a sign of God's grace. Eager to gain this reassurance, Calvinists threw themselves into a quest for success, applying rationality, discipline, and hard work to their tasks. They did not pursue wealth for its own sake, because spending money on themselves would be self-indulgent and sinful. Neither were Calvinists likely to share their wealth with the poor, because they viewed poverty as a sign of God's rejection. Calvinists' duty was pressing forward in what they saw as their personal *calling* from God, reinvesting profits for still greater success. It is easy to see how such activity—saving money, using wealth to create more wealth, and adopting new technology—became the foundation of capitalism.

Other world religions did not encourage the rational pursuit of wealth the way Calvinism did. Catholicism, the traditional religion in most of Europe, taught a passive, "otherworldly" view: Good deeds performed humbly on Earth would bring rewards in heaven. For Catholics, making money had none of the spiritual significance it had for Calvinists. Weber concluded that this was the reason that industrial capitalism developed primarily in areas of Europe where Calvinism was strong.

Weber's study of Calvinism provides striking evidence of the power of ideas to shape society. Not one to accept simple explanations, Weber knew that industrial capitalism had many causes. But by stressing the importance of ideas, Weber tried to counter Marx's strictly economic explanation of modern society.

As the decades passed, later generations of Calvinists lost much of their early religious enthusiasm. But their drive for success and personal discipline remained, and slowly a *religious* ethic was transformed into a *work* ethic. In this sense, industrial capitalism can be seen as "disenchanted" religion, with wealth now valued for its own sake. This trend is seen in the fact that the practice of "accounting," which to early Calvinists meant keeping a daily record of moral deeds, before long came to mean simply keeping track of money.

Rational Social Organization

According to Weber, rationality is the basis of modern society, giving rise to both the Industrial Revolution and capitalism. He went on to identify seven characteristics of rational social organization:

1. **Distinctive social institutions.** In hunting and gathering societies, the family is the center of all activity. Gradually, however, religious, political, and economic systems develop as separate social institutions. In modern societies, new institutions—including education and health care—also appear. Specialized social institutions are a rational strategy to meet human needs efficiently.
2. **Large-scale organizations.** Modern rationality can be seen in the spread of large-scale organizations. As early as the horticultural era, small groups of political officials made decisions

SEEING SOCIOLOGY in Everyday Life

Try to apply points 3 through 7 of the list below to life at your college or university.

MAKING THE GRADE

Weber's main claim is that modern society is defined by a rational worldview. Weber considered the rise of capitalism (Marx's focus) simply one example of this rationality, along with science and bureaucracy.

concerning religious observances, public works, and warfare. By the time Europe developed agrarian societies, the Catholic church had grown into a much larger organization with thousands of officials. In today's modern, rational society, almost everyone works for large formal organizations, and federal and state governments employ tens of millions of workers.

3. **Specialized tasks.** Unlike members of traditional societies, people in modern societies are likely to have very specialized jobs. The Yellow Pages of any city's telephone directory suggest just how many thousands of different occupations there are today.
4. **Personal discipline.** Modern societies put a premium on self-discipline. Most business and government organizations expect their workers to be disciplined, and discipline is also encouraged by our cultural values of achievement and success.
5. **Awareness of time.** In traditional societies, people measure time according to the rhythm of sun and seasons. Modern people, by contrast, schedule events precisely by the hour and even the minute. Clocks began appearing in European cities some 500 years ago, about the same time commerce began to expand. Soon people began to think (to borrow Benjamin Franklin's phrase) that "time is money."
6. **Technical competence.** Members of traditional societies size up one another on the basis of *who* they are—their family ties. Modern rationality leads us to judge people according to *what* they are, with an eye toward their education, skills, and abilities. Most workers have to keep up with the latest skills and knowledge in their field in order to be successful.
7. **Impersonality.** In a rational society, technical competence is the basis for hiring, so the world becomes impersonal. People interact as specialists concerned with particular tasks rather than as individuals concerned with one another as people. Because showing your feelings can threaten personal discipline, modern people tend to devalue emotion.

All these characteristics can be found in one important expression of modern rationality: bureaucracy.

Rationality, Bureaucracy, and Science

Weber considered the growth of large, rational organizations one of the defining traits of modern societies. Another term for this type of organization is *bureaucracy.* Weber believed that bureaucracy has much in common with capitalism—another key factor in modern social life:

> Today, it is primarily the capitalist market economy which demands that the official business of public administration be discharged precisely, unambiguously, continuously, and with as much speed as possible. Normally, the very large capitalist enterprises are themselves unequaled models of strict bureaucratic organization. (1978:974, orig. 1921)

Max Weber agreed with Karl Marx that modern society is alienating to the individual, but they identified different causes of this problem. For Marx, economic inequality is the reason; for Weber, the problem is isolating and dehumanizing bureaucracy. George Tooker's painting *Landscape with Figures* echoes Weber's sentiments.

We find aspects of bureaucracy in today's businesses, government agencies, labor unions, and universities. Weber considered bureaucracy highly rational because its elements—offices, duties, and policies—help achieve specific goals as efficiently as possible. Weber saw that capitalism, bureaucracy, and also science—the highly disciplined pursuit of knowledge—are all expressions of the same underlying factor: rationality.

Rationality and Alienation

Weber agreed with Marx that industrial capitalism was highly productive. Weber also agreed with Marx that modern society generates widespread alienation, although his reasons were different. Marx thought alienation was caused by economic inequality. Weber blamed alienation on bureaucracy's countless rules and regulations. Bureaucracies, Weber warned, treat a human being as a "number" or a "case" rather than as a unique individual. In addition, working for large organizations demands highly specialized and often tedious routines. In the end, Weber saw modern society as a vast and growing system of rules trying to regulate everything, and he feared that modern society would end up crushing the human spirit.

MAKING THE GRADE

Durkheim's view of society most clearly follows the structural-functional approach.

SEEING SOCIOLOGY in Everyday Life

Self-destructive behavior among people who experience sudden wealth is not limited to musicians. Can you think of comedians who have met a similar fate?

Magnum Photos, Inc./Elliott Landy

Magnum Photos, Inc./Elliott Landy

Magnum Photos, Inc./Elliott Landy

AP/Wide World Photos/Robert Sorbo

Durkheim's observation that people with weak social bonds are prone to self-destructive behavior stands as stark evidence of the power of society to shape individual lives. When rock-and-roll singers become famous, they are wrenched out of familiar life patterns and existing relationships, sometimes with deadly results. The history of rock-and-roll contains many tragic stories of this kind, including (from left) Janis Joplin's and Jimi Hendrix's deaths by drug overdose (both 1970) and Jim Morrison's (1971) and Kurt Cobain's (1994) suicides.

Like Marx, Weber found it ironic that modern society, meant to serve humanity, turns on its creators and enslaves them. Just as Marx described the dehumanizing effects of industrial capitalism, Weber portrayed the modern individual as "only a small cog in a ceaselessly moving mechanism that prescribes to him an endlessly fixed routine of march" (1978:988, orig. 1921). Although Weber could see the advantages of modern society, he was deeply pessimistic about the future. He feared that in the end, the rationalization of society would reduce human beings to robots.

Emile Durkheim: Society and Function

"To love society is to love something beyond us and something in ourselves." These are the words (1974:55, orig. 1924) of the French sociologist Emile Durkheim (1858–1917), another of the discipline's founders. In Durkeim's ideas we find another important vision of human society.

Structure: Society beyond Ourselves

Emile Durkheim's great insight was recognizing that society exists beyond ourselves. Society is more than the individuals who compose it. Society was here long before we were born, it shapes us while we live, and it will remain long after we are gone. Patterns of human behavior—cultural norms, values, and beliefs—exist as established structures, or *social facts,* that have an objective reality beyond the lives of individuals.

Because society is bigger than any one of us, it has the power to guide our thoughts and actions. This is why studying individuals alone (as psychologists or biologists do) can never capture the heart of the social experience. A classroom of college students taking a math exam, a family gathered around a table sharing a meal, people quietly waiting their turn in a doctor's office—all are examples of the countless situations that have a familiar organization apart from any particular individual who has ever been part of them.

Once created by people, Durkheim claimed, society takes on a life of its own and demands a measure of obedience from its creators. We experience the power of society when we see our lives falling into common patterns or when we feel the tug of morality during a moment of temptation.

Function: Society as System

Having established that society has structure, Durkheim turned to the concept of *function.* The significance of any social fact, he explained, is more than what individuals see in their immediate lives; social facts help society operate.

Consider crime. As victims of crime, individuals experience pain and loss. But taking a broader view, Durkheim saw that crime is vital to the ongoing life of society itself. Only by defining acts as wrong do people construct and defend morality, which gives direction and meaning to our collective life. For this reason, Durkheim

anomie a condition in which society provides little moral guidance to individuals

mechanical solidarity social bonds, based on common sentiments and shared moral values, that are strong among members of preindustrial societies

organic solidarity social bonds, based on specialization and interdependence, that are stong among members of industrial societies

division of labor specialized economic activity

rejected the common view of crime as abnormal. On the contrary, he concluded, crime is "normal" for the most basic of reasons: A society could not exist without it (1964a, orig. 1893; 1964b, orig. 1895).

Personality: Society in Ourselves

Durkheim said that society is not only "beyond ourselves" but also "in ourselves," helping form our personalities. How we act, think, and feel is drawn from the society that nurtures us. Society shapes us in another way as well—by providing the moral discipline that guides our behavior and controls our desires. Durkheim believed that human beings need the restraint of society because as creatures who can want more and more, we are in constant danger of being overpowered by our own desires. As he put it, "The more one has, the more one wants, since satisfactions received only stimulate instead of filling needs" (1966:248, orig. 1897).

Nowhere is the need for societal regulation better illustrated than in Durkheim's study of suicide (1966, orig. 1897). Why is it that rock stars—from Del Shannon, Elvis Presley, Janis Joplin, and Jim Morrison to Jimi Hendrix, Keith Moon, John Bonham, and Kurt Cobain—seem so prone to self-destruction? Durkheim had the answer long before the invention of the electric guitar: Now as back then, the *highest* suicide rates are found among categories of people with the *lowest* level of societal integration. In short, the enormous freedom of the young, rich, and famous carries a high price in terms of the risk of suicide.

Modernity and Anomie

Compared to traditional societies, modern societies impose fewer restrictions on everyone. Durkheim acknowledged the advantages of modern-day freedom, but he warned of increased **anomie,** *a condition in which society provides little moral guidance to individuals.* The pattern by which many celebrities are "destroyed by fame" well illustrates the destructive effects of anomie. Sudden fame tears people from their families and familiar routines, disrupts established values and norms, and breaks down society's support and regulation of the individual—sometimes with fatal results. Therefore, Durkheim explained, an individual's desires must be balanced by the claims and guidance of society—a balance that is sometimes difficult to achieve in the modern world. Durkheim would not have been surprised to see a rising suicide rate in modern societies such as the United States.

Evolving Societies: The Division of Labor

Like Marx and Weber, Durkheim lived through rapid social change in Europe during the nineteenth century. But Durkheim offered different reasons for this change.

In preindustrial societies, he explained, tradition operates as the social cement that binds people together. In fact, what he termed the *collective conscience* is so strong that the community moves quickly to punish anyone who dares to challenge conventional ways of life. Durkheim used the term **mechanical solidarity** to refer to *social bonds, based on common sentiments and shared moral values, that are strong among members of preindustrial societies.* In practice, mechanical solidarity is based on *similarity.* Durkheim called these bonds "mechanical" because people are linked together in lockstep, with a more or less automatic sense of belonging together and acting alike.

With industrialization, Durkheim continued, mechanical solidarity becomes weaker and weaker, and people are much less bound by tradition. But this does not mean that society dissolves. Modern life creates a new type of solidarity. Durkheim called this new social integration **organic solidarity,** defined as *social bonds, based on specialization and interdependence, that are strong among members of industrial societies.* The solidarity that was once rooted in likeness is now based on *differences* among people who find that their specialized work—as plumbers, college students, midwives, or sociology instructors—makes them rely on other people for most of their daily needs.

For Durkheim, then, the key to change in a society is an expanding **division of labor,** or *specialized economic activity.* Weber said that modern societies specialize in order to become more efficient, and

Photos.com

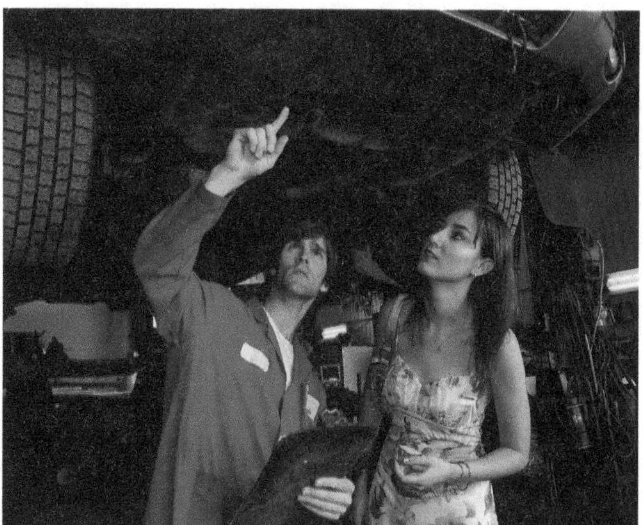

In traditional societies, everyone does much the same work. These societies are held together by strong moral beliefs. Modern societies, illustrated by urban areas in this country, are held together by a system of production in which people perform specialized work and rely on one another for all the things they cannot do for themselves.

MAKING THE GRADE

Both Marx and Weber criticized modern society for producing alienation, but in different ways. Durkheim, too, was critical, claiming that modern society created anomie. Be sure that you are able to clearly define these terms.

MAKING THE GRADE

All the sociologists discussed in this chapter have good and bad things to say about modern society. Weber was the most pessimistic, and Durkheim was the most optimistic.

Durkheim filled out the picture by showing that members of modern societies count on tens of thousands of others—most of them strangers—for the goods and services needed every day. As members of modern societies, we depend more and more on people we trust less and less. Why do we look to people we hardly know and whose beliefs may well differ from our own? Durkheim's answer was "because we can't live without them."

So modern society rests far less on *moral consensus* and far more on *functional interdependence.* Herein lies what we might call "Durkheim's dilemma": The technological power and greater personal freedom of modern society come at the cost of declining morality and the rising risk of anomie.

Like Marx and Weber, Durkheim worried about the direction society was taking. But of the three, Durkheim was the most optimistic. He saw that large, anonymous societies gave people more freedom and privacy than small towns. Anomie remains a danger, but Durkheim hoped we would be able to create laws and other norms to regulate our behavior.

How can we apply Durkheim's views to the Information Revolution? The Seeing Sociology in Everyday Life box suggests that Durkheim, as well as two of the other theorists we have considered in this chapter, would have had much to say about today's new computer technology.

PhotoEdit Inc./Jeff Greenberg

How do we understand something as complex as human society? Each of the thinkers profiled in this chapter offers insights about the meaning and importance of modern society. Each has a somewhat different view and provides a partial answer to a very complex issue.

Critical Review: Four Visions of Society

This chapter opened with several important questions about society. We will conclude by summarizing how each of the four visions of society answers these questions.

What Holds Societies Together?

How is something as complex as society possible? Lenski claims that members of a society are united by a shared culture, although cultural patterns become more diverse as a society gains more complex technology. He also points out that as technology becomes more complex, inequality divides a society more and more, although industrialization reduces inequality somewhat.

Marx saw in society not unity but social division based on class position. From his point of view, elites may force an uneasy peace, but true social unity can occur only if production becomes a cooperative process. To Weber, the members of a society share a worldview. Just as tradition joined people together in the past, so modern societies have created rational, large-scale organizations that connect people's lives. Finally, Durkheim made solidarity the focus of his work. He contrasted the mechanical solidarity of preindustrial societies, which is based on shared morality, with modern society's organic solidarity, which is based on specialization.

How Have Societies Changed?

According to Lenski's model of sociocultural evolution, societies differ mostly in terms of changing technology. Modern society stands out from past societies in terms of its enormous productive power. Marx, too, noted historical differences in productivity yet pointed to continuing social conflict (except perhaps among simple hunters and gatherers). For Marx, modern society is distinctive mostly because it brings that conflict out into the open. Weber considered the question of change from the perspective of how people look at the world. Members of preindustrial societies have a traditional outlook; modern people take a rational worldview. Finally, for Durkheim, traditional societies are characterized by mechanical solidarity based on moral likeness. In industrial societies, mechanical solidarity gives way to organic solidarity based on productive specialization.

Why Do Societies Change?

As Lenski sees it, social change comes about through technological innovation that over time transforms an entire society. Marx's materialist approach highlights the struggle between classes as the engine of change, pushing societies toward revolution. Weber, by contrast, pointed out that ideas contribute to social change. He demonstrated

SEEING SOCIOLOGY in Everyday Life

To understand how technology has changed our world, make a list of terms (e.g., e-mail, text message, Twitter, etc.) that your grandparents probably don't understand.

SEEING SOCIOLOGY IN EVERYDAY LIFE

Today's Information Revolution: What Would Durkheim, Weber, and Marx Have Thought?

COLLEEN: Didn't Marx predict there'd be a class revolution?

MASAKO: Well, yes, but in the information age, what are the classes that are supposed to be in conflict?

New technology is changing our society at a dizzying pace. Were they alive today, the founding sociologists discussed in this chapter would be eager observers of the current scene. Imagine for a moment the kinds of questions Emile Durkheim, Max Weber, and Karl Marx might ask about the effects of computer technology on our everyday lives.

Durkheim, who emphasized the increasing division of labor in modern society, would probably wonder if new information technology is pushing work specialization even further. There is good reason to think that it is. Because electronic communication (say, a Web site) gives anyone a vast market (already, about 1.2 billion people access the Internet), people can specialize far more than if they were trying to make a living in a small geographic area. For example, while most small-town lawyers have a general practice, an information age attorney, living anywhere, can provide specialized guidance on, say, prenuptial agreements or electronic copyright law. As we move into the electronic age, the number of highly specialized small businesses (some of which end up becoming very large) in all fields is increasing rapidly.

Durkheim might also point out that the Internet threatens to increase our experience of anomie. Using computers has a tendency to isolate people from personal relationships with others. In addition, although the Internet offers a flood of information, it provides little in the way of moral guidance about what is wise or good or worth knowing.

Weber believed that modern societies are distinctive because their members share a rational worldview, and nothing illustrates this worldview better than bureaucracy. But will bureaucracy be as important during the twenty-first century? Here is one reason to think it may not: Although organizations will probably continue to regulate workers performing the kinds of routine tasks that were common in the industrial era, much work in the postindustrial era involves imagination. Consider such "new age" work as designing homes, composing music, and writing software. This kind of creative work cannot be regulated in the same way as putting together automobiles as they move down an assembly line. Perhaps this is the reason many high-technology companies have done away with worker dress codes and having employees punch in and out on a time clock.

Finally, what might Marx make of the Information Revolution? Since Marx considered the earlier Industrial Revolution a *class* revolution that allowed the owners of industry to dominate society, he would probably be concerned about the emergence of a new symbolic elite. Some analysts point out that film and television writers, producers, and performers now enjoy vast wealth, international prestige, and enormous power. Just as people without industrial skills stayed at the bottom of the class system in past decades, so people without symbolic skills may well become the "underclass" of the twenty-first century. Globally, there is a "digital divide" by which most people in rich countries, but few people in poor countries, are part of the Information Revolution (United Nations Development Programme, 2008).

Durkheim, Weber, and Marx greatly improved our understanding of industrial societies. As we continue into the postindustrial age, there is plenty of room for new generations of sociologists to carry on.

WHAT DO YOU THINK?

1. Is computer technology likely to continue to increase specialization? Why or why not?
2. Can you think of examples of "creative" businesses that are less bureaucratic than industrial companies used to be? Why would you expect this to be the case?
3. What effect will the increased importance of symbolic skills have on the "earning power" of a college degree?

Stock Connection/Lucidio Studio, Inc.

how a particular worldview—Calvinism—set in motion the Industrial Revolution, which ended up reshaping all of society. Finally, Durkheim pointed to an expanding division of labor as the key dimension of social change.

The fact that these four approaches are so different does not mean that any one of them is right or wrong in an absolute sense. Society is exceedingly complex, and our understanding of society benefits from applying all four visions.

Seeing Sociology in Everyday Life

Society

Does having advanced technology make a society better?

The four thinkers discussed in this chapter all had their doubts. Here's a chance for you to do some thinking about the pros and cons of computer technology in terms of its effect on our everyday lives. For each of the three photos shown here, answer these questions: What do you see as the advantages of this technology for our everyday lives? What are the disadvantages?

HINT In the first case, being linked to the Internet allows us to stay in touch with the office, and this may help our careers. At the same time, being "connected" in this way blurs the line between work and play, just as it may allow work to come into our lives at home. In addition, employers may expect us to be on call 24-7.

In the second case, cell phones allow us to talk with others or to send and receive messages. Of course, we all know that cell phone and cars don't add up to safe driving. In addition, doesn't using cell phone in public end up reducing our privacy? And what about the other people around us? How do you feel about having to listen to the personal conversations of people sitting nearby?

In the third case, computer gaming can certainly be fun and it may develop various sensory-motor skills. At the same time, the rise of computer gaming discourages physical play and plays a part in the alarming increase of obesity, which now affects more than one in five children. Also, computers (including iPods) have the effect of isolating individuals, not only from the natural world but also from other people.

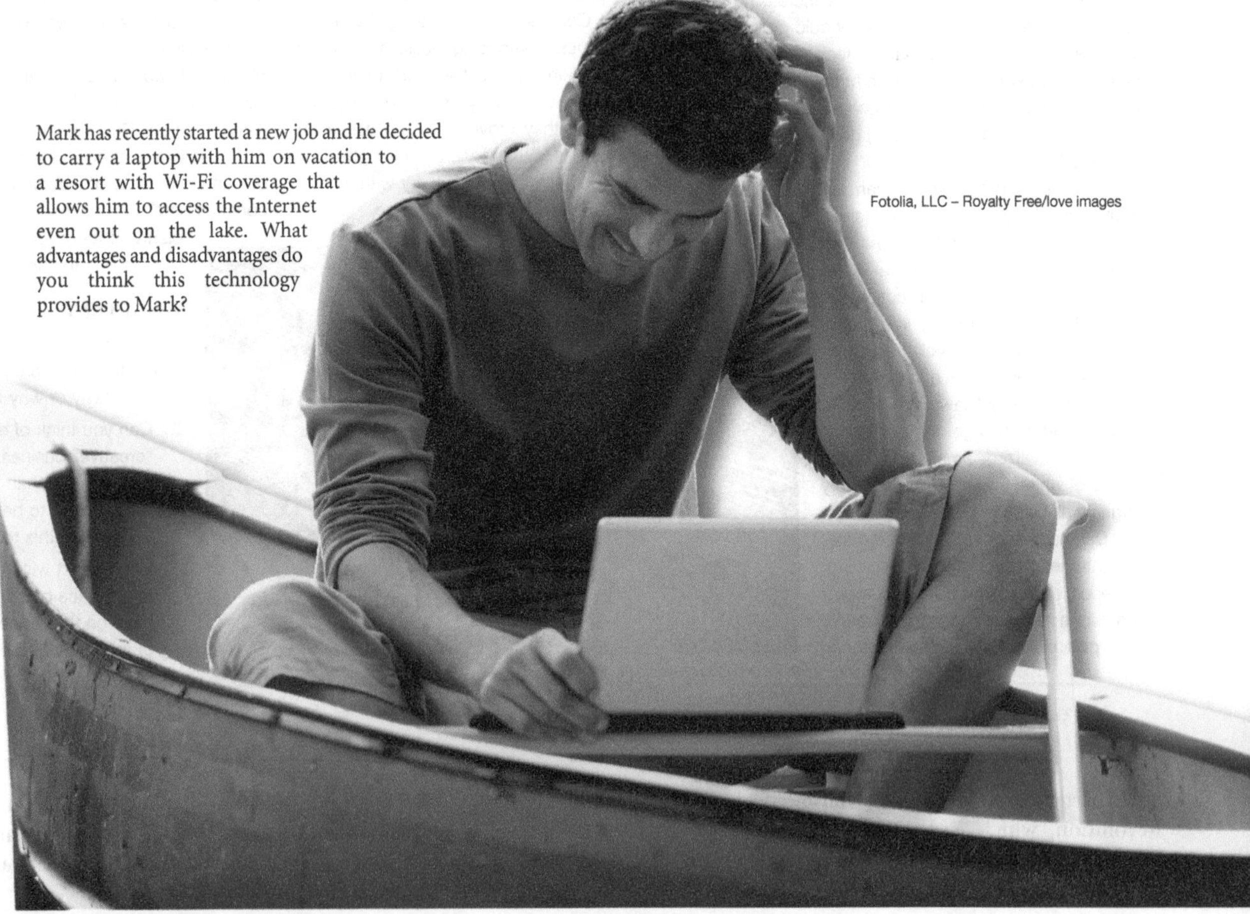

Mark has recently started a new job and he decided to carry a laptop with him on vacation to a resort with Wi-Fi coverage that allows him to access the Internet even out on the lake. What advantages and disadvantages do you think this technology provides to Mark?

Fotolia, LLC – Royalty Free/love images

Kanene likes to stay in touch with her friends when she's in the car, waiting for a flight at the airport, having dinner in a restaurant, or even while she is catching an afternoon movie in a theater. What advantages and disadvantages do you see in cell phone technology?

Getty Images/Leland Bobbe

Like children all across the United States, Andy and Trish like to play computer games and they own all the latest devices. Assess the use of computer technology as a form of recreation.

Alamy Images/Jack Sullivan

Applying SOCIOLOGY in Everyday Life

1. Spend a few minutes walking around your apartment, dorm room, or home trying to identify every device that has a computer chip in it. How many did you find? Were you surprised by the number?

2. Hunting and gathering people gazed at the stars and named the constellations in terms that reflected their way of life—mostly after animals and hunters. As a way of revealing what is important to everyday life *today*, write a short paper imagining the meanings we would give clusters of stars if people in postindustrial societies were naming them and starting frrom scratch.

3. Over the next few days, be alert for everyday evidence of these concepts: Marx's alienation, Weber's alienation, and Durkheim's anomie. What type of behavior or social pattern qualifies as an example of each in action? How are they different?

MAKING THE GRADE

Society

SOCIETY refers to people who interact in a defined territory and share a culture.
- What forces hold a society together?
- What makes societies different?
- How and why do societies change over time?

society people who interact in a defined territory and share a culture

Four Visions of Society

Gerhard Lenski: Society and Technology

Gerhard Lenski points to the importance of **TECHNOLOGY** in shaping any society. He uses the term **SOCIOCULTURAL EVOLUTION** to mean changes that occur as a society gains new technology.

In **HUNTING AND GATHERING SOCIETIES**, men use simple tools to hunt animals and women gather vegetation.

Hunting and gathering societies
- are the simplest of all societies and were the earliest type of society on Earth;
- are nomadic;
- have only a few dozen members;
- are built around the family;
- consider men and women roughly equal in social importance.

HORTICULTURAL AND PASTORAL SOCIETIES developed some 12,000 years ago as people began to use hand tools to raise crops and as they shifted to raising animals for food instead of hunting them.
Horticultural and pastoral societies
- are able to produce more food, so populations expand to hundreds;
- show greater specialization of work;
- show increasing levels of social inequality.

sociocultural evolution Lenski's term for the changes that occur as a society gains new technology

hunting and gathering making use of simple tools to hunt animals and gather vegetation for food

horticulture the use of hand tools to raise crops

pastoralism the domestication of animals

agriculture large-scale cultivation using plows harnessed to animals or more powerful energy sources

industrialism the production of goods using advanced sources of energy to drive large machinery

postindustrialism the production of information using computer technology

AGRARIAN SOCIETIES developed 5,000 years ago as the use of plows harnessed to animals or more powerful energy sources enabled large-scale cultivation.

Agrarian societies
- may expand into vast empires;
- show even greater specialization, with dozens of distinct occupations;
- have extreme social inequality;
- reduce the importance of women.

INDUSTRIAL SOCIETIES, which developed first in Europe 250 years ago, use advanced sources of energy to drive large machinery.
Industrialization
- provides many modern conveniences and advanced forms of transportation and communication;
- moves work from the home to the factory;
- reduces the traditional importance of the family;
- raises living standards.

POSTINDUSTRIAL SOCIETIES represent the most recent stage of technological development, namely, technology that supports an information-based economy.
Postindustrialization
- shifts production from heavy machinery making material things to computers and related technology processing information;
- requires a population with information-based skills;
- is the driving force behind the Information Revolution, a worldwide flow of information that now links societies with an emerging global culture.

See the Summing Up table.

Karl Marx: Society and Conflict

Karl Marx's **MATERIALIST APPROACH** claims that societies are defined by their economic systems: How humans produce material goods shapes their experiences.

CONFLICT AND HISTORY

CLASS CONFLICT is the conflict between entire classes over the distribution of a society's wealth and power.

Marx traced conflict between social classes in societies as the source of social change throughout history:

- In "ancient" societies, masters dominated slaves.
- In agrarian societies, nobles dominated serfs.
- In industrial-capitalist societies, capitalists dominate proletarians.

CAPITALISM

Marx focused on the role of **CAPITALISM** in creating inequality and class conflict in modern societies.

- Under capitalism, the ruling class (capitalists, who own the means of production) oppresses the working class (proletarians, who sell their labor).
- Capitalism alienates workers from the act of working, from the products of work, from other workers, and from their own potential.
- Marx predicted that a workers' revolution would eventually overthrow capitalism and replace it with socialism, a system of production that would provide for the social needs of all.

social conflict the struggle between segments of society over valued resources

capitalists people who own and operate factories and other businesses in pursuit of profits

proletarians people who sell their labor for wages

social institutions the major spheres of social life, or societal subsystems, organized to meet human needs

false consciousness Marx's term for explanations of social problems as the shortcomings of individuals rather than as the flaws of society

class conflict conflict between entire classes over the distribution of a society's wealth and power

class consciousness Marx's term for workers' recognition of themselves as a class unified in opposition to capitalists and ultimately to capitalism itself

alienation the experience of isolation and misery resulting from powerlessness

Max Weber: The Rationalization of Society

Max Weber's **IDEALIST APPROACH** emphasizes the power of ideas to shape society.

IDEAS AND HISTORY

Weber traced the ideas—especially beliefs and values—that have shaped societies throughout history.

- Members of preindustrial societies are bound by **TRADITION**, the beliefs and values passed from generation to generation.
- Members of industrial-capitalist societies are guided by **RATIONALITY**, a way of thinking that emphasizes deliberate, matter-of-fact calculation of the most efficient way to accomplish a particular task.

RATIONALISM

Weber focused on the growth of large, rational organizations as the defining characteristic of modern societies.

- Rationality gave rise to both the Industrial Revolution and capitalism.
- Protestantism (specifically, Calvinism) encouraged the rational pursuit of wealth, laying the groundwork for the rise of industrial-capitalism.
- Weber defined six characteristics of rational social organization, or **BUREAUCRACY**, and feared that excessive rationality would stifle human creativity.

ideal type an abstract statement of the essential characteristics of any social phenomenon

tradition values and beliefs passed from generation to generation

rationality a way of thinking that emphasizes deliberate, matter-of-fact calculation of the most efficient way to accomplish a particular task

rationalization of society Weber's term for the historical change from tradition to rationality as the main type of human thought

Emile Durkheim: Society and Function

Emile Durkheim claimed that society has an objective existence apart from its individual members.

STRUCTURE AND FUNCTION

Durkheim believed that because society is bigger than any one of us, it dictates how we are expected to act in any given social situation.

- He pointed out that social elements (such as crime) have functions that help society operate.
- Society also shapes our personalities and provides the moral discipline that guides our behavior and controls our desires.

EVOLVING SOCIETIES

Durkheim traced the evolution of social change by describing the different ways societies throughout history have guided the lives of their members.

- In preindustrial societies, **MECHANICAL SOLIDARITY**, or social bonds based on common sentiments and shared moral values, guides the social life of individuals.
- Industrialization and the **DIVISION OF LABOR** weaken traditional bonds, so that social life in modern societies is characterized by **ORGANIC SOLIDARITY**, social bonds based on specialization and interdependence.
- Durkheim warned of increased **ANOMIE** in modern societies, as society provides little moral guidance to individuals.

anomie Durkheim's term for a condition in which society provides little moral guidance to individuals

mechanical solidarity Durkheim's term for social bonds, based on common sentiments and shared moral values, that are strong among members of preindustrial societies

organic solidarity Durkheim's term for social bonds, based on specialization and interdependence, that are strong among members of industrial societies

division of labor specialized economic activity

MAKING THE GRADE

Sample Test Questions

Multiple-Choice Questions

1. **Which of the following would Lenski highlight as a cause of change in society?**
   a. new religious movements
   b. conflict between workers and factory owners
   c. the steam engine
   d. the extent to which people share moral values

2. **Horticultural societies are those in which**
   a. people hunt animals and gather vegetation.
   b. people are nomadic.
   c. people have learned to raise animals.
   d. people use simple hand tools to raise crops.

3. **Lenski claims that the development of more complex technology**
   a. has both positive and negative effects.
   b. is entirely positive.
   c. is mostly negative.
   d. has little or no effect on society.

4. **Marx believed that the industrial-capitalist economic system**
   a. was very productive.
   b. concentrated wealth in the hands of a few.
   c. created conflict between two great classes: capitalists and proletarians.
   d. All of the above are correct.

5. **Marx considered which of the following to be the "foundation" of society?**
   a. technology
   b. the economy
   c. dominant ideas
   d. type of solidarity

6. **Unlike Marx, Weber thought alienation was caused by**
   a. social change that is too rapid.
   b. extensive social inequality.
   c. the high level of rationality in modern society.
   d. All of the above are correct.

7. **What Lenski called the "industrial" society and Marx called the "capitalist" society, Weber called**
   a. the "rational" society.
   b. the "ideal" society.
   c. the "traditional" society.
   d. the "technological" society.

8. **Marx's "materialist" analysis contrasts with Weber's**
   a. "optimistic" analysis.
   b. "idealist" analysis.
   c. "traditional" analysis.
   d. "technological" analysis.

9. **Durkheim thought of society as**
   a. existing only in people's minds.
   b. constantly changing.
   c. an objective reality.
   d. having no clear existence at all.

10. **Which of the following questions might Durkheim ask about the ongoing war on terror?**
    a. Would the war on terror unite people across the United States?
    b. Which class benefits most from the war on terror?
    c. How does war lead to new kinds of technology?
    d. How does war increase the scope of bureaucracy?

ANSWERS: 1 (c); 2 (d); 3 (a); 4 (d); 5 (b); 6 (c); 7 (a); 8 (b); 9 (c); 10 (a)

Essay Questions

1. How would Marx, Weber, and Durkheim imagine U.S. society a century from now? What kinds of questions or concerns would each thinker have?
2. Link Marx, Weber, and Durkheim to one of sociology's theoretical approaches, and explain your choices.

Socialization

Veer Inc., Royalty Free/Fancy Photography

Socialization is the process by which older members of a society teach their way of life to the young. From the point of view of a young girl or boy, socialization is also the process of developing a personality.

Getty Images, Inc. – Agence France Presse/Brendan Smialowski/AFP/Getty Images

Socialization

Peter Arnold, Inc./A.Riedmiller/Das Fotoarchiv.

Getty Images Inc. - Stone Allstock/Donna Day

CHAPTER OVERVIEW

We turn now to a micro-level look at how individuals become members of society through the process of socialization.

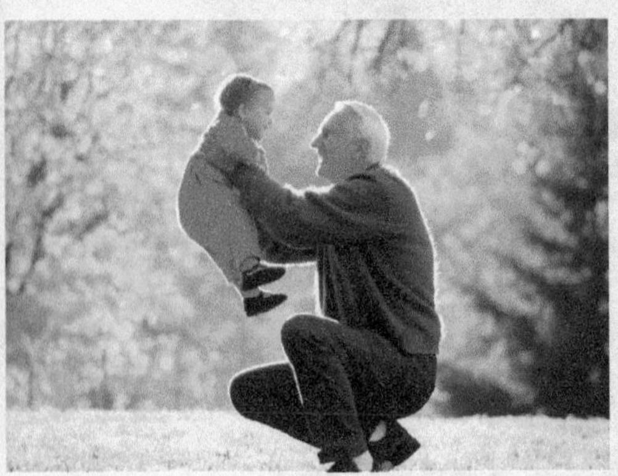

Corbis RF/Mark Karrass

On a cold winter day in 1938, a social worker walked quickly to the door of a rural Pennsylvania farmhouse. Investigating a case of possible child abuse, the social worker entered the home and soon discovered a five-year-old girl hidden in a second-floor storage room. The child, whose name was Anna, was wedged into an old chair with her arms tied above her head so that she couldn't move. She was wearing filthy clothes, and her arms and legs were as thin as matchsticks (K. Davis, 1940).

Anna's situation can only be described as tragic. She had been born in 1932 to an unmarried and mentally impaired woman of twenty-six who lived with her strict father. Angry about his daughter's "illegitimate" motherhood, the grandfather did not even want the child in his house, so for the first six months of her life, Anna was passed among several welfare agencies. But her mother could not afford to pay for her care, and Anna was returned to the hostile home of her grandfather.

To lessen the grandfather's anger, Anna's mother kept Anna in the storage room and gave her just enough milk to keep her alive. There she stayed—day after day, month after month, with almost no human contact—for five long years.

Learning of Anna's rescue, the sociologist Kingsley Davis immediately went to see the child. He found her with local officials at a county home. Davis was stunned by the emaciated girl, who could not laugh, speak, or even smile. Anna was completely unresponsive, as if alone in an empty world.

Social Experience: The Key to Our Humanity

Socialization is so basic to human development that we sometimes overlook its importance. But here, in the terrible case of an isolated child, we can see what humans would be like without social contact. Although physically alive, Anna hardly seems to have been human. We can see that without social experience, a child is not able to act or communicate in a meaningful way and seems to be as much an object as a person.

Sociologists use the term **socialization** to refer to *the lifelong social experience by which people develop their human potential and learn culture.* Unlike other living species, whose behavior is mostly or entirely set by biology, humans need social experience to learn their culture and to survive. Social experience is also the foundation of **personality,** *a person's fairly consistent patterns of acting, thinking, and feeling.* We build a personality by internalizing—taking in—our surroundings. But without social experience, as Anna's case shows, personality hardly develops at all.

Human Development: Nature and Nurture

Anna's case makes clear that humans depend on others to provide the care and nurture needed not only for physical growth but also for personality to develop. A century ago, however, people mistakenly believed that humans were born with instincts that determined their personality and behavior.

The Biological Sciences: The Role of Nature

Charles Darwin's groundbreaking 1859 study of evolution, led people to think that human behavior was instinctive, simply our "nature." Such ideas led to claims that the U.S. economic system reflects "instinctive human competitiveness," that some people are "born criminals," or that women are "naturally" emotional while men are "naturally" rational.

People trying to understand cultural diversity also misunderstood Darwin's thinking. Centuries of world exploration had taught Western Europeans that people behaved quite differently from one society to another. But Europeans linked these differences to biology

socialization the lifelong social experience by which people develop their human potential and learn culture

personality a person's fairly consistent patterns of acting, thinking, and feeling

MAKING THE GRADE

Sociologists and others have long debated the relative importance of biology (nature) and social environment (nurture). Cases of isolated children show that nurture is crucial to human development. But the text ends up avoiding a "nature versus nurture" argument in favor of linking the two concepts: It is human nature to nurture.

Corbis – NY/Ted Horowitz

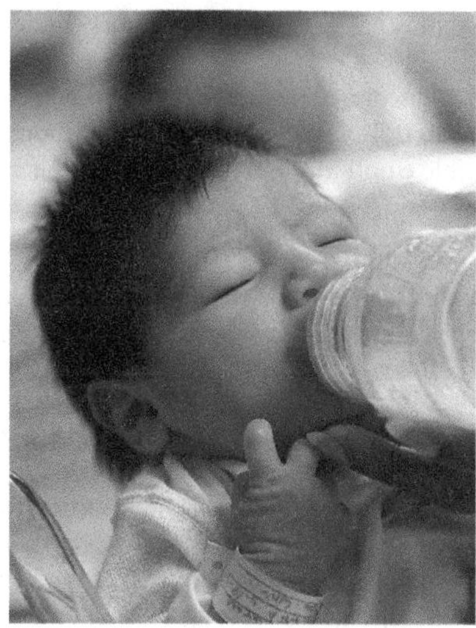

Corbis – NY/Henley & Savage

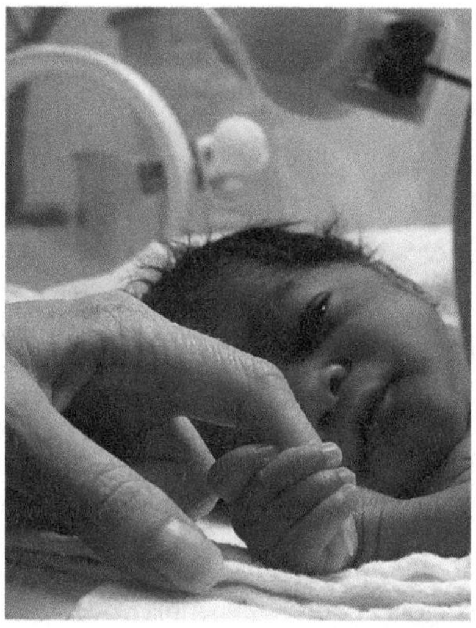

Tom Pollak

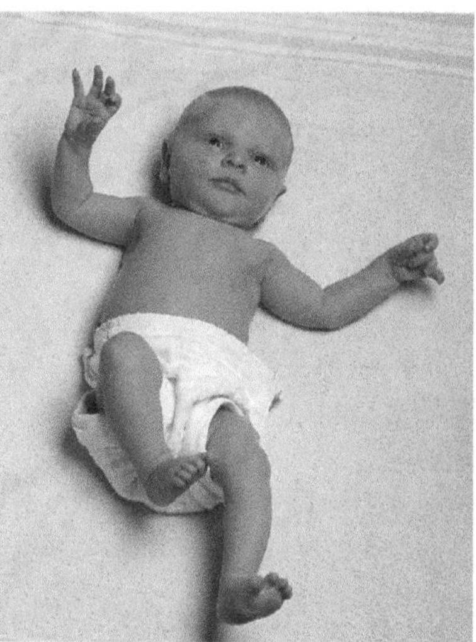

Human infants display various *reflexes*—biologically based behavior patterns that enhance survival. The sucking reflex, which actually begins before birth, enables the infant to obtain nourishment. The grasping reflex, triggered by placing a finger on the infant's palm, causing the hand to close, helps the infant maintain contact with a parent and, later on, grasp objects. The Moro reflex, activated by startling the infant, has the infant swinging both arms outward and then bringing them together across the chest. This action, which disappears after several months of life, probably developed among our evolutionary ancestors so that a falling infant could grasp the body hair of a parent.

rather than culture. It was an easy, although incorrect and very damaging, step to claim that members of technologically simple societies were biologically less evolved and therefore "less human." This ethnocentric view helped justify colonialism: Why not take advantage of others if they seem not to be human in the same sense that you are?

The Social Sciences: The Role of Nurture

In the twentieth century, biological explanations of human behavior came under fire. The psychologist John B. Watson (1878–1958) developed a theory called *behaviorism,* which holds that behavior is not instinctive but learned. Thus people everywhere are equally human, differing only in their cultural patterns. In short, Watson rooted human behavior not in nature but in *nurture.*

Today, social scientists are cautious about describing *any* human behavior as instinctive. This does not mean that biology plays no part in human behavior. Human life, after all, depends on the functioning of the body. We also know that children often share biological traits (like height and hair color) with their parents and that heredity plays a part in intelligence, musical and artistic talent, and personality (such as how you react to frustration). However, whether you develop your inherited potential depends on how you are raised. For example, unless children use their brain early in life, the brain does not fully develop (Goldsmith, 1983; Begley, 1995).

Without denying the importance of nature, then, we can correctly say that nurture matters more in shaping human behavior. More precisely, *nurture is our nature.*

Social Isolation

As the story of Anna shows, cutting people off from the social world is very harmful. For ethical reasons, researchers can never place human beings in total isolation to study what happens. But in the past, they have studied the effects of social isolation on nonhuman primates.

Research with Monkeys

In a classic study, the psychologists Harry and Margaret Harlow (1962) placed rhesus monkeys—whose behavior is in some ways surprisingly similar to that of humans—in various conditions of social isolation. They found that complete isolation (with adequate nutrition) for even six months seriously disturbed the monkeys' development. When returned to their group, these monkeys were passive, anxious, and fearful.

SEEING SOCIOLOGY in Everyday Life

An ad campaign for strengthening families used the tag line "Have you hugged your child today?" What new understanding of this line do you gain from the Harlow research?

MAKING THE GRADE

Both the cases of isolated children and the Harlow studies with rhesus monkeys lead to the same conclusion: Social experience is necessary for healthy human development.

Drawings from Dr. Annie Sparrow/Human Rights Watch

The personalities we develop depend largely on the environment in which we live. When a child's world is shredded by violence, the damage can be profound and lasting. This drawing was made by thirteen-year-old Rahid in the Darfur region of Sudan, where armed militia have killed more than 300,000 people since 2003. What are the likely effects of such experiences on a young person's self-confidence and capacity to form trusting ties with others?

Courtesy of Dr. Annie Sparrow, Human Rights Watch.

The Harlows then placed infant rhesus monkeys in cages with an artificial "mother" made of wire mesh with a wooden head and the nipple of a feeding tube where the breast would be. These monkeys also survived but were unable to interact with others when placed in a group.

But monkeys in a third category, isolated with an artificial wire mesh "mother" covered with soft terry cloth, did better. Each of these monkeys would cling to its mother closely. Because these monkeys showed less developmental damage than earlier groups, the Harlows concluded that the monkeys benefited from this closeness. The experiment confirmed how important it is that adults cradle infants affectionately.

Finally, the Harlows discovered that infant monkeys could recover from about three months of isolation. But by about six months, isolation caused irreversible emotional and behavioral damage.

Studies of Isolated Children

Tragic cases of children isolated by abusive family members show the damage caused by depriving human beings of social experience. We will review three such cases.

Anna: The Rest of the Story The rest of Anna's story squares with the Harlows' findings. After her discovery, Anna received extensive medical attention and soon showed improvement. When Kingsley Davis visited her after ten days, he found her more alert and even smiling (perhaps for the first time in her life). Over the next year, Anna made slow but steady progress, showing more interest in other people and gradually learning to walk. After a year and a half, she could feed herself and play with toys.

But as the Harlows might have predicted, five long years of social isolation had caused permanent damage. At age eight, her mental development was less than that of a two-year-old. Not until she was almost ten did she begin to use words. Because Anna's mother was mentally retarded, perhaps Anna was also. The riddle was never solved, however, because Anna died at age ten of a blood disorder, possibly related to the years of abuse she suffered (K. Davis, 1940, 1947).

Another Case: Isabelle A second case involves another girl found at about the same time as Anna and under similar circumstances. After more than six years of virtual isolation, this girl, named Isabelle, displayed the same lack of responsiveness as Anna. But Isabelle had the benefit of an intensive learning program directed by psychologists. Within a week, Isabelle was trying to speak, and a year and a half later, she knew some 2,000 words. The psychologists concluded that intensive effort had pushed Isabelle through six years of normal development in only two years. By the time she was fourteen, Isabelle was attending sixth-grade classes, damaged by her early ordeal but on her way to a relatively normal life (K. Davis, 1947).

A Third Case: Genie A more recent case of childhood isolation involves a California girl abused by her parents (Curtiss, 1977; Rymer, 1994). From the time she was two, Genie was tied to a potty chair in a dark garage. In 1970, when she was rescued at age thirteen, Genie weighed only fifty-nine pounds and had the mental development of a one-year-old. With intensive treatment, she became physically healthy, but her language ability remains that of a young child. Today, Genie lives in a home for developmentally disabled adults.

SEEING SOCIOLOGY in Everyday Life

How does the case of Anna confirm that "nurture is our nature"?

Freud's Model of Personality

id Freud's term for the human being's basic drives ← **ego** Freud's term for a person's conscious efforts to balance innate pleasure-seeking drives with the demands of society → **superego** Freud's term for the cultural values and norms internalized by an individual

CRITICAL REVIEW All evidence points to the crucial importance of social experience in personality development. Human beings can recover from abuse and short-term isolation. But there is a point—precisely when is unclear from the small number of cases studied—at which isolation in childhood causes permanent developmental damage.

CHECK YOUR LEARNING What do studies of isolated children teach us about the importance of social experience?

Understanding Socialization

Socialization is a complex, lifelong process. The following discussions highlight the work of six researchers who have made lasting contributions to our understanding of human development.

Sigmund Freud's Elements of Personality

Sigmund Freud (1856–1939) lived in Vienna at a time when most Europeans considered human behavior to be biologically fixed. Trained as a physician, Freud gradually turned to the study of personality and mental disorders and eventually developed the celebrated theory of psychoanalysis.

Basic Human Needs

Freud claimed that biology plays a major part in human development, although not in terms of specific instincts, as is the case in other species. Rather, he theorized that humans have two basic needs or drives that are present at birth. First is a need for sexual and emotional bonding, which he called the "life instinct," or *eros* (named after the Greek god of love). Second, we share an aggressive drive he called the "death instinct," or *thanatos* (the Greek word for "death"). These opposing forces, operating at an unconscious level, create deep inner tension.

Freud's Model of Personality

Freud combined basic needs and the influence of society into a model of personality with three parts: id, ego, and superego. The **id** (Latin for "it") represents *the human being's basic drives,* which are unconscious and demand immediate satisfaction. Rooted in biology, the id is present at birth, making a newborn a bundle of demands for attention, touching, and food. But society opposes the self-centered id, which is why one of the first words a child typically learns is "no."

To avoid frustration, a child must learn to approach the world realistically. This is done through the **ego** (Latin for "I"), which is *a person's conscious efforts to balance innate pleasure-seeking drives with the demands of society.* The ego arises as we become aware of our distinct existence and face the fact that we cannot have everything we want.

In the human personality, **superego** (Latin for "above or beyond the ego") is *the cultural values and norms internalized by an individual.* The superego operates as our conscience, telling us *why* we cannot have everything we want. The superego begins to form as a child becomes aware of parental demands and matures as the child comes to understand that everyone's behavior should take account of cultural norms.

Personality Development

To the id-centered child, the world is a bewildering assortment of physical sensations that bring either pleasure or pain. As the superego develops, however, the child learns the moral concepts of right and wrong. Initially, in other words, children can feel good only in a physical way (such as by being held and cuddled), but after three or four years, they feel good or bad according to how they judge their behavior against cultural norms (doing "the right thing").

The id and superego remain in conflict, but in a well-adjusted person, the ego manages these two opposing forces. If conflicts are not resolved during childhood, Freud claimed, they may surface as personality disorders later on.

Culture, in the form of the superego, *represses* selfish demands, forcing people to look beyond their own desires. Often the competing demands of self and society result in a compromise that Freud called *sublimation.* Sublimation redirects selfish drives into socially acceptable behavior. For example, marriage makes the satisfaction of sexual urges socially acceptable, and competitive sports are an outlet for aggression.

CRITICAL REVIEW In Freud's time, few people were ready to accept sex as a basic human drive. More recent critics have charged that Freud's work presents humans in male terms and devalues women (Donovan & Littenberg, 1982). Freud's theories are also difficult to test scientifically. But Freud influenced everyone who later studied human personality. Of special importance to sociology are his ideas that we internalize social norms and that childhood experiences have a lasting impact on personality.

CHECK YOUR LEARNING What are the three elements in Freud's model of personality? Explain how each one operates.

Jean Piaget's Theory of Cognitive Development

The Swiss psychologist Jean Piaget (1896–1980) studied human *cognition,* how people think and understand. As Piaget watched his own three children grow, he wondered not just what they knew but how they made sense of the world. Piaget went on to identify four stages of cognitive development.

Piaget's Stages of Development

sensorimotor stage →	preoperational stage →	concrete operational stage →	formal operational stage
Piaget's term for the level of human development at which individuals experience the world only through their senses	Piaget's term for the level of human development at which individuals first use language and other symbols	Piaget's term for the level of human development at which individuals first see causal connections in their surroundings	Piaget's term for the level of human development at which individuals think abstractly and critically

PhotoEdit Inc./David Young-Wolff

Childhood is a time to learn principles of right and wrong. According to Carol Gilligan, however, boys and girls define what is "right" in different ways. After reading about Gilligan's theory, can you suggest what these two children might be arguing about?

The Sensorimotor Stage

Stage one is the **sensorimotor stage,** *the level of human development at which individuals experience the world only through their senses.* For about the first two years of life, the infant knows the world only through the five senses: touching, tasting, smelling, looking, and listening. "Knowing" to young children amounts to what their senses tell them.

The Preoperational Stage

About age two, children enter the **preoperational stage,** *the level of human development at which individuals first use language and other symbols.* Now children begin to think about the world mentally and use imagination. But "pre-op" children between about two and six still attach meaning only to specific experiences and objects. They can identify a toy as their "favorite" but cannot explain what *types* of toys they like.

Lacking abstract concepts, a child also cannot judge size, weight, or volume. In one of his best-known experiments, Piaget placed two identical glasses containing equal amounts of water on a table. He asked several children aged five and six if the amount in each glass was the same. They nodded that it was. The children then watched Piaget take one of the glasses and pour its contents into a taller, narrower glass so that the level of the water in the glass was higher. He asked again if each glass held the same amount. The typical five- or six-year-old now insisted that the taller glass held more water. By about age seven, children are able to think abstractly and realize that the amount of water stays the same.

The Concrete Operational Stage

Next comes the **concrete operational stage,** *the level of human development at which individuals first see causal connections in their surroundings.* Between the ages of seven and eleven, children focus on how and why things happen. In addition, children now attach more than one symbol to a particular event or object. If, for example, you say to a child of five, "Today is Wednesday," she might respond, "No, it's my birthday!"—indicating that she can use just one symbol at a time. But a ten-year-old at the concrete operational stage would be able to respond, "Yes, and it's also my birthday."

The Formal Operational Stage

The last stage in Piaget's model is the **formal operational stage,** *the level of human development at which individuals think abstractly and critically.* At about age twelve, young people begin to reason abstractly rather than thinking only of concrete situations. If, for example, you were to ask a seven-year-old, "What would you like to be when you grow up?" you might receive a concrete response such as "a teacher." But most teenagers can think more abstractly and might reply, "I would like a job that helps others." As they gain the capacity for abstract thought, young people also learn to understand metaphors. Hearing the phrase "A penny for your thoughts" might lead a child to ask for a coin, but a teenager will recognize a gentle invitation to intimacy.

CRITICAL REVIEW Freud saw human beings torn by opposing forces of biology and culture. Piaget saw the mind as active and creative. He saw an ability to engage the world unfolding in stages as the result of both biological maturation and social experience.

But do people in all societies pass through all four of Piaget's stages? Living in a traditional society that changes slowly probably limits a person's capacity for abstract and critical thought. Even in the United States, perhaps 30 percent of people never reach the formal operational stage (Kohlberg & Gilligan, 1971).

CHECK YOUR LEARNING What are Piaget's four stages of cognitive development? What does his theory teach us about socialization?

SEEING SOCIOLOGY in Everyday Life

Using Piaget's concepts, can you explain why young children will reach for a nickel rather than a dime?

MAKING THE GRADE

Kohlberg's theory is similar to Piaget's theory, but Kohlberg focuses on one aspect of cognition—moral reasoning. Gilligan's theory is similar to Kohlberg's theory, but she focuses on the link between gender and moral reasoning.

THINKING ABOUT DIVERSITY: RACE, CLASS, & GENDER

The Importance of Gender in Research

Carol Gilligan (1990) has shown how gender guides social behavior. Her early work exposed the gender bias in studies by Kohlberg and others who had used only male subjects. But as her research progressed, Gilligan made a major discovery: Boys and girls actually use different standards in making moral decisions. By ignoring gender, we end up with an incomplete view of human behavior.

Gilligan has also looked at the effect of gender on self-esteem. Her research team interviewed more than 2,000 girls, aged six to eighteen, over a five-year period. She found a clear pattern: Young girls start out eager and confident, but their self-esteem slips away as they pass through adolescence.

Why? Gilligan claims that the answer lies in our society's socialization of females. In U.S. society, the ideal woman is calm, controlled, and eager to please. Then too, as girls move from the elementary grades to secondary school, they have fewer women teachers and find that most authority figures are men. As a result, by their late teens, girls struggle to regain the personal strength they had a decade earlier.

When their research was finished, Gilligan and her colleagues returned to a private girls' school where they had interviewed their subjects to share the results of their work. As their conclusions led them to expect, most younger girls who had been interviewed were eager to have their names appear in the forthcoming book. But the older girls were hesitant—many were fearful that they would be talked about.

WHAT DO YOU THINK?

1. How does Gilligan's research show the importance of gender in the socialization process?
2. Do you think boys are subject to some of the same pressures and difficulties as girls? What about the fact that a much smaller share of boys than girls make it to college? Explain your answer.
3. Can you think of ways in which your gender has shaped the development of your personality? Point out three significant ways gender has shaped your own life.

Lawrence Kohlberg's Theory of Moral Development

Lawrence Kohlberg (1981) built on Piaget's work to study *moral reasoning,* how individuals judge situations as right or wrong. Here again, development occurs in stages.

Young children who experience the world in terms of pain and pleasure (Piaget's sensorimotor stage) are at the *preconventional* level of moral development. At this early stage, in other words, "rightness" amounts to "what feels good to me." For example, a young child may simply reach for something on a table that looks shiny, which is the reason parents of young children have to "childproof" their homes.

The *conventional* level, Kohlberg's second stage, appears by the teen years (corresponding to Piaget's final, formal operational stage). At this point, young people lose some of their selfishness as they learn to define right and wrong in terms of what pleases parents and conforms to cultural norms. Individuals at this stage also begin to assess intention in reaching moral judgments instead of simply looking at what people do. For example, they understand that stealing food to feed one's hungry children is not the same as stealing an iPod to sell for pocket change.

In Kohlberg's final stage of moral development, the *postconventional* level, people move beyond their society's norms to consider abstract ethical principles. Now they think about liberty, freedom, or justice, perhaps arguing that what is legal still may not be right. When the African American activist Rosa Parks refused to give up her seat on a Montgomery, Alabama, bus in 1955, she violated that city's segregation laws in order to call attention to the racial injustice of the law.

CRITICAL REVIEW Like the work of Piaget, Kohlberg's model explains moral development in terms of distinct stages. But whether this model applies to people in all societies remains unclear. Further, many people in the United States apparently never reach the postconventional level of moral reasoning, although exactly why is still an open question.

Another problem with Kohlberg's research is that his subjects were all boys. He committed a common research error, by generalizing the results of male subjects to all people. This problem led a colleague, Carol Gilligan, to investigate how gender affects moral reasoning.

CHECK YOUR LEARNING What are Kohlberg's three stages of moral development? What does his theory teach us about socialization?

Carol Gilligan's Theory of Gender and Moral Development

Carol Gilligan, whose approach is highlighted in the Thinking About Diversity box, compared the moral development of girls and boys and concluded that the two sexes use different standards of rightness.

self George Herbert Mead's term for the part of an individual's personality composed of self-awareness and self-image

looking-glass self Charles Horton Cooley's term for a self-image based on how we think others see us

SEEING SOCIOLOGY in Everyday Life

Have you ever seen young children put on their parents' shoes, literally putting themselves "in the shoes" of another person? How does this action help children learn to "take the role of the other"?

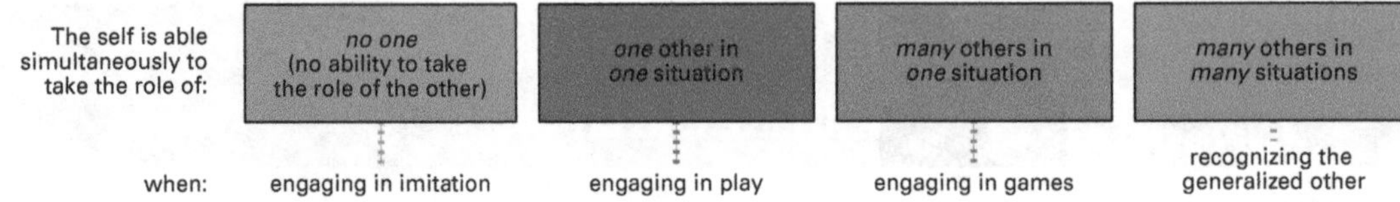

FIGURE 1 **Building on Social Experience**

George Herbert Mead described the development of the self as a process of gaining social experience. That is, the self develops as we expand our capacity to take the role of the other.

Boys, Gilligan (1982, 1990) claims, have a *justice perspective,* relying on formal rules to define right and wrong. Girls, by contrast, have a *care and responsibility perspective,* judging a situation with an eye toward personal relationships and loyalties. For example, as boys see it, stealing is wrong because it breaks the law. Girls are more likely to wonder why someone would steal and to be sympathetic toward a person who steals, say, to feed her family.

Kohlberg treats rule-based male reasoning as superior to the person-based female approach. Gilligan notes that impersonal rules dominate men's lives in the workplace, but personal relationships are more relevant to women's lives as mothers and caregivers. Why, then, Gilligan asks, should we set up male standards as the norms by which to judge everyone?

CRITICAL REVIEW Gilligan's work sharpens our understanding of both human development and gender issues in research. Yet the question remains, does nature or nurture account for the differences between females and males? In Gilligan's view, cultural conditioning is at work, a view that finds support in other research. Nancy Chodorow (1994) claims that children grow up in homes in which, typically, mothers do much more nurturing than fathers. As girls identify with mothers, they become more concerned with care and responsibility to others. By contrast, boys become more like fathers, who are often detached from the home, and develop the same formal and detached personalities. Perhaps the moral reasoning of females and males will become more similar as more women organize their lives around the workplace.

CHECK YOUR LEARNING According to Gilligan, how do boys and girls differ in their approach to understanding right and wrong?

George Herbert Mead's Theory of the Social Self

George Herbert Mead (1863–1931) developed the theory of *social behaviorism* to explain how social experience develops an individual's personality (1962, orig. 1934).

The Self

Mead's central concept is the **self,** *the part of an individual's personality composed of self-awareness and self-image.* Mead's genius was in seeing the self as the product of social experience.

First, said Mead, *the self is not there at birth; it develops.* The self is not part of the body, and it does not exist at birth. Mead rejected the idea that personality is guided by biological drives (as Freud asserted) or biological maturation (as Piaget claimed).

Second, Mead explained, *the self develops only with social experience,* as the individual interacts with others. Without interaction, as we see from cases of isolated children, the body grows, but no self emerges.

Third, Mead continued, *social experience is the exchange of symbols.* Only people use words, a wave of the hand, or a smile to create meaning. We can train a dog using reward and punishment, but the dog attaches no meaning to its actions. Human beings, by contrast, find meaning in almost every action.

Fourth, Mead stated that *seeking meaning leads people to imagine other people's intentions.* In short, we draw conclusions from people's actions, imagining their underlying intentions. A dog responds to *what you do;* a human responds to *what you have in mind* as you do it. You can train a dog to go to the hallway and bring back an umbrella, which is handy on a rainy day. But because the dog doesn't understand intention, if the dog cannot find the umbrella, it is incapable of the *human* response: to look for a raincoat instead.

Fifth, Mead explained that *understanding intention requires imagining the situation from the other's point of view.* Using symbols, we imagine ourselves "in another person's shoes" and see ourselves as that person does. We can therefore anticipate how others will respond to us even before we act. A simple toss of a ball requires stepping outside ourselves to imagine how another will catch our throw. All social interaction involves seeing ourselves as others see us—a process that Mead termed *taking the role of the other.*

The Looking-Glass Self

In effect, others are a mirror (which people used to call a "looking glass") in which we can see ourselves. What we think of ourselves,

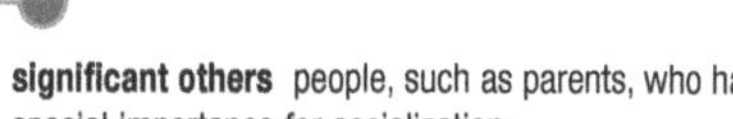

significant others people, such as parents, who have special importance for socialization

generalized other Mead's term for widespread cultural norms and values we use as a reference in evaluating ourselves

MAKING THE GRADE

Be sure you understand how Mead's concepts—the I and the me—differ from the id and superego in Freud's theory. The Critical Review section explains the difference.

then, depends on how we think others see us. For example, if we think others see us as clever, we will think of ourselves in the same way. But if we feel they think of us as clumsy, then that is how we will see ourselves. Charles Horton Cooley (1864–1929) used the phrase **looking-glass self** to mean *a self-image based on how we think others see us* (1964, orig. 1902).

The I and the Me

Mead's sixth point is that *by taking the role of the other, we become self-aware.* Another way of saying this is that the self has two parts. One part of the self operates as the subject, being active and spontaneous. Mead called the active side of the self the "I" (the subjective form of the personal pronoun). The other part of the self works as an object, that is, the way we imagine others see us. Mead called the objective side of the self the "me" (the objective form of the personal pronoun). All social experience has both components: We initiate an action (the I-phase, or subject side, of self), and then we continue the action based on how others respond to us (the me-phase, or object side, of self).

Development of the Self

According to Mead, the key to developing the self is learning to take the role of the other. Because of their limited social experience, infants can do this only through *imitation.* They mimic behavior without understanding underlying intentions, and so at this point, they have no self.

As children learn to use language and other symbols, the self emerges in the form of *play.* Play involves assuming roles modeled on **significant others,** *people, such as parents, who have special importance for socialization.* Playing "mommy and daddy" is an important activity that helps young children imagine the world from a parent's point of view.

Gradually, children learn to take the roles of several others at once. This skill lets them move from simple play (say, playing catch) with one other to complex *games* (such as baseball) involving many others. By about age seven, most children have the social experience needed to engage in team sports.

Figure 1 charts the progression from imitation to play to games. But there is a final stage in the development of the self. A game involves taking the role of specific people in just one situation. Everyday life demands that we see ourselves in terms of cultural norms as *any* member of our society might. Mead used the term **generalized other** to refer to *widespread cultural norms and values we use as references in evaluating ourselves.*

As life goes on, the self continues to change along with our social experiences. But no matter how much the world shapes us, we always remain creative beings, able to react to the world around us. Thus, Mead concluded, we play a key role in our own socialization.

CRITICAL REVIEW Mead's work explores the character of social experience itself. In the symbolic interaction of human beings, he believed he had found the root of both self and society.

Mead's view is completely social, allowing no biological element at all. This is a problem for critics who stand with Freud (who said our general drives are rooted in the body) and Piaget (whose stages of development are tied to biological maturity).

Be careful not to confuse Mead's concepts of the I and the me with Freud's id and superego. For Freud, the id originates in our biology, but Mead rejected any biological element of the self (although he never clearly spelled out the origin of the I). In addition, the id and the superego are locked in continual combat, but the I and the me work cooperatively together (Meltzer, 1978).

CHECK YOUR LEARNING Explain the meaning and importance of Mead's concepts of the I and the me. What did Mead mean by "taking the role of the other"? Why is this process so important to socialization?

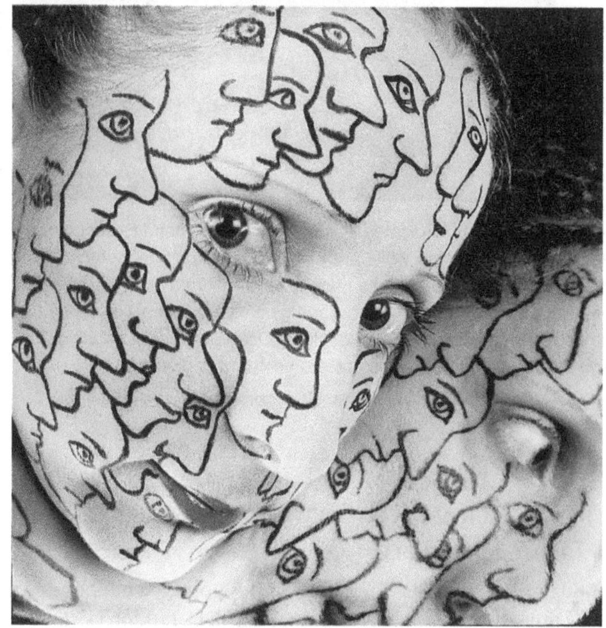

George Herbert Mead wrote, "No hard-and-fast line can be drawn between our own selves and the selves of others." The painting *Manyness* by Rimma Gerlovina and Valeriy Gerlovin conveys this important truth. Although we tend to think of ourselves as unique individuals, each person's characteristics develop in an ongoing process of interaction with others.

MAKING THE GRADE

Most theorists discussed in this chapter focus on childhood as the critical time when personality is formed. What sets Erik Erikson apart is the focus on socialization throughout the life course.

Henry Ossawa Tanner, *The Banjo Lesson*, 1893. Oil on canvas. 49" x 35 1/2". Hampton University Museum, Hampton, Virginia

Sociological research indicates that wealthy parents tend to encourage creativity in their children while poor parents tend to foster conformity. Although this general difference may be valid, parents at all class levels can and do provide loving support and guidance by simply involving themselves in their children's lives. Henry Ossawa Tanner's painting *The Banjo Lesson* stands as a lasting testament to this process.

Henry Ossawa Tanner, *The Banjo Lesson*, 1893. Oil on canvas. Hampton University Museum, Hampton, Virginia.

Erik H. Erikson's Eight Stages of Development

Although some analysts (including Freud) point to childhood as the crucial time when personality takes shape, Erik H. Erikson (1902–1994) took a broader view of socialization. He explained that we face challenges throughout the life course (1963, orig. 1950).

Stage 1: Infancy—the challenge of trust (versus mistrust). Between birth and about eighteen months, infants face the first of life's challenges: to establish a sense of trust that their world is a safe place. Family members play a key part in how any infant meets this challenge.

Stage 2: Toddlerhood—the challenge of autonomy (versus doubt and shame). The next challenge, up to age three, is to learn skills to cope with the world in a confident way. Failing to gain self-control leads children to doubt their abilities.

Stage 3: Preschool—the challenge of initiative (versus guilt). Four- and five-year-olds must learn to engage their surroundings—including people outside the family—or experience guilt at failing to meet the expectations of parents and others.

Stage 4: Preadolescence—the challenge of industriousness (versus inferiority). Between ages six and thirteen, children enter school, make friends, and strike out on their own more and more. They either feel proud of their accomplishments or fear that they do not measure up.

Stage 5: Adolescence—the challenge of gaining identity (versus confusion). During the teen years, young people struggle to establish their own identity. In part, teenagers identify with others, but they also want to be unique. Almost all teens experience some confusion as they struggle to establish an identity.

Stage 6: Young adulthood—the challenge of intimacy (versus isolation). The challenge for young adults is to form and maintain intimate relationships with others. Falling in love (as well as making close friends) involves balancing the need to bond with the need to have a separate identity.

Stage 7: Middle adulthood—the challenge of making a difference (versus self-absorption). The challenge of middle age is contributing to the lives of others in the family, at work, and in the larger world. Failing at this, people become self-centered, caught up in their own limited concerns.

Stage 8: Old age—the challenge of integrity (versus despair). As the end of life approaches, people hope to look back on what they have accomplished with a sense of integrity and satisfaction. For those who have been self-absorbed, old age brings only a sense of despair over missed opportunities.

CRITICAL REVIEW Erikson's theory views personality formation as a lifelong process, with success at one stage (say, as an infant gaining trust) preparing us to meet the next challenge. However, not everyone faces these challenges in the exact order presented by Erikson. Nor is it clear that failure to meet the challenge of one stage of life means that a person is doomed to fail later on. A broader question, raised earlier in our discussion of Piaget's ideas, is whether people in other cultures and in other times in history would define a successful life in Erikson's terms.

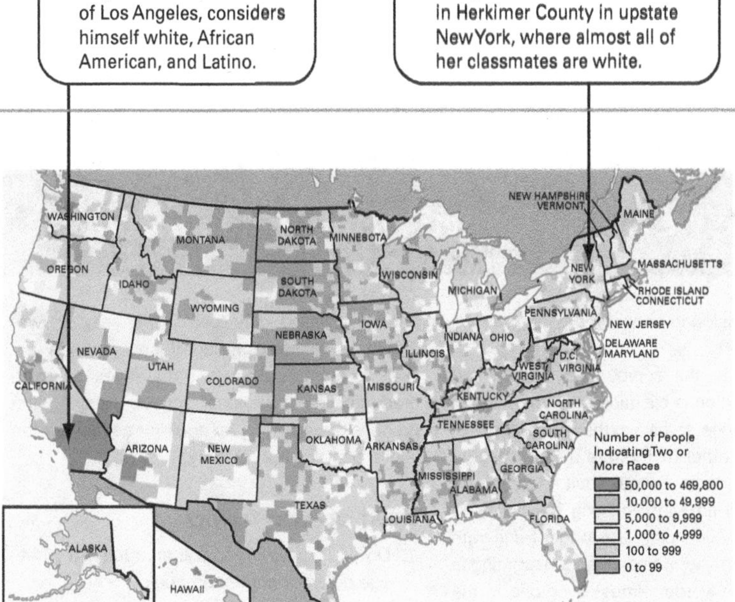

Seeing Ourselves

NATIONAL MAP 1

Racially Mixed People across the United States

This map shows the county-by-county distribution of people who described themselves as racially mixed in the 2000 census. How do you think growing up in an area with a high level of racially mixed people (such as Los Angeles or Miami) would be different from growing up in an area with few such people (for example, in upstate New York or the Plains States in the middle of the country)?

Source: U.S. Census Bureau (2001).

In sum, Erikson's model points out that many factors, including the family and school, shape our personalities. In the next section, we take a close look at these important agents of socialization.

CHECK YOUR LEARNING In what ways does Erikson take a broader view of socialization than other thinkers presented in this chapter?

Agents of Socialization

Every social experience we have affects us in at least a small way. However, several familiar settings have special importance in the socialization process.

The Family

The family affects socialization in many ways. For most people, in fact, the family may be the most important socialization agent of all.

Nurture in Early Childhood

Infants are totally dependent on others for care. The responsibility for providing a safe and caring environment typically falls on parents and other family members. For several years—at least until children begin school—the family also has the job of teaching children skills, values, and beliefs. Overall, research suggests, nothing is more likely to produce a happy, well-adjusted child than a loving family (Gibbs, 2001).

Not all family learning results from intentional teaching by parents. Children also learn from the type of environment adults create. Whether children learn to see themselves as strong or weak, smart or stupid, loved or simply tolerated—and as Erik Erikson suggests, whether they see the world as trustworthy or dangerous—depends largely on the quality of the surroundings provided by parents and other caregivers.

Race and Class

Through the family, parents give a social identity to children. In part, social identity involves race. Racial identity can be complex because societies define race in various ways. In addition, in the 2000 census, more than 7 million people (about 2.4 percent) said they consider themselves to be of two or more racial categories. This number is rising, and 3.5 percent of all births in the United States are now recorded as interracial (U.S. Census, 2008). National Map 1 shows where people who describe themselves as racially mixed live.

Social class, like race, plays a large part in shaping a child's personality. Whether born into families of high or low social position, children gradually come to realize that their family's social standing affects how others see them and, in time, how they come to see themselves.

In addition, research shows that class position affects not just how much money parents have to spend on their children but also what parents expect of them (Ellison, Bartkowski, & Segal, 1996). When people in the United States were asked to pick from a list of traits that are most desirable in a child, those with lower social standing favored obedience and conformity. Well-to-do people, by contrast, chose good judgment and creativity (NORC, 2008).

What accounts for the difference? Melvin Kohn (1977) explains that people of lower social standing usually have limited education and perform routine jobs under close supervision. Expecting that

SEEING SOCIOLOGY IN EVERYDAY LIFE

Are We Grown Up Yet? Defining Adulthood

SOLLY: *(seeing several friends walking down the dorm hallway, just returned from dinner)* Yo, guys! Jeremy's twenty-one today. We're going down to the Box Car to celebrate.

MATT: *(shaking his head)* Dunno, dude. I got a lab to finish up. It's just another birthday.

SOLLY: Not just any birthday, my friend. He's twenty-one—an *adult*!

MATT: (*sarcastically*) If turning twenty-one would make me an adult, I wouldn't still be clueless about what I want to do with my life!

Are you an adult or still an adolescent? Does turning twenty-one make you a "grown-up"? According to the sociologist Tom Smith (2003), in our society, there is no one factor that announces the onset of adulthood. In fact, the results of his survey—using a representative sample of 1,398 people over the age of eighteen—suggest that many factors play a part in our decision to consider a young person "grown up."

According to the survey, the single most important transition in claiming adult standing in the United States today is the completion of schooling. But other factors are also important: Smith's respondents linked adult standing to taking on a full-time job, gaining the ability to support a family financially, no longer living with parents, and finally, marrying and becoming a parent. In other words, almost everyone in the United States thinks a person who has done *all* of these things is fully "grown up."

At what age are these transitions likely to be completed? On average, the answer is about twenty-six. But such an average masks an important difference based on social class. People who do not attend college (more common among people growing up in lower-income families) typically finish school before age twenty, and a full-time job, independent living, marriage, and parenthood may follow in a year or two. Those from more privileged backgrounds are likely to attend college and may even go on to graduate or professional school, delaying the process of becoming an adult for as long as ten years, past the age of thirty.

WHAT DO YOU THINK?

1. Do you consider yourself an adult? At what age did your adulthood begin?
2. Consider a woman whose children are grown, who has had a recent divorce, and is now going to college getting a degree so that she can find a job. Is she likely to feel that she is suddenly not quite "grown up," now that she's back in school? Why or why not?
3. How does the research described in this box show that adulthood is a socially defined concept rather than a biological stage of life?

their children will hold similar positions, they encourage obedience and may even use physical punishment like spanking to get it. Because well-off parents have had more schooling, they usually have jobs that demand imagination and creativity, so they try to inspire the same qualities in their children. Consciously or not, all parents act in ways that encourage their children to follow in their footsteps.

Wealthier parents typically provide their children with an extensive program of leisure activities, including sports, travel, and music lessons. These enrichment activities—far less available to children growing up in low-income families—build *cultural capital,* which advances learning and creates a sense of confidence in these children that they will succeed later in life (Lareau, 2002).

Social class also affects how long the process of growing up takes, as the Seeing Sociology in Everyday Life box explains.

The School

Schooling enlarges children's social world to include people with backgrounds different from their own. It is only as they encounter people who differ from themselves that children come to understand the importance of factors such as race and social position. As they do, they are likely to cluster in playgroups made up of one class, race, and gender.

Gender

Schools join with families in socializing children into gender roles. Studies show that at school, boys engage in more physical activities and spend more time outdoors, and girls are more likely to help teachers with various housekeeping chores. Boys also engage in more aggressive behavior in the classroom, while girls are typically quieter and better behaved (Best, 1983; Jordan & Cowan, 1995).

What Children Learn

Schooling is not the same for children living in rich and poor communities. Children from well-off families typically have a far better experience in school than those whose families are poor.

For all children, the lessons learned in school include more than the formal lesson plans. Schools informally teach many things, which together might be called the *hidden curriculum.* Activities such as spelling bees teach children not only how to spell but how society divides the population into "winners" and "losers." Sports help students develop their strength and skills and also teach children important lessons in cooperation and competition.

School is also the first experience with bureaucracy for most children. The school day is based on impersonal rules and a strict

peer group a social group whose members have interests, social position, and age in common

anticipatory socialization learning that helps a person achieve a desired position

time schedule. Not surprisingly, these are also the traits of the large organizations that will employ young people later in life.

The Peer Group

By the time they enter school, children have joined a **peer group,** *a social group whose members have interests, social position, and age in common.* Unlike the family and the school, the peer group lets children escape the direct supervision of adults. Among their peers, children learn how to form relationships on their own. Peer groups also offer the chance to discuss interests that adults may not share with their children (such as clothing and popular music) or permit (such as drugs and sex).

It is not surprising, then, that parents express concern about who their children's friends are. In a rapidly changing society, peer groups have great influence, and the attitudes of young and old may differ because of a "generation gap." The importance of peer groups typically peaks during adolescence, when young people begin to break away from their families and think of themselves as adults.

Even during adolescence, however, parental influence on children remains strong. Peers may affect short-term interests such as music or films, but parents have greater influence on long-term goals, such as going to college (Davies & Kandel, 1981).

Finally, any neighborhood or school is made up of many peer groups. Individuals tend to view their own group in positive terms and put down other groups. In addition, people are influenced by peer groups they would like to join, a process sociologists call **anticipatory socialization,** *learning that helps a person achieve a desired position.* In school, for example, young people may copy the styles and slang of a group they hope will accept them. Later in life, a young lawyer who hopes to become a partner in the law firm may conform to the attitudes and behavior of the firm's partners in order to be accepted.

The Mass Media

August 30, Isle of Coll, off the west coast of Scotland. *The last time we visited this remote island, there was no electricity and most of the people spoke the ancient Gaelic language. Now that a power cable comes from the mainland, homes have lights, appliances, television, and the Internet! Almost with the flip of a switch, this tiny place has been thrust into the modern world. It is no surprise that the island's traditions are fast disappearing, with few performances of its historical dancing or music to be found. A rising share of the population now consists of mainlanders who ferry over with their cars to spend time in their vacation homes. And everyone now speaks English.*

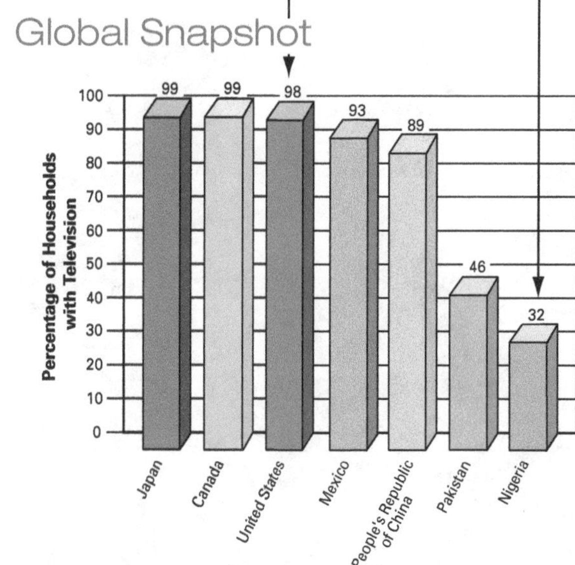

FIGURE 2 **Television Ownership in Global Perspective**

Television is popular in high- and middle-income countries, where almost every household owns at least one TV set.

Sources: U.S. Census Bureau (2008) and International Telecommunication Union (2008).

The **mass media** are *the means for delivering impersonal communications to a vast audience.* The term *media* (plural of *medium*) comes from the Latin word for "middle," suggesting that media connect people. *Mass* media arise as communications technology (first newspapers and then radio, television, films, and the Internet) spreads information on a massive scale.

In the United States today, the mass media have an enormous influence on our attitudes and behavior. Television, introduced in the 1930s, became the dominant medium after World War II, and 98 percent of U.S. households now have at least one set (by comparison, just 95 percent have telephones). Five out of six households also have cable or satellite television. As Figure 2 shows, the United States has one of the highest rates of television ownership in the world. In this country, it is people with lower incomes who spend the most time watching TV as well as using their television to watch movies and to play video games (Nielsen Media Research, 2008).

The Extent of Mass Media Exposure

Just how "glued to the tube" are we? Survey data show that the average household has at least one television set turned on for seven hours each day and that people spend almost half their free time watching television about four and a half hours a day. One study, by the Kaiser Family Foundation, found that school-age youngsters typically spend

mass media the means for delivering impersonal communications to a vast audience

PhotoEdit Inc./Raquel Ramirez

Concern with violence and the mass media extends to the world of video games, especially those popular with young boys. Among the most controversial games, which include high levels of violence, is the *Hitman* series. Do you think the current rating codes are sufficient to guide parents and children who buy video games, or would you support greater restrictions on game content?

even more time—about about six and a half hours each day—in front of video screens. Younger children favor watching television and playing video games; as children get older, music videos and Web surfing become a bigger part of the mix. At all ages, boys favor video games and girls lean toward music videos, and African American children spend more time watching television and playing video games than white children do (Rideout, Roberts, & Foehr, 2005; Nielsen Media Research, 2008).

Years before children learn to read, television watching is a regular part of their daily routine. As they grow, children spend as many hours in front of a television as they do in school or interacting with their parents. This is the case despite research suggesting that television makes children more passive and less likely to use their imagination (American Psychological Association, 1993; Fellman, 1995).

Television and Politics

The comedian Fred Allen once quipped that we call television a "medium" because it is "rarely well done." For a number of reasons, television (as well as other mass media) provokes plenty of criticism. Some liberal critics argue that for most of television's history, racial and ethnic minorities have not been visible or have been included only in stereotypical roles (such as African Americans playing butlers, Asian Americans playing gardeners, or Hispanics playing new immigrants). In recent years, however, minorities have moved closer to center stage on television. There are ten times as many Hispanic actors on prime-time television as there were a decade or two ago, and they play a far larger range of characters (Lichter & Amundson, 1997; Fetto, 2003b).

On the other side of the fence, conservative critics charge that the television and film industries are dominated by a liberal "cultural elite." In recent years, they claim, "politically correct" media have advanced liberal causes, including feminism and gay rights (Rothman, Powers, & Rothman, 1993; B. Goldberg, 2002). But not everyone agrees, with some studies suggesting that the mainstream media are fairly conservative on many issues (Adkins & Washburn, 2007). In addition, some television cable channels (such as MSNBC) have a decidedly liberal point of view, while others (such as Fox Network) are more conservative.

One study of the 2008 presidential election found that the Democratic candidate Barack Obama was endorsed by almost three times as many U.S. newspapers as Republican candidate John McCain ("Ongoing Tally," 2008). At the same time, research suggests that a wide range of political opinion is available in today's mass media and that most of us tend to focus on those media sources, whether more liberal or more conservative, that are closer to our own personal opinions (Morris, 2007).

Television and Violence

In 1996, the American Medical Association issued the startling statement that violence in television and films had reached such a high level that it posed a hazard to our health. More recently, a study found a strong link between aggressive behavior and the amount of time elementary school children spend watching television and playing video games (Robinson et al., 2001). The public is concerned about this issue: Three-fourths of U.S. adults report having walked out of a movie or turned off the television because of too much violence. About two-thirds of parents say that they are "very concerned" that their children are exposed to too much media violence. There may be reason for this concern: Almost two-thirds of television programs contain violence, and in most such scenes, violent characters show no remorse and are not punished (B. J. Wilson, 1998; Rideout, 2007).

Back in 1997, the television industry adopted a rating system. But we are left to wonder whether watching sexual or violent programming harms people as much as critics say. More important, why do the mass media contain so much sex and violence in the first place?

Television and the other mass media enrich our lives with entertaining and educational programming. The media also increase our

MAKING THE GRADE

The chapter now turns to stages of the life course. Although we think of these stages as biological (children are children because they are young and immature), comparing our society past and present and comparing various societies today show that culture shapes all stages of the life course.

SEEING SOCIOLOGY in Everyday Life

In 2005, a thirteen-year-old soccer player named Freddy Adu was offered a $1 million contract by Nike. Can you see any reasons he or his parents should be concerned about accepting this offer?

exposure to diverse cultures and provoke discussion of current issues. At the same time, the power of the media—especially television—to shape how we think remains highly controversial.

CRITICAL REVIEW This section shows that socialization is complex, with many different factors shaping our personalities as we grow. In addition, these factors do not always work together. For instance, children learn certain things from peer groups and the mass media that may conflict with what they learn at home.

Beyond family, school, peer group, and the media, other spheres of life also play a part in social learning. For most people in the United States, these include the workplace, religious organizations, the military, and social clubs. In the end, socialization proves to be not a simple matter of learning but a complex balancing act as we absorb information from a variety of sources. In the process of sorting and weighing all the information we receive, we form our own distinctive personalities.

CHECK YOUR LEARNING Identify all the major agents of socialization discussed in this section of the chapter. What are some of the unique ways that each helps us develop our individual personalities?

Socialization and the Life Course

Although childhood has special importance in the socialization process, learning continues throughout our lives. An overview of the life course reveals that our society organizes human experience according to age—childhood, adolescence, adulthood, and old age.

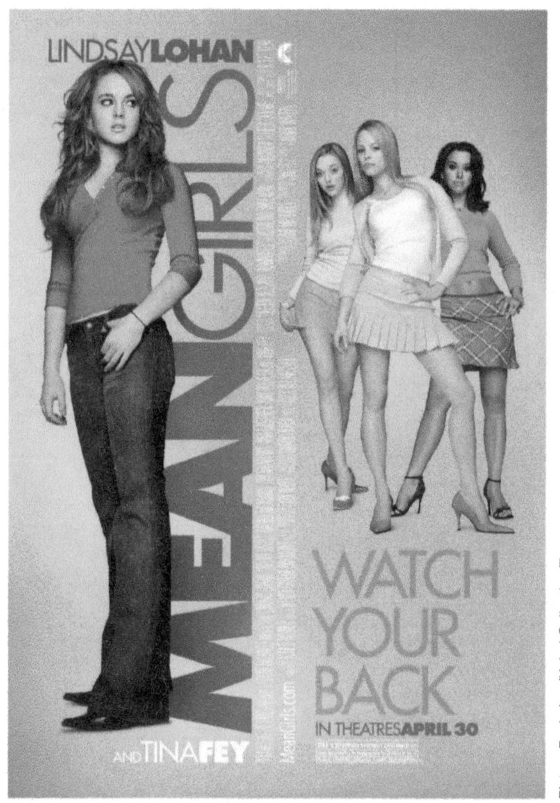

Picture Desk, Inc./Kobal Collection/Paramount

In recent decades, some people have become concerned that U.S. society is shortening childhood, pushing children to grow up faster and faster. Do films such as *Mean Girls,* starring Lindsay Lohan, which show young girls dressing and behaving as if they were much older, encourage a "hurried childhood"? Do you see this as a problem or not?

Childhood

A few years ago, the Nike Corporation, maker of popular athletic shoes, came under attack. Its shoes are made in Taiwan and Indonesia, in many cases by children who work in factories instead of going to school. As many as 160 million of the world's children work, half of them full time, and almost half of these boys and girls do work that is dangerous to their physical and mental health. For their efforts, they earn very little—typically, about 50 cents an hour (Human Rights Watch, 2006; U.S. Department of Labor, 2008). Global Map 1 shows that child labor is most common in Africa and Asia.

Criticism of Nike springs from the fact that most North Americans think of *childhood*—roughly the first twelve years of life—as a carefree time for learning and play. Yet as the historian Philippe Ariès (1965) explains, the whole idea of "childhood" is fairly new. During the Middle Ages, children of four or five were treated like adults and expected to fend for themselves.

We defend our idea of childhood because children are biologically immature. But a look back in time and around the world shows that the concept of childhood is grounded not in biology but in culture (LaRossa & Reitzes, 2001). In rich countries, not everyone has to work, so childhood can be extended to allow time for young people to learn the skills they will need in a high-technology workplace.

Because childhood in the United States lasts such a long time, some people worry when children seem to be growing up too fast. In part, this "hurried child" syndrome results from changes in the family—including high divorce rates and both parents in the labor force—that leave children with less supervision. In addition, "adult"

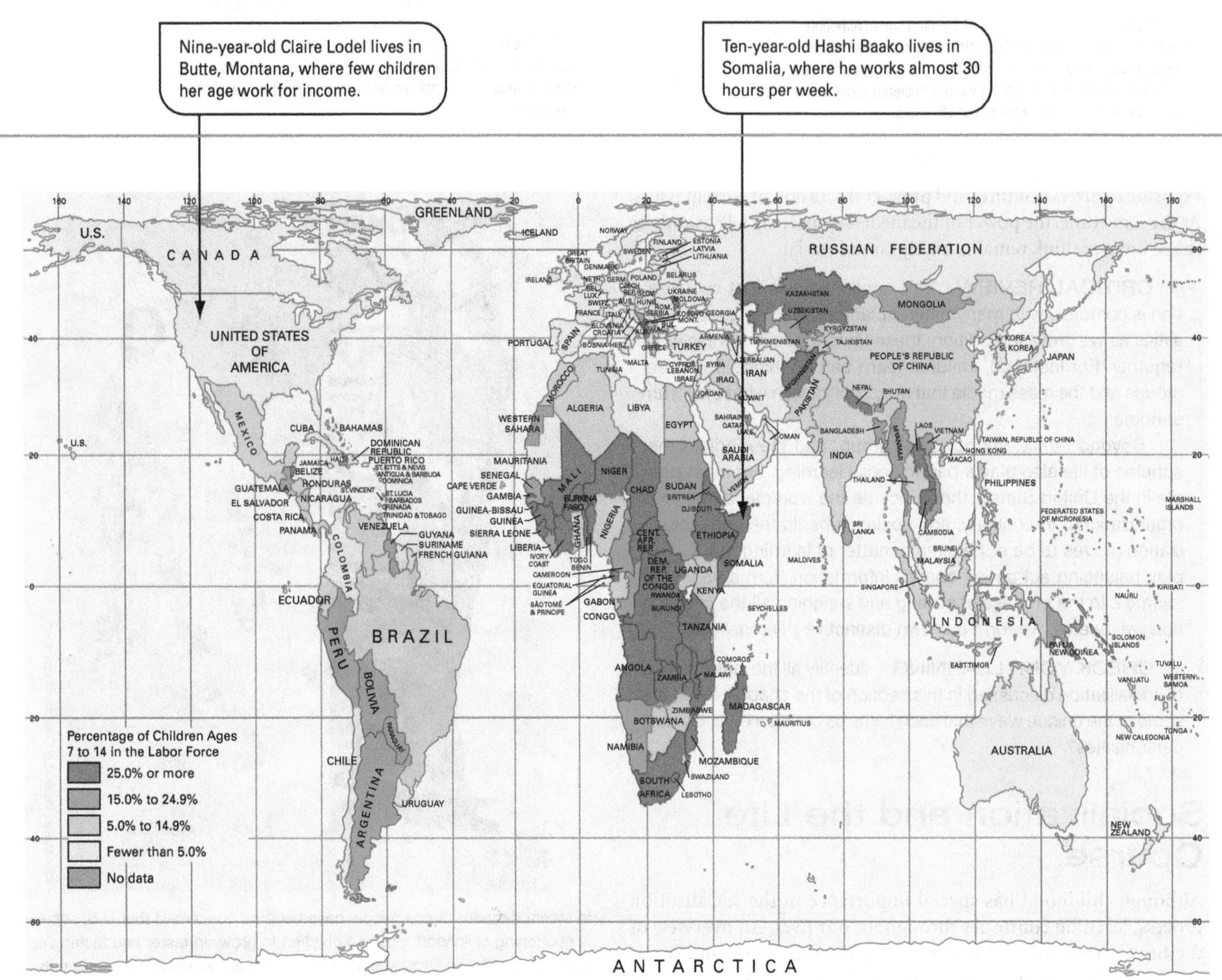

Window on the World

GLOBAL MAP 1 **Child Labor in Global Perspective**

Industrialization extends childhood and discourages children from work and other activities considered suitable only for adults. This is why child labor is uncommon in the United States and other high-income countries. In less economically developed nations of the world, however, children are a vital economic asset, and they typically begin working as soon as they are able. How would childhood in, say, the African nation of Chad or Sudan differ from that in the United States or Canada?

Sources: Global March against Child Labor (2008), UNICEF (2008), and World Bank (2008).

programming on television (not to mention in films and on the Internet) carries grown-up concerns such as sex, drugs, and violence into young people's lives. Today's ten- to twelve-year-olds, says one executive of a children's television channel, have about the same interests and experiences typical of twelve- to fourteen-year-olds a generation ago (K. S. Hymowitz, 1998). Perhaps this is why today's children, compared to kids fifty years ago, have higher levels of stress and anxiety (Gorman, 2000). Seeing Sociology in the News takes a closer look at how quickly many young children are growing up.

SEEING SOCIOLOGY in Everyday Life

Many of our soldiers in Iraq are still teenagers. Why should we not be surprised to learn that most of these young men and women performing adult jobs are from small-town, working-class families?

SEEING SOCIOLOGY in Everyday Life

What major events or trends have shaped the personalities of people your age?

THINKING ABOUT DIVERSITY: RACE, CLASS, & GENDER

The Development of Self among High School Students

Adolescence is a time when people ask questions like "Who am I?" and "What do I want to become?" In the end, we all have to answer these questions for ourselves. But race and ethnicity are likely to have an effect on what our answers turn out to be.

Grace Kao (2000) studied the identity and goals of students enrolled in Johnstown High School, a large (3,000-student) school in a Chicago suburb. Johnstown High is considered a good school, with above-average test scores. It is also racially and ethnically diverse: 47 percent of the students are white, 43 percent are African American, 7 percent are Hispanic, and 3 percent are of Asian descent.

Kao interviewed sixty-three Johnstown students, female and male, both individually and in small groups with others of the same race and ethnicity. Talking with them, she learned how important racial and ethnic stereotypes are in young people's developing sense of self.

What are these stereotypes? White students are seen as hardworking in school and concerned about getting high grades. African American students are thought to study less, either because they are not as smart or because they just don't try as hard. In any case, students see African Americans at high risk of failure in school. Because the stereotype says that Hispanics are headed for manual occupations—as gardeners or laborers—they are seen as not caring very much about doing well. Finally, Asian American students are seen as hardworking high achievers, either because they are smart or because they spend their time on academics rather than, say, sports.

From her interviews, Kao learned that most students think these stereotypes are true and take them personally. They expect people, including themselves, to perform in school more or less the way the stereotype predicts. In addition, young people—whether white, black, Hispanic, or Asian—mostly hang out with others like themselves, which gives them little chance to find out that their beliefs are wrong.

Students of all racial and ethnic categories say they *want* to do well in school. But not getting to know those who differ from themselves means that they measure success *only in relation to their own category.* To African American students, in other words, "success" means doing as well as other black students and not flunking out. To Hispanics, "success" means avoiding manual labor and ending up with any job in an office. Whites and Asians, by contrast, define "success" as earning high grades and living up to the high-achievement stereotype. For all these young people, then, "self" develops through the lens of how race and ethnicity are defined by our society.

Getty Images, Inc./Lara Jo Regan

WHAT DO YOU THINK?

1. Were you aware of racial and ethnic stereotypes similar to those described here in your high school? What about your college?
2. Do you think that gender stereotypes affect the performance of women and men in school as much as racial and ethnic stereotypes? Explain.
3. What can be done to reduce the damaging effects of racial and ethnic stereotypes?

Adolescence

At the same time that industrialization created childhood as a distinct stage of life, adolescence emerged as a buffer between childhood and adulthood. We generally link *adolescence,* or the teenage years, with emotional and social turmoil as young people struggle to develop their own identities. Again, we are tempted to attribute teenage rebelliousness and confusion to the biological changes of puberty. But it is in fact the result of cultural inconsistency. For example, the mass media glorify sex and schools hand out condoms, even as parents urge restraint. Consider, too, that an eighteen-year-old may face the adult duty of going to war but lacks the adult right to drink a beer. In short, adolescence is a time of social contradictions, when people are no longer children but not yet adults.

As is true of all stages of life, adolescence varies according to social background. Most young people from working-class families move directly from high school into the adult world of work and parenting. Wealthier teens, however, have the resources to attend college and perhaps graduate school, stretching their adolescent years into the late twenties and even the thirties (T. W. Smith, 2003). The Thinking About Diversity box provides an example of how race and ethnicity can shape the accedemic performance of high school students.

Seeing SOCIOLOGY in the 

As Kids Get Savvy, Marketers Move Down the Age Scale

By JAYNE O'DONNELL
April 11, 2007

Jill Brown almost cried the day her 9-year-old daughter sold several American Girl dolls at a yard sale so she could buy a Juicy Couture sweat suit.

It was a painful reminder that the emotional and psychological distance between childhood and the teen years is far shorter than ever. . . . .

Chalk it up to "age compression," which many marketers call "kids getting older younger" or KGOY. Retail consultant Ken Nisch says it shouldn't be a surprise or an outrage that kids are tired of toys and kid clothes by 8, considering that they are exposed to outside influences so much earlier. They are in preschool at 3 and on computers at 6.

That's why marketers now target 9-year-olds with apparel and accessories once considered only for teens, says Nisch, chairman of the retail consulting and design firm JGA.

Generation Y, those between about 8 and 26, are considered the most important generation for retailers and marketers because of their spending power and the influence they have over what their parents buy. But just as the 8- to 12-year-old "tweens" are pitched with a dizzying array of music, movie and cellphone choices, the nearly 10 million tween girls also are getting more attention from fashion, skin care and makeup businesses. Last year, NPD Group says 7- to 14-year-old girls spent $11.5 billion on apparel. . . .

With their keen but shifting senses of style, tween girls present some of the biggest rewards and challenges for retailers and brands. What's called for: a delicate marketing dance that tunes in tween girls without turning off their parents, who control both the purse strings and the car. Retailers to tween girls also must stay in close touch with the fashion pulse, because being "out" is even more painful for girls who haven't hit the teen years, say retailers and their consultants. They'll drop a brand faster than you can say Hannah Montana if the clothes become anything close to dorky. . . .

Some other tween girl traits:

• They're driven by imitation. Tweens want to look like each other but be able to call looks their own, says retail consultant Laura Evans, whose clients include Reebok and Express. Retailers that offer a lot of similar apparel—layers of shirts in a variety of colors—tend to be the most popular. . . .

• They want more of everything. Whether it's lip balm or blue jeans, "More is more," says Nita Rollins, who heads marketing intelligence at the digital marketing agency Resource Interactive. "Nothing succeeds like excess." Tweens aren't aware of "social codes of restraint," says Rollins, so they see no reason why they don't need 10 American Girl dolls or several pairs of jeans or sneakers. The average number of Lip Smacker-brand lip balm and glosses owned by Bonne Bell customers is 10, but, Bell notes, "The girls who have 100 make up for the ones who don't have 10." . .

Adulthood

If stages of the life course were based on biological changes, it would be easy to define *adulthood.* Regardless of exactly when it begins, adulthood is the time when most of life's accomplishments take place, including pursuing a career and raising a family. Personalities are largely formed by then, although marked changes in a person's environment—such as unemployment, divorce, or serious illness—may cause significant changes to the self.

Early Adulthood

During early adulthood—until about age forty—young adults learn to manage day-to-day affairs for themselves, often juggling conflicting priorities: schooling, job, partner, children, and parents. During this stage of life, many women try to "do it all," a pattern that reflects the fact that our culture gives them the major responsibility for child rearing and housework even if they have demanding jobs outside the home.

Middle Adulthood

In middle adulthood—roughly ages forty to sixty-five—people sense that their life circumstances are pretty well set. They also become more aware of the fragility of health, which the young typically take for granted. Women who have spent many years raising a family find middle adulthood emotionally trying. Children grow up and require less attention, and husbands become absorbed in their careers, leaving some women with spaces in their lives that are difficult to fill. Many women who divorce also face serious financial problems (Weitzman, 1985, 1996). For all these reasons, an increasing number of women in middle adulthood return to school and seek new careers.

For everyone, growing older means experiencing physical decline, a prospect our culture makes especially painful for women. Because good looks are considered more important for women, the appearance of wrinkles and graying hair can be traumatic. Men have their own particular difficulties as they get older. Some must admit that they are never going to reach earlier career goals. Others realize that the price of career success has been neglect of family or personal health.

Old Age

Old age—the later years of adulthood and the final stage of life itself—begins around the mid-sixties. In the United States, about one in eight people is at least age sixty-five, and the elderly now outnumber teenagers (U.S. Census Bureau, 2008).

Once again, societies attach different meanings to this stage of life. It is older members of traditional societies who typically control most of the land and other wealth. Also, since traditional societies change slowly, older people possess useful wisdom gained over their lifetime, which earns them much respect.

• They are environmentally aware. Tweens start to "feel the pain of everybody. They want to know if animals were hurt in making this," says Nisch. . . . They might even become vegetarians or vegans. Rollins agrees: "They have social consciousness at a very young age. They have great lives, and so they want to give back.". . .

• They like attention, sort of. "Our customer aspires to be like an older girl, so if she's 10 she wants to dress like a 12-year-old, and a 12-year-old wants to dress like a 14-year-old," says Atkinson. But she's also "more self-conscious" and not usually trying to attract boys, he says. . . .

A tween starts to feel more comfortable with fashions when she sees them on her older sister or the babysitter, says Atkinson. Tween Brands' challenge, he says, is to "tastefully interpret them for the younger customer. She's just literally developing into a young woman. She doesn't even want to wear spaghetti straps." The girl "has to want an item because she thinks it's the coolest thing in fashion, but if we don't pass muster with Mom, that transaction is not going to be completed."

Moms, in fact, are a big influence on tween fashions, experts say. Many tweens may get some fashion cues from celebrities, but they still look first to their moms. "They still want Mom to give them the OK," [Tween Brands spokesman Robert] Atkinson says.

What else would explain all the tweens and teens with quilted and printed cloth backpacks and purses from Vera Bradley, asks Rollins. "You can't say it's because the paisleys are particularly beautiful. It's the exposure to all the brands the parents covet." . . .

Despite the challenges, most brands want to hook kids as early as possible, which explains kid and tween lines from the likes of Lucky Brand Jeans, J. Crew and Juicy Couture. Bell calls her brand's lip balms "a rite of entry into makeup." Tweens are the brand's core customer, but they've developed products that appeal to kids starting at age 4 and then adapt them to teens and beyond. . . .

Lindsey Brown, who turned 13 last month, made almost $1,000 at the yard sale where she sold her American Girl dolls. She banked $800 and spent $200 on the Juicy Couture sweat suit, which included a skirt, pants and a jacket.

Since then, shopping has "become all about clothes," says Jill Brown.

WHAT DO YOU THINK?

1. What factors are encouraging children to grow up faster?
2. Is the fact that children are growing up faster, in your view, helpful or harmful to them? Why?
3. Are boys as well as girls growing up faster? What evidence can you point to that might help answer this question?

In industrial societies, however, most younger people work and live apart from their parents, becoming independent of their elders. Rapid change also gives our society a "youth orientation" that defines what is old as unimportant or even obsolete. To younger people, the elderly may seem out of touch with new trends and fashions, and their knowledge and experience may seem of little value.

Perhaps this anti-elderly bias will decline as the share of older people in the United States steadily increases. The percentage of the U.S. population over age sixty-five has more than tripled in the past hundred years. With life expectancy still increasing, most men and women in their mid-sixties today (the "young elderly") can look forward to living decades longer. Analysts predict that by 2030, the number of seniors will double to 72 million, and the "average" person in the United States will be close to forty (U.S. Census Bureau, 2008).

Old age differs in an important way from earlier stages in the life course. Growing up typically means entering new roles and taking on new responsibilities, but growing old is the opposite experience—leaving roles that provided both satisfaction and social identity. For some people, retirement is a period of restful activity, but for others, it can mean losing valued routines and even outright boredom. Like any life transition, retirement demands learning new patterns while at the same time letting go of habits from the past.

Death and Dying

Through most of human history, low living standards and limited medical technology meant that death from accident or disease could come at any stage of life. Today, however, 86 percent of people in the United States die after age fifty-five (Kung et al., 2008).

After observing many dying people, the psychiatrist Elisabeth Kübler-Ross (1969) described death as an orderly transition involving five distinct stages. Typically, a person first faces death with *denial,* perhaps out of fear and perhaps because our culture tends to ignore the reality of death. The second phase is *anger,* when a person facing death sees it as a gross injustice. Third, anger gives way to *negotiation* as the person imagines the possibility of avoiding death by striking a bargain with God. The fourth response, *resignation,* is often accompanied by psychological depression. Finally, a complete adjustment to death requires *acceptance.* At this point, no longer paralyzed by fear and anxiety, the person whose life is ending is able fo find peace and makes the most of whatever time remains.

As the share of women and men in old age increases, we can expect our culture to become more comfortable with the idea of death. In recent years, people in the United States have started talking about death more openly, and the trend is to view dying as natural and better than painful or prolonged suffering. More married couples now prepare for death with legal and financial planning.

MAKING THE GRADE

Each stage of life has its own joys and challenges, but in our society, early stages of life typically involve *adding* roles and responsibilities; old age differs in that it typically involves *losing* roles and responsibilities.

cohort a category of people with something in common, usually their age

total institution a setting in which people are isolated from the rest of society and manipulated by an administrative staff

resocialization radically changing an inmate's personality by carefully controlling the environment

This openness may ease somewhat the pain of the surviving spouse, a consideration for women, who, more often than not, outlive their husbands.

The Life Course: Patterns and Variations

This brief look at the life course points to two major conclusions. First, although each stage of life is linked to the biological process of aging, the life course is largely a social construction. For this reason, people in other societies may experience a stage of life quite differently or, for that matter, not at all. Second, in any society, the stages of the life course present certain problems and transitions that involve learning something new and, in many cases, unlearning familiar routines.

Societies organize the life course according to age, but other forces, such as class, race, ethnicity, and gender, also shape people's lives. This means that the general patterns described in this chapter apply somewhat differently to various categories of people within any society.

Getty Images

A cohort is a category of similar-age people who share common life experiences. Just as audiences at Rolling Stones concerts in the 1960s were mainly young people, so most of the group's fans today are over age sixty.

People's life experiences also vary, depending on when, in the history of the society, they were born. A **cohort** is *a category of people with something in common, usually their age.* Because age cohorts are generally influenced by the same economic and cultural trends, they tend to have similar attitudes and values. Women and men born in the 1940s and 1950s, for example, grew up during a time of economic expansion that gave them a sense of optimism. Today's college students, who have grown up in an age of economic uncertainty, are less confident about the future.

Resocialization: Total Institutions

A final type of socialization, experienced by more than 2.5 million people in the United States, involves being confined—usually against their will—in prisons or mental hospitals (U.S. Department of Justice, 2008). This is the world of the **total institution,** *a setting in which people are isolated from the rest of society and manipulated by an administrative staff.*

According to Erving Goffman (1961), total institutions have three important characteristics. First, staff members supervise all aspects of daily life, including when and where residents (often called "inmates") eat, sleep, and work. Second, life in a total institution is controlled and standardized, with the same food, uniforms, and activities for everyone. Third, formal rules dictate when, where, and how inmates perform their daily routines.

The purpose of such rigid routines is **resocialization,** *radically changing an inmate's personality by carefully controlling the environment.* Prisons and mental hospitals physically isolate inmates behind fences, barred windows, and locked doors and limit their access to the telephone, mail, and visitors. The institution becomes their entire world, making it easier for the staff to bring about personality change—or at least obedience—in the inmate.

Resocialization is a two-part process. First, the staff breaks down the new inmate's existing identity. For example, an inmate must give up personal possessions, including clothing and grooming articles used to maintain a distinctive appearance. Instead, the staff provides standard-issue clothes so that everyone looks alike. The staff subjects new inmates to "mortifications of self," which can include searches, head shaving, medical examinations, fingerprinting, and assignment of a serial number. Once inside the walls, individuals also give up their privacy as guards routinely inspect their living quarters.

In the second part of the resocialization process, the staff tries to build a new self in the inmate through a system of rewards and punishments. Having a book to read, watching television, or making

MAKING THE GRADE

Of the theories of human development we have considered in this chapter, Freud's probably points to the least human freedom, because we are all caught between two powerful forces—biology (id) and culture (superego).

MAKING THE GRADE

Mead's theory of human development points to the most human freedom, because he saw no biological drives as Freud did and saw humans as spontaneous and creative.

CONTROVERSY & DEBATE

Are We Free within Society?

MIKE: Sociology is an interesting course. Since my professor started telling us how to look at the world with a sociological eye, I'm realizing that a lot of who I am and where I am is because of society.

KIM: *(teasingly)* Oh, so society is responsible for you turning out so smart and witty and good-looking?

MIKE: No, that's all me. But I'm seeing that being at college and playing football is maybe not all me. What do you think? How free are we, really?

This chapter stresses one key theme: Society shapes how we think, feel, and act. If this is so, then in what sense are we free? To answer this important question, consider the Muppets, puppet stars of television and film. Watching the antics of Kermit the Frog, Miss Piggy, and the rest of the troupe, we almost believe they are real rather than objects controlled from backstage or below. As the sociological perspective points out, human beings are like puppets in that we, too, respond to backstage forces. Society, after all, gives us a culture and shapes our lives according to class, race, and gender. If this is so, can we really claim to be free?

Sociologists answer this question with many voices. The politically liberal response is that individuals are *not* free of society—in fact, as social creatures, we never could be. But if we have to live in a society with power over us, it is important to do what we can to make our world as just as possible, by working to lessen class differences and other barriers to opportunity for minorities, including women. Conservatives agree that society shapes our lives but also point out that we *are* free because society can never dictate our dreams. Our history as a nation, right from the revolutionary acts that led to its founding, is one story after another of people pursuing personal goals despite great odds.

Getty Images, Inc. – Taxi/James Porto

Does understanding more about how society shapes our lives give us greater power to "cut the strings" and choose for ourselves how to live?

Both attitudes are found in George Herbert Mead's analysis of socialization. Mead knew that society makes demands on us, sometimes limiting our options. But he also saw that human beings are spontaneous and creative, capable of continually acting on society and bringing about change. Mead noted the power of society while still affirming the human capacity to evaluate, criticize, and ultimately choose and change.

In the end, then, we may seem like puppets, but only on the surface. A crucial difference is that we can stop, look up at the "strings" that make us move, and even yank on them defiantly (Berger, 1963:176). If our pull is strong enough, we can do more than we might think. As Margaret Mead once remarked, "Never doubt that a small group of thoughtful, committed citizens can change the world. Indeed, it is the only thing that ever has."

WHAT DO YOU THINK?

1. Do you think that our society gives more freedom to males than to females? Why or why not?
2. Do you think that most people in our society feel that they have some control over their lives or not? Why?
3. Has learning about socialization increased or decreased your feeling of freedom? Why?

a telephone call may seem like minor pleasures to the outsider, but in the rigid environment of the total institution, gaining such simple privileges as these can be a powerful motivation to conform. The length of confinement typically depends on how well the inmate cooperates with the staff.

Total institutions affect people in different ways. Some inmates may end up "rehabilitated" or "recovered," but others may change little, and still others may become hostile and bitter. Over a long period of time, living in a rigidly controlled environment can leave some people *institutionalized,* without the capacity for independent living.

But what about the rest of us? Does socialization crush our individuality or empower us to reach our creative potential? The Controversy & Debate box takes a closer look at this question.

Seeing Sociology in Everyday Life

Socialization

When do we grow up and become adults?

As this chapter explains, many factors come into play in the process of moving from one stage of the life course to another. In global perspective, what makes our society unusual is that there is no one event that clearly tells everyone (and us, too) that the milestone of adulthood has been reached. We have important events that say, for example, when someone completes high school (graduation ceremony) or becomes married (wedding ceremony). Look at the photos shown here. In each case, what do we learn about how the society defines the transition from one stage of life to another?

HINT Societies differ in how they structure the life course, including which stages of life are defined as important, what years of life various stages correspond to, and how clearly movement from one stage to another is marked. Given our cultural emphasis on individual choice and freedom, many people tend to say "You're only as old as you feel" and let people decide these things for themselves. When it comes to reaching adulthood, our society is not very clear—the Seeing Sociology in Everyday Life box points out many factors that figure into becoming an adult. So there is no widespread "adult ritual" as we see in these photos. Keep in mind that, for us, class matters a lot in this process, with young people from more affluent families staying in school and delaying full adulthood until well into their twenties or even their thirties. Finally, in these tough economic times, the share of young people in their twenties living with parents goes way up, which can delay adulthood for an entire cohort.

Among the Hamer people in the Omo Valley of Ethiopia, young boys must undergo a test to mark their transition to manhood. Usually the event is triggered by the boy's expressing a desire to marry. In this ritual, witnessed by everyone in his society, the boy must jump over a line of bulls selected by the girl's family. If he succeeds in doing this three times, he is declared a man and the wedding can take place (marking the girl's transition to womanhood). Does our society have any ceremony or event similar to this?

On the San Carlos Reservation in Arizona, young Apache girls perform the Sunrise Dance to mark their transition to adulthood. Carefully painted by an elder according to Apache tradition, each girl holds a special staff, which symbolizes her hope for a long and healthy life and spiritual happiness. Why do many of the world's societies time these coming-of-age rituals to correspond to a girl's first menstrual cycle?

These young men and women in Seoul, South Korea, are participating in a Confucian ceremony to mark their becoming adults. This ritual, which takes place on the twentieth birthday, defines young people as full members of the community and also reminds them of all the responsibilities they are now expected to fulfill. If we had such a ritual in the United States, at what age would it take place?

Applying SOCIOLOGY in Everyday Life

1. Across the United States, many families plan elaborate parties to celebrate a daughter's or son's graduation from high school. In what respects is this a ritual that marks reaching adulthood? How does social class affect whether or not people define this event as the beginning of adulthood?

2. In the United States, when does the stage of life we call "old age" begin? Is there an event that marks the transition to old age? Does social class play a part in this process? If so, how?

3. Watch several hours of prime-time programming on network or cable television. Keep track of every time an act of violence is shown, and calculate the number of violent scenes per hour. On the basis of observing a small and unrepresentative sample of programs, what are your conclusions?

MAKING THE GRADE

VISUAL SUMMARY

Socialization

What Is Socialization?

Socialization is a **LIFELONG PROCESS.**
- Socialization develops our humanity as well as our particular personalities.
- The importance of socialization is seen in the fact that extended periods of social isolation result in permanent damage (cases of Anna, Isabelle, and Genie).

Socialization is a matter of **NURTURE** rather than **NATURE.**
- A century ago, most people thought human behavior resulted from biological instinct.
- For us as human beings, it is our nature to nurture.

socialization the lifelong social experience by which people develop their human potential and learn culture

personality a person's fairly consistent patterns of acting, thinking, and feeling

Important Contributions to Our Understanding of Socialization

SIGMUND FREUD'S model of the human personality has three parts:
- **id:** innate, pleasure-seeking human drives
- **superego:** the demands of society in the form of internalized values and norms
- **ego:** our efforts to balance innate, pleasure-seeking drives and the demands of society

JEAN PIAGET believed that human development involves both biological maturation and gaining social experience. He identified four stages of cognitive development:
- First, the **sensorimotor stage** involves knowing the world only through the senses.
- Next, the **preoperational stage** involves starting to use language and other symbols.
- Next, the **concrete operational stage** allows individuals to understand causal connections.
- Finally, the **formal operational stage** involves abstract and critical thought.

LAWRENCE KOHLBERG applied Piaget's approach to stages of moral development:
- We first judge rightness in **preconventional** terms, according to our individual needs.
- Next, **conventional** moral reasoning takes account of parental attitudes and cultural norms.
- Finally, **postconventional** reasoning allows us to criticize society itself.

CAROL GILLIGAN found that gender plays an important part in moral development, with males relying more on abstract standards of rightness and females relying more on the effects of actions on relationships.

To **GEORGE HERBERT MEAD,**
- the **self** is part of our personality and includes self-awareness and self-image;
- the self develops only as a result of social experience;
- social experience involves the exchange of symbols;
- social interaction depends on understanding the intention of another, which requires taking the role of the other;
- human action is partly spontaneous (the I) and partly in response to others (the me);
- we gain social experience through imitation, play, games, and understanding the **generalized other.**

CHARLES HORTON COOLEY used the term **looking-glass self** to explain that we see ourselves as we imagine others see us.

ERIK H. ERIKSON identified challenges that individuals face at each stage of life from infancy to old age.

id Freud's term for the human being's basic drives

ego Freud's term for a person's conscious efforts to balance innate pleasure-seeking drives with the demands of society

superego Freud's term for the cultural values and norms internalized by an individual

sensorimotor stage Piaget's term for the level of human development at which individuals experience the world only through their senses

preoperational stage Piaget's term for the level of human development at which individuals first use language and other symbols

concrete operational stage Piaget's term for the level of human development at which individuals first see causal connections in their surroundings

formal operational stage Piaget's term for the level of human development at which individuals think abstractly and critically

self George Herbert Mead's term for the part of an individual's personality composed of self-awareness and self-image

looking-glass self Cooley's term for a self-image based on how we think others see us

significant others people, such as parents, who have special importance for socialization

generalized other George Herbert Mead's term for widespread cultural norms and values we use as references in evaluating ourselves

Agents of Socialization

The **FAMILY** is usually the first setting of socialization.
- Family has the greatest impact on attitudes and behavior.
- A family's social position, including race and social class, shapes a child's personality.
- Ideas about gender are learned first in the family.

SCHOOLS give most children their first experience with bureaucracy and impersonal evaluation.
- Schools teach knowledge and skills needed for later life.
- Schools expose children to greater social diversity.
- Schools reinforce ideas about gender.

peer group a social group whose members have interests, social position, and age in common

anticipatory socialization learning that helps a person achieve a desired position

mass media the means for delivering impersonal communications to a vast audience

The **PEER GROUP** helps shape attitudes and behavior.
- The peer group takes on great importance during adolescence.
- The peer group frees young people from adult supervision.

The **MASS MEDIA** have a huge impact on socialization in modern, high-income societies.
- The average U.S. child spends as much time watching television and videos as attending school and interacting with parents.
- The mass media often reinforce stereotypes about gender and race.
- The mass media expose people to a great deal of violence.

Socialization and the Life Course

The concept of **CHILDHOOD** is grounded not in biology but in culture. In high-income countries, childhood is extended.

The emotional and social turmoil of **ADOLESCENCE** results from cultural inconsistency in defining people who are not children but not yet adults. Adolescence varies by social class position.

cohort a category of people with something in common, usually their age

ADULTHOOD is the stage of life when most accomplishments take place. Although personality is now formed, it continues to change with new life experiences.

OLD AGE is defined as much by culture as biology.
- Traditional societies give power and respect to elders.
- Industrial societies define elders as unimportant and out of touch.

Acceptance of **DEATH AND DYING** is part of socialization for the elderly. This process typically involves five stages: denial, anger, negotiation, resignation, and acceptance.

✓ *Every stage of life is socially constructed in ways that vary from society to society.*

Total Institutions

TOTAL INSTITUTIONS include prisons, mental hospitals, and monasteries.
- Staff members supervise all aspects of life.
- Life is standardized, with all inmates following set rules and routines.

RESOCIALIZATION is a two-part process:
- breaking down inmates' existing identity
- building a new self through a system of rewards and punishments

total institution a setting in which people are isolated from the rest of society and manipulated by an administrative staff

resocialization radically changing an inmate's personality by carefully controlling the environment

MAKING THE GRADE

Sample Test Questions

Multiple-Choice Questions

1. Kingsley Davis's study of Anna, the girl isolated for five years, shows that
  a. humans have all the same instincts found in other animal species.
  b. without social experience, a child never develops personality.
  c. personality is present in all humans at birth.
  d. many human instincts disappear in the first few years of life.

2. Most sociologists take the position that
  a. humans have instincts that direct behavior.
  b. biological instincts develop in humans at puberty.
  c. it is human nature to nurture.
  d. All of the above are correct.

3. Lawrence Kohlberg explored socialization by studying
  a. cognition.
  b. the importance of gender in socialization.
  c. the development of biological instincts.
  d. moral reasoning.

4. Carol Gilligan added to Kohlberg's findings by showing that
  a. girls and boys typically use different standards in deciding what is right and wrong.
  b. girls are more interested in right and wrong than boys are.
  c. boys are more interested in right and wrong than girls are.
  d. today's children are far less interested in right and wrong than their parents are.

5. The "self," said George Herbert Mead, is
  a. the part of the human personality made up of self-awareness and self-image.
  b. the presence of culture within the individual.
  c. basic drives that are self-centered.
  d. present in infants from birth.

6. Why is the family so important to the socialization process?
  a. Family members provide vital caregiving to infants and children.
  b. Families give children social identity in terms of class, ethnicity, and religion.
  c. Parents' behavior can greatly affect a child's self-concept.
  d. All of the above are correct.

7. Social class position affects socialization: Lower-class parents tend to stress _____, and well-to-do parents stress _____.
  a. independence; protecting children
  b. independence; dependence
  c. obedience; creativity
  d. creativity; obedience

8. In global perspective, which statement about childhood is correct?
  a. In every society, the first ten years of life are a time of play and learning.
  b. Rich societies extend childhood much longer than poor societies do.
  c. Poor societies extend childhood much longer than rich societies do.
  d. Childhood is defined by being biologically immature.

9. Modern, high-income societies typically define people in old age as
  a. the wisest of all.
  b. the most up-to-date on current fashion and trends.
  c. less socially important than younger adults.
  d. All of the above are correct.

10. According to Erving Goffman, the purpose of a total institution is
  a. to reward someone for achievement in the outside world.
  b. to give a person more choices about how to live.
  c. to encourage lifelong learning in a supervised context.
  d. to change a person's personality or behavior.

ANSWERS: 1 (b); 2 (c); 3 (d); 4 (a); 5 (a); 6 (d); 7 (c); 8 (b); 9 (c); 10 (d).

Essay Questions

1. State the two sides of the "nature-nurture" debate. In what important way are nature and nurture not opposed to each other?
2. What are common themes in the ideas of Freud, Piaget, Kohlberg, Gilligan, Mead, and Erikson? In what ways do their theories differ?

Social Interaction in Everyday Life

iStockphoto International/Royalty Free/Courtesy of www.istockphoto.com

Sociology points to the many rules that guide behavior in everyday situations. The more we learn about the rules of social interaction, the better we can play the game.

Redux Pictures/Justin Lane/*The New York Times*

Social Interaction in Everyday Life

Corbis – NY/Tom and Dee Ann McCarthy

SuperStock, Inc./Jiang Jin

CHAPTER OVERVIEW

This chapter takes a "micro-level" look at society, examining patterns of everyday social interaction. First, the chapter identifies important social structures, including status and role. Then it explains how we construct reality in social interaction. Finally, it applies the lessons learned to three everyday experiences: emotion, gender, and humor.

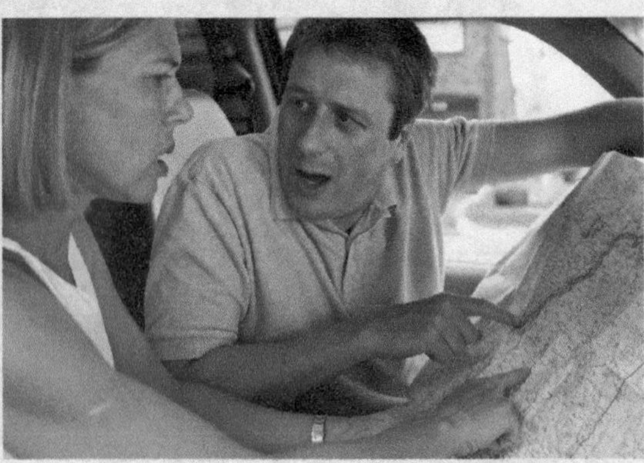

Pearson09/Frank Siteman/© www.franksiteman.com

Harold and Sybil are on their way to another couple's home in an unfamiliar area near Fort Lauderdale, Florida. For the last twenty minutes, as Sybil sees it, they have been driving in circles, searching in vain for Coconut Palm Road.

"Look, Harold," says Sybil. "There are some people up ahead. Let's ask for directions."

Harold, gripping the wheel ever more tightly, begins muttering under his breath. "I know where I am. I don't want to waste time talking to strangers. Just let me get us there."

"I'm sure you know where you are, Harold," Sybil responds, looking straight ahead. "But I don't think you know where you're going."

Harold and Sybil are lost in more ways than one: Not only can't they find where their friends live, but they also cannot understand why they are growing angrier with each other with each passing minute.

What's going on? Like most men, Harold cannot stand getting lost. The longer he drives around, the more incompetent he feels. Sybil can't understand why Harold doesn't pull over to ask someone the way to Coconut Palm Road. If she were driving, she thinks to herself, they would already be comfortably settled in with their friends.

Why don't men like to ask for directions? Because men value their independence, they are uncomfortable asking for any type of help and are reluctant to accept it. To ask another person for assistance is the same as saying, "You know something I don't know." If it takes Harold a few more minutes to find Coconut Palm Road on his own—and to keep his sense of being in control—he thinks that's the way to go.

Women are more in tune with others and strive for connectedness. From Sybil's point of view, asking for help is right because sharing information builds social bonds and at the same time gets the job done. Asking for directions seems as natural to her as searching on his own is to Harold. Obviously, getting lost is sure to create conflict for Harold and Sybil as long as neither one understands the other's point of view.

Such everyday social patterns are the focus of this chapter. The central concept is **social interaction,** *the process by which people act and react in relation to others.* We begin by presenting the rules and building blocks of everyday experience and then explore the almost magical way in which face-to-face interaction creates the reality in which we live.

Social Structure: A Guide to Everyday Living

October 21, Ho Chi Minh City, Vietnam. This morning we leave the ship and make our way along the docks toward the center of Ho Chi Minh City, known to an earlier generation as Saigon. The government security officers wave us through the heavy metal gates. Pressed against the fence are dozens of men who operate cyclos (bicycles with small carriages attached to the front), the Vietnamese version of taxicabs. We wave them off and spend the next twenty minutes shaking our heads at several drivers who pedal alongside, pleading for our business. The pressure is uncomfortable. We decide to cross the street but realize suddenly that there are no stop signs or signal lights—and the street is an unbroken stream of bicycles, cyclos, motorbikes, and small trucks. The locals don't bat an eye; they just walk at a steady pace across the street, parting waves of vehicles that immediately close in again behind them. Walk right into traffic? With our small children on our backs? Yup, we did it; that's the way it works in Vietnam.

social interaction the process by which people act and react in relation to others

status a social position that a person holds

ascribed status a social position a person receives at birth or takes on involuntarily later in life

achieved status a social position a person takes on voluntarily that reflects personal ability and effort

status set all the statuses a person holds at a given time

master status a status that has special importance for social identity, often shaping a person's entire life

Members of every society rely on social structure to make sense of everyday situations. As our family's introduction to the busy streets of Vietnam suggests, the world can be confusing, even frightening, when society's rules are unclear. Let's take a closer look at the ways in which societies set the rules of everyday life.

Status

In every society, people build their everyday lives using the idea of **status,** *a social position that a person holds.* In everyday use, the word *status* generally means "prestige," as when we say that a college president has more "status" than a newly hired assistant professor. But sociologically speaking, both "president" and "professor" are statuses, or positions, within the collegiate organization.

Status is part of our social identity and helps define our relationship to others. As Georg Simmel (1950:307, orig. 1902), one of the founders of sociology, once pointed out, before we can deal with anyone, we need to know who the person is.

Status Set

Each of us holds many statuses at once. The term **status set** refers to *all the statuses a person holds at a given time.* A teenage girl may be a daughter to her parents, a sister to her brother, a student at her school, and a goalie on her soccer team.

Status sets change over the life course. A child grows up to become a parent, a student graduates to become a lawyer, and a single person marries to become a husband or wife, sometimes becoming single again as a result of death or divorce. Joining an organization or finding a job enlarges our status set; withdrawing from activities makes it smaller. Over a lifetime, people gain and lose dozens of statuses.

In any rigidly ranked setting, no interaction can proceed until people assess each other's social standing. For this reason, military personnel wear insignia, clear symbols of their level of authority. Don't we size people up in much the same way in routine interactions, noting a person's approximate age, quality of clothing, and manner for clues about social position?

Ascribed and Achieved Status

Sociologists classify statuses in terms of how people attain them. An **ascribed status** is *a social position a person receives at birth or takes on involuntarily later in life.* Examples of ascribed statuses include being a daughter, a Cuban, a teenager, or a widower. Ascribed statuses are matters about which we have little or no choice.

By contrast, an **achieved status** refers to *a social position a person takes on voluntarily that reflects personal ability and effort.* Achieved statuses in the United States include honors student, Olympic athlete, nurse, software writer, and thief.

In the real world, of course, most statuses involve a combination of ascription and achievement. That is, people's ascribed statuses influence the statuses they achieve. People who achieve the status of lawyer, for example, are likely to share the ascribed benefit of being born into relatively well-off families. By the same token, many less desirable statuses, such as criminal, drug addict, or unemployed worker, are more easily achieved by people born into poverty.

Master Status

Some statuses matter more than others. A **master status** is *a status that has special importance for social identity, often shaping a person's entire life.* For most people, a job is a master status because it reveals a great deal about social background, education, and income. In a few cases, name is a master status; being in the Bush or Kennedy family attracts attention and creates opportunities.

A master status can be negative as well as positive. Take, for example, serious illness. Sometimes people, even longtime friends, avoid cancer patients or people with AIDS because of their illnesses. As another example, the fact that all societies limit the opportunities of women makes gender a master status.

Sometimes a physical disability serves as a master status to the point where we dehumanize people by seeing them only in terms of their disability. The Thinking About Diversity box shows how.

SEEING SOCIOLOGY in Everyday Life

Make a list of ten important statuses in your own life. Indicate whether each one is ascribed or achieved. Is this sometimes difficult to do? Why?

MAKING THE GRADE

Remember that *status* refers to a social position and *role* refers to behavior. We *hold* a status and *perform* a role.

THINKING ABOUT DIVERSITY: RACE, CLASS, & GENDER

Physical Disability as a Master Status

Physical disability works in much the same ways as class, gender, or race in defining people in the eyes of others. In the following interviews, two women explain how a physical disability can become a master status—a trait that overshadows everything else about them. The first voice is that of twenty-nine-year-old Donna Finch, who lives with her husband and son in Muskogee, Oklahoma, and holds a master's degree in social work. She is also blind.

> Most people don't expect handicapped people to grow up; they are always supposed to be children. . . . You aren't supposed to date, you aren't supposed to have a job, somehow you're just supposed to disappear. I'm not saying this is true of anyone else, but in my own case I think I was more intellectually mature than most children, and more emotionally immature. I'd say that not until the last four or five years have I felt really whole.

Rose Helman is an elderly woman who has retired and lives near New York City. She suffers from spinal meningitis and is also blind.

> You ask me if people are really different today than in the '20s and '30s. Not too much. They are still fearful of the handicapped. I don't know if *fearful* is the right word, but uncomfortable at least. But I can understand it somewhat; it happened to me. I once asked a man to tell me which staircase to use to get from the subway out to the street. He started giving me directions that were confusing, and I said, "Do you mind taking me?" He said, "Not at all." He grabbed me on the side with my dog on it, so I asked him to take my other arm. And he said, "I'm sorry, I have no other arm." And I said, "That's all right, I'll hold onto the jacket." It felt funny hanging onto the sleeve without the arm in it.

Getty Images, Inc. – Aurora/Michael Hanson

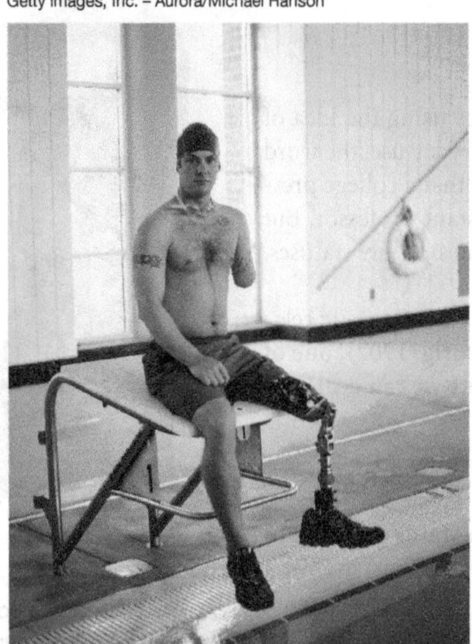

Modern technology means that most soldiers who lose limbs in war now survive. How do you think the loss of an arm or a leg affects a person's social identity and sense of self?

WHAT DO YOU THINK?

1. Have you ever had a disease or disability that became a master status? If so, how did others react?
2. How might such a master status affect someone's personality?
3. Can being very fat or very thin serve as a master status? Why or why not?

Source: Based on Orlansky & Heward (1981).

Role

A second important social structure is **role,** *behavior expected of someone who holds a particular status.* A person *holds* a status and *performs* a role (Linton, 1937b). For example, holding the status of student leads you to perform the role of attending classes and completing assignments.

Both statuses and roles vary by culture. In the United States, the status of "uncle" refers to the brother of a mother or a father. In Vietnam, the word for "uncle" is different on the mother's and father's sides of the family, and the two men have different responsibilities. In every society, actual role performance varies with an individual's unique personality, and some societies permit more individual expression of a role than others.

Role Set

Because we hold many statuses at once—a status set—everyday life is a mix of many roles. Robert Merton (1968) introduced the term **role set** to identify *a number of roles attached to a single status.*

Figure 1 shows four statuses of one person, each status linked to a different role set. First, as a professor, this woman interacts with students (the teacher role) and with other academics (the colleague role). Second, in her work as a researcher, she gathers and analyzes data (the fieldwork role) that she uses in her publications (the author role). Third, the woman occupies the status of "wife," with a marital role (such as confidante and sexual partner) toward her husband, with whom she shares household duties (domestic role). Fourth, she holds the status of "mother," with routine responsibilities for her children (the maternal role), as well as toward their school and other organizations in her community (the civic role).

A global perspective shows that the roles people use to define their lives differ from society to society. In low-income countries, people spend fewer years as students, and family roles are often very important to social identity. In high-income nations, people spend more years as students, and family roles are typically less important to social identity. Another dimension of difference involves house-

role behavior expected of someone who holds a particular status

role set a number of roles attached to a single status

role conflict conflict among the roles connected to two or more statuses

role strain tension among the roles connected to a single status

SEEING SOCIOLOGY in Everyday Life

Give one example of role conflict and one example of role strain in your own life.

work. As Global Map 1 shows, especially in poor countries, housework falls heavily on women.

Role Conflict and Role Strain

People in modern, high-income nations juggle many responsibilities demanded by their various statuses and roles. As most mothers (and more and more fathers) can testify, the combination of parenting and working outside the home is physically and emotionally draining. Sociologists thus recognize **role conflict** as *conflict among the roles connected to two or more statuses.*

We experience role conflict when we find ourselves pulled in various directions as we try to respond to the many statuses we hold. One response to role conflict is deciding that "something has to go." More than one politician, for example, has decided not to run for office because of the conflicting demands of a hectic campaign schedule and family life. In other cases, people put off having children in order to stay on the "fast track" for career success.

Even roles linked to a single status may make competing demands on us. **Role strain** refers to *tension among the roles connected to a single status.* A college professor may enjoy being friendly with students. At the same time, however, the professor must maintain the personal distance needed to evaluate students fairly. In short, performing the various roles attached to even one status can be something of a balancing act.

One strategy for minimizing role conflict is separating parts of our lives so that we perform roles for one status at one time and place and carry out roles connected to another status in a completely different setting. A familiar example of this idea is deciding to "leave the job at work" before heading home to the family.

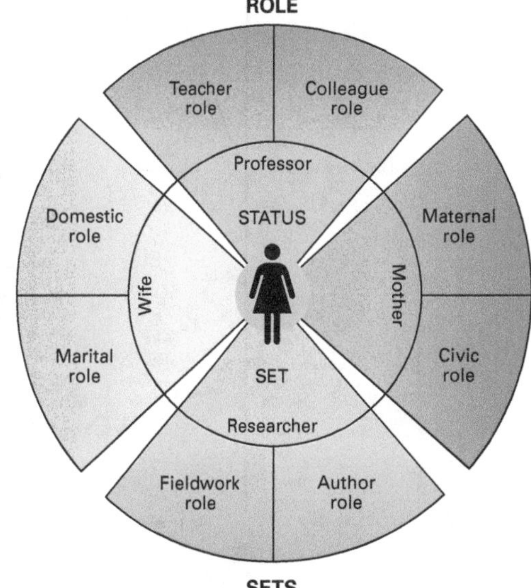

FIGURE 1 **Status Set and Role Sets**

A status set includes all the statuses a person holds at a given time. The status set defines *who we are* in society. The many roles linked to each status define *what we do.*

Role Exit

After she left the life of a Catholic nun to become a university sociologist, Helen Rose Fuchs Ebaugh began to study her own experience of *role exit,* the process by which people disengage from important social roles. Studying a range of "exes," including ex-nuns, ex-doctors, ex-husbands, and ex-alcoholics, Ebaugh identified elements common to the process of becoming an "ex."

According to Ebaugh (1988), the process begins as people come to doubt their ability to continue in a certain role. As they imagine alternative roles, they ultimately reach a tipping point when they decide to pursue a new life. Even as they are moving on, however, a past role can continue to influence their lives. Exes carry with them a self-image shaped by an earlier role, which can interfere with building a new sense of self. For example, an ex-nun may hesitate to wear stylish clothing and makeup.

Exes must also rebuild relationships with people who knew them in their earlier life. Learning new social skills is another challenge. For example, Ebaugh reports, ex-nuns who enter the dating scene after decades in the church are often surprised to learn that sexual norms are very different from those they knew when they were teenagers.

The Social Construction of Reality

In 1917, the Italian playwright Luigi Pirandello wrote a play called *The Pleasure of Honesty* about a character named Angelo Baldovino, a brilliant man with a checkered past. Baldovino enters the fashionable home of the Renni family and introduces himself in a peculiar way:

> Inevitably we construct ourselves. Let me explain. I enter this house and immediately I become what I have to become, what I can become: I construct myself. That is, I present myself to you in a form suitable to the relationship I wish to achieve with you. And, of course, you do the same with me. (1962:157–58)

Baldovino suggests that although behavior is guided by status and role, we have the ability to shape who we are and to guide what happens from moment to moment. In other words, "reality" is not as fixed as we may think.

Lucila Herrerade Nuñez is a 28-year-old mother of two in Lima, Peru, who works full time and also does all the housework.

Donna Murray, also 28, shares a Boston apartment with her fiancé. Although they agreed to share housework, she still does most of it.

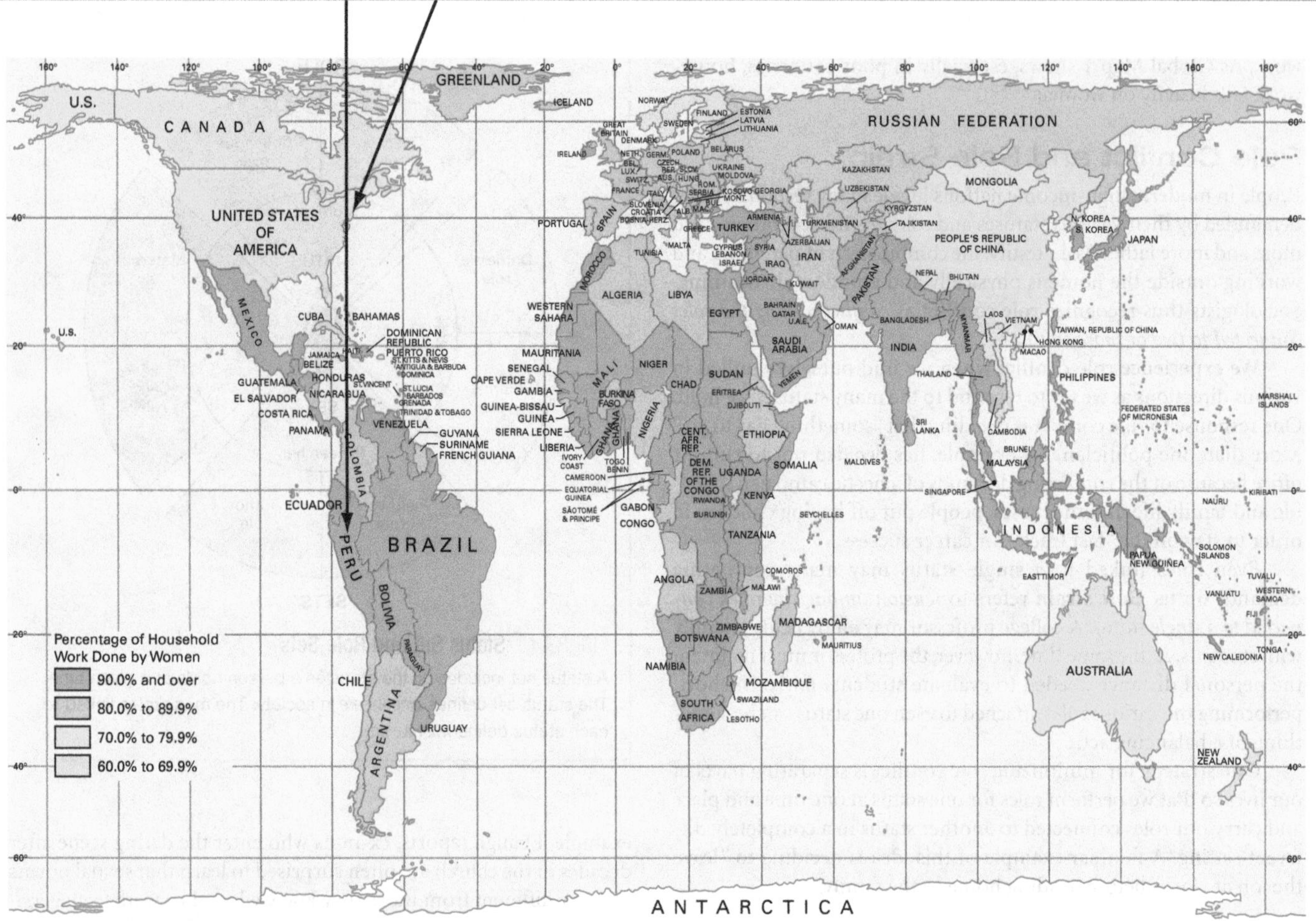

Window on the World

GLOBAL MAP 1 Housework in Global Perspective

Throughout the world, housework is a major part of women's routines and identities. This is especially true in poor nations of Latin America, Africa, and Asia, where the social position of women is far below that of men. But our society also defines housework and child care as "feminine" activities, even though women and men have the same legal rights and most women work outside the home.

Source: *Peters Atlas of the World* (1990); updated by the author.

The **social construction of reality** is *the process by which people creatively shape reality through social interaction.* This idea is the foundation of the symbolic-interaction approach. As Baldovino's remark suggests, quite a bit of "reality" remains unclear in everyone's mind, especially in unfamiliar situations. So we present ourselves in terms that suit the setting and our purposes, we try to guide what happens next, and as others do the same, reality takes shape. The Seeing Sociology in Everyday Life box looks at how this happens on the Internet at the popular Web site "Second Life."

Social interaction, then, is a complex negotiation that builds reality. Most everyday situations involve at least some agreement about what's going on. But how people see events depends on their different backgrounds, interests, and intentions.

social construction of reality the process by which people creatively shape reality through social interaction

Thomas theorem W. I. Thomas's claim that situations defined as real are real in their consequences

ethnomethodology Harold Garfinkel's term for the study of the way people make sense of their everyday surroundings

MAKING THE GRADE

"Ethnomethodology" is a long word for an easy idea: To test people's assumptions about everyday life's rules, try breaking them and observe people's reactions.

"Street Smarts"

What people commonly call "street smarts" is actually a form of constructing reality. In his autobiography *Down These Mean Streets,* Piri Thomas recalls moving to an apartment in Spanish Harlem. Returning home one evening, young Piri found himself cut off by Waneko, the leader of the local street gang, who was flanked by a dozen others.

> "Whatta ya say, Mr. Johnny Gringo," drawled Waneko.
>
> *Think man,* I told myself, *think your way out of a stomping. Make it good.* "I hear you 104th Street coolies are supposed to have heart," I said. "I don't know this for sure. You know there's a lot of streets where a whole 'click' is made out of punks who can't fight one guy unless they all jump him for the stomp." I hoped this would push Waneko into giving me a fair one. His expression didn't change.
>
> "Maybe we don't look at it that way."
>
> *Crazy, man,* I cheer inwardly, *the* cabron *is falling into my setup. . . .* "I wasn't talking to you," I said. "Where I come from, the pres is president 'cause he got heart when it comes to dealing."
>
> Waneko was starting to look uneasy. He had bit on my worm and felt like a sucker fish. His boys were now light on me. They were no longer so much interested in stomping me as seeing the outcome between Waneko and me. "Yeah," was his reply. . . .
>
> I knew I'd won. Sure, I'd have to fight; but one guy, not ten or fifteen. If I lost, I might still get stomped, and if I won I might get stomped. I took care of this with my next sentence. "I don't know you or your boys," I said, "but they look cool to me. They don't feature as punks."
>
> I had left him out purposely when I said "they." Now his boys were in a separate class. I had cut him off. He would have to fight me on his own, to prove his heart to himself, to his boys, and most important, to his turf. He got away from the stoop and asked, "Fair one, Gringo?" (1967:56–57)

This situation reveals the drama—sometimes subtle, sometimes savage—by which human beings creatively build reality. But of course, not everyone enters a situation with equal standing. If a police officer had happened to drive by when Piri and Waneko were fighting, both young men might have ended up in jail.

The Thomas Theorem

By displaying his wits and fighting with Waneko until they both tired, Piri Thomas won acceptance by the gang. What took place that evening in Spanish Harlem is an example of the **Thomas theorem,** named after W. I. Thomas (1966:301, orig. 1931): *Situations that are defined as real are real in their consequences.*

Applied to social interaction, the Thomas theorem means that although reality is initially "soft" as it is being shaped, it can become "hard" in its effects. In the case just described, local gang members saw Piri Thomas act in a worthy way, so in their eyes, he *became* worthy.

Flirting is an everyday experience in reality construction. Each person offers information to the other and hints at romantic interest. Yet the interaction proceeds with a tentative and often humorous air so that either individual can withdraw at any time without further obligation.

Ethnomethodology

Most of the time, we take social reality for granted. To become more aware of the world we help create, Harold Garfinkel (1967) devised **ethnomethodology,** *the study of the way people make sense of their everyday surroundings.* This approach begins by pointing out that everyday behavior rests on a number of assumptions. When you ask someone the simple question "How are you?" you usually want to know how the person is doing in general, but you might really be wondering how the person is dealing with a specific physical, mental, spiritual, or financial challenge. However, the person being asked probably assumes that you are not really interested in details about any of these things, that you are just "being polite."

One good way to discover the assumptions we make about reality is to break the rules. For example, the next time someone greets you by saying, "How are you?" offer details from your last physical examination or explain all the good and bad things that have happened since you woke up that morning and see how the person reacts.

The results are predictable, because we all have some idea of the "rules" of everyday interaction. The person will most likely become confused or irritated by your unexpected behavior—a reaction that

SEEING SOCIOLOGY in Everyday Life

Have you used Internet sites such as MySpace, Xanga, Facebook, or YouTube to "present" yourself to others? How "real" are these constructed realities?

SEEING SOCIOLOGY IN EVERYDAY LIFE

Performances Online? Visit "Second Life"!

A small group of young people gathers outside the Straight Talk Café to discuss the Obama administration's economic bailout program. Sophie Yates is explaining her position, "Look, all they're doing is throwing money at the people who caused the problem in the first place." Another young woman, Auryn Karu, reacts quickly. "Well, at least they're doing something. We've got to do something big and do something now to turn this country around."

This event might have played out on any college campus from New York to Los Angeles, but it actually happened nowhere at all—at least nowhere in the real world. This bit of nonreality took place in an outdoor park that is part of Second Life, the virtual world accessed through the Web site http://secondlife.com.

Invented in 2003 by Linden Research, Inc., Second Life has become a popular Web destination that has been visited by as many as 10 million people around the world. If there is anything the visitors to Second Life have in common (other than their speedy connections and very good graphics cards), it is that they tend to be creative people looking for something different from their ordinary lives.

Experiencing something new is exactly the point of Second Life, according to its inventors. Residents of this computer universe can turn loose their imagination and creativity in surroundings "teeming with people, entertainment, experiences, and opportunity."

Second Life allows you to put many of the concepts described in this chapter into action. First, to become a "resident" in the world of Second Life, you need to construct an identity. Your character is called an "avatar," which you create as you decide to be female or male (or both) and design every feature of your "body" from height to hair color, from the contours of your hips to the color of your skin. (That is, assuming you want a "humanoid" appearance at all—anything is possible, and the options are limited only by your imagination.) This virtual world contains people who look rich, poor, attractive, even scary. Whatever you can dream up becomes real in this unreal world.

Having constructed your identity, you can interact with the million or so other avatars who inhabit this virtual world at any given time. Select a setting by looking at events that are going on, and walk, skate, ride, or teleport to whatever activity interests you. There are shopping malls, dance halls, classroom lectures, open-air concerts, quiet beaches for walking, and pulsating clubs for dancing. You can choose to go to a strip club on Saturday night or attend a church service on Sunday morning. Many companies are open for business, and several real-life countries have even set up virtual embassies on the site. Volunteers for both presidential candidates actually set up campaign headquarters in Second Life, and thousands of people spent the election night in this virtual world to await the results of the voting.

Whatever your interest, once you arrive at an event, you walk up to someone (or are prepared to have someone walk up to you). As the avatars interact, "reality" is constructed. As in any society, rules guide behavior (for example, Second Life has recently banned gambling). Also as in real life, you can evaluate your own actions by seeing how others respond to what you say or do. It is not far from the truth to say that Second Life is a laboratory in which you can study many of the elements of social interaction.

Just as in the real world, many of the activities in Second Life cost money. The currency of this virtual society is Linden dollars, which can be purchased for "real" money (have your credit card ready). You can buy and sell property or services, making money or going broke in the process.

Virtual reality sites such as Second Life are gaining in popularity because they allow us to be or do what we have always dreamed about. Put another way, if you don't find everything you need in your real life (RL, for short), try a second life (SL) online. But the experience may not be quite what you would hope. For one thing, researchers who have begun studying Second Life report that the identities and behavior that people create turn out to be not so very different from those of the real world. In addition, some regular visitors to Second Life report that the experience can be lonely, raising questions about how satisfying virtual interaction is compared to the real thing.

Second Life Website

WHAT DO YOU THINK?

1. Have you ever visited Second Life? If so, what did you like about the experience? What did you not enjoy?
2. Some analysts claim that Web sites like this one are the future of entertainment because, while television turns people into a passive audience, sites such as Second Life make people active participants. Do you agree or not? Why?
3. If you were to create an online identity, in what ways would it be like your real-life identity? How would it be different? Why?

Sources: Gross (2006), Itzkoff (2007), Lagorio (2007), and Lang (2008).

SEEING SOCIOLOGY in Everyday Life

Members of every culture have rules about how close people should stand while talking. To see what the rules are in your social world, during a conversation, slowly move closer and closer to the other person and see what happens.

dramaturgical analysis Erving Goffman's term for the study of social interaction in terms of theatrical performance

presentation of self Erving Goffman's term for a person's efforts to create specific impressions in the minds of others

helps us see not only what the rules are but also how important they are to everyday reality.

Reality Building: Class and Culture

People do not build everyday experience out of thin air. In part, how we act or what we see in our surroundings depends on our interests. Gazing at the sky on a starry night, for example, lovers discover romance, and scientists see hydrogen atoms fusing into helium. Social background also affects what we see, which is why residents of Spanish Harlem experience a different world than people living on Manhattan's pricey Upper East Side.

In global perspective, reality construction varies even more. Consider these everyday situations: People waiting for a bus in London typically "queue up" in a straight line; people in New York are rarely so orderly. The law forbids women in Saudi Arabia to drive cars, a ban unthinkable in the United States. In this country, people assume that "a short walk" means a few blocks or a few minutes; in the Andes Mountains of Peru, this same phrase means a few miles.

The point is that people build reality from the surrounding culture. People the world over find different meanings in specific gestures, so inexperienced travelers can find themselves building an unexpected and unwelcome reality. Similarly, in a study of popular culture, JoEllen Shively (1992) screened western films to men of European descent and to Native American men. The men in both categories claimed to enjoy the films, but for very different reasons. White men interpreted the films as praising rugged people striking out for the West and conquering the forces of nature. Native American men saw in the same films a celebration of land and nature. Given their different cultures, it is as if people in the two categories saw two different films.

Films also have an effect on the reality we all experience. The 2007 film *Away from Her,* for example, about a woman experiencing the devastation of Alzheimer's disease, is one of a series of recent films that have changed people's awareness of the struggle of coping with serious illness for individuals and their family members.

Redux Pictures/Staton R. Winter/*The New York Times*

People build reality from their surrounding culture. Yet because cultural systems are marked by diversity and even outright conflict, reality construction always involves tensions and choices. Turkey is a nation with a mostly Muslim population, but it has also embraced Western culture. Here, women confront starkly different definitions of what is "feminine."

Staton R. Winter, *The New York Times.*

Dramaturgical Analysis: The "Presentation of Self"

Erving Goffman (1922–1982) was another sociologist who analyzed social interaction, explaining that people live their lives much like actors performing on a stage. If we imagine ourselves as directors observing what goes on in the theater of everyday life, we are doing what Goffman called **dramaturgical analysis,** *the study of social interaction in terms of theatrical performance.*

Dramaturgical analysis offers a fresh look at the concepts of status and role. A status is like a part in a play, and a role serves as a script, supplying dialogue and action for the characters. Goffman described each individual's "performance" as the **presentation of self,** *a person's efforts to create specific impressions in the minds of others.* This process, sometimes called *impression management,* begins with the idea of personal performance (Goffman, 1959, 1967).

Performances

As we present ourselves in everyday situations, we reveal information to others both consciously and unconsciously. Our performance includes the way we dress (in theatrical terms, our costume), the objects we carry (props), and our tone of voice and gestures (our demeanor). In addition, we vary our performance according to where we are (the set). We may joke loudly in a restaurant, for example, but lower our voice when entering a church or a temple. People design settings, such as homes or offices, to bring about desired reactions in others.

Seeing SOCIOLOGY in the 

The New York Times

Putting Your Best Cyberface Forward

BY STEPHANIE ROSENBLOOM
January 3, 2008

Do you bite your nails? Have you pierced your tongue? Is your tote bag emblazoned with the words "I'm not a plastic bag"?

People look and act the way they do for reasons too numerous to fit into any therapist's notebook. Yet we commonly shape our behavior or tweak our appearance in an attempt to control how others perceive us.

Some call it common sense. Social scientists call it "impression management" and attribute much of their understanding of the process to the sociologist Erving Goffman, who in a 1959 book, *The Presentation of Self in Everyday Life,* likened human interactions to a theatrical performance.

Now that first impressions are often made in cyberspace, not face-to-face, people are not only strategizing about how to virtually convey who they are, but are also grappling with how to craft an e-version of themselves that appeals to multiple audiences—co-workers, fraternity brothers, Mom and Dad.

"Which image do you present?" asked Mark R. Leary, a professor of psychology and neuroscience at Duke, who has been studying impression management in the real world for more than 20 years. . . .

People, of course, have been electronically styling themselves for as long as there has been a Web to surf. But scholars say the mainstreaming of massive social networking and dating sites, which make it easy to publicly share one's likes, dislikes, dreams and losses, . . . is prompting more people to "perform" for one another in increasingly sophisticated ways. . . .

Many of the self-presentation strategies observed by scholars will seem obvious to experienced Internet users: improving one's standing by linking to high status friends; using a screen name like "Batman" or "007" when in reality one is more like Austin Powers; referring to one's gleaming head as "shaved" not "bald"; using cutesy emoticons to charm the demographic that forwards inspirational chain mail; demonstrating leadership by being the first to adopt and turn others onto the latest Facebook applications; listing one's almost-career as a D.J. or model rather than the one that pays the bills; making calculated decisions about what to list as interests or favorite books. . . .

In one study of online dating, professors at Rutgers, Georgetown and Michigan State found that in the absence of visual and oral cues, single people develop their own presentational tactics: monitoring the length of their e-mail messages (too wordy equals too desperate); limiting the times during which they send messages (a male subject learned that writing to women in the wee hours makes them uncomfortable); and noting the day they last logged on (users who visit the site too infrequently may be deemed unavailable or, worse, undesirable).

The scholars found it common for online daters to fudge their age or weight, or to post photographs that were five years old. . . .

In general, scholars do not think of impression management as an intentionally deceptive

---

Performing for an audience is not limited to face-to-face interaction. Seeing Sociology in the News takes a close look at how people use Web sites such as Facebook.com to construct the "self" they present to others.

Source: © 2002 David Sipress from cartoonbank.com. All rights reserved.

An Application: The Doctor's Office

Consider how physicians set up their offices to convey particular information to an audience of patients. The fact that medical doctors enjoy high prestige and power in the United States is clear upon entering a doctor's office. First, the doctor is nowhere to be seen. Instead, in what Goffman describes as the "front region" of the setting, the patient encounters a receptionist, or gatekeeper, who decides whether and when the patient can meet the doctor. A simple glance around the doctor's waiting room, with patients (often impatiently) waiting to be invited into the inner sanctum, leaves little doubt that the doctor and the staff are in charge.

The "back region" is composed of the examination room plus the doctor's private office. Once inside the office, the patient can see a wide range of props, such as medical books and framed degrees, that give the impression that the doctor has the specialized knowledge necessary to call the shots. The doctor is usually seated behind a desk—the larger the desk, the greater the statement of power—and the patient is given only a chair.

The doctor's appearance and manner offer still more information. The white lab coat (costume) may have the practical function of keeping clothes from becoming dirty, but its social function is to let others know at a glance the physician's status. A stethoscope around the neck and a medical chart in hand (more props) have the same purpose. A doctor uses highly technical language that is often mystifying to the patient, again emphasizing that the doctor is in charge.

or nefarious practice. It is more like social lubrication without a drink in your hand. . . . When people misrepresent themselves, it is often because they are attempting to express an idealized or future version of themselves—someone who is thinner or has actually finished Dante's *Inferno*.

"Everyone felt pretty strongly that they tried to be honest," said Jennifer Gibbs, one of the authors of the online dating study, . . . "They justified slight misrepresentations or distortions as trying to stand out," she said, adding that online and offline, people experience tension between telling the truth and showcasing themselves in the most flattering light. . . .

Scholars do suggest, though, that the photographs people post on the sites are about more than showing what individuals look like. Rather, members carefully choose photos to display aspects of their personalities. . . .

"I use photos that describe me," said Leonard Alonge, 44, a chef and actor in Delray Beach, Fla., who is a member of Facebook. "Photos of me in the kitchen, photos of me with friends. I use it to describe my personality: friendly, outgoing, nothing very explicit. I'm a pretty conservative person. I was raised in a Roman Catholic family."

Clare Richardson, 17, of Los Angeles, is applying to colleges and is therefore mindful of what she posts on Facebook, but she knows teenagers who "want to appear to be the partying type," she said. They post pictures that seem to prove it even if it is not true. "It's clear they're trying to impress everyone out there," Ms. Richardson said.

Keith N. Hampton, an assistant professor at the Annenberg School for Communication at the University of Pennsylvania, said the notion of impressing "everyone out there" is the fundamental problem of networking sites. They are designed so that millions see the same image of a member.

For online impression management to be effective, Mr. Hampton said, the sites should be redesigned to allow people to reveal different aspects of their identity to different users. You should be able to present one face to your boss, and another to your poker buddies. "We have very real reasons for wanting to segment our social network," he said.

WHAT DO YOU THINK?

1. If you have a page on Facebook or a similar Web site, in what ways do you selectively "present" yourself to others?
2. Is presenting ourselves to others in a selective way just "putting our best foot forward," or is it dishonest? Explain.
3. Can you give an example of how you would present a different performance to your boss, your parents, and your friends?

Finally, patients use the title "doctor," but they, in turn, are often addressed by their first names, which further shows the doctor's dominant position. The overall message of a doctor's performance is clear: "I will help you, but you must allow me to take charge."

Nonverbal Communication

The novelist William Sansom describes a fictional Mr. Preedy, an English vacationer on a beach in Spain:

> He took care to avoid catching anyone's eye. First, he had to make it clear to those potential companions of his holiday that they were of no concern to him whatsoever. He stared through them, round them, over them—eyes lost in space. The beach might have been empty. If by chance a ball was thrown his way, he looked surprised; then let a smile of amusement light his face (Kindly Preedy), looked around dazed to see that there were people on the beach, tossed it back with a smile to himself and not a smile *at* the people. . . .
>
> [He] then gathered together his beach-wrap and bag into a neat sand-resistant pile (Methodical and Sensible Preedy), rose slowly to stretch his huge frame (Big-Cat Preedy), and tossed aside his sandals (Carefree Preedy, after all). (1956:230–31)

Without saying a single word, Mr. Preedy offers a great deal of information about himself to anyone watching him. This is the process of **nonverbal communication,** *communication using body movements, gestures, and facial expressions rather than speech.*

People use many parts of the body to convey information through *body language.* Facial expressions are the most important type of body language. Smiling, for instance, shows pleasure, although we distinguish among the deliberate smile of Kindly Preedy on the beach, a spontaneous smile of joy at seeing a friend, a pained smile of embarrassment after spilling a cup of coffee, and the full, unrestrained smile of self-satisfaction we often associate with winning some important contest.

Eye contact is another key element of nonverbal communication. Generally, we use eye contact to invite social interaction. Someone across the room "catches our eye," sparking a conversation. Avoiding another's eyes, by contrast, discourages communication. Hands, too, speak for us. Common hand gestures in our society convey, among other things, an insult, a request for a ride, an invitation for someone to join us, or a demand that others stop in their tracks. Gestures also supplement spoken words. For example, pointing at someone in a threatening way gives greater emphasis to a word of warning, just as shrugging the shoulders adds an air of indifference to the phrase "I don't know" and rapidly waving the arms adds urgency to the single word "Hurry!"

Body Language and Deception

As any actor knows, it is very difficult to pull off a perfect performance. In everyday interaction, unintended body language can contradict our planned meaning: A teenage boy offers an explanation for getting home late, for example, but his mother begins to doubt his words because he avoids looking her in the eye. The teenage celebrity on a television talk

SEEING SOCIOLOGY in Everyday Life

After reading the analysis of doctors' offices, try doing a similar analysis of the offices of several faculty members on your campus. What differences do you notice? How can you explain the patterns?

nonverbal communication communication using body movements, gestures, and facial expressions rather than speech

personal space the surrounding area over which a person makes some claim to privacy

show claims that her recent musical flop is "no big deal," but the nervous swing of her leg suggests otherwise. Because nonverbal communication is hard to control, it offers clues to deception, in much the same way that changes in breathing, pulse rate, perspiration, and blood pressure recorded on a lie detector indicate that a person is lying.

Detecting dishonest performances is difficult because no single bodily gesture tells us for sure that someone is lying. But because any performance involves so much body language, few people can lie without some slip-up, raising the suspicions of a careful observer. The key to detecting lies is to view the whole performance with an eye for inconsistencies.

Gender and Performances

Because women are socialized to respond to others, they tend to be more sensitive than men to nonverbal communication. Research suggests that women "read" men better than men "read" women (Farris et al., 2008). Gender is also one of the key elements in the presentation of self, as the following sections explain.

Demeanor

Demeanor—the way we act and carry ourselves—is a clue to social power. Simply put, powerful people enjoy more freedom in how they act. At the office, off-color remarks, swearing, or putting your feet on the desk may be acceptable for the boss but rarely, if ever, for employees. Similarly, powerful people can interrupt others; less powerful people are expected to show respect through silence (Smith-Lovin & Brody, 1989; Henley, Hamilton, & Thorne, 1992; C. Johnson, 1994).

Because women generally occupy positions of lesser power, demeanor is a gender issue as well. Forty percent of all working women in the United States hold clerical or service jobs under the control of supervisors who are usually men. Women, then, learn to craft their personal performances more carefully than men and to defer to men more often in everyday interaction.

Use of Space

How much space does a personal performance require? Power plays a key role here; the more power you have, the more space you use. Men typically command more space than women, whether pacing back and forth before an audience or casually sitting on a bench. Why? Our culture has traditionally measured femininity by how *little* space women occupy—the standard of "daintiness"—and masculinity by how *much* territory a man controls—the standard of "turf" (Henley, Hamilton, & Thorne, 1992).

For both sexes, the concept of **personal space** refers to *the surrounding area over which a person makes some claim to privacy*. In the United States, people typically position themselves several feet apart when speaking; throughout the Middle East, by contrast, people stand much closer. Just about everywhere, men (with their greater social power) often intrude into women's personal space. If a woman moves into a man's personal space, however, he is likely to take it as a sign of sexual interest.

Staring, Smiling, and Touching

Eye contact encourages interaction. In conversations, women hold eye contact more than men. But men have their own brand of eye contact: staring. When men stare at women, they are claiming social dominance and defining women as sexual objects.

Although it often shows pleasure, smiling can also be a sign of trying to please someone or submission. In a male-dominated world, it is not surprising that women smile more than men (Henley, Hamilton, & Thorne, 1992).

Finally, mutual touching suggests intimacy and caring. Apart from close relationships, touching is generally something men do to women (but less often, in our culture, to other men). A male physician touches the shoulder of his female nurse as they examine a report, a young man touches the back of his woman friend as he guides her across the street, or a male skiing instructor touches young women as he teaches them to ski. In such examples, the intent of touching may be harmless and may bring little response, but it amounts to a subtle ritual by which men claim dominance over women.

Idealization

People behave the way they do for many, often complex reasons. Even so, Goffman suggests, we construct performances to *idealize* our intentions. That is, we try to convince others (and perhaps ourselves) that what we do reflects ideal cultural standards rather than selfish motives.

Idealization is easily illustrated by returning to the world of doctors and patients. In a hospital, doctors engage in a performance commonly described as "making rounds." Entering the room of a patient, the doctor often stops at the foot of the bed and silently reads the patient's chart. Afterward, doctor and patient talk briefly. In ideal terms, this routine involves a doctor making a personal visit to check on a patient's condition.

In reality, the picture is not so perfect. A doctor may see several dozen patients a day and remember little about many of them. Reading the chart is a chance to recall the patient's name and medical problems, but revealing the impersonality of medical care would undermine the cultural ideal of the doctor as deeply concerned about the welfare of others.

Doctors, college professors, and other professionals typically idealize their motives for entering their chosen careers. They describe their work as "making a contribution to science," "helping others,"

SEEING SOCIOLOGY in Everyday Life

Watch female-male couples holding hands. Which person has the hand to the front and which has the hand to the rear? Can you see a pattern and offer an explanation?

SEEING SOCIOLOGY in Everyday Life

Using Goffman's approach, offer examples of performances, nonverbal communication, idealization, and tact in your own life.

Paul W. Liebhardt

Paul W. Liebhardt

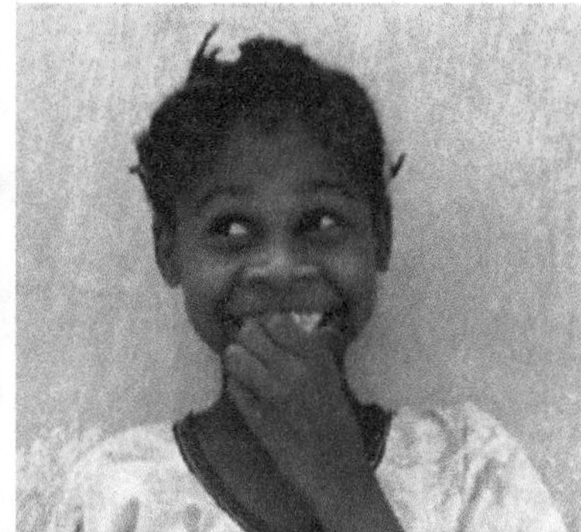

Paul W. Liebhardt

Hand gestures vary widely from one culture to another. Yet people everywhere chuckle, grin, or smirk to indicate that they don't take another person's performance seriously. Therefore, the world over, people who cannot restrain their mirth tactfully cover their faces.

"serving the community," and even "answering a calling from God." Rarely do they admit the more common, less honorable, motives: the income, power, prestige, and leisure time that these occupations provide.

We all use idealization to some degree. When was the last time you smiled and spoke politely to someone you do not like? Have you acted interested in a class that was really boring? Such little lies in our performances help us get through everyday life. Even when we suspect that others are putting on an act, we are unlikely to challenge their performances, for reasons that we shall examine next.

Embarrassment and Tact

The famous speaker giving a campus lecture keeps mispronouncing the college's name; the head coach rises to speak at the team's end-of-season banquet unaware of the napkin still tucked in her dress; the student enters the lecture hall late and soaking wet, attracting the gaze of the hundreds of classmates. As carefully as individuals may try to craft their performances, slip-ups of all kinds occur. The result is *embarrassment,* discomfort following a spoiled performance. Goffman describes embarrassment as "losing face."

Embarrassment is an ever-present danger because idealized performances usually contain some deception. In addition, most performances involve juggling so many elements that one thoughtless moment can shatter the intended impression.

A curious fact is that an audience often overlooks flaws in a performance, allowing the actor to avoid embarrassment. If we do point out a misstep ("Excuse me, but your fly is open"), we do it quietly and only to help someone avoid even greater loss of face. In Hans Christian Andersen's classic fable "The Emperor's New Clothes," the child who blurts out the truth, that the emperor is parading about naked, is scolded for being rude.

Often members of an audience actually help the performer recover from a flawed performance. *Tact* is helping someone "save face." After hearing a supposed expert make an embarrassingly inaccurate remark, for example, people may tactfully ignore the comment, as if it had never been spoken, or with mild laughter treat what was said as a joke. Or they may simply respond, "I'm sure you didn't mean that," hearing the statement but not allowing it to destroy the actor's performance. With such efforts in mind, we can understand Abraham Lincoln's comment that "tact is the ability to describe others the way they see themselves."

Why is tact so common? Because embarrassment creates discomfort not just for the actor but for everyone else as well. Just as a theater audience feels uneasy when an actor forgets a line, people who observe awkward behavior are reminded of how fragile their own performances often are. Socially constructed reality thus functions like a dam holding back a sea of chaos. When one person's performance springs a leak, others tactfully help make repairs. Everyone lends a hand in building reality, and no one wants it suddenly swept away.

In sum, Goffman's research shows that although behavior is spontaneous in some respects, it is more patterned than we like to think. Four centuries ago, William Shakespeare captured this idea in lines that still ring true:

> All the world's a stage,
> And all the men and women merely players:
> They have their exits and their entrances;
> And one man in his time plays many parts.
>
> (*As You Like It,* act 2, scene 7)

MAKING THE GRADE

Emotions are complex and reflect both biological and cultural forces. Sociologists are interested in how culture affects our emotional life.

SEEING SOCIOLOGY in Everyday Life

What emotions are (or are not) expected of a college professor in front of a class?

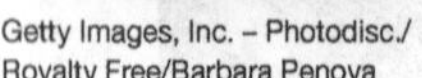

Getty Images, Inc. - Photodisc./ Royalty Free/Barbara Penoya

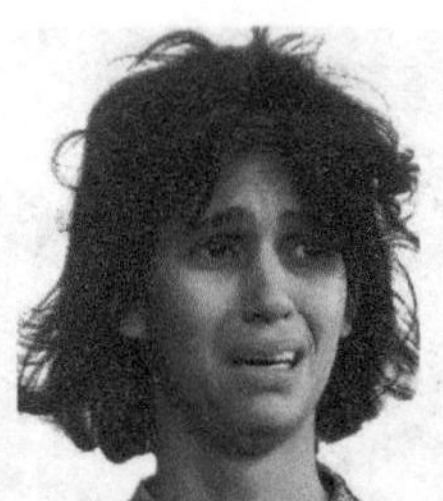

Alan S. Weiner

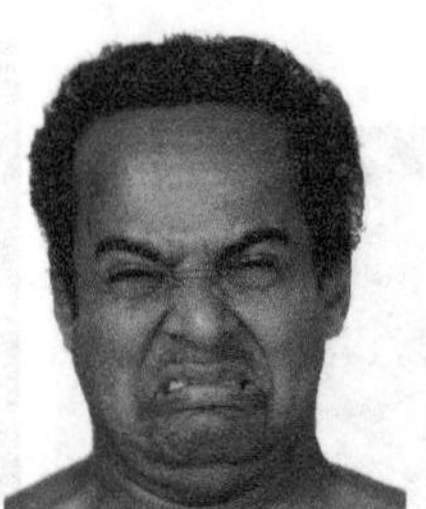

Andy Crawford © Dorling Kindersley

© Guido Alberto Rossi/TIPS Images

Corbis - NY/Chris Carroll

Magnum Photos, Inc./Costa Manos

To most people in the United States, these expressions convey anger, fear, disgust, happiness, surprise, and sadness. But do people elsewhere in the world define them in the same way? Research suggests that all human beings experience the same basic emotions and display them to others in the same basic ways. But culture plays a part by specifying the situations that trigger one emotion or another.

Interaction in Everyday Life: Three Applications

The final sections of this chapter illustrate the major elements of social interaction by focusing on three dimensions of everyday life: emotions, language, and humor.

Emotions: The Social Construction of Feeling

Emotions, more commonly called *feelings,* are an important element of human social life. In truth, what we *do* often matters less than how we *feel* about it. Emotions seem very personal because they are "inside." Even so, just as society guides our behavior, it guides our emotional life.

The Biological Side of Emotions

Studying people all over the world, Paul Ekman (1980a, 1980b, 1998, 2003) reports that people everywhere express six basic emotions: happiness, sadness, anger, fear, disgust, and surprise. In addition, Ekman found that people in every society use much the same facial expressions to show these emotions. Ekman believes that some emotional responses are "wired" into human beings; that is, they are biologically programmed in our facial features, muscles, and central nervous system.

Why might this be so? Over centuries of evolution, emotions developed in the human species because they serve a social purpose: supporting group life. Emotions are powerful forces that allow us to overcome our self-centeredness and build connections with others. Thus the capacity for emotion arose in our ancestors along with the capacity for culture (Turner, 2000).

The Cultural Side of Emotions

But culture does play an important role in guiding human emotions. First, Ekman explains, culture defines *what triggers* an emotion. Whether people define the departure of an old friend as joyous (causing happiness), insulting (arousing anger), a loss (producing sadness), or mystical (provoking surprise and awe) has a lot to do with culture. Second, culture provides rules for the *display* of emotions. For example, most people in the United States express emotions more freely with family members than with colleagues in the workplace. Similarly, we expect children to express emotions freely to parents, but parents tend to hide their emotions from their children. Third, culture guides how we *value* emotions. Some societies encourage the expression of emotion; others expect members to control their feelings and maintain a "stiff upper lip." Gender also plays a part; traditionally, at least, many cultures expect women to show emotions, but they discourage emotional expression by men as a sign of weakness. In some cultures, of course, this pattern is less pronounced or even reversed.

Emotions on the Job

In the United States, most people are freer to express their feelings at home than on the job. The reason, as Arlie Russell Hochschild (1979, 1983) explains, is that the typical company tries to regulate not only the behavior of its employees but also their emotions. Take the case of an airline flight attendant who offers passengers a drink, a bag of pretzels, and a smile. Although this smile may convey real pleasure at serving the customer, Hochschild's study points to a different conclusion: The smile is an emotional script demanded by the airline management as the right way to perform the job. Therefore, we see that the "presentation of self" described by Erving Goffman can involve not just surface acting but also the "deep acting" of emotions.

SEEING SOCIOLOGY in Everyday Life

What are the "emotional scripts" that students might apply to college graduation? That is, why might people see this event in positive or negative terms?

CONTROVERSY & DEBATE

Managing Feelings: Women's Abortion Experiences

LIZ: I just *can't* be pregnant! I'm going to see my doctor tomorrow about an abortion. There's no way I can deal with a baby at this point in my life!

JEN: I can't believe you'd do that, Liz! How are you going to feel a few years from now when you think about what that *child* would be doing if you'd let it live?

Few issues today generate as much emotion as abortion. In a study of women's abortion experiences, the sociologist Jennifer Keys (2002) discovered emotional scripts or "feeling rules" that guided how women feel about ending a pregnancy.

Keys explains that emotional scripts arise from the political controversy surrounding abortion. The antiabortion movement defines abortion as a personal tragedy, the "killing of an unborn child." Given this definition, women who terminate a pregnancy through abortion are doing something morally wrong and can expect to feel grief, guilt, and regret. So intense are these feelings, according to supporters of this position, that such women often suffer from "postabortion syndrome."

Those who take the pro-choice position have an opposing view of abortion. From this point of view, the woman's problem is the *unwanted pregnancy*; abortion is an acceptable medical solution. Therefore, the emotion common to women who terminate a pregnancy should be not guilt but relief.

In her research, Keys conducted in-depth interviews with forty women who had recently had abortions and found that all of them used such scripts to "frame" their situation in an antiabortion or pro-choice manner. In part, this construction of reality reflected the women's own attitudes about abortion. In addition, however, the women's partners and friends typically encouraged specific feelings about the event. Ivy, one young woman in the study, had a close friend who was also pregnant. "Congratulations!" she exclaimed when she learned of Ivy's condition. "We're going to be having babies together!" Such a statement established one "feeling rule"—having a baby is *good*—which sent the message to Ivy that her planned abortion should trigger guilt. Working in the other direction, Jo's partner was horrified by the news that she was pregnant. Doubting his own ability to be a father, he blurted out, "I would rather put a gun to my head than have this baby!" His panic not only defined having the child as a mistake but alarmed Jo as well. Clearly, her partner's reaction made the decision to end the pregnancy a matter of relief from a terrible problem.

Medical personnel also play a part in this process of reality construction by using specific terms. Nurses and doctors who talk about "the baby" encourage the antiabortion framing of abortion and provoke grief and guilt. On the other hand, those who use language such as "pregnancy tissue," "fetus," or "the contents of the uterus" encourage the pro-choice framing of abortion as a fairly routine medical procedure leading to relief. Olivia began using the phrase "products of conception," which she picked up from her doctor. Denise spoke of her procedure as "taking the extra cells out of my body. Yeah, I did feel some guilt when I thought that this was the beginning of life, but my body is full of life—you have lots of cells in you."

After the procedure, most women reported actively trying to manage their feelings. Explained Ivy, "I never used the word 'baby.' I kept saying to myself that it was not formed yet. There was nothing there yet. I kept that in my mind." On the other hand, Keys found that all of the women in her study who leaned toward the antiabortion position did use the term "baby." Gina explained, "I do think of it as a baby. The truth is that I ended my baby's life. . . . Thinking that makes me feel guilty. But—considering what I did—maybe I *should* feel guilty." Believing that what she had done was wrong, in other words, Gina actively called out the feeling of guilt—in part, Keys concluded, to punish herself.

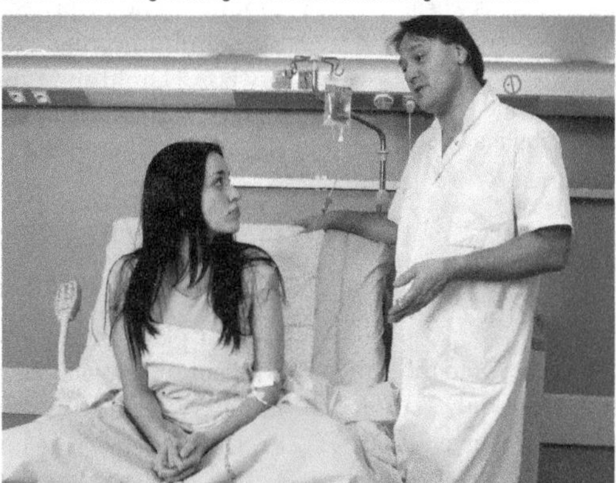

The words that doctors and nurses use guide whether a woman having an abortion defines the experience in positive or negative terms.

WHAT DO YOU THINK?

1. In your own words, what are "emotional scripts" or "feeling rules"?
2. Can you apply the idea of "feeling rules" to the experience of getting married?
3. In light of this discussion, how accurate is it to say that our feelings are not as personal as we may think they are?

With these patterns in mind, it is easy to see that we socially construct our emotions as part of our everyday reality, a process sociologists call *emotion management.* The Controversy & Debate box links the emotions displayed by women who decide to have an abortion to their political views and to their personal view of terminating a pregnancy.

SEEING SOCIOLOGY in Everyday Life

List words that people use to describe a very sexually active female. How many such terms are there? Are they positive or negative in meaning? Repeat this exercise for a very sexually active male. What differences do you notice?

Getty Images/Erik Dreyer

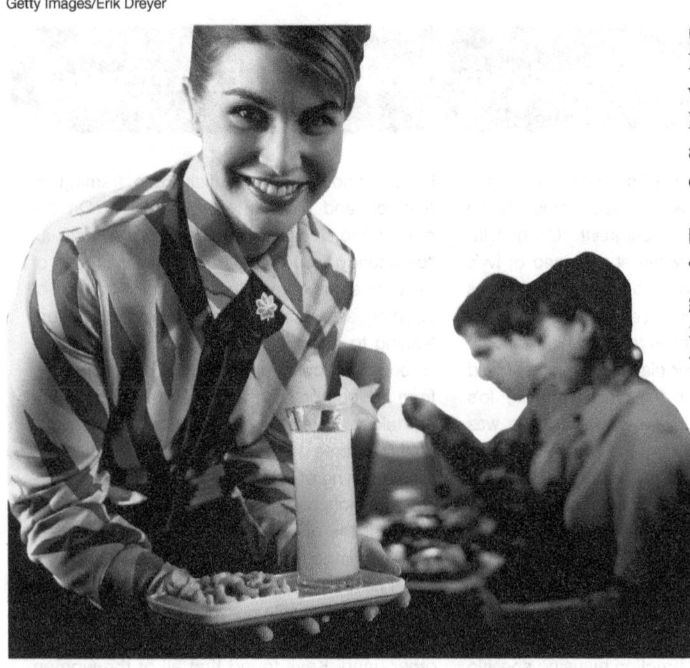

Many of us think emotions are simply part of our biological makeup. While there is a biological foundation to human emotion, sociologists have demonstrated that what triggers an emotion—as well as when, where, and to whom the emotion is displayed—is shaped by culture. For example, many jobs not only regulate a worker's behavior but also expect workers to display a particular emotion, as in the case of the always-smiling airline flight attendant. Can you think of other jobs that regulate emotions in this way?

Language: The Social Construction of Gender

Language is the thread that weaves members of a society into the symbolic web we call culture. Language communicates not only a surface reality but also deeper levels of meaning. One such level involves gender. Language defines men and women differently in terms of both power and value (Henley, Hamilton, & Thorne, 1992; Thorne, Kramarae, & Henley, 1983).

Language and Power

A young man proudly rides his new motorcycle up his friend's driveway and boasts, "Isn't she a beauty?" On the surface, the question has little to do with gender. Yet why does he use the pronoun *she* instead of *he* or *it* to refer to his prized possession?

The answer is that men often use language to establish control over their surroundings. A man attaches a female pronoun to a motorcycle (or car, boat, or other object) because it reflects the power of *ownership*. Perhaps this is also why, in the United States and elsewhere, a woman who marries traditionally takes the last name of her husband. Because many of today's married women value their independence, an increasing share (about 18 percent) now keep their own name or combine the two family names.

Language and Value

Typically, the English language treats as masculine whatever has greater value, force, or significance. For instance, the word *virtuous*, meaning "morally worthy" or "excellent," comes from the Latin word *vir*, meaning "man." On the other hand, the adjective *hysterical*, meaning "emotionally out of control," comes from the Greek word *hystera*, meaning "uterus."

In many familiar ways, language also confers different value on the two sexes. Traditional masculine terms such as *king* and *lord* have a positive meaning, while comparable feminine terms, such as *queen*, *madam*, and *dame*, can have negative meanings. Similarly, use of the suffixes *-ette* and *-ess* to denote femininity usually devalues the words to which they are added. For example, a *major* has higher standing than a *majorette*, as does a *host* in relation to a *hostess* or a *master* in relation to a *mistress*. Language both mirrors social attitudes and helps perpetuate them.

Given the importance of gender in everyday life, perhaps we should not be surprised that women and men sometimes have trouble communicating with each other. In the Thinking About Diversity box, Harold and Sybil, whose misadventures in trying to find their friends' home opened this chapter, return to illustrate how the two sexes often seem to be speaking different languages.

Reality Play: The Social Construction of Humor

Humor plays an important part in everyday life. Everyone laughs at a joke, but few people stop to think about what makes something funny. We can apply many of the ideas developed in this chapter to explain how, by using humor, we "play with reality" (Macionis, 1987).

The Foundation of Humor

Humor is produced by the social construction of reality; it arises as people create and contrast two different realities. Generally, one reality is *conventional*, that is, what people expect in a specific situation. The other reality is *unconventional*, an unexpected violation of cultural patterns. Humor arises from the contradictions, ambiguities, and double meanings found in differing definitions of the same situation.

There are countless ways to mix realities and generate humor. Contrasting realities are found in statements that contradict

MAKING THE GRADE

The foundation of humor follows from the earlier discussion of the social construction of reality—building and contrasting two different definitions of reality.

THINKING ABOUT DIVERSITY: RACE, CLASS, & GENDER

Gender and Language: "You Just Don't Understand!"

In the story that opened this chapter, Harold and Sybil faced a situation that rings true to many people: When they are lost, men grumble to themselves and perhaps blame their partners but avoid asking for directions. For their part, women can't understand why men refuse help when they need it.

Deborah Tannen (1990) explains that men typically define most everyday encounters as competitive. Therefore, getting lost is bad enough without asking for help, which lets someone else get "one up." By contrast, because women have traditionally had a subordinate position, they find it easy to ask for help. Sometimes, Tannen points out, women ask for assistance even when they don't need it.

A similar gender-linked problem common to couples involves what women consider "trying to be helpful" and men call "nagging." Consider the following exchange (adapted from Adler, 1990:74):

SYBIL: What's wrong, honey?

HAROLD: Nothing.

SYBIL: Something is bothering you. I can tell.

HAROLD: I told you nothing is bothering me. Leave me alone.

SYBIL: But I can see that there is a problem.

HAROLD: OK. Just why do you think there is a problem?

SYBIL: Well, for one thing, you're bleeding all over your shirt.

HAROLD: *(now irritated)* Yeah, well, it doesn't bother me.

SYBIL: *(losing her temper)* WELL, IT SURE IS BOTHERING ME!

HAROLD: Fine. I'll go change my shirt.

The problem here is that what one partner *intends* by a comment is not always what the other *hears* in the words. To Sybil, her opening question is an effort at cooperative problem solving. She can see that something is wrong with Harold (who has cut himself while doing yard work), and she wants to help him. But Harold interprets her pointing out his problem as belittling him, and he tries to close off the discussion. Sybil, believing that Harold would be more positive if he understood that she just wants to be helpful, repeats her question. This reaction sets in motion a vicious circle in which Harold, who feels his wife is thinking that he cannot take care of himself, responds by digging in his heels. This response, in turn, makes Sybil all the more sure that she needs to get through to him. And around it goes until somebody gets really angry.

Photodisc/Getty Images/Ryan McVay/Photodisc

In the end, Harold agrees to change his shirt but still refuses to discuss the original problem. Defining his wife's concern as "nagging," Harold just wants Sybil to leave him alone. For her part, Sybil fails to understand her husband's view of the situation and walks away convinced that he is a stubborn grouch.

WHAT DO YOU THINK?

1. Have you noticed differences in the way men and women communicate? Explain.
2. In your opinion, what are the reasons for any gender differences in how people use language?
3. Do you think that understanding Tannen's conclusions would help couples communicate better? Why or why not?

themselves, such as "Nostalgia is not what it used to be"; statements that repeat themselves, such as Yogi Berra's line "It's *déjà vu* all over again"; or statements that mix up words, such as Oscar Wilde's line "Work is the curse of the drinking class." Even switching around syllables does the trick, as in the case of the country song "I'd Rather Have a Bottle in Front of Me than a Frontal Lobotomy."

A comedian can also build a joke the other way around, leading the audience to expect an unconventional answer and then delivering a very ordinary one. When a reporter asked the famous gangster Willy Sutton why he continued to rob banks, for example, he replied dryly, "Because that's where the money is." Regardless of how a joke is constructed, the greater the opposition or difference is between the two definitions of reality, the greater the humor that is produced.

When telling jokes, the comedian uses various strategies to strengthen this opposition and make the joke funnier. One common technique is to present the first, or conventional, remark in conversation with another actor and then to turn toward the audience (or the camera) to deliver the second, unexpected line. In a Marx Brothers movie, Groucho remarks, "Outside of a dog, a book is a man's best friend." Then, raising his voice and turning to the camera, he adds, "And *inside* of a dog, it's too dark to read!" Such "channel switching" emphasizes the difference between the two realities. Following the same logic, stand-up comedians may "reset" the audience

SEEING SOCIOLOGY in Everyday Life

Here is a joke about sociologists: How many sociologists does it take to change a light bulb? Answer: None. There is nothing wrong with the light bulb; it's *the system* that needs to be changed! What makes this joke funny? What sort of people are likely to get it? What kind of people probably won't? Why?

to conventional expectations by interjecting the phrase, "But seriously, folks, . . ." between jokes. Monty Python comedian John Cleese did this with his trademark line, "And now for something completely different."

Comedians pay careful attention to their performances—the precise words they use and the timing of their delivery. A joke is well told if the comedian creates the sharpest possible opposition between the realities; in a careless performance, the joke falls flat. Because the key to humor lies in the collision of realities, we can see why the climax of a joke is termed the "*punch* line."

The Dynamics of Humor: "Getting It"

After hearing a joke, did you ever say, "I don't get it"? To "get" humor, you must understand both the conventional and the unconventional realities well enough to appreciate their difference. A comedian may make getting a joke harder by leaving out some important information. In such cases, listeners must pay attention to the stated elements of the joke and then fill in the missing pieces on their own. A simple example is the comment of the movie producer Hal Roach on his one hundredth birthday: "If I had known I would live to be one hundred, I would have taken better care of myself!" Here, getting the joke depends on realizing that Roach must have taken pretty good care of himself because he did make it to one hundred. Or take one of W. C. Fields's lines: "Some weasel took the cork out of my lunch." What a lunch! we think to ourselves to "finish" the joke.

Here is an even more complex joke: What do you get if you cross an insomniac, a dyslexic, and an agnostic? Answer: A person who stays up all night wondering if there is a dog. To get this one, you must know that insomnia is an inability to sleep, that dyslexia causes a person to reverse the letters in words, and that an agnostic doubts the existence of God.

Why would a comedian want the audience to make this sort of effort to understand a joke? Our enjoyment of a joke is increased by the pleasure of figuring out all the pieces needed to "get it." In addition, getting the joke makes you an "insider" compared to those who don't get it. We have all experienced the frustration of *not* getting a joke: fear of being judged stupid, along with a sense of being excluded from a pleasure shared by others. Sometimes someone may tactfully explain the joke so that the other person doesn't feel left out. But as the old saying goes, if a joke has to be explained, it isn't very funny.

The Topics of Humor

All over the world, people smile and laugh, making humor a universal element of human culture. But because the world's people live in different cultures, humor rarely travels well.

October 1, Kobe, Japan. Can you share a joke with people who live halfway around the world? At dinner, I ask two Japanese college women to tell me a joke. "You know 'crayon'?" Asako asks. I nod. "How do you ask for a crayon in Japanese?" I respond that I have no idea. She laughs out loud as she says what sounds like "crayon crayon." Her companion Mayumi laughs too. My wife and I sit awkwardly, straight-faced. Asako relieves some of our embarrassment by explaining that the Japanese word for "give me" is <u>kureyo</u>, which sounds like "crayon." I force a smile.

What is humorous to the Japanese may be lost on the Chinese, South Africans, or people in the United States. Even the social diversity of our own country means that different types of people will find humor in different situations. New Englanders, southerners, and westerners have their own brands of humor, as do Latinos and Anglos, fifteen- and fifty-year-olds, construction workers and rodeo riders.

But for everyone, topics that lend themselves to double meanings or controversy generate humor. In the United States, the first jokes many of us learned as children concerned bodily functions kids are not supposed to talk about. The mere mention of "unmentionable acts" or even certain parts of the body can dissolve young faces in laughter.

Are there jokes that do break through the culture barrier? Yes, but they must touch on universal human experiences such as, say, turning on a friend:

I think of a number of jokes, but none seems likely to work. Understanding jokes about the United States is difficult for people who know little of our culture. Is there something more universal? Inspiration: "Two fellows are walking in the woods and come upon a huge bear. One guy leans over and tightens up the laces on his running shoes. 'Jake,' says the other, 'what are you doing? You can't outrun this bear!' 'I don't have to outrun the bear,' responds Jake. 'All I have to do is outrun <u>you</u>!' " Smiles all around.

Humor often walks a fine line between what is funny and what is "sick" or offensive. During the Middle Ages, people used the word *humors* (derived from the Latin *humidus,* meaning "moist") to refer to the various bodily fluids believed to regulate a person's health. Researchers today document the power of humor to reduce stress and improve health. One recent study of cancer patients, for example, found that the greater people's sense of humor, the greater their odds of surviving the disease. Such findings confirm the old saying

SEEING SOCIOLOGY in Everyday Life

Humor is most common among people with roughly the same social standing. Why is it risky to joke with people who have more power than you do? What about joking with people who have less power?

that "laughter is the best medicine" (Bakalar, 2005; Svebak, cited in M. Elias, 2007). At the extreme, however, people who always take conventional reality lightly risk being defined as deviant or even mentally ill (a common stereotype shows insane people laughing uncontrollably, and for a long time mental hospitals were known as "funny farms").

Then, too, every social group considers certain topics too sensitive for humorous treatment, and joking about them risks criticism for having a "sick" sense of humor (and being labeled "sick" yourself). People's religious beliefs, tragic accidents, or appalling crimes are some of the topics of sick jokes or no jokes at all. Even all these years later, no one jokes about the September 11, 2001, terrorist attacks.

The Functions of Humor

Humor is found everywhere because it works as a safety valve for potentially disruptive sentiments. Put another way, humor provides an acceptable way to discuss a sensitive topic without appearing to be serious or offending anyone. Having said something controversial, people can use humor to defuse the situation by simply stating, "I didn't mean anything by what I said—it was just a joke!"

People also use humor to relieve tension in uncomfortable situations. One study of medical examinations found that most patients try to joke with doctors to ease their own nervousness (Baker et al., 1997).

AP Wide World Photos/Dana Edelson/NBCU Photo Bank

Because humor involves challenging established conventions, people everywhere make fun of those in power. During the 2008 presidential campaign, Tina Fey delighted audiences with her impersonations of Sarah Palin.

Humor and Conflict

Humor may be a source of pleasure, but it can also be used to put down other people. Men who tell jokes about women, for example, are typically expressing some measure of hostility toward them (Powell & Paton, 1988; Benokraitis & Feagin, 1995). Similarly, jokes about gay people reveal tensions about sexual orientation. Real conflict can be masked by humor in situations where one or both parties choose not to bring the conflict out into the open (Primeggia & Varacalli, 1990).

"Put-down" jokes make one category of people feel good at the expense of another. After collecting and analyzing jokes from many societies, Christie Davies (1990) confirmed that ethnic conflict is one driving force behind humor in most of the world. The typical ethnic joke makes fun of some disadvantaged category of people, at the same time making the joke teller feel superior. Given the Anglo-Saxon traditions of U.S. society, Poles and other ethnic and racial minorities have long been the butt of jokes in the United States, as have Newfoundlanders in eastern Canada, the Irish in Scotland, Sikhs in India, Turks in Germany, Hausas in Nigeria, Tasmanians in Australia, and Kurds in Iraq.

Disadvantaged people also make fun of the powerful, although usually with some care. Women in the United States joke about men, just as African Americans find humor in white people's ways and poor people poke fun at the rich. Throughout the world, people target their leaders with humor, and officials in some countries take such jokes seriously enough to arrest those who do not show proper respect (Speier, 1998).

In sum, humor is much more important than we may think. It is a means of mental escape from a conventional world that is never entirely to our liking (Flaherty, 1984, 1990; Yoels & Clair, 1995). This fact helps explain why so many of our nation's comedians are from the ranks of historically marginalized peoples, including Jews and African Americans. As long as we maintain a sense of humor, we assert our freedom and are not prisoners of reality. By putting a smile on our faces, we can change ourselves and the world just a little and for the better.

Seeing Sociology in Everyday Life

Social Interaction in Everyday Life

How do we construct the reality we experience?

This chapter suggests that Shakespeare may have had it right when he said, "All the world's a stage." And if so, then the Internet may be the latest and greatest stage so far. When we use Web sites such as Facebook, as Goffman explains, we present ourselves as we want others to see us. Everything we write about ourselves as well as how we arrange our page creates an impression in the mind of anyone interested in "checking us out." Take a look at the Facebook page below, paying careful attention to all the details. What is the young man explicitly saying about himself? What can you read "between the lines"? That is, what information can you identify that he may be trying to conceal, or at least purposely not be mentioning? How honest do you think his "presentation of self" is? Why? Do a similar analysis of the young woman's Facebook profile shown on the next page.

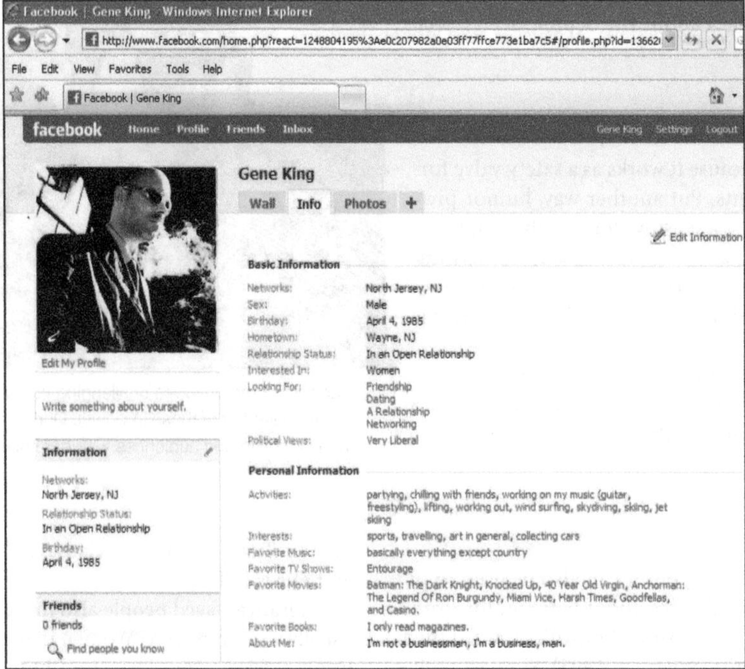

HINT Just about every element of a presentation conveys information about us to others, so all the information found on a Web site like this one is significant. Some information is intentional—for example, what people write about themselves and the photos they choose to post. Other information may be unintentional but is nevertheless picked up by the careful viewer who may be noting such things as these:

- The length and tone of the person's profile. Is it a long-winded list of talents and accomplishments or humorous and modest?
- The language used. Poor grammar may be a clue to educational level.
- What hour of the day or night the person wrote the material. A person creating his profile at 11 P.M. on a Saturday night may not be quite the party person he describes himself to be.

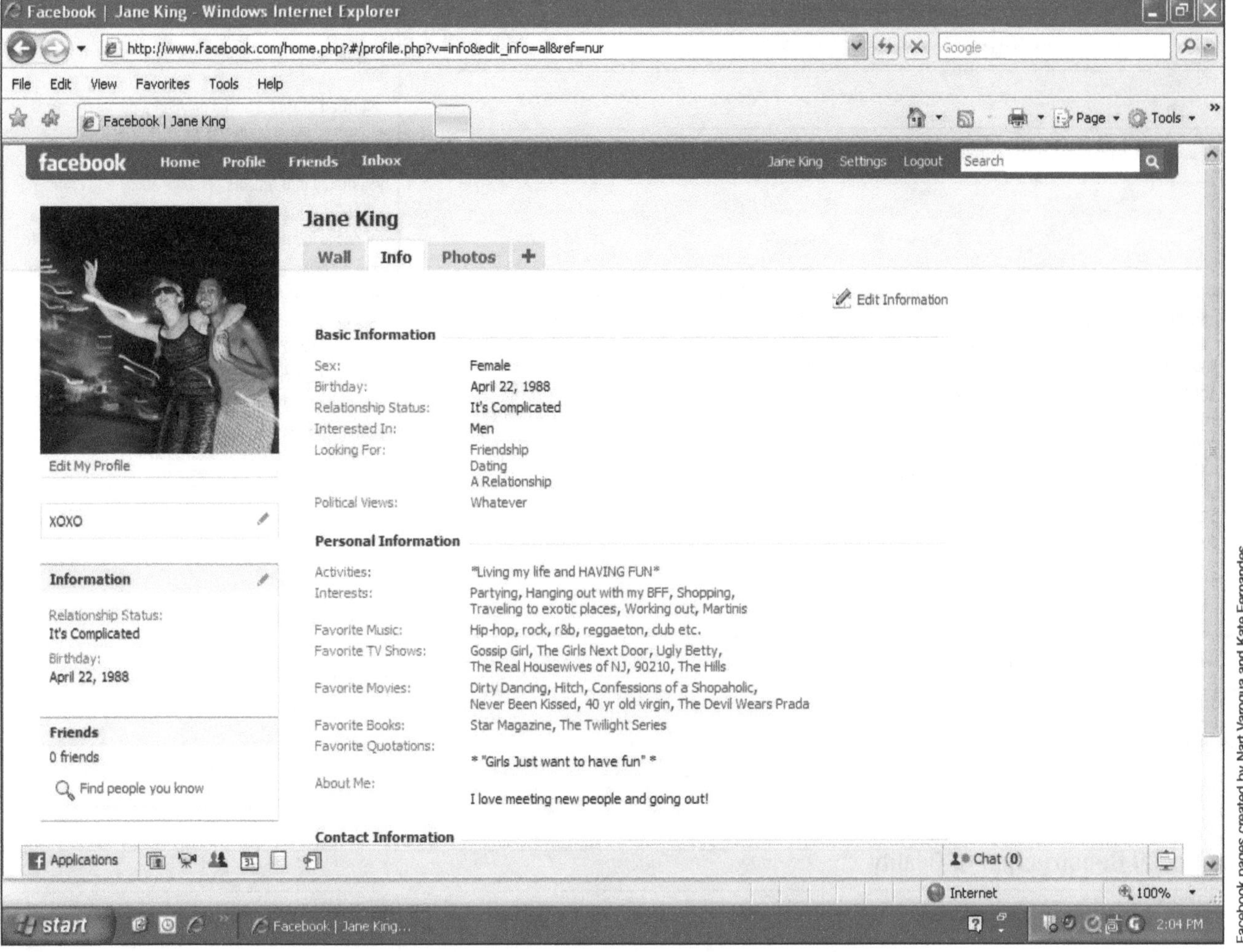

Getty Images – Stockbyte

Facebook pages created by Nart Varoqua and Kate Fernandes

Applying SOCIOLOGY in Everyday Life

1. Identify five important ways in which you "present yourself" to others, including, for example, the way you decorate your dorm room, apartment, or house; the way you dress; and the way you behave in the classroom. In each case, think about what you are trying to say about yourself. Have your presentations changed in recent years? If so, how and why?
2. During one full day, every time somebody asks, "How are you?" or "How's it goin'?" stop and actually give a complete, truthful answer. What happens when you respond to a polite question in an honest way? Listen to how people respond, and also watch their body language. What can you conclude?
3. Stroll around downtown or at a local mall. Pay attention to how many women and men you find at each location. From your observations, are there stores that are "gendered" so that there are "female spaces" and "male spaces"? How and why are spaces "gendered"?

MAKING THE GRADE

Social Interaction in Everyday Life

What Is Social Structure?

SOCIAL STRUCTURE refers to social patterns that guide our behavior in everyday life. The building blocks of social structure are
- **STATUS**—a social position that is part of our social identity and that defines our relationships to others
- **ROLE**—the action expected of a person who holds a particular status

✓ *A person* holds *a status and* performs *a role.*

A status can be either an
- **ASCRIBED STATUS**, which is involuntary (for example, being a teenager, an orphan, or a Mexican American), or an
- **ACHIEVED STATUS**, which is earned (for example, being an honors student, a pilot, or a thief).

A **MASTER STATUS**, which can be either ascribed or achieved, has special importance for a person's identity (for example, being blind, a doctor, or a Kennedy).

ROLE CONFLICT results from tension among roles linked to two or more statuses (for example, a woman who juggles her responsibilities as a mother and a corporate CEO).

ROLE STRAIN results from tension among roles linked to a single status (for example, the college professor who enjoys personal interaction with students but at the same time knows that social distance is necessary in order to evaluate students fairly).

✓ *A person's status set changes over the life course.*

✓ *The role sets attached to a single status vary from society to society around the world.*

social interaction the process by which people act and react in relation to others

status a social position that a person holds

status set all the statuses a person holds at a given time

ascribed status a social position a person receives at birth or takes on involuntarily later in life

achieved status a social position a person takes on voluntarily that reflects personal ability and effort

master status a status that has special importance for social identity, often shaping a person's entire life

role behavior expected of someone who holds a particular status

role set a number of roles attached to a single status

role conflict conflict among the roles connected to two or more statuses

role strain tension among the roles connected to a single status

The Social Construction of Reality

Through **SOCIAL INTERACTION**, we construct the reality we experience.
- For example, two people interacting both try to shape the reality of their situation.

The **THOMAS THEOREM** says that the reality people construct in their interaction has real consequences for the future.
- For example, a teacher who believes a certain student to be intellectually gifted may well encourage exceptional academic performance.

ETHNOMETHODOLOGY is a strategy to reveal the assumptions people have about their social world.
- We can expose these assumptions by intentionally breaking the "rules" of social interaction and observing the reactions of other people.

Both **CULTURE** and **SOCIAL CLASS** shape the reality people construct.
- For example, a "short walk" for a New Yorker is a few city blocks, but for a peasant in Latin America, it could be a few miles.

✓ *Through the social construction of reality, people creatively shape their social world.*

social construction of reality the process by which people creatively shape reality through social interaction

Thomas theorem W. I. Thomas's observation that situations defined as real are real in their consequences

ethnomethodology Harold Garfinkel's term for the study of the way people make sense of their everyday surroundings

Dramaturgical Analysis: The "Presentation of Self"

DRAMATURGICAL ANALYSIS explores social interaction in terms of theatrical performance: A status operates as a part in a play, and a role is a script.

PERFORMANCES are the way we present ourselves to others.

- Performances are both conscious (intentional action) and unconscious (nonverbal communication).
- Performances include costume (the way we dress), props (objects we carry), and demeanor (tone of voice and the way we carry ourselves).

GENDER affects performances because men typically have greater social power than women. Gender differences involve *demeanor, use of space,* and *staring, smiling, and touching.*

- **DEMEANOR**—With greater social power, men have more freedom in how they act.
- **USE OF SPACE**—Men typically command more space than women.
- **STARING** and **TOUCHING** are generally done by men to women.
- **SMILING**, as a way to please another, is more commonly done by women.

IDEALIZATION of performances means we try to convince others that our actions reflect ideal culture rather than selfish motives.

EMBARRASSMENT is the "loss of face" in a performance. People use **TACT** to help others "save face."

dramaturgical analysis Erving Goffman's term for the study of social interaction in terms of theatrical performance

presentation of self Erving Goffman's term for a person's efforts to create specific impressions in the minds of others

nonverbal communication communication using body movements, gestures, and facial expressions rather than speech

personal space the surrounding area over which a person makes some claim to privacy

Interaction in Everyday Life: Three Applications

EMOTIONS: The Social Construction of **FEELING**

The same basic emotions are biologically programmed into all human beings, but culture guides what triggers emotions, how people display emotions, and how people value emotions. In everyday life, the presentation of self involves managing emotions as well as behavior.

LANGUAGE: The Social Construction of **GENDER**

Gender is an important element of everyday interaction. Language defines women and men as different types of people, reflecting the fact that society attaches greater power and value to what is viewed as masculine.

REALITY PLAY: The Social Construction of **HUMOR**

Humor results from the difference between conventional and unconventional definitions of a situation. Because humor is a part of culture, people around the world find different situations funny.

MAKING THE GRADE

Sample Test Questions

Multiple-Choice Questions

1. **Which term defines who and what we are in relation to others?**
   a. role
   b. status
   c. role set
   d. master status

2. **In U.S. society, which of the following is often a master status?**
   a. occupation
   b. physical or mental disability
   c. race or color
   d. All of the above are correct.

3. **"Role set" refers to**
   a. a number of roles found in any one society.
   b. a number of roles attached to a single status.
   c. a number of roles that are more or less the same.
   d. a number of roles within any one organization.

4. **Frank excels at football at his college, but he doesn't have enough time to study as much as he wants to. This problem is an example of**
   a. role set.
   b. role strain.
   c. role conflict.
   d. role exit.

5. **The Thomas theorem states that**
   a. our statuses and roles are the keys to our personality.
   b. most people rise to their level of incompetence.
   c. people know the world only through their language.
   d. situations defined as real are real in their consequences.

6. **Which of the following is the correct meaning of "presentation of self"?**
   a. efforts to create impressions in the minds of others
   b. acting out a master status
   c. thinking back over the process of role exit
   d. trying to take attention away from others

7. **Paul Ekman points to what as an important clue to deception by another person?**
   a. smiling
   b. using tact
   c. inconsistencies in a presentation
   d. All of the above are correct.

8. **In terms of dramaturgical analysis, tact is understood as**
   a. helping someone take on a new role.
   b. helping another person "save face."
   c. making it hard for someone to perform a role.
   d. negotiating a situation to get your own way.

9. **In her study of human emotion, Arlie Hochschild explains that companies typically**
   a. try to regulate the emotions of workers.
   b. want workers to be unemotional.
   c. encourage people to express their true emotions.
   d. profit from making customers more emotional.

10. **People are likely to "get" a joke when they**
    a. know something about more than one culture.
    b. have a different social background than the joke teller.
    c. understand the two different realities being presented.
    d. know why someone wants to tell the joke.

ANSWERS: 1 (b); 2 (d); 3 (b); 4 (c); 5 (d); 6 (a); 7 (c); 8 (b); 9 (a); 10 (c).

Essay Questions

1. Explain Erving Goffman's idea that we engage in a "presentation of self." What are the elements of this presentation? Apply this approach to an analysis of a professor teaching a class.
2. In what ways are human emotions rooted in biology? In what ways are emotions guided by culture?

Groups and Organizations

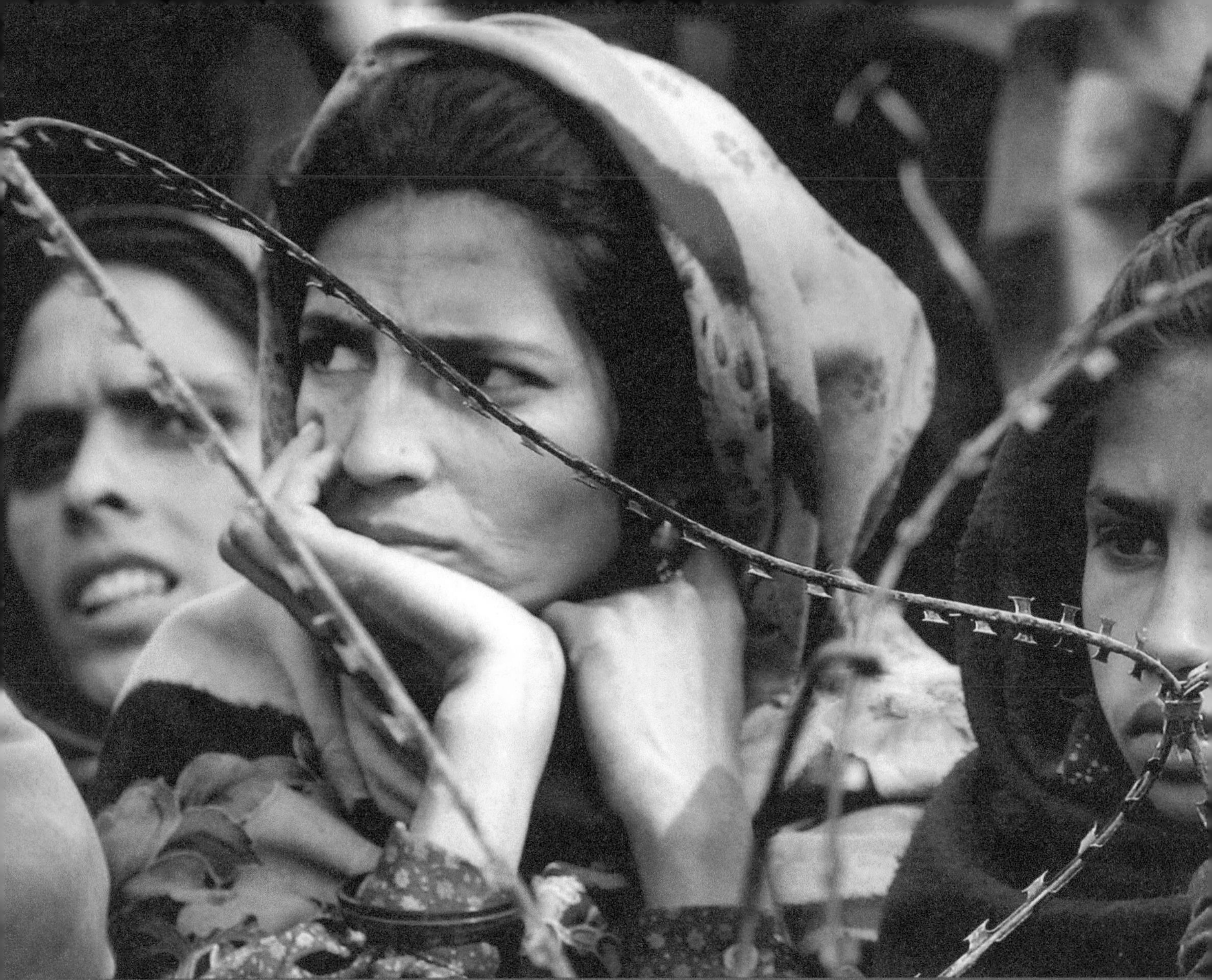

Corbis – NY/© Amit Bhargava/Corbis, All Rights Reserved

We carry out much of our daily lives as members of small groups, such as sports teams, and large organizations, such as the businesses where we work. Both small groups and large organizations operate according to general rules, which this chapter explains.

Corbis – NY/© Sherwin Crasto/Reuters/Corbis

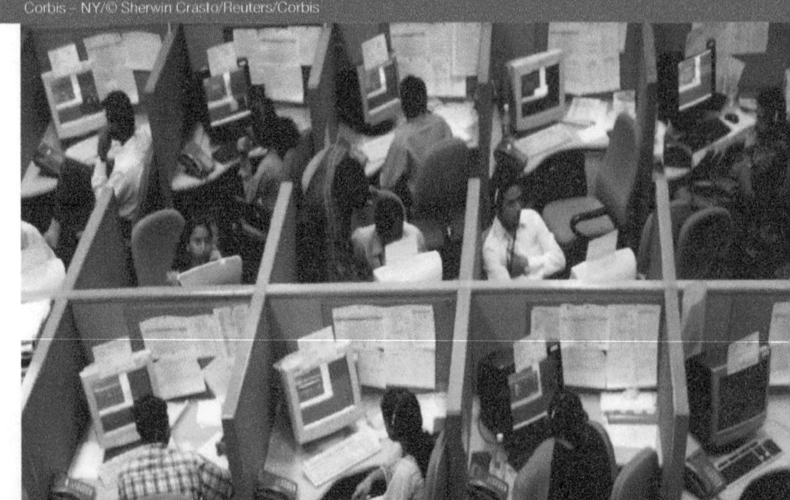

Groups and Organizations

Omni-Photo Communications, Inc./Esbin/Anderson

PhotoEdit Inc./Tony Freeman

CHAPTER OVERVIEW

This chapter analyzes social groups, both small and large, highlighting the differences between them. Then the focus shifts to formal organizations that carry out various tasks in our modern society.

Historic Site of the Original McDonald's

With the workday over, Juan and Jorge pushed through the doors of the local McDonald's restaurant. "Man, am I hungry," announced Juan, heading right into line. "Look at all the meat I'm gonna eat." But Jorge, a recent immigrant from a small village in Guatemala, is surveying the room with a sociological eye. "There is much more than food to see here. This place is all about America!"

And so it is, as we shall see. Back in 1948, people in Pasadena, California, paid little attention to the opening of a new restaurant by brothers Maurice and Richard McDonald. The McDonald brothers' basic concept, which was soon called "fast food," was to serve meals quickly and cheaply to large numbers of people. The brothers trained employees to do specialized jobs: One person grilled hamburgers while others "dressed" them, made French fries, whipped up milkshakes, and presented the food to the customers in assembly-line fashion.

As the years went by, the McDonald brothers prospered, and they opened several more restaurants, including one in San Bernardino. It was there, in 1954, that Ray Kroc, a traveling blender and mixer salesman, paid them a visit.

Kroc was fascinated by the efficiency of the brothers' system and saw the potential for a whole chain of fast-food restaurants. The three launched the plan as partners. In 1961, in the face of rapidly increasing sales, Kroc bought out the McDonalds (who returned to running their original restaurant) and went on to become one of the great success stories of all time. Today, McDonald's is one of the most widely known brand names in the world, with more than 31,500 restaurants serving 52 million people daily throughout the United States and in 118 other countries (McDonald's, 2008).

The success of McDonald's points to more than just the popularity of burgers and fries. The organizational principles that guide this company have come to dominate social life in the United States and elsewhere.

We begin this chapter with an examination of *social groups,* the clusters of people with whom we interact in everyday life. As you will learn, the scope of group life in the United States expanded greatly during the twentieth century. From a world of families, local neighborhoods, and small businesses, our society now turns on the operation of huge corporations and other bureaucracies that sociologists describe as *formal organizations.* Understanding this expanding scale of social life and appreciating what it means for us as individuals are the main objectives of this chapter.

Social Groups

Almost everyone wants a sense of belonging, which is the essence of group life. A **social group** is *two or more people who identify with and interact with one another.* Human beings come together in couples, families, circles of friends, churches, clubs, businesses, neighborhoods, and large organizations. Whatever its form, a group is made up of people with shared experiences, loyalties, and interests. In short, while keeping their individuality, members of social groups also think of themselves as a special "we."

Not every collection of individuals forms a group. People all over the country with a status in common, such as women, homeowners, soldiers, millionaires, college graduates, and Roman Catholics, are not a group but a *category.* Though they know that others hold the same status, most are strangers to one another. Similarly, students sitting in a large stadium interact to a very limited extent. Such a loosely formed collection of people in one place is a *crowd* rather than a group.

However, the right circumstances can quickly turn a crowd into a group. Unexpected events, from power failures to terrorist attacks, can make people bond quickly with strangers.

Primary and Secondary Groups

Friends often greet one another with a smile and the simple phrase "Hi! How are you?" The response is usually "Fine, thanks. How about

social group two or more people who identify with and interact with one another

primary group a small social group whose members share personal and lasting relationships

secondary group a large and impersonal social group whose members pursue a specific goal or activity

SEEING SOCIOLOGY in Everyday Life

List all the groups in your life that you think of in terms of "we."

you?" This answer is often more scripted than sincere. Explaining how you are *really* doing might make people feel so awkward that they would beat a hasty retreat.

Social groups are of two types, depending on their members' degree of personal concern for one another. According to Charles Horton Cooley (1864–1929), a **primary group** is *a small social group whose members share personal and lasting relationships.* Joined by *primary relationships,* people spend a great deal of time together, engage in a wide range of activities, and feel that they know one another pretty well. In short, they show real concern for one another. The family is every society's most important primary group.

Cooley called personal and tightly integrated groups "primary" because they are among the first groups we experience in life. In addition, family and friends have primary importance in the socialization process, shaping our attitudes, behavior, and social identity.

Members of primary groups help one another in many ways, but they generally think of the group as an end in itself rather than as a means to some goal. In other words, we prefer to think that family and friendship link people who "belong together." Members of a primary group also tend to view each other as unique and irreplaceable. Especially in the family, we are bound to others by emotion and loyalty. Brothers and sisters may not always get along, but they always remain "family."

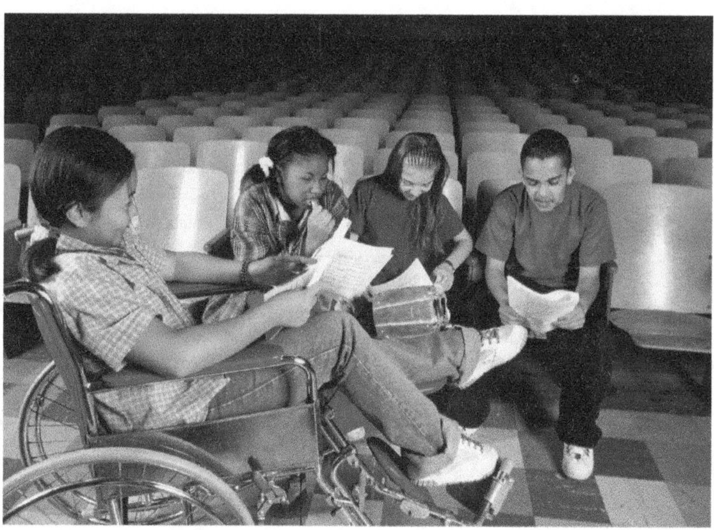
PhotoEdit Inc./Michael Newman

As human beings, we live our lives as members of groups. Such groups may be large or small, temporary or long-lasting, and can be based on kinship, cultural heritage, or some shared interest.

In contrast to the primary group, the **secondary group** is *a large and impersonal social group whose members pursue a specific goal or activity.* In most respects, secondary groups have characteristics opposite to those of primary groups. *Secondary relationships* involve weak emotional ties and little personal knowledge of one another. Many secondary groups exist for only a short time, beginning and ending without particular significance. Students in a college course, who may or may not see one another again after the semester ends, are one example of a secondary group.

Secondary groups include many more people than primary groups. For example, dozens or even hundreds of people may work together in the same company, yet most of them pay only passing attention to one another. In some cases, time may transform a group from secondary to primary, as with co-workers who share an office for many years and develop closer relationships. But generally, members of a secondary group do not think of themselves as "we." Secondary ties need not be hostile or cold, of course. Interactions among students, co-workers, and business associates are often quite pleasant even if they are impersonal.

Unlike members of primary groups, who display a *personal orientation,* people in secondary groups have a *goal orientation.* Primary group members define each other according to *who* they are in terms of family ties or personal qualities, but people in secondary groups look to one another for *what* they are, that is, what they can do for each other. In secondary groups, we tend to "keep score," aware of what we give others and what we receive in return. This goal orientation means that secondary-group members usually remain formal and polite. In a secondary relationship, therefore, we ask the question "How are you?" without expecting a truthful answer.

The Summing Up table reviews the characteristics of primary and secondary groups. Keep in mind that these traits define two types of groups in ideal terms; most real groups contain elements of both. For example, a women's group on a university campus may be quite large (and therefore secondary), but its members may identify strongly with one another and provide lots of mutual support (making it seem primary).

Many people think that small towns and rural areas have mostly primary relationships and that large cities are characterized by more secondary ties. This generalization is partly true, but some urban neighborhoods—especially those populated by people of a single ethnic or religious category—are very tightly knit.

Group Leadership

How do groups operate? One important element of group dynamics is leadership. Though a small circle of friends may have no leader at all, most large secondary groups place leaders in a formal chain of command.

SEEING SOCIOLOGY in Everyday Life

List five social groups on campus that you belong to. In each case, is the group more primary or more secondary?

instrumental leadership group leadership that focuses on the completion of tasks

expressive leadership group leadership that focuses on the group's well-being

SUMMING UP

Primary Groups and Secondary Groups

	Primary Group ⟵	⟶ Secondary Group
Quality of relationships	Personal orientation	Goal orientation
Duration of relationships	Usually long-term	Variable; often short-term
Breadth of relationships	Broad; usually involving many activities	Narrow; usually involving few activities
Perception of relationships	Ends in themselves	Means to an end
Examples	Families, circles of friends	Co-workers, political organizations

Two Leadership Roles

Groups typically benefit from two kinds of leadership. **Instrumental leadership** refers to *group leadership that focuses on the completion of tasks.* Members look to instrumental leaders to make plans, give orders, and get things done. **Expressive leadership,** by contrast, is *group leadership that focuses on the group's well-being.* Expressive leaders take less interest in achieving goals than in raising group morale and minimizing tension and conflict among members.

Because they concentrate on performance, instrumental leaders usually have formal secondary relationships with other members. These leaders give orders and reward or punish members according to how much the members contribute to the group's efforts. Expressive leaders build more personal primary ties. They offer sympathy to a member going through tough times, keep the group united, and lighten serious moments with humor. Typically, successful instrumental leaders enjoy more *respect* from members, and expressive leaders generally receive more personal *affection.*

Three Leadership Styles

Sociologists also describe leadership in terms of decision-making style. *Authoritarian leadership* focuses on instrumental concerns, takes personal charge of decision making, and demands that group members obey orders. Although this leadership style may win little affection from the group, a fast-acting authoritarian leader is appreciated in a crisis.

Democratic leadership is more expressive and makes a point of including everyone in the decision-making process. Although less successful in a crisis situation, democratic leaders generally draw on the ideas of all members to develop creative solutions to problems.

Laissez-faire leadership allows the group to function more or less on its own (*laissez-faire* in French means "leave it alone"). This style is typically the least effective in promoting group goals (White & Lippitt, 1953; Ridgeway, 1983).

Group Conformity

Groups influence the behavior of their members by promoting conformity. "Fitting in" provides a secure feeling of belonging, but at the extreme, group pressure can be unpleasant and even dangerous. As experiments by Solomon Asch and Stanley Milgram showed, even strangers can encourage conformity.

Asch's Research

Solomon Asch (1952) recruited students for what he told them was a study of visual perception. Before the experiment began, he explained to all but one member in a small group that their real purpose was to put pressure on the remaining person. Arranging six to eight students around a table, Asch showed them a "standard" line, as drawn on Card 1 in Figure 1, and asked them to match it to one of three lines on Card 2.

Anyone with normal vision could easily see that the line marked "A" on Card 2 is the correct choice. At the beginning of the experiment, everyone made the matches correctly. But then Asch's secret accomplices began answering incorrectly, leaving the uninformed student (seated at the table so as to answer next to last) bewildered and uncomfortable.

What happened? Asch found that one-third of all subjects chose to conform by answering incorrectly. Apparently, many of us are willing to compromise our own judgment to avoid the discomfort of being seen as different, even by people we do not know.

SEEING SOCIOLOGY in Everyday Life

Do you think that sociologists today would consider Milgram's research ethical? Why or why not?

groupthink the tendency of group members to conform, resulting in a narrow view of some issue

Milgram's Research

Stanley Milgram, a former student of Solomon Asch's, conducted conformity experiments of his own. In Milgram's controversial study (1963, 1965; A. G. Miller, 1986), a researcher explained to male recruits that they would be taking part in a study of how punishment affects learning. One by one, he assigned the subjects to the role of teacher and placed another person—actually an accomplice of Milgram's—in a connecting room to pose as a learner.

The teacher watched as the learner was seated in what looked like an electric chair. The researcher applied electrode paste to one of the learner's wrists, explaining that this would "prevent blisters and burns." The researcher then attached an electrode to the wrist and secured the leather straps, explaining that these would "prevent excessive movement while the learner was being shocked." The researcher assured the teacher that although the shocks would be painful, they would cause "no permanent tissue damage."

The researcher then led the teacher back to the next room, explaining that the "electric chair" was connected to a "shock generator," actually a phony but realistic-looking piece of equipment with a label that read "Shock Generator, Type ZLB, Dyson Instrument Company, Waltham, Mass." On the front was a dial that appeared to regulate electric shock from 15 volts (labeled "Slight Shock") to 300 volts (marked "Intense Shock") to 450 volts (marked "Danger: Severe Shock").

Seated in front of the "shock generator," the teacher was told to read aloud pairs of words. Then the teacher was to repeat the first word of each pair and wait for the learner to recall the second word. Whenever the learner failed to answer correctly, the teacher was told to apply an electric shock.

The researcher directed the teacher to begin at the lowest level (15 volts) and to increase the shock by another 15 volts every time the learner made a mistake. And so the teacher did. At 75, 90, and 105 volts, the teacher heard moans from the learner; at 120 volts, shouts of pain; at 270 volts, screams; at 315 volts, pounding on the wall; after that, dead silence. None of forty subjects assigned to the role of teacher during the initial research even questioned the procedure before reaching 300 volts, and twenty-six of the subjects—almost two-thirds—went all the way to 450 volts. Even Milgram was surprised at how readily people obeyed authority figures.

Milgram (1964) then modified his research to see if groups of ordinary people—not authority figures—could pressure people to administer electrical shocks, as Asch's groups had pressured individuals to match lines incorrectly.

This time, Milgram formed a group of three teachers, two of whom were his accomplices. Each of the three teachers was to suggest a shock level when the learner made an error; the rule was that the group would then administer the *lowest* of the three suggested levels. This arrangement gave the person not "in" on the experiment the power to deliver a lesser shock regardless of what the others said.

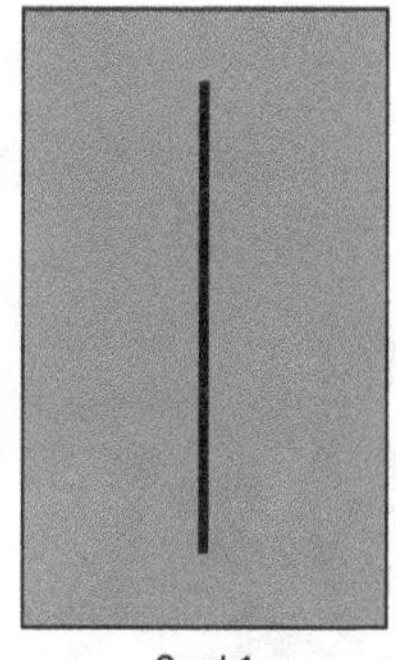

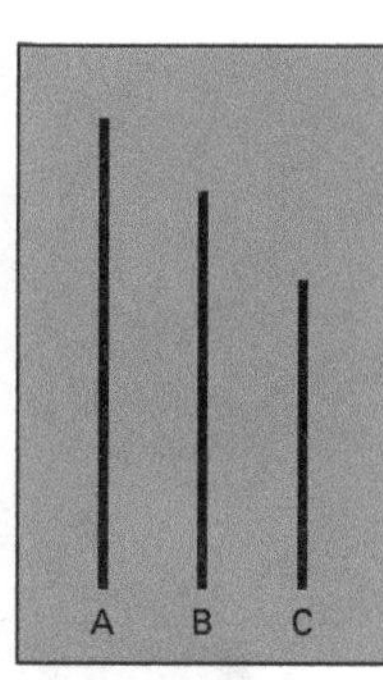

FIGURE 1 **Cards Used in Asch's Experiment in Group Conformity**

In Asch's experiment, subjects were asked to match the line on Card 1 to one of the lines on Card 2. Many subjects agreed with the wrong answers given by others in their group.

Source: Asch (1952).

The accomplices suggested increasing the shock level with each error, putting pressure on the third member to do the same. The subjects in these groups applied voltages three to four times higher than the levels applied by subjects acting alone. In this way, Milgram showed that people are likely to follow the lead of not only legitimate authority figures but also groups of ordinary individuals, even when it means harming another person.

Janis's "Groupthink"

Experts also cave in to group pressure, says Irving L. Janis (1972, 1989). Janis argues that a number of U.S. foreign policy errors, including the failure to foresee Japan's attack on Pearl Harbor during World War II and our ill-fated involvement in the Vietnam War, resulted from group conformity among our highest-ranking political leaders.

Common sense tells us that group discussion improves decision making. Janis counters that group members often seek agreement that closes off other points of view. Janis called this process **groupthink,** *the tendency of group members to conform, resulting in a narrow view of some issue.*

A classic example of groupthink led to the failed invasion of Cuba at the Bay of Pigs in 1961. Looking back, Arthur Schlesinger Jr., an adviser to President John F. Kennedy, confessed to feeling guilty for "having kept so quiet during those crucial discussions in the Cabinet Room," adding that the group discouraged anyone from

reference group a social group that serves as a point of reference in making evaluations and decisions

in-group a social group toward which a member feels respect and loyalty

out-group a social group toward which a person feels a sense of competition or opposition

The triad, illustrated by Jonathan Green's painting *Friends,* includes three people. A triad is more stable than a dyad because conflict between any two persons can be mediated by the third member. Even so, should the relationship between any two become more intense in a positive sense, those two are likely to exclude the third.

Jonathan Green, *Friends,* 1992. Oil on masonite, 14 in. × 11 in. © Jonathan Green, Naples, Florida. Collection of Patric McCoy.

challenging what, in hindsight, Schlesinger considered "nonsense" (quoted in Janis, 1972:30, 40). Groupthink may also have been a factor in 2003 when U.S. leaders went to war on the assumption that Iraq had stockpiles of weapons of mass destruction.

Reference Groups

How do we assess our own attitudes and behavior? Frequently, we use a **reference group,** *a social group that serves as a point of reference in making evaluations and decisions.*

A young man who imagines his family's response to a woman he is dating is using his family as a reference group. A supervisor who tries to predict her employees' reaction to a new vacation policy is using them in the same way. As these examples suggest, reference groups can be primary or secondary. In either case, our need to conform shows how others' attitudes affect us.

We also use groups that we do *not* belong to for reference. Being well prepared for a job interview means showing up dressed the way people in that company dress for work. Conforming to groups we do not belong to is a strategy to win acceptance and illustrates the process of *anticipatory socialization.*

Stouffer's Research

Samuel Stouffer and his colleagues (1949) conducted a classic study of reference group dynamics during World War II. Researchers asked soldiers to rate their own or any competent soldier's chances of promotion in their army unit. You might guess that soldiers serving in outfits with a high promotion rate would be optimistic about advancement. Yet Stouffer's research pointed to the opposite conclusion: Soldiers in army units with low promotion rates were actually more positive about their chances to move ahead.

The key to understanding Stouffer's results lies in the groups against which soldiers measured themselves. Those assigned to units with lower promotion rates looked around them and saw people making no more headway than they were. That is, although they had not been promoted, neither had many others, so they did not feel slighted. However, soldiers in units with a higher promotion rate could easily think of people who had been promoted sooner or more often than they had. With such people in mind, even soldiers who had been promoted were likely to feel shortchanged.

The point is that we do not make judgments about ourselves in isolation, nor do we compare ourselves with just anyone. Regardless of our situation in *absolute* terms, we form a subjective sense of our well-being by looking at ourselves *relative* to specific reference groups.

In-Groups and Out-Groups

Each of us favors some groups over others, based on political outlook, social prestige, or even just manner of dress. On the college campus, for example, left-leaning student activists may look down on fraternity members, whom they consider too conservative; fraternity members, in turn, may snub the "nerds," who they feel work too hard. People in every social setting make positive and negative evaluations of members of other groups.

Such judgments illustrate another important element of group dynamics: the opposition of in-groups and out-groups. An **in-group** is *a social group toward which a member feels respect and loyalty.* An in-group exists in relation to an **out-group,** *a social group toward which a person feels a sense of competition or opposition.* In-groups

SEEING SOCIOLOGY in Everyday Life

In terms of in-groups and out-groups, explain what happens when people who may not like each other discover that they have a common enemy.

dyad a social group with two members

triad a social group with three members

and out-groups are based on the idea that "we" have valued traits that "they" lack.

Tensions between groups sharpen the groups' boundaries and give people a clearer social identity. However, members of in-groups generally hold overly positive views of themselves and unfairly negative views of various out-groups.

Power also plays a part in intergroup relations. A powerful in-group can define others as a lower-status out-group. Historically, in countless U.S. towns and cities, many white people viewed people of color as an out-group and subordinated them socially, politically, and economically. Minorities who internalize these negative attitudes often struggle to overcome negative self-images. In this way, in-groups and out-groups foster loyalty but also generate conflict (Tajfel, 1982; Bobo & Hutchings, 1996).

Group Size

The next time you go to a party, try to arrive first. If you do, you will be able to watch some fascinating group dynamics. Until about six people enter the room, every person who arrives shares a single conversation. As more people arrive, the group divides into two clusters, and it divides again and again as the party grows. Size plays an important role in how group members interact.

To understand why, note the mathematical number of relationships among two to seven people. As shown in Figure 2, two people form a single relationship; adding a third person results in three relationships; adding a fourth person yields six. Increasing the number of people one at a time, then, expands the number of relationships much more rapidly since every new individual can interact with everyone already there. Thus by the time seven people join one conversation, twenty-one "channels" connect them. With so many open channels, some people begin to feel left out, and the group usually divides.

The Dyad

The German sociologist Georg Simmel (1858–1918) studied social dynamics in the smallest groups. Simmel (1950, orig. 1902) used the term **dyad** (Greek for "pair") to designate *a social group with two members.* Simmel explained that social interaction in a dyad is usually more intense than in larger groups because neither member shares the other's attention with anyone else. In the United States, love affairs, marriages, and the closest friendships are typically dyadic.

But like a stool with only two legs, dyads are unstable. Both members of a dyad must work to keep the relationship going; if either withdraws, the group collapses. Because the stability of marriages is important to society, the marital dyad is supported by legal, economic, and often religious ties.

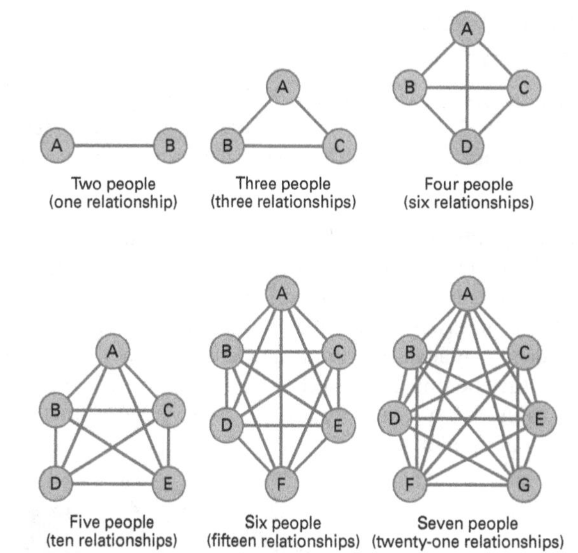

FIGURE 2 **Group Size and Relationships**

As the number of people in a group increases, the number of relationships that link them increases much faster. By the time six or seven people share a conversation, the group usually divides into two. Why are relationships in smaller groups typically more intense?

Source: Created by the author.

The Triad

Simmel also studied the **triad,** *a social group with three members,* which contains three relationships, each uniting two of the three people. A triad is more stable than a dyad because one member can act as a mediator should the relationship between the other two become strained. Such group dynamics help explain why members of a dyad (say, a married couple) often seek out a third person (such as a counselor) to discuss tensions between them.

On the other hand, two of the three can pair up at times to press their views on the third, or two may intensify their relationship, leaving the other feeling left out. For example, when two of the three develop a romantic interest in each other, they will come to understand the meaning of the old saying, "Two's company, three's a crowd."

As groups grow beyond three people, they become more stable and capable of withstanding the loss of one or more members. At the same time, increases in group size reduce the intense personal interaction possible only in the smallest groups. This is why larger groups are based less on personal attachment and more on formal rules and regulations.

MAKING THE GRADE

Is a network a group? No, because there is no common identification or frequent interaction among members. But fuzzy or not, networks are a valuable resource, which is probably the best reason to understand a little about how they work.

network a web of weak social ties

Social Diversity: Race, Class, and Gender

Race, ethnicity, class, and gender each play a part in group dynamics. Peter Blau (1977; Blau, Blum, & Schwartz, 1982; South & Messner, 1986) points out three ways in which social diversity influences intergroup contact:

1. **Large groups turn inward.** Blau explains that the larger a group is, the more likely its members are to have relationships just among themselves. Say a college is trying to enhance social diversity by increasing the number of international students. These students may add a dimension of difference, but as their numbers rise, they become more likely to form their own social group. Thus efforts to promote social diversity may have the unintended effect of promoting separatism.

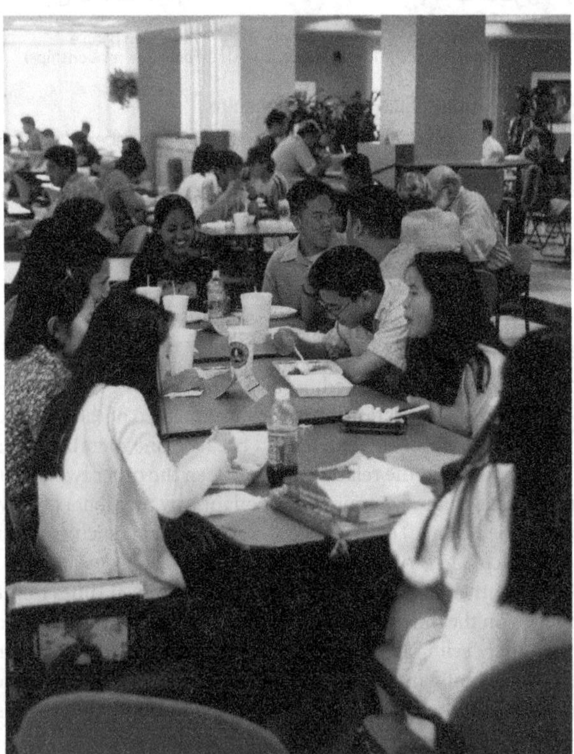

Today's college campuses value social diversity. One of the challenges of this movement is ensuring that all categories of students are fully integrated into campus life. This is not always easy. Following Blau's theory of group dynamics, as the number of minority students increases, these men and women are able to form a group unto themselves, perhaps interacting less with others.

2. **Heterogeneous groups turn outward.** The more internally diverse a group is, the more likely its members are to interact with outsiders. Members of campus groups that recruit people of both sexes and various social backgrounds typically have more intergroup contact than those with members of one social category.
3. **Physical boundaries create social boundaries.** To the extent that a social group is physically segregated from others (by having its own dorm or dining area, for example), its members are less likely to interact with other people.

Networks

A **network** is *a web of weak social ties.* Think of a network as a "fuzzy" group containing people who come into occasional contact but who lack a sense of boundaries and belonging. If you think of a *group* as a "circle of friends," think of a network as a "social web" expanding outward, often reaching great distances and including large numbers of people.

The largest network of all is the World Wide Web of the Internet. But the Internet has expanded much more in some global regions than in others. Global Map 1 shows that Internet use is high in rich countries and far less common in poor nations.

Closer to home, some networks come close to being groups, as is the case with college classmates who stay in touch after graduation through class newsletters and reunions. More commonly, however, a network includes people we know of or who know of us but with whom we interact rarely, if at all. As one woman known as a community organizer explains, "I get calls at home, [and] someone says, 'Are you Roseann Navarro? Somebody told me to call you. I have this problem. . . .'" (quoted in Kaminer, 1984:94).

Network ties often give us the sense that we live in a "small world." In a classic experiment, Stanley Milgram (1967; Watts, 1999) gave letters to subjects in Kansas and Nebraska intended for a few specific people in Boston who were unknown to the original subjects. No addresses were supplied, and the subjects in the study were told to send the letters to others they knew personally who might know the target people. Milgram found that the target people received the letters with, on average, six subjects passing them on. This result led Milgram to conclude that just about everyone is connected to everyone else by "six degrees of separation." Later research, however, has cast doubt on Milgram's conclusions. Examining Milgram's original data, Judith Kleinfeld points out that most of Milgram's letters (240 out of 300) never arrived at their destinations (Wildavsky, 2002). Those that did were typically given to people who were wealthy, a fact that led Kleinfeld to conclude that rich people are far better connected across the country than ordinary women and men.

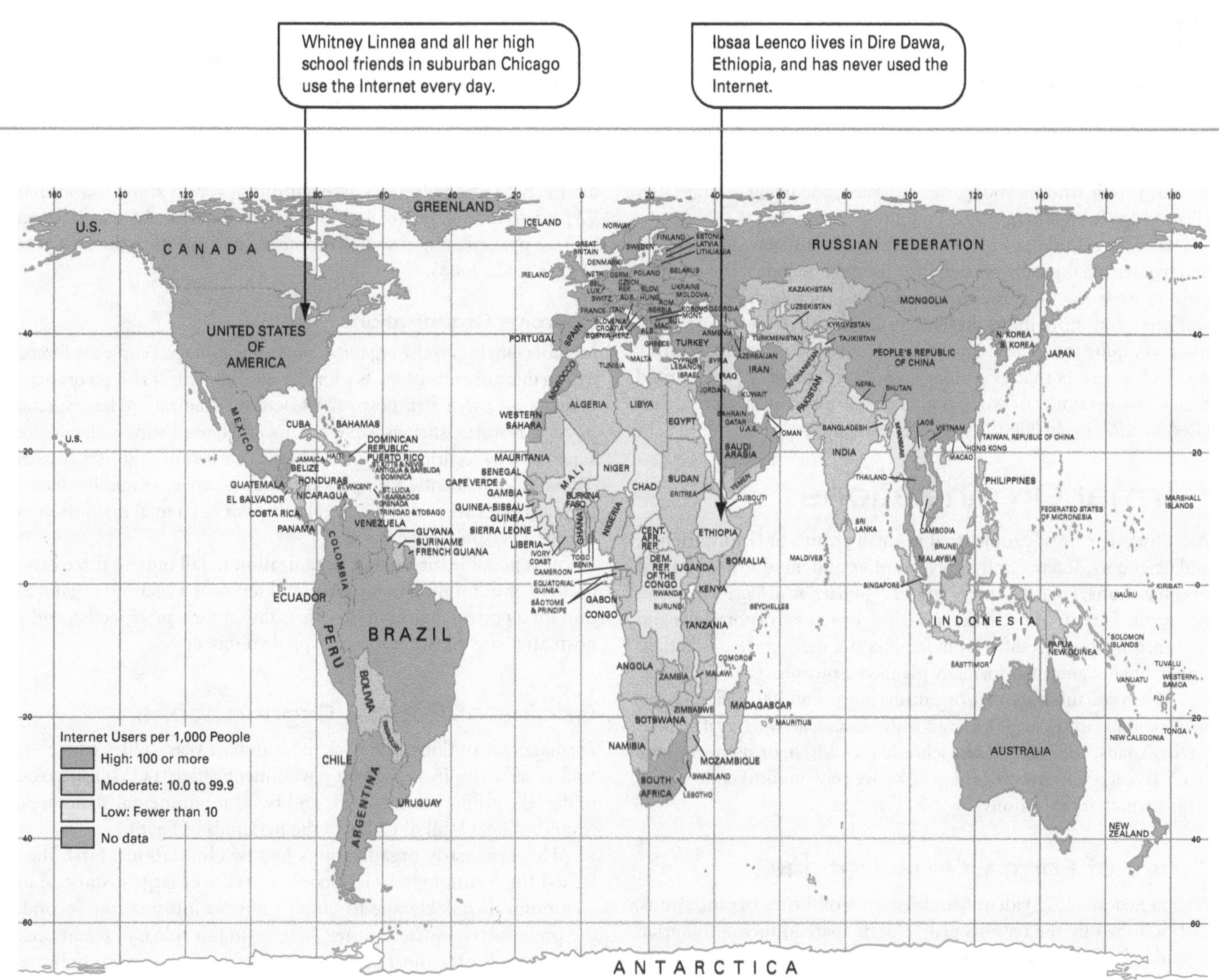

Window on the World

GLOBAL MAP 1 **Internet Users in Global Perspective**

This map shows how the Information Revolution has affected countries around the world. In most high-income nations, at least one-third of the population uses the Internet. By contrast, only a small share of people in low-income nations does so. What effect does this pattern have on people's access to information? What does this mean for the future in terms of global inequality?

Source: United Nations Statistics Division (2008).

Network ties may be weak, but they can be a powerful resource. For immigrants who are trying to become established in a new community, businesspeople seeking to expand their operations, or new college graduates looking for a job, *whom* you know is often as important as *what* you know (Hagan, 1998; Petersen, Saporta, & Seidel, 2000).

Networks are based on people's colleges, clubs, neighborhoods, political parties, and personal interests. Obviously, some networks contain people with considerably more wealth, power, and prestige than others; that explains the importance of being "well connected." The networks of more privileged categories of people—such as the members of an expensive country club—are a valuable form of "social capital," which is more likely to lead people to higher-paying jobs (Green, Tigges, & Diaz, 1999; Lin, Cook, & Burt, 2001).

Some people also have denser networks than others; that is, they are connected to more people. Typically, the largest social networks

formal organizations large secondary groups organized to achieve their goals efficiently

bureaucracy an organizational model rationally designed to perform tasks efficiently

organizational environment factors outside an organization that affect its operation

SEEING SOCIOLOGY in Everyday Life

Today's world has so many large organizations that we identify them just by initials: IRS, FBI, IBM, CIA, NATO, CNN, PTA, WWF, and so on. How many more examples can you think of?

include people who are young, well educated, and living in large cities (Fernandez & Weinberg, 1997; Podolny & Baron, 1997).

Gender also shapes networks. Although the networks of men and women are typically the same size, women include more relatives (and more women) in their networks, and men include more co-workers (and more men). Research suggests that women's ties do not carry quite the same clout as typical "old boy" networks. Even so, research suggests that as gender equality increases in the United States, the networks of women and men are becoming more alike (Reskin & McBrier, 2000; Torres & Huffman, 2002).

Formal Organizations

A century ago, most people lived in small groups of family, friends, and neighbors. Today, our lives revolve more and more around **formal organizations,** *large secondary groups organized to achieve their goals efficiently.* Formal organizations, such as business corporations and government agencies, differ from families and neighborhoods in their impersonality and their formally planned atmosphere.

When you think about it, organizing more than 300 million people in this country into a single society is truly remarkable, whether it involves paving roads, collecting taxes, schooling children, or delivering the mail. To carry out most of these tasks, we rely on different types of large formal organizations.

Types of Formal Organizations

Amitai Etzioni (1975) identified three types of formal organizations, distinguished by the reasons people participate in them: utilitarian organizations, normative organizations, and coercive organizations.

Utilitarian Organizations

Just about everyone who works for income belongs to a *utilitarian organization,* one that pays people for their efforts. Large businesses, for example, generate profits for their owners and income for their employees. Becoming part of a utilitarian organization such as a business or government agency is usually a matter of individual choice, although most people must join one or another such organization to make a living.

Normative Organizations

People join *normative organizations* not for income but to pursue some goal they think is morally worthwhile. Sometimes called *voluntary associations,* these include community service groups (such as the PTA, the Lions Club, the League of Women Voters, and the Red Cross), as well as political parties and religious organizations. In global perspective, people living in the United States and other high-income nations with relatively democratic political systems are likely to join voluntary associations. A recent study found that 72 percent of first-year college students in the United States claimed to have participated in some volunteer activity within the past year (Pryor et al., 2008).

Coercive Organizations

Membership in *coercive organizations* is involuntary. People are forced to join these organizations as a form of punishment (prisons) or treatment (some psychiatric hospitals). Coercive organizations have special physical features, such as locked doors and barred windows, and are supervised by security personnel. They isolate people, whom they label "inmates" or "patients," for a period of time in order to radically change their attitudes and behavior. Recall the power of a total institution to change a person's sense of self.

It is possible for a single organization to fall into all three categories. For example, a mental hospital serves as a coercive organization for a patient, a utilitarian organization for a psychiatrist, and a normative organization for a hospital volunteer.

Origins of Formal Organizations

Formal organizations date back thousands of years. Elites who controlled early empires relied on government officials to collect taxes, undertake military campaigns, and build monumental structures, from the Great Wall of China to the pyramids of Egypt.

However, early organizations had two limitations. First, they lacked the technology to let people travel over large distances, to communicate quickly, and to gather and store information. Second, the preindustrial societies they were trying to rule had traditional cultures, so for the most part, ruling organizations tried to preserve cultural systems, not change them. But during the last few centuries, what Max Weber called a "rational worldview" emerged in parts of the world. In Europe and North America, the Industrial Revolution ushered in a new structure for formal organizations concerned with efficiency that Weber called "bureaucracy."

Characteristics of Bureaucracy

Bureaucracy is *an organizational model rationally designed to perform tasks efficiently.* Bureaucratic officials regularly create and revise policy to increase efficiency. To appreciate the power and scope of bureaucratic organization, consider that any one of the almost 400 million telephones in the United States can connect you within seconds to any other phone in a home, business, automobile, or even a hiker's backpack on a remote trail in the Rocky Mountains. Such instant communication was beyond the imagination of people who lived in the ancient world.

SEEING SOCIOLOGY in Everyday Life

Give an example of each of the factors listed here in the operation of your college or university bureaucracy.

MAKING THE GRADE

The six traits listed here defined, for Weber, the *ideal* bureaucracy. This means that in its pure form, bureaucracy has all these traits.

Our telephone system depends on technology such as electricity, fiber optics, and computers. But the system could not exist without the bureaucracy that keeps track of every telephone call—noting which phone calls which other phone, when, and for how long—and then presents the relevant information to more than 250 million telephone users in the form of a monthly bill (CTIA, 2008).

What specific traits promote organizational efficiency? Max Weber (1978, orig. 1921) identified six key elements of the ideal bureaucratic organization:

1. **Specialization.** Our ancestors spent most of their time looking for food and shelter. Bureaucracy, by contrast, assigns people highly specialized jobs.
2. **Hierarchy of positions.** Bureaucracies arrange workers in a vertical ranking. Each person is supervised by someone "higher up" in the organization while in turn supervising others in lower positions. Usually, with few people at the top and many at the bottom, bureaucratic organizations take the form of a pyramid.
3. **Rules and regulations.** Cultural tradition counts for little in a bureaucracy. Instead, rationally enacted rules and regulations guide a bureaucracy's operation. Ideally, a bureaucracy operates in a completely predictable way.
4. **Technical competence.** Bureaucratic officials have the technical competence to carry out their duties. Bureaucracies typically hire new members according to set standards and then monitor their performance. Such impersonal evaluation contrasts with the ancient custom of favoring relatives, whatever their talents, over strangers.
5. **Impersonality.** Bureaucracy puts rules ahead of personal whim so that both clients and workers are treated in the same way. From this impersonal approach comes the image of the "faceless bureaucrat."
6. **Formal, written communications.** It is said that the heart of bureaucracy is not people but paperwork. Instead of the casual, face-to-face talk that characterizes interaction within small groups, bureaucracy relies on formal, written memos and reports, which accumulate in vast files.

Bureaucratic organization promotes efficiency by carefully hiring workers and limiting the unpredictable effects of personal taste and opinion. The Summing Up table reviews the differences between small social groups and large bureaucratic organizations.

PhotoEdit Inc./Spencer Grant

Weber described the operation of the ideal bureaucracy as rational and highly efficient. In real life, actual large organizations often operate very differently from Weber's model, as can be seen on the television show *The Office.*

Organizational Environment

No organization operates in a vacuum. The performance of any organization depends not only on its own goals and policies but also on the **organizational environment,** *factors outside an organization that affect its operation.* These factors include technology, economic and political trends, current events, the available workforce, and other organizations.

Modern organizations are shaped by *technology,* including copiers, fax machines, telephones, and computers. This technology gives employees access to more information and more people than ever before. At the same time, modern technology allows managers to monitor worker activities much more closely than in the past (Markoff, 1991).

Economic and political trends affect organizations. All organizations are helped or hurt by periodic economic growth or recession. Most industries also face competition from abroad as well as changes in laws—such as new environmental standards—at home.

Current events can have significant effects on organizations that are far removed from the location of the events themselves. A regional conflict that sends oil prices spiking upward or the election of a new president affects both government agencies and business organizations.

Population patterns also affect organizations. The average age, typical level of education, social diversity, and size of a local community

MAKING THE GRADE

Just because an organization is efficient doesn't mean that people enjoy being part of it or that it is actually good for people. Weber feared the opposite: The more rational and bureaucratic society became, the less it would advance human well-being.

SUMMING UP

Small Groups and Formal Organizations

	Small Groups	Formal Organizations
Activities	Much the same for all members	Distinct and highly specialized
Hierarchy	Often informal or nonexistent	Clearly defined according to position
Norms	General norms, informally applied	Clearly defined rules and regulations
Membership criteria	Variable; often based on personal affection or kinship	Technical competence to carry out assigned tasks
Relationships	Variable and typically primary	Typically secondary, with selective primary ties
Communications	Typically casual and face to face	Typically formal and in writing
Focus	Person-oriented	Task-oriented

determine the available workforce and sometimes the market for an organization's products or services.

Other organizations also contribute to the organizational environment. To be competitive, a hospital must be responsive to the insurance industry and to organizations representing doctors, nurses, and other health care workers. It must also be aware of the equipment and procedures available at nearby facilities, as well as their prices.

The Informal Side of Bureaucracy

Weber's ideal bureaucracy deliberately regulates every activity. In actual organizations, however, human beings are creative (and stubborn) enough to resist bureaucratic regulation. Informality may amount to simply cutting corners on your job, but it can also provide the flexibility needed to adapt and prosper.

In part, informality comes from the personalities of organizational leaders. Studies of U.S. corporations document that the qualities and quirks of individuals—including personal charisma, interpersonal skills, and the willingness to recognize problems—can have a great effect on organizational outcomes (Halberstam, 1986; Baron, Hannan, & Burton, 1999).

Authoritarian, democratic, and laissez-faire types of leadership (described earlier in this chapter) reflect individual personality as much as any organizational plan. In the "real world" of organizations, leaders sometimes seek to benefit personally by abusing organizational power. Many of the corporate leaders of banks and insurance companies that collapsed during the financial meltdown of 2008 walked off with huge "golden parachutes." Throughout the business world, leaders take credit for the efforts of the people who work for them, at least when things go well. In addition, the importance of many secretaries to how well a boss performs is often much greater than most people think (and greater than a secretary's official job title and salary suggest).

Communication offers another example of organizational informality. Memos and other written communications are the formal way to spread information throughout an organization. Typically, however, individuals also create informal networks, or "grapevines," that spread information quickly, if not always accurately. Grapevines, using both word of mouth and e-mail, are particularly important to rank-and-file workers because higher-ups often try to keep important information from them.

The spread of e-mail has "flattened" organizations somewhat, allowing even the lowest-ranking employee to bypass immediate superiors and communicate directly with the organization's leader or with all fellow employees at once. Some organizations object to such "open-channel" communication and limit the use of e-mail. Microsoft Corporation (whose founder, Bill Gates, has an unlisted e-mail address that helps him limit his mail to a few hundred messages a day) pioneered the development of screens that filter out messages from everyone except certain approved people (Gwynne & Dickerson, 1997).

SEEING SOCIOLOGY in Everyday Life

Do you think FEMA or other large government organizations are inherently inefficient, or do you think their leaders sometimes make bad decisions? Explain your answer.

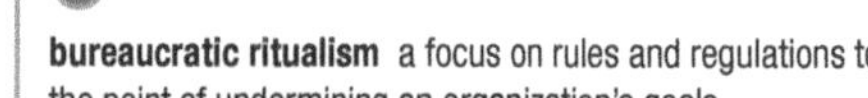

bureaucratic ritualism a focus on rules and regulations to the point of undermining an organization's goals

bureaucratic inertia the tendency of bureaucratic organizations to perpetuate themselves

oligarchy the rule of the many by the few

Using new information technology as well as age-old human ingenuity, members of organizations often try to break free of rigid rules in order to personalize procedures and surroundings. Such efforts suggest that we should take a closer look at some of the problems of bureaucracy.

George Tooker, *Government Bureau*, 1956, egg tempera on gesso panel, 19 5/8 x 29 5/8 inches. The Metropolitan Museum of Art, George A. Hearn Fund, 1956 (56.78). Photograph courtesy of The Metropolitan Museum of Art/Art Resource, NY

George Tooker's painting *Government Bureau* is a powerful statement about the human costs of bureaucracy. The artist paints members of the public in a drab sameness—reduced from human beings to mere "cases" to be disposed of as quickly as possible. Set apart from others by their positions, officials are "faceless bureaucrats" concerned more with numbers than with providing genuine assistance (notice that the artist places the fingers of the officials on calculators).

George Tooker, *Government Bureau*, 1956. Egg tempera on gesso panel, $19\frac{5}{8} \times 29\frac{5}{8}$ inches. The Metropolitan Museum of Art, George A. Hearn Fund, 1956 (56.78). Photograph © 1984 The Metropolitan Museum of Art.

Problems of Bureaucracy

We rely on bureaucracy to manage everyday life efficiently, but many people are uneasy about large organizations. Bureaucracy can dehumanize and manipulate us, and some say it poses a threat to political democracy. These dangers are discussed in the following sections.

Bureaucratic Alienation

Max Weber held up bureaucracy as a model of productivity. However, Weber was keenly aware of bureaucracy's ability to *dehumanize* the people it is supposed to serve. The same impersonality that fosters efficiency also keeps officials and clients from responding to one another's unique personal needs. Typically, officials at large government and corporate agencies must treat each client impersonally as a standard "case." In 2008, for example, the U.S. Army accidently sent letters to family members of soldiers killed in Iraq and Afghanistan, addressing the recipients as "John Doe" ("Army Apologizes," 2009).

Formal organizations breed *alienation*, according to Weber, by reducing the human being to "a small cog in a ceaselessly moving mechanism" (1978:988, orig. 1921). Although formal organizations are designed to benefit people, Weber feared that people might well end up serving formal organizations.

Bureaucratic Inefficiency and Ritualism

On Labor Day 2005, as people in New Orleans and other coastal areas were battling to survive in the wake of Hurricane Katrina, 600 firefighters from around the country assembled in a hotel meeting room in Atlanta awaiting deployment. Officials of the Federal Emergency Management Agency (FEMA) explained to the crowd that they were first going to be given a lecture on "equal opportunity, sexual harassment, and customer service." Then, the official continued, they would each be given a stack of FEMA pamphlets with the agency's phone number to distribute to people in the devastated areas. A firefighter stood up and shouted, "This is ridiculous! Our fire departments and mayors sent us down here to save lives, and you've got us doing *this*?" The FEMA official thundered back, "You are now employees of FEMA, and you will follow orders and do what you are told!" ("Places," 2005:39)

Criticism of the government response to the hurricane disaster of 2005 was widespread and pointed to the problem of bureaucratic *inefficiency*, the failure of an organization to carry out the work that it exists to perform. Even four years later, as Seeing Sociology in the News explains, the complaints continue.

People sometimes describe this inefficiency as too much "red tape," a reference to the ribbon used by slow-working eighteenth-century English administrators to wrap official parcels and records (Shipley, 1985).

To Robert Merton (1968), red tape amounts to a new twist on the already familiar concept of group conformity. He coined the term **bureaucratic ritualism** to describe *a focus on rules and regulations to the point of undermining an organization's goals*. In short, rules and regulations should be a means to an end, not an end in themselves that takes the focus away from the organization's stated goals. After the terrorist attacks of September 11, 2001, for example, the U.S. Postal Service continued to help deliver mail addressed to Osama bin Laden at a post office in Afghanistan, despite the objections of the FBI. It took an act of Congress to change the policy (Bedard, 2002).

CBS News

FEMA's "Toxic Bureaucracy": Are FEMA Managers Holding Up Aid to Hold onto Their Jobs?

By ARMEN KETEYIAN
February 25, 2009

(CBS) FEMA's been under fire from critics who claim the Gulf Coast recovery is moving too slowly. Now FEMA officials said they're investigating allegations of serious misconduct at the New Orleans office. CBS News has learned workers there accuse their bosses of intentionally holding up Katrina aid.

The day Hurricane Katrina hit Slidell, La., in 2005, more than six feet of tidal surge flooded the city's downtown. Today Slidell mayor Ben Morris is still running city hall—out of a trailer.

"When the train goes by, it shakes," Morris said.

All because of endless delays, caused by FEMA, he says, which just last month delayed money for rebuilding yet again, CBS News chief investigative correspondent Armen Keteyian reports exclusively.

"It's been an indescribable nightmare that most people would not believe," Morris explained.

Today, nearly $4 billion intended to rebuild the Gulf Coast remains unspent. That's 68 percent of the $6 billion promised by FEMA.

This is leaving hundreds of projects, like a police station in New Orleans, and the Charity Hospital, waiting.

Now, a CBS News investigation has uncovered what more than a dozen current and former employees say is one key reason help isn't getting to those in need.

They point to a FEMA office in downtown New Orleans, which is responsible for distributing the money. They say the way the office is managed is itself a disaster.

Three senior level staff people—who still work for FEMA—fear they will lose their jobs for speaking out. CBS News agreed to protect their identities.

Keteyian asked one employee to describe the atmosphere in the office.

Keteyian: Cronyism?
FEMA employee: Yes.
Keteyian: Sexual harassment?
FEMA employee: Yes.
Keteyian: Racial discrimination?
FEMA employee: Yes.
Keteyian: Intimidation?
FEMA employee: Yes.
Keteyian: Retaliation?
FEMA employee: Yes.

Bureaucratic Inertia

If bureaucrats sometimes have little reason to work very hard, they have every reason to protect their jobs. Officials typically work to keep an organization going even after its original goal has been realized. As Weber put it, "Once fully established, bureaucracy is among the social structures which are hardest to destroy" (1978:987, orig. 1921).

Bureaucratic inertia refers to *the tendency of bureaucratic organizations to perpetuate themselves.* Formal organizations tend to take on a life of their own beyond their formal objectives. For example, the U.S. Department of Agriculture has offices in nearly every county in all fifty states, even though only one county in seven has any working farms. Usually, an organization stays in business by redefining its goals. For example, the Agriculture Department now performs a broad range of work not directly related to farming, including nutritional and environmental research.

Oligarchy

Early in the twentieth century, Robert Michels (1876–1936) pointed out the link between bureaucracy and political **oligarchy**, *the rule of the many by the few* (1949, orig. 1911). According to what Michels called the "iron law of oligarchy," the pyramid shape of bureaucracy places a few leaders in charge of the resources of the entire organization.

Weber believed that a strict hierarchy of responsibility resulted in high organizational efficiency. But Michels countered that this hierarchical structure also concentrates power and thus threatens democracy because officials can and often do use their access to information, resources, and the media to promote their own personal interests.

Furthermore, bureaucracy helps distance officials from the public, as in the case of the corporate president or public official who is "unavailable for comment" to the local press or the U.S. president who withholds documents from Congress claiming "executive privilege." Oligarchy, then, thrives in the hierarchical structure of bureaucracy and reduces leaders' accountability to the people.

Political competition, term limits, and a legal system that includes various checks and balances prevent the U.S. government from becoming an out-and-out oligarchy. Even so, incumbents, who generally have more visibility, power, and money than their challengers, enjoy a significant advantage in U.S. politics. In recent congressional elections, more than 90 percent of congressional officeholders on the ballot were able to win reelection.

The Evolution of Formal Organizations

The problems of bureaucracy—especially the alienation it produces and its tendency toward oligarchy—stem from two organizational traits: hierarchy and rigidity. To Weber, bureaucracy was a top-down system: Rules and regulations made at the top guide every facet of people's lives down the chain of command. A century ago in the United States, Weber's ideas took hold in an organizational model called *scientific management.* We take a look at this model and then examine three challenges over the course of the twentieth century that gradually led to a new model: the *flexible organization.*

CBS News has learned that since January 1, nearly 80 employment-related complaints have been filed by staff at the office. . . .

"The harassment, the equal rights—violations that are currently taking place over there, this office is slowing down the recovery in this region." said one former FEMA employee.

And slowing down the recovery—these former employees charge—is exactly what some senior managers at the New Orleans FEMA office want.

Keteyian: But what's in it for them? To slow this process . . .

Former FEMA employee: They're making . . . over $100,000 plus a pension in some cases.

Keteyian: So they've taken a natural disaster and turned it into a huge boondoggle for themselves?

Former FEMA employee: In my opinion, yes.

"Shame on FEMA," said Rep. Joseph Cao of Lousiana. Cao said the New Orleans FEMA office needs to be investigated.

"They're more worried about their own positions in FEMA, their own salaries," Cao said, "than the recovery process down here."

CBS News wanted to speak with Doug Whitmer or Jim Stark, his boss. Stark opened up this morning in Washington. He denied there was any intentional slow down of the recovery process.

"I find that pretty offensive, Armen," said Stark. "I live in New Orleans. I've lived there for six years. I joined FEMA to help my community to recover." . . .

"The word that has been used with us is 'toxic.' That the atmosphere in your office right now is toxic," Keteyian said.

"Then we'll take steps to fix it," Stark said.

Gulf Coast residents shouldn't expect FEMA's recovery work to end here anytime soon.

Employees say they've been told to expect it to go on for as long as 15 years.

WHAT DO YOU THINK?

1. Which of the "problems of bureaucracy" discussed in this section of the chapter do you find in this article?
2. Do the problems described here appear to be the failings of individuals or failings of large organizations? Explain.
3. What might be the solution to the problems described here?

Scientific Management

Frederick Winslow Taylor (1911) had a simple message: Most businesses in the United States were sadly inefficient. Managers had little idea of how to increase their business's output, and workers relied on the same tired skills of earlier generations. To increase efficiency, Taylor explained, business should apply the principles of science. **Scientific management** is thus *the application of scientific principles to the operation of a business or other large organization.*

Scientific management involves three steps. First, managers carefully observe the task performed by each worker, identifying all the operations involved and measuring the time needed for each. Second, managers analyze their data, trying to discover ways for workers to perform each job more efficiently. For example, managers might decide to give the worker different tools or to reposition various work operations within the factory. Third, management provides guidance and incentives for workers to do their jobs more quickly. If a factory worker moves 20 tons of pig iron in one day, for example, management shows the worker how to do the job more efficiently and then provides higher wages as the worker's productivity rises. Taylor concluded that if scientific principles were applied in this way, companies would become more profitable, workers would earn higher wages, and consumers would pay lower prices.

A century ago, the auto pioneer Henry Ford put it this way: "Save ten steps a day for each of 12,000 employees, and you will have saved fifty miles of wasted motion and misspent energy" (Allen & Hyman, 1999:209). In the early 1900s, the Ford Motor Company and many other businesses followed Taylor's lead and made improvements in efficiency.

The principles of scientific management suggested that workplace power should reside with owners and executives, who paid little attention to the ideas of their workers. As the decades passed, formal organizations faced important challenges, involving race and gender, rising competition from abroad, and the changing nature of work. We now take a brief look at each of these challenges.

The First Challenge: Race and Gender

In the 1960s, critics pointed out that big businesses and other organizations engaged in unfair hiring practices. Rather than hiring on the basis of competence as Weber had proposed, organizations had excluded women and other minorities, especially from positions of power. Hiring on the basis of competence is only partly a matter of fairness; it is also a matter of enlarging the talent pool to promote efficiency.

Patterns of Privilege and Exclusion

Even in the early twenty-first century, as shown in Figure 3, non-Hispanic white men in the United States—33 percent of the working-age population—still held 54 percent of management jobs. Non-Hispanic white women made up 34 percent of the population but held just 29 percent of managerial positions (U.S. Equal Employment Opportunity Commission, 2008). The members of other minorities lagged further behind.

Rosabeth Moss Kanter (1977; Kanter & Stein, 1979) points out that excluding women and minorities from the workplace ignores the talents of more than half the population. Furthermore,

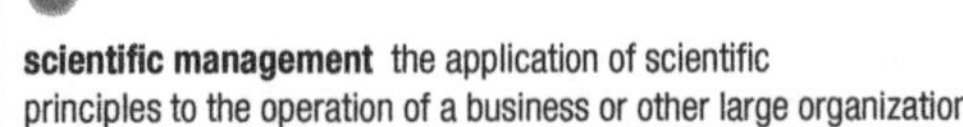

scientific management the application of scientific principles to the operation of a business or other large organization

Compared to their percentage of the total population, white men are over-represented in management positions.

Diversity Snapshot

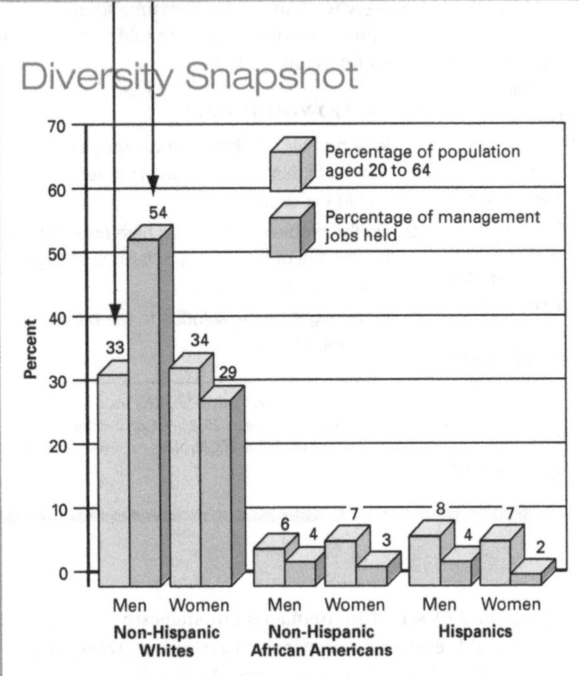

FIGURE 3 **U.S. Managers in Private Industry by Race, Sex, and Ethnicity, 2006**

White men are more likely than their population size suggests to be managers in private industry. The opposite is true for white women and other minorities. What factors do you think may account for this pattern?

Sources: U.S. Census Bureau (2008) and U.S. Equal Employment Opportunity Commission (2008).

underrepresented people in an organization often feel like socially isolated out-groups—uncomfortably visible, taken less seriously, and given fewer chances for promotion. Sometimes what passes for "merit" or good work in an organization is simply being of the right social category (Castilla, 2008).

Opening up an organization so that change and advancement happen more often, Kanter claims, improves everyone's on-the-job performance by motivating employees to become "fast-trackers" who work harder and are more committed to the company. By contrast, an organization with many dead-end jobs turns workers into less productive "zombies" who are never asked for their opinion on anything. An open organization encourages leaders to seek out the input of all employees, which usually improves decision making.

The "Female Advantage"

Some organizational researchers argue that women bring special management skills that strengthen an organization. According to Deborah Tannen (1994), women have a greater "information focus" and more readily ask questions in order to understand an issue. Men, by contrast, have an "image focus" that makes them wonder how asking questions in a particular situation will affect their reputation.

In another study of women executives, Sally Helgesen (1990) found three other gender-linked patterns. First, women place greater value on communication skills than men and share information more than men do. Second, women are more flexible leaders who typically give their employees greater freedom. Third, compared to men, women tend to emphasize the interconnectedness of all organizational operations. These patterns, which Helgesen dubbed the *female advantage,* help make companies more flexible and democratic.

In sum, one challenge to conventional bureaucracy is to become more open and flexible in order to take advantage of the experience, ideas, and creativity of everyone, regardless of race or gender. The result goes right to the bottom line: greater profits.

The Second Challenge: The Japanese Work Organization

In 1980, the U.S. corporate world was shaken to discover that the most popular automobile model sold in this country was not a Chevrolet, Ford, or Plymouth but the Honda Accord, made in Japan. Recently, the Japanese corporation Toyota passed General Motors to become the largest carmaker in the world (Fowler, 2008). This is quite a change. As late as the 1950s, U.S. automakers dominated car production, and the label "Made in Japan" was generally found on products that were cheap and poorly made. The success of the Japanese auto industry, as well as companies making cameras and other products, drew attention to the "Japanese work organization." How was so small a country able to challenge the world's economic powerhouse?

Japanese organizations reflect that nation's strong collective spirit. In contrast to the U.S. emphasis on rugged individualism, the Japanese value cooperation. In effect, formal organizations in Japan are more like large primary groups. A generation ago, William Ouchi (1981) highlighted five differences between formal organizations in Japan and those in the United States. First, Japanese companies hired new workers in groups, giving everyone the same salary and responsibilities. Second, many Japanese companies hired workers for life, fostering a strong sense of loyalty. Third, with the idea that employees would spend their entire careers there, many Japanese companies trained workers in all phases of their operations. Fourth, although Japanese corporate leaders took final responsibility for their organization's performance, they involved workers in "quality circles" to discuss decisions that affected them. Fifth, Japanese companies played a large role in the lives of workers, providing home mortgages, sponsoring recreational activities, and scheduling social events. Together, such policies encourage much more loyalty among members of Japanese organizations than is typically the case in their U.S. counterparts.

SEEING SOCIOLOGY in Everyday Life

Have you ever had a "dead-end" job? A job that demanded creativity? Which would you prefer and why?

Not everything has worked well for Japan's corporations. About 1990, the Japanese economy entered a recession that lasted more than a decade, and recent years have seen another wave of economic setbacks. Pressured by the need to cut costs, many Japanese companies have changed their policies, no longer offering workers jobs for life or many of the other benefits noted by Ouchi. But the long-term outlook for Japan's business organizations remains bright.

The Third Challenge: The Changing Nature of Work

Beyond rising global competition and the need to provide equal opportunity for all, pressure to modify conventional organizations is coming from changes in the nature of work itself. Recall the shift from industrial to postindustrial production. Rather than working in factories using heavy machinery to make *things,* more and more people are using computers and other electronic technology to create or process *information.* The postindustrial society, then, is characterized by information-based organizations.

Frederick Taylor developed his concept of scientific management at a time when jobs involved tasks that, though often backbreaking, were routine and repetitive. Workers shoveled coal, poured liquid iron into molds, welded body panels to automobiles on an assembly line, or shot hot rivets into steel girders to build skyscrapers. In addition, many of the industrial workers in Taylor's day were immigrants, most of whom had little schooling and many of whom knew little English. The routine nature of industrial jobs, coupled with the limited skills of the labor force, led Taylor to treat work as a series of fixed tasks, set down by management and followed by employees.

Many of today's information age jobs are very different: The work of designers, artists, writers, composers, programmers, business owners, and others now demands individual creativity and imagination. Here are several ways in which today's organizations differ from those of a century ago:

1. **Creative freedom.** As one Hewlett-Packard executive put it, "From their first day of work here, people are given important responsibilities and are encouraged to grow" (cited in Brooks, 2000:128). Today's organizations now treat employees with information age skills as a vital resource. Executives can set production goals but cannot dictate how a worker is to accomplish tasks that require imagination and discovery. This gives highly skilled workers *creative freedom,* which means less day-to-day supervision as long as they generate good results in the long run.
2. **Competitive work teams.** Organizations typically give several groups of employees the freedom to work on a problem, offering the greatest rewards to those who come up with the best solution. Competitive work teams, a strategy first used by Japanese organizations, draw out the creative contributions of everyone and at the same time reduce the alienation often found in conventional organizations (Maddox, 1994; Yeatts, 1994).
3. **A flatter organization.** By spreading responsibility for creative problem solving throughout the workforce, organizations take on a flatter shape. That is, the pyramid shape of conventional bureaucracy is replaced by an organizational form with fewer levels in the chain of command, as shown in Figure 4.
4. **Greater flexibility.** The typical industrial age organization was a rigid structure guided from the top. Such organizations may accomplish a large amount of work, but they are not especially creative or able to respond quickly to changes in the larger environment. The ideal model in the information age is a more open, *flexible* organization that both generates new ideas and, in a rapidly changing global marketplace, adapts quickly.

Fotolia, LLC – Royalty Free

During the last fifty years in the United States, women have moved into management positions throughout the corporate world. While some men initially opposed women's presence in the executive office, it is now clear that women bring particular strengths to the job, including leadership flexibility and communication skills. Thus, some analysts speak of women offering a "female advantage."

What does all this mean for formal organizations? As David Brooks puts it, "The machine is no longer held up as the standard that

SEEING SOCIOLOGY in Everyday Life

Is your college or university a top-down bureaucracy or a flatter, more flexible organization? How might you find out?

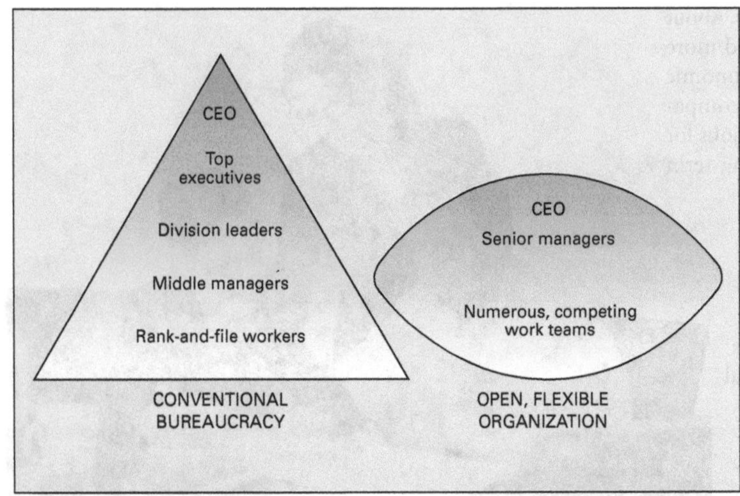

FIGURE 4 Two Organizational Models

The conventional model of bureaucratic organizations has a pyramid shape, with a clear chain of command. Orders flow from the top down, and reports of performance flow from the bottom up. Such organizations have extensive rules and regulations, and their workers have highly specialized jobs. More open and flexible organizations have a flatter shape, more like a football. With fewer levels in the hierarchy, responsibility for generating ideas and making decisions is shared throughout the organization. Many workers do their jobs in teams and have a broad knowledge of the entire organization's operation.

Source: Created by the author.

healthy organizations should emulate. Now it's the ecosystem" (2000:128). Today's "smart" companies seek out intelligent, creative people (AOL's main building is called "Creative Center 1") and nurture the growth of their talents.

Keep in mind, however, that many of today's jobs do not involve creative work at all. More correctly, the postindustrial economy has created two very different types of work: high-skill creative work and low-skill service work. Work in the fast-food industry, for example, is routine and highly supervised and thus has much more in common with the factory work of a century ago than with the creative teamwork typical of today's information organizations. Therefore, at the same time that some organizations have taken on a flexible, flatter form, others continue to use the rigid chain of command.

The "McDonaldization" of Society

As noted in the opening to this chapter, McDonald's has enjoyed enormous success, now operating more than 31,000 restaurants in the United States and around the world. Japan has more than 3,700 Golden Arches, and the world's largest McDonald's, which seats more than 1,000 customers, is located in China's capital city of Beijing.

McDonald's is far more than a restaurant chain; it is a symbol of U.S. culture. Not only do people around the world associate McDonald's with the United States, but here at home, one poll found that 98 percent of schoolchildren could identify Ronald McDonald, making him as well known as Santa Claus.

Even more important, the organizational principles that underlie McDonald's are coming to dominate our entire society. Our culture is becoming "McDonaldized," an awkward way of saying that we model many aspects of life on this restaurant chain: Parents buy toys at worldwide chain stores all carrying identical merchandise; we drop in for a ten-minute oil change while running errands; face-to-face communication is being replaced more and more by e-mail, voice mail, and instant messaging; more vacations take the form of resorts and tour packages; television packages the news in the form of ten-second sound bites; college admissions officers size up students they have never met by glancing at their GPA and SAT scores; and professors assign ghost-written textbooks[1] and evaluate students with tests mass-produced for them by publishing companies. The list goes on and on.

Four Principles

What do all these developments have in common? According to George Ritzer (1993), the McDonaldization of society rests on four organizational principles:

1. **Efficiency.** Ray Kroc, the marketing genius behind the expansion of McDonald's back in the 1950s, set out to serve a hamburger, French fries, and a milkshake to a customer in exactly fifty seconds. Today, one of the company's most popular menu items is the Egg McMuffin, an entire breakfast in a single sandwich. In the restaurant, customers dispose of their trash and stack their own trays as they walk out the door or, better still, drive away from the pickup window taking whatever mess they make with them. Such efficiency is now central to our way of life. We tend to think that anything done quickly is, for that reason alone, good.
2. **Predictability.** An efficient organization wants to make everything it does as predictable as possible. McDonald's prepares all food using set formulas. Company policies guide the performance of every job.

[1]A number of popular sociology books were not written by the person whose name appears on the cover. The book this chapter comes from is not one of them. Even the test bank that accompanies this text was written by the author.

SEEING SOCIOLOGY in Everyday Life

Can you point to examples of McDonaldization beyond those noted below? What are they?

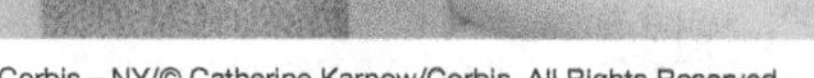

The best of today's information age jobs—including working at Google, the popular search engine Web site—allow people lots of personal freedom as long as they produce good ideas. At the same time, many other jobs, such as working the counter at McDonald's, involve the same routines and strict supervision found in factories a century ago.

3. **Uniformity.** The first McDonald's operating manual set the weight of a regular raw hamburger at 1.6 ounces, its size at 3.875 inches across, and its fat content at 19 percent. A slice of cheese weighs exactly half an ounce. Fries are cut precisely 9/32 of an inch thick.

   Think about how many objects around your home, the workplace, and the campus are designed and mass-produced according to a standard plan. Not just our environment but our life experiences—from traveling the nation's interstates to sitting at home viewing television—are more standardized than ever before.

   Almost anywhere in the world, a person can walk into a McDonald's restaurant and purchase the same sandwiches, drinks, and desserts prepared in precisely the same way.[2] Uniformity results from a highly rational system that specifies every action and leaves nothing to chance.

4. **Control.** The most unreliable element in the McDonald's system is the human beings who work there. After all, people have good and bad days, sometimes let their minds wander, or simply decide to try something a different way. To minimize the unpredictable human element, McDonald's has automated its equipment to cook food at a fixed temperature for a set length of time. Even the cash register at McDonald's is keyed to pictures of the items so that ringing up a customer's order is as simple as possible.

   Similarly, automatic teller machines are replacing bank tellers, highly automated bakeries now produce bread while people stand back and watch, and chickens and eggs (or is it eggs and chickens?) emerge from automated hatcheries. In supermarkets, laser scanners at self-checkouts are phasing out human checkers. We do most of our shopping in malls, where everything from temperature and humidity to the kinds of stores and products is carefully controlled and supervised (Ide & Cordell, 1994).

Can Rationality Be Irrational?

There is no doubt about the popularity or efficiency of McDonald's. But there is another side to the story.

Max Weber was alarmed at the increasing rationalization of the world, fearing that formal organizations would cage our imaginations and crush the human spirit. As Weber saw it, rational systems were efficient but dehumanizing. McDonaldization bears him out. Each of the four principles just discussed limits human creativity, choice, and freedom. Echoing Weber, Ritzer states that "the ultimate irrationality of McDonaldization is that people could lose control

[2] As McDonald's has "gone global," a few products have been added or changed according to local tastes. For example, in Uruguay, customers enjoy the McHuevo (hamburger with poached egg on top); Norwegians can buy McLaks (grilled salmon sandwiches); the Dutch favor the Groenteburger (vegetable burger); in Thailand, McDonald's serves Samurai pork burgers (pork burgers with teriyaki sauce); the Japanese can purchase a Chicken Tatsuta Sandwich (chicken seasoned with soy and ginger); Filipinos eat McSpaghetti (spaghetti with tomato sauce and bits of hot dog); and in India, where Hindus eat no beef, McDonald's sells a vegetarian Maharaja Mac (B. Sullivan, 1995).

MAKING THE GRADE

The McDonaldization thesis is that rational organization is coming to define our way of life and this trend is in important ways harmful to our well-being.

CONTROVERSY & DEBATE

Computer Technology, Large Organizations, and the Assault on Privacy

JAKE: I'm doing MySpace. It's really cool.

DUNCAN: Why do you want to put your whole life out there for everyone to see?

JAKE: I'm famous, man!

DUNCAN: Famous? Ha! You're throwing away whatever privacy you have left.

Jake completes a page on MySpace.com, which includes his name and college, e-mail address, photo, biography, and current personal interests. It can be accessed by billions of people around the world.

Late for a meeting with a new client, Sarah drives her car through a yellow light as it turns red at a main intersection. A computer linked to a pair of cameras notes the violation and takes one picture of her license plate and another of her sitting in the driver's seat. In seven days, she receives a summons to appear in traffic court.

Julio looks through his mail and finds a letter from a Washington, D.C., data services company telling him that he is one of about 145,000 people whose name, address, Social Security number, and credit file have recently been sold to criminals in California posing as businesspeople. With this information, other people can obtain credit cards or take out loans in his name.

These are all cases showing that today's organizations—which know more about us than ever before and more than most of us realize—pose a growing threat to personal privacy. Large organizations are necessary for today's society to operate. In some cases, organizations using information about us may actually be helpful. But cases of identity theft are on the rise, and personal privacy is on the decline.

In the past, small-town life gave people little privacy. But at least if people knew something about you, you were just as likely to know something about them. Today, unknown people "out there" can access information about each of us all the time without our learning about it.

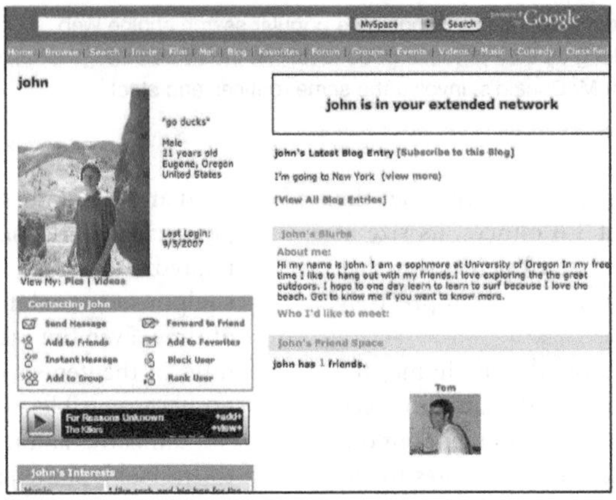

In part, the loss of privacy is a result of more and more complex computer technology. Are you aware that every e-mail you send and every Web site you visit leaves a record in one or more computers? These records can be retrieved by people you don't know, as well as by employers and other public officials.

Another part of today's loss of privacy reflects the number and size of formal organizations. As explained in this chapter, large organizations tend to treat people impersonally, and they have a huge appetite for information. Mix large organizations with ever more complex computer technology, and it is no wonder that

Lillian Graeble

over the system and it would come to control us" (1993:145). Perhaps even McDonald's understands this—the company has now expanded its more upscale offerings to include premium roasted coffee and salad selections that are more sophisticated, fresh, and healthful (Philadelphia, 2002).

The Future of Organizations: Opposing Trends

Early in the twentieth century, ever-larger organizations arose in the United States, most taking on the bureaucratic form described by Max Weber. In many respects, these organizations resembled armies led by powerful generals who issued orders to their captains and lieutenants. Foot soldiers, working in the factories, did what they were told.

With the emergence of a postindustrial economy around 1950, as well as rising competition from abroad, many organizations evolved toward a flatter, more flexible model that prizes communication and creativity. Such "intelligent organizations" (Pinchot & Pinchot, 1993; Brooks, 2000) have become more productive than ever. Just as important, for highly skilled people who now enjoy creative freedom, these organizations cause less of the alienation that so worried Weber.

But this is only half the story. Although the postindustrial economy has created many highly skilled jobs over the past

SEEING SOCIOLOGY in Everyday Life

Have large organizations reduced your privacy in ways you don't like? Explain.

most people in the United States are concerned about who knows what about them and what people are doing with this information.

For decades, the level of personal privacy in the United States has been declining. Early in the twentieth century, when state agencies began issuing driver's licenses, for example, they generated files for every licensed driver. Today, officials can send this information at the touch of a button not only to the police but to all sorts of other organizations. The Internal Revenue Service and the Social Security Administration, as well as government agencies that benefit veterans, students, the unemployed, and the poor, all collect mountains of personal information.

Business organizations now do much the same thing, and many of the choices we make end up in a company's database. Most of us use credit—the U.S. population now has more than 1 billion credit cards, an average of five per adult—but the companies that do "credit checks" collect and distribute information about us to almost anyone who asks, including criminals planning to steal our identity.

Then there are the small cameras found not only at traffic intersections but also in stores, public buildings, and parking garages and across college campuses. The number of surveillance cameras that monitor our movements is rapidly increasing with each passing year. So-called security cameras may increase public safety in some ways—say, by discouraging a mugger or even a terrorist—at the cost of the little privacy we have left. In the United Kingdom, probably the world leader in the use of security camera, the typical resident of London appears on closed-circuit television about 300 times every day, and all this "tracking" is stored in computer files.

In terms of government monitoring of the population, the United States is not far behind. After the September 11, 2001, terrorist attacks, the federal government took steps (including passage of the USA PATRIOT Act) to strengthen national security. Today, government officials closely monitor not only people entering the country but also the activities of all of us. It is possible that these efforts increase national security, but it is certain that they erode personal privacy.

Some legal protections remain. Each of the fifty states has laws that give citizens the right to examine some records about themselves kept by employers, banks, and credit bureaus. The federal Privacy Act of 1974 also limits the exchange of personal information among government agencies and permits citizens to examine and correct most government files. In response to rising levels of identity theft, Congress is likely to pass more laws to regulate the sale of credit information. But so many organizations, private as well as public, now have information about us—experts estimate that 90 percent of U.S. households are profiled in databases somewhere—that current laws simply cannot effectively address the privacy problem.

WHAT DO YOU THINK?

1. Do you think that the use of surveillance cameras in public places enhances our personal security? Does it threaten our privacy? Would you limit such surveillance? Why or why not?
2. Do you use Internet sites such as MySpace.com? Why do you think so many young people are eager to spread personal information in this way?
3. Automatic toll payment technology allows traffic to move more quickly through toll gates on our highways but also collects information on which cars are where and when they get there. Do you have any concerns that such technology will be used in ways no one now expects?

Sources: "Online Privacy" (2000), A. Hamilton (2001), Heymann (2002), O'Harrow (2005), Tingwall (2008), and Werth (2008).

half-century, it has created even more routine service jobs, such as those offered by McDonald's. Fast-food companies now represent the largest pool of low-wage labor, aside from migrant workers, in the United States (Schlosser, 2002). Work of this kind, which Ritzer terms "McJobs," offers few of the benefits that today's highly skilled workers enjoy. On the contrary, the automated routines that define work in the fast-food industry, telemarketing, and similar fields are very much the same as those that Frederick Taylor described a century ago.

Today, organizational flexibility gives better-off workers more freedom but often means the threat of "downsizing" and job loss for many rank-and-file employees. Organizations facing global competition seek out creative employees, but they are also eager to cut costs by eliminating as many routine jobs as possible. The net result is that some people are better off than ever, while others worry about holding their jobs and struggle to make ends meet.

U.S. organizations are the envy of the world for their productive efficiency. For example, there are few places on Earth where the mail arrives as quickly and dependably as it does in this country. But we should remember that the future is far brighter for some workers than for others. In addition, as the Controversy & Debate box explains, organizations pose an increasing threat to our privacy—something to keep in mind as we envision our organizational future.

Seeing Sociology in Everyday Life

Groups and Organizations

What have we learned about the way modern society is organized?

This chapter explains that since the opening of the first McDonald's restaurant in 1948, the principles that underlie the fast food industry—efficiency, predictability, uniformity, and control—have spread to many aspects of our everyday lives. Here is a chance to identify aspects of McDonaldization in several familiar routines. In each of the two photos on the facing page, can you identify specific elements of McDonaldization? That is, in what ways does the organizational pattern or the technology involved increase efficiency, predictability, uniformity, and control? In the photo below, what elements do you see that are clearly not McDonaldization? Why?

HINT This process, which is described as the "McDonaldization of society," has made our lives easier in some ways, but it has also made our society ever more impersonal, gradually diminishing our range of human contact. Also, although this organizational pattern is intended to serve human needs, it may end up doing the opposite by forcing people to live according to the demands of machines. Max Weber feared that our future would be an overly rational world in which we all might lose much of our humanity.

Small, privately owned stores like this one were once the rule in the United States. But the number of "mom and pop" businesses is declining as "big box" discount stores expand. Why are small stores disappearing? What social qualities of these stores are we losing in the process?

PhotoEdit Inc./Don Smetzer

Automated teller machines became common in the United States in the early 1970s. A customer with an electronic identification card can complete certain banking operations (such as withdrawing cash) without having to deal with a human bank teller. What makes the ATM one example of McDonaldization? Do you enjoy using an ATM? Why or why not?

Robert Harbison

At checkout counters in many supermarkets, customers lift each product through a laser scanner linked to a computer in order to identify what the product is and what it costs. The customer then inserts a credit or debit card to pay for the purchases.

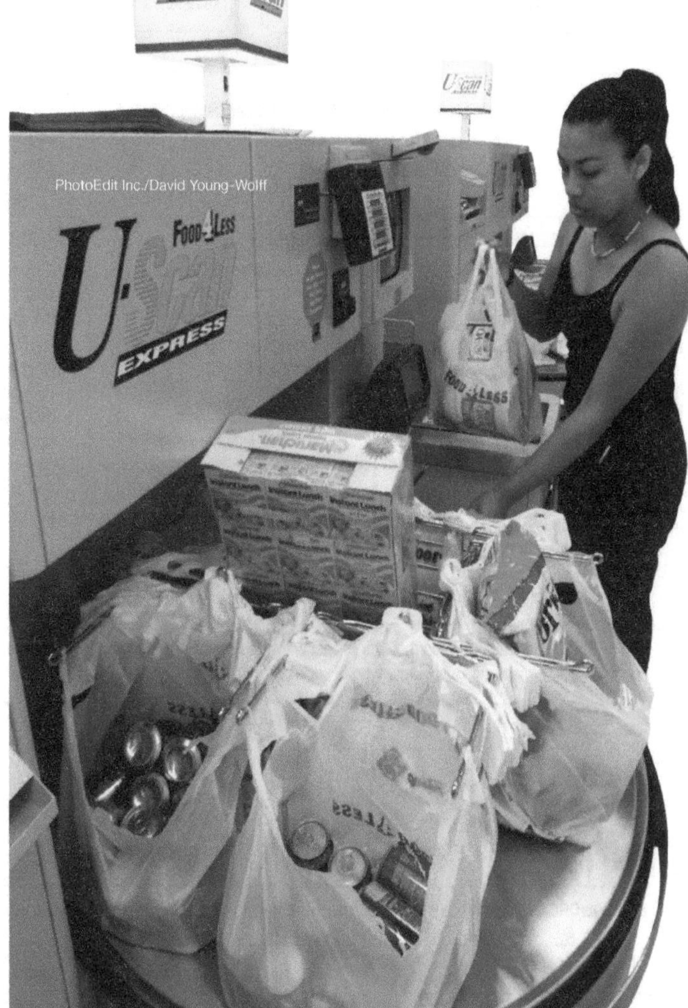

PhotoEdit Inc./David Young-Wolff

Applying SOCIOLOGY in Everyday Life

1. Have colleges and universities been affected by the process called McDonaldization? Do large, anonymous lecture courses qualify as an example? Why? What other examples of McDonaldization can you identify on the college campus?
2. Visit any large public building with an elevator. Observe groups of people as they approach the elevator, and enter the elevator with them. Watch their behavior: What happens to conversations as the elevator doors close? Where do people fix their eyes? Can you explain these patterns?
3. Using campus publications or your school's Web page (and some assistance from an instructor), try to draw an organizational pyramid for your college or university. Show the key offices and how they supervise and report to one another.

VISUAL SUMMARY

MAKING THE GRADE

Groups and Organizations

What Are Social Groups?

SOCIAL GROUPS are two or more people who identify with and interact with one another.

A **PRIMARY GROUP** is small, personal, and lasting (examples include family and close friends).

A **SECONDARY GROUP** is large, impersonal and goal-oriented, and often of shorter duration (examples include a college class or a corporation).

See the Summing Up table. "Primary Groups and Secondary Groups."

Elements of Group Dynamics

GROUP LEADERSHIP
- *Instrumental leadership* focuses on completing tasks.
- *Expressive leadership* focuses on a group's well-being.
- *Authoritarian leadership* is a "take charge" style that demands obedience; *democratic leadership* includes everyone in decision making; *laissez-faire leadership* lets the group function mostly on its own.

GROUP CONFORMITY
- The Asch, Milgram, and Janis research shows that group members often seek agreement and may pressure one another toward conformity.
- Individuals use *reference groups*—including both *in-groups* and *out-groups*—to form attitudes and make evaluations.

GROUP SIZE and **DIVERSITY**
- Georg Simmel described the *dyad* as intense but unstable; the *triad*, he said, is more stable but can dissolve into a dyad by excluding one member.
- Peter Blau claimed that larger groups turn inward, socially diverse groups turn outward, and physically segregated groups turn inward.

NETWORKS are relational webs that link people with little common identity and limited interaction. Being "well connected" in networks is a valuable type of social capital.

social group two or more people who identify with and interact with one another

primary group a small social group whose members share personal and lasting relationships

secondary group a large and impersonal social group whose members pursue a specific goal or activity

instrumental leadership group leadership that focuses on the completion of tasks

expressive leadership group leadership that focuses on the group's well-being

groupthink the tendency of group members to conform, resulting in a narrow view of some issue

reference group a social group that serves as a point of reference in making evaluations and decisions

in-group a social group toward which a member feels respect and loyalty

out-group a social group toward which a person feels a sense of competition or opposition

dyad a social group with two members

triad a social group with three members

network a web of weak social ties

What Are Formal Organizations?

FORMAL ORGANIZATIONS are large secondary groups organized to achieve their goals efficiently.

UTILITARIAN ORGANIZATIONS pay people for their efforts (examples include a business or government agency).

NORMATIVE ORGANIZATIONS have goals people consider worthwhile (examples include voluntary associations such as the PTA).

COERCIVE ORGANIZATIONS are organizations people are forced to join (examples include prisons and mental hospitals).

formal organization a large secondary group organized to achieve its goals efficiently

What Are Formal Organizations? *(continued)*

All formal organizations operate in an **ORGANIZATIONAL ENVIRONMENT,** which is influenced by
- technology
- political and economic trends
- current events
- population patterns
- other organizations

organizational environment factors outside an organization that affect its operation

See the Summing Up table, "Small Groups and Formal Organizations."

Modern Formal Organizations: Bureaucracy

BUREAUCRACY, which Max Weber saw as the dominant type of organization in modern societies, is based on
- specialization
- hierarchy of positions
- rules and regulations
- technical competence
- impersonality
- formal, written communications

PROBLEMS OF BUREAUCRACY include
- bureaucratic alienation
- bureaucratic inefficiency and ritualism
- bureaucratic inertia
- oligarchy

bureaucracy an organizational model rationally designed to perform tasks efficiently

bureaucratic ritualism a focus on rules and regulations to the point of undermining an organization's goals

bureaucratic inertia the tendency of bureaucratic organizations to perpetuate themselves

oligarchy the rule of the many by the few

scientific management Frederick Taylor's term for the application of scientific principles to the operation of a business or other large organization

The Evolution of Formal Organizations

CONVENTIONAL BUREAUCRACY

In the early 1900s, Frederick Taylor's **SCIENTIFIC MANAGEMENT** applied scientific principles to increase productivity.

MORE OPEN, FLEXIBLE ORGANIZATIONS

In the 1960s, Rosabeth Moss Kanter proposed that opening up organizations for all employees, especially women and other minorities, increased organizational efficiency.

In the 1980s, global competition drew attention to the Japanese work organization's collective orientation.

THE CHANGING NATURE OF WORK

Recently, the rise of a postindustrial economy has created two very different types of work:
- highly skilled and creative work (examples include designers, consultants, programmers, and executives)
- low-skilled service work associated with the "McDonaldization" of society, based on efficiency, uniformity, and control (examples include jobs in fast-food restaurants and telemarketing)

MAKING THE GRADE

Sample Test Questions

Multiple-Choice Questions

1. **What term did Charles Cooley give to a small social group whose members share personal and lasting relationships?**
   a. expressive group
   b. in-group
   c. primary group
   d. secondary group
2. **Which type of group leadership is concerned with getting the job done?**
   a. laissez-faire leadership
   b. secondary group leadership
   c. expressive leadership
   d. instrumental leadership
3. **The research done by Solomon Asch, in which subjects were asked to pick lines of the same length, showed that**
   a. groups encourage their members to conform.
   b. most people are stubborn and refuse to change their minds.
   c. groups often generate conflict.
   d. group members rarely agree on everything.
4. **What term refers to a social group that someone uses as a point of reference in making an evaluation or decision?**
   a. out-group
   b. reference group
   c. in-group
   d. primary group
5. **A network is correctly thought of as**
   a. the most close-knit social group.
   b. a category of people with something in common.
   c. a social group in which most people know one another.
   d. a web of weak social ties.
6. **From the point of view of a nurse, a hospital is a**
   a. normative organization.
   b. coercive organization.
   c. utilitarian organization.
   d. All of the above are correct.
7. **Bureaucracy is a type of social organization characterized by**
   a. specialized jobs.
   b. offices arranged in a hierarchy.
   c. lots of rules and regulations.
   d. All of the above are correct.
8. **According to Robert Michels, bureaucracy always means**
   a. inefficiency.
   b. oligarchy.
   c. alienation.
   d. specialization.
9. **Rosabeth Moss Kanter claims that large business organizations**
   a. need to "open up" opportunity to encourage workers to perform well.
   b. must have clear and stable rules to survive in a changing world.
   c. do well or badly depending on how talented the leader is.
   d. suffer if they do not adopt the latest technology.
10. **The "McDonaldization of society" implies that**
    a. organizations can provide food for people more efficiently than families can.
    b. impersonal organizations concerned with efficiency, uniformity, and control are becoming more and more common.
    c. it is possible for organizations to both do their job and meet human needs.
    d. society today is one vast social network.

ANSWERS: 1 (c); 2 (d); 3 (a); 4 (b); 5 (d); 6 (c); 7 (d); 8 (b); 9 (a); 10 (b).

Essay Questions

1. How do primary groups differ from secondary groups? Give examples of each in your own life.
2. According to Max Weber, what are the six traits that define bureaucracy? What is the advantage of this organizational form? What are several problems that often go along with it?

Deviance

Getty Images/Digital Vision/Chase Jarvis

We are all familiar with the experience of being "different." Deviance—standing out by not conforming to what is normal or expected—results not just from individual choice but also from the operation and norms of society.

© 2007 Ron Chapple Stock

Deviance

Getty Images/Digital Vision/James Lauritz

Getty Images, Inc. – Stockbyte Royalty Free

CHAPTER OVERVIEW

This chapter investigates how society encourages both conformity and deviance and also provides an introduction to crime and the criminal justice system.

© Santa Fabio Photography

"I was like the guy lost in another dimension, a stranger in town, not knowing which way to go." With these words, Bruce Glover recalls the day he returned to his hometown of Detroit, Michigan, after being away for twenty-six years—a long stretch in a state prison. Glover was a young man of thirty when he was arrested for running a call girl ring. Found guilty at trial, he was given a stiff jail sentence.

"My mother passed while I was gone," Glover continues, shaking his head. "I lost everything." On the day he walked out of prison, he realized just how true that statement was. He had nowhere to go and no way to get there. He had no valid identification, which he would need to find a place to live and a job. He had no money to buy the clothes he needed to go out and start looking. He turned to a prison official and asked for help. A state agency finally provided some money and temporary housing to get him started on his journey (C. Jones, 2007).

This chapter explores crime, criminals, and punishment, showing that individuals convicted of wrongdoing do not always fit the common stereotype of the "street criminal." The chapter also tackles the larger question of why societies develop standards of right and wrong in the first place. As you will see, law is simply one part of a complex system of social control: Society teaches us all to conform, at least most of the time, to countless rules. We begin our investigation by defining several basic concepts.

What Is Deviance?

Deviance is *the recognized violation of cultural norms.* Norms guide almost all human activities, so the concept of deviance is quite broad. One category of deviance is **crime**, *the violation of a society's formally enacted criminal law.* Even criminal deviance spans a wide range, from minor traffic violations to prostitution, sexual assault, and murder.

Most familiar examples of nonconformity are negative instances of rule breaking, such as stealing from a campus bookstore, assaulting a fellow student, or driving while intoxicated. But we also define especially righteous people—students who speak up too much in class or people who are overly enthusiastic about new computer technology—as deviant, even if we give them a measure of respect. What deviant actions or attitudes, whether negative or positive, have in common is some element of *difference* that causes us to think of another person as an "outsider" (H. S. Becker, 1966).

Not all deviance involves action or even choice. The very *existence* of some categories of people can be troublesome to others. To the young, elderly people may seem hopelessly "out of it," and to some whites, the mere presence of people of color may cause discomfort. Able-bodied people often view people with disabilities as an out-group, just as rich people may shun the poor for falling short of their standards.

Social Control

All of us are subject to **social control**, *attempts by society to regulate people's thoughts and behavior.* Often this process is informal, as when parents praise or scold their children or when friends make fun of a classmate's choice of music or style of dress. Cases of serious deviance, however, may involve the **criminal justice system**, *the organizations—police, courts, and prison officials—that respond to alleged violations of the law.*

How a society defines deviance, who is branded as deviant, and what people decide to do about deviance all have to do with the way society is organized. Only gradually, however, have people recognized that deviance is much more than a matter of individual choice.

The Biological Context

A century ago, most people assumed—incorrectly, as it turns out—that human behavior was the result of biological instincts. Early interest in criminality thus focused on biological causes. In 1876, Cesare

deviance the recognized violation of cultural norms

crime the violation of a society's formally enacted criminal law

social control attempts by society to regulate people's thoughts and behavior

criminal justice system the organizations—police, courts, and prison officials—that respond to alleged violations of the law

Lombroso (1835–1909), an Italian physician who worked in prisons, theorized that criminals stand out physically, with low foreheads, prominent jaws and cheekbones, hairiness, and unusually long arms. In other words, Lombroso claimed that criminals look like our ape-like ancestors.

Had Lombroso looked more carefully, he would have found the physical features he linked to criminality throughout the entire population. We now know that no physical traits distinguish criminals from noncriminals.

In the middle of the twentieth century, William Sheldon took a different approach, suggesting that general body structure might predict criminality (Sheldon, Hartl, & McDermott, 1949). He cross-checked hundreds of young men for body type and criminal history and concluded that criminality was most likely among boys with muscular, athletic builds. Sheldon Glueck and Eleanor Glueck (1950) confirmed Sheldon's conclusion but cautioned that a powerful build does not necessarily *cause* criminality. Parents, they suggested, tend to be somewhat distant from powerfully built sons, who in turn grow up to show less sensitivity toward others. Moreover, in a self-fulfilling prophecy, people who expect muscular boys to be bullies may act in ways that bring about the aggressive behavior they expect.

Today, genetics research seeks possible links between biology and crime. In 2003, scientists at the University of Wisconsin reported results of a twenty-five-year study of crime among 400 boys. The researchers collected DNA samples from each boy and noted any trouble he had had with the law. The researchers concluded that genetic factors (especially defective genes that, say, make too much of an enzyme) together with environmental factors (especially abuse early in life) were strong predictors of adult crime and violence. They noted, too, that these factors together were a better predictor of crime than either one alone (Lemonick, 2003; Pinker, 2003).

CRITICAL REVIEW Biological theories offer a limited explanation of crime. The best guess at present is that biological traits in combination with environmental factors explain some serious crime. But the biggest problem with this approach is that most of the actions we define as deviant are carried out by people who are biologically quite normal.

In addition, because a biological approach looks at the individual, it offers no insight into how some kinds of behaviors come to be defined as deviant in the first place. Therefore, although there is much to be learned about how human biology may affect behavior, research currently puts far greater emphasis on social influences.

CHECK YOUR LEARNING What does biological research add to our understanding of crime? What are the limitations of this approach?

The Image Works/Melissa Moore

Deviance is always a matter of difference. Deviance emerges in everyday life as we encounter people whose appearance or behavior differs from what we consider "normal." Who is the "deviant" in this photograph? From whose point of view?

Personality Factors

Like biological theories, psychological explanations of deviance focus on abnormality in the individual personality. Some personality traits are inherited, but most psychologists think that personality is shaped primarily by social experience. Deviance, then, is viewed as the result of "unsuccessful" socialization.

Classic research by Walter Reckless and Simon Dinitz (1967) illustrates the psychological approach. Reckless and Dinitz began by asking a number of teachers to categorize twelve-year-old male students as either likely or unlikely to get into trouble with the law. They then interviewed both the boys and their mothers to assess each boy's self-concept and how he related to others. Analyzing their results, Reckless and Dinitz found that the "good boys" displayed a strong conscience (what Freud called superego), could handle frustration, and identified with cultural norms and values. The "bad boys," by

MAKING THE GRADE

Deviance, the violation of norms, is a broad concept. Crime, the violation of formally enacted law, is one type of deviance.

contrast, had a weaker conscience, displayed little tolerance of frustration, and felt out of step with conventional culture.

As we might expect, the "good boys" went on to have fewer run-ins with the police than the "bad boys." Because all the boys lived in an area where delinquency was widespread, the investigators attributed staying out of trouble to a personality that controlled deviant impulses. Based on this conclusion, Reckless and Dinitz called their analysis *containment theory.*

CRITICAL REVIEW Psychologists have shown that personality patterns have some connection to deviance. Some serious criminals are psychopaths who do not feel guilt or shame, have no fear of punishment, and have little or no sympathy for the people they harm (Herpertz & Sass, 2000). However, as noted in the case of the biological approach, most serious crimes are committed by people whose psychological profiles are normal.

Both the biological and psychological approaches view deviance as a trait of individuals. The reason that these approaches have had limited value in explaining deviance is that wrongdoing has more to do with the organization of society. We now turn to a sociological approach, which explores where ideas of right and wrong come from, why people define some rule breakers but not others as deviant, and what role power plays in this process.

CHECK YOUR LEARNING Why do biological and psychological analyses not explain deviance very well?

Aurora Photos, Inc./Jose Azel

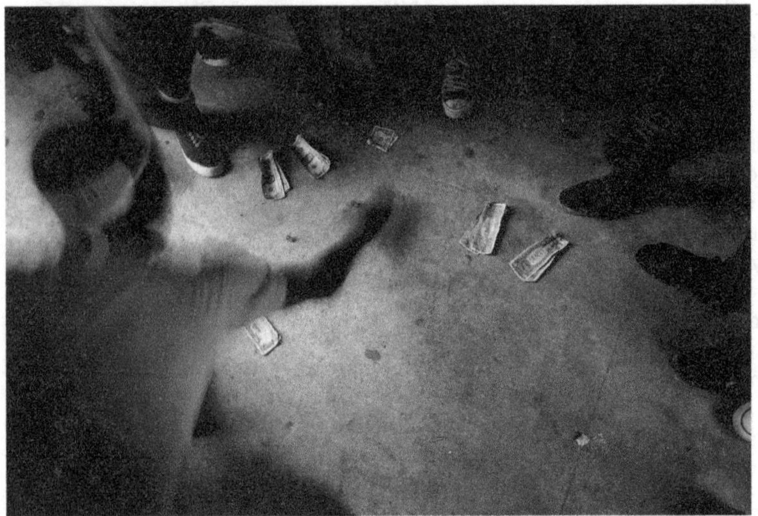

Why is it that street-corner gambling like this is usually against the law but playing the same games in a fancy casino is not?

The Social Foundations of Deviance

Although we tend to view deviance as the free choice or personal failings of individuals, all behavior—deviance as well as conformity—is shaped by society. Three social foundations of deviance identified here will be detailed later in this chapter:

1. **Deviance varies according to cultural norms.** No thought or action is inherently deviant; it becomes deviant only in relation to particular norms. Because norms vary from place to place, deviance also varies. State law permits prostitution in rural areas of Nevada, although the practice is outlawed in the rest of the United States. Twelve states have gambling casinos, twenty-nine permit casinos but only on Indian reservations, and four other states have casinos at race tracks. In all other states, casino gambling is illegal. Text messaging while driving is legal in forty-one states but against the law in six others (three other states forbid the practice for young drivers). Until the end of 2008, when a court struck down the law, only Florida legally banned gay men and lesbians from adopting a child (Csere, 2008; National Conference of State Legislatures, 2008c; Ruggeri, 2008; American Gaming Association, 2009).

   Further, most cities and towns have at least one unique law. For example, Mobile, Alabama, outlaws the wearing of stiletto-heeled shoes; Pine Lawn, Missouri, bans saggy, "low-rider" pants; in Juneau, Alaska, it is illegal to bring a flamingo into a barbershop; South Padre Island, Texas, bans the wearing of neckties; Mount Prospect, Illinois, has a law against keeping pigeons or bees; Topeka, Kansas, bans snowball fights; Hoover, South Dakota, does not allow fishing by the light of a kerosene lantern; and Beverly Hills, California, regulates the number of tennis balls allowed on the court at one time (R. Steele, 2000; Wittenauer, 2007).

   Around the world, deviance is even more diverse. Albania outlaws any public display of religious faith, such as crossing oneself; Cuba bans citizens from owning personal computers; Vietnam can prosecute citizens for meeting with foreigners; Malaysia does not allow women to wear tight-fitting jeans; Saudi Arabia bans the sale of red flowers on Valentine's Day; and Iran bans wearing makeup by women and forbids anyone from playing rap music (Chopra, 2008).

2. **People become deviant as others define them that way.** Everyone violates cultural norms at one time or another. Have you ever walked around talking to yourself or "borrowed" a pen from your workplace? Whether such behavior defines us as mentally ill or criminal depends on how others perceive, define, and respond to it.

MAKING THE GRADE

Notice that Durkheim considered deviance to be a natural and necessary part of all social organization.

SEEING SOCIOLOGY in Everyday Life

Keeping in mind Durkheim's claim that society creates deviance to mark moral boundaries, why do we often define people only in terms of their deviance by calling someone an "addict" or a "thief"?

3. **How societies set norms and how they define rule-breaking both involve social power.** The law, declared Karl Marx, is the means by which powerful people protect their interests. A homeless person who stands on a street corner speaking out against the government risks arrest for disturbing the peace; a mayoral candidate during an election campaign who does exactly the same thing gets police protection. In short, norms and how we apply them reflect social inequality.

AP Wide World Photos/Jim Cole

Durkheim claimed that deviance is a necessary element of social organization, serving several important functions. After a man convicted of killing a child settled in their New Hampshire town, residents came together to affirm their community ties as well as their understanding of right and wrong. Has any event on your campus caused a similar reaction?

The Functions of Deviance: Structural-Functional Analysis

The key insight of the structural-functional approach is that deviance is a necessary part of social organization. This point was made a century ago by Emile Durkheim.

Durkheim's Basic Insight

In his pioneering study of deviance, Emile Durkheim (1964a, orig. 1893; 1964b, orig. 1895) made the surprising claim that there is nothing abnormal about deviance. In fact, it performs four essential functions:

1. **Deviance affirms cultural values and norms.** As moral creatures, people must prefer some attitudes and behaviors to others. But any definition of virtue rests on an opposing idea of vice: There can be no good without evil and no justice without crime. Deviance is needed to define and support morality.
2. **Responding to deviance clarifies moral boundaries.** By defining some individuals as deviant, people draw a boundary between right and wrong. For example, a college marks the line between academic honesty and cheating by punishing students who cheat on exams.
3. **Responding to deviance brings people together.** People typically react to serious deviance with shared outrage. In doing so, Durkheim explained, they reaffirm the moral ties that bind them. For example, after the September 11, 2001, terrorist attacks, people across the United States were joined by a common desire to protect the country and bring those responsible to justice.
4. **Deviance encourages social change.** Deviant people push a society's moral boundaries, suggesting alternatives to the status quo and encouraging change. Today's deviance, declared Durkheim, can become tomorrow's morality (1964b:71, orig. 1895). For example, rock-and-roll, condemned as immoral in the 1950s, became a multibillion-dollar industry just a few years later; in recent years, hip-hop music has followed the same path.

An Illustration: The Puritans of Massachusetts Bay

Kai Erikson's classic study of the Puritans of Massachusetts Bay brings Durkheim's theory to life. Erikson (2005b, orig. 1966) shows that even the Puritans, a disciplined and highly religious group, created deviance to clarify their moral boundaries. In fact, Durkheim might well have had the Puritans in mind when he wrote this:

> Imagine a society of saints, a perfect cloister of exemplary individuals. Crimes, properly so called, will there be unknown; but faults which appear [insignificant] to the layman will create there the same scandal that the ordinary offense does in ordinary consciousness. . . . For the same reason, the perfect and upright man judges his smallest failings with a severity that the majority reserve for acts more truly in the nature of an offense. (1964b:68–69, orig. 1895)

Deviance is thus not a matter of a few "bad apples" but a necessary condition of "good" social living.

Deviance may be found in every society, but the *kind* of deviance people generate depends on the moral issues they seek to clarify. The Puritans, for example, experienced a number of "crime waves,"

MAKING THE GRADE

Merton's strain theory shows how people's opportunities (or lack of opportunities) to achieve cultural goals can encourage both deviance and conformity. In addition, what sociologists call people's "structure of opportunities" helps explain the type of deviance they engage in.

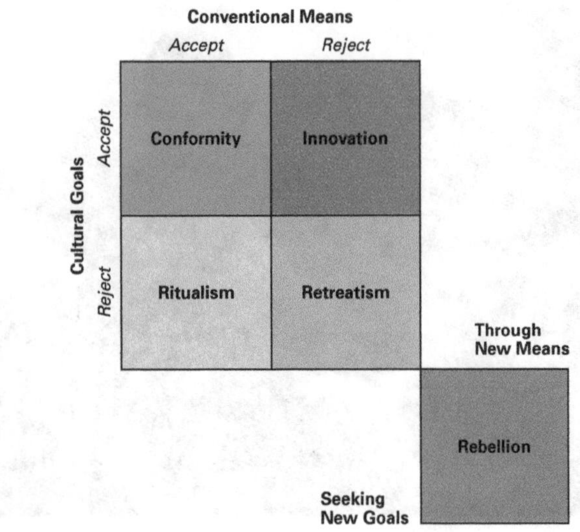

FIGURE 1 **Merton's Strain Theory of Deviance**

Combining a person's view of cultural goals and the conventional means to obtain them allowed Robert Merton to identify various types of deviance.

Source: Merton (1968).

including the well-known outbreak of witchcraft in 1692. With each response, the Puritans answered questions about the range of proper beliefs by celebrating some of their members and condemning others as deviant.

Erikson discovered that even though the offenses changed, the proportion of people the Puritans defined as deviant remained steady over time. This stability, he concluded, confirms Durkheim's claim that society creates deviants to mark its changing moral boundaries. In other words, by constantly defining a small number of people as deviant, the Puritans maintained the moral shape of their society.

Merton's Strain Theory

Some deviance may be necessary for a society to function, but Robert Merton (1938, 1968) argued that society can be set up in a way that encourages too much deviance. In addition, he explained, the type of deviance people engage in depends on whether a society provides them the *means* (such as schooling and job opportunities) to achieve cultural *goals* (such as financial success). Merton's strain theory is illustrated in Figure 1.

Conformity lies in pursuing cultural goals through approved means. Thus the U.S. "success story" is someone who gains wealth and prestige through talent, schooling, and hard work. But not everyone who wants conventional success has the opportunity to attain it. For example, people raised in poverty may have little hope of becoming successful if they play by the rules. According to Merton, the strain between our culture's emphasis on wealth and the lack of opportunities to get rich may encourage some people, especially the poor, to engage in stealing, drug dealing, or other forms of street crime. Merton called this type of deviance *innovation*—using unconventional means (street crime) rather than conventional means (hard work at a "straight" job) to achieve a culturally approved goal (wealth).

The inability to reach a cultural goal may also prompt another type of deviance that Merton calls *ritualism*. For example, many people may not care much about becoming rich but rigidly stick to the rules (the conventional means) anyway in order to at least feel "respectable."

A third response to the inability to succeed is *retreatism*: rejecting both cultural goals and conventional means so that a person in effect "drops out." Some alcoholics, drug addicts, and street people can be described as retreatists. The deviance of retreatists lies in their unconventional lifestyle and also in what seems to be their willingness to live this way.

The fourth response to failure is *rebellion*. Like retreatists, rebels such as radical "survivalists" reject both the cultural definition of success and the conventional means of achieving it, but they go one step further by forming a counterculture supporting alternatives to the existing social order.

Deviant Subcultures

Richard Cloward and Lloyd Ohlin (1966) extended Merton's theory, proposing that crime results not simply from limited legitimate (legal) opportunity but also from readily accessible illegitimate (illegal) opportunity. In short, deviance or conformity arises from the *relative opportunity structure* that frames a person's life.

The life of Al Capone, a notorious gangster, illustrates Cloward and Ohlin's theory. As the son of poor immigrants, Capone faced barriers of poverty and ethnic prejudice, which lowered his odds of achieving success in conventional terms. Yet as a young man during Prohibition (when alcoholic beverages were banned in the United States between 1920 and 1933), Capone found in his neighborhood people who could teach him how to sell alcohol illegally—a source of illegitimate opportunity. Where the structure of opportunity favors criminal activity, Cloward and Ohlin predict the development of *criminal subcultures*, such as Capone's criminal organization or today's inner-city street gangs.

But what happens when people are unable to find *any* opportunity, legal or illegal? Then deviance may take one of two forms. One is *conflict subcultures*, such as armed street gangs that engage in violence out of frustration and a desire for respect. Another possible

MAKING THE GRADE

Study the definition of labeling theory, which is the key idea of the symbolic-interaction approach. Be sure you understand this statement: Deviance results not so much from what people do as from how others respond to what they do.

outcome is the development of *retreatist subcultures,* in which deviants drop out and abuse alcohol or other drugs.

Albert Cohen (1971, orig. 1955) suggests that delinquency is most common among lower-class youths because they have the least opportunity to achieve conventional success. Neglected by society, they seek self-respect by creating a delinquent subculture that defines as worthy the traits these youths do have. Being feared on the street may not win many points with society as a whole, but it may satisfy a young person's desire to "be somebody" in the local neighborhood.

Walter Miller (1970, orig. 1958) adds that delinquent subcultures are characterized by (1) *trouble,* arising from frequent conflict with teachers and police; (2) *toughness,* the value placed on physical size and strength, especially among males; (3) *smartness,* the ability to succeed on the streets, to outsmart or "con" others, and to avoid being similarly taken advantage of; (4) a *need for excitement,* the search for thrills, risk, or danger; (5) a *belief in fate,* a sense that people lack control over their own lives; and (6) a *desire for freedom,* often expressed as anger toward authority figures.

Getty Images, Inc. – Agence France Presse/Hector Mata

Young people cut off from legitimate opportunity often form subcultures that many people view as deviant. Gang subcultures are one way young people gain the sense of belonging and respect denied to them by the larger culture.

Finally, Elijah Anderson (1994, 2002; Kubrin, 2005) explains that in poor urban neighborhoods, most people manage to conform to conventional or "decent" values. Yet faced with neighborhood crime and violence, indifference or even hostility from police, and sometimes neglect by their own parents, some young men decide to live by the "street code." To show that they can survive on the street, a young man displays "nerve," a willingness to stand up to any threat. Following this street code, which is also evident in much recent rap music, the young man believes that a violent death is better than being "dissed" (disrespected) by others. Some manage to escape the dangers, but the risk of ending up in jail—or worse—is very high for these young men, who have been pushed to the margins of our society.

CRITICAL REVIEW Durkheim made an important contribution by pointing out the functions of deviance. However, there is evidence that a community does not always come together in reaction to crime; sometimes fear of crime causes people to withdraw from public life (Liska & Warner, 1991; Warr & Ellison, 2000).

Merton's strain theory has been criticized for explaining some kinds of deviance (stealing, for example) better than others (such as crimes of passion or mental illness). In addition, not everyone seeks success in the conventional terms of wealth, as strain theory suggests.

The general argument of Cloward and Ohlin, Cohen, Miller, and Anderson—that deviance reflects the opportunity structure of society—has been confirmed by subsequent research (Allan & Steffensmeier, 1989; Uggen, 1999). However, these theories fall short by assuming that everyone shares the same cultural standards for judging right and wrong. In addition, if we define crime to include not only burglary and auto theft but also fraud and other crimes carried out by corporate executives and Wall Street tycoons, then more high-income people will be counted among criminals. There is evidence that people of all social backgrounds are becoming more casual about breaking the rules, as the Seeing Sociology in Everyday Life box explains.

Finally, all structural-functional theories suggest that everyone who breaks important rules will be labeled deviant. However, becoming deviant is actually a highly complex process, as the next section explains.

CHECK YOUR LEARNING Why do you think many of the theories just discussed seem to say that crime is more common among people with lower social standing?

Labeling Deviance: Symbolic-Interaction Analysis

The symbolic-interaction approach explains how people define deviance in everyday situations. From this point of view, definitions of deviance and conformity are surprisingly flexible.

SEEING SOCIOLOGY in Everyday Life

An old saying goes, "Sticks and stones can break my bones, but names can never hurt me." What might labeling theory have to say about this idea?

MAKING THE GRADE

The development of secondary deviance is one application of the Thomas theorem, which states that situations people define as real become real in their consequences.

SEEING SOCIOLOGY IN EVERYDAY LIFE

Deviant Subculture: Has It Become OK to Break the Rules?

Astrid: Simon! You're downloading that music illegally. You'll get us both into trouble!

Simon: Look, everyone cheats. Rich CEOs cheat in business. Ordinary people cheat on their taxes. Politicians lie. What else is new?

Astrid: So it's OK to steal? Is that what you really believe?

Simon: I'm not saying it's OK. I'm just saying everyone does it. . . .

It's been a bad couple of years for the idea of playing by the rules. First, we learn that the executives of not just one but many U.S. corporations are guilty of fraud and outright stealing on a scale most of us cannot even imagine. More recently, we realize that the Wall Street leaders running the U.S. economy not only did a pretty bad job of it but paid themselves tens of millions of dollars for doing so. And of course, even the Catholic church, which we hold up as a model of moral behavior, is still trying to recover from the charges that hundreds of priests have sexually abused parishioners (most of them teens and children) for decades while church officials covered up the crimes.

There are plenty of ideas about what is causing this widespread wrongdoing. Some people suggest that the pressure to win—by whatever means necessary—in today's highly competitive world of business and politics can be overwhelming. As one analyst put it, "You can get away with your embezzlements and your lies, but you can never get away with *failing*."

Such thinking helps explain the wrongdoing among many CEOs in the world of business and finance and the conviction of several members of Congress for ethics violations, but it offers little insight into the problem of abusive priests. In some ways at least, wrongdoing seems to have become a way of life for just about everybody.

Getty Images/Yellow Dog Productions

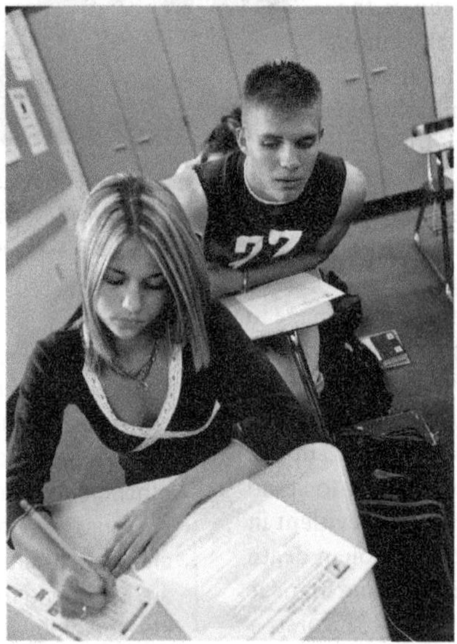

Do you consider cheating in school wrong? Would you turn in someone you saw cheating? Why or why not?

For example, the Internal Revenue Service reports that many U.S. taxpayers cheat on their taxes, failing to pay an estimated $345 billion each year. The music industry claims that it has lost billions of dollars to illegal piracy of recordings, a practice especially common among young people. Perhaps most disturbing of all, in surveys about half of high school and college students say that they have cheated on a test at least once during the past year (Gallup, 2004).

Emile Durkheim viewed society as a moral system built on a set of rules about what people should and should not do. Years earlier, another French thinker named Blaise Pascal made the contrasting claim that "cheating is the foundation of society." Today, which of the two statements is closer to the truth?

WHAT DO YOU THINK?

1. In your opinion, how widespread is wrongdoing in U.S. society today? Have you downloaded music illegally? What about cheating on your college assignments or tests?
2. Do you think people who break the rules usually think that their actions are wrong? Why or why not?
3. What do you think are the reasons for the apparent increase in dishonesty?

Sources: "Our Cheating Hearts" (2002), Bono (2006), and Lohr (2008).

Labeling Theory

The main contribution of symbolic-interaction analysis is **labeling theory**, *the idea that deviance and conformity result not so much from what people do as from how others respond to those actions.* Labeling theory stresses the relativity of deviance, meaning that people may define the same behavior in any number of ways.

Consider these situations: A college student takes a sweater off the back of a roommate's chair and packs it for a weekend trip, a married woman at a convention in a distant city has sex with an old boyfriend, and a city mayor gives a big contract to a major campaign contributor. We might define the first situation as carelessness, borrowing, or theft. The consequences of the second case depend largely on whether the woman's behavior becomes known back home. In the third situation, is the official choosing the best contractor or paying off a political debt? The social construction of reality is a highly variable process of detection, definition, and response.

Primary and Secondary Deviance

Edwin Lemert (1951, 1972) observed that some norm violations—say, skipping school or underage drinking—provoke slight reaction from

labeling theory the idea that deviance and conformity result not so much from what people do as from how others respond to those actions

stigma a powerfully negative label that greatly changes a person's self-concept and social identity

medicalization of deviance the transformation of moral and legal deviance into a medical condition

Explain in your own words sociologist Howard Becker's (1966) statement that deviance is nothing more than behavior that people define as deviant.

others and have little effect on a person's self-concept. Lemert calls such passing episodes *primary deviance.*

But what happens if people take notice of someone's deviance and really make something of it? After an audience has defined some action as primary deviance, the individual may begin to change, taking on a deviant identity by talking, acting, or dressing in a different way, rejecting the people who are critical, and repeatedly breaking the rules. Lemert (1951:77) calls this change of self-concept *secondary deviance.* He explains that "when a person begins to employ . . . deviant behavior as a means of defense, attack, or adjustment to the . . . problems created by societal reaction," deviance becomes secondary. For example, say that people have begun describing a young man as an "alcohol abuser," which establishes primary deviance. These people may then exclude him from their friendship network. His response may be to become bitter toward them, start drinking even more, and seek the company of others who approve of his drinking. These actions mark the beginning of secondary deviance, a deeper deviant identity.

Stigma

Secondary deviance marks the start of what Erving Goffman (1963) calls a *deviant career.* As people develop a stronger commitment to deviant behavior, they typically acquire a **stigma,** *a powerfully negative label that greatly changes a person's self-concept and social identity.*

A stigma operates as a master status, overpowering other aspects of social identity so that a person is discredited in the minds of others and becomes socially isolated. Often a person gains a stigma informally as others begin to see the individual in deviant terms. Sometimes, however, an entire community formally stigmatizes an individual through what Harold Garfinkel (1956) calls a *degradation ceremony.* A criminal trial is one example, operating much like a high school graduation ceremony in reverse: A person stands before the community and is labeled in negative rather than positive terms.

Retrospective and Projective Labeling

Once people stigmatize an individual, they may engage in *retrospective labeling,* interpreting someone's past in light of some present deviance (Scheff, 1984). For example, after discovering that a priest has sexually molested a child, others rethink his past, perhaps musing, "He always did want to be around young children." Retrospective labeling, which distorts a person's biography by being highly selective, typically deepens a deviant identity.

Similarly, people may engage in *projective labeling* of a stigmatized person, using the person's deviant identity to predict future actions. Regarding the priest, people might say, "He's going to keep at it until he gets caught." The more people in someone's social world think such things, the more these definitions affect the individual's self-concept, increasing the chance that they will come true.

Labeling Difference as Deviance

Is a homeless man who refuses to allow police to take him to a city shelter on a cold night simply trying to live independently, or is he "crazy"? People have a tendency to treat behavior that irritates or threatens them not simply as different but as deviance or even mental illness.

The psychiatrist Thomas Szasz (1961, 1970, 2003, 2004) charges that people are too quick to apply the label of mental illness to conditions that simply amount to a difference we don't like. The only way to avoid this troubling practice, Szasz continues, is to abandon the idea of mental illness entirely. The world is full of people who think or act differently in ways that may irritate us, but such differences are not grounds for defining someone as mentally ill. Such labeling, Szasz claims, simply enforces conformity to the standards of people powerful enough to impose their will on others.

Most mental health care professionals reject the idea that mental illness does not exist. But they agree that it is important to think critically about how we define "difference." First, people who are mentally ill are no more to blame for their condition than people who suffer from cancer or some other physical problem. Therefore, having a mental or physical illness is not grounds for being labeled deviant. Second, ordinary people without the medical knowledge to diagnose mental illness should avoid using such labels just to make people conform to their own standards of behavior.

The Medicalization of Deviance

Labeling theory, particularly the ideas of Szasz and Goffman, helps explain an important shift in the way our society understands deviance. Over the past fifty or sixty years, the growing influence of psychiatry and medicine in the United States has led to the **medicalization of deviance,** *the transformation of moral and legal deviance into a medical condition.*

Medicalization amounts to swapping one set of labels for another. In moral terms, we evaluate people or their behavior as "bad" or "good." However, the scientific objectivity of medicine passes no moral judgment, instead using clinical diagnoses such as "sick" or "well."

To illustrate, until the mid-twentieth century, people generally viewed alcoholics as morally weak people easily tempted by the pleasure of drink. Gradually, however, medical specialists redefined alcoholism so that most people now consider it a disease, rendering people "sick" rather than "bad." In the same way, obesity, drug addiction, child abuse, sexual promiscuity, and other behaviors that used to be strictly moral matters are widely defined today as illnesses for which people need help rather than punishment.

The Difference Labels Make

Whether we define deviance as a moral or a medical issue has three consequences. First, it affects *who responds* to deviance. An offense

MAKING THE GRADE

Deviance can be defined as either a moral or a medical issue. Be sure you understand the three key differences between defining deviance one way or the other.

AP Wide World Photos/Northern Star/Jim Killan

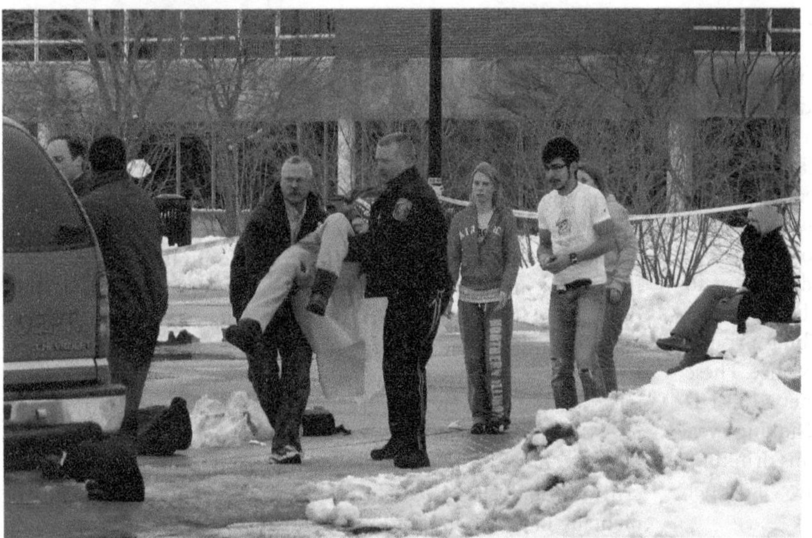

The nation was stunned by the 2008 rampage on the Northern Illinois University campus that left six people dead and eighteen injured. It is easy to imagine that a person who commits such a crime might be "crazy" or "sick." Or might you view the offender as "evil" or just very misguided?

against common morality usually brings about a reaction from members of the community or the police. A medical label, however, places the situation under the control of clinical specialists, including counselors, psychiatrists, and physicians.

A second issue is *how people respond* to deviance. A moral approach defines deviants as offenders subject to punishment. Medically, however, they are patients who need treatment. Punishment is designed to fit the crime, but treatment programs are tailored to the patient and may involve virtually any therapy that a specialist thinks might prevent future deviance.

Third, and most important, the two labels differ on the *personal competence of the deviant person.* From a moral standpoint, whether we are right or wrong, at least we take responsibility for our own behavior. Once we are defined as sick, however, we are seen as unable to control (or if "mentally ill," even to understand) our actions. People who are labeled incompetent are in turn subjected to treatment, often against their will. For this reason alone, attempts to define deviance in medical terms should be made with extreme caution.

Sutherland's Differential Association Theory

Learning any behavioral pattern, whether conventional or deviant, is a process that takes place in groups. According to Edwin Sutherland (1940), a person's tendency toward conformity or deviance depends on the amount of contact with others who encourage or reject conventional behavior. This is Sutherland's theory of *differential association.*

A number of research studies confirm the idea that young people are more likely to engage in delinquency if they believe members of their peer groups encourage such activity (Akers et al., 1979; Miller & Mathews, 2001). One investigation focused on sexual activity among eighth-grade students. Two strong predictors of such behavior for young girls was having a boyfriend who encouraged sexual relations and having girlfriends they believed would approve of such activity. Similarly, boys were encouraged to become sexually active by friends who rewarded them with high status in their peer group (Little & Rankin, 2001).

Hirschi's Control Theory

The sociologist Travis Hirschi (1969; Gottfredson & Hirschi, 1995) developed *control theory,* which states that social control depends on people anticipating the consequences of their behavior. Hirschi assumes that everyone finds at least some deviance tempting. But the thought of a ruined career keeps most people from breaking the rules; for some, just imagining the reactions of family and friends is enough. On the other hand, individuals who feel they have little to lose by deviance are likely to become rule breakers.

Specifically, Hirschi links conformity to four different types of social control:

1. **Attachment**. Strong social attachments encourage conformity. Weak family, peer, and school relationships leave people freer to engage in deviance.
2. **Opportunity**. The greater a person's access to legitimate opportunity, the greater the advantages of conformity. By contrast, someone with little confidence in future success is more likely to drift toward deviance.
3. **Involvement**. Extensive involvement in legitimate activities—such as holding a job, going to school, or playing sports—inhibits deviance (Langbein & Bess, 2002). By contrast, people who simply "hang out" waiting for something to happen have time and energy to engage in deviant activity.
4. **Belief**. Strong belief in conventional morality and respect for authority figures restrain tendencies toward deviance. People who have a weak conscience (and who are left unsupervised) are more open to temptation (Stack, Wasserman, & Kern, 2004).

SEEING SOCIOLOGY in Everyday Life

Why do you think that politicians and other well-known people who get into trouble with the law often claim they have a problem with alcohol or other drugs and check into "rehab"?

Hirschi's analysis combines a number of earlier ideas about the causes of deviant behavior. Note that a person's relative social privilege as well as family and community environment are likely to affect the risk of deviant behavior (Hope, Grasmick, & Pointon, 2003).

CRITICAL REVIEW The various symbolic-interaction theories all see deviance as a process. Labeling theory links deviance not to action but to the *reaction* of others. Thus some people are defined as deviant but others who think or behave in the same way are not. The concepts of secondary deviance, deviant career, and stigma show how being labeled deviant can become a lasting self-concept.

Yet labeling theory has several limitations. First, because it takes a highly relative view of deviance, labeling theory ignores the fact that some kinds of behavior—such as murder—are condemned just about everywhere. Therefore, labeling theory is most usefully applied to less serious issues, such as sexual promiscuity or mental illness. Second, research on the consequences of deviant labeling does not clearly show whether deviant labeling produces further deviance or discourages it (Smith & Gartin, 1989; Sherman & Smith, 1992). Third, not everyone resists being labeled deviant; some people actively seek it out (Vold & Bernard, 1986). For example, people take part in civil disobedience and willingly subject themselves to arrest in order to call attention to social injustice.

Sociologists consider Sutherland's differential association theory and Hirschi's control theory important contributions to our understanding of deviance. But why do society's norms and laws define certain kinds of activities as deviant in the first place? This question is addressed by social-conflict analysis, the focus of the next section.

CHECK YOUR LEARNING Clearly define primary deviance, secondary deviance, deviant career, and stigma.

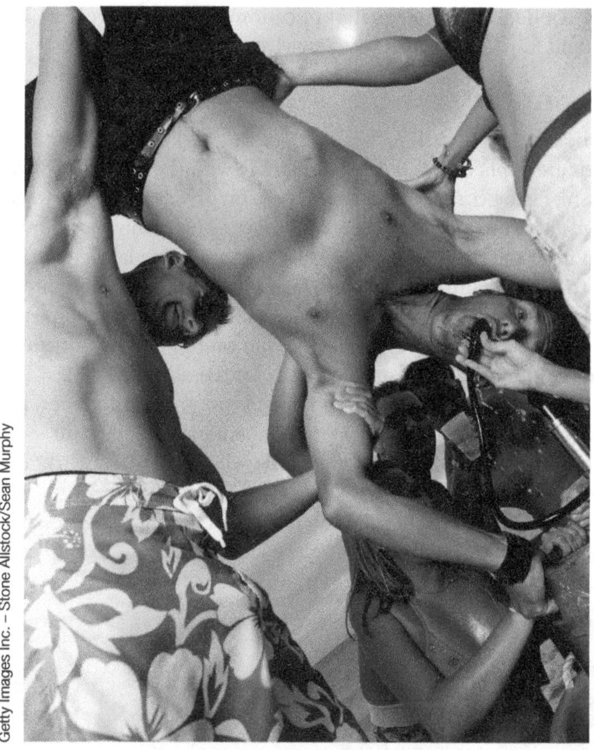

Getty Images Inc. - Stone Allstock/Sean Murphy

All social groups teach their members skills and attitudes that encourage certain behavior. In recent years, discussion on college campuses has focused on the dangers of binge drinking, which results in several dozen deaths each year among young people in the United States. How much of a problem is binge drinking on your campus?

Deviance and Inequality: Social-Conflict Analysis

The social-conflict approach links deviance to social inequality. That is, who or what is labeled deviant depends on which categories of people hold power in a society.

Deviance and Power

Alexander Liazos (1972) points out that the people we tend to define as deviants—the ones we dismiss as "nuts" and "sluts"—are typically not as bad or harmful as they are *powerless*. Bag ladies and unemployed men on street corners, not corporate polluters or international arms dealers, carry the stigma of deviance.

Social-conflict theory explains this pattern in three ways. First, all norms—especially the laws of any society—generally reflect the interests of the rich and powerful. People who threaten the wealthy are likely to be labeled deviant, either for taking people's property ("common thieves") or for advocating a more egalitarian society ("political radicals"). Karl Marx argued that the law and all other social institutions support the interests of the rich. Or as Richard Quinney puts it, "Capitalist justice is by the capitalist class, for the capitalist class, and against the working class" (1977:3).

Second, even if their behavior is called into question, the powerful have the resources to resist deviant labels. The majority of the executives involved in recent corporate scandals have yet to be arrested; only a few have gone to jail.

Third, the widespread belief that norms and laws are natural and good masks their political character. For this reason, although we

SEEING SOCIOLOGY in Everyday Life

How would a Marxist analysis explain the fact that hundreds of miners have died in coal mines in West Virginia and other states in recent decades without anyone being charged with any crime?

white-collar crime crime committed by people of high social position in the course of their occupations

corporate crime the illegal actions of a corporation or people acting on its behalf

organized crime a business supplying illegal goods or services

may condemn the unequal application of the law, we give little thought to whether the laws themselves are really fair or not.

Deviance and Capitalism

In the Marxist tradition, Steven Spitzer (1980) argues that deviant labels are applied to people who interfere with the operation of capitalism. First, because capitalism is based on private control of wealth, people who threaten the property of others—especially the poor who steal from the rich—are prime candidates for being labeled deviant. On the other hand, the rich who take advantage of the poor are less likely to be labeled deviant. For example, landlords who charge poor tenants high rents and evict anyone who cannot pay are not considered criminals; they are simply "doing business."

Second, because capitalism depends on productive labor, people who cannot or will not work risk being labeled deviant. Many members of our society think people who are out of work, even through no fault of their own, are somehow deviant.

Third, capitalism depends on respect for authority figures, causing people who resist authority to be labeled deviant. Examples are children who skip school or talk back to parents and teachers and adults who do not cooperate with employers or police.

Getty Images, Inc. - Agence France Presse/Christine Cornell

Perhaps no one better symbolized the greed that drove the Wall Street meltdown of 2008 than Bernard Madoff, who swindled thousands of people and organizations out of some $50 billion. In 2009, after pleading guilty to eleven felony counts, Madoff was sentenced to 150 years in prison. Do you think white-collar offenders are treated fairly by our criminal justice system? Why or why not?

Fourth, anyone who directly challenges the capitalist status quo is likely to be defined as deviant. Such has been the case with labor organizers, radical environmentalists, and antiwar activists.

On the other side of the coin, society positively labels whatever supports the operation of capitalism. For example, winning athletes enjoy celebrity status because they express the values of individual achievement and competition, both vital to capitalism. Also, Spitzer notes, we condemn using drugs of escape (marijuana, psychedelics, heroin, and crack) as deviant but encourage drugs (such as alcohol and caffeine) that promote adjustment to the status quo.

The capitalist system also tries to control people who are not economically productive. The elderly, people with mental or physical disabilities, and Robert Merton's retreatists (people addicted to alcohol or other drugs) are a "costly yet relatively harmless burden" on society. Such people, claims Spitzer, are subject to control by social welfare agencies. But people who openly challenge the capitalist system, including the inner-city underclass and revolutionaries—Merton's innovators and rebels—are controlled by the criminal justice system and, in times of crisis, military forces such as the National Guard.

Note that both the social welfare and criminal justice systems blame individuals, not the system, for social problems. Welfare recipients are considered unworthy freeloaders, poor people who express rage at their plight are labeled rioters, anyone who challenges the government is branded a radical or a communist, and those who try to gain illegally what they will never get legally are rounded up as common criminals.

White-Collar Crime

In a sign of things to come, a Wall Street stockbroker named Michael Milken made headlines back in 1987 when he was jailed for business fraud. Milken attracted attention because not since the days of Al Capone had anyone made so much money in one year: $550 million—about $1.5 million a day (Swartz, 1989).

Milken engaged in **white-collar crime**, defined by Edwin Sutherland (1940) as *crime committed by people of high social position in the course of their occupations*. White-collar crimes do not involve violence and rarely attract police to the scene with guns drawn. Rather, white-collar criminals use their powerful offices to illegally enrich themselves and others, often causing significant public harm in the process. For this reason, sociologists sometimes call white-collar offenses that occur in government offices and corporate boardrooms "crime in the suites" as opposed to "crime in the streets."

The most common white-collar crimes are bank embezzlement, business fraud, bribery, and antitrust violations. Sutherland (1940)

SEEING SOCIOLOGY in Everyday Life

Imagine police holding a street gang, but not its individual members, responsible for an outbreak of violence. What does this suggest about the link between crime and power?

MAKING THE GRADE

White-collar crime and corporate crime are similar concepts, and there is not always a clear line separating the two. White-collar criminals are *individuals* of high social position who commit crimes while doing their jobs. Corporate crime occurs when a *company* acts in violation of the law.

explains that such white-collar offenses typically end up in a civil hearing rather than a criminal courtroom. *Civil law* regulates business dealings between private parties, and *criminal law* defines the individual's moral responsibilities to society. In practice, then, someone who loses a civil case pays for damage or injury but is not labeled a criminal. Corporate officials are also protected by the fact that most charges of white-collar crime target the organization rather than individuals.

When white-collar criminals are charged and convicted, they usually escape punishment. A government study found that those convicted of fraud and punished with a fine ended up paying less than 10 percent of what they owed; most managed to hide or transfer their assets to avoid paying up. Among white-collar criminals convicted of the more serious crime of embezzlement, only about half ever served a day in jail. One accounting found that just 57 percent of the embezzlers convicted in the U.S. federal courts served prison sentences; the rest were put on probation or issued a fine (U.S. Bureau of Justice Statistics, 2008). As some analysts see it, until courts impose more prison terms, we should expect white-collar crime to remain widespread (Shover & Hochstetler, 2006).

Corporate Crime

Sometimes whole companies, not just individuals, break the law. **Corporate crime** is *the illegal actions of a corporation or people acting on its behalf.*

Corporate crime ranges from knowingly selling faulty or dangerous products to deliberately polluting the environment (Derber, 2004). The collapse of a number of major U.S. corporations in recent years cost tens of thousands of people their jobs and their pensions. Even more seriously, 111 people died in underground coal mines in 2006, 2007, and 2008; hundreds more died from "black lung" disease caused by years of inhaling coal dust. The death toll for all job-related hazards in the United States probably exceeds 50,000 each year (Frank, 2007; Jafari, 2008; U.S. Census Bureau, 2009).

Organized Crime

Organized crime is *a business supplying illegal goods or services.* Sometimes criminal organizations force people to do business with them, as when a gang extorts money from shopkeepers for "protection." In most cases, however, organized crime involves the sale of illegal goods and services—often sex, drugs, and gambling—to willing buyers.

Organized crime has flourished in the United States for more than a century. The scope of its operations expanded among immigrants, who found that this society was not willing to share its opportunities with them. Some ambitious individuals (such as Al Capone, mentioned earlier) made their own success, especially during Prohibition, when the government banned the production and sale of alcohol.

Everett Collection/Paramount Pictures, Inc.

The *Godfather* films offered an inside look at the world of organized crime. How accurately do you think the mass media portray organized crime? Explain.

The Italian Mafia is a well-known example of organized crime. But other criminal organizations involve African Americans, Chinese, Colombians, Cubans, Haitians, Nigerians, and Russians, as well as others of almost every racial and ethnic category. Today, organized crime involves a wide range of activities, from selling illegal drugs to prostitution to credit-card fraud to selling false identification papers to illegal immigrants (Valdez, 1997; Federal Bureau of Investigation, 2008).

CRITICAL REVIEW According to social-conflict theory, a capitalist society's inequality in wealth and power shapes its laws and how they are applied. The criminal justice and social welfare systems thus act as political agents, controlling categories of people who are a threat to the capitalist system.

Like other approaches to deviance, social-conflict theory has its critics. First, this approach implies that laws and other cultural norms are created directly by the rich and powerful. At the very least, this is an oversimplification, as laws also protect workers, consumers, and the environment, sometimes opposing the interests of corporations and the rich.

Second, social-conflict analysis argues that criminality springs up only to the extent that a society treats its members unequally. However, as Durkheim noted, deviance exists in all societies, whatever their economic system and their degree of inequality.

hate crime a criminal act against a person or a person's property by an offender motivated by racial or other bias

MAKING THE GRADE

The section "Deviance, Race, and Gender" is an extension of the social-conflict approach, which shows how inequality based on race and gender can affect the way we understand deviance.

APPLYING THEORY

Deviance

	Structural-Functional Approach	Symbolic-Interaction Approach	Social-Conflict Approach
What is the level of analysis?	Macro-level	Micro-level	Macro-level
What is deviance? What part does it play in society?	Deviance is a basic part of social organization. By defining deviance, society sets its moral boundaries.	Deviance is part of socially constructed reality that emerges in interaction. Deviance comes into being as individuals label something deviant.	Deviance results from social inequality. Norms, including laws, reflect the interests of powerful members of society.
What is important about deviance?	Deviance is universal: It exists in all societies.	Deviance is variable: Any act or person may or may not be labeled deviant.	Deviance is political: People with little power are at high risk of being labeled deviant.

The sociological explanations for crime and other types of deviance that we have discussed are summarized in the Applying Theory table.

CHECK YOUR LEARNING Define white-collar crime, corporate crime, and organized crime.

Deviance, Race, and Gender

What people consider deviant reflects the relative power and privilege of different categories of people. The following sections offer two examples: how racial and ethnic hostility motivates hate crimes and how gender is linked to deviance.

Hate Crimes

A **hate crime** is *a criminal act against a person or a person's property by an offender motivated by racial or other bias.* A hate crime may express hostility toward someone's race, religion, ancestry, sexual orientation, or physical disability. The federal government recorded 7,624 hate crimes in 2007 (U.S. Department of Justice, 2008).

In 1998, people across the country were stunned by the brutal killing of Matthew Shepard, a gay student at the University of Wyoming, by two men filled with hatred toward homosexuals. The National Gay and Lesbian Task Force reported 2,430 hate crimes against gay and lesbian people in 2007 and estimates that one in five lesbians and gay men will become a victim of physical assault based on sexual orientation (Dang & Vianney, 2007; National Coalition of Anti-Violence Programs, 2007). People who contend with multiple stigmas, such as gay men of color, are especially likely to be victims. Yet it can happen to anyone: In 2007, 18 percent of hate crimes based on race targeted white people (Federal Bureau of Investigation, 2008).

By 2008, forty-five states and the federal government had enacted legislation that increased penalties for crimes motivated by hatred (Anti-Defamation League, 2008). Supporters are gratified, but opponents charge that such laws, which increase penalties based on the attitudes of the offender, punish "politically incorrect" thoughts. The Thinking About Diversity box takes a closer look at the issue of hate crime laws.

The Feminist Perspective: Deviance and Gender

Virtually every society in the world places stricter controls on women than on men. Historically, our own society has centered the lives of women on the home. In the United States even today, women's opportunities in the workplace, in politics, in athletics, and in the military are more limited than men's. Elsewhere in the world, the constraints on women are greater still. In Saudi Arabia, women cannot vote or legally operate motor vehicles; in Iran, women who dare to expose their hair or wear makeup in public can be whipped; and not long

SEEING SOCIOLOGY in Everyday Life

Why do you think that women are much less likely than men to be arrested for a serious crime?

THINKING ABOUT DIVERSITY: RACE, CLASS, & GENDER

Hate Crime Laws: Should We Punish Attitudes as Well as Actions?

On a cool October evening, nineteen-year-old Todd Mitchell, an African American, was standing with some friends in front of their apartment complex in Kenosha, Wisconsin. They had just seen the film *Mississippi Burning* and were fuming over a scene that showed a white man beating a young black boy while he knelt in prayer.

"Do you feel hyped up to move on some white people?" asked Mitchell. Minutes later, they saw a young white boy walking toward them on the other side of the street. Mitchell commanded, "There goes a white boy; go get him!" The group swarmed around the youngster, beating him bloody and leaving him on the ground in a coma. The attackers took the boy's tennis shoes as a trophy.

Police soon arrested the teenagers and charged them with the beating. Mitchell went to trial as the ringleader, and the jury found him guilty of aggravated battery *motivated by racial hatred.* Instead of the usual two-year sentence, Mitchell went to jail for four years.

As this case illustrates, hate crime laws punish a crime more severely if the offender is motivated by bias against some category of people. Supporters make three arguments in favor of hate crime legislation. First, as noted in the text discussion of crime, the offender's intentions are always important in weighing criminal responsibility, so considering hatred an intention is nothing new. Second, victims of hate crimes typically suffer greater injury than victims of crimes with other motives. Third, a crime motivated by racial or other bias is more harmful because it inflames the public mood more than a crime carried out, say, for money.

Critics counter that while some hate crime cases involve hard-core racism, most are impulsive acts by young people. Even more important, critics maintain, hate crime laws are a threat to First Amendment guarantees of free speech. Hate crime laws allow courts to sentence offenders not just for their actions but for their attitudes. As the Harvard University law professor Alan Dershowitz cautions, "As much as I hate bigotry, I fear much more the Court attempting to control the minds of its citizens." In short, according to critics, hate crime statutes open the door to punishing beliefs rather than behavior.

Newscom/Zuma Press

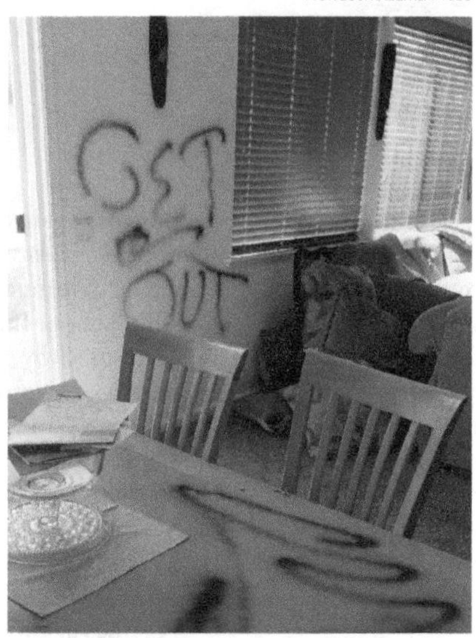

Do you think this example of vandalism should be prosecuted as a hate crime? In other words, should the punishment be more severe than if the spray painting were just "normal" graffiti? Why or why not?

In 1993, the U.S. Supreme Court upheld the sentence handed down to Todd Mitchell. In a unanimous decision, the justices stated that the government should not punish an individual's beliefs. But, they reasoned, a belief is no longer protected when it becomes the motive for a crime.

WHAT DO YOU THINK?

1. Do you think crimes motivated by hate are more harmful than those motivated by greed? Why or why not?
2. Do you think minorities such as African Americans should be subject to the same hate crime laws as white people? Why or why not?
3. Do you favor or oppose hate crime laws? Why?

Sources: Terry (1993), A. Sullivan (2002), and Hartocollis (2007).

ago, a Nigerian court convicted a divorced woman of bearing a child out of wedlock and sentenced her to death by stoning; her life was later spared out of concern for her child (Eboh, 2002; Jefferson, 2009).

Gender also figures in the theories of deviance you read about earlier in the chapter. Robert Merton's strain theory, for example, defines cultural goals in terms of financial success. Traditionally, at least, this goal has had more to do with the lives of men because women have been taught to define success in terms of relationships, particularly marriage and motherhood (E. B. Leonard, 1982). A more woman-focused theory might recognize the "strain" that results from the cultural ideal of equality clashing with the reality of gender-based inequality.

According to labeling theory, gender influences how we define deviance because people commonly use different standards to judge the behavior of females and males. Further, because society puts men in positions of power over women, men often escape direct responsibility for actions that victimize women. In the past, at least, men who sexually harassed or assaulted women were labeled only mildly deviant and sometimes escaped punishment entirely.

Sam Pearson, who lives in Renville County, North Dakota, rarely locks his doors when he leaves the house.

Serge Shuman, who lives in Mecklenburg County, North Carolina, knows many people who have been victims of crime and avoids going out at night.

SEEING SOCIOLOGY in Everyday Life

Do you think a student who downloads music in violation of the law is guilty of theft? Why or why not?

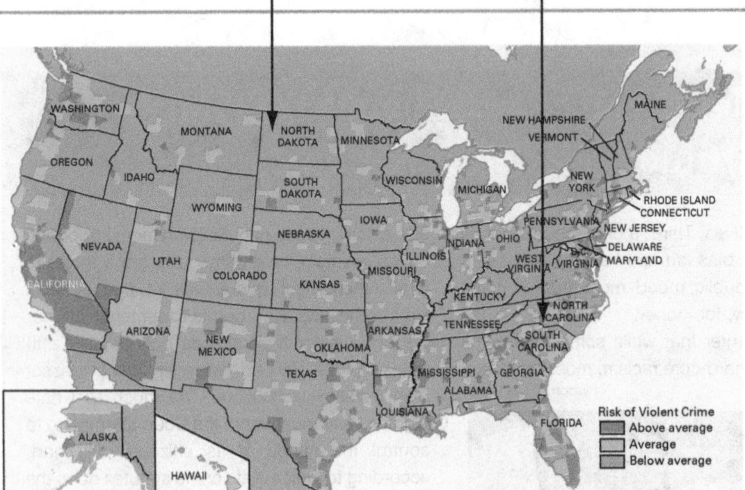

Seeing Ourselves

NATIONAL MAP 1

The Risk of Violent Crime across the United States

This map shows the risk of becoming a victim of violent crime. In general, the risk is highest in low-income, rural counties that have a large population of men between the ages of fifteen and twenty-four. After reading this section of the text, see whether you can explain this pattern.

Source: CAP Index, Inc., 2009.

By contrast, women who are victimized may have to convince others—even members of a jury—that they were not to blame for their own sexual harassment or assault. Research confirms an important truth: Whether people define a situation as deviance—and, if so, who the deviant is—depends on the sex of both the audience and the actors (King & Clayson, 1988).

Finally, despite its focus on social inequality, much social-conflict analysis does not address the issue of gender. If economic disadvantage is a primary cause of crime, as conflict theory suggests, why do women (whose economic position is much worse than men's) commit far *fewer* crimes than men?

Crime

Crime is the violation of criminal laws enacted by a locality, a state, or the federal government. All crimes are composed of two elements: the *act* itself (or in some cases, the failure to do what the law requires) and *criminal intent* (in legal terminology, *mens rea*, or "guilty mind"). Intent is a matter of degree, ranging from willful conduct to negligence. Someone who is negligent does not deliberately set out to hurt anyone but acts in a way that results in harm. Prosecutors weigh the degree of intent in deciding whether, for example, to charge someone with first-degree murder, second-degree murder, or negligent manslaughter. Alternatively, they may consider a killing justifiable, as in self-defense.

Types of Crime

In the United States, the Federal Bureau of Investigation (FBI) gathers information on criminal offenses and regularly reports the results in a publication called *Crime in the United States.* Two major types of crime make up the FBI "crime index."

Crimes against the person, also called *violent crimes*, are *crimes that direct violence or the threat of violence against others.* Violent crimes include murder and manslaughter (legally defined as "the willful killing of one human being by another"), aggravated assault ("an unlawful attack by one person upon another for the purpose of inflicting severe or aggravated bodily injury"), forcible rape ("the carnal knowledge of a female forcibly and against her will"), and robbery ("taking or attempting to take anything of value from the care, custody, or control of a person or persons by force or threat of force or violence and/or putting the victim in fear"). National Map 1 shows a person's risk of becoming a victim of violent crime in counties all across the United States.

Crimes against property, also called *property crimes*, are *crimes that involve theft of property belonging to others.* Property crimes include burglary ("the unlawful entry of a structure to commit a [serious crime] or a theft"), larceny-theft ("the unlawful taking, carrying, leading, or riding away of property from the possession of another"), auto theft ("the theft or attempted theft of a motor vehicle"), and arson ("any willful or malicious burning or attempt to burn the personal property of another").

A third category of offenses, not included in major crime indexes, is **victimless crimes**, *violations of law in which there are no obvious victims.* Also called *crimes without complaint,* they include illegal drug use, prostitution, and gambling. The term "victimless crime" is misleading, however. How victimless is a crime when young people steal to support a drug habit? What about a young pregnant woman who, by smoking crack, permanently harms her baby? Perhaps it is more correct to say that people who commit such crimes are both offenders and victims.

Because public views of victimless crimes vary greatly, laws differ from place to place. In the United States, although gambling and

crimes against the person (violent crimes) crimes that direct violence or the threat of violence against others

crimes against property (property crimes) crimes that involve theft of money or property belonging to others

victimless crimes violations of law in which there are no obvious victims

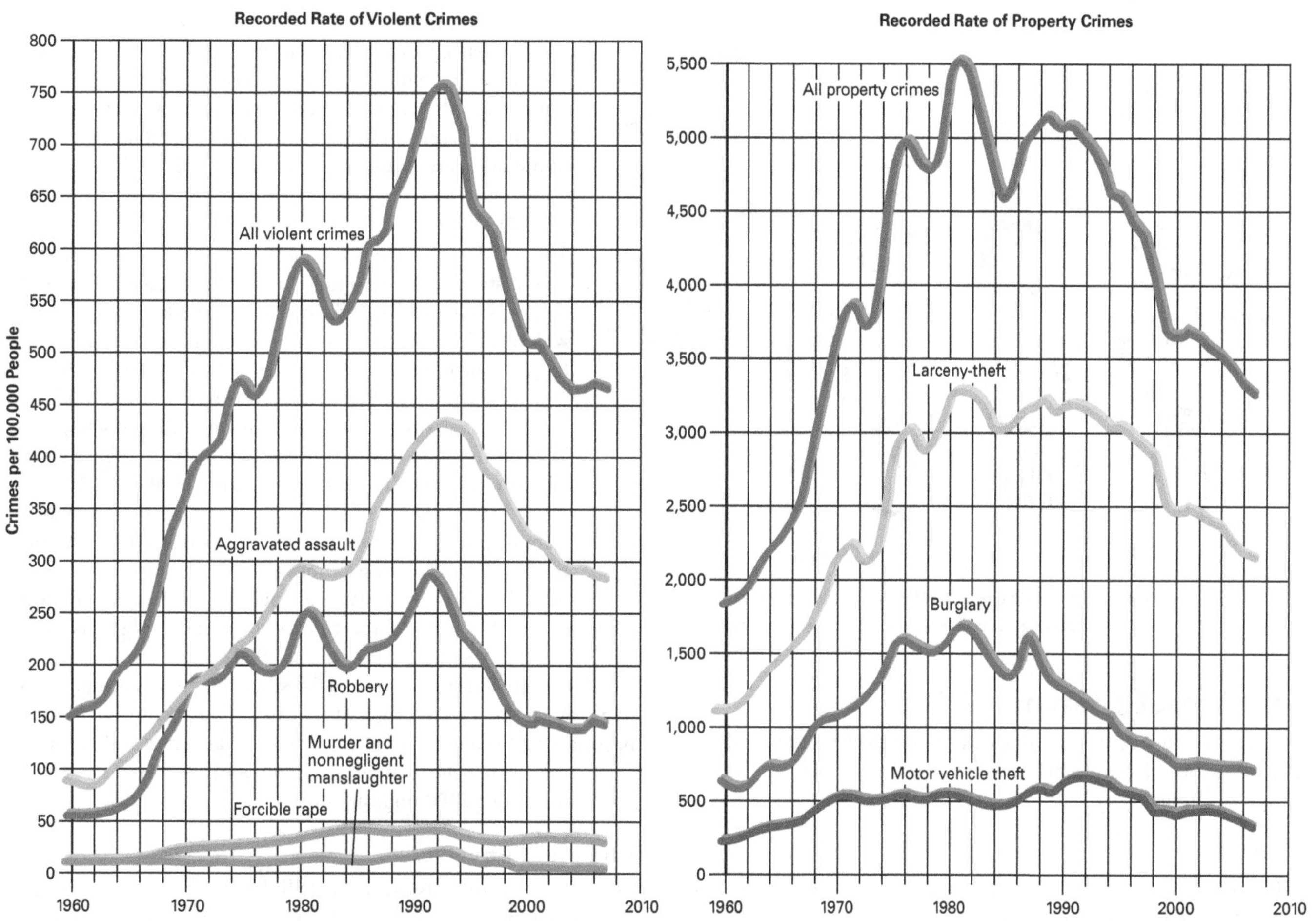

FIGURE 2 **Crime Rates in the United States, 1960–2006**

The graphs show the rates for various violent crimes and property crimes during recent decades. Since about 1990, the trend has been downward.

Source: Federal Bureau of Investigation (2008).

prostitution are legal in only limited areas, both activities are common across the country.

Criminal Statistics

Statistics gathered by the FBI show crime rates rising from 1960 to 1990 and then declining. Even so, police count more than 11 million serious crimes each year. Figure 2 shows the trends for various serious crimes.

Always read crime statistics with caution, because they include only crimes known to the police. Almost all homicides are reported, but assaults—especially among people who know one another—often are not. Police records include an even smaller share of the property crimes that occur, especially when the crime involves losses that are small.

Researchers check official crime statistics using *victimization surveys,* in which they ask a representative sample of people if they have had any experience with crime. According to such surveys, the overall crime rate is about three times higher than official reports indicate (Russell, 1995b).

SEEING SOCIOLOGY in Everyday Life

The 2009 arrest of Harvard professor Henry Louis Gates Jr., an African American, by a white police officer sparked a national debate over racial profiling.

MAKING THE GRADE

Remember that the profile of a criminal depends on the type of crime. Street crime involves a larger share of lower-income people; corporate crime involves mostly high-income people. With regard to race, most street crime is committed by whites.

"You look like this sketch of someone who's thinking about committing a crime."

The Street Criminal: A Profile

Using government crime reports, we can gain a general description of the categories of people most likely to be arrested for violent and property crimes.

Age

Official crime rates rise sharply during adolescence, peak in the late teens, and then fall as people get older. People between the ages of fifteen and twenty-four represent just 14 percent of the U.S. population, but in 2007, they accounted for 40.9 percent of all arrests for violent crimes and 46.8 percent of arrests for property crimes (Federal Bureau of Investigation, 2008).

Gender

Although each sex makes up roughly half the population, police collared males in 66.6 percent of all property crime arrests in 2007; the other 33.4 percent of arrests involved women. In other words, men are arrested more than twice as often as women for property crimes. In the case of violent crimes, the difference is even greater, with 81.8 percent of arrests involving males and just 18.2 percent females (more than a four-to-one ratio).

It may be that law enforcement officials are reluctant to define women as criminals. In fact, all over the world, the greatest gender differences in crime rates occur in societies that most severely limit the opportunities of women. In the United States, however, the difference in arrest rates for women and men is narrowing, which probably indicates increasing sexual equality in our society. Between 1998 and 2007, there was a 6.6 percent *increase* in arrests of women and a 6.1 percent *drop* in arrests of men (Federal Bureau of Investigation, 2008).

Social Class

The FBI does not assess the social class of arrested persons, so no statistical data of the kind given for age and gender are available. But research has long indicated that street crime is more widespread among people of lower social position (Thornberry & Farnsworth, 1982; Wolfgang, Thornberry, & Figlio, 1987).

Yet the link between class and crime is more complicated than it appears on the surface. For one thing, many people look on the poor as less worthy than the rich, whose wealth and power confer "respectability" (Tittle, Villemez, & Smith, 1978; Elias, 1986). And although crime—especially violent crime—is a serious problem in the poorest inner-city communities, most of these crimes are committed by a few repeat offenders. The majority of the people who live in poor communities have no criminal record at all (Wolfgang, Figlio, & Sellin, 1972; Elliott & Ageton, 1980; Harries, 1990).

The connection between social standing and criminality also depends on the type of crime. If we expand our definition of crime beyond street offenses to include white-collar crime and corporate crime, the "common criminal" suddenly looks much more affluent and may live in a $100 million home.

Race and Ethnicity

Both race and ethnicity are strongly linked to crime rates, although the reasons are many and complex. Official statistics show that 69.7 percent of arrests for FBI index crimes in 2007 involved white people. However, the African American arrest rate was higher than the rate for whites in proportion to their representation in the general population. African Americans make up 12.8 percent of the population but account for 29.8 percent of arrests for property crimes (versus 67.9 percent for whites) and 39.0 percent of arrests for violent crimes (versus 58.9 percent for whites) (Federal Bureau of Investigation, 2008).

There are several reasons for the disproportionate number of arrests among African Americans. First, race in the United States closely relates to social standing, which, as already explained, affects the likelihood of engaging in street crimes. Many poor people living in the midst of wealth come to perceive society as unjust and are therefore more likely to turn to crime to get their share (Blau & Blau, 1982; E. Anderson, 1994; Martinez, 1996).

Second, black and white family patterns differ: More than two-thirds of non-Hispanic black children (compared to one-fourth of

MAKING THE GRADE

The profile of the street criminal is based on arrest data and not on convictions in a court of law. This is because the data made available by the FBI are based on arrests.

SEEING SOCIOLOGY in Everyday Life

Do you think stricter gun control laws would lower the level of deadly violence in the United States? Why or why not?

non-Hispanic white children) are born to single mothers. Single parenting carries two risks: Children receive less supervision and are at greater risk of living in poverty. With more than one-third of African American children growing up poor (compared to one in ten white children), no one should be surprised at the proportionately higher crime rates for African Americans (Hamilton, Martin, & Ventura, 2007; U.S. Census Bureau, 2008).

Third, prejudice prompts white police to arrest black people more readily and leads citizens to report African Americans more willingly, so people of color are overly criminalized (Chiricos, McEntire, & Gertz, 2001; Quillian & Pager, 2001; Demuth & Steffensmeier, 2004).

Fourth, remember that the official crime index does not include arrests for offenses ranging from drunk driving to white-collar violations. This omission contributes to the view of the typical criminal as a person of color. If we broaden our definition of crime to include drunk driving, business fraud, embezzlement, stock swindles, and cheating on income tax returns, the proportion of white criminals rises dramatically.

Keep in mind, too, that categories of people with high arrest rates are also at higher risk of being victims of crime. In the United States, for example, African Americans are six times as likely as white people to die as a result of homicide (Rogers et al., 2001; Kung et al., 2008).

Finally, some categories of the population have unusually low rates of arrest. People of Asian descent, who account for about 4 percent of the population, figure in only 1 percent of all arrests. Asian Americans enjoy higher than average educational achievement and income. Also, Asian American culture emphasizes family solidarity and discipline, both of which keep criminality down.

Crime in Global Perspective

By world standards, the crime rate in the United States is high. Although recent crime trends are downward, there were 16,929 murders in the United States in 2007, which amounts to one every half hour around the clock. In large cities such as New York, rarely does a day pass without someone being killed.

The rate of violent crime (but not property crime) in the United States is several times higher than in Europe. The contrast is even greater between our country and the nations of Asia, including India and Japan, where rates of violent and property crime are among the lowest in the world.

Elliott Currie (1985) suggests that crime stems from our culture's emphasis on individual economic success, frequently at the expense of strong families and neighborhoods. The United States also has extraordinary cultural diversity—a result of centuries of immigration—that can lead to conflict. In addition, economic inequality is higher in this country than in most other high-income nations. Thus our society's relatively weak social fabric, combined with considerable frustration among the poor, increases the level of criminal behavior.

Another factor contributing to violence in the United States is extensive private ownership of guns. About two-thirds of murder victims in the United States die from shootings. The U.S. rate of handgun deaths is about six times higher than the rate in Canada, a country that strictly limits handgun ownership (Statistics Canada, 2008).

Surveys suggest that about one-third of U.S. households have at least one gun. In fact, there are more guns (about 285 million) than adults in this country, and 40 percent of these weapons are handguns, commonly used in violent crimes. In large part, gun ownership reflects people's fear of crime, yet the easy availability of guns in this country also makes crime more deadly (NORC, 2007; Brady Campaign, 2008).

Supporters of gun control claim that restricting gun ownership would reduce the number of murders in the United States. For example, the number of murders each year in Canada, where the law prevents most people from owning guns, is about the same as in just the city of New York in this country. But as critics of gun control point out, laws regulating gun ownership do not keep guns out of the hands of criminals, who almost always obtain guns illegally. They also claim that gun control is no magic bullet in the war on crime: The number of people in the United States killed each year by knives alone is three times the number of Canadians killed by weapons of all kinds (Currie, 1985; J. D. Wright, 1995; Munroe, 2007; Federal Bureau of Investigation, 2008).

By the end of 2008, gun sales to private citizens was up sharply, reflecting fears on the part of many gun owners that the Obama administration would act to curtail gun ownership. Changes in law may or may not occur in the next few years, but debate over the consequences of widespread gun ownership will continue (Potter, 2008).

December 24–25, traveling through Peru. In Lima, Peru's capital city, the concern with crime is obvious. Almost every house is fortified with gates, barbed wire, or broken glass embedded in cement at the top of a wall. Private security forces are everywhere in the rich areas along the coast, where we find the embassies, expensive hotels, and the international airport.

The picture is very different as we pass through small villages high in the Andes to the east. The same families have lived in these communities for generations, and people know one another. No gates and fences here. And we've seen only one police car all afternoon.

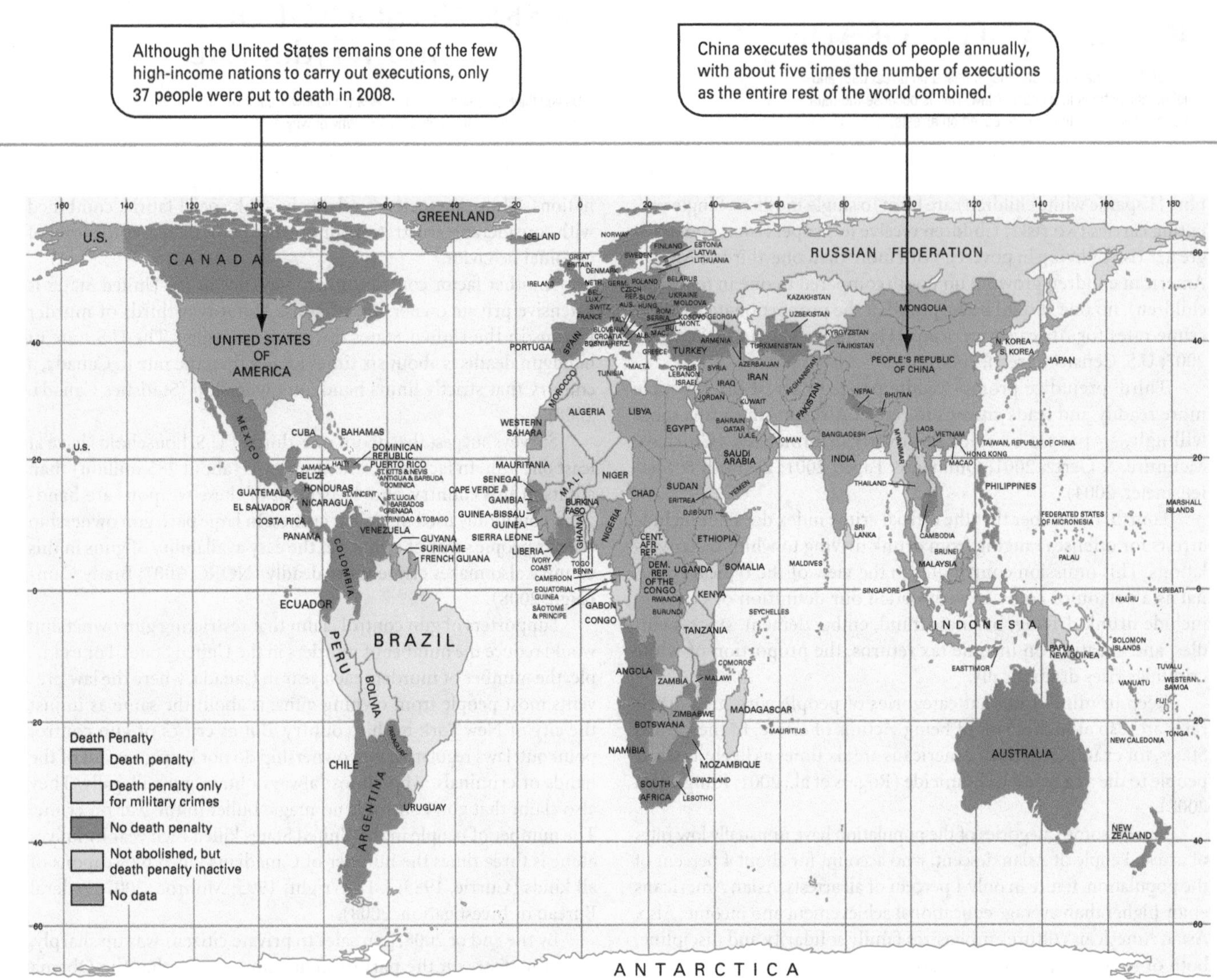

Window on the World

GLOBAL MAP 1 Capital Punishment in Global Perspective

The map identifies sixty-five countries in which the law allows the death penalty for ordinary crimes; in nine more, the death penalty is reserved for exceptional crimes under military law or during times of war. The death penalty does not exist in ninety-three countries; in thirty-five more, although the death penalty remains in law, no execution has taken place in more than ten years. Compare rich and poor nations: What general pattern do you see? In what way are the United States and Japan exceptions to this pattern?

Source: Amnesty International (2008a).

Crime rates are high in some of the largest cities of the world, including Lima, Peru; São Paulo, Brazil; and Manila, Philippines—all of which have rapid population growth and millions of desperately poor people. Outside of big cities, however, the traditional character of low-income societies and their strong families allow local communities to control crime informally.

Some types of crime have always been multinational, such as terrorism, espionage, and arms dealing (Martin & Romano, 1992). But today, the globalization we are experiencing on many fronts also extends to crime. A recent case in point is the illegal drug trade. In part, the problem of illegal drugs in the United States is a *demand* issue. That is, the demand for cocaine and other drugs in this country is high, and many people risk arrest or even a violent death for a chance to get rich in the drug trade. But the *supply* side of the issue is just as important. In the South American nation of Colombia, at least 20 percent of the people depend on cocaine production for their

MAKING THE GRADE

Due process—the idea that the criminal justice system should operate under the rule of law—guides the actions of police, court officials, and corrections officers.

livelihood. Not only is cocaine Colombia's most profitable export, but it outsells all other exports combined—including coffee. Clearly, drug dealing and many other crimes are closely related to social and economic conditions both in the United States and elsewhere.

Different countries have different strategies for dealing with crime. The use of the death penalty provides a case in point. According to Amnesty International (2008b), five nations (China, Iran, Pakistan, Saudi Arabia, and the United States) account for 93 percent of the world's executions carried out by governments. Global Map 1 shows which countries currently use capital punishment. The global trend is toward abolishing the death penalty: Amnesty International (2008a) reports that since 1985, sixty-two nations have ended this practice.

The U.S. Criminal Justice System

The criminal justice system is a society's formal system of social control. We shall briefly examine the key elements of the U.S. criminal justice system: police, courts, and the system of punishment and corrections. First, however, we must understand an important principle that underlies the entire system, the idea of due process.

Due Process

Due process is a simple but very important idea: The criminal justice system must operate according to law. This principle is grounded in the first ten amendments to the U.S. Constitution—known as the Bill of Rights—adopted by Congress in 1791. The Constitution offers various protections to any person charged with a crime, including the right to counsel, the right to refuse to testify against oneself, the right to confront all accusers, freedom from being tried twice for the same crime, and freedom from being "deprived of life, liberty, or property without due process of law." Furthermore, the Constitution gives all people the right to a speedy and public trial by jury and freedom from excessive bail and from "cruel and unusual" punishment.

In general terms, the concept of due process means that anyone charged with a crime must receive (1) fair notice of legal proceedings, (2) the opportunity to present a defense during a hearing on the charges, which must be conducted according to law, and (3) a judge or jury that weighs evidence impartially (Inciardi, 2000).

Due process limits the power of government, with an eye toward this nation's cultural support of individual rights and freedoms. Deciding exactly how far government can go is an ongoing process that makes up much of the work of the judicial system, especially the U.S. Supreme Court.

Police

The police generally serve as the primary point of contact between a society's population and the criminal justice system. In principle, the police maintain public order by enforcing the law. Of course, there is only so much that the 699,850 full-time police officers in the United States can do to monitor the activities of 300 million people. As a result, the police use a great deal of personal judgment in deciding which situations warrant their attention and how to handle them.

How do police officers carry out their duties? In a study of police behavior in five cities, Douglas Smith and Christy Visher (1981; D.

PhotoEdit Inc./Kayte M. Deioma

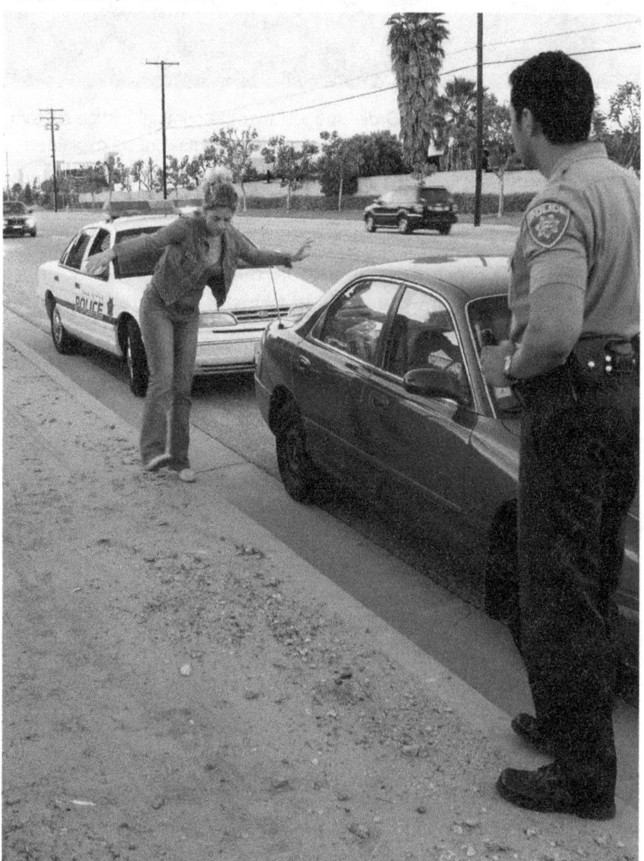

Police must be allowed discretion if they are to handle effectively the many different situations they face every day. At the same time, it is important that the police treat people fairly. Here we see a police officer deciding whether or not to charge a young woman with driving while intoxicated. What factors do you think enter into this decision?

plea bargaining a legal negotiation in which a prosecutor reduces a charge in exchange for a defendant's guilty plea

Picture Desk, Inc./Kobal Collection/Universal TV/Wolf Film

Television shows like *Law & Order* suggest that the criminal justice system carefully weighs the guilt and innocence of defendants. But as explained below, only 5 percent of criminal cases are actually resolved through a formal trial.

A. Smith, 1987) concluded that because they must act swiftly, police officers quickly size up situations in terms of six factors. First, the more serious they think the situation is, the more likely they are to make an arrest. Second, officers take account of the victim's wishes in deciding whether or not to make an arrest. Third, the odds of arrest go up the more uncooperative a suspect is. Fourth, officers are more likely to take into custody someone they have arrested before, presumably because this suggests guilt. Fifth, the presence of observers increases the chances of arrest. According to Smith and Visher, the presence of observers prompts police to take stronger control of a situation, if only to move the encounter from the street (the suspect's turf) to the police department (where law officers have the edge). Sixth, all else being equal, police officers are more likely to arrest people of color than whites, perceiving suspects of African or Latino descent as either more dangerous or more likely to be guilty.

Courts

After arrest, a court determines a suspect's guilt or innocence. In principle, U.S. courts rely on an adversarial process involving attorneys—one representing the defendant and another the state—in the presence of a judge, who monitors legal procedures.

In practice, however, about 95 percent of criminal cases are resolved prior to court appearance through **plea bargaining**, *a legal negotiation in which a prosecutor reduces a charge in exchange for a defendant's guilty plea.* For example, the state may offer a defendant charged with burglary a lesser charge, perhaps possession of burglary tools, in exchange for a guilty plea (U.S. Department of Justice, 2008).

Plea bargaining is widespread because it spares the system the time and expense of trials. A trial is usually unnecessary if there is little disagreement over the facts of the case. In addition, because the number of cases entering the system annually has doubled over the past decade, prosecutors could not bring every case to trial even if they wanted to. By quickly resolving most of their work, the courts channel their resources into the most important cases.

But plea bargaining pressures defendants (who are presumed innocent) to plead guilty. A person can exercise the right to a trial, but only at the risk of receiving a more severe sentence if found guilty. Furthermore, low-income defendants enter the process with the guidance of a public defender—typically an overworked and underpaid attorney who may devote little time to even the most serious cases (Novak, 1999). Plea bargaining may be efficient, but it undercuts both the adversarial process and the rights of defendants.

Punishment

In 2008, as he approached the city hall in Kirkwood, Missouri, a man pulled a handgun and shot and killed a police officer. He then entered a city council meeting and killed another police officer and three council members. The city's mayor was critically wounded (C. Leonard, 2008).

Such cases force us to wonder about the reasons for such extreme violence and also to ask how a society should respond to such acts. In the case of the Kirkwood shootings, police shot and killed the man at the crime scene. But typically, of course, a suspect is apprehended and put on trial. If found guilty, the next step is punishment.

What does a society gain through the punishment of wrongdoers? Scholars answer with four basic reasons: retribution, deterrence, rehabilitation, and societal protection.

Retribution

The oldest justification for punishment is to satisfy people's need for **retribution**, *an act of moral vengeance by which society makes the offender suffer as much as the suffering caused by the crime.* Retribution rests on a view of society as a moral balance. When criminality upsets this balance, punishment in equal measure restores the moral order, as suggested in the ancient code calling for "an eye for an eye, a tooth for a tooth."

In the Middle Ages, most Europeans viewed crime as sin—an offense against God as well as society that required a harsh response. Today, although critics point out that retribution does little to reform the offender, many people consider vengeance reason enough for punishment.

Four Justifications for Punishment

retribution an act of moral vengeance by which society makes the offender suffer as much as the suffering caused by the crime

deterrence the attempt to discourage criminality through the use of punishment

rehabilitation a program for reforming the offender to prevent later offenses

societal protection rendering an offender incapable of further offenses temporarily through imprisonment or permanently by execution

SUMMING UP

Four Justifications for Punishment

Retribution	The oldest justification for punishment. Punishment is society's revenge for a moral wrong. In principle, punishment should be equal in severity to the crime itself.
Deterrence	An early modern approach. Crime is considered social disruption, which society acts to control. People are viewed as rational and self-interested; deterrence works because the pain of punishment outweighs the pleasure of crime.
Rehabilitation	A modern strategy linked to the development of social sciences. Crime and other deviance are viewed as the result of social problems (such as poverty) or personal problems (such as mental illness). Social conditions are improved; treatment is tailored to the offender's condition.
Societal protection	A modern approach easier to carry out than rehabilitation. Even if society is unable or unwilling to rehabilitate offenders or reform social conditions, people are protected by the imprisonment or execution of the offender.

Deterrence

A second justification for punishment is **deterrence,** *the attempt to discourage criminality through the use of punishment.* Deterrence is based on the eighteenth-century Enlightenment idea that humans, as calculating and rational creatures, will not break the law if they think that the pain of punishment will outweigh the pleasure of the crime.

Deterrence emerged as a reform measure in response to the harsh punishments based on retribution. Why put someone to death for stealing if theft can be discouraged with a prison sentence? As the concept of deterrence gained acceptance in industrial nations, the execution and physical mutilation of criminals in most high-income societies were replaced by milder forms of punishment such as imprisonment.

Punishment can deter crime in two ways. *Specific deterrence* is used to convince an individual offender that crime does not pay. Through *general deterrence,* the punishment of one person serves as an example to others.

Rehabilitation

The third justification for punishment is **rehabilitation,** *a program for reforming the offender to prevent later offenses.* Rehabilitation arose along with the social sciences in the nineteenth century. Since then, sociologists have claimed that crime and other deviance spring from a social environment marked by poverty or a lack of parental supervision. Logically, then, if offenders learn to be deviant, they can also learn to obey the rules; the key is controlling their environment. *Reformatories* or *houses of correction* provided controlled settings where people could learn proper behavior.

Like deterrence, rehabilitation motivates the offender to conform. In contrast to deterrence and retribution, which simply make the offender suffer, rehabilitation encourages constructive improvement. Unlike retribution, which demands that the punishment fit the crime, rehabilitation tailors treatment to each offender. Thus identical crimes would prompt similar acts of retribution but different rehabilitation programs.

Societal Protection

A final justification for punishment is **societal protection,** *rendering an offender incapable of further offenses temporarily through imprisonment or permanently by execution.* Like deterrence, societal protection is a rational approach to punishment intended to protect society from crime.

Currently, about 2.3 million people are jailed in the United States. Although the crime rate has gone down in recent years, the number of offenders locked up across the country has gone up, tripling since 1980. This rise in the prison population reflects both tougher public attitudes toward crime and punishing offenders and an increasing number of drug-related arrests. As a result, the United States now incarcerates a larger share of its population than any other

Seeing SOCIOLOGY in the 

The New York Times

More Than 1 in 100 Adults Are Now in Prison in United States

By ADAM LIPTAK
February 29, 2008

For the first time in the nation's history, more than one in 100 American adults are behind bars, according to a new report.

Nationwide, the prison population grew by 25,000 last year, bringing it to almost 1.6 million, after three decades of growth that has seen the prison population nearly triple. Another 723,000 people are in local jails.

The number of American adults is about 230 million, meaning that one in every 99.1 adults is behind bars.

Incarceration rates are even higher for some groups. One in 36 adult Hispanic men is behind bars, based on Justice Department figures for 2006. One in 15 adult black men is, too, as is one in nine black men ages 20 to 34.

The report, from the Pew Center on the States, also found that one in 355 white women ages 35 to 39 is behind bars, compared with one in 100 black women. . . .

The increase in the number of prisoners over the last 18 months, the Pew report says, pushed the national adult incarceration rate to just over one in 100.

"We aren't really getting the return in public safety from this level of incarceration," said Susan Urahn, the center's managing director.

But Paul Cassell, a law professor at the University of Utah and a former federal judge, said the Pew report considered only half of the cost-benefit equation and overlooked the "very tangible benefits: lower crime rates."

In the past 20 years, according to the Federal Bureau of Investigation, rates of violent crimes fell by 25 percent, to 464 per 100,000 people in 2007 from 612.5 in 1987.

"While we certainly want to be smart about who we put into prisons," Professor Cassell said, "it would be a mistake to think that we can release any significant number of prisoners without increasing crime rates. One out of every 100 adults is behind bars because one out of every 100 adults has committed a serious criminal offense."

The United States imprisons more people than any other nation in the world. China is second, with 1.5 million people behind bars. The gap is even wider in percentage terms.

Germany imprisons 93 out of every 100,000 people, according to the International Center for Prison Studies at King's College in London. The comparable number for the United States is roughly eight times that, or 750 out of 100,000.

Ms. Urahn said the nation could not afford the incarceration rate documented in the report.

"We tend to be a country in which incarceration is an easy response to crime," she said. "Being tough on crime is an easy position to take, particularly if you have the money. And we did have the money in the '80s and '90s."

Now, with fewer resources available, the report said, "prison costs are blowing a hole in state budgets." On average, states spend almost 7 percent

country in the world (Pew Center on the States, 2008; Sentencing Project, 2008). Seeing Sociology in the News provides details about the rising rate of incarceration in the United States.

CRITICAL REVIEW The Summing Up table reviews the four justifications for punishment. However, an accurate assessment of the consequences of punishment is no simple task.

The value of retribution lies in Durkheim's claim that punishing the deviant person increases society's moral awareness. For this reason, punishment was traditionally a public event. Although the last public execution in the United States took place in Kentucky more than seventy years ago, today's mass media ensure public awareness of executions carried out inside prison walls (Kittrie, 1971).

Does punishment deter crime? Despite our extensive use of punishment, our society has a high rate of **criminal recidivism**, *later offenses by people previously convicted of crimes.* About three-fourths of prisoners in state penitentiaries have been jailed before, and about two-thirds of people released from prison are arrested again within three years (DeFina & Arvanites, 2002; U.S. Department of Justice, 2008). So does punishment really deter crime? Only about one-third of all crimes are known to police, and of these, only about one in five results in an arrest. Most crimes, therefore, go unpunished, so the old saying that "crime doesn't pay" rings hollow.

Prisons provide short-term societal protection by keeping offenders off the streets, but they do little to reshape attitudes or behavior in the long term (Carlson, 1976; R. A. Wright, 1994). Perhaps rehabilitation is an unrealistic expectation, because according to Sutherland's theory of differential association, locking up criminals together for years probably strengthens criminal attitudes and skills. Imprisonment also stigmatizes prisoners, making it harder for them to find legitimate employment later on (Pager, 2003). Finally, prison breaks the social ties inmates may have in the outside world, which, following Hirschi's control theory, makes inmates more likely to commit new crimes upon release.

CHECK YOUR LEARNING What are society's four justifications for punishment? Does sending offenders to prison accomplish each of them? Why?

The Death Penalty

Perhaps the most controversial issue involving punishment is the death penalty. Between 1977 and 2009, more than 7,000 people were sentenced to death in U.S. courts; 1,136 executions were carried out.

In thirty-six states, the law allows the state to execute offenders convicted of very serious crimes such as first-degree murder. But while a majority of states do permit capital punishment, only a few states are likely to carry out executions. Across the United States, half of the 3,220 people on death row at the end of 2007 were in just four of their budgets on corrections, trailing only health care, education and transportation.

In 2007, according to the National Association of State Budget Officers, states spent $44 billion in tax dollars on corrections. That is up from $10.6 billion in 1987, a 127 percent increase when adjusted for inflation. . . . By 2011, the Pew report said, states are on track to spend an additional $25 billion.

It cost an average of $23,876 to imprison someone in 2005, the most recent year for which data were available. But state spending varies widely, from $45,000 a year in Rhode Island to $13,000 in Louisiana.

"Getting tough on crime has gotten tough on taxpayers," said Adam Gelb, the director of the public safety performance project at the Pew Center. "They don't want to spend $23,000 on a prison cell for a minor violation any more than they want a bridge to nowhere."

The cost of medical care is growing by 10 percent annually, the report said, and will accelerate as the prison population ages.

About one in nine state government employees works in corrections, and some states are finding it hard to fill those jobs. California spent more than $500 million on overtime alone in 2006.

The number of prisoners in California dropped by 4,000 last year, making Texas's prison system the nation's largest, at about 172,000. But the Texas Legislature last year approved broad changes to the state's corrections system, including expansions of drug treatment programs and drug courts and revisions to parole practices.

"Our violent offenders, we lock them up for a very long time—rapists, murderers, child molesters," said State Senator John Whitmire, Democrat of Houston and the chairman of the Senate's Criminal Justice Committee. "The problem was that we weren't smart about nonviolent offenders. . . ."

The Pew report recommended diverting nonviolent offenders away from prison and using punishments short of reincarceration for minor or technical violations of probation or parole. It also urged states to consider earlier release of some prisoners. . . .

WHAT DO YOU THINK?

1. How does the United States differ from other countries in terms of incarceration rates? Why do you think this country makes such widespread use of prison as a response to crime?
2. In light of the high costs of locking up offenders, what other policies might be implemented to hold down the crime rate?
3. Do you support the idea that prison should be used to protect society from only violent offenders? What about white-collar criminals?

states: California, Texas, Florida, and Pennsylvania (U.S. Bureau of Justice Statistics, 2008).

Opponents of capital punishment point to research suggesting that the death penalty has limited value as a crime deterrent. Countries such as Canada, where the death penalty has been abolished, have not seen a rise in the number of murders. Critics also point out that the United States is the only Western, high-income nation that routinely executes offenders. As public concern about the death penalty has increased, the use of capital punishment has declined, falling from 74 executions in 1997 to 37 in 2008.

Public opinion surveys reveal that the share of U.S. adults who claim to support the death penalty as a punishment for murder remains high (63 percent) and has been fairly stable over time (NORC, 2007:159). College students hold about the same attitudes as everyone else, with about two-thirds of first-year students expressing support for the death penalty (Pryor et al., 2008).

But judges, criminal prosecutors, and members of trial juries are less and less likely to call for the death penalty. One reason is that because the crime rate has come down in recent years, the public now has less fear of crime and is less interested in applying the most severe punishment.

A second reason is public concern that the death penalty may be applied unjustly. The analysis of DNA evidence—a recent advance—from old crime scenes has shown that many people were wrongly convicted of a crime. Across the country, between 1975 and 2008, 131 people who had been sentenced to death were released from death row after new DNA evidence demonstrated their innocence. Such findings were one reason that in 2000, the governor of Illinois stated he could no longer support the death penalty, leading him to commute the death sentences of every person on that state's death row (S. Levine, 2003; Death Penalty Information Center, 2008).

A third reason for the decline in the use of the death penalty is that more states now permit judges and juries to sentence serious offenders to life in prison without the possibility of parole. Such punishment offers to protect society from dangerous criminals who can be "put away" forever without requiring an execution.

Fourth and finally, many states now shy away from capital punishment because of the high cost of prosecuting capital cases. Death penalty cases require more legal work and demand superior defense lawyers, often at public expense. In addition, such cases commonly include testimony by various paid "experts," including physicians and psychiatrists, which also runs up the costs of trial. Then there is the cost of many appeals that almost always follow a conviction leading to the sentence of death. When all these factors are put together, the cost of a death penalty case typically exceeds the cost of sending an offender to prison for life. So it is easy to see why states often choose not to seek the death penalty. One accounting, for example, reveals that the state of New Jersey has been spending more than $10 million a year prosecuting death penalty cases that have yet to result in a single execution (Thomas & Brant, 2007).

Organizations opposed to the death penalty are challenging this punishment in court. In 2008, for example, the U.S. Supreme Court

criminal recidivism later offenses by people previously convicted of crimes

community-based corrections correctional programs operating within society at large rather than behind prison walls

MAKING THE GRADE

"Community-based corrections" refers to ways of dealing with offenders without sending them to prison.

US Information Agency

To increase the power of punishment to deter crime, capital punishment was long carried out in public. Here is a photograph from the last public execution in the United States, with twenty-two-year-old Rainey Bethea standing on the scaffold moments from death in Owensboro, Kentucky, on August 16, 1937. Children as well as adults were in the crowd. Now that the mass media report the story of executions across the country, states carry out capital punishment behind closed doors.

upheld the use of lethal injection against the charge that this procedure amounts to cruel and unusual punishment, which would be unconstitutional (Greenhouse, 2008). There is no indication at present that the United States will end the use of the death penalty, but the trend is away from this type of punishment.

Community-Based Corrections

Prisons keep convicted criminals off the streets, but the evidence suggests that they do little to rehabilitate most offenders. Furthermore, prisons are expensive, costing more than $25,000 per year to support each inmate, in addition to the initial costs of building the facilities.

One alternative to the traditional prison that has been adopted by cities and states across the country is **community-based corrections**, *correctional programs operating within society at large rather than behind prison walls.* Community-based corrections have three main advantages: They reduce costs, reduce overcrowding in prisons, and allow for supervision of convicts while eliminating the hardships of prison life and the stigma that accompanies going to jail. In general, the idea of community-based corrections is not so much to punish as to reform; such programs are therefore usually offered to individuals who have committed less serious offenses and appear to be good prospects for avoiding future criminal violations (Inciardi, 2000).

Probation

One form of community-based corrections is *probation,* a policy permitting a convicted offender to remain in the community under conditions imposed by a court, including regular supervision. Courts may require that a probationer receive counseling, attend a drug treatment program, hold a job, avoid associating with "known criminals," or anything else a judge thinks is appropriate. Typically, a probationer must check in with an officer of the court (the probation officer) on a regular schedule to make sure the guidelines are being followed. Should the probationer fail to live up to the conditions set by the court or commit a new offense, the court may revoke probation and send the offender to jail.

Shock Probation

A related strategy is *shock probation,* a policy by which a judge orders a convicted offender to prison for a short time but then suspends the remainder of the sentence in favor of probation. Shock probation is thus a mix of prison and probation, used to impress on the offender the seriousness of the situation without resorting to full-scale imprisonment. In some cases, shock probation takes place in a special "boot camp" facility where offenders might spend one to three months in a military-style setting intended to teach discipline and respect for authority (Cole & Smith, 2002).

Parole

Parole is a policy of releasing inmates from prison to serve the remainder of their sentences in the local community under the supervision of a parole officer. Although some sentences specifically deny the possibility of parole, most inmates become eligible for parole after serving a certain portion of their sentences. At that time, a parole board evaluates the risks and benefits of the inmate's early release from prison. If parole is granted, the parole board monitors the offender's conduct until the sentence is completed. Should the offender not comply with the conditions of parole or be arrested for another crime, the board can revoke parole and return the offender to prison to complete the sentence.

CRITICAL REVIEW Evaluations of probation and parole are mixed. There is little question that probation and parole programs are much less expensive than conventional imprisonment; they also free up room in prisons for people who commit more serious crimes. Yet research suggests that although probation and shock probation do seem to work for some people, they do not significantly reduce recidivism. Parole is also useful to prison officials as a means to encourage good behavior among inmates. But levels of crime among those released on parole are so high that a number of states have ended their parole programs entirely (Inciardi, 2000).

CONTROVERSY & DEBATE

Violent Crime Is Down—but Why?

Duane: I'm a criminal justice major, and I want to be a police officer. Crime is a huge problem in America, and police are what keep the crime rate low.

Sandy: I'm a sociology major. As for the crime rate, I'm not sure it's quite that simple. . . .

During the 1980s, crime rates shot upward. Just about everyone lived in fear of violent crime, and in many large cities, the numbers killed and wounded made whole neighborhoods seem like war zones. There seemed to be no solution to the problem.

Yet in the 1990s, serious crime rates began to fall, until by 2000, they were at levels not seen in more than a generation. Why? Researchers point to several reasons:

1. **A reduction in the youth population.** It was noted earlier that young people (particularly males) are responsible for much violent crime. During the 1990s, the population aged fifteen to twenty-four dropped by 5 percent (in part because of the legalization of abortion in 1973).
2. **Changes in policing.** Much of the drop in crime (as well as the earlier rise in crime) took place in large cities. In New York City, the number of murders fell from 2,245 in 1990 to just 500 in 2007 (the lowest figure since the city began keeping reliable records in 1963). Part of the reason for the decline is that the city has adopted a policy of *community policing,* which means that police are concerned not just with making arrests but with preventing crime before it happens. Officers get to know the areas they patrol and stop young men for jaywalking or other minor infractions so they can check them for concealed weapons (the word has gotten around that you can be arrested for carrying a gun). There are also more police at work in large cities. Los Angeles added more than 2,000 police officers in the 1990s, which contributed to its drop in violent crime during that period. Milwaukee assigned more police officers to foot patrols across the city and saw a sharp decline in deadly violence.
3. **More prisoners.** Between 1985 and 2008, the number of inmates in jails and prisons soared from 750,000 to more than 2.3 million. The main reason for this increase is tough laws that demand prison time for certain crimes, such as drug offenses. Mass incarceration has consequences. As one analyst put it, "When you lock up an extra million people, it's got to have some effect on the crime rate" (Franklin Zimring, quoted in Witkin, 1998:31).
4. **A better economy.** The U.S. economy boomed during the 1990s. Unemployment was down, reducing the likelihood that some people would turn to crime out of economic desperation. The logic here is simple: More jobs equal fewer crimes. By the same token, the recent economic downturn may well send crime rates back upward.
5. **The declining drug trade.** Many analysts agree that the most important factor in reducing rates of violent crime was the decline of crack cocaine. Crack came on the scene about 1985, and violence spread as young people—especially in the inner cities and increasingly armed with guns—became part of a booming drug trade. By the early 1990s, however, the popularity of crack began to fall as people saw the damage it was causing to entire communities. This realization, coupled with steady economic improvement and stiffer sentences for drug offenses, helped bring about the turnaround in violent crime.

PhotoEdit Inc./A. Ramey

One reason that crime has gone down is that there are more than 2 million people incarcerated in this country. This has caused severe overcrowding of facilities such as this Maricopa County, Arizona, prison.

The current picture looks better relative to what it was a decade or two ago. But one researcher cautions, "It looks better . . . only because the early 1990s were so bad. So let's not fool ourselves into thinking everything is resolved. It's not."

WHAT DO YOU THINK?

1. Do you support the policy of community policing? Why or why not?
2. What do you see as the pros and cons of building more prisons?
3. Which of the factors mentioned here do you think is the most important in crime control? Which is least important? Why?

Sources: Winship & Berrien (1999), Donahue & Leavitt (2000), Rosenfeld (2002), Liptak (2008), C. Mitchell (2008), and Antlfinger (2009).

Such evaluations point to a sobering truth: The criminal justice system cannot eliminate crime. As the Controversy & Debate box explains, although police, courts, and prisons do affect crime rates, crime and other forms of deviance are not just the acts of "bad people" but reflect the operation of society itself.

CHECK YOUR LEARNING What are three types of community-based corrections? What are their advantages?

Seeing Sociology in Everyday Life

Deviance

Why do most of us—at least most of the time—obey the rules?

As this chapter has explained, every society is a system of social control that encourages conformity to certain norms and discourages deviance or norm breaking. One way society does this is through the construction of heroes and villains. Heroes, of course, are people we are supposed to "look up to" and use as role models. Villains are people whom we "look down on" and reject their example. Organizations of all types create heroes that serve as guides to everyday behavior. In each case below, who is being made into a hero? Why? What are the values or behaviors that we are encouraged to copy in our own lives?

HINT A society without heroes and villains would be one in which no one cared what people thought or how they acted. Societies create heroes as role models that should inspire us to be more like them. Societies create heroes by emphasizing one aspect of someone's life and ignoring lots of other things. For example, Babe Ruth was a great ball player, but his private life was sometimes less than inspiring. Perhaps this is why the Catholic church never considers anyone a candidate for sainthood until after—usually long after—the person has died.

AP Wide World Photos/Charlie Campbell/*The Star-Democrat*

Colleges and universities create heroes in various ways. Here we see the president of Washington College (Maryland) awarding the Sophie Kerr Prize at a recent graduation ceremony. This prize, which included a check for more than $50,000, recognized English major Claire Tompkins's ability to write outstanding short stories. What is heroic in this case? What does graduating with honors or Latin praise (*cum laude* and so on) define as heroic? What about villains—how do colleges and universities create them, too?

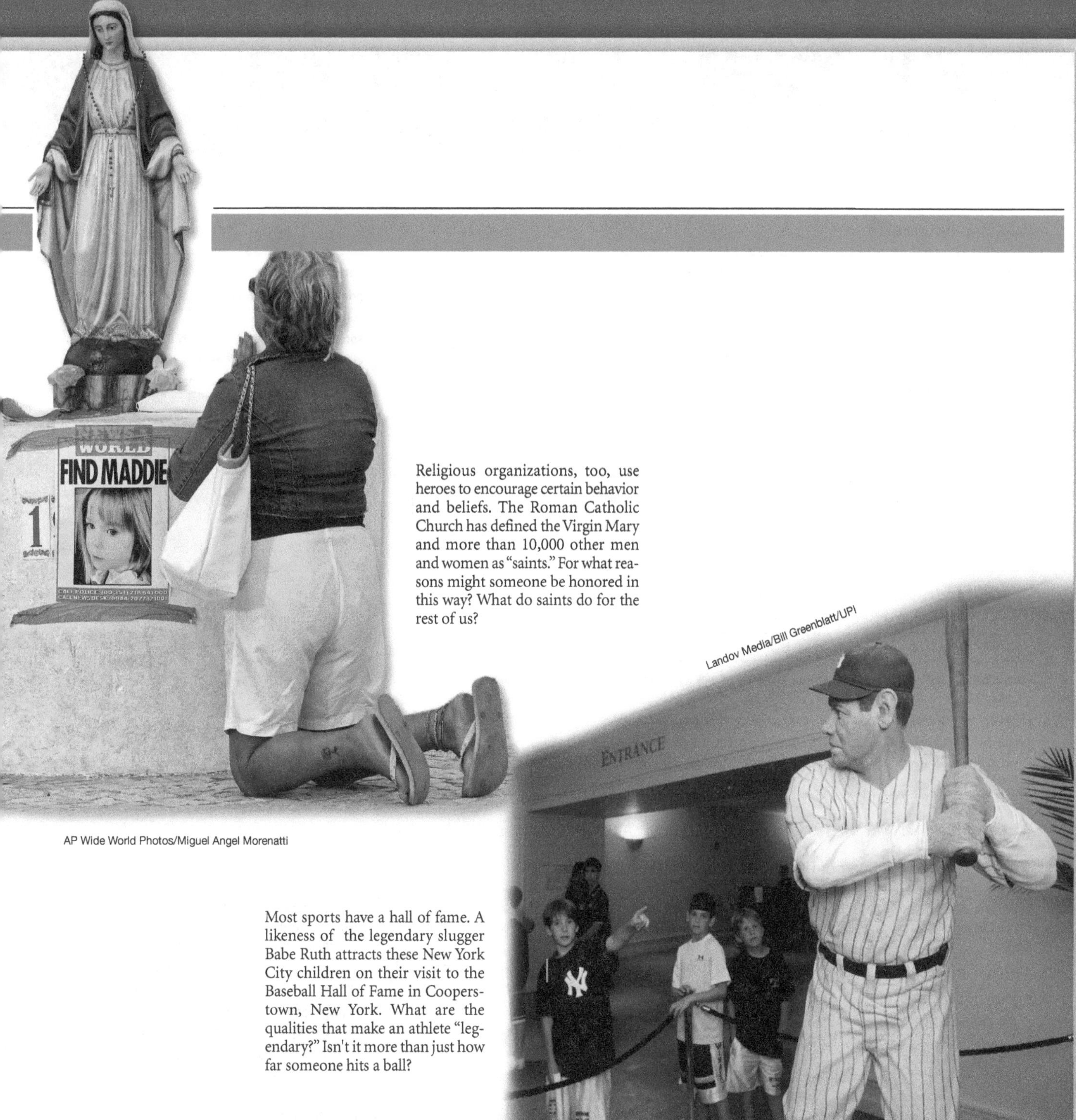

Religious organizations, too, use heroes to encourage certain behavior and beliefs. The Roman Catholic Church has defined the Virgin Mary and more than 10,000 other men and women as "saints." For what reasons might someone be honored in this way? What do saints do for the rest of us?

AP Wide World Photos/Miguel Angel Morenatti

Most sports have a hall of fame. A likeness of the legendary slugger Babe Ruth attracts these New York City children on their visit to the Baseball Hall of Fame in Cooperstown, New York. What are the qualities that make an athlete "legendary?" Isn't it more than just how far someone hits a ball?

Landov Media/Bill Greenblatt/UPI

Applying SOCIOLOGY in Everyday Life

1. Do athletic teams, fraternities and sororities, and even people in a college classroom create heroes and villains? Explain how and why.
2. Identity theft is a new type of crime that victimizes as many as 10 million people each year in the United States. Research this phenomenon, and explain how this offense differs from property crime that takes place "on the street." (Consider differences in the crime, the offenders, and the victims.)
3. Watch an episode of any real-action police show such as *Cops*. Based on what you see, how would you profile the people who commit crimes?

MAKING THE GRADE

Deviance

What Is Deviance?

DEVIANCE refers to norm violations ranging from minor infractions, such as bad manners, to major infractions, such as serious violence.

Theories of Deviance

BIOLOGICAL THEORIES

- focus on individual abnormality
- explain human behavior as the result of biological instincts

Lombroso claimed that criminals have apelike physical traits; later research links criminal behavior to certain body types and genetics.

PSYCHOLOGICAL THEORIES

- focus on individual abnormality
- see deviance as the result of "unsuccessful socialization"

Reckless and Dinitz's *containment theory* links delinquency to weak conscience.

✓ *Biological and psychological theories provide a limited understanding of crime and other deviance because most violations are carried out by people who are normal.*

SOCIOLOGICAL THEORIES view all behavior—deviance as well as conformity—as products of society. Sociologists point out that

- what is deviant varies from place to place according to cultural norms
- behavior and individuals become deviant as others define them that way
- what and who a society defines as deviant reflect who has and does not have social power

deviance the recognized violation of cultural norms

crime the violation of a society's formally enacted criminal law

social control attempts by society to regulate people's thoughts and behavior

criminal justice system the organizations—police, courts, and prison officials—that respond to alleged violations of the law

Theoretical Analysis of Deviance

The Functions of Deviance: Structural-Functional Analysis

Durkheim claimed that deviance is a normal element of society that

- affirms cultural norms and values
- clarifies moral boundaries
- brings people together
- encourages social change

Merton's **strain theory** explains deviance in terms of a society's cultural goals and the means available to achieve them.

Deviant subcultures are discussed by Cloward and Ohlin, Cohen, Miller, and Anderson.

Labeling Deviance: Symbolic-Interaction Analysis

Labeling theory claims that deviance depends less on what someone does than on how others react to that behavior. If people respond to primary deviance by stigmatizing a person, secondary deviance and a deviant career may result.

The **medicalization of deviance** is the transformation of moral and legal deviance into a medical condition. In practice, this means a change in labels, replacing "good" and "bad" with "sick" and "well."

Sutherland's **differential association theory** links deviance to how much others encourage or discourage such behavior.

Hirschi's **control theory** states that imagining the possible consequences of deviance often discourages such behavior. People who are well integrated into society are less likely to engage in deviant behavior.

labeling theory the idea that deviance and conformity result not so much from what people do as from how others respond to those actions

stigma a powerfully negative label that greatly changes a person's self-concept and social identity

medicalization of deviance the transformation of moral and legal deviance into a medical condition

white-collar crime crime committed by people of high social position in the course of their occupations

corporate crime the illegal actions of a corporation or people acting on its behalf

organized crime a business supplying illegal goods or services

hate crime a criminal act against a person or a person's property by an offender motivated by racial or other bias

 *See the Applying Theory table.*

Deviance and Inequality: Social-Conflict Analysis

Based on Karl Marx's ideas, social-conflict theory holds that laws and other norms operate to protect the interests of powerful members of any society.

- **White-collar offenses** are committed by people of high social position as part of their jobs. Sutherland claimed that such offenses are rarely prosecuted and are most likely to end up in civil rather than criminal court.
- **Corporate crime** refers to illegal actions by a corporation or people acting on its behalf. Although corporate crimes cause considerable public harm, most cases of corporate crime go unpunished.
- **Organized crime** has a long history in the United States, especially among categories of people with few legitimate opportunities.

Deviance, Race, and Gender

- What people consider deviant reflects the relative power and privilege of different categories of people.
- **Hate crimes** are crimes motivated by racial or other bias; they target people with disadvantages based on race, gender, or sexual orientation.
- In the United States and elsewhere, societies control the behavior of women more closely than that of men.

What Is Crime?

CRIME is the violation of criminal laws enacted by local, state, or federal governments. There are two major categories of serious crime:

- crimes against the person (violent crime), including murder, aggravated assault, forcible rape, and robbery
- crimes against property (property crime), including burglary, larceny-theft, auto theft, and arson

PATTERNS OF CRIME IN THE UNITED STATES

- Official statistics show that arrest rates peak in late adolescence and drop steadily with age.
- About 67% of people arrested for property crimes and 82% of people arrested for violent crimes are male.
- Street crime is more common among people of lower social position. Including white-collar and corporate crime makes class differences in criminality smaller.
- More whites than African Americans are arrested for street crimes. However, African Americans are arrested more often than whites in relation to their population size. Asian Americans have a lower-than-average rate of arrest.
- By world standards, the U.S. crime rate is high.

crimes against the person crimes that direct violence or the threat of violence against others; also known as *violent crimes*

crimes against property crimes that involve theft of property belonging to others; also known as *property crimes*

victimless crimes violations of law in which there are no obvious victims

The U.S. Criminal Justice System

Police

The police maintain public order by enforcing the law.

- Police use personal discretion in deciding whether and how to handle a situation.
- Research suggests that police are more likely to make an arrest if the offense is serious, if bystanders are present, or if the suspect is African American or Latino.

Courts

Courts rely on an adversarial process in which attorneys—one representing the defendant and one representing the state—present their cases in the presence of a judge who monitors legal procedures.

- In practice, U.S. courts resolve most cases through plea bargaining. Though efficient, this method puts less powerful people at a disadvantage.

Punishment

There are four justifications for punishment:

- retribution
- deterrence
- rehabilitation
- societal protection

The **death penalty** remains controversial in the United States, the only high-income Western nation that routinely executes serious offenders. The trend is toward fewer executions.

Community-based corrections include probation and parole. These programs lower the cost of supervising people convicted of crimes and reduce prison overcrowding but have not been shown to reduce recidivism.

See the Summing Up table.

plea bargaining a legal negotiation in which a prosecutor reduces a charge in exchange for a defendant's guilty plea

retribution an act of moral vengeance by which society makes the offender suffer as much as the suffering caused by the crime

deterrence the attempt to discourage criminality through the use of punishment

rehabilitation a program for reforming the offender to prevent later offenses

societal protection rendering an offender incapable of further offenses temporarily through imprisonment or permanently by execution

criminal recidivism later offenses by people previously convicted of crimes

community-based corrections correctional programs operating within society at large rather than behind prison walls

MAKING THE GRADE

Sample Test Questions

Multiple-Choice Questions

1. **Crime is a special type of deviance that**
   a. refers to violations of law.
   b. involves punishment.
   c. refers to any violation of a society's norms.
   d. always involves a particular person as the offender.

2. **Emile Durkheim explains that deviance is**
   a. defined by the rich and used against the poor.
   b. harmful not just to victims but to society as a whole.
   c. often at odds with public morality.
   d. found in every society.

3. **Applying Robert Merton's strain theory, a person selling illegal drugs for a living would be an example of which of the following categories?**
   a. conformist
   b. innovator
   c. retreatist
   d. ritualist

4. **Labeling theory states that deviance**
   a. is a normal part of social life.
   b. always changes people's social identity.
   c. arises not from what people do as much as how others respond.
   d. All of the above are correct.

5. **When Jake's friends began calling him a "dope-head," he left the group and spent more time smoking marijuana. He also began hanging out with others who used drugs, and by the end of the term, he had dropped out of college. Edwin Lemert would call this situation an example of**
   a. primary deviance.
   b. the development of secondary deviance.
   c. the formation of a deviant subculture.
   d. the beginning of retreatism.

6. **A social-conflict approach claims that who a society calls deviant depends on**
   a. who has and does not have power.
   b. a society's moral values.
   c. how often the behavior occurs.
   d. how harmful the behavior is.

7. **Stealing a laptop computer from the study lounge in a college dorm is an example of which criminal offense?**
   a. burglary
   b. motor vehicle theft
   c. robbery
   d. larceny-theft

8. **The FBI's criminal statistics used in this chapter to create a profile of the street criminal reflect**
   a. all crimes that occur.
   b. offenses known to the police.
   c. offenses that involve violence.
   d. offenses resulting in a criminal conviction.

9. **Most people arrested for a violent crime in the United States are**
   a. white.
   b. African American.
   c. Hispanic.
   d. Asian.

10. **Which of the following is the oldest justification for punishing an offender?**
    a. deterrence
    b. retribution
    c. societal protection
    d. rehabilitation

ANSWERS: 1 (a); 2 (d); 3 (b); 4 (c); 5 (b); 6 (a); 7 (d); 8 (b); 9 (a); 10 (b).

Essay Questions

1. How does a sociological view of deviance differ from the common-sense idea that bad people do bad things?
2. Research (Mauer, 1999) shows that one in three black men between the ages of twenty and twenty-nine is in jail, on probation, or on parole. What factors, noted in this chapter, help explain this pattern?

Social Stratification

Jay Directo/Agence France Presse/Getty Images

All societies rank people so that some have far greater opportunities and resources than others. What the specific inequalities are and how great they are vary from place to place and over time.

Getty Images/Abid Katib

Social Stratification

Getty Images/Lori Adamski Peek/Stone

Alamy Images/Homer Sykes

CHAPTER OVERVIEW

This chapter introduces the central concept of social stratification. Social stratification is important because our social standing affects almost everything about our lives.

Illustration by Ken Marschall © 1992

On April 10, 1912, the ocean liner *Titanic* slipped away from the docks of Southampton, England, on its maiden voyage across the North Atlantic to New York. A proud symbol of the new industrial age, the towering ship carried 2,300 men, women, and children, some enjoying more luxury than most travelers today could imagine. Poor passengers crowded the lower decks, journeying to what they hoped would be a better life in the United States.

Two days out, the crew received radio warnings of icebergs in the area but paid little notice. Then, near midnight, as the ship steamed swiftly westward, a lookout was stunned to see a massive shape rising out of the dark ocean directly ahead. Moments later, the *Titanic* collided with a huge iceberg, as tall as the ship itself, which split open its side as if the grand vessel were a giant tin can.

Seawater flooded into the ship's lower levels. Within twenty-five minutes of impact, people were rushing for the lifeboats. By 2:00 A.M., the bow was completely submerged, and the stern rose high above the water. Minutes later, all the lights went out. Clinging to the deck, quietly observed by those huddled in lifeboats, hundreds of helpless passengers and crew solemnly passed their final minutes before the ship disappeared into the frigid Atlantic (W. Lord, 1976).

The tragic loss of more than 1,600 lives when the *Titanic* sank made news around the world. Looking back at this terrible accident with a sociological eye, we note that some categories of passengers had much better odds of survival than others. Reflecting that era's traditional ideas about gender, women and children were allowed to board the lifeboats first, with the result that 80 percent of the people who died were men. Class, too, was at work. More than 60 percent of people holding first-class tickets were saved because they were on the upper decks, where warnings were sounded first and lifeboats were accessible. Only 36 percent of the second-class passengers survived, and of the third-class passengers on the lower decks, only 24 percent escaped drowning. On board the *Titanic,* class turned out to mean much more than the quality of accommodations—it was a matter of life or death.

The fate of the passengers on the *Titanic* dramatically illustrates how social inequality affects the way people live and sometimes whether they live at all. This chapter explores the important concept of social stratification.

What Is Social Stratification?

For tens of thousands of years, humans lived in small hunting and gathering societies. Although members of these bands might single out one person as swifter, stronger, or more skillful in collecting food, everyone had roughly the same social standing. As societies became more complex a major change came about. Societies began to elevate specific categories of people above others, giving some parts of the population more wealth, power, and prestige than others.

Social stratification, *a system by which a society ranks categories of people in a hierarchy,* is based on four important principles:

1. **Social stratification is a trait of society, not simply a reflection of individual differences.** Many of us think of social standing in terms of personal talent and effort, and as a result, we often exaggerate the extent to which we control our own fate. Did a higher percentage of the first-class passengers on the *Titanic* survive because they were better swimmers than second- and third-class passengers? No. They did better because of their privileged position on the ship, which gave them first access to the lifeboats. Similarly, children born into wealthy families are more likely than children born into poverty to enjoy good health, do well in school, succeed in a career, and live a long life. Neither the rich nor the poor created social stratification, yet this system shapes the lives of us all.
2. **Social stratification carries over from generation to generation.** We have only to look at how parents pass their social position

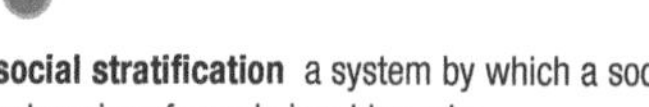

social stratification a system by which a society ranks categories of people in a hierarchy

social mobility a change in position within the social hierarchy

SEEING SOCIOLOGY in Everyday Life

Are there elements of caste in U.S. society? To what extent do parents pass on their social position to children? What about the idea that there are "women's jobs" and "men's jobs"?

on to their children to see that stratification is a trait of societies rather than individuals. Some individuals, especially in high-income societies, do experience **social mobility**, *a change in position within the social hierarchy.* Social mobility may be upward or downward. We celebrate the achievements of rare individuals such as Christina Aguilera and Michael Jordan, both of whom rose from modest beginnings to fame and fortune. Some people move downward because of business failures, unemployment, or illness. More often people move *horizontally;* they switch from one job to another at about the same social level. The social standing of most people remains much the same over their lifetime.

3. **Social stratification is universal but variable.** Social stratification is found everywhere. Yet *what* is unequal and *how* unequal it is varies from one society to another. In some societies, inequality is mostly a matter of prestige; in others, wealth or power is the key element of difference. In addition, some societies contain more inequality than others.
4. **Social stratification involves not just inequality but beliefs as well.** Any system of inequality not only gives some people more than others but also defines these arrangements as fair. Just as the details of inequality vary, the explanations of *why* people should be unequal differ from society to society.

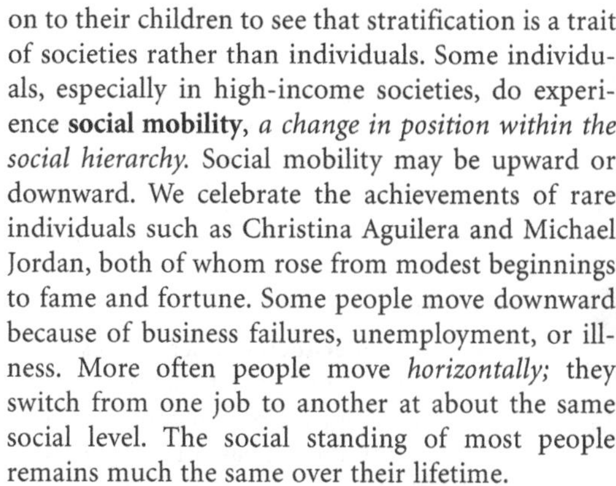

The personal experience of poverty is clear in this photograph of mealtime in a homeless shelter. The main sociological insight is that although we feel the effects of social stratification personally, our social standing is largely the result of the way society (or a world of societies) structures opportunity and reward. To the core of our being, we are all products of social stratification.

Caste and Class Systems

Sociologists distinguish between *closed systems,* which allow for little change in social position, and *open systems,* which permit much more social mobility. Closed systems are called *caste systems,* and more open systems are called *class systems.*

The Caste System

A **caste system** is *social stratification based on ascription, or birth.* A pure caste system is closed because birth alone determines a person's entire future, allowing little or no social mobility based on individual effort. People live out their lives in the rigid categories assigned to them, without the possibility of change for the better or worse.

An Illustration: India

Many of the world's societies, most of them agrarian, are caste systems. In India, for example, much of the population still lives in traditional villages where the caste system persists. The Indian system identifies four major castes (or *varnas,* from a Sanskrit word that means "color"): Brahman, Kshatriya, Vaishya, and Sudra. On the local level, each of these is composed of hundreds of subcaste groups (*jatis*).

From birth, a caste system determines the direction of a person's life. First, with the exception of farming, which is open to everyone, families in each caste perform one type of work, as priests, soldiers, barbers, leather workers, street sweepers, and so on.

Second, a caste system demands that people marry others of the same ranking. If people were to enter into "mixed" marriages with members of other castes, what rank would their children hold? Sociologists call this pattern of marrying within a social category *endogamous* marriage (*endo-* stems from the Greek word for "within"). According to tradition—this practice is now rare today and it is found only in remote rural areas—Indian parents select their children's future marriage partners, often before the children reach their teens.

Third, caste guides everyday life by keeping people in the company of "their own kind." Norms reinforce this practice by teaching, for example, that a "purer" person of a higher caste is "polluted" by contact with someone of lower standing.

Fourth, caste systems rest on powerful cultural beliefs. Indian culture is built on the Hindu tradition that doing the caste's life work and accepting an arranged marriage are moral duties.

Caste and Class Systems

caste system social stratification based on ascription, or birth

class system social stratification based on both birth and individual achievement

meritocracy social stratification based on personal merit

William Albert Allard/National Geographic Image Collection

In rural India, the traditional caste system still shapes people's lives. This girl is a member of the "untouchables," a category below the four basic castes. She and her family are clothes washers, people who clean material "polluted" by blood or human waste. Such work is defined as unclean for people of higher caste position.

Caste and Agrarian Life

Caste systems are typical of agrarian societies because agriculture demands a lifelong routine of hard work. By teaching a sense of moral duty, a caste system ensures that people are disciplined for a lifetime of work and are willing to perform the same jobs as their parents. Thus the caste system has hung on in rural areas of India some seventy years after being formally outlawed. Seeing Sociology in the News later in this chapter provides another example of caste in the Middle Eastern nation of Yemen.

Another country long dominated by caste is South Africa, although the system of *apartheid,* or separation of the races, is no longer legal and is now in decline. The Thinking Globally box takes a closer look.

The Class System

Because a modern economy must attract people to work in many occupations other than farming, it depends on developing people's talents in diverse fields. This gives rise to a **class system**, *social stratification based on both birth and individual achievement.*

Class systems are more open than caste systems, so people who gain schooling and skills may experience social mobility. As a result, class distinctions become blurred, and even blood relatives may have different social standings. Categorizing people according to their color, sex, or social background comes to be seen as wrong in modern societies as all people gain political rights and, in principle, equal standing before the law. In addition, work is no longer fixed at birth but involves some personal choice. Greater individuality also translates into more freedom in selecting a marriage partner.

Meritocracy

The concept of **meritocracy** refers to *social stratification based on personal merit.* Because industrial societies need to develop a broad range of abilities beyond farming, stratification is based not just on the accident of birth but also on *merit* (from a Latin word meaning "earned"), which includes a person's knowledge, abilities, and effort. A rough measure of merit is a person's job and how well it is done. To increase meritocracy, industrial societies expand equality of opportunity and teach people to expect unequal rewards based on individual performance.

In a pure meritocracy, which has never existed, social position would depend entirely on a person's ability and effort. Such a system would have ongoing social mobility, blurring social categories as individuals continuously move up or down in the system, depending on their latest performance.

Caste societies define merit in terms of loyalty to the system—that is, dutifully performing whatever job comes with a person's birth. Caste systems waste human potential, but they are very orderly. A need for some amount of order is one reason industrial and postindustrial societies keep some elements of caste—such as letting wealth pass from generation to generation—rather than becoming complete meritocracies. A pure meritocracy would weaken families and other social groupings. After all, economic performance is not everything: Would we want to evaluate our family members solely on how successful they are in their jobs outside the home? Probably not. Class systems in industrial societies develop some meritocracy to promote productivity and efficiency, but they keep caste elements, such as family, to maintain order and social unity.

Status Consistency

Status consistency is *the degree of uniformity in a person's social standing across various dimensions of social inequality.* A caste system has limited social mobility and high status consistency, so the typical person has the same relative ranking with regard to wealth, power, and prestige. The greater mobility of class systems produces less status

SEEING SOCIOLOGY in Everyday Life

How much of your social position is due to merit (personal ability and effort), and how much is due to caste (passed on from your parents)?

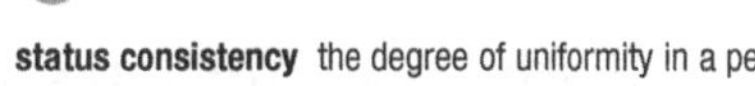

status consistency the degree of uniformity in a person's social standing across various dimensions of social inequality

THINKING GLOBALLY

Race as Caste: A Report from South Africa

Jerome: Wow. I've been reading about racial caste in South Africa. I'm glad that's history.

Reggie: But racial inequality is far from over. . . .

At the southern tip of the African continent lies South Africa, a country about the size of Alaska with a population of more than 48 million. For 300 years, the native Africans who lived there were ruled by white people, first by the Dutch traders and farmers who settled there in the mid-seventeenth century and then by the British, who colonized the area early in the nineteenth century. By the early 1900s, the British had taken over the entire country, naming it the Union of South Africa.

In 1961, the nation declared its independence from Britain, calling itself the Republic of South Africa, but freedom for the black majority was still decades away. To ensure their political control over the black population, whites instituted the policy of *apartheid*, or racial separation. Apartheid, written into law in 1948, denied blacks national citizenship, ownership of land, and any voice in the nation's government. As a lower caste, blacks received little schooling and performed menial, low-paying jobs. White people with even average wealth had at least one black household servant.

The members of the white minority claimed that apartheid protected their cultural traditions from the influence of people they considered inferior. When blacks resisted apartheid, whites used brutal military repression to maintain their power. Even so, steady resistance—especially from younger blacks, who demanded a political voice and economic opportunity—gradually forced the country to change. Criticism from other industrial nations added to the pressure. By the mid-1980s, the tide began to turn as the South African government granted limited political rights to people of mixed race and Asian ancestry. Next came the right of all people to form labor unions, to enter occupations once limited to whites, and to own property. Officials also repealed apartheid laws that separated the races in public places.

The pace of change increased in 1990 with the release from prison of Nelson Mandela, who led the fight against apartheid. In 1994, the first national election open to all races made Mandela president, ending centuries of white minority rule.

Despite this dramatic political change—and strong economic growth during the last decade—social stratification in South Africa is still based on race. Even with the right to own property, one-fourth of black South Africans have no work, and half the population lives below the poverty line. The worst off are some 7 million *ukuhleleleka,* which means "marginal people" in the Xhosa language. Soweto-by-the-Sea may sound like a summer getaway, but this cluster of townships is home to thousands of people who live crammed into shacks made of packing crates, corrugated metal, cardboard, and other discarded materials. There is no electricity for lights or refrigeration. Without plumbing, people use buckets to haul sewerage. The community's women line up to take a turn at a single water tap that serves more than 1,000 people. Jobs are hard to come by, and those who do find work are lucky to earn $250 a month.

South Africa's current president, Jacob Zuma, who was elected in 2009, leads a nation still crippled by its history of racial caste. Tourism is up and holds the promise of an economic boom in years to come, but the country can break from the past only by providing real opportunity to all its people.

Tomasz Tomaszewski/National Geographic Image Collection

WHAT DO YOU THINK?

1. How has race been a form of caste in South Africa?
2. Although apartheid is no longer law, why does racial inequality continue to shape South African society?
3. Does race operate as an element of caste in the United States? Explain your answer.

Sources: Mabry & Masland (1999), Murphy (2002), and Perry (2009).

consistency, so people are ranked higher on some dimensions of social standing and lower on others. In the United States, for example, most college professors with advanced academic degrees enjoy high social prestige but earn only modest incomes. Low status consistency means that it is harder to define people's social position. Therefore, *classes* are much harder to define than *castes.*

Caste and Class: The United Kingdom

The mix of caste and meritocracy in class systems is well illustrated by the United Kingdom (Great Britain—consisting of England, Wales, and Scotland—and Northern Ireland), an industrial nation with a long agrarian history.

Seeing SOCIOLOGY in the 

The New York Times

Languishing at the Bottom of Yemen's Ladder

By ROBERT F. WORTH
February 27, 2008

By day, they sweep the streets of the Old City, ragged, dark-skinned men in orange jump suits. By night, they retreat to fetid slums on the edge of town.

They are known as "Al Akhdam"—the servants. Set apart by their African features, they form a kind of hereditary caste at the very bottom of Yemen's social ladder.

Degrading myths pursue them: they eat their own dead, and their women are all prostitutes. Worst of all, they are reviled as outsiders in their own country, descendants of an Ethiopian army that is said to have crossed the Red Sea to oppress Yemen before the arrival of Islam.

"We are ready to work, but people say we are good for nothing but servants; they will not accept us," said Ali Izzil Muhammad Obaid, a 20-year-old man who lives in a filthy Akhdam shantytown on the edge of this capital. "So we have no hope."

In fact, the Akhdam—who prefer to be known as "Al Muhamasheen," or the marginalized ones—may have been in this southern corner of the Arabian Peninsula for as long as anyone, and their ethnic origins are unclear. Their debased status is a remnant of Yemen's old social hierarchy, which collapsed after the 1962 revolution struck down the thousand-year-old Imamate.

But where Yemen's other hereditary social classes, the sayyids and the judges and the sheiks, and even the lower orders like butchers and ironworkers, slowly dissolved, the Akhdam retained their separate position. There are more than a million of them among Yemen's fast-growing population of 22 million, concentrated in segregated slums in the major cities.

"All the doors are closed to us except sweeping streets and begging," Mr. Obaid said. "We are surviving, but we are not living."

The Akhdam have not been offered the kind of affirmative action programs India's government has used to improve the lot of the Dalits, or untouchables, there. In part, that is because Yemen never had a formal caste system like India's.

As a result, the Akhdam have languished at the margins of society, suffering a persistent discrimination that flouts the egalitarian maxims of the Yemeni state.

Even the recent waves of immigrants from Ethiopia and Somalia, many of them desperately poor, have fared better than the Akhdam, and do not share their stigma.

The Akhdam who work as street sweepers, for instance, are rarely granted contracts even after decades of work, despite the fact that all Yemeni civil servants are supposed to be granted contracts after six months, said Suha Bashren, a relief official with Oxfam here. They receive no benefits, and almost no time off.

"If supervisors want to dismiss them, they can do that," said Ali Abdullah Saeed Hawdal, who started working as a street sweeper in 1968. "The supervisors use violence against them with no fear of penalties. They treat them as people with no rights."

The living conditions of the Akhdam are appalling. . . . In one Akhdam shantytown on the edge of Sana, more than 7,000 people live crammed into a stinking warren of low concrete

Aristocratic England

In the Middle Ages, England had a castelike system of aristocracy. The aristocracy included the leading members of the church, who were thought to speak with the authority of God. Some clergy were local priests who were not members of the aristocracy and who lived simple lives. But the highest church officials lived in palaces and presided over an organization that owned much land, which was the major source of wealth. Church leaders, typically referred to as the *first estate* in France and other European countries, also had a great deal of power to shape the political events of the day.

The rest of the aristocracy, which in France and other European countries was known as the *second estate,* was a hereditary nobility that made up barely 5 percent of the population. The royal family—the king and queen at the top of the power structure—as well as lesser nobles (including several hundred families headed by men titled as dukes, earls, and barons) together owned most of the nation's land. Most of the men and women within the aristocracy were wealthy due to their holdings of land, and they had many servants for their homes as well as ordinary farmers to work their fields. With all their work done for them by others, members of the aristocracy had no occupation and came to believe that engaging in a trade or any other work for income was beneath them. Aristocrats used their leisure time to develop skills in horseback riding and warfare and to cultivate refined tastes in art, music, and literature.

To prevent their vast landholdings from being divided by heirs when they died, aristocrats devised the law of *primogeniture* (from the Latin meaning "firstborn"), which required that all property pass to the oldest son or other male relation. Younger sons had to find other means of support. Some of these men became leaders in the church—where they would live as well as they were used to—and helped tie together the church and the state by having members of the same families running both. Other younger sons within the aristocracy became military officers or judges or took up other professions considered honorable for gentlemen. In an age when no woman could inherit her father's property and few women had the opportunity to earn a living on their own, a noble daughter depended for her security on marrying well.

Below the high clergy and the rest of the aristocracy, the vast majority of men and women were simply called *commoners* or, in France and other European countries, the *third estate.* Most commoners were serfs working land owned by nobles or the church. Unlike members of the aristocracy, most commoners had little schooling and were illiterate.

As the Industrial Revolution expanded England's economy, some commoners living in cities made lots of money and were able to challenge the nobility. More emphasis on meritocracy, the growing importance of money, and the expansion of schooling and legal rights eventually blurred the difference between aristocrats and commoners and gave rise to a class system.

blocks next to a mountain of trash. Young children, many of them barefoot, run through narrow, muddy lanes full of human waste and garbage.

A young woman named Nouria Abdullah stood outside the tiny cubicle—perhaps 6 feet by 8 feet, with a ceiling too low to allow her to stand up—where she lives with her husband and six children. Inside, a thin plastic sheet covered a dirt floor. A small plastic mirror hung on the wall, and a single filthy pillow lay in the corner.

Nearby, a single latrine, in a room approximately 3 feet by 3 feet, serves about 50 people. The residents must carry water in plastic jugs from a tank on the edge of the slum, supplied by a charity group. . . .

Ms. Abdullah said she and her family brought in no more than 1,000 Yemeni riyals a week, about $5. She begs for change, while her husband, Muhammad, gathers metal and electrical components from trash heaps and sells them.

Like most people in the shantytown, they have no documents, and they do not know how old they are. "We are living like animals," Ms. Abdullah said. "We cook and sleep and live in the same room. We need other shelters."

When the winter rains come, the houses are flooded, she said. On the cold days in winter, the family burns trash to stay warm.

Richard Bramble, a British doctor who works in a charity-sponsored clinic inside the shantytown, said half of the deaths there over the past year were of children under the age of 5, and one-quarter were in the first month of life. . . .

Part of the problem, many members of the community say, is that most of the Akhdam have internalized their low status and do not try to better themselves, find real jobs or seek an education. . . .

"They do not even push their children to become soldiers," said Muhammad Abdu Ali, the director of the medical clinic in the shantytown and one of the Akhdam. "They have given up on changing their situation." . . .

Mr. Hawdal pointed proudly to a plaque on the wall commemorating his long service as a sweeper. He has sent all of his children to school, unlike most of the Akhdam, and one of them made it as far as ninth grade.

But Mr. Hawdal acknowledged sadly that all of his children had since dropped out. He was running out of money, he said. But that was not the only reason.

"They had no hope of doing anything except street sweeping," he said.

WHAT DO YOU THINK?

1. Castes are set apart with cues visible in everyday life. What indicators of low-caste standing identify the people known as Al Akhdam?
2. What common stereotypes are used by people in Yemen to justify marginalizing Al Akhdam?
3. What, if anything, would you suggest the government do to assist the people known as Al Akhdam? Explain.

Adapted from the original article, "Languishing at the Bottom of Yemen's Ladder," by Robert F. Worth from *The New York Times*, Global Edition Section, February 27, 2008.

Perhaps it is a sign of the times that these days, traditional titles are put up for sale by aristocrats who need money. In 1996, for example, Earl Spencer—the brother of the late Princess Diana—sold one of his titles, Lord of Wimbledon, to raise the $300,000 he needed to redo the plumbing in one of his large homes (McKee, 1996).

The United Kingdom Today

The United Kingdom has a class system, but caste elements from England's aristocratic past are still evident. A small number of British families still hold considerable inherited wealth and enjoy high prestige, schooling at excellent universities, and substantial political influence. A traditional monarch, Queen Elizabeth II, is the United Kingdom's head of state, and Parliament's House of Lords is composed of "peers," about half of whom are aristocrats of noble birth. However, control of government has passed to the House of Commons, where the prime minister and other leaders reach their positions by achievement—winning an election—rather than by birth.

Lower in the class hierarchy, roughly one-fourth of the British people form the middle class. Many earn comfortable incomes from professions and business and are likely to have investments in the form of stocks and bonds. Below the middle class, perhaps half of all Britons consider themselves "working-class," earning modest incomes through manual labor. The remaining one-fourth of the British people make up the lower class, the poor who lack steady work or who work full time but are paid too little to live comfortably. Most lower-class Britons live in the nation's northern and western regions, which have been further impoverished by the closings of mines and factories.

The British mix of caste elements and meritocracy has produced a highly stratified society with some opportunity to move upward or downward, much the same as exists in the United States (Long & Ferrie, 2007). One result of centuries of aristocracy in the United Kingdom is great importance attached to linguistic accent. Distinctive patterns of speech develop in any society when people are set off from one another over several generations. People in the United States treat accent as a clue to where a person lives or grew up (we can easily identify a midwestern "twang" or a southern "drawl"). In the United Kingdom, however, accent is a mark of social class, with upper-class people speaking "the King's English" but most people speaking "like commoners." So different are these two accents that the British seem to be, as the saying goes, "a single people divided by a common language."

Another Example: Japan

Social stratification in Japan also mixes caste and meritocracy. Japan is both the world's oldest continuously operating monarchy and a modern society where wealth follows individual achievement.

Aristocratic Japan

By the fifth century C.E., Japan was an agrarian society with a rigid caste system, ruled by an imperial family, containing both aristocrats

SEEING SOCIOLOGY in Everyday Life

Are there any aristocratic elements of U.S. society? What are they?

SEEING SOCIOLOGY in Everyday Life

In modern Japan, notice how elements of meritocracy (such as people going to school in order to get a better job) mix with elements of caste (such as the continuing importance of people's social background and differences in opportunities for women and men).

Getty Images, Inc. – Getty News/Tim Graham Picture Library

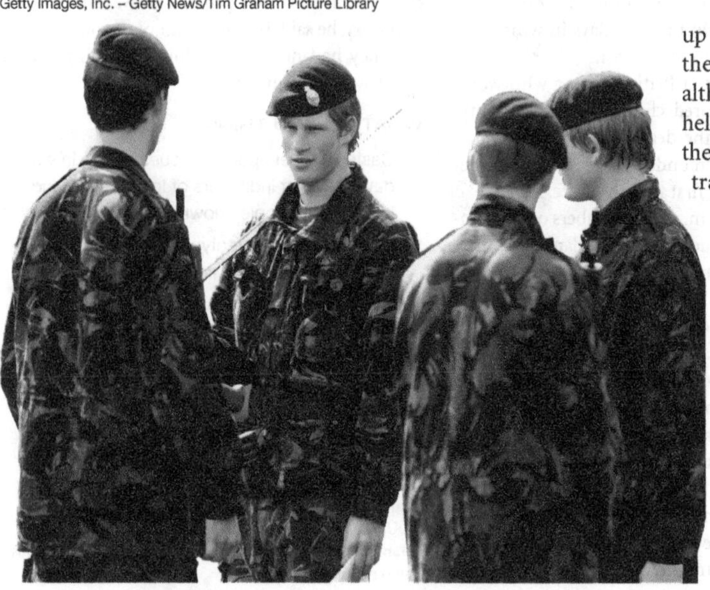

Following the centuries-old practice among aristocratic men in England, Prince Harry completed military training as part of his studies at Eton. He is part of a royal family that traces its ancestry back more than a thousand years—an element of caste that remains in the British class system.

and commoners. The emperor ruled by divine right (meaning that he claimed that God intended him to rule), and his military leader (*shogun*) enforced the emperor's rule with the help of regional nobles or warlords.

Below the nobility were the *samurai*, a warrior caste whose name means "to serve." This second rank of Japanese society was made up of soldiers who learned martial arts and who lived by a code of honor based on absolute loyalty to their leaders.

As in Great Britain, most people in Japan at this time in history were commoners who worked very hard to live from day to day. Unlike their European counterparts, however, Japanese commoners were not lowest in rank. At the bottom were the *burakumin*, or "outcasts," looked down on by both lord and commoner. Like the lowest-caste groups in India, these outcasts lived apart from others, performed the most distasteful work, and could not change their social standing.

Modern Japan

By the 1860s (the time of the Civil War in the United States), the nobles realized that Japan's traditional caste system would prevent the country from entering the modern industrial era. Besides, as in Britain, some nobles were happy to have their children marry wealthy commoners who had more money than they did. As Japan opened up to the larger world, the traditional caste system weakened. In 1871, the Japanese legally banned the social category of *burakumin*, although some people still looked down on those whose ancestors held this rank. After Japan's defeat in World War II, the nobles lost their privileges, so only the emperor remains as a symbol of Japan's traditions, but he has little real power.

Social stratification in Japan is very different from the rigid caste system of centuries ago. Today, Japanese society consists of "upper," "upper-middle," "lower-middle," and "lower" classes. The exact lines between these classes are unclear to most Japanese, and many people do move between classes over time. But because Japanese culture tends to respect tradition, family background is never far from the surface when sizing up someone's social standing. Officially, everyone is equal before the law, but in reality, many people still look at one another through the centuries-old lens of caste.

Finally, traditional ideas about gender continue to shape Japanese society. Legally, the two sexes are equal, but men dominate women in many ways. Because Japanese parents are more likely to send sons than daughters to college, there is a significant gender gap in education. With the recent economic downturn in Japan, many more women have entered the labor force. But most working women fill lower-level support positions in the corporate world, only rarely assuming leadership roles. In short, individual achievement in Japan's modern class system operates in the shadow of centuries of traditional male privilege (Norbeck, 1983; Brinton, 1988; H. W. French, 2002).

Classless Societies? The Former Soviet Union

Nowhere in the world do we find a society without some degree of social inequality. Yet some nations have claimed to be classless.

The Second Russian Revolution

The Union of Soviet Socialist Republics (USSR), which rivaled the United States as a military superpower in the mid- to late twentieth century, was born out of a revolution in Russia in 1917. The Russian Revolution ended the feudal aristocracy in which a nobility ruled the country and transferred farms, factories, and other productive property from private ownership to a new centralized state government.

The Russian Revolution was guided by the ideas of Karl Marx, who believed that private ownership of productive property was the basis of social classes. When the state took control of the economy, Soviet officials boasted that they had created the first modern classless society.

Critics, however, pointed out that based on their jobs, the Soviet people were actually stratified into four unequal categories. At the top

structual social mobility a shift in the social position of large numbers of people due more to changes in society itself than to individual efforts

were high government officials, known as *apparatchiks.* Next came the Soviet intelligentsia, including lower government officials, college professors, scientists, physicians, and engineers. Below them were manual workers and, at the lowest level, the rural peasantry.

In reality, the Soviet Union was not classless at all. But putting factories, farms, colleges, and hospitals under state control did create more economic equality (although with sharp differences in power) than in capitalist societies such as the United States.

The Modern Russian Federation

In 1985, Mikhail Gorbachev came to power in the Soviet Union with a new economic program known as *perestroika* ("restructuring"). Gorbachev saw that although the Soviet system had reduced economic inequality, living standards were far behind those of other industrial nations. He tried to generate economic growth by reducing the inefficient centralized control of the economy.

Gorbachev's economic reforms turned into one of the most dramatic social movements in history. People in the Soviet Union and in other socialist countries of Eastern Europe blamed their poverty and their lack of basic freedoms on the repressive ruling class of Communist party officials. Beginning in 1989, people throughout Eastern Europe toppled their socialist governments, and at the end of 1991, the Soviet Union itself collapsed, with its largest republic remaking itself as the Russian Federation.

The Soviet Union's story shows that social inequality involves more than economic resources. Soviet society did not have the extremes of wealth and poverty found in the United Kingdom, Japan, and the United States. But an elite class existed all the same, based on political power rather than wealth.

What about social mobility in so-called classless societies? During the twentieth century, there was as much upward social mobility in the Soviet Union as in the United States. Rapidly expanding industry and government drew many poor rural peasants into factories and offices. This trend illustrates what sociologists call **structural social mobility**, *a shift in the social position of large numbers of people due more to changes in society itself than to individual efforts.*

Getty Images/De Agostini Editore Picture Library

One of the major events of the twentieth century was the socialist revolution in Russia, which led to the creation of the Soviet Union. Following the ideas of Karl Marx, the popular uprising overthrew a feudal aristocracy, as depicted in the 1920 painting *Bolshevik* by Boris Mikhailovich Kustodiev.

November 24, Odessa, Ukraine. The first snow of our voyage flies over the decks as our ship docks at Odessa, the former Soviet Union's southernmost port on the Black Sea. A short distance away, we gaze up the Potemkin Steps, the steep stairway up to the city, where bloody violence that eventually led to the Russian Revolution took place. It has been several years since our last visit, and much has changed; in fact, the Soviet Union itself has collapsed. Has life improved? For some people, certainly: There are now chic boutiques where well-dressed shoppers buy fine wines, designer clothes, and imported perfumes. But for most people, life seems much worse. Flea markets line the curbs as families sell their home furnishings. When meat costs $4 a pound and the average person earns about $30 a month, people become desperate. Even the city has to save money by turning off street lights after 8:00 p.m. The spirits of most people seem as dim as Odessa's streets.

During the 1990s, the forces of structural social mobility in the new Russian Federation turned downward. One indicator is that the average life span for Russian men dropped by eight years and for women by two years. Many factors are involved in this decline, including Russia's poor health care system, but the Russian people clearly have suffered in the turbulent period of economic change that began in 1991 (Gerber & Hout, 1998; Mason, 2003).

The hope was that in the long run, closing inefficient state industries would improve the nation's economic performance. The economy has expanded, but for many Russians, living standards have fallen, and millions face hard times. The few people who made huge fortunes have seen much of their new wealth vanish in the recent recession. This fact, along with more government control over the Russian economy, has caused economic inequality to decline. At the same time, however, many people wonder what a return to a more socialist society will mean for their living standards and political freedoms (Zuckerman, 2006; Wendle, 2009).

China: Emerging Social Classes

Sweeping political and economic change has affected not just the former Soviet Union but also the People's Republic of China. After the Communist revolution in 1949, the state took control of all farms, factories, and other productive property. Communist party leader Mao Zedong declared all types of work to be equally important, so officially, social classes no longer existed.

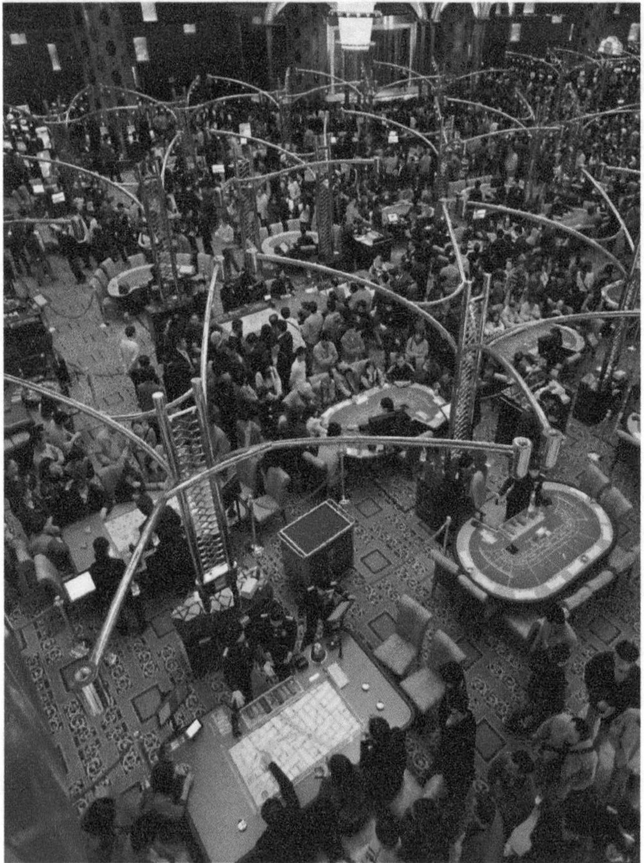

By allowing a market economy to expand, especially in the coastal regions, China has experienced remarkable economic growth. The gambling industry in Macao now rivals that of Las Vegas.

The new program greatly reduced economic inequality. But as in the Soviet Union, social differences remained. The country was ruled by a political elite with enormous power and considerable privilege; below them were managers of large factories as well as skilled professionals; next came industrial workers; at the bottom were rural peasants, who were not even allowed to leave their villages and migrate to cities.

Further economic change came in 1978 when Mao died and Deng Xiaoping became China's leader. The state gradually loosened its hold on the economy, allowing a new class of business owners to emerge. Communist party leaders remain in control of the country, and some have prospered as they have joined the ranks of the small but wealthy elite who control new privately run industries. Much of this new economic growth has been concentrated in cities, especially in coastal areas, where living standards have soared far above those in China's rural interior (United Nations, 2008).

Since the late 1990s, the booming cities along China's coast have become home to many thousands of people made rich by the expanding economy. In addition, these cities have attracted more than 100 million young migrants from rural areas in search of better jobs and a better life. Many more have wanted to move to the booming cities, but the government still restricts movement, which has the effect of slowing upward social mobility. For those who have been able to move, the jobs that are available are generally better than the work that people knew before. But many of these new jobs are dangerous, and most pay wages that barely meet the higher costs of living in the city, so that the majority of the migrants remain poor. To make matters worse, the weakening global economy has caused many Chinese factories to lay off workers or even to shut down. As a result, beginning in 2008, some people began to migrate from cities back to the countryside—a case of downward social mobility (Atlas, 2007; Wu & Treiman, 2007; Chang, 2008; Powell, 2008).

A new category in China's social hierarchy consists of the *hai gui*, a term derived from words meaning "returned from overseas" or "sea turtles." The ranks of the "sea turtles" are increasing by tens of thousands each year as young women and men return from education in other countries, in many cases from college and university campuses in the United States. These young people, most of whom were from privileged families to begin with, typically return to China to find many opportunities and soon become very influential (Liu & Hewitt, 2008).

In sum, China displays a new and emerging class system that is a mix of the old political hierarchy and a new business hierarchy. Economic inequality in China has increased, and as Figure 1 shows, it is now about the same as in the United States. With so much change

ideology cultural beliefs that justify particular social arrangements, including patterns of inequality

Davis-Moore thesis the functional analysis claiming that social stratification has beneficial consequences for the operation of society

in China, that country's social stratification is likely to remain dynamic for some time to come (Bian, 2002).

Ideology: The Power behind Stratification

How do societies persist without sharing resources more equally? The highly stratified British aristocracy and the caste system in Japan each survived for centuries, and for 2,000 years, people in India accepted the idea that they should be privileged or poor based on the accident of birth.

A major reason that social hierarchies endure is **ideology**, *cultural beliefs that justify particular social arrangements, including patterns of inequality.* A belief—for example, the idea that rich people are smart and poor people are lazy—is ideological to the extent that it supports inequality by defining it as fair.

Plato and Marx on Ideology

According to the ancient Greek philosopher Plato (427–347 B.C.E.), every culture considers some type of inequality just. Although Karl Marx understood this, he was far more critical of inequality than Plato. Marx criticized capitalist societies for defending wealth and power in the hands of a few as "a law of the marketplace." Capitalist law, he continued, defines the right to own property and ensures that money stays within the same families from one generation to the next. In short, Marx concluded, culture and institutions combine to support a society's elite, which is why established hierarchies last such a long time.

Historical Patterns of Ideology

Ideology changes along with a society's economy and technology. Because agrarian societies depend on most people's lifelong labor, they develop caste systems that make carrying out the duties of a person's social position or "station" a moral responsibility. With the rise of industrial capitalism, an ideology of meritocracy emerges, defining wealth and power as prizes to be won by the individuals who perform the best. This change means that the poor—often given charity under feudalism—come to be looked down on as personally undeserving. This harsh view is found in the ideas of the early sociologist Herbert Spencer, as explained in the Thinking About Diversity box.

History shows how difficult it is to change social stratification. However, challenges to the status quo always arise. The traditional idea that "a woman's place is in the home," for example, has given way to increased economic opportunities for women in many societies today. The continuing progress toward racial equality in South Africa reflects widespread rejection of the ideology of apartheid.

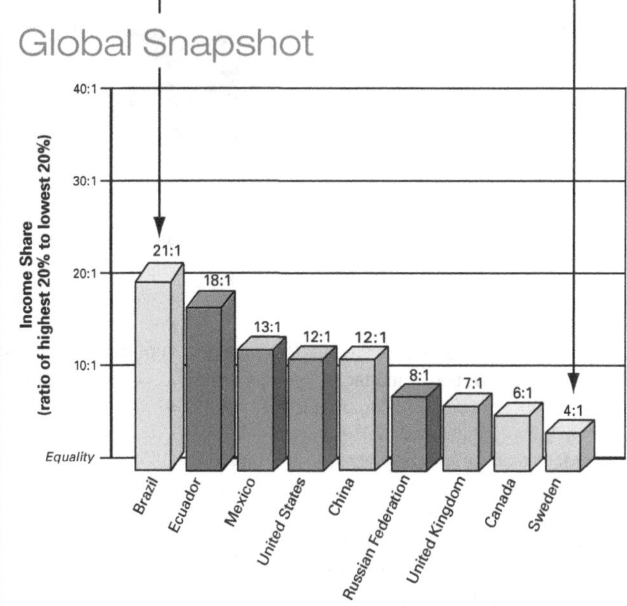

FIGURE 1 Economic Inequality in Selected Countries, 2007

Many low- and middle-income countries have greater economic inequality than the United States. But the United States has more economic inequality than most high-income nations.

Sources: U.S. Census Bureau (2008) and World Bank (2008).

The Functions of Social Stratification

Why does social stratification exist at all? One answer, consistent with the structural-functional approach, is that social inequality plays a vital part in the smooth operation of society. This argument was set forth more than sixty years ago by Kingsley Davis and Wilbert Moore (1945).

The Davis-Moore Thesis

The **Davis-Moore thesis** states that *social stratification has beneficial consequences for the operation of society.* How else, ask Davis and Moore, can we explain the fact that some form of social stratification has been found in every society?

Davis and Moore note that modern societies have hundreds of occupational positions of varying importance. Certain jobs—say, washing windows, cutting grass, or answering a telephone—are fairly easy and can be performed by almost anyone. Other jobs—such as designing new generations of computers or transplanting human

MAKING THE GRADE

Stratification systems produce ideas and beliefs that define their operation as just. In short, stratification involves not just who has what but also beliefs about justice—why people should have what they have.

THINKING ABOUT DIVERSITY: RACE, CLASS, & GENDER

The Meaning of Class: Is Getting Rich "the Survival of the Fittest"?

Jake: "My dad is amazing. He's really smart!"

Frank: "You mean he's rich. He owns I don't know how many businesses."

Jake: "Do you think people get rich without being smart?"

It's a question we all wonder about. How much is our social position a matter of intelligence? What about hard work? Being born to the "right family"? Even "dumb luck"?

More than in most societies, in the United States we link social standing to personal abilities including intelligence. This idea goes back a long time. We have all heard the words "the survival of the fittest," which describes our society as a competitive jungle in which the "best" survive and the rest fall behind. The phrase was coined by one of sociology's pioneers, Herbert Spencer (1820–1903), whose ideas about social inequality are still widespread today.

Spencer, who lived in England, eagerly followed the work of the natural scientist Charles Darwin (1809–1882). Darwin's theory of biological evolution held that a species changes physically over many generations as it adapts to the natural environment. Spencer incorrectly applied Darwin's theory to the operation of society, which does not operate according to biological principles. In Spencer's distorted view, society became the "jungle," with the "fittest" people rising to wealth and the "failures" sinking into miserable poverty.

It is no surprise that Spencer's views, wrong as they were, were popular among the rising U.S. industrialists of the day. John D. Rockefeller (1839–1937), who made a vast fortune building the oil industry, recited Spencer's "social gospel" to young children in Sunday school. As Rockefeller saw it, the growth of giant corporations—and the astounding wealth of their owners—was merely the result of the survival of the fittest, a basic fact of nature. Neither Spencer nor Rockefeller had much sympathy for the poor, seeing poverty as evidence of individuals' failing to measure up in a competitive world. Spencer opposed social welfare programs because he thought they penalized society's "best" people (through taxes) and rewarded its "worst" members (through welfare benefits). By incorrectly using Darwin's theory, the rich could turn their backs on everyone else, assuming that inequality was inevitable and somehow "natural."

Today, sociologists point out that our society is far from a meritocracy, as Spencer claimed. And it is not the case that companies or individuals who generate lots of money necessarily benefit society. The people who made hundreds of millions of dollars selling subprime mortgages in recent years certainly ended up hurting just about everyone. But Spencer's view that the "fittest" rise to the top remains widespread in our very unequal and individualistic culture.

WHAT DO YOU THINK?

1. How much do you think inequality in our society can correctly be described as "the survival of the fittest"? Why?
2. Why do you think Spencer's ideas are still popular in the United States today?
3. Is how much you earn a good measure of your importance to society? Why or why not?

organs—are difficult and demand the scarce talents of people with extensive and expensive training.

Therefore, Davis and Moore explain, the greater the functional importance of a position, the more rewards a society attaches to it. This strategy promotes productivity and efficiency because rewarding important work with income, prestige, power, and leisure encourages people to do these jobs and to work better, longer, and harder. In short, unequal rewards (which is what social stratification is) benefit society as a whole.

Davis and Moore claim that any society could be egalitarian, but only to the extent that people are willing to let *anyone* perform *any* job. Equality would also demand that someone who carries out a job poorly be rewarded the same as someone who performs it well. Such a system would clearly offer little incentive for people to try their best, reducing the society's productive efficiency.

The Davis-Moore thesis suggests the reason stratification exists; it does not state what rewards a society should give to any occupational position or how unequal the rewards should be. It merely points out that positions a society considers more important must offer enough rewards to draw talented people away from less important work.

CRITICAL REVIEW Although the Davis-Moore thesis is an important contribution to understanding social stratification, it has provoked criticism. Melvin Tumin (1953) wondered, first, how we assess the importance of a particular occupation. Perhaps the high rewards our society gives to physicians results partly from deliberate efforts by the medical profession to limit the supply of physicians and thereby increase the demand for their services.

SEEING SOCIOLOGY in Everyday Life

Following Davis and Moore's thinking, why do professors give grades from A to F? What would happen if they gave every student the same grade? Explain.

Furthermore, do rewards actually reflect the contribution someone makes to society? With income of about $275 million per year, Oprah Winfrey earns more in one day than President Obama earns all year. Would anyone argue that hosting a talk show is more important than leading a country? And what about members of the U.S. military serving in Iraq or Afghanistan? Facing the risks of combat, a private first-class in the U.S. Army earned only $19,000 in 2008 (Defense Finance and Accounting Service, 2008; Kroll, 2008).

And what about the heads of the big Wall Street financial firms that collapsed in 2008? It seems reasonable to conclude that these corporate leaders made some bad decisions, yet their salaries were astronomical. Even after finishing its worst year ever, with losses of $27 billion, Merrill Lynch paid bonuses of more than $1 million to more than 700 employees (Fox, 2009). The top people in the financial industry made out even better. In 2007, James Dimon, head of JP Morgan Chase, had earnings of more than $55 million; the same year, Lloyd Blankfein, head of Goldman Sachs, made more than $70 million—an amount it would take the typical U.S. Army private more than 3,500 years to earn.

Even top executives who lose their jobs do surprisingly well. Chuck Prince was forced to resign as head at Citigroup, but not before receiving a "severance package" worth more than $30 million. When insurance giant AIG failed, corporate leader Martin Sullivan left the company, receiving $47 million on the way out (Beck & Simon, 2008; Scherer, 2008). Do corporate executives deserve such megasalaries for their contributions to society?

Second, Tumin claimed that Davis and Moore ignore how caste elements of social stratification can prevent the development of individual talent. Born to privilege, rich children have opportunities to develop their abilities that many gifted poor children never have.

Third, living in a society that places so much emphasis on money, we tend to overestimate the importance of high-paying work; what do stockbrokers or people who trade international currencies really contribute to society? For the same reason, it is difficult for us to see the value of work that is not oriented toward making money, such as parenting, creative writing, playing music in a symphony, or just being a good friend to someone in need (Packard, 2002).

Finally, by suggesting that social stratification benefits all of society, the Davis-Moore thesis ignores how social inequality promotes conflict and even outright revolution. This criticism leads us to the social-conflict approach, which provides a very different explanation for social inequality.

CHECK YOUR LEARNING State the Davis-Moore thesis in your own words. What are Tumin's criticisms of this thesis?

Getty Images/Kevin Winter

Oprah Winfey reported income of $275 million in 2008 and enjoys fame to match her fortune. Guided by the Davis-Moore thesis, why would societies reward some people so much more than others? How would Karl Marx answer this question differently?

Stratification and Conflict

Social-conflict analysis argues that rather than benefiting society as a whole, social stratification benefits some people and disadvantages others. This analysis draws heavily on the ideas of Karl Marx, with contributions from Max Weber.

Karl Marx: Class Conflict

Karl Marx, explained that most people have one of two basic relationships to the means of production: They either own productive property or labor for others. Different productive roles arise from different social classes. In medieval Europe, aristocratic families, including high church officials and titled nobles, owned the land on which peasants labored as farmers. In industrial class systems, the capitalists

blue-collar occupations lower-prestige jobs that involve mostly manual labor

white-collar occupations higher-prestige jobs that involve mostly mental activity

(or the bourgeoisie) own the factories, which use the labor of workers (the proletarians).

Marx lived during the nineteenth century, a time when a small number of industrialists in the United States were amassing great fortunes. Andrew Carnegie, J. P. Morgan, John D. Rockefeller, and John Jacob Astor (one of the few very rich passengers to drown on the *Titanic*) lived in fabulous mansions staffed by dozens of servants. Even by today's standards, their incomes were staggering. For example, Carnegie earned about $20 million a year in 1900 (more than $500 million in today's dollars), when the average worker earned roughly $500 a year (Baltzell, 1964; Pessen, 1990; Williamson, 2008).

Marx explained that capitalist society *reproduces the class structure* in each new generation. This happens as families gain wealth and pass it down from generation to generation. But, he predicted, oppression and misery would eventually drive the working majority to come together to overthrow capitalism in favor of a socialist system that would end class differences.

CRITICAL REVIEW Marx has had enormous influence on sociological thinking. But his revolutionary ideas, calling for the overthrow of capitalist society, also make his work highly controversial.

One of the strongest criticisms of Marxism is that it denies a central idea of the Davis-Moore thesis: that a system of unequal rewards is necessary to place talented people in the right jobs and to motivate them to work hard. Marx separated reward from performance; his egalitarian ideal was based on the principle "from each according to his ability; to each according to his needs" (Marx & Engels, 1972:388, orig. 1848). However, failure to reward individual performance may be precisely what caused the low productivity of the former Soviet Union and other socialist economies around the world. Defenders of Marxism respond to such criticism by asking why we assume that humanity is inherently selfish rather than social, noting that individual rewards are not the only way to motivate people to perform their social roles (M. S. Clark, 1991).

A second problem is that the revolutionary change Marx predicted has failed to happen, at least in advanced capitalist societies. The next section explains why.

CHECK YOUR LEARNING How does Marx's view of social stratification differ from the Davis-Moore thesis?

Why No Marxist Revolution?

Despite Marx's prediction, capitalism is still thriving. Why have industrial workers not overthrown capitalism? Ralf Dahrendorf (1959) suggested four reasons:

1. **Fragmentation of the capitalist class.** Today, millions of stockholders, rather than single families, own most large companies. Day-to-day corporate operations are in the hands of a large class of managers, who may or may not be major stockholders. With stock widely held—about half of U.S. households own stocks—more and more people have a direct stake in the capitalist system (U.S. Census Bureau, 2008).
2. **A higher standard of living.** A century ago, most workers were in factories or on farms employed in **blue-collar occupations**, *lower-prestige jobs that involve mostly manual labor.* Today, most workers are engaged in **white-collar occupations**, *higher-prestige jobs that involve mostly mental activity.* These jobs are in sales, management, and other service fields. Most of today's white-collar workers do not think of themselves as an "industrial proletariat." Just as important, the average income

Redux Pictures/Kristen Schmid/*The New York Times*

What is the main cause of social inequality? The Davis-Moore thesis suggests that societies attach unequal rewards to tasks of unequal importance. The social-conflict approach offers a different insight, claiming that the economic system determines the extent of stratification. Times have been tough in Galesburg, Illinois, since the Maytag corporation closed its factory in 2004. How would each theoretical approach explain the economic troubles of many of this town's people?

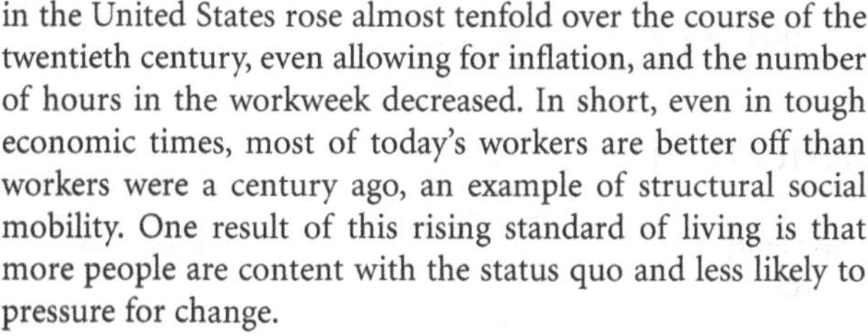

SEEING SOCIOLOGY in Everyday Life

Using what you have learned so far about social inequality in the United States, how correct do you think Marx was about capitalism? Explain your answer.

socioeconomic status (SES) a composite ranking based on various dimensions of social inequality

in the United States rose almost tenfold over the course of the twentieth century, even allowing for inflation, and the number of hours in the workweek decreased. In short, even in tough economic times, most of today's workers are better off than workers were a century ago, an example of structural social mobility. One result of this rising standard of living is that more people are content with the status quo and less likely to pressure for change.

3. **More worker organizations.** Workers today have the right to form labor unions, to make demands of management, and to back up their demands with threats of work slowdowns and strikes. As a result, labor disputes are settled without threatening the capitalist system.
4. **Greater legal protections.** Over the past century, the government passed laws to make workplaces safer. In addition, unemployment insurance, disability protection, and Social Security now provide workers with greater financial security.

A Counterpoint

These developments suggest that U.S. society has smoothed many of capitalism's rough edges. Yet some observers claim that Marx's analysis of capitalism is still largely valid (Domhoff, 1983; Boswell & Dixon, 1993; Hout, Brooks, & Manza, 1993). First, wealth remains highly concentrated, with 35 percent of all privately owned property in the hands of just 1 percent of the U.S. population (Keister, 2000; Wolff, 2007). Second, many of today's white-collar jobs offer no more income, security, or satisfaction than factory work did a century ago. Third, many benefits enjoyed by today's workers came about through the class conflict Marx described. Workers still struggle to hold on to what they have, and in recent years, many workers have actually lost pensions and other benefits. Fourth, although workers have gained some legal protections, ordinary people still face disadvantages that the law cannot overcome. Therefore, social-conflict theorists conclude, even without a socialist revolution in the United States, Marx was still mostly right about capitalism.

Max Weber: Class, Status, and Power

Max Weber, agreed with Karl Marx that social stratification causes social conflict, but he viewed Marx's economics-based model as simplistic. Instead, he claimed that social stratification involves three distinct dimensions of inequality.

The first dimension is economic inequality—the issue so important to Marx—which Weber termed *class position.* Weber did not think of classes as well-defined categories but as a continuum ranging from

Shutterstock/Aleksandar Todorovic

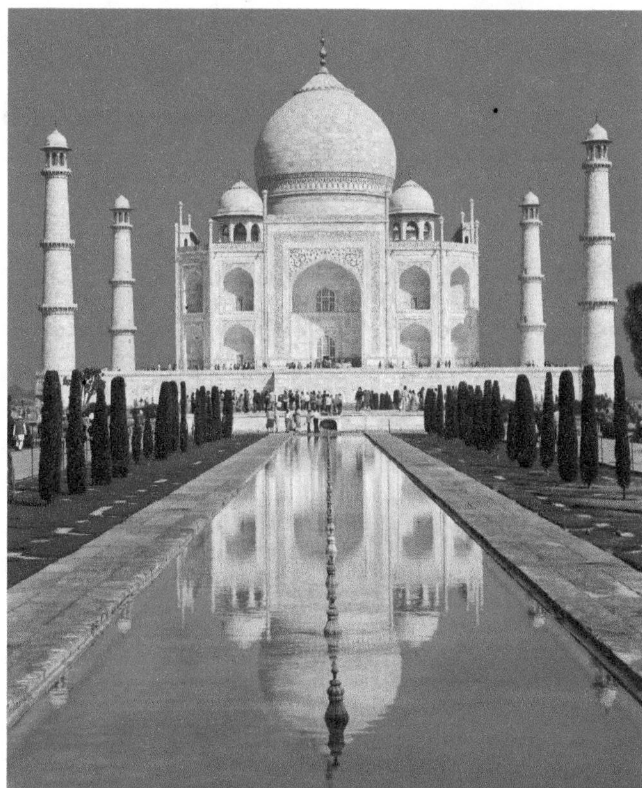

The extent of social inequality in agrarian systems is greater than that found in industrial societies. One indication of the unchallenged power of rulers is the monumental structures built over years with the unpaid labor of common people. Although the Taj Mahal in India is among the world's most beautiful buildings, it was built as a tomb for a single individual.

high to low. Weber's second dimension is *status,* or social prestige, and the third is *power.*

Weber's Socioeconomic Status Hierarchy

Marx viewed social prestige and power as simple reflections of economic position and did not treat them as distinct dimensions of inequality. But Weber noted that status consistency in modern societies is often quite low: A local official might exercise great power yet have little wealth or social prestige.

Weber, then, portrays social stratification in industrial societies as a multidimensional ranking rather than a hierarchy of clearly defined classes. In line with Weber's thinking, sociologists use the term **socioeconomic status (SES)** to refer to *a composite ranking based on various dimensions of social inequality.*

MAKING THE GRADE

Marx viewed social stratification in terms of classes. Weber viewed inequality in terms of a socioeconomic status hierarchy with multiple dimensions. Individuals stand higher on some dimensions and lower on others, so there are no clear-cut classes.

MAKING THE GRADE

Be sure you understand Weber's claim about the changing basis of stratification in agrarian (prestige), industrial-capitalist (money), and socialist (power) societies.

APPLYING THEORY

Social Stratification

	Structural-Functional Approach	Social-Conflict Approach	Symbolic-Interaction Approach
What is the level of analysis?	Macro-level	Macro-level	Micro-level
What is social stratification?	Stratification is a system of unequal rewards that benefits society as a whole.	Stratification is a division of a society's resources that benefits some people and harms others.	Stratification is a factor that guides people's interactions in everyday life.
What is the reason for our social position?	Social position reflects personal talents and abilities in a competitive economy.	Social position reflects the way society divides resources.	The products we consume all say something about social position.
Are unequal rewards fair?	Yes. Unequal rewards boost economic production by encouraging people to work harder and try new ideas. Linking greater rewards to more important work is widely accepted.	No. Unequal rewards only serve to divide society, creating "haves" and "have-nots." There is widespread opposition to social inequality.	Maybe. People may or may not define inequality as fair. People may view their social position as a measure of self-worth, justifying inequality in terms of personal differences.

Inequality in History

Weber claimed that each of his three dimensions of social inequality stands out at different points in the evolution of human societies. Status or social prestige is the main difference in agrarian societies, taking the form of honor. Members of these societies (whether nobles or servants) gain status by conforming to cultural norms that apply to their particular rank.

Industrialization and the development of capitalism eliminate traditional rankings based on birth but create striking financial inequality. Thus in an industrial society, the crucial difference between people is the economic dimension of class.

Over time, industrial societies witness the growth of a bureaucratic state. Bigger government and the spread of all sorts of other organizations make power more important in the stratification system. Especially in socialist societies, where government regulates many aspects of life, high-ranking officials become the new ruling elite.

This historical analysis points to a final difference between Weber and Marx. Marx thought societies could eliminate social stratification by abolishing the private ownership of productive property that is the basis of capitalism. Weber doubted that overthrowing capitalism would significantly lessen social stratification. It might reduce economic differences, he reasoned, but socialism would increase inequality by expanding government and concentrating power in the hands of a political elite. Popular uprisings against socialist bureaucracies in Eastern Europe and the former Soviet Union show that discontent can be generated by socialist political elites and thus support Weber's position.

CRITICAL REVIEW Max Weber's multidimensional view of social stratification has greatly influenced sociological thinking. But critics (particularly those who favor Marx's ideas) argue that although social class boundaries may have blurred, industrial and postindustrial societies still show striking patterns of social inequality.

Income inequality has been increasing in the United States. Although some people still favor Weber's multidimensional hierarchy, in light of this trend, others think that Marx's view of the rich versus the poor is closer to the truth.

CHECK YOUR LEARNING What are Weber's three dimensions of social inequality? According to Weber, which of them would you expect to be most important in the United States? Why?

conspicuous consumption buying and using products because of the "statement" they make about social position

SEEING SOCIOLOGY IN EVERYDAY LIFE

When Class Gets Personal: Picking (with) Your Friends

The sound of banjo music drifted across the field late one summer afternoon. I lay down my brush, climbed over the fence I had been painting, and walked toward the sound of the music to see what was going on. That's how I met my neighbor Max, a retired factory worker who lived just up the road. Max was a pretty good "picker," and within an hour, I was back on his porch with my guitar. I called Howard, a friend who teaches at the college, and he showed up a little while later, six-string in hand. The three of us jammed for a couple of hours, smiling all the while.

The next morning, I was mowing the grass in front of the house when Max came walking down the road. I turned off the mower as he got closer. "Hi, Max," I said. "Thanks for having us over last night. I really had fun."

"Don't mention it," Max responded with a wave. Then he stopped and shook his head a little and added, "Ya know, I was thinkin' after you guys left. I mean, it was really somethin' how you guys looked like you were having a great time. With somebody like *me!*"

Getty Images, Inc – Liaison/Aaron J.H. Walker

"Well, yeah," I replied, not sure of what he meant. "You sure played better than we did."

Max looked down at the ground, embarrassed by the compliment. Then he added, "What I mean is that you guys were having a good time with somebody like *me.* You're both professors, right? *Doctors,* even . . ."

WHAT DO YOU THINK?

1. Why did Max assume that two college teachers would not enjoy spending time with him?
2. How does his reaction suggest that people take social position personally?
3. Can you think of a similar experience you have had with someone of a different social position?

Stratification and Interaction

Because social stratification has to do with the way an entire society is organized, sociologists (Marx and Weber included) typically treat it as a macro-level issue. But a micro-level analysis of social stratification is also important because people's social standing affects their everyday interactions. The Applying Theory table summarizes the contributions of the three approaches to an understanding of social stratification.

In most communities, people interact primarily with others of about the same social standing. To some extent, this is because we tend to live with others like ourselves. As we observe people during the course of our everyday activities, such as walking in a downtown shopping area, we see that couples or groups tend to be made up of individuals whose appearance and shopping habits are similar. People with very different social standing commonly keep their distance from one another. Well-dressed people walking down the street on their way to an expensive restaurant, for example, might move across the sidewalk or even cross the street to avoid getting close to others they think are homeless people. The Seeing Sociology in Everyday Life box gives another example of how differences in social class position can affect interaction.

Finally, just about everyone realizes that the way we dress, the car we drive (or the bus we ride), and even the food and drink we order at the campus snack bar say something about our budget and personal tastes. Sociologists use the term **conspicuous consumption** to refer to *buying and using products because of the "statement" they make about social position.* Ignoring the water fountain in favor of paying for bottled water tells people you have extra money to spend. And no one needs a $100,000 automobile to get around, of course, but driving up in such a vehicle says "I have arrived" in more ways than one.

Stratification and Technology: A Global Pespective

We can weave together a number of observations made in this chapter to show that a society's technology affects its type of social stratification. This analysis draws on Gerhard Lenski's model of sociocultural evolution.

SEEING SOCIOLOGY in Everyday Life

Can you identify aspects of everyday life that seem to suggest that economic inequality is increasing? Explain.

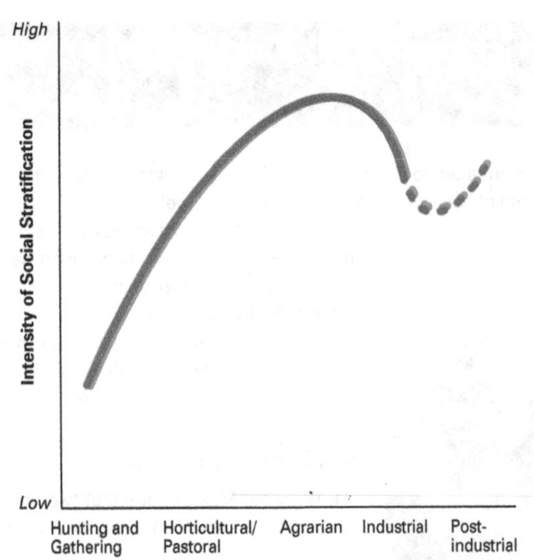

FIGURE 2 **Social Stratification and Technological Development: The Kuznets Curve**

The Kuznets curve shows that greater technological sophistication is generally accompanied by more pronounced social stratification. The trend reverses itself as industrial societies relax rigid, castelike distinctions in favor of greater opportunity and equality under the law. Political rights are more widely extended, and there is even some leveling of economic differences. However, the emergence of postindustrial society has brought an upturn in economic inequality, as indicated by the broken line added by the author.

Sources: Based on Kuznets (1955) and Lenski (1966).

Hunting and Gathering Societies

With simple technology, members of hunting and gathering societies produce only what is necessary for day-to-day living. Some people may produce more than others, but the group's survival depends on all sharing what they have. Thus no categories of people are better off than others.

Horticultural, Pastoral, and Agrarian Societies

As technological advances create a surplus, social inequality increases. In horticultural and pastoral societies, a small elite controls most of the surplus. Large-scale agriculture is more productive still, and striking inequality—as great as at any time in history—places the nobility in an almost godlike position over the masses.

Industrial Societies

Industrialization turns the tide, pushing inequality downward. Prompted by the need to develop individual talents, meritocracy takes hold and weakens the power of traditional aristocracy. Industrial productivity also raises the standard of living of the historically poor majority. Specialized work demands schooling for all, sharply reducing illiteracy. A literate population, in turn, presses for a greater voice in political decision making, reducing social inequality and lessening men's domination of women.

Over time, even wealth becomes somewhat less concentrated (contradicting Marx's prediction). In the 1920s, the richest 1 percent of the U.S. population owned about 40 percent of all wealth, a figure that fell to 30 percent by the 1980s as higher taxes on the rich paid for new government programs benefiting the poor (Williamson & Lindert, 1980; Beeghley, 1989; U.S House of Representatives, 1991). Such trends help explain why Marxist revolutions occurred in *agrarian* societies—such as Russia (1917), Cuba (1959), and Nicaragua (1979)—where social inequality is most pronounced, rather than in industrial societies as Marx had predicted. However, wealth inequality in the United States turned upward again after 1990 and is once again about the same as it was in the 1920s (Keister, 2000; Wolff & Zacharias, 2006). With the goal of reducing this trend, the Obama administration has acted to raise federal income tax rates on high-income individuals.

The Kuznets Curve

In human history, then, technological advances first increase but then moderate the extent of social stratification. Greater inequality is functional for agrarian societies, but industrial societies benefit from a less unequal system. This historical trend, recognized by the Nobel Prize–winning economist Simon Kuznets (1955, 1966), is illustrated by the Kuznets curve, shown in Figure 2.

Social inequality around the world generally supports the Kuznets curve. Global Map 1 shows that high-income nations that have passed through the industrial era (including the United States, Canada, and the nations of Western Europe) have somewhat less income inequality than nations in which a larger share of the labor force remains in farming (as is common in Latin America and Africa). At the same time, it is important to remember that income inequality reflects not just technological development but also the political and economic priorities of a country. Income disparity in the United States may have declined during much of the last century, but this country still has more economic inequality than Canada, European nations, and Japan (although less than some other high-income nations, including Argentina, Saudi Arabia, and South Africa).

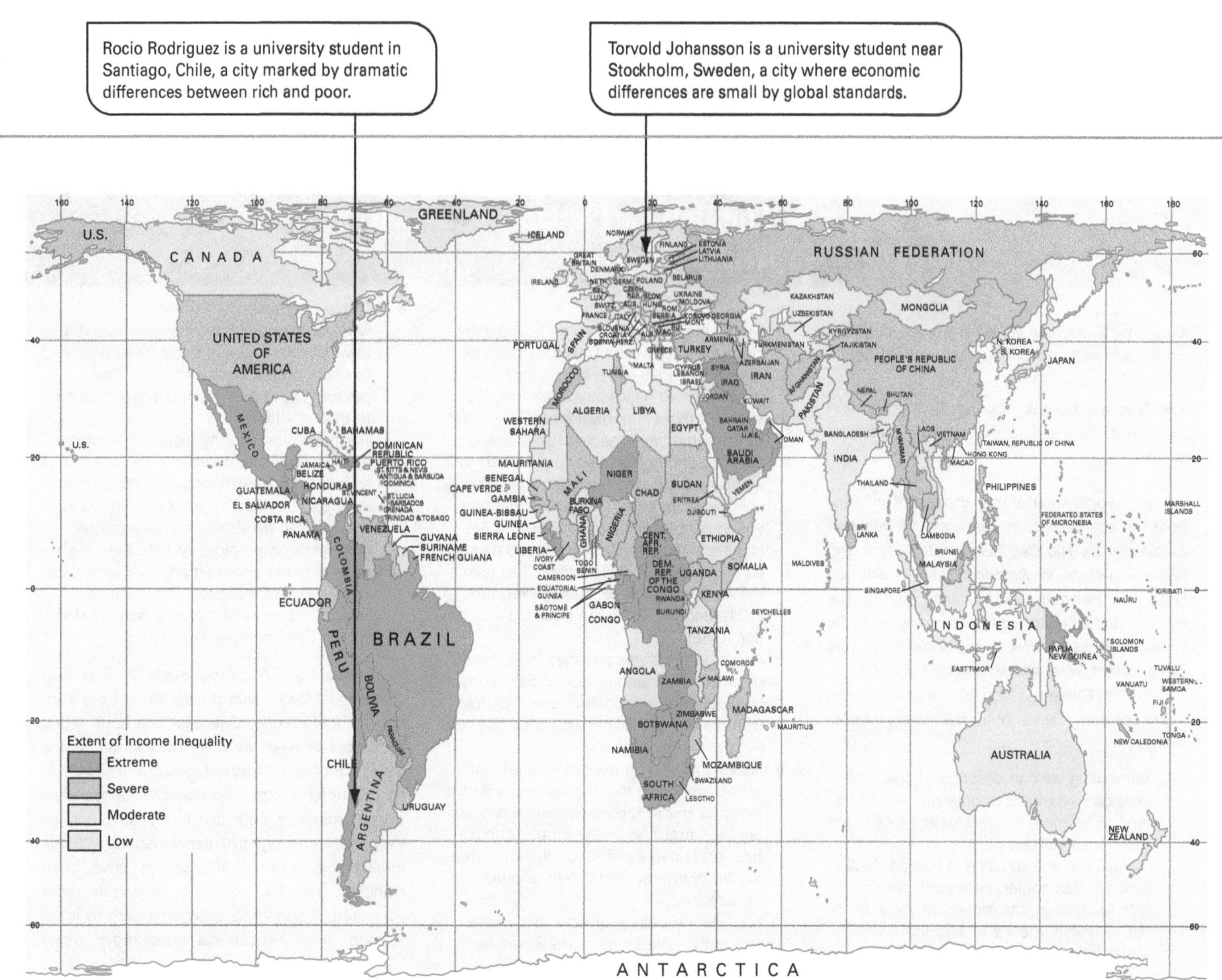

Window on the World

GLOBAL MAP 1 **Income Inequality in Global Perspective**

Societies throughout the world differ in the rigidity and extent of their social stratification and their overall standard of living. This map highlights income inequality. Generally speaking, the United States stands out among high-income nations, such as Great Britain, Sweden, Japan, and Australia, as having greater income inequality. The less economically developed countries of Latin America and Africa, including Colombia, Brazil, and the Central African Republic, as well as much of the Arab world, exhibit the most pronounced inequality of income. Is this pattern consistent with the Kuznets curve?

Source: Based on Gini coefficients obtained from World Bank (2008).

Another criticism of the Kuznets curve is that it was developed by comparing societies at different levels of economic development (what sociologists call "cross-sectional data"). Such data do not tell us about the future of any one society. In the United States, recent trends showing increases in economic inequality suggest that the Kuznets curve may require serious revision—represented by the broken line in Figure 2. The fact that U.S. society is experiencing greater economic inequality as the Information Revolution moves forward suggests that the long-term trend may differ from what Kuznets projected half a century ago.

CONTROVERSY & DEBATE

The Bell Curve Debate: Are Rich People Really Smarter?

Elena: (*with a smile*) So what do you think? Is going out with me giving you upward social mobility?

Joe: Give me a break. Your family is richer than mine. But that doesn't mean you're better or smarter. . . .

Are rich people smarter than the rest of us? Few books in sociology have taken on this question as directly as *The Bell Curve: Intelligence and Class Structure in American Life* (1994), by Richard J. Herrnstein and Charles Murray. The book ignited a firestorm of controversy over why social stratification divides our society and, just as important, what should be done about it.

The Bell Curve is a long book that addresses many complex issues, but it makes eight major claims:

1. Something we can describe as "general intelligence" exists; people with more of it tend to be more successful in their careers than those with less.
2. At least half the variation in human intelligence is transmitted genetically from parents to children; the remaining variability is due to environmental factors that affect socialization.
3. During the past century—and especially since the Information Revolution began several decades ago—intelligence has become more necessary to perform our society's most important jobs.
4. At the same time, the most selective U.S. colleges and universities have shifted their admissions policies away from favoring children of inherited wealth to admitting young people with high grades and the highest scores on standardized tests such as the Scholastic Assessment Test (SAT), the American College Testing Program (ACT), and the Graduate Record Examination (GRE).
5. As a result of these changes in the workplace and on campus, our society is now dominated by a "cognitive elite," people who are not only better educated but actually more intelligent.
6. As very intelligent people interact with others similar to themselves, both on the campus and in the workplace, the odds are high that they will pair up, get married, and have intelligent children, extending the "cognitive elite" into another generation.
7. A similar process is at work at the other end of the social ladder: Poor people, who, on average, have lower intelligence, have become socially segregated and tend to marry others like themselves, thus passing along their more modest abilities to their children.
8. Herrnstein and Murray therefore conclude that because membership in the affluent elite or the impoverished underclass is at least partly rooted in genetically inherited intelligence, we should not be surprised that the poor are more likely to have higher rates of crime and drug abuse. Further, we should expect that programs such as Head Start and affirmative action will do little to help the poor.

Evaluating the claims made in *The Bell Curve* must begin with a hard look at the concept of intelligence. Critics of the book argue that most of what we call "intelligence" is the result not of genetic inheritance but of socialization. In other words, so-called intelligence tests do not measure cognitive *ability* as much as they measure cognitive *performance.* Average intelligence quotient (IQ) scores have been rising as the U.S. population becomes more educated. If schooling is so important to intelligence, then educational advantages alone

Social Stratification: Facts and Values

> The year was 2081 and everybody was finally equal. They weren't only equal before God and the law. They were equal every which way. Nobody was smarter than anybody else. Nobody was better looking than anybody else. Nobody was stronger or quicker than anybody else. All this equality was due to the 211th, 212th, and 213th Amendments to the Constitution and the unceasing vigilance of agents of the Handicapper General.

With these words, the novelist Kurt Vonnegut Jr. (1968:7) begins the story of Harrison Bergeron, an imaginary account of a future United States in which all social inequality has been abolished. Vonnegut warns that although attractive in principle, equality can be a dangerous concept in practice. His story describes a nightmare of social engineering in which every individual talent that makes one person different from another is systematically neutralized by the government.

To eliminate differences that make one person "better" than another, Vonnegut's state requires that physically attractive people wear masks that make them average-looking, that intelligent people wear earphones that generate distracting noise, and that the best athletes and dancers be fitted with weights to make them as clumsy as everyone else. In short, although we may imagine that social equality would liberate people to make the most of their talents, Vonnegut concludes that an egalitarian society could exist only if everyone is reduced to the lowest common denominator. In Vonnegut's view, this would amount not to liberation but to oppression.

would explain why rich children perform better on such tests.

Most researchers who study intelligence agree that genetics plays a part in children's intelligence, but most conclude that only 25 to 40 percent of intelligence is inherited—less than Herrnstein and Murray claim. *The Bell Curve* therefore misleads readers when it states that social stratification is a natural product of differences in inherited intelligence. Critics claim that this book echoes the social Darwinism popular a century ago, which justified the great wealth of industrial tycoons as "the survival of the fittest."

Could it be that the more today's competitive society seems like a jungle, the more people think of stratification as a matter of nature rather than nurture? But even if it is flawed, *The Bell Curve* raises important issues. If some people are smarter than others, shouldn't we expect them to end up in higher social positions? Shouldn't we expect the people who rise to the top in most fields to be at least a little smarter than the rest of us? If this is true, is it fair? Finally, what can our society do to ensure that all people will have the opportunity to develop their abilities as fully as possible?

Getty Images, Inc. - Agence France Presse/Jim Watson

How closely linked are social class position and personal intelligence? According to Herrnstein and Murray, in today's society birth matters less than in the past and personal ability matters more. Do you think the remarkable life story of Barack Obama, who was born to a single mother and went on to be president, reflects a more general trend? Why or why not?

WHAT DO YOU THINK?

1. Do you think there is such a thing as "general intelligence"? Why or why not?
2. Do you think that well-off people are, on average, more intelligent than people of low social position? If so, how do you know which factor is the cause and which the effect?
3. Do you think social scientists should study issues such as differences in human intelligence if their results could justify social inequality? Why or why not?

Sources: Herrnstein & Murray (1994), Jacoby & Glauberman (1995), Kohn (1996), and Arrow, Bowles, & Durlauf (2000).

Like Vonnegut's story, all of this chapter's explanations of social stratification involve value judgments. The Davis-Moore thesis states not only that social stratification is universal but also that it is necessary to make society highly productive. Class differences in U.S. society, from this point of view, reflect both variation in human abilities and the relatively unequal importance of different jobs. Taken together, these facts lead us to see complete equality as undesirable, because it could be achieved only in a rigid and inefficient society that cared little for developing individual talent and rewarding excellence.

Social-conflict analysis, advocated by Karl Marx, takes a much more positive view of equality. Marx thought that inequality is harmful because it causes both human suffering and conflict between haves and have-nots. As he saw it, social stratification springs from injustice and greed. As a result, Marx wanted people to share resources equally.

The Controversy & Debate box addresses the connection between intelligence and social class. This issue is among the most troublesome in social science, partly because of the difficulty in defining and measuring "intelligence" but also because the idea that elites are somehow "better" than others challenges our democratic culture.

At all levels, the study of social stratification involves a mix of facts and values about the shape of a just society.

Seeing Sociology in Everyday Life

Social Stratificattion

Can you find elements of caste and meritocracy in U.S. society?

This chapter explains that modern societies are class systems that combine elements of caste and meritocracy. Using the sociological perspective, you can see both caste and meritocracy in operation in many everyday situations. Here are three examples to get you started. Look at the photos below and then start your own list.

HINT The fact that parenting is not paid work means that people should not raise children for money but out of moral duty. "Fathering a child" may suggest only biological paternity; "mothering a child" implies deep involvement in a child's life, suggesting that gender has long been a caste element linking women to nurturing. Careers that emphasize merit, on the other hand, are typically those jobs that that are regarded as especially important and that require rare talents; even so, most successful musical performers are male. Judge Sotomayor is the first Hispanic and just the third woman (along with Sandra Day O'Connor and Ruth Bader Ginsburg) to serve on the U.S. Supreme Court. There have been just two African American justices (Thurgood Marshall and Clarence Thomas).

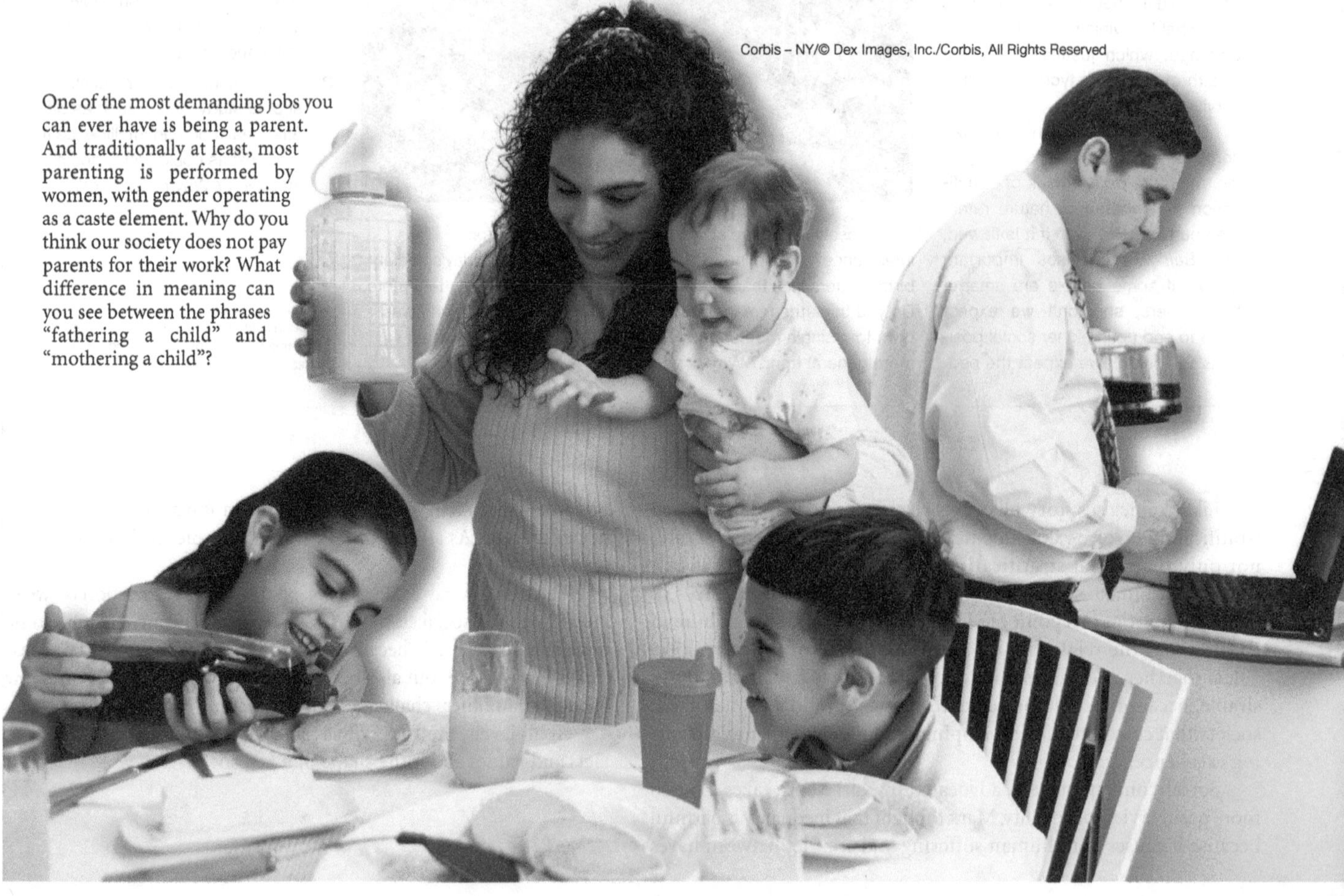

One of the most demanding jobs you can ever have is being a parent. And traditionally at least, most parenting is performed by women, with gender operating as a caste element. Why do you think our society does not pay parents for their work? What difference in meaning can you see between the phrases "fathering a child" and "mothering a child"?

AP Wide World Photos/Matt Sayles

Joel and Benji Madden grew up poor in a single-parent family and went on to find success in the band "Good Charlotte." Some careers, such as being a musician, an athlete, or an actor or actress, allow for a good deal of meritocracy. What do these careers have in common that explains the importance of meritocracy? Can you see elements of caste, as well, in these careers?

Corbis - NY/© White House/CNP/Corbis, All Rights Reserved

In 2009, Judge Sonia Sotomayor became the first Hispanic woman to join the U.S. Supreme Court. Her record of achievement began at Cardinal Spellman High School in the Bronx (New York), where she was valedictorian. Of more than 100 justices who have served on the Supreme Court, how many do you think have been Hispanic? How many have been women?

Applying SOCIOLOGY in Everyday Life

1. Identify three ways in which social stratification is evident in the everyday lives of students on your campus. In each case, explain exactly what is unequal and what difference it makes. Do you think individual talent or family background is more important in creating these social differences?
2. Sit down with parents, grandparents, or other relatives, and talk about how your family's social position has changed over the last three generations. Has social mobility taken place? If so, describe the change. Was it caused by the effort of individuals or changes in society itself?
3. The "seven deadly sins," the human failings recognized by the Roman Catholic Church during the Middle Ages, were pride, greed, envy, anger, lust, gluttony, and sloth. Why are these traits dangerous to an agrarian caste system? Are they a threat to a modern, capitalist class system? Why or why not?

VISUAL SUMMARY

MAKING THE GRADE

Social Stratification

What Is Social Stratification?

SOCIAL STRATIFICATION is a system by which a society ranks categories of people in a hierarchy, so that some people have more money, power, and prestige than others.

Social stratification

- is a trait of society, not simply a reflection of individual differences
- is found in all societies but varies according to *what* is unequal and *how* unequal it is
- carries over from one generation to the next
- is supported by a system of cultural beliefs that defines certain kinds of inequality as just
- takes two general forms: caste systems and class systems

✓ *Although some people, especially in high-income countries, may experience* ***social mobility,*** *the social standing of most people remains pretty much the same over their lifetime.*

social stratification a system by which a society ranks categories of people in a hierarchy

social mobility a change in position within the social hierarchy

Caste and Class Systems

CASTE SYSTEMS

- are based on birth (ascription)
- permit little or no social mobility
- shape a person's entire life, including occupation and marriage
- are common in traditional, agrarian societies

AN ILLUSTRATION: INDIA

Although the caste system is formally outlawed in India, it is still observed in rural areas, where agriculture demands a lifetime of hard work and discipline.

- In traditional villages, people's caste determines the type of work they perform.
- People must interact with and marry others of the same ranking.
- Powerful cultural beliefs make observing caste rules a moral duty.

CLASS SYSTEMS

- are based on both birth (ascription) and **MERITOCRACY** (individual achievement)
- permit some social mobility based on individual achievement
- are common in modern industrial and postindustrial societies

- Class systems include elements of both caste and meritocracy.
- Class systems advance meritocracy to promote specialization, productivity, and efficiency.
- Class systems keep caste elements, such as family, to maintain order and social unity.
- **Status consistency** in class systems is low due to increased social mobility.

CASTE AND CLASS: THE UNITED KINGDOM

- In the Middle Ages, England had a castelike aristocracy, including the leading clergy and a hereditary nobility. The vast majority of people were commoners.
- Today's British class system mixes caste and meritocracy, producing a highly stratified society with some social mobility.

CASTE AND CLASS: JAPAN

- In the Middle Ages, Japan had a rigid caste system in which an imperial family ruled over nobles and commoners.
- Today's Japanese class system still places great importance on family background and traditional gender roles.

caste system social stratification based on ascription, or birth

class system social stratification based on both birth and individual achievement

meritocracy social stratification based on personal merit

status consistency the degree of uniformity in a person's social standing across various dimensions of social inequality

structural social mobility a shift in the social position of large numbers of people due more to changes in society itself than to individual efforts

ideology cultural beliefs that justify particular social arrangements, including patterns of inequality

CLASSLESS SOCIETIES? THE FORMER SOVIET UNION

- Although the Russian Revolution in 1917 attempted to abolish social classes, the new Soviet Union was still stratified based on unequal job categories and the concentration of power in the new political elite. Economic development created new types of jobs, which resulted in **structural social mobility**.
- Since the collapse of the Soviet Union in the early 1990s, the forces of structural social mobility have turned downward and the gap between rich and poor has increased.

CHINA: EMERGING SOCIAL CLASSES

- Economic reforms introduced after the Communist revolution in 1949—including state control of factories and productive property—greatly reduced economic inequality, although social differences remained.
- In the last thirty years, China's government has loosened control of the economy, causing the emergence of a new class of business owners and an increase in economic inequality.

✓ *Both caste and class systems are supported by* ***ideology****—cultural values and beliefs—that defines certain kinds of inequality as just.*

Theoretical Analysis of Social Stratification

The **STRUCTURAL-FUNCTIONAL APPROACH** points to ways social stratification helps society operate.

- The Davis-Moore thesis states that social stratification is universal because of its functional consequences.
- In caste systems, people are rewarded for performing the duties of their position at birth.
- In class systems, unequal rewards attract the ablest people to the most important jobs and encourage effort.

The **SOCIAL-CONFLICT APPROACH** claims that stratification divides societies in classes, benefiting some categories of people at the expense of others and causing social conflict.

- Karl Marx claimed that capitalism places economic production under the ownership of capitalists, who exploit the proletarians who sell their labor for wages.
- Max Weber identified three distinct dimensions of social stratification: economic class, social status or prestige, and power. Conflict exists between people at various positions on a multidimensional hierarchy of **Socioeconomic status (SES)**.

Davis-Moore thesis the functional analysis claiming that social stratification has beneficial consequences for the operation of society

blue-collar occupations lower-prestige jobs that involve mostly manual labor

white-collar occupations higher-prestige jobs that involve mostly mental activity

socioeconomic status (SES) a composite ranking based on various dimensions of social inequality

conspicuous consumption buying and using products because of the "statement" they make about social position

The **SYMBOLIC-INTERACTION APPROACH**, a micro-level analysis, explains that we size up people by looking for clues to their social standing. **Conspicuous consumption** refers to buying and displaying products that make a "statement" about social class. Most people tend to socialize with others whose social standing is similar to their own.

See the Applying Theory table.

Social Stratification and Technology: A Global Perspective

Hunting and Gathering → **Horticultural and Pastoral** → **Agrarian** → **Industrial** → **Postindustrial**

- Gerhard Lenski explains that advancing technology initially increases social stratification, which is most intense in agrarian societies.
- Industrialization reverses the trend, reducing social stratification.
- In postindustrial societies, social stratification again increases.

See the Kuznets curve (Figure 2).

Stratification: Facts and Values

People's beliefs about social inequality reflect not just facts but also politics and values concerning how a society should be organized.

MAKING THE GRADE

Sample Test Questions

Multiple-Choice Questions

1. ***Social stratification* refers to**
   a. job specialization.
   b. ranking categories of people in a hierarchy.
   c. the fact that some people work harder than others.
   d. inequality of personal talent and individual effort.

2. **Looking back in history and around the world today, we see that social stratification may involve differences in**
   a. how unequal people are.
   b. what resources are unequally distributed.
   c. why a society claims people should be unequal.
   d. All of the above are correct.

3. **A caste system is social stratification**
   a. based on individual achievement.
   b. based on meritocracy.
   c. based on birth.
   d. in which a person's social position is likely to change over time.

4. **Sally has two advanced degrees, earns an average salary, and is working at a low-prestige job. Which concept best describes her situation?**
   a. low status consistency
   b. horizontal social mobility
   c. upward social mobility
   d. high status consistency

5. **According to the Davis-Moore thesis,**
   a. equality is functional for society.
   b. the more inequality a society has, the more productive it is.
   c. more important jobs must offer enough rewards to draw talent from less important work.
   d. societies with more meritocracy are less productive than those with caste systems.

6. **Karl Marx claimed that society "reproduces the class structure." By this, he meant that**
   a. society benefits from inequality.
   b. class differences are passed on from one generation to the next.
   c. class differences are the same everywhere.
   d. a society without classes is impossible.

7. **Max Weber claimed that social stratification is based on**
   a. economic class.
   b. social status or prestige.
   c. power.
   d. All of the above are correct.

8. **A society with which type of productive technology has the least amount of social stratification?**
   a. hunting and gathering
   b. horticultural/pastoral
   c. industrial
   d. postindustrial

9. **Keeping the Kuznets curve in mind, which type of society has the most social stratification?**
   a. hunting and gathering
   b. horticultural/pastoral
   c. agrarian
   d. industrial

10. **The "bell curve" thesis suggests that which of the following is more important than ever to social position in the United States?**
    a. family background
    b. intelligence
    c. hard work
    d. whom you know

ANSWERS: 1 (b); 2 (d); 3 (c); 4 (a); 5 (c); 6 (b); 7 (d); 8 (a); 9 (c); 10 (b).

Essay Questions

1. Explain why social stratification is a creation of society, not just a reflection of individual differences.
2. How do caste and class systems differ? How are they the same? Why does industrialization introduce a measure of meritocracy into social stratification?

Social Class in the United States

Jupiter Images/Creatas

Many people think of the United States as a "middle-class society." But social inequality in our society is greater than in most other high-income nations, and it is increasing.

iStockphoto International/Royalty Free/Sharon Dominick Photography/Courtesy of www.istockphoto.com

Social Class in the United States

PhotoEdit Inc./Michael Newman

Getty Images, Inc. – PhotoDisc/C Lee

CHAPTER OVERVIEW

This chapter surveys social stratification in the United States, beginning with a look at important measures of inequality. Many dimensions of inequality exist in our society, and inequality is greater than many people imagine.

PhotoEdit Inc./Mary Kate Denny

Rosa Urias leans forward, pushing and pulling the vacuum cleaner across the hardwood floors, a motion she has repeated hundreds of times to the point that her right wrist and elbow are sore. It is now almost five o'clock in the afternoon, and this forty-five-year-old single mother of two is on her third cleaning job of the day. She works with her cousin Melitsa Sermiento, thirty-six, cleaning nine apartments and five houses each week. The two women, who both came to the United States from El Salvador, divide the money they earn, giving each one an annual income of about $28,000, barely enough to pay the bills in New York City.

But there is no shortage of work cleaning homes. Hundreds of thousands of New Yorkers make more than enough money to hire people like Rosa and Melitsa to dust their tables, mop their floors, and scrub their sinks and toilets while they are out doing their high-paying jobs, working out at the health club, or having lunch with friends.

Rosa reaches up over the bathroom sink to turn on a light so she can see better. She pulls the silver chain, but it breaks and she stands there with part of the chain hanging from her hand. She looks over at Melitsa, and both do their best to laugh it off. Then Rosa turns serious and says softly, in Spanish, "My daughter tells me I need some new dreams" (Eisenstadt, 2004).

New York may be a single large city, but the social world in which Rosa and Melitsa live is not the same as the social world of the people who hire these women. How different are the lives of the richest people in the United States and the lives of those who work hard all day just to get by? What about the lives of those who do not even have the security of work? This chapter answers all these questions, explaining some of the different "worlds" found in U.S. society, how different we are, and why the differences are getting bigger.

Dimensions of Social Inequality

The United States differs from most European nations and Japan in never having had a titled nobility. With the significant exception of our racial history, we have never known a caste system that rigidly ranks categories of people.

Even so, U.S. society is highly stratified. Not only do the rich have most of the money, but they also receive the most schooling, enjoy the best health, and consume the most goods and services. Such privilege contrasts sharply with the poverty of millions of women and men who worry about paying next month's rent or a doctor's bill when a child becomes ill. Many people think of the United States as a middle-class society, but is this really the case?

Income

One important dimension of inequality is **income,** *earnings from work or investments*. The Census Bureau reports that the median U.S. family income in 2007 was $61,355. The pie chart in the middle of Figure 1 illustrates the distribution of income among all U.S. families.[1] The richest 20 percent of families (earning at least $113,000 annually, with a mean of about $187,000) received 47.3 percent of all income, while the bottom 20 percent (earning less than $28,000, with a mean of about $16,000) received only 4.1 percent (U.S. Census Bureau, 2008).

The table at the left in Figure 1 provides a closer look at income distribution. In 2007, the highest-paid 5 percent of U.S. families earned at least $197,000 (averaging almost $317,000), or 20.1 percent of all income, more than the total earnings of the lowest-paid 40 percent. At the very top of the income pyramid, the richest half of 1 percent earned at least $1.8 million.

[1]The Census Bureau reports both mean and median incomes for families ("two or more persons related by blood, marriage, or adoption") and households ("two or more persons sharing a living unit"). In 2007, mean family income was $78,845, higher than the median ($61,355) because high-income families pull up the mean but not the median. For households, these figures are somewhat lower—a mean of $67,609 and a median of $50,233—largely because families average 3.15 people and households average 2.56.

income earnings from work or investments

wealth the total value of money and other assets, minus outstanding debts

SEEING SOCIOLOGY in Everyday Life

Why do you think so many people view the United States as a middle-class society in which most people have more or less equal social standing?

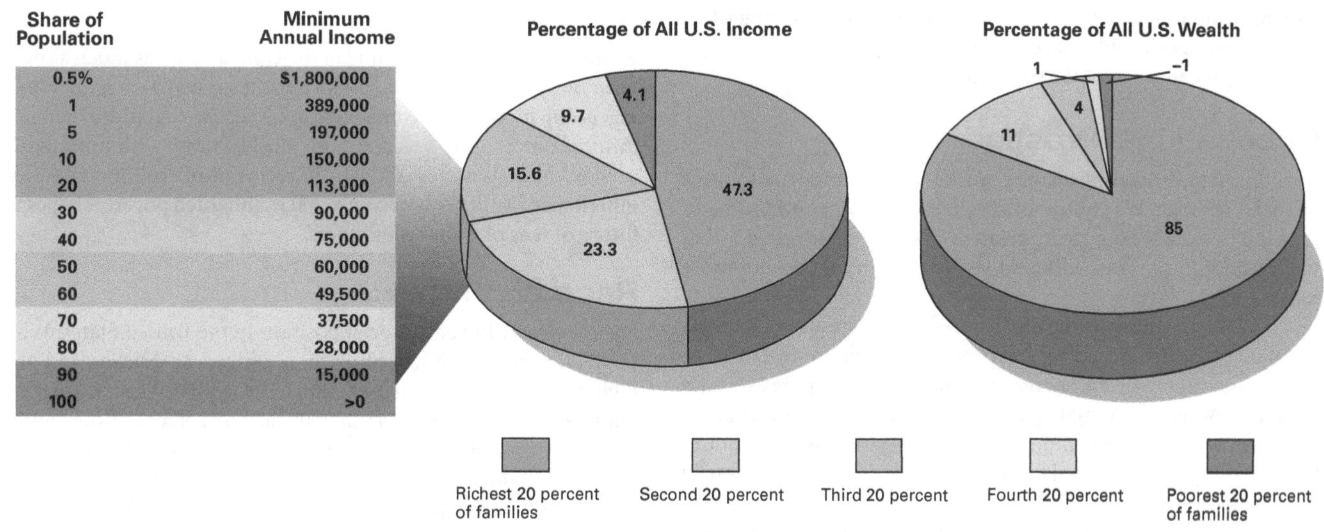

FIGURE 1 **Distribution of Income and Wealth in the United States, 2007**

Income, and especially wealth, is divided unequally in U.S. society.

Sources: Income data from U.S. Census Bureau (2008); wealth data based on Keister (2000), Bucks, Kennickell, & Moore (2006), Wolff (2007), and author estimates.

During recent decades, income inequality has increased. One part of this trend is that the very richest people now receive a much larger share of all income. For example, in 1978, the highest-paid 0.1 percent of all earners received 2.7 percent of all income. By 2007, this elite category (people making $7 million or more a year) took home more than four times as much, equaling 11.6 percent of all income (Internal Revenue Service, 2008; Fox, 2009).

Wealth

Income is only a part of a person's or family's **wealth,** *the total value of money and other assets, minus outstanding debts.* Wealth—including stocks, bonds, and real estate—is distributed more unequally than income. Recent reductions in taxes on income earned by individuals and on wealth passed from one generation to the next are likely to make this inequality even greater (Wahl, 2003).

The pie chart on the right in Figure 1 shows the distribution of wealth. The richest 20 percent of U.S. families own roughly 85 percent of the country's wealth. High up in this privileged category are the wealthiest 5 percent of families—the "very rich," who own 60 percent of all private property. Richer still, with wealth in the tens of millions of dollars, are the 1 percent of families that qualify as "super-rich" and possess about 35 percent of this nation's privately held resources (Keister, 2000; Keister & Moller, 2000; Bucks, Kennickell, & Moore, 2006; Davies et al., 2006; Wolff, 2007). At the top of the wealth pyramid, the ten richest U.S. families have a combined net worth of more than $285 billion (Kroll, 2008). This amount equals the total property of 3 million average families, including enough people to fill the cities of Chicago, Houston, Philadelphia, Phoenix, and San Diego.

The wealth of the average U.S. family is currently about $100,000 (Bucks, Kennickell, & Moore, 2006; Federal Reserve Board, 2007). Family wealth reflects the value of homes, cars, investments, insurance policies, retirement pensions, furniture, clothing, and all other personal property, minus a home mortgage and other debts. The wealth of average people is not only less than that of the rich, however, but also different in kind. Most people's wealth centers on a home and a car—that is, property that generates no income—but the wealth of the rich is mostly in the form of stocks and other income-producing investments.

When financial assets are balanced against debts, the lowest-ranking 40 percent of U.S. families have virtually no wealth at all. The negative percentage shown in Figure 1 for the poorest 20 percent of the population means that these families actually live in debt.

Power

In the United States, wealth is an important source of power. The small proportion of families that control most of the nation's wealth

SEEING SOCIOLOGY in Everyday Life

People of all social classes have the same right to vote. But can you think of ways in which the rich have more power to shape U.S. society than the rest of us?

MAKING THE GRADE

Notice in the sections below how ancestry, race and ethnicity, and gender can operate as caste elements.

also shape the agenda of the entire society. Some sociologists argue that such concentrated wealth weakens democracy because the political system serves the interests of the super-rich.

Occupational Prestige

In addition to generating income, work is also an important source of social prestige. We commonly evaluate each other according to the kind of work we do, giving greater respect to those who do what we consider important work and less respect to others with more modest jobs.

Sociologists measure the relative prestige of various occupations (NORC, 2007). Table 1 shows that people give high prestige to occupations such as physician, lawyer, and engineer that require extensive training and generate high income. By contrast, less prestigious work—as a waitress or janitor, for example—pays less and requires less schooling. Occupational prestige rankings are much the same in all high-income nations (Lin & Xie, 1988).

In any society, high-prestige occupations go to privileged categories of people. In Table 1, for example, the highest-ranking occupations are dominated by men. We have to go more than a dozen jobs down the list to find "secondary school teacher" and "registered nurse," careers chosen mostly by women. Similarly, many of the lowest-prestige jobs are commonly performed by people of color.

Schooling

Industrial societies have expanded opportunities for schooling, but some people still receive much more education than others. More than 85 percent of women and men aged twenty-five and older have completed high school. But just 29 percent of men and 30 percent of women have completed a four-year college degree.

Schooling affects both occupation and income, since most (but not all) of the better-paying white-collar jobs shown in Table 1 require a college degree or other advanced study. Most blue-collar jobs, which bring lower income and social prestige, require less schooling.

U.S. Stratification: Merit and Caste

The U.S. class system is partly a meritocracy in that social position reflects individual talent and effort. But it also has caste elements, because birth plays a part in what we become later in life.

Ancestry

Nothing affects social standing in the United States as much as being born into a particular family, which has a strong bearing on schooling, occupation, and income. Research suggests that more than one-third of our country's richest individuals—those with hundreds of millions of dollars in wealth—acquired some of their fortunes from inheritance (Miller & Newcomb, 2005). Inherited poverty shapes the future of tens of millions of others.

Race and Ethnicity

Race is closely linked to social position in the United States. White people receive more schooling than African Americans and have higher overall occupational standing. The median African American family's income was $40,143 in 2007, just 57 percent of the $69,937 earned by non-Hispanic white families. This inequality in income makes a real difference in people's lives. For example, non-Hispanic white families are more likely to own their homes (75 percent do) than black families (47 percent) (U.S. Census Bureau, 2008).

Families that include married couples earn more than families with a single parent. With this fact in mind, some of the racial difference in income results from the larger share of single-parent families among African Americans. Comparing only families headed by married couples, African Americans earned 80 percent as much as non-Hispanic white families.

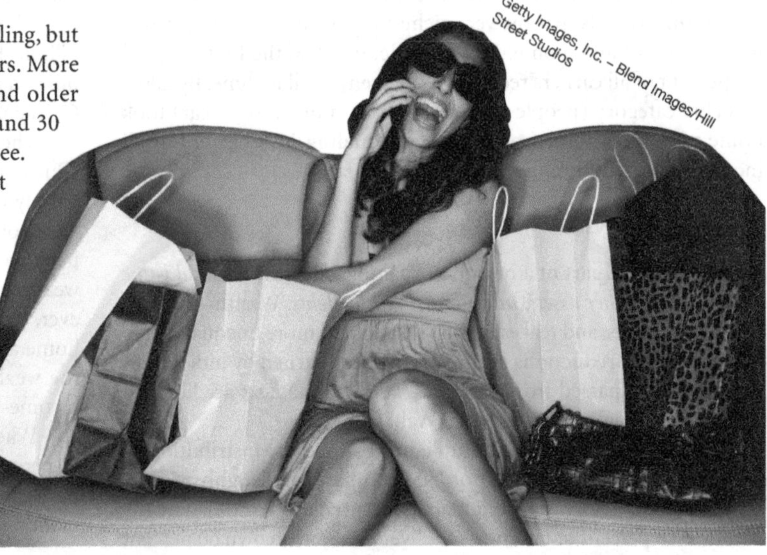

Getty Images, Inc. - Blend Images/Hill Street Studios

Members of our society tend to think of social class in terms of income and wealth, as if to say "I am what I own." For this reason, conspicuous consumption—buying and displaying various goods partly with an eye toward gaining social standing in the eyes of others—is a common pattern. How have you engaged in conspicuous consumption?

SEEING SOCIOLOGY in Everyday Life

Identify the jobs in Table 1 that have traditionally been performed by people of color. What pattern do you discover?

SEEING SOCIOLOGY in Everyday Life

Reading down from the top of Table 1, how far do you have to go before you see a job in which most workers would be women?

Table 1 The Relative Social Prestige of Selected Occupations in the United States

White-Collar Occupations	Prestige Score	Blue-Collar Occupations
Physician	82	
College or university professor	78	
Lawyer	76	
Dentist	74	
Physicist, astronomer	74	
Architect	71	
Psychologist	71	
Airline pilot	70	
Electrical engineer	69	
Member of the clergy	69	
Sociologist	66	
Secondary school teacher	63	
Optometrist	62	
Registered nurse	62	
Dental hygienist	61	
Pharmacist	61	
Elementary school teacher	60	
Veterinarian	60	
Actor	58	
Accountant	57	
Economist	57	
Painter, sculptor	56	
Librarian	55	
	53	Aircraft mechanic
	53	Firefighter
Social worker	52	
Athlete	51	
Computer programmer	51	
Editor, reporter	51	
Radio or TV announcer	51	
	49	Electrician

White-Collar Occupations	Prestige Score	Blue-Collar Occupations
Real estate agent	49	
Bookkeeper	48	
	48	Machinist
	48	Police officer
Musician, composer	46	
	46	Secretary
Real estate agent or broker	44	
	42	Mail carrier
Photographer	41	
	41	Tailor
	40	Carpenter
	37	Auto body repairer
	36	Bricklayer, stonemason
	33	Baker
	33	Bulldozer operator
	33	Hairdresser
	32	Truck driver
Cashier	31	
File clerk	30	
Retail salesperson	29	
	28	Waiter, waitress
	25	Bartender
	25	Child care worker
	23	Farm laborer
	23	Household laborer
	22	Door-to-door salesperson
	22	Janitor
	22	Taxi driver
	17	Garbage collector
	14	Bellhop
	9	Shoe shiner

Source: Adapted from *General Social Surveys, 1972–2007: Cumulative Codebook* (Chicago: National Opinion Research Center, 2008).

Over time, the income difference builds into a huge wealth gap (Altonji, Doraszelski, & Segal, 2000). A recent survey of families by the Federal Reserve found that median wealth for minority families, including African Americans, Hispanics, and Asian Americans ($27,100), is just 19 percent of the median ($142,700) for non-Hispanic white families (Bucks, Kennickell, & Moore, 2006).

Social ranking involves ethnicity as well. People of English ancestry have always enjoyed the most wealth and the greatest power in

SEEING SOCIOLOGY in Everyday Life

To what extent is gender still an element of caste? That is, as you look around you, do women seem to have the same opportunities and privileges as men?

MAKING THE GRADE

Pay attention to a key difference between the small number of "upper-uppers," who are almost always born (or occasionally marry) into "old money," and the much larger number of "lower-uppers," who move upward socially as they earn lots of "new money."

Corbis – NY/Patrick Wallet

Magnum Photos, Inc./Burt Glinn

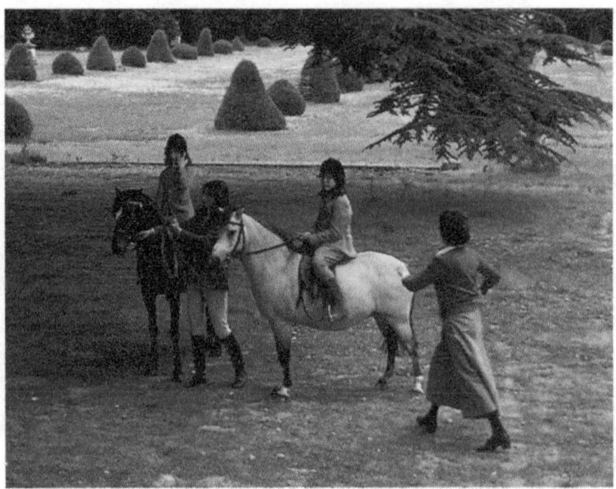

People often distinguish between the "new rich" and families with "old money." Men and women who suddenly begin to earn high incomes tend to spend their money on status symbols because they enjoy the new thrill of high-roller living and they want others to know of their success. Those who grow up surrounded by wealth, by contrast, are used to a privileged way of life and are more quiet about it. Thus the conspicuous consumption of the lower-upper class (*left*) can differ dramatically from the more private pursuits and understatement of the upper-upper class (*right*).

U.S. society. The Latino population—the largest U.S. racial or ethnic minority—has long been disadvantaged. In 2007, the median income among Hispanic families was $40,500, which is 58 percent of the median income for non-Hispanic white families.

Gender

Of course, both men and women are found in families at every class level. Yet on average, women have less income, wealth, and occupational prestige than men. Among single-parent families, those headed by a woman are more than twice as likely to be poor than those headed by a man.

Social Classes in the United States

Rankings in a caste system are rigid and obvious to all. Defining social categories in a more fluid class system such as ours, however, is not so easy.

There is an old joke about two guys who order a pizza, asking that it be cut into six slices because they aren't hungry enough to eat eight. Sociologists do the same thing with social class: Some divide the population into more classes than others. At one extreme, people find as many as six or even seven social classes; at the other, some follow Karl Marx and see two major classes: capitalists and proletarians. Still others side with Max Weber, claiming that stratification creates not clear-cut classes but a multidimensional status hierarchy.

Defining classes in U.S. society is difficult because of our relatively low level of status consistency. Especially toward the middle of the hierarchy, people's standing in one dimension may not be the same as their standing in another. For example, a government official may have the power to administer a multimillion-dollar budget yet may earn only a modest personal income. Similarly, many members of the clergy enjoy ample prestige but only moderate power and low pay. Or consider a lucky casino poker player who wins no special respect but makes a lot of money.

Finally, the social mobility characteristic of class systems—again, most pronounced around the middle—means that social position may change during a person's lifetime, further blurring class boundaries. With these issues in mind, we will examine four general rankings: the upper class, the middle class, the working class, and the lower class.

The Upper Class

Families in the upper class—5 percent of the U.S. population—earn at least $197,000 a year, and some earn ten times that much or more. As a general rule, the more a family's income comes from inherited

SEEING SOCIOLOGY in Everyday Life

When you think about the "American dream," you imagine rising to which part of the upper class? Explain your answer.

wealth in the form of stocks and bonds, real estate, and other investments, the stronger a family's claim to being upper-class.

In 2008, *Forbes* magazine profiled the richest 400 people in the country, who were worth at least $1.3 billion (and as much as $57 billion) (Miller & Greenberg, 2008). These people are the core of the upper class, or Karl Marx's "capitalists"—the owners of the means of production or most of the nation's private wealth. Many upper-class people are business owners, executives in large corporations, or senior government officials. Historically, the upper class has been composed mostly of white Anglo-Saxon Protestants, but this is less true today (Pyle & Koch, 2001).

Upper-Uppers

The *upper-upper class,* sometimes called "blue bloods" or simply "society," includes less than 1 percent of the U.S. population (Coleman & Neugarten, 1971; Baltzell, 1995). Membership is almost always the result of birth, as suggested by the joke that the easiest way to become an upper-upper is to be born one. Most of these families possess enormous wealth, which is primarily inherited. For this reason, members of the upper-upper class are said to have "old money."

Set apart by their wealth, upper-uppers live in old, exclusive neighborhoods, such as Beacon Hill in Boston, Rittenhouse Square in Philadelphia, the Gold Coast of Chicago, and Nob Hill in San Francisco. Their children typically attend private schools with others of similar background and complete their schooling at high-prestige colleges and universities. In the tradition of European aristocrats, they study liberal arts rather than vocational skills.

Women of the upper-upper class do volunteer work for charitable organizations. Such activities serve a dual purpose: They help the larger community, and they build networks that broaden this elite's power (Ostrander, 1980, 1984).

For decades, U.S. farm families who worked hard could expect to end up in the middle class. But the trend toward large-scale agribusiness has put the future of the small family farm in doubt. Although many young people in rural areas are turning away from farming toward other careers, some carry on, incorporating high technology into their farm management in their determined efforts to succeed.

Lower-Uppers

Most upper-class people actually fall into the *lower-upper class.* The queen of England is in the upper-upper class based not on her fortune of $650 million but on her family tree. J. K. Rowling, author of the Harry Potter books, is probably worth twice as much—more than $1 billion—but this woman (who was once on welfare) is a member of the lower-upper class. The major difference, in other words, is that lower-uppers are the "working rich" who get their money mostly by earning it rather than inheritance. These well-to-do families—who make up 3 or 4 percent of the U.S. population—generally live in large homes in expensive neighborhoods, own vacation homes near the water or in the mountains, and send their children to private schools and good colleges. Yet most of the "new rich" do not gain entry into the clubs and associations of "old money" families.

In the United States, what we often call the American dream has been to earn enough to join the ranks of the lower-upper class. The athlete who signs a multimillion-dollar contract, the actress who lands a starring role in a Hollywood film, the computer whiz who creates the latest Internet site to capture the public's attention, and even the person who hits it big by winning a huge lottery jackpot are the talented achievers and lucky people who reach the lower-upper class.

The Middle Class

Made up of 40 to 45 percent of the U.S. population, the large middle class has a tremendous influence on our culture. Television programs and movies usually show middle-class people, and most commercial advertising is directed at these average consumers. The middle class contains far more racial and ethnic diversity than the upper class.

Upper-Middles

People in the top half of this category are called the *upper-middle class,* based on above-average income in the range of $113,000 to $197,000 a year. Such income allows upper-middle-class families to

The Waehner family lives in Marin County, California, one of the highest-income communities in the United States, where annual household income averages more than $100,000.

Mitakuye Oyasin lives on the Pine Ridge Indian Reservation, one of the poorest communities in the United States, where annual household income averages less than $4,000.

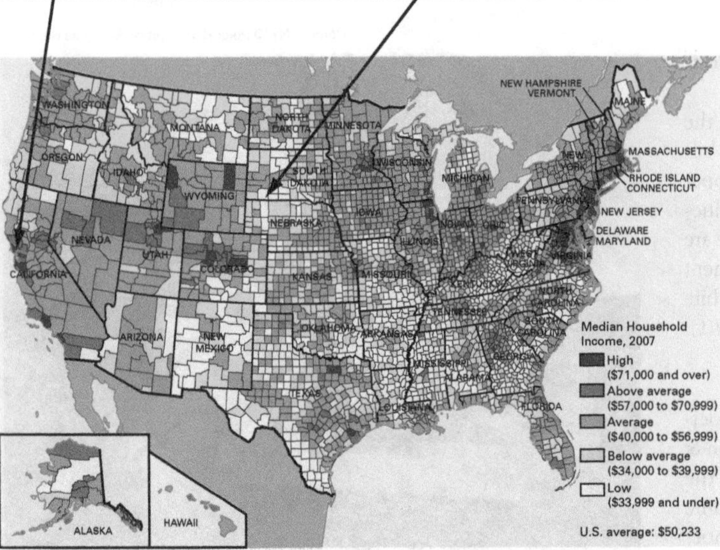

Seeing Ourselves

NATIONAL MAP 1

Household Income across the United States, 2007

This map shows the median household income (that is, how much money, on average, a household earned) in the more than 3,000 counties that make up the United States, for the year 2007. The richest counties, shown in the darker shades of green, are not spread randomly across the country. Nor are the poorest U.S. counties, which are shown in the lightest green. Looking at the map, what patterns do you see in the distribution of wealth and poverty across the United States? What can you say about wealth and poverty in urban and rural areas?

Source: U.S. Census Bureau (2008).

live in comfortable homes in fairly expensive areas, own several automobiles, and build investments. Two-thirds of upper-middle-class children graduate from college, and postgraduate degrees are common. Many go on to high-prestige careers as physicians, engineers, lawyers, accountants, and business executives. Lacking the power of the richest people to influence national or international events, upper-middles often play an important role in local political affairs.

Average-Middles

The rest of the middle class falls close to the center of the U.S. class structure. *Average-middles* typically work at less prestigious white-collar jobs as bank branch managers, high school teachers, and government office workers or in highly skilled blue-collar jobs such as electrical work and carpentry. Family income is between $50,000 and $112,000 a year, which is roughly the national average.[2] Middle-class people typically build up a small amount of wealth over the course of their working lives, mostly in the form of a house and a retirement account. Middle-class men and women are likely to be high school graduates, but the odds are just fifty-fifty that they will complete a college degree, usually at a less expensive, state-supported school.

The Working Class

About one-third of the population falls within the working class (sometimes called the *lower-middle class*). In Marxist terms, the working class forms the core of the industrial proletariat. The blue-collar jobs held by members of the working class yield a family income of between $25,000 and $50,000 a year, somewhat below the national average. Working-class families have little or no wealth and are vulnerable to financial problems caused by unemployment or illness.

Many working-class jobs provide little personal satisfaction, require discipline but rarely imagination, and subject workers to continual supervision. These jobs also offer fewer benefits, such as medical insurance and pension plans. About two-thirds of working-class families own their own homes, usually in lower-cost neighborhoods. College becomes a reality for only about one-third of working-class children.

The Lower Class

The remaining 20 percent of our population make up the lower class. Low income makes their lives insecure and difficult. In 2007, the federal government classified 37 million people (12.5 percent of the population) as poor. Millions more—called the "working poor"—are slightly better off, holding low-prestige jobs that provide little satisfaction and minimal income. Barely half manage to complete high school, and only one in four ever reaches college.

Society segregates the lower class, especially when the poor are racial or ethnic minorities. About 45 percent of lower-class families own their own homes, typically in the least desirable neighborhoods. Although poor neighborhoods are usually found in our inner cities, lower-class families also live in rural communities, especially in the South.

Most communities contain people of various class levels. In the country as a whole, however, some areas are wealthier than others. National Map 1 shows one measure of social class—median household income—for all the counties in the United States.

[2]In some parts of the United States where the cost of living is very high (say, San Francisco), a family might need $150,000 or more in annual income to reach the middle class.

SEEING SOCIOLOGY in Everyday Life

If you wanted to assess someone's social class position and could ask only one question, what would it be? Explain your decision.

MAKING THE GRADE

Be sure you understand how social class position involves not only money but also "cultural capital."

The Difference Class Makes

Social stratification affects nearly every dimension of our lives. We will briefly examine some of the ways social standing is linked to our health, values, politics, and family life.

Health

Health is closely related to social standing. Children born into poor families are three times more likely to die from disease, neglect, accidents, or violence during their first years of life than children born into privileged families. Among adults, people with above-average incomes are almost twice as likely as low-income people to describe their health as excellent. In addition, richer people live, on average, five years longer because they eat more nutritious food, live in safer and less stressful environments, and receive better medical care (Adams, Lucas, & Barnes, 2008).

Values and Attitudes

Some cultural values vary from class to class. The "old rich" have an unusually strong sense of family history because their social position is based on wealth passed down from generation to generation. Secure in their birthright privileges, upper-uppers also favor understated manners and tastes; many "new rich" engage in conspicuous consumption, using homes, cars, and even airplanes as status symbols to make a statement about their social position.

Affluent people with greater education and financial security are also more tolerant of controversial behavior such as homosexuality. Working-class people, who grow up in an atmosphere of greater supervision and discipline and are less likely to attend college, tend to be less tolerant (Lareau, 2002; NORC, 2007).

Social class has a great deal to do with self-concept. People with higher social standing experience more confidence in everyday interaction for the simple reason that others tend to view them as having greater importance. The Thinking About Diversity box describes the challenges faced by one young woman from a poor family attending a college where most students are from elite families.

Politics

Do political attitudes follow class lines? The answer is yes, but the pattern is complex. A desire to protect their wealth prompts well-off people to be more conservative on *economic* issues, favoring, for example, lower taxes. But on *social* issues such as abortion and gay rights, highly educated, more affluent people are more liberal. People of lower social standing, by contrast, tend to be economic liberals, favoring government social programs that benefit them, but typically hold more conservative views on social issues (NORC, 2007).

A simple pattern emerges when it comes to political involvement. Higher-income people, who are better served by the system, are more likely to vote and to join political organizations than people with low incomes. In presidential elections, 80 percent of adults with family incomes of $75,000 vote, compared to about 60 percent of those with family incomes of $35,000 (U.S. Census Bureau, 2008).

Family and Gender

Social class also shapes family life. Generally, lower-class families are somewhat larger than middle-class families because of earlier marriage and less use of birth control. Another family pattern is that working-class parents encourage children to conform to conventional norms and to respect authority figures. Parents of higher social standing pass on different "cultural capital" to their children, teaching them to express their individuality and use their imagination more freely. In both cases, parents are looking to the future: The odds are that less privileged children will have jobs that require them to follow rules and that more privileged children will have careers that require more creativity (Kohn, 1977; McLeod, 1995; Lareau, 2002).

The more money a family has, the more parents can develop their children's talents and abilities. An affluent family earning an average

Corbis – NY/Russell Lee

Compared to high-income people, low-income people are half as likely to report good health and, on average, live about five fewer years. The toll of low income—played out in inadequate nutrition, little medical care, and high stress—is easy to see on the faces of the poor, who look old before their time.

SEEING SOCIOLOGY in Everyday Life

After reading the box below, think about times when you have felt out of place in some setting based on your social class position. Why did you feel this way? How do such feelings show that we often understand class differences in terms of personal worthiness?

THINKING ABOUT DIVERSITY: RACE, CLASS, & GENDER

The Power of Class: A Low-Income Student Asks, "Am I as Good as You?"

Marcella grew up without the privileges that most other students on the campus of this private, liberal arts college take for granted. During her senior year, she and I talked at length about her college experiences and why social class presented a huge challenge to her. Marcella is not her real name; she wishes to remain anonymous. I have summarized what she has said about her college life in the story that follows.

> When I came here, I entered a new world. I found myself in a strange and dangerous place. All around me were people with habits and ideas I did not understand. A thousand times, I thought to myself, I hope all of you will realize that there are other worlds out there and that I am from one of them. Will you accept me?
>
> I am a child of poverty, a young woman raised in a world of want and violence. I am now on the campus of an elite college. I may have a new identity as a college student. But my old life is still going on in my head. I have not been able to change how I think of myself.
>
> Do you want to find out more about me? Learn more about the power of social class to shape how we feel about ourselves? Here is what I want to say to you.
>
> When I was growing up, I envied most of you. You lived in a middle-class bubble, a world that held you, protected you, and comforted you. Not me. While your parents were discussing current events, planning family trips, and looking out for you, my father and mother were screaming at each other. I will never be able to forget summer nights when I lay in my bed, sticky with sweat, biting my fingernails as a telephone crashed against the wall that separated my room from theirs. My father was drunk and out of control; my mother ducked just in time.
>
> Your fathers and mothers work in office buildings. They have good jobs, as doctors, lawyers, and architects; they are corporate managers; they run small businesses. Your mothers and fathers are people who matter. My mom takes the bus to a hospital where she works for $10 an hour cleaning up after people. She spends her shift doing what she is told. My dad? Who knows. He was a deadbeat, a drunk, a drug addict. I don't know if he still is or not. I haven't heard from him in eight years.
>
> You grew up in a neighborhood and probably lived for many years in one house. My family lived in low-cost rental housing. We moved a lot. When there was no money for rent, we packed up our stuff and moved to a new place. It seemed like we were always running away from something.
>
> You grew up with books, with trips to the library, with parents who read to you. You learned how to speak well and have an impressive vocabulary. I never heard a bedtime story, and I had maybe one inspiring teacher. Most of what I know I had to learn on my own. Maybe that's why I always feel like I am trying to catch up to you.
>
> You know how to use forks, knives, and spoons the right way. You know how to eat Chinese food and what to order at a Thai restaurant. You have favorite Italian dishes. You know how to order wine. You know about German beers, Danish cheeses, and French sauces. Me? I grew up having Thanksgiving dinner on paper plates, eating turkey served by social service volunteers. When you ask me to go with you to some special restaurant, I make some excuse and stay home. I can't afford it. I am afraid you will find out how little I know about things you take for granted.
>
> How did I ever get to this college? I remember one of my teachers telling me that I "have promise." The college admission office accepted me. But I am not sure why. I was given a scholarship that covers most of my tuition. That solved one big problem, and now I am here. But sometimes I am not sure I will stay. I have to study more than many of you to learn things you already know. I have to work two part-time jobs to make the money I needed to buy a used computer, clothes, and the occasional pizza at the corner place where many of you spend so much time.
>
> It's amazing to me that I am here. I realize how lucky I am. But now that I am here, I realize that the road is so much longer than I thought it would be. Getting to this college was only part of the journey. The scholarship was only part of the answer. The biggest challenge for me is what goes on every day—the thousands of ways in which you live a life that I still don't really understand, the thousands of things that I won't know or that I will do wrong that will blow my cover, and show me up for the fraud I am.

Getty Images Inc. – Stone Allstock/Penny Tweedie

WHAT DO YOU THINK?

1. How does this story show that social class involves much more than how much money a person has?
2. Why does Marcella worry that other people will think she is a "fraud"? If you could speak to her about this fear, what would you say?
3. Have you ever had similar feelings about being less important than—or better than—someone else based on social class position? Explain.

intragenerational social mobility a change in social position occurring during a person's lifetime

intergenerational social mobility upward or downward social mobility of children in relation to their parents

SEEING SOCIOLOGY in Everyday Life

One reason for the increasing gap between high- and low-paid workers is the increasing value of a college degree in our postindustrial society.

of $115,400 a year will spend $298,680 raising a child born in 2007 to the age of eighteen. Middle-class people, with an average annual income of $61,000, will spend $204,060, and a lower-income family, earning less than $45,800, will spend $148,320 (Lino, 2008). Privilege leads to privilege as family life reproduces the class structure in each generation.

Class also shapes our world of relationships. In a classic study of married life, Elizabeth Bott (1971, orig. 1957) found that most working-class couples divide their responsibilities according to gender roles; middle-class couples, by contrast, are more egalitarian, sharing more activities and expressing greater intimacy. More recently, Karen Walker (1995) discovered that working-class friendships typically serve as sources of material assistance; middle-class friendships are likely to involve shared interests and leisure pursuits.

Social Mobility

Ours is a dynamic society marked by quite a bit of social movement. Earning a college degree, landing a higher-paying job, or marrying someone who earns a good income contributes to *upward social mobility;* dropping out of school, losing a job, or becoming divorced (especially for women) may result in *downward social mobility.*

Over the long term, social mobility is not so much a matter of changes in individuals as changes in society itself. In the first half of the twentieth century, for example, industrialization expanded the U.S. economy, pushing up living standards. Even people who were not good swimmers rode the rising tide of prosperity. In recent decades, the closing of U.S. factories has pushed *structural social mobility* in a downward direction, dealing economic setbacks to many people. The economic downturn that hit hard in 2008 and 2009 reduced the income and economic opportunities of millions of people.

Sociologists distinguish between shorter- and longer-term changes in social position. **Intragenerational social mobility** is *a change in social position occurring during a person's lifetime* (*intra* is Latin for "within"). **Intergenerational social mobility,** *upward or downward social mobility of children in relation to their parents,* is important because it usually reveals long-term changes in society, such as industrialization, that affect everyone (*inter* is Latin for "between").

Research on Mobility

In few societies do people think about "getting ahead" as much as in the United States. Moving up, after all, is the American dream. But is there as much social mobility as we like to think?

One recent study of intergenerational mobility shows that about 32 percent of U.S. men have the same type of work as their fathers, 37 percent have been upwardly mobile (for example, a son born to a father with a blue-collar job now does white-collar work), and 32 percent have been downwardly mobile (for example, the father has a white-collar job and the son does blue-collar work). Among women, 27 percent showed no change in relation to their fathers, 46 percent were upwardly mobile, and 28 percent were downwardly mobile (Beller & Hout, 2006).

Horizontal social mobility—changing jobs at the same class level—is even more common; overall, about 80 percent of children show at least some type of social mobility in relation to their fathers (Hout, 1998; Beller & Hout, 2006).

Research points to four general conclusions about social mobility in the United States:

1. **Social mobility over the past century has been fairly high.** A high level of mobility is what we would expect in an industrial class system.

FIGURE 2 **Mean Annual Income, U.S. Families, 1980–2007 (in 2007 dollars, adjusted for inflation)**

The gap between high-income and low-income families is wider today than it was in 1980.

Source: U.S. Census Bureau (2008).

Seeing SOCIOLOGY in the 

Newsweek

The End of Upward Mobility?

By JOEL KOTKIN
January 26, 2009

Barack Obama's ascension to the presidency won't end racism, but it does mean race is no longer the dominant issue in American politics. Instead, over the coming decades, class will likely constitute the major dividing line in our society—and the greatest threat to America's historic aspirations. This is a fundamental shift from the last century. Writing in the early 1900s, W.E.B. DuBois observed, "The problem of the 20th century is the problem of the color line." Developments in the ensuing years bore out this assertion. Indeed, before the 1960s, the decade of Barack Obama's birth, even the most talented people of color faced often insurmountable barriers to reaching their full potential. Today in a multiracial America, the path to success has opened up to an extent unimaginable in DuBois's time.

Obama's ascent reflects in particular the rise of the black bourgeoisie from tokens to a force at the heart of the meritocracy. Since the late 1960s, the proportion of African-American households living in poverty has shrunk from 70 percent to 46 percent, while the black middle class has grown from 27 percent to 37 percent. Perhaps more remarkable, the percentage who are considered prosperous—earning more than $107,000 a year in 2007 dollars—expanded from 3 percent to 17 percent.

Yet as racial equity has improved, class disparities between rich and poor, between the ultra-affluent and the middle class, have widened. This gap transcends race. African-Americans and Latinos may tend, on average, to be poorer than whites or Asians, but stagnant or even diminishing incomes affect all ethnic groups. (Most housecleaners are white, for instance—and the same goes for other low-wage professions.) Divisions may not be as visible as during the Gilded Age.

As Irving Kristol once noted, "Who doesn't wear blue jeans these days?" You can walk into a film studio or software firm and have trouble distinguishing upper management from midlevel employees.

But from the 1940s to the 1970s, the American middle class enjoyed steadily increasing incomes that stayed on a par with those in the upper classes. Since then, wages for most workers have lagged behind. As a result, the relatively small number of Americans with incomes seven times or more above the poverty level have achieved almost all the recent gains in wealth. Most disturbingly, the rate of upward mobility has stagnated overall, which means it is no easier for the poor to move up today than it was in the 1970s.

This disparity is strikingly evident in income data compiled by Citigroup, which shows that the top 1 percent of U.S. households now account for as much of the nation's total wealth . . . as they did

2. **Within a single generation, social mobility is usually small.** Most young families increase their income over time as they gain education and skills. For example, a typical family headed by a thirty-year-old earned about $57,000 in 2007; a typical family headed by a fifty-year-old earned $80,000 (U.S. Census Bureau, 2008). Yet only a few people move "from rags to riches" (the way J. K. Rowling did) or lose a lot of money (a number of rock stars who made it big had little money a few years later). Most social mobility involves limited movement within one class level rather than striking moves between classes.
3. **The long-term trend in social mobility has been upward.** Industrialization, which greatly expanded the U.S. economy, and the growth of white-collar work over the course of the twentieth century have raised living standards.
4. **Social mobility since the 1970s has been uneven.** Real income (adjusted for inflation) rose during the twentieth century until the 1970s. Between 1975 and 1985, gains were far smaller. During the 1980s, real income changed little for many people, rising slowly during the 1990s and falling slightly after 2000. The economic recession that began in 2008 is likely to result in downward social mobility for most U.S. families. Seeing Sociology in the News reports evidence that fewer people in this country are getting ahead.

Mobility by Income Level

The experience of social mobility depends on where in the social class system you happen to be. Figure 2 shows how U.S. families at different income levels made out between 1980 and 2007. Well-to-do families (the highest 20 percent, but not all the same families over the entire period) saw their incomes jump 58 percent, from an average $117,986 in 1980 to $186,529 in 2007. People in the middle of the population also had gains, but more modest ones. The lowest-income 20 percent saw only a 4.6 percent increase in earnings.

For families at the top of the income scale (the highest 5 percent), recent decades have brought a windfall. These families, with average income of more than $168,000 in 1980, were making $317,000 in 2007—almost twice as much (U.S. Census Bureau, 2008).

Mobility: Race, Ethnicity, and Gender

White people in the United States have always been in a more privileged position than people of African or Hispanic descent. Through the economic expansion of the 1980s and 1990s, many more African Americans entered the ranks of the wealthy. But overall, the real income of African Americans has changed little in three decades. African American family income as a percentage of white family income has fallen slightly to 57 percent in 2007 from 62 percent back in 1975. Compared with white families, Latino families in the United States lost even more ground, earning 66 percent as much as white families in 1975 and just 58 percent as much in 2007 (U.S. Census Bureau, 2008).

Feminists point out that historically, women in U.S. society have had limited opportunity for upward mobility because the clerical jobs (such as secretary) and service positions (such as food server) widely held by women offer few opportunities for advancement.

in 1913, when monopolistic business practices were the order of the day. Their net worth is now greater than that of the bottom 90 percent of the nation's households combined. The top 20 percent of taxpayers realized nearly three quarters of all income gains from 1979 to 2000.

Even getting a colleges degree no longer guarantees upward mobility. The implicit American contract has always been that with education and hard work, anyone can get ahead. But since 2000, young people with college educations—except those who go to elite colleges and graduate schools—have seen their wages decline. The deepening recession will make this worse. According to a 2008 survey by the National Association of Colleges and Employers, half of all companies plan to cut the number of new graduates they hire this year, compared with last. But the problem goes well beyond the current crisis. For one thing, the growing number of graduates has flooded the job market at a time when many financially pressed boomers are postponing retirement. And college-educated workers today face unprecedented competition from skilled labor in other countries, particularly in the developing world.

The greatest challenge for Obama will be to change this trajectory for Americans under 30, who supported him by two to one. The promise that "anyone" can reach the highest levels of society is the basis of both our historic optimism and the stability of our political system. Yet even before the recession, growing inequality was undermining Americans' optimism about the future. In a 2006 Zogby poll, for example, nearly two thirds of adults did not think life would be better for their children. However inspirational the story of his ascent, Barack Obama will be judged largely by whether he can rebuild a ladder of upward mobility for the rest of America, too.

WHAT DO YOU THINK?

1. Do you think that class differences are emerging as the big issue of this century? Why or why not?
2. Most people in this country think it is only fair that, with schooling and hard work, people should be able to get ahead. How true is that idea today? Explain.
3. In your opinion, how optimistic or pessimistic are young people in the United States about their chances to get ahead in the years to come? Why?

Adapted from the original article, "The End of Upward Mobility?" by Joel Kotkin, published in *Newsweek*, January 26, 2009,

Over time, however, the earnings gap between women and men has been narrowing. Women working full time in 1980 earned 60 percent as much as men working full time; by 2007, women were earning 78 percent as much (U.S. Census Bureau, 2008).

Mobility and Marriage

Research points to the conclusion that marriage has an important effect on social standing. In a study of women and men in their forties, Jay Zagorsky (2006) found that people who marry and stay married accumulate about twice as much wealth as people who remain single or who divorce. Reasons for this difference include the fact that couples who live together typically enjoy double incomes and also pay only half the bills they would have if they were single and living in separate households.

It is also likely that compared to single people, married men and women work harder in their jobs and save more money. Why? The main reason is that they are working not just for themselves but to support others who are counting on them (Popenoe, 2006).

Just as marriage pushes social standing upward, divorce usually makes social position go down. Couples who divorce take on the financial burden of supporting two households. After divorce, women are hurt more than men because it is typically the man who earns more. Many women who divorce lose not only most of their income but also benefits such as health care and insurance coverage (Weitzman, 1996).

Everett Collection/Columbia Pictures

Social mobility is a common theme in popular culture, including films. In *The Pursuit of Happyness,* Will Smith plays a man who struggles to "make it" and faces many challenges, such as caring for his son while he tries to succeed at a new job. In most such films, the main character eventually reaches his goal. In your opinion, how much truth is there in the idea that "everyone can get ahead through hard work"?

SEEING SOCIOLOGY in Everyday Life

Do you feel that you are likely to end up with a higher social position than your parents? The same? Lower? Why? How much of the mobility you expect is due to changes in U.S. society?

SEEING SOCIOLOGY in Everyday Life

Big houses are an example of conspicuous consumption. Can you point to other examples of conspicuous consumption in everyday life?

SEEING SOCIOLOGY IN EVERYDAY LIFE

As CEOs Get Richer, the Great Mansions Return

I grew up in Elkins Park, Pennsylvania, an older suburban community just north of Philadelphia. Elkins Park was at that time and still is a mostly middle-class community, although, like most of suburbia, some neighborhoods boast bigger houses than others. What made Elkins Park special was that scattered over the area were a handful of great mansions, built a century ago by early Philadelphia industrialists. Back then, just about all there was to the town was these great "estates," along with fields and meadows. By about 1940, however, most of the land was split off into lots for the homes of newer middle-class suburbanites. The great mansions suddenly seemed out of place, with heirs trying to figure out how to pay the rising property taxes. As a result, many of the great mansions were sold, the buildings taken down, and the land subdivided.

In the 1960s, when I was a teenager, a short ride on my bicycle could take me past the Breyer estate (built by the founder of the ice-cream company, now the township police building), the Curtis estate (built by a magazine publisher and transformed into a community park), and the Wanamaker estate (built by the founder of a large Philadelphia department store, now the site of high-rise apartments). Probably the grandest of them all was the Wiedner estate, modeled after a French chateau, complete with doorknobs and window pulls covered in gold; it now stands empty.

In their day, these structures were not just homes to families with many servants; they also served as monuments to a time when the rich were, well, *really* rich. By contrast, the community that emerged on the grounds once owned by these wealthy families is middle-class, with modest homes on small lots.

But did the so-called Gilded Age of great wealth disappear forever? Hardly. By the 1980s, a new wave of great mansions was being built in the United States. Take the architect Thierry Despont, who designs huge houses for the super-rich. One of Despont's smaller homes might be 20,000 square feet (about ten times the size of the average U.S. house), and the larger ones go all the way up to 60,000 square feet (as big as any of the Elkins Park mansions built a century ago and almost the size of the White House). These megahomes have kitchens as large as college classrooms, exercise rooms, indoor swimming pools, and even indoor tennis courts (Krugman, 2002).

Most of these megahouses have been built by newly rich chief executive officers (CEOs) of large corporations. CEOs have always made more money than most people, but recent years have seen executive pay soar. Between 1970 and 2007, the average U.S. family saw only a modest increase in income (about 30 percent after inflation is taken into account). Yet according to *Fortune* magazine, during the same period, the average annual compensation for the 100 highest-paid CEOs skyrocketed from $1.3 million (about 40 times the earnings of an average worker of that time) to $37.5 million (roughly a 2,800 percent increase and equal to 1,000 times as much as the earnings of today's average worker). Richer still, the twenty highest-earning investment fund managers in 2008 (a terrible year for the stock market) had, on average, $465 million *each* in income, earning more in ten minutes than the average worker made all year (Story, 2009).

AP Wide World Photos/*Indianapolis Star*, Charlie Nye

WHAT DO YOU THINK?

1. Do you consider increasing economic inequality a problem? Why or why not?
2. How many times more than an average worker should a CEO earn? Explain your answer.
3. In light of the economic recession that began in 2008, with so many companies struggling, do you think we will enter an era of lower CEO pay or not? Explain your answer.

The American Dream: Still a Reality?

The expectation of upward social mobility is deeply rooted in U.S. culture. Through most of our history, the economy has grown steadily, raising living standards. Even today, for some people at least, the American dream is alive and well. In 2007, about one in four U.S. families earned $100,000 or more, compared with just one in twenty back in 1967 (in dollars controlled for inflation). There are now about 9 million millionaires in the United States, more than four times the number a decade ago (L. Eisenberg, 2007; R. Frank, 2008; U.S. Census Bureau, 2008).

Yet not all indicators are positive. Note these disturbing trends:

1. **For many workers, earnings have stalled.** The annual income of a fifty-year-old man working full time climbed by about 50 percent between 1958 and 1974 in constant dollars. Between 1974 and 2007, however, this worker's income rose by only 32 percent, even as the number of hours worked increased and the cost of

MAKING THE GRADE

The changes in median family income shown below in Figure 3 are examples of structural social mobility.

SEEING SOCIOLOGY in Everyday Life

In your opinion, how significantly has the recent economic downturn affected people's optimism about their ability to realize the "American dream"?

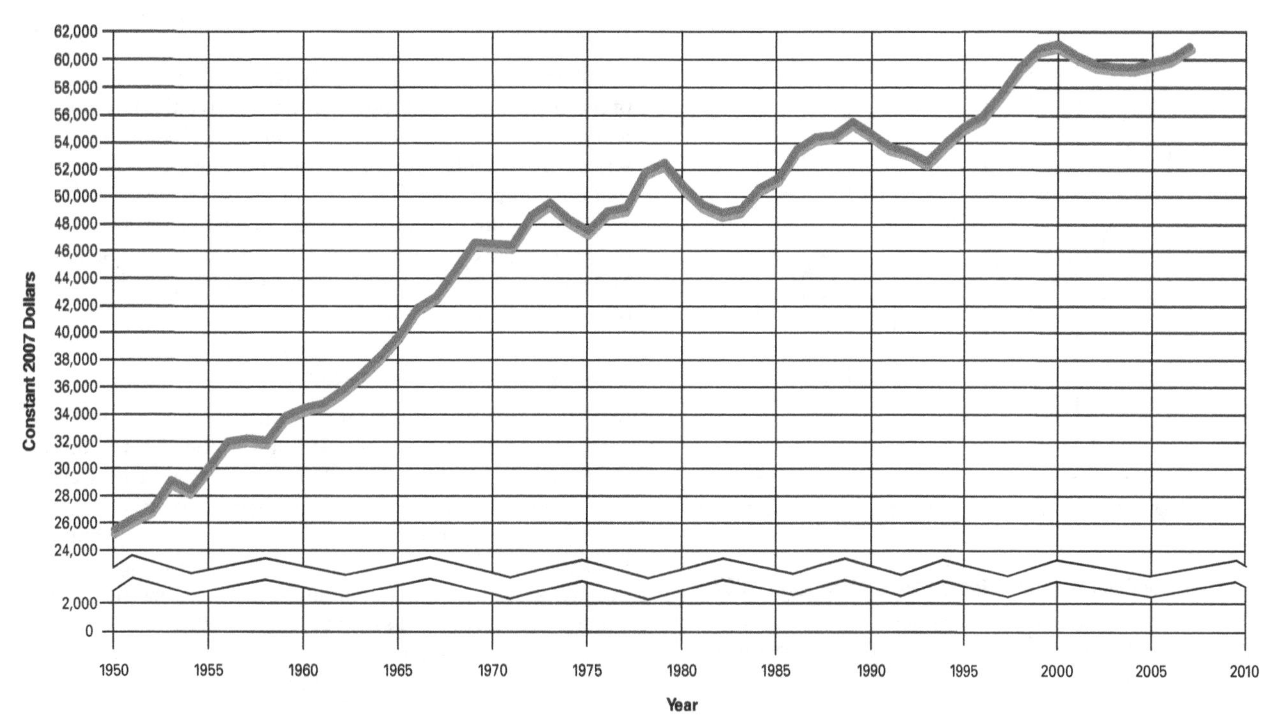

FIGURE 3 **Median Annual Income, U.S. Families, 1950–2007**

Average family income in the United States grew rapidly between 1950 and 1970. Since then, however, the increase has been smaller.

Source: U.S. Census Bureau (2008).

necessities like housing, education, and medical care went way up (Russell, 1995a; U.S. Census Bureau, 2008).

2. **More jobs offer little income.** The expanding global economy has moved many industrial jobs overseas, reducing the number of high-paying factory jobs here in the United States. At the same time, the expansion of our service economy means that more of today's jobs—in fast-food restaurants or large discount stores—offer relatively low wages.
3. **Young people are remaining at home.** Currently, more than half of young people aged eighteen to twenty-four are living with their parents. Since 1975, the average age at marriage has moved upward four years (to 25.6 years for women and 27.5 years for men).

Over the past generation, more people have become rich, and the rich have become richer. At the very top of the pile, as the Seeing Sociology in Everyday Life box explains, the highest-paid corporate executives have enjoyed a runaway rise in their earnings. Yet the increasing share of low-paying jobs has also brought downward mobility for millions of families, feeding the fear that the chance to enjoy a middle-class lifestyle is slipping away. As Figure 3 shows, although median income doubled between 1950 and 1973, it has grown by only 22 percent since then (U.S. Census Bureau, 2008).

The Global Economy and the U.S. Class Structure

Underlying the shifts in U.S. class structure is global economic change. Much of the industrial production that gave U.S. workers high-paying jobs a generation ago has moved overseas. With less industry at home, the United States now serves as a vast market for industrial goods such as cars and popular items like stereos, cameras, and computers made in China, Japan, South Korea, and elsewhere.

relative poverty the lack of resources of some people in relation to those who have more

absolute poverty a lack of resources that is life-threatening

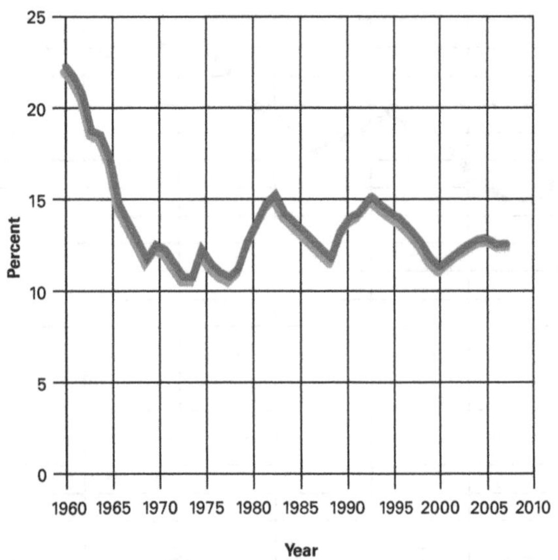

FIGURE 4 **The Poverty Rate in the United States, 1960–2007**

The share of our population in poverty fell dramatically between 1960 and 1970. Since then, the poverty rate has remained between 10 and 15 percent of the population.

Source: U.S. Census Bureau (2008).

High-paying jobs in manufacturing, held by 28 percent of the U.S. labor force in 1960, support only 10 percent of workers today (U.S. Department of Labor, 2008b). In their place, the economy now offers service work, which often pays far less. A traditionally high-paying corporation like USX (formerly United States Steel) now employs fewer people than the expanding McDonald's chain, and fast-food clerks make only a fraction of what steelworkers earn.

The global reorganization of work has not been bad news for everyone. On the contrary, the global economy is driving upward social mobility for educated people who specialize in law, finance, marketing, and computer technology. Even allowing for the downturn in 2008 and 2009, the global economic expansion helped push up the stock market about eightfold between 1980 and 2008, reaping profits for families with money to invest over this period.

But the same trend has hurt many average workers, who have lost their factory jobs and now perform low-wage service work. In addition, many companies (General Motors and Ford are recent examples) have downsized, cutting the ranks of their workforce in their efforts to stay competitive in world markets. As a result, even though more than 50 percent of all families contain two or more workers—more than twice the share in 1950—many families are working harder simply to hold on to what they have (U.S. Census Bureau, 2008).

Poverty in the United States

Social stratification creates both "haves" and "have-nots." All systems of social inequality create poverty, or at least **relative poverty,** *the lack of resources of some people in relation to those who have more.* A more serious but preventable problem is **absolute poverty,** *a lack of resources that is life-threatening.*

About 1 billion human beings—one person in six—are at risk of absolute poverty. Even in the affluent United States, families go hungry, live in inadequate housing, and suffer poor health because of a serious lack of resources.

The Extent of Poverty

In 2007, the government classified 37 million men, women, and children—12.5 percent of the population—as poor. This count of relative poverty refers to families with incomes below an official poverty line, which for a family of four in that year was set at $21,203. The poverty line is about three times what the government estimates people must spend for food. But the income of the average poor family was just 60 percent of this amount. This means that the typical poor family had to get by on less than $13,000 in 2007 (U.S. Census Bureau, 2008). Figure 4 shows that the official poverty rate fell during the 1960s and has stayed about the same since then.

Who Are the Poor?

Although no single description fits all poor people, poverty is pronounced among certain categories of our population. Where these categories overlap, the problem is especially serious.

Age

A generation ago, the elderly were at greatest risk for poverty. But thanks to better retirement programs offered today by private employers and the government, the poverty rate for people over age sixty-five fell from 30 percent in 1967 to 9.7 percent—well below the national average—in 2007. Looking at it from another angle, about 9.5 percent (3.6 million) of the poor are elderly (U.S. Census Bureau, 2008).

Today the burden of poverty falls more heavily on children. In 2007, 18.0 percent of people under age eighteen (13.3 million children) and 17.3 percent of people age eighteen to twenty-four (5 million young adults) were poor. Put another way, 49 percent of the U.S. poor are young people no older than twenty-four.

Race and Ethnicity

Two-thirds of all poor people are white; 25 percent are African Americans. But in relation to their overall numbers, African Americans are about three times as likely as non-Hispanic whites to be poor. In 2007,

Anna Mae Peters lives in Nitta Yuma, Mississippi. Almost everyone she knows lives below the government's poverty line.

Julie Garland lives in Greenwich, Connecticut, where people have very high income and there is little evidence of poverty.

feminization of poverty the trend of women making up an increasing proportion of the poor

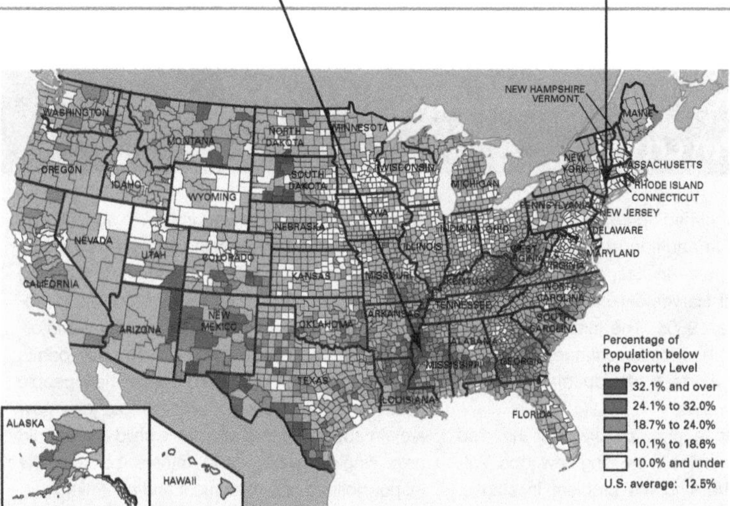

Seeing Ourselves

NATIONAL MAP 2

Poverty across the United States, 2007

This map shows that the poorest counties in the United States—where the poverty rate is more than twice the national average—are in Appalachia, across the Deep South, along the border with Mexico, near the Four Corners region of the Southwest, and in the Dakotas. Can you suggest some reasons for this pattern?

Source: U.S. Census Bureau (2008).

24.5 percent of African Americans (9.2 million people) lived in poverty, compared to 21.5 percent of Hispanics (9.9 million), 10.2 percent of Asians and Pacific Islanders (1.3 million), and 8.2 percent of non-Hispanic whites (16 million). The poverty gap between whites and minorities has changed little since 1975.

People of color have especially high rates of child poverty. Among African American children, 34.5 percent are poor; the comparable figures are 28.6 percent among Hispanic children and 10.1 percent among non-Hispanic white children (U.S. Census Bureau, 2008).

Gender and Family Patterns

Of all poor people age eighteen or older, 56 percent are women and 44 percent are men. This difference reflects the fact that women who head households are at high risk of poverty. Of all poor families, 51 percent are headed by women with no husband present; just 8 percent of poor families are headed by single men.

The United States has thus experienced a **feminization of poverty**, *the trend of women making up an increasing proportion of the poor*. In 1960, only 25 percent of all poor households were headed by women; the majority of poor families had both wives and husbands in the home. By 2007, however, the share of poor households headed by a single woman had more than doubled to 51 percent.

The feminization of poverty is one result of a larger trend: the rapidly increasing number of households at all class levels headed by single women. This trend, coupled with the fact that households headed by women are at high risk of poverty, helps explain why women and their children make up an increasing share of the U.S. poor.

Urban and Rural Poverty

In the United States, the greatest concentration of poverty is found in central cities, where the 2007 poverty rate stood at 16.5 percent. The poverty rate in suburbs is 9 percent. Thus the poverty rate for urban areas as a whole is 11.9 percent—somewhat lower than the 15.4 percent found in rural areas. National Map 2 shows that most of the counties with the highest poverty rate in the United States are rural.

Explaining Poverty

The richest nation on Earth contains tens of millions of poor people, a fact that raises serious questions. It is true, as some analysts remind us, that most poor people in the United States are far better off than the poor in other countries: 35 percent of U.S. poor families own a home, 70 percent own a car, and only about 15 percent say they often go without food (U.S. Bureau of Agriculture, 2008; U.S. Census Bureau, 2008). But there is little doubt that poverty harms the overall well-being of millions of people in this country.

Why is there poverty in the first place? We will examine two opposing explanations for poverty that lead to a lively and important political debate.

One View: Blame the Poor

One approach holds that *the poor are mostly responsible for their own poverty.* Throughout this nation's history, people have placed a high value on self-reliance, convinced that social standing is mostly a matter of individual talent and effort. According to this view, society offers plenty of opportunities to anyone who is able and willing to take advantage of them, and the poor are those

MAKING THE GRADE

Reading the box below, can you point to elements of structural social mobility—in this case, in a downward direction?

SEEING SOCIOLOGY in Everyday Life

From what you know about President Obama's economic program, how does he hope to put people back to work? Do you think William Julius Wilson would support the president's approach to unemployment and poverty?

SEEING SOCIOLOGY IN EVERYDAY LIFE

When Work Disappears, the Result Is Poverty

The U.S. economy has created tens of millions of new jobs in recent decades. Yet African Americans who live in inner cities have faced a catastrophic loss of work. William Julius Wilson points out that although people continue to talk about welfare reform, neither major political party (Democrats or Republicans) has said anything about the lack of work in central cities.

With the loss of inner-city jobs, Wilson continues, for the first time in U.S. history a large majority of the adults in our inner cities are not working. Studying the Washington Park area of Chicago, Wilson found a troubling trend. Back in 1950, most adults in this African American community had jobs, but by the mid-1990s, two-thirds did not. As one elderly woman who moved to the neighborhood in 1953 explained:

> When I moved in, the neighborhood was intact. It was intact with homes, beautiful homes, mini-mansions, with stores, laundromats, with Chinese cleaners. We had drugstores. We had hotels. We had doctors over on 39th Street. We had doctors' offices in the neighborhood. We had the middle class and the upper-middle class. It has gone from affluent to where it is today. (W.J. Wilson, 1996b:28)

Why has this neighborhood declined? Wilson's eight years of research point to one answer: There are barely any jobs. It is the loss of work that has pushed people into desperate poverty, weakened families, and made people turn to welfare. In nearby Woodlawn, Wilson identified more than 800 businesses that had operated in 1950; today, just 100 remain. In addition, a number of major employers in the past—including Western Electric and International Harvester—closed their plant doors in the late 1960s. The inner cities have fallen victim to economic change, including downsizing and the loss of industrial jobs that have moved overseas.

Wilson paints a grim picture. But he also believes the answer lies in creating new jobs. Wilson proposes attacking the problem in stages. First, the government could hire people to do all kinds of work, from clearing slums to putting up new housing. Such a program, modeled on the Works Progress Administration (WPA) created in 1935 during the Great Depression, would move people from welfare to work and in the process create much-needed hope. In addition, federal and state governments must improve schools by enacting performance standards and providing more funding. Of special importance is teaching children language skills and computer skills to prepare them for the jobs being created by the Information Revolution. Improved regional public transportation would connect cities (where people need work) and suburbs (where most jobs now are). In addition, more affordable child care would help single mothers and fathers balance the responsibilities of employment and parenting.

Wilson claims that his proposals are well grounded in research. But he knows that politics revolves around other considerations as well. For one thing, if the public *thinks* there are jobs available, it is hard to change the perception that the poor are simply avoiding work. He also concedes that his proposals, at least in the short term, are more expensive than continuing to funnel welfare assistance to jobless communities.

But what are the long-term costs of allowing our cities to decay while suburbs prosper? On the other hand, what would be the benefits of giving everyone the hope and satisfaction that are supposed to define our way of life?

Newscom/Carl Wagner/*Chicago Tribune*

William Julius Wilson spent years studying neighborhoods like this one in Chicago. He now teaches at Harvard University in Cambridge, Massachusetts.

WHAT DO YOU THINK?

1. If Wilson were running for public office, do you think he would be elected? Why or why not?
2. In your opinion, why are people so reluctant to see inner-city poverty as a problem?
3. Where do you agree with Wilson's analysis of poverty? Where do you disagree?

people who cannot or will not work due to a lack of skills, schooling, or motivation.

In his study of poverty in Latin American cities, the anthropologist Oscar Lewis (1961) noted that many poor become trapped in a *culture of poverty,* a lower-class subculture that can destroy people's ambition to improve their lives. Raised in poor families, children become resigned to their situation, producing a self-perpetuating cycle of poverty.

In 1996, hoping to break the cycle of poverty in the United States, Congress changed the welfare system, which had provided federal funds to assist poor people since 1935. The federal government continues to send money to the states to distribute to needy people, but

SEEING SOCIOLOGY in Everyday Life

Our society has been more generous with the "worthy" poor (such as elderly people) than with the "unworthy" poor (such as able-bodied people who, we assume, should take care of themselves). Why do you think we have not done more to reduce poverty among children, who surely fall into the "worthy" category?

benefits carry strict time limits—in most cases, no more than two years at a stretch and a total of five years as an individual moves in and out of the welfare system. The stated purpose of this reform was to force people to be self-supporting and move them away from dependency on government.

Another View: Blame Society

A different position, argued by William Julius Wilson (1996a, 1996b; Mouw, 2000), holds that *society is mostly responsible for poverty.* Wilson points to the loss of jobs in the inner cities as the main cause of poverty, claiming that there is simply not enough work to support families. Wilson sees any apparent lack of trying on the part of poor people as a result of little opportunity rather than a cause of poverty. From Wilson's point of view, Lewis's analysis amounts to blaming the victims for their own suffering. The Seeing Sociology in Everyday Life box provides a closer look at Wilson's argument and how it would shape public policy.

CRITICAL REVIEW The U.S. public is evenly divided over whether the government or people themselves should take responsibility for reducing poverty (NORC, 2007). And here's what we know about poverty and work: Government statistics show that 52 percent of the heads of poor households did not work at all during 2007, and an additional 29 percent worked only part time (U.S. Census Bureau, 2008). Such facts seem to support the "blame the poor" side of the argument, because one major cause of poverty is not holding a job.

But the *reasons* that people do not work seem more in step with the "blame society" position. Middle-class women may be able to combine working and child rearing, but this is much harder for poor women who cannot afford child care, and few employers provide child care programs. As Wilson explains, many people are idle not because they are avoiding work but because there are not enough jobs to go around. In short, the most effective way to reduce poverty is to ensure a greater supply of jobs as well as child care for parents who work (W. J. Wilson, 1996a; Bainbridge, Meyers, & Waldfogel, 2003).

CHECK YOUR LEARNING Explain the view that the poor should take responsibility for poverty and the view that society is responsible for poverty. Which is closer to your own view?

The Working Poor

Not all poor people are jobless. The *working poor* command the sympathy and support of people on both sides of the poverty debate. In 2007, some 18 percent of heads of poor families (1.4 million women and men) worked at least fifty weeks of the year and yet could not escape poverty. Another 30 percent of these heads of families (2.2 million people) remained poor despite part-time employment. Put differently, 3.3 percent of full-time workers earn so little that they remain poor (U.S. Census Bureau, 2008). Congress set the minimum wage at $6.55 per hour in 2008, raising it to $7.25 per hour in July 2009. But even this increase cannot end working poverty—even at $8.00 an hour, a full-time worker still cannot lift an urban family of four above the poverty line.

Individual ability and personal effort do play a part in shaping social position. However, the weight of sociological evidence points to society, not individual character traits, as the primary cause of poverty because more and more of the jobs that are available offer only low wages. In addition, the poor are *categories* of people—female heads of families, people of color, people isolated from the larger society in inner-city areas—who face special barriers and limited opportunities.

The Controversy & Debate box takes a closer look at current welfare policy. Understanding this important social issue can help us

The African American artist Henry Ossawa Tanner captured the humility and humanity of impoverished people in his painting *The Thankful Poor.* This insight is important in a society that tends to define poor people as morally unworthy and deserving of their bitter plight.

Henry Ossawa Tanner (1859–1937), *The Thankful Poor.* Private collection. Art Resource, New York.

SEEING SOCIOLOGY in Everyday Life

Do you see evidence of homelessness in your community? Has the problem become worse during the recent economic recession?

SEEING SOCIOLOGY in Everyday Life

Do you think people in the United States consider homelessness to be a serious problem? Why or why not?

CONTROVERSY & DEBATE

The Welfare Dilemma

Marco: *(rushing in the door)* Sorry I'm late. I stopped at the store and got stuck behind some welfare mother in the checkout line.

Sergi: *(looking back with a confused grin)* Exactly what does a person on welfare look like?

What is *your* image of a "welfare recipient"? If you are like many people in the United States, you might think of a middle-aged African American woman. But you would be wrong. In truth, the typical person receiving welfare in this country is a child who is white.

There is a lot of confusion about welfare. There is also disagreement about whether this type of assistance is a good or bad idea. In 1996, Congress debated the issue and enacted new law that ended the federal government's role in providing income assistance to poor households. In place of this federal program, new state-run programs now offer limited help to the poor, but they require people who receive aid to get job training or find work—or have their benefits cut off.

To understand how we got to where we are, let's begin by explaining what, exactly, welfare is. The term "welfare" refers to an assortment of policies and programs designed to improve the well-being of some low-income people. Until the welfare reform of 1996, most people used the term to refer to just one part of the overall system, Aid for Families with Dependent Children (AFDC), a federal program of monthly financial support for parents (mostly single women) to care for themselves and their children. In 1996, about 5 million households received AFDC for some part of the year.

Conservatives opposed AFDC, claiming that rather than reducing child poverty, AFDC made the problem worse, in two ways. First, they claimed that AFDC weakened families, because for years after the program began, it paid benefits to poor mothers only if no husband lived in the home. As a result, the government was actually providing an economic incentive to women to have children outside of marriage, and they blame it for the rapid rise of out-of-wedlock births among poor people. To conservatives, marriage is one key to reducing poverty: Fewer than one in ten married-couple families are poor; more than nine in ten AFDC families were headed by an unmarried woman.

PhotoEdit Inc./David Urbina

Is society responsible for poverty or are individuals themselves to blame? When it comes to homeless families, most people think society should do more.

Second, conservatives believe that welfare encourages poor people to become dependent on government handouts, the main reason that eight out of ten poor heads of households did not have full-time jobs. Furthermore, only 5 percent of single mothers receiving AFDC worked full time, compared to more than half of nonpoor single mothers. Conservatives say that welfare gradually moved well beyond its original purpose of short-term help to nonworking women with children (say, after divorce or death of a husband) and gradually became a way of life. Once trapped

decide how our society should respond to the problem of poverty, as well as the problem of homelessness, discussed next.

Homelessness

In 2005, the government's Department of Housing and Urban Development conducted a national survey of cities and towns to find out how many people in the United States were homeless at some time during that year. The answer was about 754,000, including people living in shelters, in transitional housing, and on the street (Ohlemacher, 2007). As with earlier estimates of the homeless population, critics claimed that the HUD survey undercounted the homeless, who may well number several million people. In addition, they add, evidence suggests that the number of homeless people in the United States is increasing (L. Kaufman, 2004; National Coalition for the Homeless, 2007).

The familiar stereotypes of homeless people—men sleeping in doorways and women carrying everything they own in a shopping bag—have been replaced by the "new homeless": people thrown out of work because of plant closings, women who take their children and leave home to escape domestic violence, women and men forced out of apartments by rent increases, and others unable to meet mortgage or rent payments because of low wages or no work at all. Today, no stereotype paints a complete picture of the homeless.

The large majority of homeless people report that they do not work, although about 20 percent have at least a part-time job (U.S. Conference of Mayors, 2007). Working or not, all homeless people

SEEING SOCIOLOGY in Everyday Life

What are the arguments typically made by Democratic and Republican politicians on the issue of poverty?

in dependency, poor women would raise children who were themselves likely to be poor as adults.

Liberals have a different view. Why, they ask, do people object to government money going to poor mothers and children when most "welfare" actually goes to richer people? The cost of AFDC was as high as $25 billion annually—no small sum, to be sure, but much less than the $580 billion in annual Social Security benefits Uncle Sam provides to senior citizens, most of whom are not poor. And it is just a small fraction of the more than $1 trillion "bailout money" Congress voted in 2008 and 2009 to assist the struggling financial industry.

Liberals insist that most poor families who turn to public assistance are truly needy. Most of the people who are helped in this way are children. And they don't get very much. The typical household receives only about $400 per month in assistance, hardly enough to attract people to a life of welfare dependency. Even adding some additional money in the form of food stamps, households assisted by welfare still struggle well below the poverty line everywhere in the country. Therefore, liberals see public assistance as a "Band-Aid approach" to the serious social problems of too few jobs and too much income inequality in the United States. As for the charge that public assistance weakens families, liberals agree that the share of families with one parent has gone up, but they see single parenting as a broad trend found at all class levels in many countries.

Back in 1996, the conservative arguments carried the day, ending the AFDC program. Our society's individualistic culture has always encouraged us to blame people themselves (rather than society) for poverty, which becomes a sign not of need but of laziness and personal failure. This view of the poor is probably the biggest reason that led Congress to replace the federal AFDC program with state-run programs called Temporary Assistance for Needy Families (TANF), requiring poor adults to get job training and limiting income assistance to two consecutive years with a lifetime limit of five years.

By 2008, the new TANF policy had reduced the number of households receiving income assistance by about 60 percent. This means that many single parents who were once on welfare have taken jobs or are receiving job training. In addition, the rate of out-of-wedlock births has fallen. With these facts in mind, conservatives who supported welfare reform see the new program as a huge success. The welfare rolls have been cut by more than half, and more people have moved from receiving a check to working in order to support themselves. But liberals claim that the reform is far from successful. They point out that many of the people who are now working earn so little pay that they are hardly better off than before. In addition, half of these workers have no health insurance. In other words, the reform has greatly reduced the number of people receiving welfare but has done little to reduce the extent of poverty.

WHAT DO YOU THINK?

1. How does our cultural emphasis on self-reliance help explain the controversy surrounding public assistance? Why do people not criticize benefits (such as home mortgage interest deductions) for people who are better off?
2. Do you approve of the time limits on benefits built into the TANF program? Why or why not?
3. Do you think the Obama administration will reduce poverty? Explain your answer.

Sources: Lichter & Crowley (2002), Lichter & Jayakody (2002), U.S. Census Bureau (2008), and Von Drehle (2008).

have one thing in common: *poverty.* For that reason, the explanations of poverty just presented also apply to homelessness. Some (more conservative) people blame the *personal traits* of the homeless themselves. One-third of homeless people are substance abusers, and one-fourth are mentally ill. More broadly, a fraction of 1 percent of our population, for one reason or another, seems unable to cope with our complex and highly competitive society (U.S. Conference of Mayors, 2007; U.S. Department of Housing and Urban Development, 2007).

Other (more liberal) people see homelessness as resulting from *societal factors,* including low wages and a lack of low-income housing (Kozol, 1988; Bohannan, 1991; L. Kaufman, 2004). Supporters of this position note that one-third of the homeless consists of entire families, and they point to children as the fastest-growing category of the homeless.

No one disputes that a large proportion of homeless people are personally impaired to some degree, but cause and effect are difficult to untangle. Long-term, structural changes in the U.S. economy, cutbacks in social service budgets, and the recent economic downturn have all contributed to the problem of homelessness.

Finally, social stratification extends far beyond the borders of the United States. In fact, the most striking social inequality is found not within any one nation but in the different living standards from nation to nation around the world.

Seeing Sociology in Everyday Life

Social Class in the United States

How do we understand inequality in our society?

This chapter sketches the class structure of the United States and also explains how factors such as race are linked to social standing. You already know, for example, that the rate of poverty is three times higher for African Americans than for whites, and you have also learned that the typical black family earns just 57 percent as much as the typical (non-Hispanic) white family. But rich people—here, we'll define "rich" as a family earning more than $75,000 a year—come in all colors. Here's a chance to test your sociological thinking by answering several questions about how race affects being rich. Look at each of the statements below: Does the statement reflect reality, or is it a myth?

Getty Images Inc. – PhotoDisc/David De Lossy

Q

1. **In the United States, all rich people are white.** *Reality or myth?*
2. **Rich white families are actually richer than rich African American families.** *Reality or myth?*
3. **People in rich black families don't work as hard as members of rich white families.** *Reality or myth?*
4. **When you are rich, color doesn't matter.** *Reality or myth?*

A

1. *Of course, in a nation that has an African American president, this is a myth.* But when it comes to being rich, race does matter: About 20 percent of African American families are affluent (Hispanic families, too), compared to about 46 percent of non-Hispanic white families.
2. *Reality.* Rich white, non-Hispanic families have a mean (average) income of almost $200,000 per year. Rich African American families average about $130,000 per year.
3. *Myth.* On average, rich black families are more likely to rely on multiple incomes (that is, they have more people working) than their white counterparts. In addition, rich white families receive more unearned income—that is, income from investments—than rich African American families.
4. *Myth.* Rich African Americans still face social barriers based on their race, just as rich whites benefit from the privileges linked to their color.

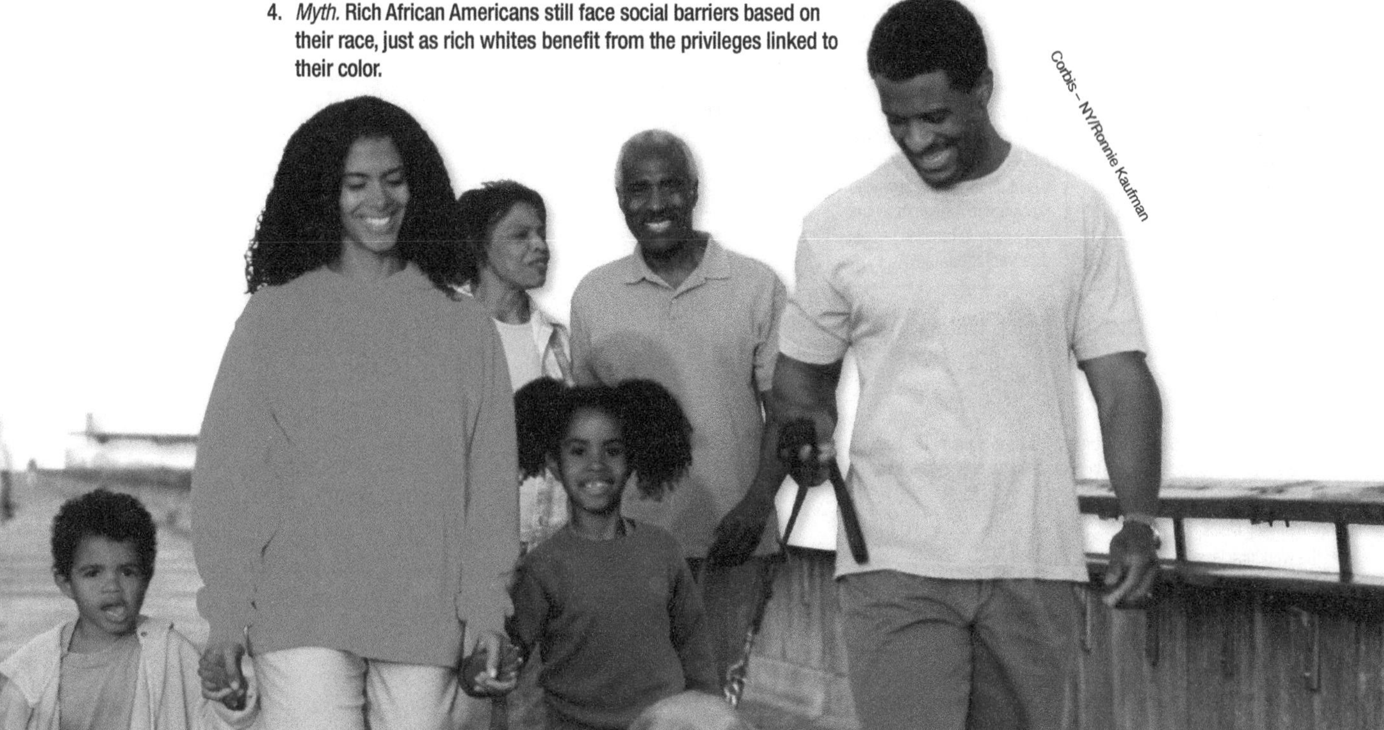

Corbis – NY/Ronnie Kaufman

Applying SOCIOLOGY in Everyday Life

1. Develop several questions that together will let you measure social class position. The trick is to decide what you think social class really means. Then try your questions on several adults, refining the questions as you proceed.
2. During an evening of television viewing, assess the social class level of the characters you see on various shows. In each case, explain why you assign someone a particular social position. Do you find many clearly upper-class people? Middle-class people? Working-class people? Poor people? Describe the patterns you find.
3. Governor Arnold Schwarzenegger of California said, "In this country, it doesn't make any difference where you were born. It doesn't make any difference if, like me, you couldn't even speak English until you were in your twenties. America gave me opportunities, and my immigrant dreams came true. I want other people to get the same chances I did, the same opportunities. And I believe they can." Ask a number of people who came to the United States from another country the extent to which they agree or disagree with this statement.

MAKING THE GRADE

Social Class in the United States

Dimensions of Social Inequality

SOCIAL STRATIFICATION involves many dimensions:

- *Income*—Earnings from work and investments are unequal, with the richest 20% of families earning twelve times as much as the poorest 20% of families.
- *Wealth*—The total value of all assets minus debts, wealth is distributed more unequally than income, with the richest 20% of families holding 85% of all wealth.
- *Power*—Income and wealth are important sources of power.
- *Schooling*—Schooling affects both occupation and income. Some categories of people have greater opportunities for schooling than others.
- *Occupational prestige*—Work generates not only income but also prestige. White-collar jobs generally offer more income and prestige than blue-collar jobs. Many lower-prestige jobs are performed by women and people of color.

income earnings from work or investments

wealth the total value of money and other assets, minus outstanding debts

U.S. Stratification: Merit and Caste

Although the United States is a meritocracy, social position in this country involves some caste elements.

ANCESTRY
Being born into a particular family affects a person's opportunities for schooling, occupation, and income.

RACE AND ETHNICITY
Non-Hispanic white families enjoy high social standing based on income and wealth. By contrast, African American and Hispanic families remain disadvantaged.

GENDER
On average, women have less income, wealth, and occupational prestige than men.

Social Classes in the United States

Defining **SOCIAL CLASSES** in the United States is difficult because of low status consistency and relatively high social mobility. But we can describe four general rankings:

- the upper class
- the middle class
- the working class
- the lower class

Income range	Class
$197,000 ↑	**UPPER CLASS**—5% of the population. Most members of the *upper-upper class*, or "old rich," inherited their wealth; the *lower-upper class*, or "new rich," work at high-paying jobs.
$197,000 – $60,000	**MIDDLE CLASS**—40% to 45% of the population. People in the *upper-middle class* have significant wealth; *average-middles* have less prestige, do white-collar work, and most attend college.
$60,000 – $28,000	**WORKING CLASS**—30% to 35% of the population. People in the *lower-middle class* do blue-collar work; only about one-third of children attend college.
$28,000 ↓	**LOWER CLASS**—20% of the population. Most people in the lower class lack financial security due to low income; many live below the poverty line; half do not complete high school.

The Difference Class Makes

HEALTH

- Rich people, on average, live longer and receive better health care than poor people.

VALUES AND ATTITUDES

- Affluent people, with greater education and financial security, display greater tolerance than working-class people.

POLITICS

- Affluent people tend to be more conservative on economic issues and more liberal on social issues than poor people.
- Affluent people, who are better served by the political system, are more likely to vote than poor people.

FAMILY AND GENDER

- Affluent families pass on advantages in the form of "cultural capital" to their children.
- Class also shapes the division of family responsibilities, with lower-class people maintaining more traditional gender roles.

Social Mobility

- Social mobility is common in the United States, as it is in other high-income countries, but typically only small changes occur from one generation to the next.
- Between 1980 and 2007, the richest 20% of U.S. families enjoyed a 58% jump in annual income, while the 20% of families with the lowest income saw only a 4.6% increase.
- Historically, African Americans, Hispanic Americans, and women have had less opportunity for upward mobility in U.S. society than white men.
- The American dream—the expectation of upward social mobility—is deeply rooted in our culture. Although high-income families are earning more and more, many average families are struggling to hold on to what they have.
- Marriage encourages upward social mobility. Divorce lowers social standing.
- The global reorganization of work has created upward social mobility for educated people in the United States but has hurt average workers, whose factory jobs have moved overseas and who are forced to take low-wage service work.

intragenerational social mobility a change in social position occurring during a person's lifetime

intergenerational social mobility upward or downward social mobility of children in relation to their parents

Poverty in the United States

POVERTY PROFILE

- The government classifies 37 million people, 12.5% of the population, as poor.
- About 49% of the poor are under age twenty-four.
- Two-thirds of the poor are white, but in relation to their population, African Americans and Hispanics are more likely to be poor.
- The **feminization of poverty** means that more poor families are headed by women.
- About 48% of the heads of poor families are among the "working poor" who work at least part time but do not earn enough to lift a family of four above the poverty line.
- An estimated 750,000 people are homeless at some time during the course of a year.

EXPLANATIONS OF POVERTY

- Blame individuals: The *culture of poverty* thesis states that poverty is caused by shortcomings in the poor themselves (Oscar Lewis).
- Blame society: Poverty is caused by society's unequal disbribution of wealth and lack of good jobs (William Julius Wilson).

relative poverty the lack of resources of some people in relation to those who have more

absolute poverty a lack of resources that is life-threatening

feminization of poverty the trend of women making up an increasing proportion of the poor

MAKING THE GRADE

Sample Test Questions

Multiple-Choice Questions

1. **Which of the following terms refers to earnings from work or investments?**
   a. income
   b. assets
   c. wealth
   d. power

2. **The wealthiest 20 percent of people in the United States own about how much of the country's privately owned wealth?**
   a. 35 percent
   b. 55 percent
   c. 85 percent
   d. 95 percent

3. **About what share of U.S. adults over the age of twenty-five are college graduates?**
   a. 10 percent
   b. 29 percent
   c. 40 percent
   d. 68 percent

4. **In the United States, average income for African American families is what share of average income for non-Hispanic white families?**
   a. 87 percent
   b. 77 percent
   c. 67 percent
   d. 57 percent

5. **Which of the following is another term for the "working class"?**
   a. upper-middle class
   b. average-middle class
   c. lower-middle class
   d. lower class

6. **In terms of health, people living in high-income families**
   a. live in safer and less stressful environments.
   b. are more likely to describe their own health as "excellent."
   c. live longer lives.
   d. All of the above are correct.

7. **Which quintile (20 percent) of the U.S. population has seen the greatest change in income over the last generation?**
   a. the top quintile
   b. the middle quintile
   c. the lowest quintile
   d. All quintiles have seen the same change.

8. **Change in social position during a person's own lifetime is called**
   a. intergenerational social mobility.
   b. intragenerational social mobility.
   c. structural social mobility.
   d. horizontal social mobility.

9. **In 2006, about what share of the U.S. population was officially counted as poor?**
   a. 42.3 percent
   b. 22.3 percent
   c. 12.3 percent
   d. 2.3 percent

10. **Which age category of the U.S. population has the highest percentage of people in poverty?**
    a. seniors over age sixty-five
    b. middle-aged people
    c. young people aged eighteen to twenty-four
    d. children under age eighteen

ANSWERS: 1 (a); 2 (c); 3 (b); 4 (d); 5 (c); 6 (d); 7 (a); 8 (b); 9 (c); 10 (c).

Essay Questions

1. We often hear people say that the United States is a "middle-class society." Where does this idea come from? Based on what you have read in this chapter, how true do you think this claim is? Why?
2. What is the extent of poverty in the United States? Who are the poor in terms of age, race and ethnicity, and gender?

Gender Stratification

Stock Connection/Gilbert Martinez

Gender is more than differences in the ways society expects women and men to behave. It is also a matter of social stratification, placing men in positions of power over women.

PhotoEdit Inc./Paul Conklin

Gender Stratification

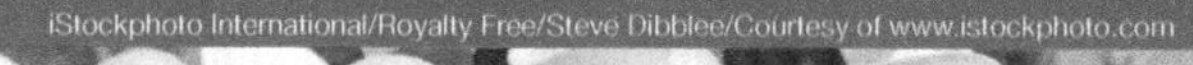

iStockphoto International/Royalty Free/Alex Brosa/Courtesy of www.istockphoto.com

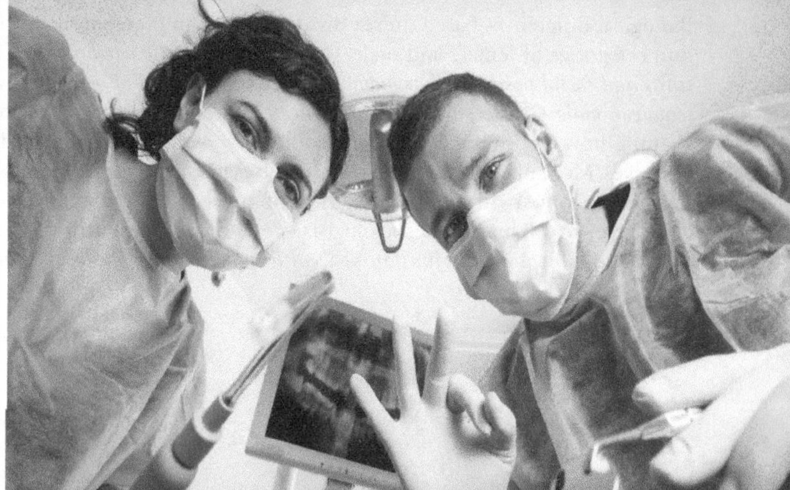

CHAPTER OVERVIEW

This chapter examines gender, the meaning societies attach to being female or male, and explains how gender is an important dimension of social stratification.

Corbis – NY

At first we traveled quite alone . . . but before we had gone many miles, we came on other wagon-loads of women, bound in the same direction. As we reached different cross-roads, we saw wagons coming from every part of the country and, long before we reached Seneca Falls, we were a procession.

So wrote Charlotte Woodward in her journal as she made her way along the rutted dirt roads leading to Seneca Falls, a small town in upstate New York. The year was 1848, a time when slavery was legal in much of the United States and the social standing of all women, regardless of color, was far below that of men. Back then, in much of the country, women could not own property, keep their wages if they were married, draft a will, file lawsuits in a court (including lawsuits seeking custody of their children), or attend college, and husbands were widely viewed as having unquestioned authority over their wives and children.

Some 300 women gathered at Wesleyan Chapel in Seneca Falls to challenge this second-class citizenship. They listened as their leader, Elizabeth Cady Stanton, called for expanding women's rights and opportunities, including the right to vote. At that time, most people considered such a proposal absurd and outrageous. Even many attending the conference were shocked by the idea: Stanton's husband, Henry, rode out of town in protest (Gurnett, 1998).

Much has changed since the Seneca Falls convention, and many of Stanton's proposals are now widely accepted as matters of basic fairness. But as this chapter explains, women and men still lead different lives, in the United States and elsewhere in the world; in most respects, men are still in charge. This chapter explores the importance of gender and explains that gender, like class position, is a major dimension of social stratification.

Gender and Inequality

Biological differences based on sex divide the human population into categories of female and male. **Gender** refers to *the personal traits and social positions that members of a society attach to being female or male.* Gender, then, is a dimension of social organization, shaping how we interact with others and how we think about ourselves. More important, gender also involves *hierarchy,* ranking men and women differently in terms of power, wealth, and other resources. This is why sociologists speak of **gender stratification**, *the unequal distribution of wealth, power, and privilege between men and women.* In short, gender affects the opportunities and challenges we face throughout our lives.

Male-Female Differences

Many people think there is something "natural" about gender distinctions because biology does make one sex different from the other. But we must be careful not to think of social differences in biological terms. In 1848, for example, women were denied the vote because many people assumed that women did not have enough intelligence or interest in politics. Such attitudes had nothing to do with biology; they reflected the *cultural* patterns of that time and place.

Another example is athletic performance. In 1925, most people—women and men—believed that the best women runners could never compete with men in a marathon. Today, as Figure 1 shows, the gender gap has greatly narrowed, and the fastest women routinely post better times than the fastest men of decades past. Even here, most of the differences between men and women turn out to be socially created.

There are some differences in physical ability between the sexes. On average, males are 10 percent taller, 20 percent heavier, and

gender the personal traits and social positions that member of a society attach to being female or male

gender stratification the unequal distribution of wealth, power, and privilege between men and women

30 percent stronger, especially in the upper body. On the other hand, women outperform men in the ultimate game of life itself: Life expectancy for men in the United States is 75.4 years, and women can expect to live 80.7 years (Ehrenreich, 1999; Heron et al., 2008; McDowell et al., 2008).

In adolescence, males do a bit better in mathematics, and females show slightly stronger verbal skills, a difference that reflects both biology and socialization. However, research does not point to any difference in overall intelligence between males and females (Tavris & Wade, 2001; Lewin, 2008).

Biologically, then, men and women differ in limited ways; neither one is naturally superior. But culture can define the two sexes very differently, as the global study of gender described in the next section shows.

Gender in Global Perspective

The best way to see the cultural foundation of gender is by comparing one society to another. Three important studies highlight how societies can define "masculine" and "feminine" very differently.

The Israeli Kibbutz

In Israel, collective settlements are called *kibbutzim.* The *kibbutz* (the singular form of the word) has been an important setting for research because gender equality is one of its stated goals; men and women share in both work and decision making.

In recent decades, kibbutzim have become less collective and thus less distinctive organizations. But through much of their history, both sexes shared most everyday jobs. Many men joined women in taking care of children, and women joined men in repairing buildings and providing armed security. Both sexes made everyday decisions for the group. Girls and boys were raised in the same way; in many cases, young children were raised together in dormitories away from parents. Women and men in the kibbutzim have achieved remarkable (although not complete) social equality, evidence that cultures define what is feminine and what is masculine.

Margaret Mead's Research

The anthropologist Margaret Mead carried out groundbreaking research on gender. If gender is based on the biological differences between men and women, she reasoned, people everywhere should define "feminine" and "masculine" in the same way; if gender is cultural, these concepts should vary.

Mead (1963, orig. 1935) studied three societies in New Guinea. In the mountainous home of the Arapesh, Mead observed men and women with remarkably similar attitudes and behavior. Both sexes, she reported, were cooperative and sensitive to others—in short, what our culture would label "feminine."

The women's movement of the 1960s encouraged women to show their true abilities.

Diversity Snapshot

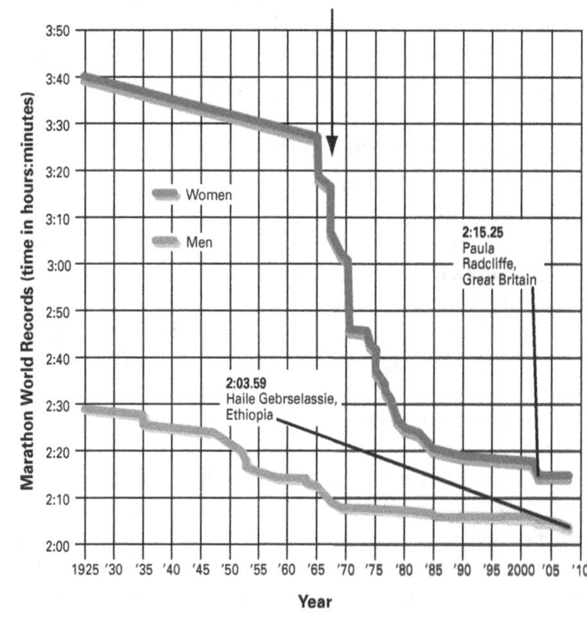

FIGURE 1 **Men's and Women's Athletic Performance**

Do men naturally outperform women in athletic competition? The answer is not obvious. Early in the twentieth century, men outpaced women by more than an hour in marathon races. But as opportunities for women in athletics have increased, women have been closing the performance gap. Only eleven minutes separate the current world marathon records for women (set in 2003) and for men (set in 2008).

Source: Marathonguide.com (2008).

Moving south, Mead then studied the Mundugumor, whose headhunting and cannibalism stood in striking contrast to the gentle ways of the Arapesh. In this culture, both sexes were typically selfish and aggressive, traits we define as "masculine."

Finally, traveling west to the Tchambuli, Mead discovered a culture that, like our own, defined females and males differently. But, Mead reported, the Tchambuli *reversed* many of our notions of gender: Females were dominant and rational, and males were submissive, emotional, and nurturing toward children. Based on her observations, Mead concluded that culture is the key to gender differences, because what one society defines as masculine another may see as feminine.

Some critics view Mead's findings as "too neat," as if she saw in these three societies just the patterns she was looking for. Deborah Gewertz (1981) challenged what she called Mead's "reversal hypothesis,"

SEEING SOCIOLOGY in Everyday Life

Do you think female and male athletes should compete on the same teams? Why or why not? Do you think men and women see this issue differently?

matriarchy a form of social organization in which females dominate males

patriarchy a form of social organization in which males dominate females

sexism the belief that one sex is innately superior to the other

pointing out that Tchambuli males are really the more aggressive sex. Gewertz explains that Mead visited the Tchambuli (who themselves spell their name Chambri) during the 1930s, after they had lost much of their property in tribal wars, and observed men rebuilding their homes, a temporary role for Chambri men.

George Murdock's Research

In a broader review of research on more than 200 preindustrial societies, George Murdock (1937) found some global agreement about which tasks are feminine and which are masculine. Hunting and warfare, Murdock concluded, generally fall to men, and home-centered tasks such as cooking and child care tend to be women's work. With their simple technology, preindustrial societies apparently assign roles reflecting men's and women's physical characteristics. With their greater size and strength, men hunt game and protect the group; because women bear children, they do most of the work in the home.

But beyond this general pattern, Murdock found much variety. Consider agriculture: Women did the farming in about the same number of societies as men; in most, the two sexes shared this work. When it came to many other tasks, from building shelters to tattooing the body, Murdock found that societies of the world were as likely to turn to one sex as the other.

Robert Estall Photo Agency/Carol Beckwith

In every society, people assume that certain jobs, patterns of behavior, and ways of dressing are "naturally" feminine while others are just as obviously masculine. But in global perspective, we see remarkable variety in such social definitions. These men, Wodaabe pastoral nomads who live in the African nation of Niger, are proud to engage in a display of beauty most people in our society would consider feminine.

CRITICAL REVIEW Global comparisons show that overall, societies do not consistently define tasks as either feminine or masculine. With industrialization, the importance of muscle power declines, further reducing gender differences (Nolan & Lenski, 2007). In sum, gender is too variable across cultures to be a simple expression of biology; what it means to be female and male is mostly a creation of society.

CHECK YOUR LEARNING By comparing many cultures, what do we learn about the origin of gender differences?

Patriarchy and Sexism

Conceptions of gender vary, and there is evidence of societies in which women have greater power than men. One example is the Musuo, a very small society in China's Yunnan province, in which women control most property, select their sexual partners, and make most decisions about everyday life. The Musuo appear to be a case of **matriarchy** ("rule of mothers"), *a form of social organization in which females dominate males,* which has only rarely been documented in human history.

The pattern found almost everywhere in the world is **patriarchy** ("rule of fathers"), *a form of social organization in which males dominate females.* Global Map 1 shows the great variation in the relative power and privilege of women that exists from country to country. According to the United Nations, Iceland, Australia, and Norway give women the highest social standing; by contrast, women in the African nations of Burkina Faso, Niger, Guinea-Bissau, and Sierra Leone have the lowest social standing in comparison to to men. Of all the world's nations, the United States ranks sixteenth in terms of gender equality (United Nations Development Programme, 2008).

The justification for patriarchy is **sexism**, *the belief that one sex is innately superior to the other.* Sexism is not just a matter of individual attitudes; it is built into the institutions of society. *Institutional sexism* is found throughout the economy, with women concentrated in low-paying jobs. Similarly, the legal system has long excused violence against women, especially on the part of boyfriends, husbands, and fathers.

The Costs of Sexism

Sexism limits the talents and ambitions of the half of the human population who are women. Although men benefit in some respects from sexism, their privilege comes at a high price. Masculinity in our culture encourages men to engage in many high-risk behaviors: using tobacco and alcohol, playing dangerous sports, and even driving recklessly. As Marilyn

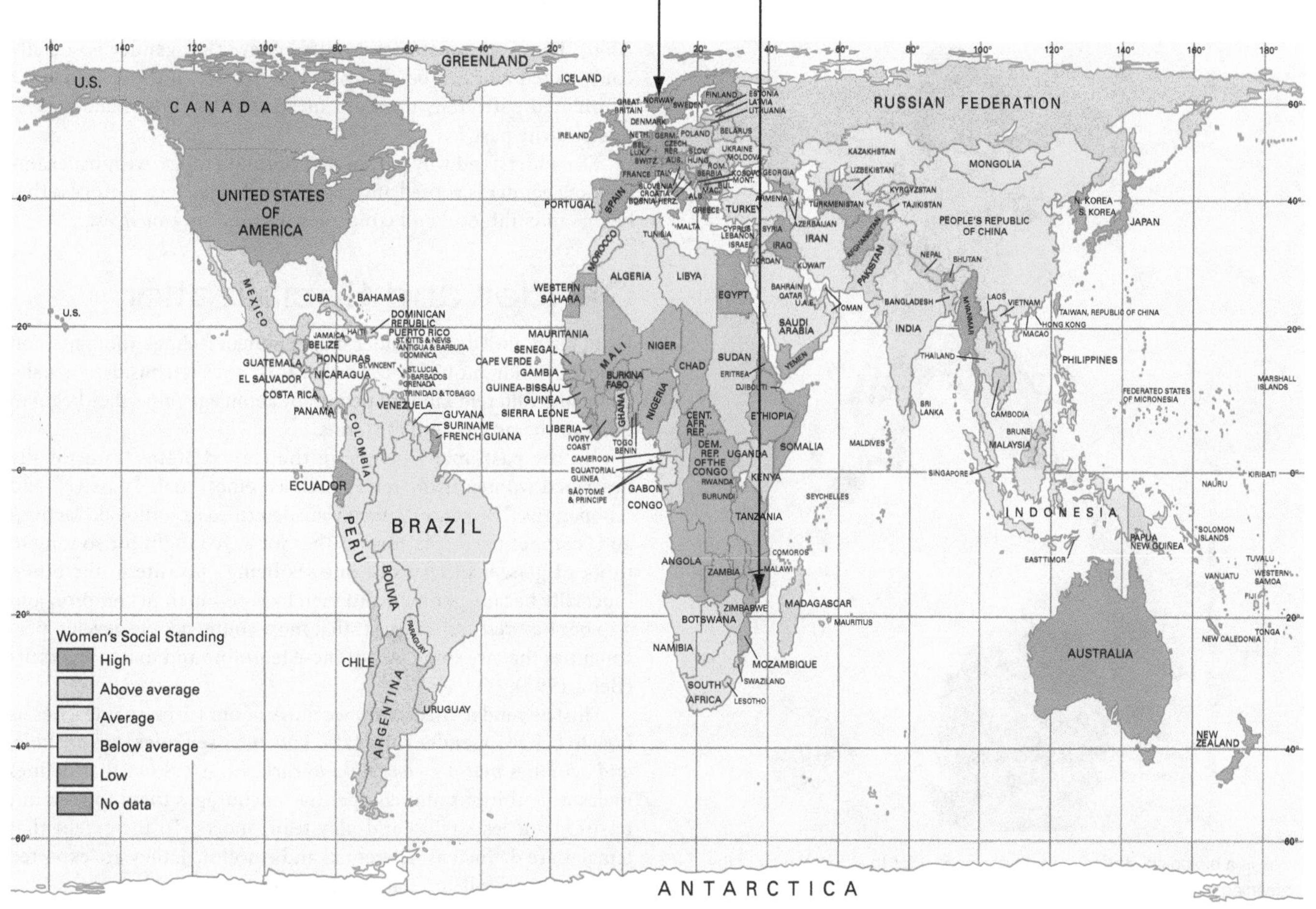

Window on the World

GLOBAL MAP 1 Women's Power in Global Perspective

Women's social standing in relation to men's varies around the world. In general, women live better in rich countries than in poor countries. Even so, some nations stand out: In Iceland, Australia, and Norway, women come closest to social equality with men.

Source: Data from United Nations Development Programme (2008).

French (1985) argues, patriarchy leads men to seek control, not only of women but also of themselves and their world. This is why masculinity is closely linked not only to accidents but also to suicide, violence, and stress-related diseases. The *Type A personality*—marked by chronic impatience, driving ambition, competitiveness, and free-floating hostility—is a recipe for heart disease and almost perfectly matches the behavior that our culture considers masculine (Ehrenreich, 1983).

Finally, as men seek control over others, they lose opportunities for intimacy and trust. As one analyst put it, competition is supposed to "separate the men from the boys." In practice, however, it separates men from men and everyone else (Raphael, 1988).

Must Patriarchy Go On?

In preindustrial societies, women have little control over pregnancy and childbirth, which limits the scope of their lives. In those same

gender roles (also known as **sex roles**) attitudes and activities that a society links to each sex

SEEING SOCIOLOGY in Everyday Life

Did you grow up in a home in which females and males had different jobs and responsibilities? How did this affect your view of gender?

Getty Images Inc. – Stone Allstock/Jean Louis Batt

Sex is a biological distinction that develops prior to birth. Gender is the meaning that a society attaches to being female or male. Gender differences are a matter of power, because what is defined as masculine typically has more importance than what is defined as feminine. Infants begin to learn the importance of gender by the way parents treat them. Do you think this child is a girl or a boy? Why?

societies, men's greater size and physical strength are valued resources that give them power. But industrialization, including birth control technology, increases people's choices about how to live. In societies like our own, biological differences offer little justification for patriarchy.

But males are dominant in the United States and elsewhere. Does this mean that patriarchy is inevitable? Some researchers claim that biological factors such as differences in hormones and slight differences in brain structure "wire" the two sexes with different motivations and behaviors—especially aggressiveness in males—making patriarchy difficult or perhaps even impossible to change (S. Goldberg, 1974; Rossi, 1985; Popenoe, 1993b; Udry, 2000). However, most sociologists believe that gender is socially constructed and *can* be changed. Just because no society has yet eliminated patriarchy does not mean that we must remain prisoners of the past.

To understand why patriarchy continues today, we must examine how gender is rooted and reproduced in society, a process that begins in childhood and continues throughout our lives.

Gender and Socialization

From birth until death, gender shapes human feelings, thoughts, and actions. Children quickly learn that their society considers females and males different kinds of people; by about age three, they begin to think of themselves in these terms.

In the past, many people in the United States traditionally described women using terms such as "emotional," "passive," and "cooperative." By contrast, men were described as "rational," "active," and "competitive." It is curious that we were taught for so long to think of gender in terms of one sex being opposite to the other, especially because women and men have so much in common and also because research suggests that most young people develop personalities that are some mix of these feminine and masculine traits (Bem, 1993).

Just as gender affects how we think of ourselves, so it teaches us how to behave. **Gender roles** (also known as **sex roles**) are *attitudes and activities that a society links to each sex.* A culture that defines males as ambitious and competitive encourages them to seek out positions of leadership and play team sports. To the extent that females are defined as deferential and emotional, they are expected to be supportive helpers and quick to show their feelings.

Gender and the Family

The first question people usually ask about a newborn—"Is it a boy or a girl?"—has great importance because the answer involves not just sex but the likely direction of the child's life. In fact, gender is at work even before the birth of a child, because especially in lower-income nations, parents hope that their firstborn will be a boy rather than a girl.

Soon after birth, family members welcome infants into the "pink world" of girls or the "blue world" of boys (Bernard, 1981). Parents even send gender messages in the way they handle infants. One researcher at an English university presented an infant dressed as either a boy or a girl to a number of women; her subjects handled the "female" child tenderly, with frequent hugs and caresses, and treated the "male" child more roughly, often lifting him up high in the air or bouncing him on a knee (Bonner, 1984; Tavris & Wade, 2001). The lesson is clear: The female world revolves around cooperation and emotion, and the male world puts a premium on independence and action.

SEEING SOCIOLOGY in Everyday Life

Consider the statements "He fathered the child" and "She mothered the child." How do you think gender shapes the meaning of parenting?

SEEING SOCIOLOGY in Everyday Life

What is your declared or likely major? Based on the classes you have taken, what share of students in this major are female and what share are male? Does this pattern agree with those described here?

Gender and the Peer Group

About the time they enter school, children begin to move outside the family and make friends with others of the same age. Considerable research shows that young children tend to form single-sex play groups (Martin & Fabes, 2001).

Peer groups teach additional lessons about gender. After spending a year observing children at play, Janet Lever (1978) concluded that boys favor team sports that have complex rules and clear objectives such as scoring runs or making touchdowns. Such games nearly always have winners and losers, reinforcing masculine traits of aggression and control.

Girls, too, play team sports. But, Lever explains, girls also play hopscotch, jump rope, or simply talk, sing, or dance. These activities have few rules, and rarely is victory the ultimate goal. Instead of teaching girls to be competitive, Lever explains, female peer groups promote the interpersonal skills of communication and cooperation, presumably the basis for girls' future roles as wives and mothers.

The games we play offer important lessons for our later lives. Lever's observations recall Carol Gilligan's gender-based theory of moral reasoning. Boys, Gilligan (1982) claims, reason according to abstract principles. For them, "rightness" amounts to "playing by the rules." By contrast, girls consider morality a matter of responsibility to others.

Picture Desk, Inc./Kobal Collection/Marvel/Sony Pictures

The mass media typically present men in action, with women providing romantic interest. Can you find gender at work in the *Spiderman* films? What about other films?

Gender and Schooling

Gender shapes our interests and beliefs about our own abilities, guiding areas of study and, eventually, career choices (Correll, 2001). In high school, for instance, more girls than boys learn secretarial skills and take vocational classes such as cosmetology and food services. Classes in woodworking and auto mechanics attract mostly young men.

Women have now become a majority (57 percent) of the students on college campuses across the United States. As their numbers have increased, women have become well represented in many fields of study that once excluded them, including mathematics, chemistry, and biology. But men still predominate in many fields, including engineering, physics, and philosophy, and women cluster in the visual and performing arts (including music, dance, and drama), English, foreign languages, and the social sciences (including psychology, anthropology, and sociology). Newer areas of study are also gender-typed: More men than women take computer science, and courses in gender studies enroll mostly women (U.S. Department of Education, 2008).

Gender and the Mass Media

Since television first captured the public imagination in the 1950s, white males have held center stage; racial and ethnic minorities were all but absent from television until the early 1970s. Even when both sexes appeared on camera, men generally played the brilliant detectives, fearless explorers, and skilled surgeons. Women played the less capable characters, often unnecessary except for the sexual interest they added to the story.

Historically, advertisements have shown women in the home, cheerfully using cleaning products, serving food, and modeling clothes. Men predominate in ads for cars, travel, banking services, and alcoholic beverages. The authoritative voiceover—the faceless voice that describes a product on television and radio—is almost always male (D. M. Davis, 1993).

A careful study of gender in advertising reveals that men usually appear taller than women, implying male superiority. Women are more frequently presented lying down (on sofas and beds) or, like children, seated on the floor. Men's facial expressions and behavior give off an air of competence and imply dominance; women often appear childlike, submissive, and sexual. Men focus on the products being advertised; women often focus on the men (Goffman, 1979; Cortese, 1999).

Advertising also actively perpetuates what Naomi Wolf calls the "beauty myth." The Seeing Sociology in Everyday Life box takes a closer look.

SEEING SOCIOLOGY in Everyday Life

Do you think women on your campus are overly concerned with looking thin? Explain.

SEEING SOCIOLOGY IN EVERYDAY LIFE

The Beauty Myth

BETH: "I can't eat lunch. I need to be sure I can get into that black dress for tonight."

SARAH: "Maybe eating is more important than looking good for Tom."

BETH: "That's easy for you to say. You're a size 2 and Jake adores you!"

The Duchess of Windsor once remarked, "A woman cannot be too rich or too thin." The first half of her observation might apply to men as well, but certainly not the second. The answer lies in the fact that the vast majority of ads placed by the $10-billion-a-year cosmetics industry and the $35-billion diet industry target women.

According to Naomi Wolf (1990), certain cultural patterns create a "beauty myth" that is damaging to women. The beauty myth arises, first, because society teaches women to measure their worth in terms of physical appearance. Yet the standards of beauty embodied in the *Playboy* centerfold or the 100-pound New York fashion model are out of reach for most women.

The way society teaches women to prize relationships with men, whom they presumably attract with their beauty, also contributes to the beauty myth. Striving for beauty drives women to be extremely disciplined but also forces them to be highly attentive to and responsive to men. In short, beauty-minded women try to please men and avoid challenging male power.

Belief in the beauty myth is one reason that so many young women are focused on body image, particularly being as thin as possible, often to the point of endangering their health. During the past several decades, the share of young women who develop an eating disorder such as anorexia nervosa (dieting to the point of starvation) or bulimia (binge eating followed by vomiting) has risen dramatically.

AP Wide World Photos

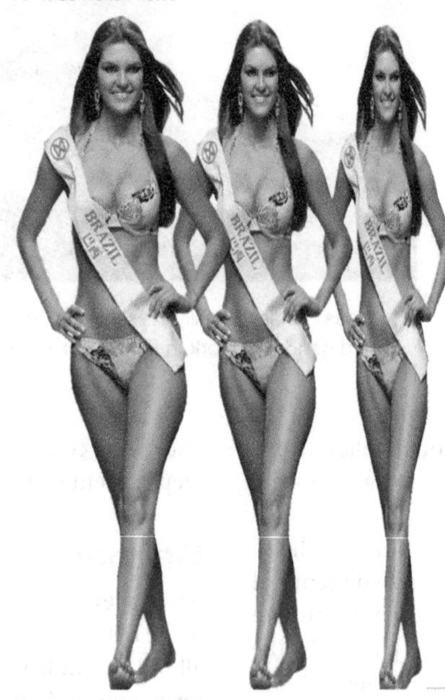

One way our culture supports the beauty myth is through beauty pageants for women; over the years, contestants have become thinner and thinner.

The beauty myth affects males as well: Men are told repeatedly that they should want to possess beautiful women. Such ideas about beauty reduce women to objects and motivate thinking about women as if they were dolls or pets rather than human beings.

There can be little doubt that the idea of beauty is important in everyday life. The question, according to Wolf, is whether beauty is about how we look or how we act.

WHAT DO YOU THINK?

1. Is there a "money myth" that states that people's income is a reflection of their worth? Does it apply more to one sex than to the other?
2. Can you see a connection between the beauty myth and the rise of eating disorders in young women in the United States? Explain the link.
3. Among people with physical disabilities, do you think that issues of "looking different" are more serious for women or for men? Why?

Gender and Social Stratification

Gender affects more than how people think and act. It is also about social hierarchy. The reality of gender stratification can be seen, first, in the world of working women and men.

Working Women and Men

Back in 1900, just 20 percent of U.S. women were in the labor force. Today, the figure has tripled to 60 percent, and 72 percent of these working women work full time (U.S. Department of Labor, 2008). The once common view that earning income is a man's role no longer holds true.

Factors that have changed the U.S. labor force include the decline of farming, the growth of cities, shrinking family size, and a rising divorce rate. The United States, along with most other nations, considers women working for income the rule rather than the exception. Women make up almost half the U.S. paid labor force, and 52 percent of U.S. married couples depend on two incomes.

In the past, many women in the U.S. labor force were childless. But today, 60 percent of married women with children under age six are in the labor force, as are 73 percent of married women with children between six and seventeen years of age. For widowed, divorced,

SEEING SOCIOLOGY in Everyday Life

As you look at Table 1, think about which jobs have a high concentration of men (some are noted in the text). How do they differ from the jobs in Table 1?

or separated women with children, the comparable figures are 65 percent of women with younger children and 78 percent of women with older children (U.S. Department of Labor, 2008).

Gender and Occupations

Although women are closing the gap with men as far as working for income is concerned, the work done by the two sexes remains very different. The U.S. Department of Labor (2008) reports a high concentration of women in two job types. Administrative support work draws 24 percent of working women, most of whom are secretaries or other office workers. These are often called "pink-collar jobs" because 75 percent are filled by women. Another 16 percent of employed women do service work. Most of these jobs are in food service industries, child care, and health care.

Table 1 shows the ten occupations with the highest concentrations of women. These jobs tend to be at the low end of the pay scale, with limited opportunities for advancement and with men as supervisors (U.S. Department of Labor, 2008).

Men dominate most other job categories, including the building trades, where 98 percent of brickmasons, stonemasons, and heavy equipment operators are men. Likewise, men make up 86 percent of police officers, 86 percent of engineers, 70 percent of physicians and surgeons, 67 percent of lawyers, and 67 percent of corporate managers. According to a recent survey, just twelve of the *Fortune* 500 companies in the United States have a woman chief executive officer, and just 15 percent of the seats of corporate boards of directors are held by women. The twenty-five highest-paid executives in the United States do not include any women at all. Even so, increasing the leadership role of women in the business world is not just a matter of fairness; research into the earnings of this country's 500 largest corporations showed that the companies with more women on the board are also the most profitable (Dickler, 2007; Graybow, 2007; Loomis, 2007; Catalyst, 2008; U.S. Department of Labor, 2008).

Gender stratification in everyday life is easy to see: Female nurses assist male physicians, female secretaries serve male executives, and female flight attendants are under the command of male airplane pilots. In any field, the greater the income and prestige associated with a job, the more likely it is to be held by a man. For example, women represent 97 percent of kindergarten teachers, 81 percent of elementary school teachers, 57 percent of secondary school educators, 46 percent of professors in colleges and universities, and 23 percent of college and university presidents (U.S. Department of Labor, 2008).

How are women kept out of certain jobs? By defining some kinds of work as "men's work," companies define women as less competent than men. In a study of coal mining in southern West Virginia, Suzanne Tallichet (2000) found that most men considered it "unnatural" for women to work in the mines. Women who did so were defined as deviant and subject to labeling as "sexually loose" or as lesbians. Such labeling made these women outcasts, presented a challenge to their holding the job, and made advancement all but impossible.

In the corporate world, as already noted, the higher in the company we look, the fewer women we find. You hardly ever hear anyone say that women don't belong at the top levels of a company. But many people seem to feel this way, which can prevent women from being promoted. Sociologists describe this barrier as a *glass ceiling* that is not easy to see but blocks women's careers all the same.

One challenge to male domination in the workplace comes from women who are entrepreneurs. In 2008, there were more than 10 million women-owned businesses in the United States, double the number of a decade ago; they employed more than 13 million people and generated $2 trillion in sales. Through starting their own businesses, women have shown that they can make opportunities for themselves apart from large, male-dominated companies (Center for Women's Business Research, 2008).

Men, too, are guided into some work and away from other jobs by gender. In Seeing Sociology in the News one man explains the challenge of having a job that many people in our society define as feminine.

Gender, Income, and Wealth

In 2007, the median earnings of women working full time were $35,241, and men working full time earned $45,159. This means that for every dollar earned by men, women earned about 78 cents. This

Table 1 Jobs with the Highest Concentrations of Women, 2007

Occupation	Number of Women Employed	Percentage in Occupation Who Are Women
1. Dental hygienist	156,000	99.2
2. Speech-language pathologist	122,000	98.0
3. Preschool or kindergarten teacher	649,000	97.3
4. Secretary or administrative assistant	3,289,000	96.7
5. Dental assistant	265,000	96.3
6. Child care worker	1,269,000	94.6
7. Licensed practical or licensed vocational nurse	497,000	93.2
8. Receptionist or information clerk	1,340,000	93.0
9. Hairdresser, hairstylist, or cosmetologist	723,000	93.0
10. Medical records and health information technician	77,000	93.0

Source: U.S. Department of Labor (2008).

Seeing SOCIOLOGY in the 

Newsweek

Don't Judge Me by My Tights

BY SASCHA RADETSKY
March 17, 2008

My business attire is a pair of tights. All right, there it is. I wear makeup onstage, and some of my colleagues are gay. Can we move on now? Can we leave behind the tired male-ballet-dancer stigma—that ballet is not a masculine pursuit—in order to move toward an appreciation of the athleticism and artistry involved in this line of work?

On an average day at the job, I handle lithe, lovely women, engage in duels and delight in the experience of an exotic locale. I move like a gymnast or martial artist and embody the vilest of pimps or the most chivalrous and passionate of lovers. I constantly expand the borders of my physical capabilities, and I hone my mind to a quick-learning, focused edge. Come 8 P.M., I'll fuse dynamic movement and storytelling with the grandeur of a full live orchestra.

Yes, I'm proud of my profession. Yet I find myself slightly guarded when I tell people what I do. Like some sort of incurable blight, the male-dancer stereotype has taken root . . . in our cultural consciousness. Pioneers like Baryshnikov or Nureyev might have opened some minds, but their days have long passed, and despite the noble efforts of a handful of current ballet leaders to expose fresh audiences to our art form, a whole new generation looks at male dancing with skewed vision. Some of my peers are foreigners; in many other countries male dancers are held in higher esteem. I studied in Russia for a year and always marveled at the way Russians celebrated their artists, whether their medium was dance, music or the written word. But I'm American, and I want to live in my own country, as a dancer, with some respect.

The most irritating aspect of the male-dancer stereotype is the underlying insinuation that we in some way lack strength of character or a courageous spirit. Male and female, all dancers undergo strenuous training from a very young age, and constantly wrestle with injuries and fatigue. But male dancers must possess a special type of will and fortitude if they are to become professionals. . . . In our culture, girls are encouraged to take ballet; boys receive no such endorsement, except of course from ballet teachers or exceptionally supportive parents. The boy who perseveres in dance must have a genuine hunger for it, must be uniquely motivated and dedicated, and must develop a truly thick skin.

I started taking ballet when I was 5. My open-minded parents thought it was a good way to channel my rambunctious behavior. A few years later I was hooked. I loved the physicality and, of course, the girls, but I also learned that not everyone recognized the value of dance the way I did. I don't remember the first fight I got into for being a kid who took ballet, but I remember fighting a lot before I realized that maybe I should keep my extracurricular activities to myself. But ballet was rewarding enough to be worth a fat lip or a black eye, and I emerged from my years of dance training more focused than ever. . . . My American colleagues share similar stories of discouragement, harassment and even violence. But these experiences served to harden resolve and develop courage, and I know I can always count on several of my dancer buddies for steadfast support—they got my back! Ironically, the stereotype of the sissy male dancer has given rise to a male dancer who is anything but. . . .

Exposure to ballet is all that is needed to open minds, for the combination of athletic movement, ardent drama and beautiful music can instill a profound appreciation in an audience. But for you out there who still feel compelled to malign male dancers with half-truths and petty stereotypes, well, maybe we need to step outside. I'll leave my tights on.

WHAT DO YOU THINK?

1. In the article, what qualities does the writer associate with being masculine?
2. Are you surprised at how difficult it can be for a man to do a job that many people see as not masculine? Explain.
3. Are there jobs that create similar problems for women? What jobs? Why?

difference is greater among older workers because older working women typically have less education and seniority than older working men. Earning differences are smaller among younger workers because younger men and women tend to have similar schooling and work experience.

Among all full-time workers of all ages, 26 percent of women earned less than $25,000 in 2006, compared with 17 percent of men. At the upper end of the income scale, men were more than twice as likely as women (20 percent versus 9 percent) to earn more than $75,000 (U.S. Census Bureau, 2008).

The main reason women earn less is the *type* of work they do, largely clerical and service jobs. In effect, jobs and gender interact. People still perceive jobs with less clout as "women's work," just as people devalue certain work simply because it is performed by women (England, Hermsen, & Cotter, 2000; Cohen & Huffman, 2003).

In recent decades, supporters of gender equality have proposed a policy of "comparable worth," paying people not according to the historical double standard but according to the level of skill and responsibility involved in the work. Several nations, including Great Britain and Australia, have adopted comparable worth policies, but such policies have found limited acceptance in the United States. As a result, women in this country lose as much as $1 billion in income annually.

A second cause of gender-based income disparity has to do with the family. Both men and women have children, of course, but our culture gives more responsibility for parenting to women. Pregnancy and raising small children keep many young women out of the labor force at a time when their male peers are making significant career advancements. When women workers return to the labor force, they have less job seniority than their male counterparts (Stier, 1996; Waldfogel, 1997).

SEEING SOCIOLOGY in Everyday Life

How is gender related to doing housework in your current home or in the home in which you grew up?

In addition, women who choose to have children may be unable or unwilling to take on demanding jobs that tie up their evenings and weekends. To avoid role strain, they may take jobs that offer shorter commuting distances, more flexible hours, and employer-provided child care services. Women pursuing both a career and a family are often torn between their dual responsibilities in ways that men are not. One study found that almost half of women in competitive jobs took time off to have children, compared to about 12 percent of men (Hewlett & Luce, 2005). Role conflict is also experienced by women on campus: One study concluded that young female professors with at least one child were at least 20 percent less likely to have tenure than male professors in the same field (Shea, 2002).

The two factors noted so far—type of work and family responsibilities—account for about two-thirds of the earnings difference between women and men. A third factor—discrimination against women—accounts for most of the remainder (Fuller & Schoenberger, 1991). Because overt discrimination is illegal, it is practiced in subtle ways. Women on their way up the corporate ladder often run into the glass ceiling described earlier; company officials may deny its existence, but it effectively prevents many women from rising above middle management.

For all these reasons, women earn less than men in all major occupational categories. Even so, many people think that women own most of this country's wealth, perhaps because women typically outlive men. Government statistics tell a different story: Fifty-seven percent of individuals with $1.5 million or more in assets are men, although widows are highly represented in this elite club (Johnson & Raub, 2006; Internal Revenue Service, 2008). Just 10 percent of the individuals identified in 2008 by *Forbes* magazine as the richest people in the United States were women (Miller & Greenberg, 2008).

Housework: Women's "Second Shift"

In the United States, we have always been of two minds about housework: We say that it is important to family life, but people get little reward for doing it (Bernard, 1981). Here, as around the world, taking care of the home and children has always been considered "women's work". As women have entered the labor force, the amount of housework women do has gone down, but the *share* done by women has stayed the same. Figure 2 shows that overall, women average 16.1 hours a week of housework, compared to 10.5 hours for men. As the figure shows, women in all categories do significantly more housework than men (Bureau of Labor Statistics, 2009).

Men do support the idea of women entering the paid labor force, and most husbands count on the money their wives earn. But many men resist taking on a more equal share of household duties (Heath & Bourne, 1995; Harpster & Monk-Turner, 1998; Stratton, 2001).

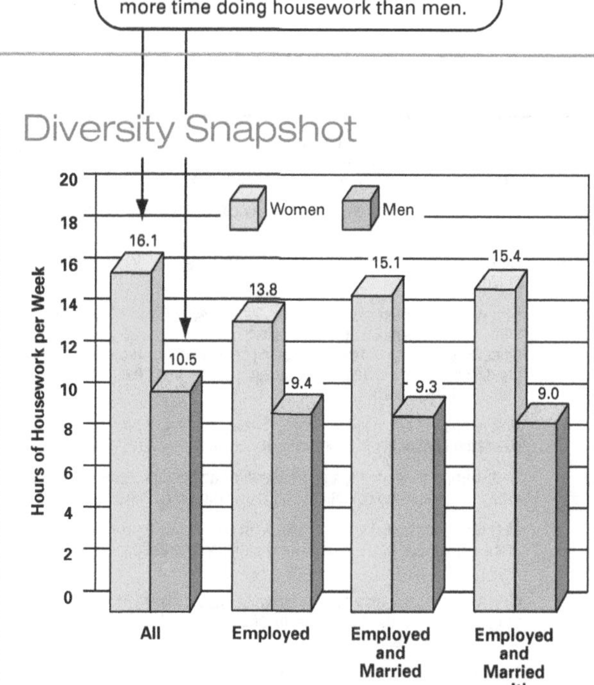

FIGURE 2 **Housework: Who Does How Much?**

Regardless of employment or family status, women do more housework than men. What effect do you think the added burden of housework has on women's ability to advance in the workplace?

Source: Adapted from Bureau of Labor Statistics (2009).

Gender and Education

In the past, our society considered schooling more necessary for men, who worked outside the home, than for women, who worked in the home. But times have changed. By 1980, women earned a majority of all associate's and bachelor's degrees; in 2007, that share was 59 percent (National Center for Education Statistics, 2009).

In recent decades, college doors have opened wider to women, and the differences in men's and women's majors are becoming smaller. In 1970, for example, women earned just 17 percent of bachelor's degrees in the natural sciences, computer science, and engineering; by 2007, their proportion had more than doubled to 36 percent.

In 1992, for the first time, women also earned a majority of postgraduate degrees, which often serve as a springboard to high-prestige jobs. In all areas of study in 2007, women earned 61 percent of master's degrees and 50 percent of doctorates (including 64 percent of all Ph.D. degrees in sociology). Women have also broken into many graduate fields that used to be almost all male. For example, in 1970, only a few hundred women earned a master's of business administration

SEEING SOCIOLOGY in Everyday Life

Sweden, Norway, Finland, and Denmark have laws that require at least 25 percent of candidates for elected office to be women. Do you think the United States should enact such a law? Why or why not?

Table 2 Significant "Firsts" for Women in U.S. Politics

Year	Event
1869	Law allows women to vote in Wyoming territory.
1872	First woman to run for the presidency (Victoria Woodhull) represents the Equal Rights party.
1917	First woman elected to the House of Representatives (Jeannette Rankin of Montana).
1924	First women elected state governors (Nellie Taylor Ross of Wyoming and Miriam "Ma" Ferguson of Texas); both followed their husbands into office. First woman to have her name placed in nomination for the vice-presidency at the convention of a major political party (Lena Jones Springs, a Democrat).
1931	First woman to serve in the Senate (Hattie Caraway of Arkansas); completed the term of her husband upon his death and won reelection in 1932.
1932	First woman appointed to the presidential cabinet (Frances Perkins, secretary of labor in the cabinet of President Franklin D. Roosevelt).
1964	First woman to have her name placed in nomination for the presidency at the convention of a major political party (Margaret Chase Smith, a Republican).
1972	First African American woman to have her name placed in nomination for the presidency at the convention of a major political party (Shirley Chisholm, a Democrat).
1981	First woman appointed to the U.S. Supreme Court (Sandra Day O'Connor).
1984	First woman to be successfully nominated for the vice-presidency (Geraldine Ferraro, a Democrat).
1988	First woman chief executive to be elected to a consecutive third term (Madeleine Kunin, governor of Vermont).
1992	Political "Year of the Woman" yields record number of women in the Senate (six) and the House (forty-eight), as well as (1) first African American woman to win election to the U.S. Senate (Carol Moseley-Braun of Illinois), (2) first state (California) to be served by two women senators (Barbara Boxer and Dianne Feinstein), and (3) first woman of Puerto Rican descent elected to the U.S. House of Representatives (Nydia Velazquez of New York).
1996	First woman appointed secretary of state (Madeleine Albright).
2000	First First Lady to win elected political office (Hillary Rodham Clinton, senator from New York).
2001	First woman to serve as national security adviser (Condoleezza Rice); first Asian American woman to serve in a presidential cabinet (Elaine Chao, secretary of labor).
2005	First African American woman appointed secretary of state (Condoleezza Rice).
2007	First woman elected as speaker of the House (Nancy Pelosi).
2008	For the first time, women make up a majority of a state legislature (New Hampshire).
2009	Record number of women in the Senate (seventeen) and the House (seventy-three).

Source: Compiled by the author.

(M.B.A.) degree, compared to almost 66,000 in 2007 (44 percent of all such degrees) (National Center for Education Statistics, 2009).

Despite these advances for women, men still predominate in some professional fields. In 2007, men received 51 percent of medical (M.D.) degrees, 52 percent of law (LL.B. and J.D.) degrees, and 55 percent of dental (D.D.S. and D.M.D.) degrees (National Center for Education Statistics, 2009). Our society once defined high-paying professions (and the drive and competitiveness needed to succeed in them) as masculine. But the share of women in all these professions has risen and is now close to half. When will parity be reached? It may not be in the next few years. For example, the American Bar Association (2008) reports that men still account for 53 percent of law school students across the United States.

Gender and Politics

A century ago, almost no women held elected office in the United States. In fact, women were legally barred from voting in national elections until the passage of the Nineteenth Amendment to the Constitution in 1920. However, a few women were candidates for political office even before they could vote. The Equal Rights party supported Victoria Woodhull for the U.S. presidency in 1872; perhaps it was a sign of the times that she spent election day in a New York City jail. Table 2 identifies milestones in women's gradual movement into U.S. political life.

Today, thousands of women serve as mayors of cities and towns across the United States, and tens of thousands hold responsible administrative posts in the federal government. At the state level, 24 percent of state legislators in 2009 were women (up from just 6 percent in 1970). National Map 1 shows where in the United States women have made the greatest political gains.

Change is coming more slowly at the highest levels of politics, although a majority of U.S. adults claim they would support a qualified woman for any office. In 2008, Hillary Clinton came close to gaining the presidential nomination of the Democratic party, losing out to Barack Obama, who became the nation's first African American president. In 2008, eight of fifty state governors were women (16 percent), and in Congress, women held 73 of 435 seats in the House of Representatives (17 percent) and 17 of 100 seats in the Senate (17 percent) (Center for American Women and Politics, 2009a).

Women make up half the world's population, but they hold just 18 percent of seats in the world's 188 parliaments. Although this percentage represents a rise from 3 percent fifty years ago, in only fourteen countries, among them Sweden and Norway, do women represent more than one-third of the members of parliament (Paxton, Hughes, & Green, 2006; Inter-Parliamentary Union, 2008).

Gender and the Military

Since colonial times, women have served in the U.S. armed forces. Yet in 1940, at the outset of World War II, just 2 percent of armed forces personnel were women. By the time of the war in Iraq, women represented about 14 percent of all U.S. military personnel, including deployed troops.

minority any category of people distinguished by physical or cultural difference that a society sets apart and subordinates

intersection theory analysis of the interplay of race, class, and gender, often resulting in multiple dimensions of disadvantage

In general, the western states have a higher percentage of legislators who are women than the southern states.

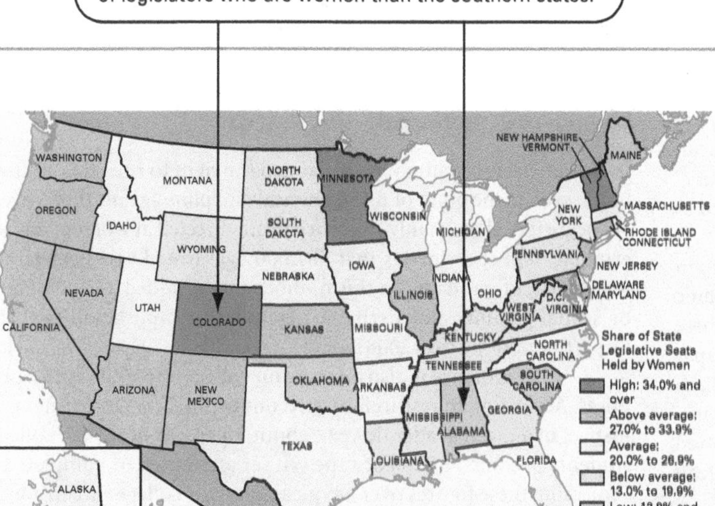

Seeing Ourselves

NATIONAL MAP 1

Women in State Government across the United States

Although women make up half of U.S. adults, just 24 percent of the seats in state legislatures are held by women. Look at the state-by-state variations in the map. In which regions of the country have women gained the greatest political power? What do you think accounts for this pattern?

Source: Center for American Women and Politics (2009).

Clearly, women make up a growing share of the U.S. military, and almost all military assignments are now open to both women and men. But law prevents women from engaging in offensive warfare. Even so, the line between troop support and outright combat is easily crossed, as the women serving in Iraq have learned. In fact, between March 2003 and March 2009, the war in Iraq claimed the lives of 101 women soldiers.

The debate on women's role in the military has been going on for centuries. Some people object to opening doors in this way, claiming that women lack the physical strength of men. Others reply that military women are better educated and score higher on intelligence tests than military men. But the heart of the issue is our society's deeply held view of women as *nurturers*—people who give life and help others—which clashes with the image of women trained to kill.

Whatever our views of women and men, the reality is that military women are in harm's way. In part, this fact reflects the strains experienced by a military short of personnel. In addition, the type of insurgency that surrounds our troops in Iraq can bring violent combat to any soldier at any time. Finally, our modern warfare technology blurs the distinction between combat and noncombat personnel. A combat pilot can fire missiles by radar at a target miles away; by contrast, noncombat medical evacuation teams routinely travel directly into the line of fire (Segal & Hansen, 1992; Kaminer, 1997; McGirk, 2006).

Are Women a Minority?

A **minority** is *any category of people distinguished by physical or cultural difference that a society sets apart and subordinates.* Given the economic disadvantage of being a woman in our society, it seems reasonable to say that U.S. women are a minority even though they outnumber men.[1]

Even so, most white women do not think of themselves in this way (Lengermann & Wallace, 1985). This is partly because, unlike racial minorities (including African Americans) and ethnic minorities (say, Hispanics), white women are well represented at all levels of the class structure, including the very top.

Bear in mind, however, that at every class level, women typically have less income, wealth, education, and power than men. Patriarchy makes women dependent on men—first their fathers and later their husbands—for their social standing (Bernard, 1981).

Minority Women: Intersection Theory

If women are defined as a minority, what about minority women? Are they doubly handicapped? This question lies at the heart of **intersection theory**, *analysis of the interplay of race, class, and gender, often resulting in multiple dimensions of disadvantage.* Research shows that disadvantages linked to gender and race often combine to produce especially low social standing (Ovadia, 2001).

Income data illustrate the validity of this theory. Looking first at race and ethnicity, the median income in 2007 for African American women working full time was $31,114, which is 84 percent as much as the $36,891 earned by non-Hispanic white women

[1]Sociologists use the term "minority" instead of "minority group" because, women make up a *category*, not a group. People in a category share a status or identity but generally do not know one another or interact.

MAKING THE GRADE

Feminists argue that rape is not about sex but about power. It is this claim that makes sexual violence against women not just a crime but a matter of gender stratification.

working full time; Hispanic women earned $26,695—just 72 percent as much as their white counterparts. Looking at gender, African American women earned only 86 percent as much as African American men, and Hispanic women earned only 89 percent as much as Hispanic men.

Combining these disadvantages, African American women earned 62 percent as much as non-Hispanic white men, and Hispanic women earned 53 percent as much (U.S. Census Bureau, 2008). These differences reflect minority women's lower positions in the occupational and educational hierarchies. These data confirm that although gender has a powerful effect on our lives, it does not operate alone. Class position, race and ethnicity, and gender form a multilayered system of disadvantage for some and privilege for others (Saint Jean & Feagin, 1998).

PhotoEdit Inc./Michael Newman

The basic insight of intersection theory is that various dimensions of social stratification—including race and gender—can add up to great disadvantages for some categories of people. Just as African Americans earn less than whites, women earn less than men. Thus African American women confront a "double disadvantage," earning just 62 cents for every dollar earned by non-Hispanic white men. How would you explain the fact that some categories of people are much more likely to end up in low-paying jobs like this one?

Violence against Women

In the nineteenth century, men claimed the right to rule their households, even to the point of using physical discipline against their wives, and a great deal of "manly" violence is still directed at women. A government report estimates that 587,000 aggravated assaults against women occur annually. To this number can be added 233,000 rapes or sexual assaults and perhaps 1.8 million simple assaults (U.S. Department of Justice, 2008).

Gender violence is also an issue on college and university campuses. According to research carried out by the U.S. Department of Justice, in a given academic year, about 3 percent of female college students become victims of rape (either attempted or completed). Projecting these figures over a typical five-year college career, about 20 percent of college women experience rape. In 90 percent of all cases, the victim knew the offender, and most of the assaults took place in the woman's living quarters (Karjane, Fisher, & Cullen, 2005).

Off campus, most gender-linked violence also occurs where most interaction between women and men takes place: in the home. Richard Gelles (cited in Roesch, 1984) argues that with the exception of the police and the military, the family is the most violent organization in the United States, and women suffer most of the injuries. The risk of violence is especially great for low-income women living in families that face a great deal of stress; low-income women also have fewer options to get out of a dangerous home (Gelles & Cornell, 1990; Smolowe, 1994; Frias & Angel, 2007).

Violence against women also occurs in casual relationships. Most rapes involve men known, and often trusted, by the victims. Dianne Herman (2001) claims that abuse of women is built into our way of life. All forms of violence against women—from the catcalls that intimidate women on city streets to a pinch in a crowded subway to physical assaults that occur at home—express what she calls a "rape culture" of men trying to dominate women. Sexual violence is fundamentally about *power,* not sex, and therefore should be understood as a dimension of gender stratification.

In global perspective, violence against women is built into different cultures in different ways. One case in point is the practice of female genital mutilation, a painful and often dangerous surgical procedure performed in more than forty countries and known to occur in the United States, as shown in Global Map 2. The Thinking About Diversity box later in this chapter highlights a case of genital mutilation that took place in California and asks whether this practice, which some people defend as promoting "morality," amounts to a case of violence against women.

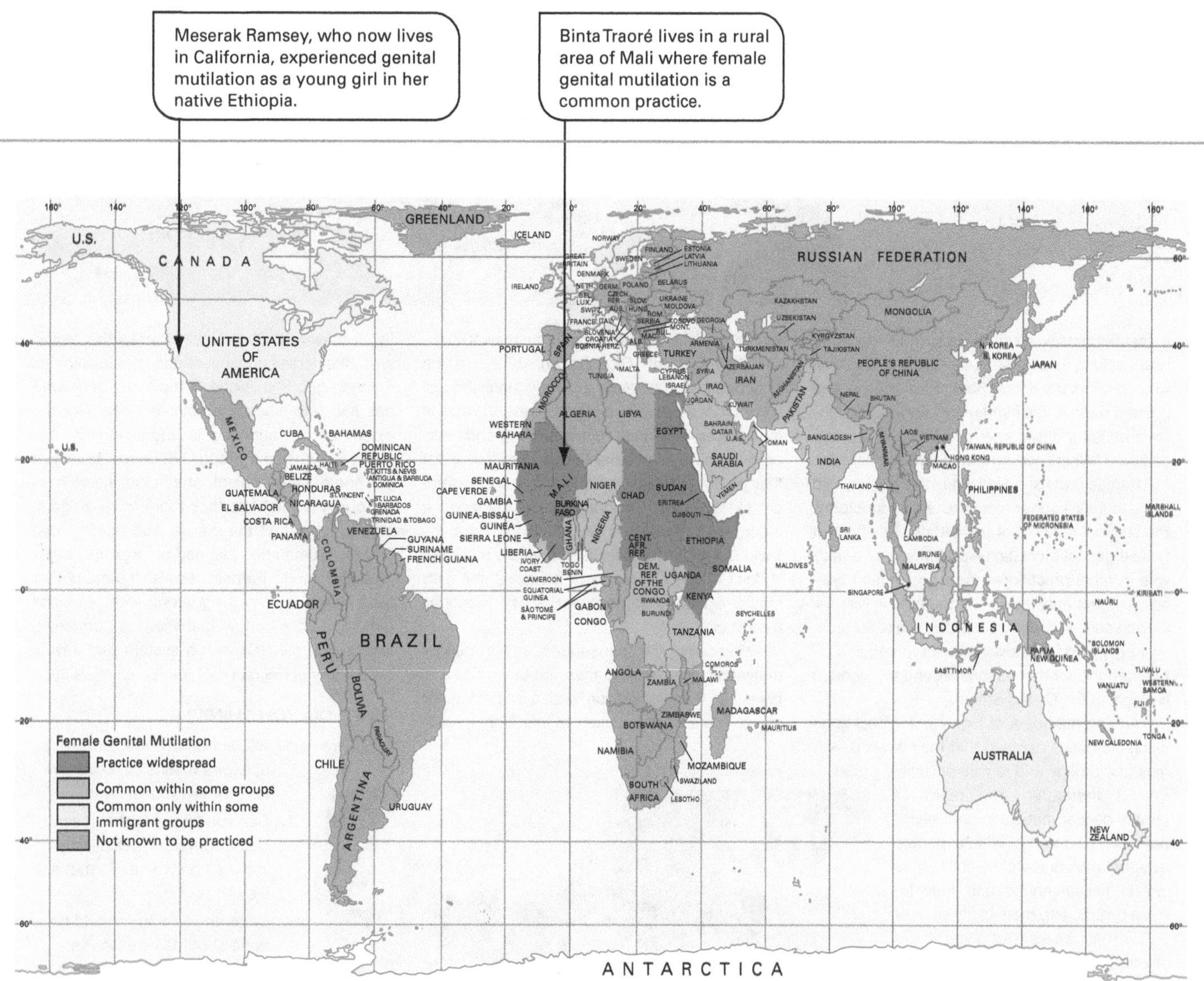

Window on the World

GLOBAL MAP 2 **Female Genital Mutilation in Global Perspective**

Female genital mutilation is known to be performed in more than forty countries around the world. Across Africa, the practice is common and affects a majority of girls in the eastern African nations of Sudan, Ethiopia, and Somalia. In several Asian nations, including India, the practice is limited to a few ethnic minorities. In the United States, Canada, several European nations, and Australia, there are reports of the practice among some immigrants.

Sources: Data from Seager (2003), World Health Organization (2006), and UNICEF (2008).

Violence against Men

If our way of life encourages violence against women, it may encourage even more violence against men. In more than 80 percent of cases in which police make an arrest for a violent crime, including murder, robbery, and physical assault, the person arrested is a male. In addition, 53 percent of all victims of violent crime are also men (U.S. Department of Justice, 2008).

Our culture tends to define masculinity in terms of aggression and violence. "Real men" work and play hard, speed on the highways, and let nothing stand in their way. A higher crime rate is one result. But even when no laws are broken, men's lives involve more stress and isolation than women's lives, which is one reason that the suicide rate for

sexual harassment comments, gestures, or physical contacts of a sexual nature that are deliberate, repeated, and unwelcome

THINKING ABOUT DIVERSITY: RACE, CLASS, & GENDER

Female Genital Mutilation: Violence in the Name of Morality

Meserak Ramsey, a woman born in Ethiopia and now working as a nurse in California, paid a visit to an old friend's home. Soon after arriving, she noticed her friend's eighteen-month-old daughter huddled in the corner of a room in obvious distress. "What's wrong with her?" she asked.

Ramsey was shocked when the woman said her daughter had recently had a clitoridectomy, the surgical removal of the clitoris. This type of female genital mutilation—performed by a midwife, a tribal practitioner, or a doctor, and typically without anesthesia—is common in Nigeria, Sierra Leone, Senegal, Sudan, Ethiopia, Somalia, and Egypt and is known to exist in certain cultural groups in other nations around the world. It is illegal in the United States.

Among members of highly patriarchal societies, husbands demand that their wives be virgins at marriage and remain sexually faithful thereafter. The point of female genital mutilation is to eliminate sexual feeling, which, people assume, makes the girl less likely to violate sexual norms and thus be more desirable to men. In about one-fifth of all cases, an even more severe procedure, called infibulation, is performed, in which the entire external genital area is removed and the surfaces are stitched together, leaving only a small hole for urination and menstruation. Before marriage, a husband retains the right to open the wound and ensure himself of his bride's virginity.

How many women have undergone genital mutilation? Worldwide, estimates place the number at more than 100 million (World Health Organization, 2006). In the United States, hundreds or even thousands of such procedures are performed every year. In most cases, immigrant mothers and grandmothers who have themselves been mutilated insist that young girls in their family follow their example. Indeed, many immigrant women demand the procedure *because* their daughters now live in the United States, where sexual mores are more lax. "I don't have to worry about her now," the girl's mother explained to Meserak Ramsey. "She'll be a good girl."

Medically, the consequences of genital mutilation include more than the loss of sexual pleasure. Pain is intense and can persist for years. There is also danger of infection, infertility, and even death. Ramsey knows this all too well: She herself underwent genital mutilation as a young girl. She is one of the lucky ones who has had few medical problems since. But the extent of her suffering is suggested by this story: She invited a young U.S. couple to stay at her home. Late at night, she heard the woman cry out and burst into their room to investigate, only to learn that the couple was making love and the woman had just had an orgasm. "I didn't understand," Ramsey recalls. "I thought that there must be something wrong with American girls. But now I know that there is something wrong with me." Or with a system that inflicts such injury in the name of traditional morality.

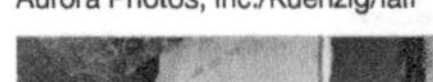

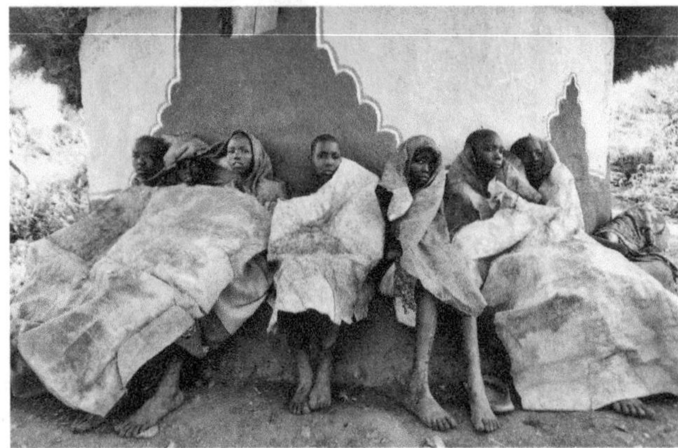

Aurora Photos, Inc./Kuenzig/laif

These young women have just undergone female genital mutilation. What do you think should be done about this practice?

WHAT DO YOU THINK?

1. Is female genital mutilation a medical procedure or a means of social control? Explain your answer.
2. Can you think of other examples of physical mutilation imposed on women? What are they?
3. What do you think should be done about female genital mutilation in places where it is widespread? Do you think respect for human rights should override respect for cultural differences in this case? Explain your answer.

Sources: Crossette (1995) and Boyle, Songora, & Foss (2001).

men is four times higher than for women. In addition, as noted earlier, men live, on average, about five fewer years than women.

Violence is not simply a matter of choices made by individuals. It is built into our way of life, with resulting harm to both men and women. In short, the way any culture constructs gender plays an important part in how violent or peaceful a society will be.

Sexual Harassment

Sexual harassment refers to *comments, gestures, or physical contacts of a sexual nature that are deliberate, repeated, and unwelcome.* During the 1990s, sexual harassment became an issue of national importance that rewrote the rules for workplace interaction between women and men.

SEEING SOCIOLOGY in Everyday Life

The Internet has made pornography more accessible; do you think it has become more acceptable as well? Why or why not?

Corbis RF/Sven Hagolani/Zefa

In recent decades, our society has recognized sexual harassment as an important problem. As a result, at least officially, unwelcome sexual attention is no longer tolerated in the workplace. To what extent do you think sexual comments, off-color jokes, and unnecessary touching still take place on the job?

Most (but not all) victims of sexual harassment are women. The reason is that, first, our culture encourages men to be sexually assertive and to see women in sexual terms. As a result, social interaction in the workplace, on campus, and elsewhere can easily take on sexual overtones. Second, most people in positions of power—including business executives, doctors, bureau chiefs, assembly-line supervisors, professors, and military officers—are men who oversee the work of women. Surveys carried out in widely different work settings show that 5 percent of women claim that they have been harassed on the job during the past year and about half of women say they receive unwanted sexual attention (NORC, 2007).

Sexual harassment is sometimes obvious and direct: A supervisor may ask for sexual favors from an employee and make threats if the advances are refused. Courts have declared such *quid pro quo* sexual harassment (the Latin phrase means "one thing in return for another") to be a violation of civil rights.

More often, however, sexual harassment is a matter of subtle behavior—suggestive teasing, off-color jokes, comments about someone's looks—that may not even be intended to harass anyone. But based on the *effect* standard favored by many feminists, such actions add up to creating a *hostile environment.* Incidents of this kind are far more complex because they involve different perceptions of the same behavior. For example, a man may think that repeatedly complimenting a co-worker on her appearance is simply being friendly. The co-worker may believe that the man is thinking of her in sexual terms and is not taking her work seriously, an attitude that could harm her job performance and prospects for advancement.

Pornography

Defined *pornography* as sexually explicit material that causes sexual arousal. Keep in mind, however, that people take different views of what is and what is not pornographic. The law gives local communities the power to define what sexually explicit materials violate "community standards of decency" and "lack any redeeming social value."

Traditionally, people have raised concerns about pornography as a *moral* issue. But pornography also plays a part in gender stratification. From this point of view, pornography is really a *power* issue because most pornography dehumanizes women, depicting them as the playthings of men.

In addition, there is widespread concern that pornography promotes violence against women by portraying them as weak and undeserving of respect. Men may show contempt for women defined this way by striking out against them. Surveys show that about half of U.S. adults think that pornography encourages men to commit rape (NORC, 2007:300).

Like sexual harassment, pornography raises complex and conflicting issues. Despite the fact that some material may offend just about everybody, many people defend the rights of free speech and artistic expression. Pressure to restrict pornography has increased in recent decades, reflecting both the long-standing concern that pornography weakens morality and more recent concerns that it is demeaning and threatening to women.

Theoretical Analysis of Gender

Why does gender exist in the first place? Sociology's three main approaches offer insights about the importance of gender in social organization. The Applying Theory table summarizes the important insights offered by these approaches.

Structural-Functional Analysis

The structural-functional approach views society as a complex system of many separate but integrated parts. From this point of view, gender serves as a means to organize social life.

Members of hunting and gathering societies had little power over the forces of biology. Lacking effective birth control, women were frequently pregnant, and the responsibilities of child care kept them close to home. At the same time, men's greater strength made

APPLYING THEORY

Gender

	Structural-Functional Approach	Symbolic-Interaction Approach	Social-Conflict Approach
What is the level of analysis?	Macro-level	Micro-level	Macro-level
What does gender mean?	Parsons described gender in terms of two complementary patterns of behavior: masculine and feminine.	Numerous sociologists have shown that gender is part of the reality that guides social interaction in everyday situations.	Engels described gender in terms of the power of one sex over the other.
Is gender helpful or harmful?	Helpful. Gender gives men and women distinctive roles and responsibilities that help society operate smoothly. Gender builds social unity as men and women come together to form families.	Hard to say; gender is both helpful and harmful. In everyday life, gender is one of the factors that helps us relate to one another. At the same time, gender shapes human behavior, placing men in control of social situations. Men tend to initiate most interactions, while women typically act in a more deferential manner.	Harmful. Gender limits people's personal development. Gender divides society by giving power to men to control the lives of women. Capitalism makes patriarchy stronger.

them more suited for warfare and hunting game. Over the centuries, this sexual division of labor became institutionalized and largely taken for granted (Lengermann & Wallace, 1985; Freedman, 2002).

Industrial technology opens up a much greater range of cultural possibilities. With human muscles no longer the main energy source, the physical strength of men becomes less important. In addition, the ability to control reproduction gives women greater choices about how to live. Modern societies relax traditional gender roles as they become more meritocratic because such rigid roles waste an enormous amount of human talent. Yet change comes slowly because gender is deeply rooted in culture.

Gender and Social Integration

As Talcott Parsons (1942, 1951, 1954) observed, gender helps integrate society, at least in its traditional form. Gender establishes a *complementary* set of roles that link men and women into family units and give each sex responsibility for carrying out important tasks. Women take the lead in managing the household and raising children. Men connect the family to the larger world as they participate in the labor force.

Thus gender plays an important part in socialization. Society teaches boys—presumably destined for the labor force—to be rational, self-assured, and competitive. Parsons called this complex of traits *instrumental* qualities. To prepare girls for child rearing, their socialization stresses *expressive* qualities, such as emotional responsiveness and sensitivity to others.

Society encourages gender conformity by instilling in men and women a fear that straying too far from accepted standards of masculinity or femininity will cause rejection by the other sex. In simple terms, women learn to reject nonmasculine men as sexually unattractive, and men learn to reject unfeminine women. In sum, gender integrates society both structurally (in terms of what we do) and morally (in terms of what we believe).

CRITICAL REVIEW Influential in the 1950s, this approach has lost much of its standing today. First, functionalism assumes a singular vision of society that is not shared by everyone. Historically, many women have worked outside the home because of economic need, a fact not reflected in Parsons's conventional, middle-class view of family life. Second, Parsons's analysis ignores the personal strains and social costs of rigid, traditional gender

MAKING THE GRADE

The structural-functional approach is a more "horizontal" view of gender that emphasizes complementarity. The social-conflict approach is a more "vertical" view of gender that emphasizes inequality. The symbolic-interaction approach is the micro-level look at gender in everyday life.

roles. Third, in the eyes of those seeking sexual equality, Parsons's gender "complementarity" amounts to little more than women submitting to male domination.

CHECK YOUR LEARNING In Parsons's analysis, what functions does gender perform for society?

Symbolic-Interaction Analysis

The symbolic-interaction approach takes a micro-level view of society, focusing on face-to-face interaction in everyday life. Gender affects everyday interaction in a number of ways.

Gender and Everyday Life

If you watch women and men interacting, you will probably notice that women typically engage in more eye contact than men do. Why? Holding eye contact is a way of encouraging the conversation to continue; in addition, looking directly at someone clearly shows the other person that you are paying attention.

This pattern is an example of sex roles, defined earlier as the way a society defines how women and men should think and behave. To understand such patterns, consider the fact that people with more power tend to take charge of social encounters. When men and women engage one another, as they do in families and in the workplace, it is men who typically initiate the interaction. That is, men speak first, set the topics of discussion, and control the outcomes. With less power, women are expected to be more *deferential,* meaning that they show respect for others of higher social position. In many cases, this means that women (just like children or others with less power) spend more time being silent and also encouraging men (or others with more power) not just with eye contact but by smiling or nodding in agreement. As a technique to control a conversation, men often interrupt others, just as they typically feel less need to ask the opinions of other people, especially those with less power (Tannen, 1990, 1994; Henley, Hamilton, & Thorne, 1992; Ridgeway & Smith-Lovin, 1999).

Getty Images Inc. – Hulton Archive Photos/FPG

In the 1950s, Talcott Parsons proposed that sociologists interpret gender as a matter of *differences.* As he saw it, masculine men and feminine women formed strong families and made for an orderly society. In recent decades, however, social-conflict theory has reinterpreted gender as a matter of *inequality.* From this point of view, U.S. society places men in a position of dominance over women.

CRITICAL REVIEW The strength of the symbolic-interaction approach is helping us see how gender plays a part in shaping almost all our everyday experiences. Because our society defines men (and everything that is defined as masculine) as having more value than women (and what is defined as feminine), just about every familiar social encounter is "gendered," so that men and women interact in distinctive and unequal ways.

The symbolic-interaction approach suggests that individuals socially construct the reality they experience as they interact, using gender as one element of their personal "performances." Gender can be a useful guide to how we behave. Yet gender, as a structural dimension of society, is beyond the immediate control of any of us as individuals and also gives some people power over others. Therefore, patterns of everyday social interaction reflect our society's gender stratification. Everyday interaction also helps reinforce this inequality. For example, to the extent that fathers take the lead in family discussions, the entire family learns to expect men to "display leadership" and "show their wisdom."

A limitation of the symbolic-interaction approach is that by focusing on situational social experience, it says little about the broad patterns of inequality that set the rules for our everyday lives. To understand the roots of gender stratification, we have to "look up" to see more closely how society makes men and women unequal. We will do this using the social-conflict approach.

CHECK YOUR LEARNING Point to ways that gender shapes the everyday face-to-face interactions of individuals.

Social-Conflict Analysis

From a social-conflict point of view, gender involves differences not just in behavior but in power as well. Consider the striking similarity between the way ideas about gender benefit men and the way

feminism support of social equality for women and men, in opposition to patriarchy and sexism

Landov Media/UPI

NASCAR racing has always been a masculine world. But Danica Patrick has made a name for herself as an outstanding driver. At the same time, she has made much of her income from trading on her good looks, including the 2009 *Sports Illustrated* swimsuit edition. Are men as likely to do the same? Why or why not?

oppression of racial and ethnic minorities benefits white people. Conventional ideas about gender do not make society operate smoothly; they create division and tension, with men seeking to protect their privileges as women challenge the status quo.

The social-conflict approach draws heavily on the ideas of Karl Marx. Yet as far as gender is concerned, Marx was a product of his time, and his writings focused almost entirely on men. However, his friend and collaborator Friedrich Engels did develop a theory of gender stratification.

Gender and Class Inequality

Looking back through history, Engels saw that in hunting and gathering societies, the activities of women and men, although different, had equal importance. A successful hunt brought men great prestige, but the vegetation gathered by women provided most of a group's food supply. As technological advances led to a productive surplus, however, social equality and communal sharing gave way to private property and ultimately a class hierarchy, and men gained significant power over women. With surplus wealth to pass on to heirs, upper-class men needed to be sure their sons were their own, which led them to control the sexuality of women. The desire to control property brought about monogamous marriage and the family. Women were taught to remain virgins until marriage, to remain faithful to their husbands thereafter, and to build their lives around bearing and raising one man's children.

According to Engels (1902, orig. 1884), capitalism makes male domination even stronger. First, capitalism creates more wealth, which gives greater power to men as income earners and owners of property. Second, an expanding capitalist economy depends on turning people, especially women, into consumers who seek personal fulfillment through buying and using products. Third, society assigns women the task of maintaining the home to free men to work in factories. The double exploitation of capitalism, as Engels saw it, lies in paying men low wages for their labor and paying women no wages at all.

CRITICAL REVIEW Social-conflict analysis is critical of conventional ideas about gender, claiming that society would be better off if we minimized or even did away with this dimension of social structure. That is, this approach regards conventional families, which traditionalists consider personally and socially positive, as a social evil. A problem with social-conflict analysis, then, is that it minimizes the extent to which women and men live together cooperatively and often happily in families. A second problem lies in the assertion that capitalism is the basis of gender stratification. In fact, agrarian societies are typically more patriarchal than industrial-capitalist societies. Although socialist nations, including the People's Republic of China and the former Soviet Union, did move women into the workforce, by and large they provided women with very low pay in sex-segregated jobs (Rosendahl, 1997; Haney, 2002).

CHECK YOUR LEARNING According to Friedrich Engels, how does gender support social inequality in a capitalist class system?

Feminism

Feminism is *support of social equality for women and men, in opposition to patriarchy and sexism.* The first wave of feminism in the United States began in the 1840s as women opposed to slavery, including Elizabeth Cady Stanton and Lucretia Mott, drew parallels between

SEEING SOCIOLOGY in Everyday Life

On your campus, do men's organizations (such as fraternities and athletic teams) enjoy any special privileges? What about women's organizations?

the oppression of African Americans and the oppression of women. Their main objective was obtaining the right to vote, which was finally achieved in 1920. But other disadvantages persisted, causing a second wave of feminism to arise in the 1960s that continues today.

Basic Feminist Ideas

Feminism views the personal experiences of women and men through the lens of gender. How we think of ourselves (gender identity), how we act (gender roles), and our sex's social standing (gender stratification) are all rooted in the operation of society.

Although feminists disagree about many things, most support five general principles:

1. **Working to increase equality.** Feminist thinking is political; it links ideas to action. Feminism is critical of the status quo, pushing for change toward social equality for women and men.
2. **Expanding human choice.** Feminists argue that cultural conceptions of gender divide the full range of human qualities into two opposing and limiting spheres: the female world of emotions and cooperation and the male world of rationality and competition. As an alternative, feminists propose a "reintegration of humanity" by which all individuals can develop all human traits (M. French, 1985).
3. **Eliminating gender stratification.** Feminism opposes laws and cultural norms that limit the education, income, and job opportunities of women. For this reason, feminists have long supported passage of the Equal Rights Amendment (ERA) to the U.S. Constitution, which states, in its entirety, "Equality of rights under the law shall not be denied or abridged by the United States or any State on account of sex." The ERA was first proposed in Congress in 1923. Although it has widespread support, it has yet to become law.
4. **Ending sexual violence.** Today's women's movement seeks to eliminate sexual violence. Feminists argue that patriarchy distorts the relationships between women and men, encouraging violence against women in the form of rape, domestic abuse, sexual harassment, and pornography (A. Dworkin, 1987; Freedman, 2002).
5. **Promoting sexual freedom.** Finally, feminism supports women's control over their sexuality and reproduction. Feminists support the free availability of birth control information. As Figure 3 shows, sixty-eight percent of married women of childbearing age in the United States use contraception; the use of contraceptives is far less common in many lower-income nations. Most feminists also support a woman's right to choose whether to bear children or end a pregnancy, rather than allowing men—husbands, physicians, and legislators—to control their reproduction. Many feminists also support gay people's efforts to end prejudice and discrimination in a largely heterosexual culture (Ferree & Hess, 1995; Armstrong, 2002).

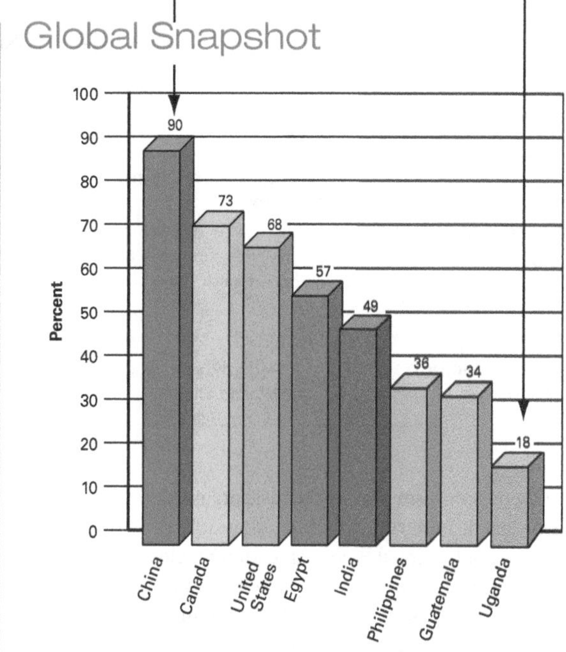

FIGURE 3 Use of Contraception by Married Women of Childbearing Age

In the United States, most married women of childbearing age use contraception. In many lower-income countries, however, most women do not have the opportunity to make this choice.

Source: Population Reference Bureau (2009).

Types of Feminism

Although feminists agree on the importance of gender equality, they disagree on how to achieve it: through liberal feminism, socialist feminism, or radical feminism (Stacey, 1983; L. Vogel, 1983; Ferree & Hess, 1995; Armstrong, 2002; Freedman, 2002). The Applying Theory table highlights the key arguments made by each type of feminist thinking.

Liberal Feminism

Liberal feminism is rooted in the classic liberal thinking that individuals should be free to develop their own talents and pursue their own

MAKING THE GRADE

Feminism is one type of social-conflict approach to understanding gender.

MAKING THE GRADE

The three types of feminism all agree on the importance of gender and the need to make women and men more socially equal. They disagree on the way to do that, with liberal feminism involving the least societal change and radical feminism involving the most.

APPLYING THEORY

Feminism

	Liberal Feminism	Socialist Feminism	Radical Feminism
Does it accept the basic order of society?	Yes. Liberal feminism seeks change only to ensure equality of opportunity.	No. Socialist feminism supports an end to social classes and to family gender roles that encourage "domestic slavery."	No. Radical feminism supports an end to the family system.
How do women improve their social standing?	Individually, according to personal ability and effort.	Collectively, through socialist revolution.	Collectively, by working to eliminate gender itself.

interests. Liberal feminism accepts the basic organization of our society but seeks to expand the rights and opportunities of women, in part through passage of the Equal Rights Amendment. Liberal feminists also support reproductive freedom for all women. They respect the family as a social institution but seek changes, including more widely available maternity and paternity leave and child care for parents who work.

Given their belief in the rights of individuals, liberal feminists think that women should advance according to their own efforts, rather than working collectively for change. Both women and men, through their individual achievement, are capable of improving their lives, as long as society removes legal and cultural barriers.

Socialist Feminism

Socialist feminism evolved from the ideas of Karl Marx and Friedrich Engels. From this point of view, capitalism strengthens patriarchy by concentrating wealth and power in the hands of a small number of men. Socialist feminists do not think the reforms supported by liberal feminism go far enough. The family form created by capitalism must change if we are to replace "domestic slavery" with some collective means of carrying out housework and child care. Replacing the traditional family can come about only through a socialist revolution that creates a state-centered economy to meet the needs of all.

Radical Feminism

Like socialist feminism, *radical feminism* finds liberal feminism inadequate. Radical feminists believe that patriarchy is so deeply rooted in society that even a socialist revolution would not end it. Instead, reaching the goal of gender equality means that society must eliminate gender itself.

One possible way to achieve this goal is to use new reproductive technology to separate women's bodies from the process of childbearing. With an end to motherhood, radical feminists reason, society could leave behind the entire family system, liberating women, men, and children from the oppression of family, gender, and sex itself (A. Dworkin, 1987). Radical feminism seeks an egalitarian and gender-free society, a revolution more sweeping than that sought by Marx.

Opposition to Feminism

Because feminism calls for significant change, it has always been controversial. But today, just 20 percent of U.S. adults say they oppose feminism, a share that has declined over time (NORC, 2007). Figure 4 shows a similar downward trend in opposition to feminism among college students after 1970. Note, however, that there has been little change in attitudes in recent years and that more men than women express antifeminist attitudes.

Feminism provokes criticism and resistance from both men and women who hold conventional ideas about gender. Some men oppose sexual equality for the same reason that many white people have historically opposed social equality for people of color: They do not want to give up their privileges. Other men and women, including those who are neither rich nor powerful, distrust a social movement (especially its radical expressions) that attacks the traditional family and rejects patterns that have guided male-female relations for centuries.

Men who have been socialized to value strength and dominance may feel uneasy about the feminist ideal of men as gentle and warm (Doyle, 1983). Similarly, some women whose lives center on their husbands and children may think that feminism does not value the social roles that give meaning to their lives. In general, resistance to feminism is strongest among women who have the least education and those who do not work outside the home (Marshall, 1985; Ferree & Hess, 1995; CBS News, 2005).

SEEING SOCIOLOGY in Everyday Life

Do you think women should get ahead through individual effort or by collective action? Explain.

Race and ethnicity play some part in shaping people's attitudes toward feminism. In general, African Americans (especially African American women) express the greatest support of feminist goals, followed by whites, with Hispanic Americans holding somewhat more traditional attitudes regarding gender (Kane, 2000).

Resistance to feminism is also found in academic circles. Some sociologists charge that feminism ignores a growing body of evidence that men and women do think and act in somewhat different ways, which may make complete gender equality impossible. Furthermore, say critics, with its drive to increase women's presence in the workplace, feminism undervalues the crucial and unique contribution women make to the development of children, especially in the first years of life (Baydar & Brooks-Gunn, 1991; Popenoe, 1993b; Gibbs, 2001).

Finally, there is the question of *how* women should go about improving their social standing. A large majority of U.S. adults believe that women should have equal rights, but 70 percent also say that women should advance individually, according to their abilities; only 10 percent favor women's rights groups or collective action (NORC, 2007: 430).

For these reasons, most opposition to feminism is directed toward its socialist and radical forms, while support for liberal feminism is widespread. In addition, there is an unmistakable trend toward greater gender equality. In 1977, some 65 percent of all adults endorsed the statement "It is much better for everyone involved if the man is the achiever outside the home and the woman takes care of the home and family." By 2006, the share supporting this statement had dropped sharply, to 36 percent (NORC, 2007:321).

Student Snapshot

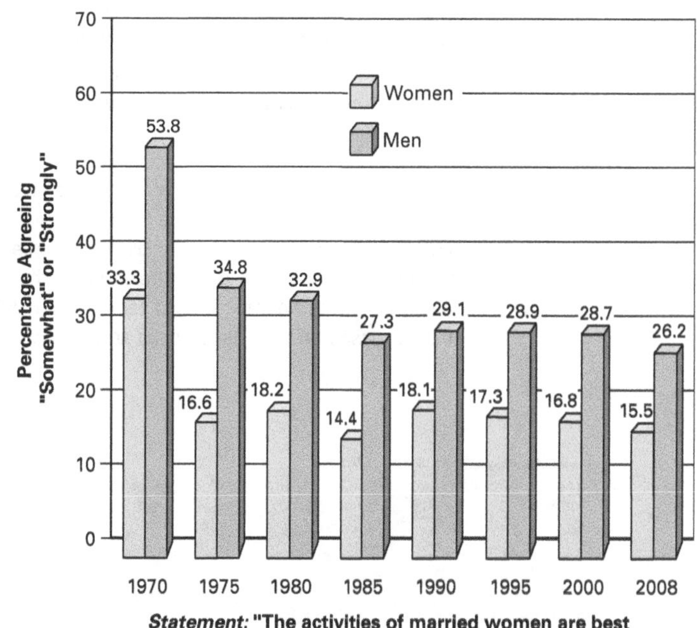

FIGURE 4 **Opposition to Feminism among First-Year College Students, 1970–2008**

The share of college students expressing antifeminist views declined after 1970. Men are still more likely than women to hold such attitudes.

Sources: Astin et al. (2002) and Pryor et al. (2008).

Gender: Looking Ahead

Predictions about the future are no more than educated guesses. Just as economists disagree about what the employment rate will be a year from now, sociologists can offer only general observations about the likely future of gender and society.

Change so far has been remarkable. A century ago, women were second-class citizens, without access to many jobs, barred from political office, and with no right to vote. Although women remain socially disadvantaged, the movement toward equality has surged ahead. Two-thirds of people entering the workforce during the 1990s were women, and in 2000, for the first time, a majority of U.S. families had both husband and wife in the paid labor force. Today's economy depends a great deal on the earnings of women.

Many factors have contributed to this transformation. Perhaps most important, industrialization and recent advances in computer technology have shifted the nature of work from physically demanding tasks that favor male strength to jobs that require thought and imagination. This change puts women and men on an even footing. Also, because birth control technology has given us greater control over reproduction, women's lives are less constrained by unwanted pregnancies.

Many women and men have also deliberately pursued social equality. For example, complaints of sexual harassment in the workplace are now taken much more seriously than they were a generation ago. As more women assume positions of power in the corporate and political worlds, social changes in the twenty-first century may be as great as those that have already taken place.

Seeing Sociology in Everyday Life

Gender Stratification

Can you spot "gender messages" in the world around you?

As this chapter makes clear, gender is one of the basic organizing principles of everyday life. Most of the places we go and most of the activities we engage in as part of our daily routines are "gendered," meaning that they are defined as either more masculine or more feminine. Understanding this fact, corporations keep gender in mind when they market products to the public. Take a look at the ads below. In each case, can you explain how gender is at work in selling these products?

HINT Looking for "gender messages" in ads is a process that involves several levels of analysis. Start on the surface by noting everything obvious in the ad, including the setting, the background, and especially the people. Then notice how the people are shown—what they are doing, how they are situated, their facial expressions, how they are dressed, and how they appear to relate to each other. Finally, state what you think is the message of the ad, based on both the ad itself and also what you know about the surrounding society.

Images courtesy of The Advertising Archives

There are a lot of gender dynamics going on in this ad. What do you see?

Generally, our society defines cosmetics as feminine because most cosmetics are marketed toward women. How and why is this ad different?

What gender messages do you see in this ad?

Images courtesy of The Advertising Archives

Applying SOCIOLOGY in Everyday Life

1. Look through some recent magazines and select three advertisements that involve gender. In each case, provide analysis of how gender is used in the ad.

2. Watch several hours of children's television programming on a Saturday morning. Notice the advertising, which mostly sells toys and breakfast cereal. Keep track of what share of toys are "gendered," that is, aimed at one sex or the other. What traits do you associate with toys intended for boys and those intended for girls?

3. Do some research on the history of women's issues in your state. When was the first woman sent to Congress? What laws once existed that restricted the work women could do? Do any such laws exist today? Did your state support the passage of the Equal Rights Amendment or not? What share of political officials today are women?

MAKING THE GRADE

Gender Stratification

Gender and Inequality

GENDER refers to the meaning a culture attaches to being female or male.

- Evidence that gender is rooted in culture includes global comparisons by Margaret Mead and others showing how societies define what is feminine and masculine in various ways.
- Gender is not only about difference: Because societies give more power and other resources to men than to women, gender is an important dimension of social stratification. **Sexism** is built into the operation of social institutions.
- Although some degree of **patriarchy** is found almost everywhere, it varies throughout history and from society to society.

gender the personal traits and social positions that members of a society attach to being female or male

gender stratification the unequal distribution of wealth, power, and privilege between men and women

matriarchy a form of social organization in which females dominate males

patriarchy a form of social organization in which males dominate females

sexism the belief that one sex is innately superior to the other

Gender and Socialization

Through the socialization process, gender becomes part of our personalities (**gender identity**) and our actions (**gender roles**). All the major agents of socialization—family, peer groups, schools, and the mass media—reinforce cultural definitions of what is feminine and masculine.

gender roles (sex roles) attitudes and activities that a society links to each sex

Gender and Social Stratification

Gender stratification shapes **THE WORKPLACE**:

- A majority of women are now in the paid labor force, but 40% hold clerical or service jobs.
- Comparing full-time U.S. workers, women earn 78% as much as men.
- This gender difference in earnings results from differences in jobs, differences in family responsibilities, and discrimination.

Gender stratification shapes **FAMILY LIFE**:

- Most unpaid housework is performed by women, whether or not they hold jobs outside the home.
- Pregnancy and raising small children keep many women out of the labor force at a time when their male peers are making important career gains.

Gender stratification shapes **EDUCATION:**

- Women now earn 59% of all associate's and bachelor's degrees.
- Women make up 47% of law school students and are an increasing share of graduates in professions traditionally dominated by men, including medicine and business administration.

minority any category of people distinguished by physical or cultural difference that a society sets apart and subordinates

intersection theory analysis of the interplay of race, class, and gender, often resulting in multiple dimensions of disadvantage

sexual harassment comments, gestures, or physical contacts of a sexual nature that are deliberate, repeated, and unwelcome

Gender stratification shapes **POLITICS**:

- Until a century ago, almost no women held any elected office in the United States.
- In recent decades, the number of women in politics has increased significantly.
- Even so, the vast majority of elected officials, especially at the national level, are men.
- Women make up only about 14% of U.S. military personnel.

INTERSECTION THEORY investigates the factors of race, class, and gender, which combine to cause special disadvantages for some categories of people.

- Women of color encounter greater social disadvantages than white women and earn much less than white men.
- Because all women have a distinctive social identity and are disadvantaged, they are a minority, although most white women do not think of themselves this way.

VIOLENCE AGAINST WOMEN AND MEN is a widespread problem that is linked to how a society defines gender. Related issues include

- **sexual harassment**, which mostly victimizes women because our culture encourages men to be assertive and to see women in sexual terms.
- **pornography**, which portrays women as sexual objects. Many see pornography as a moral issue; because pornography dehumanizes women, it is also a power issue.

Theoretical Analysis of Gender

The **STRUCTURAL-FUNCTIONAL APPROACH** suggests that

- in preindustrial societies, distinctive roles for males and females reflect biological differences between the sexes.
- in industrial societies, marked gender inequality becomes dysfunctional and gradually decreases.

Talcott Parsons described gender differences in terms of complementary roles that promote the social integration of families and society as a whole.

The **SYMBOLIC-INTERACTION APPROACH** suggests that

- individuals use gender as one element of their personal performances as they socially construct reality through everyday interactions.
- gender plays a part in shaping almost all our everyday experiences.

Because our society defines men as having more value than women, the sex roles that define how women and men should behave place men in control of social situations; women play a more deferential role.

The **SOCIAL-CONFLICT APPROACH** suggests that

- gender is an important dimension of social inequality and social conflict.
- gender inequality benefits men and disadvantages women.

Friedrich Engels tied gender stratification to the rise of private property and a class hierarchy. Marriage and the family are strategies by which men control their property through control of the sexuality of women. Capitalism exploits everyone by paying men low wages and assigning women the task of maintaining the home.

See the Applying Theory table, "Gender" .

Feminism

FEMINISM

- endorses the social equality of women and men and opposes patriarchy and sexism.
- seeks to eliminate violence against women.
- advocates giving women control over their reproduction.

There are three types of feminism:

- Liberal feminism seeks equal opportunity for both sexes within the existing society.
- Socialist feminism claims that gender equality will come about by replacing capitalism with socialism.
- Radical feminism seeks to eliminate the concept of gender itself and to create an egalitarian and gender-free society.

Today, only 20% of U.S. adults say they oppose feminism. Most opposition is directed toward socialist and radical feminism. Support for liberal feminism is widespread.

feminism support of social equality for women and men, in opposition to patriarchy and sexism

See the Applying Theory table, "Feminism".

MAKING THE GRADE

Sample Test Questions

Multiple-Choice Questions

1. Gender is not just a matter of difference but also a matter of

a. power.
b. wealth.
c. prestige.
d. All of the above are correct.

2. The anthropologist Margaret Mead studied gender in three societies in New Guinea and found that

a. all societies define femininity in much the same way.
b. all societies define masculinity in much the same way.
c. what is feminine in one society may be masculine in another.
d. the meaning of gender is changing everywhere toward greater equality.

3. For all of us raised in U.S. society, gender shapes our

a. feelings.
b. thoughts.
c. actions.
d. All of the above are correct.

4. There is a "beauty myth" in U.S. society that encourages

a. women to believe that their personal importance depends on their looks.
b. beautiful women to think that they do not need men.
c. men to improve their physical appearance to get the attention of women.
d. women to think they are as physically attractive as today's men are.

5. In the United States, what share of women work for income?

a. 80 percent
b. 60 percent
c. 50 percent
d. 30 percent

6. In the U.S. labor force,

a. men and women have the same types of jobs.
b. men and women have the same pay.
c. women are still concentrated in several types of jobs.
d. almost all working women hold "pink-collar jobs."

7. For which of the following categories of people in the United States is it true that women do more housework than men?

a. people who work for income
b. people who are married
c. people who have children
d. All of the above are correct.

8. In the United States, women in the labor force working full time earn how much for every dollar earned by men working full time?

a. 78 cents
b. 86 cents
c. 90 cents
d. 98 cents

9. After the 2008 elections, women held about what percentage of seats in Congress?

a. 7 percent
b. 17 percent
c. 37 percent
d. 57 percent

10. Which type of feminism accepts U.S. society as it is but wants to give women the same rights and opportunities as men?

a. socialist feminism
b. liberal feminism
c. radical feminism
d. All of the above are correct.

ANSWERS: 1 (d); 2 (c); 3 (d); 4 (a); 5 (b); 6 (c); 7 (d); 8 (a); 9 (b); 10 (b).

Essay Questions

1. How do the concepts "sex" and "gender" differ? In what ways are they related?
2. Why is gender considered a dimension of social stratification? How does gender intersect with other dimensions of inequality such as class, race, and ethnicity?

Race and Ethnicity

Shutterstock/Monkey Business Images

Ours is among the most racially and ethnically diverse of all societies. Racial and ethnic differences reflect people's traditional heritage and are a source of pride. At the same time, they are also an important foundation of social stratification.

Shutterstock

Race and Ethnicity

iStockphoto International/Royalty Free/Radu Razvan/Courtesy of www.istockphoto.com

PhotoEdit Inc./Tony Freeman

CHAPTER OVERVIEW

This chapter explains how race and ethnicity are created by society. Both race and ethnicity are not only matters of difference but also dimensions of social inequality.

Bryant Mason

On a cool November morning in New York City, the instructor of a sociology class at Bronx Community College is leading a small-group discussion of race and ethnicity. He explains that the meaning of both concepts is far less clear than most people think. Then he asks, "How do you describe yourself?"

Eva Rodriguez leans forward in her chair and is quick to respond. "Who am I? Or should I say what am I? This is hard for me to answer. Most people think of race as black and white. But it's not. I have both black and white ancestry in me, but you know what? I don't think of myself in that way. I don't think of myself in terms of race at all. It would be better to call me Puerto Rican or Hispanic. Personally, I prefer the term 'Latina.' Calling myself Latina says I have a mixed racial heritage, and that's what I am. I wish more people understood that race is not clear-cut."

This chapter examines the meaning of race and ethnicity. There are now millions of people in the United States who, like Eva Rodriguez, do not think of themselves in terms of a single category but as having a mix of ancestry.

The Social Meaning of Race and Ethnicity

As the opening to this chapter suggests, people frequently confuse race and ethnicity. For this reason, we begin with some definitions.

Race

A **race** is *a socially constructed category of people who share biologically transmitted traits that members of a society consider important.* People may classify one another racially based on physical characteristics such as skin color, facial features, hair texture, and body shape.

Racial diversity appeared among our human ancestors as the result of living in different geographic regions of the world. In regions of intense heat, for example, humans developed darker skin (from the natural pigment melanin) as protection from the sun; in regions with moderate climates, people have lighter skin. Such differences are literally only skin deep because human beings the world over are members of a single biological species.

The striking variety of physical traits found today is also the product of migration; genetic characteristics once common to a single place (such as light skin or curly hair) are now found in many lands. Especially pronounced is the racial mix in the Middle East (that is, western Asia), historically a crossroads of migration. Greater physical uniformity characterizes more isolated people, such as the island-dwelling Japanese. But every population has some genetic mixture, and increasing contact among the world's people ensures even more blending of physical characteristics in the future.

Although we think of race in terms of biological elements, race is a socially constructed concept. It is true that human beings differ in any number of ways involving physical traits, but a "race" comes into being only when the members of a society decide that some physical trait (such as skin color or eye shape) actually *matters.*

Because race is a matter of social definitions, it is a highly variable concept. For example, the members of U.S. society consider racial differences more important than people of many other countries. We also tend to "see" three racial categories—typically, black, white, and Asian—while people in other societies identify many more categories. People in Brazil, for example, distinguish between *branca* (white), *parda* (brown), *morena* (brunette), *mulata* (mulatto), *preta* (black), and *amarela* (yellow) (Inciardi, Surratt, & Telles, 2000).

In addition, race may be defined differently by various categories of people within a society. In the United States, for example, research shows that white people "see" black people as having darker skin than black people do (Hill, 2002).

The meanings and importance of race not only differ from place to place but also change over time. Back in 1900, for example, it was common in the United States to consider people of Irish, Italian, or

race a socially constructed category of people who share biologically transmitted traits that members of a society consider important

ethnicity a shared cultural heritage

SEEING SOCIOLOGY in Everyday Life

Researchers have found that biracial and multiracial people choose different racial identities in different settings, depending on whom they are with (Harris & Sim, 2002). Have you ever experienced such a "racial shift"? Explain.

Joel Gordon Photography

Leong Ka Tai

Corbis – NY/Owen Franken

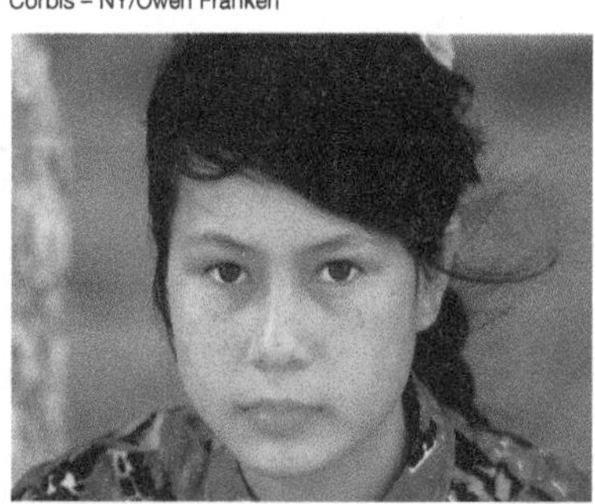

Corbis – NY/Charles O'Rear

Paul W. Liebhardt

Lisl Dennis

The range of biological variation in human beings is far greater than any system of racial classification allows. This fact is made obvious by trying to place all of the people pictured here into simple racial categories.

Jewish ancestry as "nonwhite." By 1950, however, this was no longer the case, and such people today are considered part of the "white" category (Loveman, 1999; Brodkin, 2007).

Today, the Census Bureau allows people to describe themselves using more than one racial category (offering six single-race options and fifty-seven multiracial options). Our society officially recognizes a wide range of multiracial people (U.S. Census Bureau, 2008).

Racial Types

Scientists invented the concept of "race" more than a century ago as they tried to organize the world's physical diversity into three racial types. They called people with relatively light skin and fine hair *Caucasoid,* people with darker skin and coarse hair *Negroid,* and people with yellow or brown skin and distinctive folds on the eyelids *Mongoloid.*

Sociologists consider such terms misleading at best and harmful at worst. For one thing, no society contains biologically "pure" people. The skin color of people we might call "Caucasoid" (or "Indo-European," "Caucasian," or more commonly, "white") ranges from very light (typical in Scandinavia) to very dark (in southern India). The same variation exists among so-called "Negroids" ("Africans" or more commonly, "black" people) and "Mongoloids"("Asians"). In fact, many "white" people (say, in southern India) actually have darker skin than many "black" people (the Aborigines of Australia). Overall, the three racial categories differ in just 6 percent of their genes, and there is actually more genetic variation *within* each category than *between* categories. This means that two people in the European nation of Sweden, randomly selected, are likely to have at least as much genetic difference as a Swede and a person in the African nation of Senegal (Harris & Sim, 2002; American Sociological Association, 2003; California Newsreel, 2003).

So how important is race? From a biological point of view, knowing people's racial category allows us to predict almost nothing about them. Why, then, do societies make so much of race? Such categories allow societies to rank people in a hierarchy, giving some people more money, power, and prestige than others and allowing some people to feel that they are inherently "better" than others. Because race may matter so much, societies may construct racial categories in extreme ways. Throughout much of the twentieth century, for example, many southern states labeled as "colored" anyone with as little as one thirty-second African ancestry (that is, one African American great-great-great-grandparent). Today, the law allows parents to declare the race of a child (or not) as they wish. Even so, most members of U.S. society are still very sensitive to people's racial backgrounds.

SEEING SOCIOLOGY in Everyday Life

Do you think all U.S. people of color, rich and poor alike, should be considered minorities? Why or why not?

minority any category of people distinguished by physical or cultural difference that a society sets apart and subordinates

prejudice a rigid and unfair generalization about an entire category of people

stereotype a simplified description applied to every person in some category

Table 1 Racial and Ethnic Categories in the United States, 2007

Racial or Ethnic Classification*	Approximate U.S. Population	Share of Total Population
Hispanic descent	**45,427,437**	**15.1%**
Mexican	29,166,981	9.7
Puerto Rican	4,120,205	1.4
Cuban	1,611,478	0.5
Other Hispanic	10,528,773	3.5
African descent	**38,756,452**	**12.8**
Nigerian	225,284	0.1
Ethiopian	159,809	0.1
Somalian	90,363	<
Other African	38,280,996	12.7
Native American descent	**2,365,347**	**0.8**
American Indian	1,922,043	0.6
Alaska Native Tribes	110,556	<
Other Native American	332,748	0.1
Asian or Pacific Island descent	**13,667,962**	**4.4**
Chinese	3,045,592	1.0
Asian Indian	2,570,166	0.9
Filipino	2,412,446	0.8
Vietnamese	1,508,489	0.5
Korean	1,344,171	0.4
Japanese	803,092	0.3
Cambodian	218,624	0.1
Other Asian or Pacific Islander	1,765,382	0.6
West Indian descent	**2,231,842**	**0.7**
Arab descent	**1,545,982**	**0.5**
Non-Hispanic European descent	**198,696,006**	**65.9**
German	50,756,529	16.8
Irish	36,495,800	12.1
English	28,178,670	9.3
Italian	17,849,848	5.9
Polish	9,976,358	3.3
French	9,616,662	3.2
Scottish	6,019,281	2.0
Dutch	5,071,425	1.7
Norwegian	4,655,711	1.5
Two or more races	**6,509,013**	**2.2**

*People of Hispanic descent may be of any race. Many people also identify with more than one ethnic category. Therefore, figures total more than 100 percent.

< indicates less than 1/10 of 1 percent.

Source: U.S. Census Bureau (2008).

A Trend toward Mixture

Over many generations and throughout the Americas, the genetic traits from around the world have become mixed. Many "black" people have a significant Caucasoid ancestry, just as many "white" people have some Negroid genes. Whatever people may think, race is not a black-and-white issue.

Today, people are more willing to define themselves as multiracial. On the most recent (2007) U.S. Census survey, almost 7 million people described themselves by checking two or more racial categories. And the official number of interracial births has tripled over the past twenty years to about 175,000 annually, almost 4 percent of all births.

Living in a multiracial family surely encourages people to think about the meaning of race. Seeing Sociology in the News later in this chapter provides one example.

Ethnicity

Ethnicity is *a shared cultural heritage.* People define themselves—or others—as members of an *ethnic category* based on common ancestry, language, or religion that gives them a distinctive social identity. The United States is a multiethnic society. Even though we favor the English language, more than 56 million people (20 percent of the U.S. population) speak Spanish, Italian, German, French, Chinese, or some other language in their homes. In California, about 45 percent of the population does so (U.S. Census Bureau, 2008).

With regard to religion, the United States is a predominantly Protestant nation, but most people of Spanish, Italian, and Polish descent are Roman Catholic, and many of Greek, Ukrainian, and Russian descent belong to the Eastern Orthodox church. More than 6 million Jewish Americans have ancestral ties to various nations around the world. The population of Muslim men and women is rapidly increasing and is generally estimated at between 2 and 3 million (Pew Research Center, 2007b).

Like race, the concept of "ethnicity" is socially constructed, becoming important only because society defines it that way. For example, U.S. society defines people of Spanish descent as "Latin," even though Italy probably has a more "Latin" culture than Spain. People of Italian descent are not viewed as Latin but as "European" and therefore less different (Camara, 2000; Brodkin, 2007). Like racial differences, the importance of ethnic differences can change over time. A century ago, Catholics and Jews were considered "different" in the mostly Protestant United States. This is much less true today.

Keep in mind that *race* is constructed from *biological* traits and *ethnicity* is constructed from *cultural* traits. However, the two often go hand in hand. For example, Japanese Americans have distinctive physical traits and, for those who hold to a traditional way of life, a

Marcos Chapa attends college in San Diego and lives in a community where most people are in some minority category.

Marianne Blumquist attends a community college in a small town an hour west of Minneapolis, where there are few racial or ethnic minorities.

SEEING SOCIOLOGY in Everyday Life

Do you see stereotypes in common phrases such as "French kiss," "Dutch treat," "Indian giver," or being "gypped" (a reference to Gypsies)? Explain.

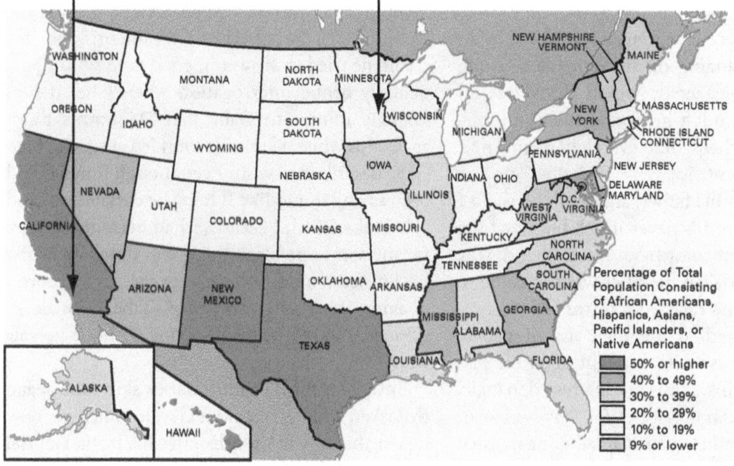

Seeing Ourselves

NATIONAL MAP 1

Where the Minority Majority Already Exists

Minorities are now in the majority in four states—Hawaii, California, New Mexico, and Texas—and the District of Columbia. At the other extreme, Vermont and Maine have the lowest share of racial and ethnic minorities (about 5 percent each). Why do you think states with high minority populations are located in the South and Southwest?

Source: U.S. Census Bureau (2008).

distinctive culture as well. Table 1 presents the most recent data on the racial and ethnic diversity of the United States.

On an individual level, people play up or play down cultural traits, depending on whether they want to fit in or stand apart from the surrounding society. Immigrants may drop their cultural traditions or, like many people of Native American descent in recent years, try to revive their heritage. For most people, ethnicity is more complex than race because they identify with several ethnic backgrounds. The golf star Tiger Woods describes himself as one-eighth American Indian, one-fourth Thai, and one-fourth Chinese, as well as one-eighth white and one-fourth black (J. E. White, 1997).

Minorities

March 3, Dallas, Texas. *The lobby of just about any hotel in a major U.S. city presents a lesson in contrasts: The majority of the guests checking in are white; the majority of hotel employees who carry luggage, serve food, and clean the rooms are racial or ethnic minorities.*

A **minority** is *any category of people distinguished by physical or cultural difference that a society sets apart and subordinates.* Minority standing can be based on race, ethnicity, or both. As shown in Table 1, nonHispanic white people (66 percent of the total) are still a majority of the U.S. population. But the share of minorities is increasing. Today, minorities are a majority in four states (California, New Mexico, Texas, and Hawaii) and in sixteen of the country's 100 largest cities. By about 2050, minorities are likely to form a majority of the entire U.S. population. National Map 1 shows where a minority majority already exists.

Minorities have two important characteristics. First, they share a *distinctive identity,* which may be based on physical or cultural traits. Second, minorities experience *subordination.* As the rest of this chapter shows, U.S. minorities typically have lower income, lower occupational prestige, and limited schooling. These facts mean that class, race, and ethnicity, as well as gender, are overlapping and reinforcing dimensions of social stratification. The Thinking About Diversity box later in this chapter profiles the struggles of recent Latin American immigrants.

Of course, not all members of any minority category are disadvantaged. Some Latinos are quite wealthy, certain Chinese Americans are celebrated business leaders, and African Americans are among our nation's political leaders. But even job success rarely allows individuals to escape their minority standing. Race or ethnicity often serves as a *master status* that overshadows personal accomplishments.

Minorities usually make up a small proportion of a society's population, but this is not always the case. Black South Africans are disadvantaged even though they are a numerical majority in their country. In the United States, women represent slightly more than half the population but are still struggling for all the opportunities and privileges enjoyed by men.

Prejudice and Stereotypes

November 19, Jerusalem, Israel. *We are driving along the outskirts of this historical city—a holy place to Jews, Christians, and Muslims—when Razi, our taxi driver, spots a small group of Falasha—Ethiopian Jews—on a street corner. "Those people over there," he points as he*

Seeing SOCIOLOGY in the 

Newsweek

Beyond Just Black and White: Why I Was So Eager to Claim My Biracial Son for My Own Side

By RAINA KELLEY
February 2, 2009

When I took my newly born son from the nurse's arms, I did the expected counting of his fingers and toes. I checked under his cap for hair and flexed his little limbs. Once confident he was whole and healthy, I began to wonder how dark his skin would get. As a black woman married to one of the world's fairest men, I worried that our son would be so light-skinned as to appear Caucasian, and I wanted him to look black. After we all came home from the hospital this past June, I Googled newborn eye color to reassure myself that Gabriel's eyes wouldn't change from my shade of brown to my husband's green. I brushed up on my genetics, and though I discovered that curly hair is a dominant trait, Gabe has straight brown locks that stick up in a cowlick just like his dad's—not the wild curls I struggle to keep under control. Undaunted by these failures to find Gabe's blackness, I inspected my son's skin daily for the Mongolian spots common in African-American babies, but his skin was as smooth as . . . alabaster.

It was time to face facts. One day, I would be an old black lady hanging on the arm of a young white man who passersby would think was an obliging stranger but who was actually my offspring. It didn't help that everywhere my new nuclear family went, we were told that our son was the picture of his father, and, well, he is. So I began to wonder, if it's never much bothered me that I'm a different color from my husband, why was I as rigid as a Klan member when it came to identifying my son's race from birth?

It never occurred to me then that if people thought my son was white, it might make life easier on him. Obviously, I was not interested in logic. I just wanted to claim Gabriel for "my" side—in league with his mother against small minds, casual racism and discrimination. So even though Gabe still appeared Caucasian, I grew more obsessive in my racial cataloging. I'd ask my spouse embarrassingly leading questions: "Do you think you have a black son?" "Is it weird having a black kid?" "Would it be strange for you if Gabe became the second African-American president?" To his credit, he tried to answer in good faith until a particularly brutal interrogation when I heard him jokingly mutter to Gabe that "Mommy's racist against us white people." It sounded absurd to hear Gabe described as white even though I myself had been saying things like "I hope he darkens up" and "He looks Dutch." Clearly, I had become so eager for my son to be black that I was tiptoeing across the line from mildly offensive to racist. . . . Can you imagine the reverse scenario? Gabe born dark-skinned and my husband saying, "I hope he gets whiter"?

But by his third month, Gabe's skin tone began to darken and my hormones leveled off; I can now report that, seven months after his birth, Gabriel is the exact shade you'd get if you mixed his father and me up in a paint can—a color I call golden. This has made me realize that I want Gabe to be

---

speaks, "they are different. They don't drive cars. They don't want to improve themselves. Even when our country offers them schooling, they don't take it." He shakes his head at the Ethiopians and drives on.

Prejudice is *a rigid and unfair generalization about an entire category of people*. Prejudice is unfair because *all* people in some category are described as the same, based on little or no direct evidence. Prejudice may target people of a particular social class, sex, sexual orientation, age, political affiliation, physical disability, race, or ethnicity.

Prejudices are *prejudgments* that can be either positive or negative. Our positive prejudices tend to exaggerate the virtues of people like ourselves, and our negative prejudices condemn those who differ from us. Negative prejudice can be expressed as anything from mild dislike to outright hostility. Because such attitudes are rooted in culture, everyone has at least some prejudice.

Prejudice often takes the form of a **stereotype** (*stereo* is derived from a Greek word meaning "solid"), *a simplified description applied to every person in some category*. Many white people hold stereotypical views of minorities. Stereotyping is especially harmful to minorities in the workplace. If company officials see workers only in terms of a stereotype, they will make assumptions about their abilities, steering them toward certain jobs and limiting their access to better opportunities (R. L. Kaufman, 2002).

Minorities, too, stereotype whites and other minorities (T. W. Smith, 1996; Cummings & Lambert, 1997). Surveys show, for example, that more African Americans than whites express the belief that Asians engage in unfair business practices and that more Asians than whites criticize Hispanics for having too many children (Perlmutter, 2002).

Measuring Prejudice: The Social Distance Scale

One measure of prejudice is *social distance*, how closely people are willing to interact with members of some category. In the 1920s, Emory Bogardus developed the *social distance scale* shown in Figure 1. Bogardus (1925) asked students at U.S. colleges and universities to look at this scale and indicate how closely they were willing to interact with people in thirty racial and ethnic categories. People express the greatest social distance (most negative prejudice) by declaring that a particular category of people should be barred from the country entirely (point 7); at the other extreme, people express the least social distance (most social acceptance) by saying they would accept members of a particular category into their family through marriage (point 1).

Bogardus (1925, 1967; Owen, Elsner, & McFaul, 1977) found that people felt much more social distance from some categories than from others. In general, students in his surveys expressed the most social distance from Hispanics, African Americans, Asians, and Turks, indicating that they would be willing to tolerate such people as co-workers but not as neighbors, friends, or family members. Students expressed the least social distance from those from northern and western Europe, including English and Scottish people, and also Canadians, indicating that they were willing to include them in their families by marriage.

proud of his entire heritage. Why does my son have to bear the legacy of a one-drop rule that is the direct intellectual descendant of slavery and Jim Crow? The very concept, that even the smallest amount of black blood in your ancestry makes you African-American, harks back to the early 20th century when states including Texas and Virginia passed laws to protect the "purity" of the white race. Is this really a concept that needs to be perpetuated? . . .

For Gabriel's sake, I'm going to try to stop playing the black-vs.-white game, since my son is actually neither white nor black. He's biracial, and there are hundreds of thousands of little golden children out there just like him. One of them even grew up to be president of the United States. The latest U.S. Census numbers indicate that there are [almost 7] million biracial Americans. . . .

New mothers being insecure, I've now begun to wonder whether my constant harping about skin tone warped my infant son for life. Did I already doom him to rebel against my dichotomous racial regime, reject his blackness altogether and move to the Netherlands, the land of his father's people? Or maybe he'll grow up to look upon his father as the Man, his mother as a race traitor, and move to Namibia to start a new black-separatist movement? Or maybe he'll just be himself, because when you juxtapose Obama's comments about society with the reality of his election, isn't the real secret of American freedom that we don't have to accept the roles that society assigns us? Our newly elected president ignored the racial stereotyping that seemed to limit what he could accomplish in this country—and he didn't do it by passively accepting society's assessment of his skin tone. Perhaps as the number of multiracial Americans continues to grow, there will be a plurality of golden people who are impossible to positively identify as one race or the other. And the rest of us who can be easily categorized will be forced to accept that color does not contribute to the content of one's character because we won't know which set of stereotypes to apply to whom. I want my son to grow up wearing his biracial heritage like an invisibility cloak, able to move unseen among people's prejudices—impervious to racial profiling. But I will prepare him for a world that may think he is black or white, even though he is golden.

WHAT DO YOU THINK?

1. When her son was born, did this mother make too much of trying to determine his race? Why or why not?
2. How is thinking about race a special challenge for mixed-race couples? Explain.
3. Do you think that as he goes through life, Gabe will decide to be one race at some times and another race at others? Explain.

Adapted from the original article, "Beyond Just Black and White" by Raina Kelley, published in *Newsweek*, February 2, 2009.

What patterns of social distance do we find among college students today? A recent study using the same social distance scale reported three major findings (Parrillo & Donoghue, 2005):[1]

1. **Student opinion shows a trend toward greater social acceptance.** Today's students express less social distance from all minorities than students did several decades ago. Figure 1 shows that the mean (average) score on the social distance scale declined from 2.14 in 1925 to 1.93 in 1977 and 1.44 in 2001. Respondents (81 percent of whom were white) showed notably greater acceptance of African Americans, a category that moved up from near the bottom in 1925 to the top one-third in 2001.
2. **People see less difference between various minorities.** The earliest studies found the difference between the highest- and lowest-ranked minorities (the range of averages) equal to almost three points on the scale. As the figure shows, the most recent research produced a range of averages of less than one point, indicating that today's students see fewer differences between various categories of people.
3. **The terrorist attacks of September 11, 2001, may have reduced social acceptance of Arabs and Muslims.** The most recent study was conducted just a few weeks after September 11, 2001. Perhaps the fact that the nineteen men who attacked the World Trade Center and the Pentagon were Arabs and Muslims is part of the reason that students ranked these categories last on the social distance scale. However, not a single student gave Arabs or Muslims a 7, indicating that they should be barred from the country. On the contrary, the 2001 mean scores (1.94 for Arabs and 1.88 for Muslims) show higher social acceptance than students in 1977 expressed toward eighteen of the thirty categories of people studied.

Racism

A powerful and harmful form of prejudice, **racism** is *the belief that one racial category is innately superior or inferior to another.* Racism has existed throughout world history. Despite their many achievements, the ancient Greeks, the peoples of India, and the Chinese all regarded people unlike themselves as inferior.

Racism has also been widespread throughout the history of the United States, where ideas about racial inferiority supported slavery. Today, overt racism in this country has decreased because more people believe in evaluating others, in Martin Luther King Jr.'s words, "not by the color of their skin but by the content of their character."

Even so, racism remains a serious social problem, as some people think that certain racial and ethnic categories are smarter than

[1]Parrillo and Donoghue dropped seven of the categories used by Bogardus (Armenians, Czechs, Finns, Norwegians, Scots, Swedes, and Turks), claiming they were no longer visible minorities. They added nine new categories (Africans, Arabs, Cubans, Dominicans, Haitians, Jamaicans, Muslims, Puerto Ricans, and Vietnamese), claiming that these are visible minorities today. This change probably encouraged higher social distance scores, making the trend toward decreasing social distance all the more significant.

racism the belief that one racial category is innately superior or inferior to another

scapegoat a person or category of people, typically with little power, whom people unfairly blame for their own troubles

SEEING SOCIOLOGY in Everyday Life

Do you think students on your campus have become more accepting of social diversity? Explain why or why not.

THINKING ABOUT DIVERSITY: RACE, CLASS, & GENDER

Hard Work: The Immigrant Life in the United States

Early in the morning, it is already hot on the streets of Houston as a line of pickup trucks snakes slowly into a dusty yard, where 200 laborers have been gathering since dawn, each hoping for a day's work. The driver of the first truck opens his window and tells the foreman that he is looking for a crew to spread boiling tar on a roof. Abdonel Cespedes, the foreman, turns to the crowd, and after a few minutes, three workers step forward and climb into the back of the truck. The next driver is looking for two experienced housepainters. The scene is repeated over and over as men and a few women leave to dig ditches, spread cement, hang drywall, open clogged septic tanks, or crawl under houses to poison rats.

As each driver pulls into the yard, the foreman asks, "How much?" Most offer $5 an hour. Cespedes automatically responds, "$7.25; the going rate is $7.25 for an hour's hard work." Sometimes he convinces them to pay that much, but usually not. The workers, who come from Mexico, El Salvador, and Guatemala, know that dozens of them will end up with no work at all this day. Most accept $5 or $6 an hour because they know that when the day is over, $50 is better than nothing.

Labor markets like this one are common in large cities, especially across the southwestern United States. The surge in immigration in recent years has brought millions of people to this country in search of work, and most have little schooling and speak little English.

Manuel Barrera has taken a day's work moving the entire contents of a store to a storage site. He arrives at the boarded-up building and gazes at the mountains of heavy furniture that he must carry out to a moving van, drive across town, and then carry again. He sighs when he thinks about how hot it is outside and realizes that it is even hotter inside the building. He will have no break for lunch. No one says anything about toilets. Barrera shakes his head: "I will do this kind of work because it puts food on the table. But I did not foresee it would turn out like this."

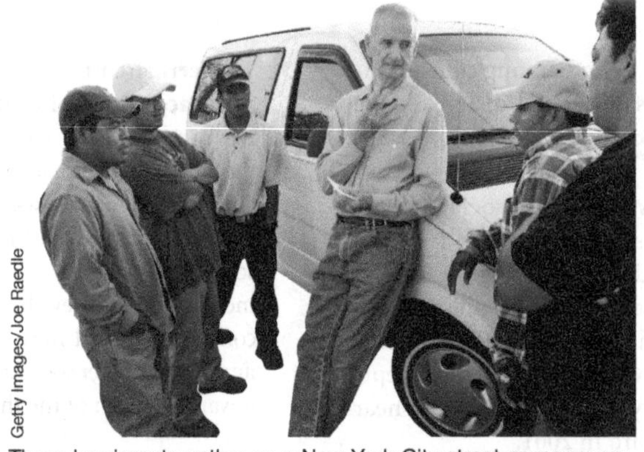

Getty Images/Joe Raedle

These immigrants gather on a New York City street corner every morning hoping to be hired for construction work that pays about $60 a day with no benefits.

The hard truth is that immigrants to the United States do the jobs that no one else wants. At the bottom level of the national economy, they perform low-skill jobs in restaurants and hotels and on construction crews, and they work in private homes cooking, cleaning, and caring for children. Across the United States, about half of all housekeepers, household cooks, tailors, and restaurant waiters are men or women born abroad. Few immigrants make much more than the official minimum wage ($7.25 in 2009), and rarely do immigrant workers receive any health or pension benefits. Many well-off families take the labor of immigrants as much for granted as their air-conditioned cars and comfortable homes.

WHAT DO YOU THINK?

1. In what ways do you or members of your family depend on the low-paid labor of immigrants?
2. Do you favor allowing the 12 million people who entered this country illegally to earn citizenship? What should be done?
3. Should the U.S. government act to reduce the number of immigrants entering this country in the future? Why or why not?

Sources: Booth (1998), Tumulty (2006), and U.S. Department of Labor (2008a).

others. As the Seeing Sociology in Everyday Life box later in this chapter explains, however, racial differences in mental abilities result from environment rather than biology.

Theories of Prejudice

Where does prejudice come from? Social scientists provide several answers to this question, focusing on frustration, personality, culture, and social conflict.

Scapegoat Theory

Scapegoat theory holds that prejudice springs from frustration among people who are themselves disadvantaged (Dollard et al., 1939). For instance, take the case of a white woman who is frustrated by the low pay she receives from her assembly-line job in a textile factory. Directing hostility at the powerful factory owners carries the obvious risk of being fired; therefore, she may blame her low pay on the presence of minority co-workers. Her prejudice does not improve her situation, but it is a relatively safe way to express anger, and it

MAKING THE GRADE

On the social distance scale, the higher the number, the greater the social distance, meaning more negative prejudice.

MAKING THE GRADE

The text presents four theories of prejudice. Check your understanding of each by completing this sentence: "This theory explains that prejudice is caused by . . ."

Student Snapshot

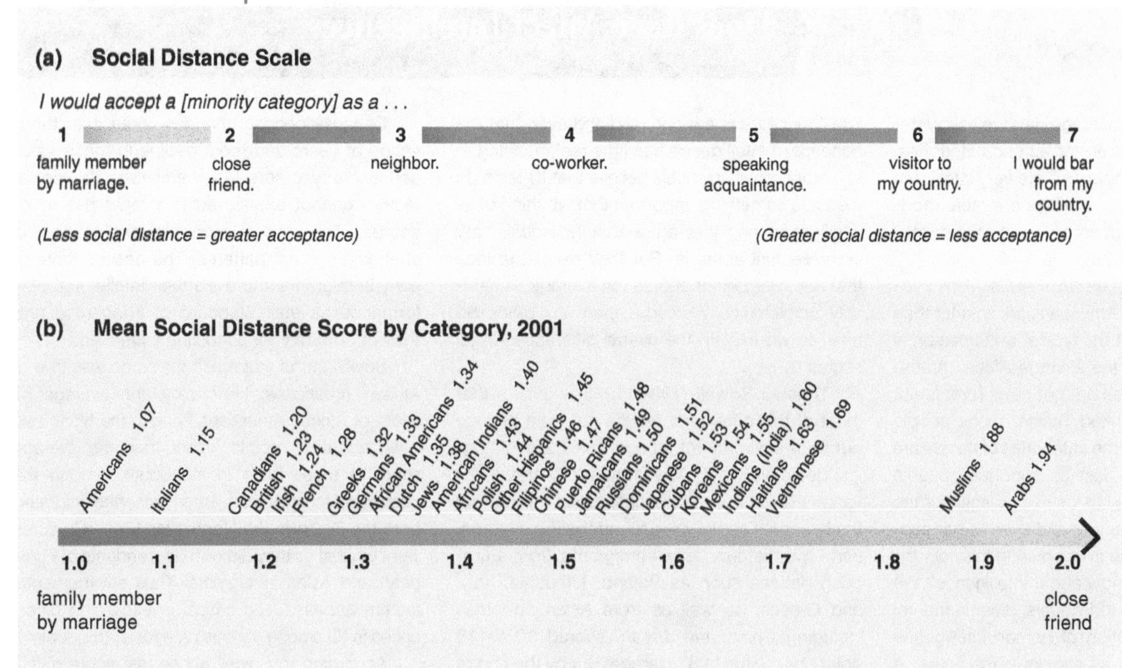

	1925	1946	1956	1966	1977	2001
(c) Mean Score for All Categories:	2.14	2.14	2.08	1.92	1.93	1.44
(d) Range of Averages:	2.85	2.57	1.75	1.55	1.38	0.87

FIGURE 1 **Bogardus Social Distance Research**

The social distance scale is a good way to measure prejudice. Part (a) illustrates the complete social distance scale, from least social distance at the far left to greatest social distance at the far right. Part (b) shows the mean (average) social distance score received by each category of people in 2001. Part (c) presents the overall mean score (the average of the scores received by all racial and ethnic categories) in specific years. These scores have fallen from 2.14 in 1925 to 1.44 in 2001, showing that students express less social distance toward minorities today than they did in the past. Part (d) shows the range of averages, the difference between the highest and lowest scores in given years (in 2001, for instance, it was 0.87, the difference between the high score of 1.94 for Arabs and the low score of 1.07 for Americans). This figure has also become smaller since 1925, indicating that today's students tend to see fewer differences between various categories of people.

Source: Parrillo & Donoghue (2005).

may give her the comforting feeling that at least she is superior to someone.

A **scapegoat,** then, is *a person or category of people, typically with little power, whom people unfairly blame for their own troubles.* Because they have little power and thus are usually "safe targets," minorities often are used as scapegoats.

Authoritarian Personality Theory

Theodor Adorno and colleagues (1950) considered extreme prejudice a personality trait of certain individuals. This conclusion is supported by research showing that people who show strong prejudice toward one minority are usually intolerant of all minorities. These *authoritarian personalities* rigidly conform to conventional cultural

MAKING THE GRADE

The box links differences in intelligence between categories of people to culture, not biology. The point is that such differences are not genetic, and culture matters in the types of human achievement that figure into intelligence.

SEEING SOCIOLOGY IN EVERYDAY LIFE

Does Race Affect Intelligence?

As we go through an average day, we encounter people of various racial and ethnic categories. We also deal with people who are very intelligent as well as those whose abilities are more modest. Is there a connection between race or ethnicity and intelligence?

Common stereotypes say there is. Many people believe that Asian Americans are smarter than white people and that the typical white person is more intelligent than the average African American. These stereotypes are not new. Throughout the history of the United States, many people have assumed that some categories of people are smarter than others. Just as important, people have used this thinking to justify privileges for the allegedly superior category and even to bar supposedly inferior people from entering this country.

So what do we know about intelligence? We know that people, as individuals, differ in mental abilities. The distribution of human intelligence forms a "bell curve," as shown in the figure. A person's *intelligence quotient* (IQ) is calculated as the person's mental age in years, as measured by a test, divided by the person's actual age in years, with the result multiplied by 100. An eight-year-old who performs like a ten-year-old has an IQ of $10 \div 8 = 1.25 \times 100 = 125$. Average performance yields an IQ of 100.

In a controversial study of intelligence and social inequality, Richard Herrnstein and Charles Murray (1994) claimed that race was related to measures of intelligence. They said that the average IQ for people with European ancestry was 100; for people with East Asian ancestry, 103; and for people with African ancestry, 90.

Such assertions go against our democratic and egalitarian beliefs that no racial type is naturally better than another. Because these findings can increase prejudice, critics charge that intelligence tests are not valid and even that the concept of intelligence has little real meaning.

Most social scientists believe that IQ tests do measure something important that we think of as intelligence, and they agree that *individuals* vary in intellectual aptitude. But they reject the idea that any *category* of people, on average, is naturally or biologically smarter than any other. So how do we explain the overall differences in IQ scores by race?

Thomas Sowell (1994, 1995) explains that most of this difference results not from biology but from environment. In some skillful sociological detective work, Sowell traced IQ scores for various racial and ethnic categories throughout the twentieth century. He found that on average, early-twentieth-century immigrants from European nations such as Poland, Lithuania, Italy, and Greece, as well as from Asian countries including China and Japan, scored 10 to 15 points below the U.S. average. But by the end of the twentieth century, people in these same categories had IQ scores that were average or above average. Among Italian Americans, for example, average IQ jumped almost 10 points; among Polish and Chinese Americans, the increase was almost 20 points.

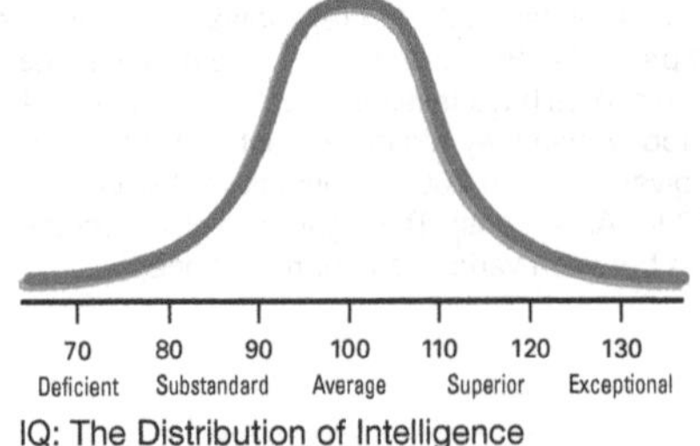

IQ: The Distribution of Intelligence

Because genetic changes occur over thousands of years and most people in these categories marry others like themselves, biological factors cannot explain such a rapid rise in IQ scores. The only reasonable explanation is changing cultural patterns. The descendants of early immigrants improved their intellectual performance as their standard of living rose and their opportunity for schooling increased.

Sowell found that much the same was true of African Americans. Historically, the average IQ score of African Americans living in the North has been about 10 points higher than the average score of those living in the South. Among the descendants of African Americans who migrated from the South to the North after 1940, IQ scores went up, just as they did with descendants of European and Asian immigrants. Thus environmental factors appear to be critical in explaining differences in IQ among various categories of people.

According to Sowell, these test score differences tell us that *cultural patterns matter.* Asians who score high on tests are no smarter than other people, but they have been raised to value learning and pursue excellence. African Americans are no less intelligent than anyone else, but they carry a legacy of disadvantage that can undermine self-confidence and discourage achievement.

WHAT DO YOU THINK?

1. If IQ scores reflect people's environment, are they valid measures of intelligence? Could they be harmful?
2. According to Thomas Sowell, why do some racial and ethnic categories show dramatic short-term gains in average IQ scores?
3. Do you think parents and schools influence a child's IQ score? If so, how?

values and see moral issues as clear-cut matters of right and wrong. People with authoritarian personalities also view society as naturally competitive and hierarchical, with "better" people (like themselves) inevitably dominating those who are weaker (all minorities).

Adorno and his colleagues also found the opposite pattern to be true: People who express tolerance toward one minority are likely to be accepting of all. They tend to be more flexible in their moral judgments and treat all people as equals.

prejudice a rigid and unfair generalization about an entire category of people

discrimination unequal treatment of various categories of people

institutional prejudice and discrimination bias built into the operation of society's institutions

MAKING THE GRADE

The importance of institutional prejudice and discrimination can be summed up like this: Prejudice and discrimination are found in individuals but are rooted in society itself.

Adorno thought that people with little schooling and those raised by cold and demanding parents tend to develop authoritarian personalities. Filled with anger and anxiety as children, they grow into hostile, aggressive adults who seek out scapegoats.

Culture Theory

A third theory claims that although extreme prejudice may be found in some people, some prejudice is found in everyone. Why? Because prejudice is part of the culture in which we all live and learn. The Bogardus social distance studies help prove the point. Bogardus found that students across the country had much the same attitudes toward specific racial and ethnic categories, feeling closer to some and more distant from others.

More evidence that prejudice is rooted in culture is the fact that minorities express the same attitudes as white people toward categories other than their own. Such patterns suggest that individuals hold prejudices because we live in a "culture of prejudice" that has taught us all to view certain categories of people as "better" or "worse" than others.

Conflict Theory

A fourth explanation proposes that prejudice is used as a tool by powerful people to oppress others. Anglos who look down on Latino immigrants in the Southwest, for example, can get away with paying the immigrants low wages for hard work. Similarly, all elites benefit when prejudice divides workers along racial and ethnic lines and discourages them from working together to advance their common interests (Geschwender, 1978; Olzak, 1989; Rothenberg, 2008).

According to another conflict-based argument, made by Shelby Steele (1990), minorities themselves encourage *race consciousness* to win greater power and privileges. Because of their historical disadvantage, minorities claim that they are victims entitled to special consideration based on their race. This strategy may bring short-term gains, but Steele cautions that such thinking often sparks a backlash from whites or others who oppose "special treatment" on the basis of race or ethnicity.

Discrimination

Closely related to prejudice is **discrimination,** *unequal treatment of various categories of people. Prejudice* refers to *attitudes,* but *discrimination* is a matter of *action.* Like prejudice, discrimination can be either positive (providing special advantages) or negative (creating obstacles) and ranges from subtle to extreme.

Institutional Prejudice and Discrimination

We typically think of prejudice and discrimination as the hateful ideas or actions of specific people. But Stokely Carmichael and Charles Hamilton (1967) pointed out that far greater harm results from **institutional prejudice and discrimination,** *bias built into the operation of society's institutions,* including schools, hospitals, the police, and the workplace. For example, researchers have found that banks reject home mortgage applications from minorities at a higher rate than those from white people, even when income and quality of neighborhood are held constant (Gotham, 1998; Blanton, 2007).

According to Carmichael and Hamilton, people are slow to condemn or even recognize institutional prejudice and discrimination because it often involves respected public officials and long-established traditions. A case in point is *Brown* v. *Board of Education of Topeka,* the 1954 Supreme Court decision that ended the legal segregation of schools. The principle of "separate but equal" schooling had been the law of the land, supporting racial inequality by allowing school segregation. Despite this change in the law, half a century later, most U.S. students still attend schools in which one race overwhelmingly predominates (KewalRamani et al., 2007). In 1991, the courts pointed

PhotoEdit Inc./David Young-Wolff

Recent research measuring student attitudes confirms the trend of declining prejudice toward all racial and ethnic categories. On your campus, does race or ethnicity guide people's choice in romantic attachments? Do some racial and ethnic categories mix more often than others? Explain your answer.

Patterns of Majority and Minority Interaction

pluralism a state in which people of all races and ethnicities are distinct but have equal social standing

assimilation the process by which minorities gradually adopt patterns of the dominant culture

segregation the physical and social separation of categories of people

genocide the systematic killing of one category of people by another

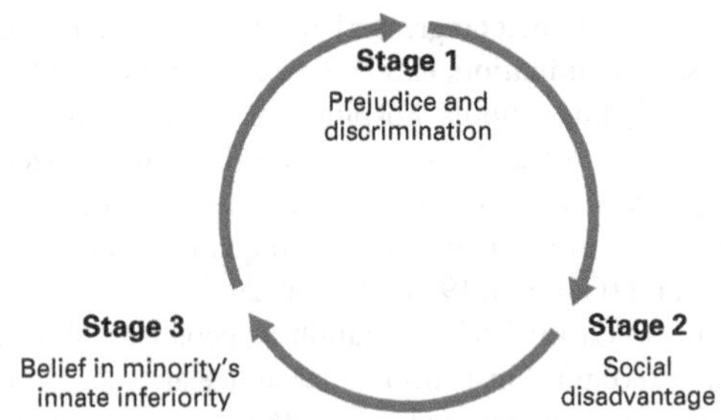

Stage 1: Prejudice and discrimination begin, often as an expression of ethnocentrism or an attempt to justify economic exploitation.

Stage 2: As a result of prejudice and discrimination, a minority is socially disadvantaged, occupying a low position in the system of social stratification.

Stage 3: This social disadvantage is then interpreted not as the result of earlier prejudice and discrimination but as evidence that the minority is innately inferior, unleashing renewed prejudice and discrimination by which the cycle repeats itself.

FIGURE 2 **Prejudice and Discrimination: The Vicious Circle**
Prejudice and discrimination can form a vicious circle, perpetuating themselves.

out that neighborhood schools will never provide equal education as long as our population is segregated, with most African Americans living in central cities and most white people and Asian Americans living in suburbs.

Prejudice and Discrimination: The Vicious Circle

Prejudice and discrimination reinforce each other. The Thomas theorem offers a simple explanation of this fact: *Situations that are defined as real become real in their consequences* (W. I. Thomas, 1966:301, orig. 1931).

As Thomas recognized, stereotypes become real to people who believe them and sometimes even to those who are victimized by them. Prejudice on the part of white people toward people of color does not produce *innate* inferiority, but it can produce *social* inferiority, pushing minorities into low-paying jobs, inferior schools, and racially segregated housing. Then, as white people interpret that social disadvantage as evidence that minorities do not measure up, they unleash a new round of prejudice and discrimination, giving rise to a vicious circle in which each perpetuates the other, as shown in Figure 2.

Majority and Minority: Patterns of Interaction

Sociologists describe patterns of interaction among racial and ethnic categories in a society in terms of four models: pluralism, assimilation, segregation, and genocide.

Pluralism

Pluralism is *a state in which people of all races and ethnicities are distinct but have equal social standing.* In other words, people who differ in appearance or social heritage all share resources roughly equally.

The United States is pluralistic to the extent that all people have equal standing under the law. In addition, large cities contain countless "ethnic villages," where people proudly display the traditions of their immigrant ancestors. These include New York's Spanish Harlem, Little Italy, and Chinatown; Philadelphia's Italian "South Philly"; Chicago's Little Saigon; and Latino East Los Angeles. New York City alone has more than 300 magazines, newspapers, and radio stations that publish in more than ninety languages (Logan, Alba, & Zhang, 2002; *Many Voices,* 2008; U.S. Department of Homeland Security, 2008b).

But the United States is not truly pluralistic, for three reasons. First, although most people value their cultural heritage, few want to live exclusively with others exactly like themselves (NORC, 2007). Second, our tolerance of social diversity goes only so far. One reaction to the rising number of U.S. minorities is a social movement to make English the nation's official language. Third, as you will see later in this chapter, people of various colors and cultures do *not* have equal social standing.

Assimilation

Many people think of the United States as a "melting pot" in which different nationalities blend together. But rather than everyone "melting" into some new cultural pattern, most minorities have adopted the dominant culture established by our earliest settlers. Why? Because doing so is both the path to upward social mobility and a way to escape the prejudice and discrimination directed at more visible foreigners. Sociologists use the term **assimilation** to describe *the process by which minorities gradually adopt patterns of the dominant culture.* Assimilation can involve changing modes of dress, values, religion, language, and friends.

The amount of assimilation varies by category. For example, Canadians have "melted" more than Cubans, the Dutch more than Dominicans, Germans more than the Japanese. Multiculturalists oppose making assimilation a goal because it suggests that minorities are a problem and the ones who need to do all the changing.

Note that assimilation involves changes in ethnicity but not in race. For example, many descendants of Japanese immigrants discard their ethnic traditions but retain their racial identity. For racial traits

miscegenation biological reproduction by partners of different racial categories

to diminish over generations, **miscegenation,** or *biological reproduction by partners of different racial categories,* must occur. Although interracial marriage is becoming more common, it still amounts to only 4 percent of all U.S. marriages (U.S. Census Bureau, 2008).

Segregation

Segregation is *the physical and social separation of categories of people.* Some minorities, especially religious orders like the Amish, voluntarily segregate themselves. However, majorities usually segregate minorities by excluding them. Residential neighborhoods, schools, occupations, hospitals, and even cemeteries may be segregated. Pluralism encourages distinctiveness without disadvantage, but segregation enforces separation that harms a minority.

Racial segregation has a long history in the United States, beginning with slavery and evolving into racially separated housing, schools, buses, and trains. Court decisions such as the 1954 *Brown* case have reduced *de jure* (Latin, "by law") discrimination in this country. However, *de facto* ("in actual fact") segregation continues in the form of countless neighborhoods that are home to people of a single race.

Despite some recent decline, segregation persists in the United States. For example, Livonia, Michigan, is 91 percent white, and neighboring Detroit is 83 percent African American. Kurt Metzger (2001) explains, "Livonia was pretty much created by white flight [from Detroit]." Further, research shows that across the country, whites (especially those with young children) avoid neighborhoods where African Americans live (Emerson, Yancey, & Chai, 2001; Krysan, 2002). At the extreme, Douglas Massey and Nancy Denton (1989) document the *hypersegregation* of poor African Americans in some inner cities. Hypersegregation means having little contact of any kind with people outside the local community. Hypersegregation is the daily experience of about 20 percent of poor African Americans and is a pattern found in about twenty-five large U.S. cities (Wilkes & Iceland, 2004).

Genocide

Genocide is *the systematic killing of one category of people by another.* This deadly form of racism and ethnocentrism violates nearly every recognized moral standard, yet it has occurred time and again in human history.

Genocide was common in the history of contact between Europeans and the original inhabitants of the Americas. From the sixteenth century on, the Spanish, Portuguese, English, French, and Dutch forcibly colonized vast empires. Although most native people died from diseases brought by Europeans, against which they had no natural defenses, many who opposed the colonizers were killed deliberately (Matthiessen, 1984; Sale, 1990).

Genocide also occurred during the twentieth century. During World War I, at least 1 million Armenians in Eastern Europe per-

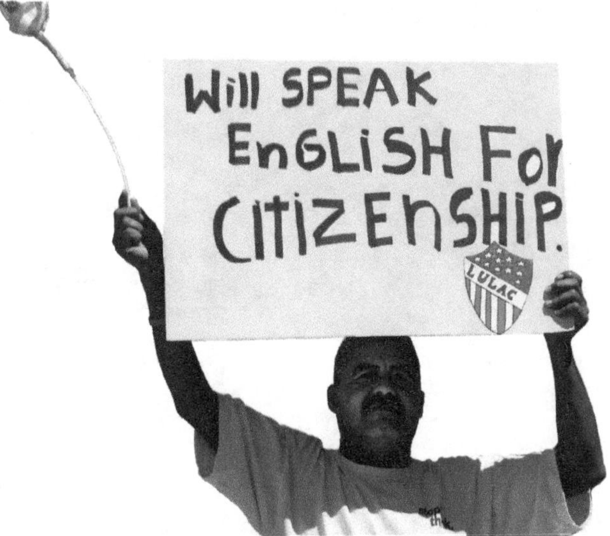

Should we expect people who come to the United States to change their language and other cultural patterns in order to "fit in," or should we expect them to hold onto their own traditions? Why?

ished under the rule of the Ottoman Empire. Soon after that, European Jews experienced a reign of terror known as the Holocaust during Adolf Hitler's rule in Germany. From about 1935 to 1945, the Nazis murdered more than 6 million Jewish men, women, and children, along with gay people, Gypsies, and people with handicaps. During the same period, the Soviet dictator Josef Stalin murdered on an even greater scale, killing perhaps 30 million real and imagined enemies during decades of violent rule. Between 1975 and 1980, Pol Pot's Communist regime in Cambodia butchered all "capitalists," a category that included anyone able to speak a Western language. In all, some 2 million people (one-fourth of the population) perished in the Cambodian "killing fields."

Tragically, genocide continues in the modern world. Recent examples include Hutus killing Tutsis in the African nation of Rwanda, Serbs killing Bosnians in the Balkans of Eastern Europe, and the killing of hundreds of thousands of people in the Darfur region of Sudan in Africa.

These four patterns of minority-majority interaction have all been played out in the United States. Although many people proudly point to patterns of pluralism and assimilation, it is also important to recognize the degree to which U.S. society has been built on segregation (of African Americans) and genocide (of Native Americans). The remainder of this chapter examines how these four patterns have shaped the history and present social standing of major racial and ethnic categories in the United States.

SEEING SOCIOLOGY in Everyday Life

In your city or town, are there minority neighborhoods? Which categories of people live there? To what degree is your community racially or ethnically segregated?

Western History Collections, University of Oklahoma Libraries. Phillips Collection

In an effort to force assimilation, the U.S. Bureau of Indian Affairs took American Indian children from their families and placed them in boarding schools like this one, Oklahoma's Riverside Indian School. There they were taught to speak English by non-Indian teachers with the goal of making them into "Americans."

Race and Ethnicity in the United States

Give me your tired, your poor,
Your huddled masses yearning to breathe free,
The wretched refuse of your teeming shore,
Send these, the homeless, tempest-tossed to me:
I lift my lamp beside the golden door.

These words by Emma Lazarus, inscribed on the Statue of Liberty, express cultural ideals of human dignity, personal freedom, and economic opportunity. The United States has provided more of the "good life" to more immigrants than any other nation. About 1.5 million immigrants come to this country every year, and their many ways of life create a social mosaic that is especially evident in large cities with many distinctive racial and ethnic neighborhoods.

However, as a survey of this country's racial and ethnic minorities will show, our country's golden door has opened more widely for some than for others. We turn next to the history and current social standing of the major categories of the U.S. population.

Native Americans

The term "Native Americans" refers to the hundreds of societies—including the Aztec, Inca, Aleuts, Cherokee, Zuni, Sioux, and Mohawk—that first settled the Western Hemisphere. Some 30,000 years before Christopher Columbus landed in the Americas in 1492, migrating peoples crossed a land bridge from Asia to North America where the Bering Strait (off the coast of Alaska) lies today. Gradually, they spread throughout North and South America.

When the first Europeans arrived late in the fifteenth century, Native Americans numbered in the millions. But by 1900, after centuries of conflict and even acts of genocide, the "vanishing Americans" numbered just 250,000 (Dobyns, 1966; Tyler, 1973). The land they controlled also shrank dramatically, as National Map 2 shows.

Columbus first referred to Native Americans that he encountered as "Indians" because he mistakenly thought he had reached the coast of India. Columbus found the native people passive and peaceful, in stark contrast to the materialistic and competitive Europeans. Yet Europeans justified the seizure of Native American land by calling their victims thieves and murderers (Josephy, 1982; Matthiessen, 1984; Sale, 1990).

After the Revolutionary War, the new U.S. government took a pluralistic approach to Native American societies, seeking to gain more land through treaties. Payment for the land was far from fair, however, and when Native Americans resisted the surrender of their homelands, the U.S. government simply used its superior military power to evict them. By the early 1800s, few Native Americans remained east of the Mississippi River.

In 1871, the United States declared Native Americans wards of the government and adopted a strategy of forced assimilation. Relocated to specific territories designated as "reservations," Native Americans continued to lose their land and were well on their way to losing their culture as well. Reservation life encouraged dependency, replacing ancestral languages with English and traditional religion with Christianity. Officials of the Bureau of Indian Affairs took children from their parents and put them in boarding schools, where they were resocialized as "Americans." Authorities gave local control of reservation life to the few Native Americans who supported government policies, and they distributed reservation land, traditionally held collectively, as private property to individual families (Tyler, 1973).

Not until 1924 were Native Americans entitled to U.S. citizenship. After that, many migrated from reservations, adopting mainstream cultural patterns and marrying non–Native Americans. Today, almost half of Native Americans consider themselves biracial or multiracial (U. S. Census Bureau, 2008), and many large cities now contain sizable Native American populations. However, as Table 2 shows, Native American income is far below the U.S. average, and relatively few Native Americans earn a college degree.[2]

SEEING SOCIOLOGY in Everyday Life

People tend to think about race and ethnicity when they deal with categories of people whom they think of as "other." WASPs have race and ethnicity, too, of course, but U.S. society does not construct these into a minority identity.

SEEING SOCIOLOGY in Everyday Life

In what ways does being a WASP (or simply being white) confer privilege on people?

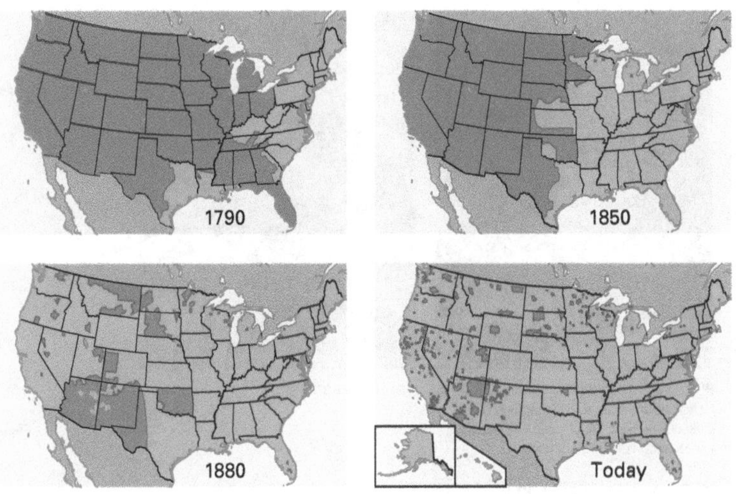

Seeing Ourselves

NATIONAL MAP 2

Land Controlled by Native Americans, 1790 to Today

In 1790, Native Americans controlled three-fourths of the land (blue-shaded areas) that eventually became the United States. Today, Native Americans control 304 reservations, scattered across the United States, that account for just 2 percent of the country's land area. How would you characterize these locations?

Source: Published in *The New York Times* on March 18, 1998.

From in-depth interviews with Native Americans in a western city, Joan Albon (1971) linked low Native American social standing to a range of cultural factors, including a noncompetitive view of life and a reluctance to pursue higher education. In addition, she noted, many Native Americans have dark skin, which makes them targets of prejudice and discrimination.

Members of more than 200 American Indian nations today are reclaiming pride in their cultural heritage. Traditional cultural organizations report a surge in new membership applications, and many children can speak native languages better than their parents. The legal right of Native Americans to govern their reservations has enabled some tribes to build profitable gaming casinos. But the wealth produced from gambling has enriched relatively few Native peoples, and most profits go to non-Indian investors (Bartlett & Steele, 2002). While some prosper, most Native Americans remain severely disadvantaged and share a profound sense of the injustice they have suffered at the hands of white people.

White Anglo-Saxon Protestants

White Anglo-Saxon Protestants (WASPs) were not the first people to inhabit the United States, but they soon dominated after European settlement began. Most WASPs are of English ancestry, but the category also includes people from Scotland and Wales. With some 36 million people claiming English, Scottish, or Welsh ancestry, 12 percent of our society has some WASP background, and WASPs are found at all class levels (U.S. Census Bureau, 2008).

Many people associate WASPs with elite communities along the East and West Coasts. But the highest concentrations of WASPs are in Utah (because of migrations of Mormons with English ancestry), Appalachia, and northern New England (also due to historical patterns of immigration).

Looking back in time, WASP immigrants were highly skilled and motivated to achieve by what we now call the Protestant work ethic. Because of their high social standing, WASPs were not subject to the prejudice and discrimination experienced by other categories of immigrants. In fact, the historical dominance of WASPs has led others to want to become more like them (K. W. Jones, 2001).

WASPs were never one single group; especially in colonial times, considerable hostility separated English Anglicans and Scottish Presbyterians (Parrillo, 1994). But in the nineteenth century, most WASPs joined together to oppose the arrival of "undesirables" such as Germans in the 1840s and Italians in the 1880s. Those who could afford

Table 2 The Social Standing of Native Americans, 2007

	Native Americans	Entire U.S. Population
Median family income	$40,310	$61,355
Percentage in poverty	21.4%	12.5%
Completion of four or more years of college (age 25 and over)	12.7%	29.4%

Source: U.S. Census Bureau (2008).

[2]In making comparisons of education and especially income, keep in mind that various categories of the U.S. population have different median ages. In 2007, the median age for all U.S. people was 36.6 years; for Native Americans, the figure was 32.1 years. Because people's schooling and income increase over time, this age difference accounts for some of the disparities seen in Table 2.

SEEING SOCIOLOGY in Everyday Life

Do you think that Marian Anderson, who broke a "color line" by being invited to the White House, would have imagined our nation having an African American president?

SEEING SOCIOLOGY in Everyday Life

In your opinion, how much change has there been in racial prejudice and discrimination against African Americans during your lifetime? Explain your position.

Corbis – NY

Culver Pictures, Inc.

Photographs and Prints Division, Schomburg Center for Research in Black Culture/The New York Public Library/Astor, Lenox and Tilden Foundations

Corbis – NY/UPI

The efforts of these four women greatly advanced the social standing of African Americans in the United States. Pictured from left to right: Sojourner Truth (1797–1883), born a slave, became an influential preacher and outspoken abolitionist who was honored by President Lincoln at the White House. Harriet Tubman (1820–1913), after escaping from slavery herself, masterminded the flight from bondage of hundreds of African American men and women via the "Underground Railroad." Ida Wells-Barnett (1862–1931), born to slave parents, became a partner in a Memphis newspaper and served as a tireless crusader against the terror of lynching. Marian Anderson (1902–1993), an exceptional singer whose early career was restrained by racial prejudice, broke symbolic "color lines" by singing in the White House in 1936 and on the steps of the Lincoln Memorial to a crowd of almost 100,000 people in 1939.

it sheltered themselves in exclusive suburbs and restrictive clubs. Thus the 1880s—the decade when the Statue of Liberty first welcomed immigrants to the United States—also saw the founding of the first country club with exclusively WASP members (Baltzell, 1964).

By about 1950, however, WASP wealth and power had peaked, as indicated by the 1960 election of John Fitzgerald Kennedy, the first Irish Catholic president. Yet the WASP cultural legacy remains. English is this country's dominant language and Protestantism its majority religion. Our legal system also reflects our English origins. But the historical dominance of WASPs is most evident in the widespread assumption that the terms "race" and "ethnicity" apply to everyone but them.

African Americans

Africans accompanied European explorers to the New World in the fifteenth century. But most accounts date the beginning of black history in the United States to 1619, when a Dutch trading ship brought twenty Africans to Jamestown, Virginia. Many more ships filled with African laborers followed. Whether these people arrived as slaves or as indentured servants (who paid for their passage by agreeing to work for a period of time), being of African descent on these shores soon became virtually synomymous with being a slave. In 1661, Virginia enacted the first law in the new colonies recognizing slavery (Sowell, 1981).

Slavery was the foundation of the southern colonies' plantation system. White people ran plantations using slave labor, and until 1808, some were also slave traders. Traders—Europeans, Africans, and North Americans—forcibly transported some 10 million Africans to various countries in the Americas, including 400,000 to the United States. On small sailing ships, hundreds of slaves were chained together for the several weeks it took to cross the Atlantic Ocean. Filth and disease killed many and drove others to suicide. Overall, perhaps half died en route (Franklin, 1967; Sowell, 1981).

The reward for surviving the miserable journey was a lifetime of servitude. Although some slaves worked in cities at various trades, most labored in the fields, often from daybreak until sunset and even longer during the harvest. The law allowed owners to use whatever disciplinary measures they deemed necessary to ensure that slaves were obedient and hardworking. Even killing a slave rarely prompted legal action. Owners also divided slave families at public auctions, where human beings were bought and sold as property. Unschooled and dependent on their owners for all their basic needs, slaves had little control over their lives (Franklin, 1967; Sowell, 1981).

Some free persons of color lived in both the North and the South, laboring as small-scale farmers, skilled workers, and small business owners. But the lives of most African Americans stood in glaring contradiction to the principles of equality and freedom on which the United States was founded. The Declaration of Independence states:

> We hold these Truths to be self-evident, that all Men are created equal, that they are endowed by their Creator with certain unalienable Rights, that among these are Life, Liberty, and the Pursuit of Happiness.

MAKING THE GRADE

Jim Crow laws are a clear example of institutional discrimination.

However, most white people did not apply these ideals to black people, and certainly not to slaves. In the *Dred Scott* case of 1857, the U.S. Supreme Court addressed the question "Are slaves citizens?" by writing, "We think they are not, and that they are not included, and were not intended to be included, under the word 'citizens' in the Constitution, and can therefore claim none of the rights and privileges which that instrument provides for and secures for citizens of the United States" (quoted in Blaustein & Zangrando, 1968:160). Thus arose what the Swedish sociologist Gunnar Myrdal (1944) called the "American dilemma": a democratic society's denial of basic rights and freedoms to one category of people. People would speak of equality, in other words, but do little to make all categories of people equal. Many white people resolved this dilemma by defining black people as naturally inferior and undeserving of equality (Leach, 2002).

In 1865, the Thirteenth Amendment to the Constitution outlawed slavery. Three years later, the Fourteenth Amendment reversed the *Dred Scott* ruling, giving citizenship to all people born in the United States. The Fifteenth Amendment, ratified in 1870, stated that neither race nor previous condition of servitude could deprive anyone of the right to vote. However, so-called *Jim Crow laws*—classic cases of institutional discrimination—segregated U.S. society into two racial castes. Especially in the South, white people beat and lynched black people (and some white people) who challenged the racial hierarchy.

The twentieth century brought dramatic changes for African Americans. After World War I, tens of thousands of men, women, and children left the rural South for jobs in northern factories. Although most did find economic opportunities, few escaped racial prejudice and discrimination, which placed them lower in the social hierarchy than white immigrants arriving from Europe.

In the 1950s and 1960s, a national civil rights movement led to landmark judicial decisions outlawing segregated schools and overt discrimination in employment and public accommodations. The Black Power movement gave African Americans a renewed sense of pride and purpose.

Despite these gains, people of African descent continue to occupy a lower social position in the United States, as shown in Table 3. The median income of African American families in 2007 ($40,143) was only 57 percent of non-Hispanic white family income ($69,937), a ratio that has changed little in thirty years.[3] Black families remain three times as likely as white families to be poor.

The number of African Americans securely in the middle class rose by more than half between 1980 and 2008; 41 percent earn $50,000 or more. This means that the African American community is now economically diverse. Even so, a majority of African Americans are still working-class or poor. In recent years, many have seen earnings slip as urban factory jobs, vital to residents of central cities, have been lost to other countries where labor costs are lower. This is one reason that black unemployment is more than twice as high as white unemployment; among African American teenagers in many cities, the figure exceeds 40 percent (R. A. Smith, 2002; Pattillo, 2007; U.S. Department of Labor, 2008).

Table 3 The Social Standing of African Americans, 2007

	African Americans	Entire U.S. Population
Median family income	$40,143	$61,355
Percentage in poverty	24.5%	12.5%
Completion of four or more years of college (age 25 and over)	19.6%	29.4%

Source: U.S. Census Bureau (2008).

Since 1980, African Americans have made remarkable educational progress. The share of adults completing high school rose from half to more than three-fourths, nearly closing the gap between whites and blacks. Between 1980 and 2007, the share of African American adults with at least a college degree rose from 8 to 20 percent. But as Table 3 shows, African Americans are still well below the national standard when it comes to completing four years of college.

The political clout of African Americans has also increased. As a result of black migration to the cities and white flight to the suburbs, African Americans have gained greater political power in urban places, and half of this country's ten largest cities have elected African American mayors (Marshall & Ruhil, 2006). At the national level, the election of Barack Obama as this country's forty-fourth president—the first African American to hold this office—is a historic and hugely important event. It demonstrates that our society has moved beyond the assumption that race is a barrier to the highest office in the land (West, 2008). Yet in 2009, African Americans accounted for just 39 members of the House of Representatives (9 percent of the 435), one member of the Senate (out of 100), and only two of fifty state governors (National Governors Association, 2008).

In sum, for nearly 400 years, people of African ancestry in the United States have struggled for social equality. As a nation, we have come far in this pursuit. Overt discrimination is now illegal, and research documents a long-term decline in prejudice against African Americans (Firebaugh & Davis, 1988; J. Q. Wilson, 1992; NORC, 2007).

Fifty years after the abolition of slavery, W. E. B. Du Bois (1913) pointed to the extent of black achievement but cautioned that racial caste remained strong in the United States. Almost a century later, this racial hierarchy persists.

---

[3]Here again, a median age difference (non-Hispanic whites, 40.8; blacks, 31.1) accounts for some of the income and educational disparities. More important is a higher proportion of one-parent families among blacks than whites. If we compare only married-couple families, African Americans (median income $62,163 in 2007) earned 80 percent as much as non-Hispanic whites ($77,340).

SEEING SOCIOLOGY in Everyday Life

Don't assume that all Asian Americans (or Hispanics or members of any other minority category) are the same. The tables in this chapter highlight important differences among members of each minority category.

Table 4 The Social Standing of Asian Americans, 2007

	All Asian Americans	Chinese Americans	Japanese Americans	Asian Indian Americans	Filipino Americans	Entire U.S. Population
Median family income	$77,133	$78,258	$88,037	$92,925	$83,126	$61,355
Percentage in poverty	10.2%	12.0%	8.5%	8.1%	5.5%	12.5%
Completion of four or more years of college (age 25 and over)	52.6%	51.6%	46.5%	68.3%	48.0%	29.4%

Source: U.S. Census Bureau (2008).

Asian Americans

Although Asian Americans share some racial traits, enormous cultural diversity characterizes this category of people with ancestors from dozens of nations. In 2007, the total number of Asian Americans exceeded 13 million, or about 4.4 percent of the U.S. population. The largest category of Asian Americans is people of Chinese ancestry (3.1 million), followed by those of Asian Indian (2.6 million), Filipino (2.4 million), Vietnamese (1.5 million), Korean (1.3 million), and Japanese (800,000) descent. More than one-third of Asian Americans live in California.

Young Asian Americans command attention and respect as high achievers and are disproportionately represented at our country's best colleges and universities. Many of their elders, too, have made economic and social gains; most Asian Americans now live in middle-class suburbs, and an increasing number of Asian Americans live in some of the highest-income neighborhoods in the country. Yet despite (and sometimes because of) this achievement, Asian Americans often find that others are aloof or outright hostile toward them (O'Hare, Frey, & Fost, 1994; Chua-Eoan, 2000; Lee & Marlay, 2007).

The achievement of some Asian Americans has given rise to a "model minority" stereotype that is misleading because it hides the sharp differences in class standing found among their ranks. We will focus first on the history and current standing of Chinese Americans and Japanese Americans—the longest-established Asian American minorities—and conclude with a brief look at the more recent arrivals.

Chinese Americans

Chinese immigration to the United States began in 1849 with the economic boom of California's Gold Rush. New towns and businesses sprang up overnight, and the demand for cheap labor attracted some 100,000 Chinese immigrants. Most Chinese workers were young men willing to take difficult, low-status jobs that whites did not want. But the economy soured in the 1870s, and desperate whites began to compete with the Chinese for whatever work could be found. Suddenly, the hardworking Chinese were seen as a threat. Economic hard times led to prejudice and discrimination (Ling, 1971; Boswell, 1986). Soon laws were passed barring Chinese people from many occupations, and public opinion turned strongly against the "Yellow Peril."

In 1882, the U.S. government passed the first of several laws limiting Chinese immigration. This action caused domestic hardship because in the United States, Chinese men outnumbered Chinese women by twenty to one. This sex imbalance drove the Chinese population down to only 60,000 by 1920. Because Chinese women already in the United States were in high demand, they soon lost much of their traditional submissiveness to men (Hsu, 1971; Lai, 1980; Sowell, 1981).

Responding to racial hostility, some Chinese moved east; many more sought the relative safety of urban Chinatowns. There Chinese traditions flourished, and kinship networks, called *clans,* provided financial assistance to individuals and represented the interests of all. At the same time, however, living in an all-Chinese community discouraged residents from learning English, which limited their job opportunities (Wong, 1971).

A renewed need for labor during World War II prompted President Franklin Roosevelt to end the ban on Chinese immigration in 1943 and to extend the rights of citizenship to Chinese Americans born abroad. Many responded by moving out of Chinatowns and pursuing cultural assimilation. In Honolulu in 1900, for example, 70 percent of Chinese people lived in Chinatown; today, the figure is below 20 percent.

By 1950, many Chinese Americans had experienced upward social mobility. Today, people of Chinese ancestry are no longer limited to self-employment in laundries and restaurants; many hold high-prestige positions, especially in fields related to science and technology.

As shown in Table 4, the median family income of Chinese Americans in 2007 was $78,258, which is above the national average of $61,355. However, the higher income of all Asian Americans reflects a larger number of family members in the labor force.[4] Chinese Americans also have a record of educational achievement, with almost twice the national average of college graduates.

Despite their successes, many Chinese Americans still deal with subtle (and sometimes blatant) prejudice and discrimination. Such hostility is one reason that poverty remains a problem for many Chi-

[4]Median age for all Asian Americans in 2007 was 35.4 years, somewhat below the national median of 36.6 and the non-Hispanic white median of 40.8. But specific categories vary widely in median age: Japanese, 45.6; Filipino, 38.3; Chinese, 38.0; Korean, 35.8; Asian Indian, 32.2; Cambodian, 27.1; Hmong, 20.0 (U.S. Census Bureau, 2008).

SEEING SOCIOLOGY in Everyday Life

On your campus, do students of any one race or ethnic category tend to hang out together? Explain the patterns you see.

SEEING SOCIOLOGY in Everyday Life

Recent research on social distance indicates that most of today's college students say they are more accepting of African Americans than Asian Americans. Does this square with your experiences? What about white people in the country as a whole—are they more accepting of Asian Americans or African Americans? Why?

nese Americans. The problem of poverty is most common among people who remain in the socially isolated Chinatowns working in restaurants or other low-paying jobs, raising the question of whether racial and ethnic enclaves help their residents or exploit them (Portes & Jensen, 1989; Kinkead, 1992; Gilbertson & Gurak, 1993).

Japanese Americans

Japanese immigration to the United States began slowly in the 1860s, reaching only 3,000 by 1890. Most were men who came to the Hawaiian Islands (annexed by the United States in 1898 and made a state in 1959) as a source of cheap labor. After 1900, however, as the number of Japanese immigrants to California rose (reaching 140,000 by 1915), white hostility increased (Takaki, 1998). In 1907, the United States signed an agreement with Japan curbing the entry of men—the chief economic threat—while allowing women to enter this country to ease the Japanese sex ratio imbalance. In the 1920s, state laws in California and elsewhere segregated the Japanese and banned interracial marriage, just about ending further Japanese immigration. Not until 1952 did the United States extend citizenship to foreign-born Japanese.

Immigrants from Japan and China differed in three important ways. First, there were fewer Japanese immigrants, so they escaped some of the hostility directed toward the more numerous Chinese. Second, the Japanese knew more about the United States than the Chinese did, which helped them assimilate (Sowell, 1981). Third, Japanese immigrants preferred rural farming to clustering in cities, which made them less visible. But many white people objected to Japanese ownership of farmland, so in 1913, California barred further purchases. Many foreign-born Japanese (called *Issei*) responded by placing farmland in the names of their U.S.-born children (*Nisei*), who were constitutionally entitled to citizenship.

Japanese Americans faced their greatest crisis after Japan bombed the U.S. naval fleet at Hawaii's Pearl Harbor on December 7, 1941. Rage was directed at the Japanese living in the United States. Some people feared that Japanese Americans would spy for Japan or commit acts of sabotage. Within a year, President Franklin Roosevelt signed Executive Order 9066, an unprecedented action designed to ensure national security by detaining people of Japanese ancestry in military camps. Authorities soon relocated 120,000 people of Japanese descent (90 percent of all U.S. Japanese) to remote inland reservations (Sun, 1998; Ewers, 2008).

Concern about national security always rises in times of war, but Japanese internment was sharply criticized. First, it targeted an entire category of people, not a single one of whom was known to have committed a disloyal act. Second, most of those imprisoned were *Nisei*, U.S. citizens by birth. Third, the United States was also at war with Germany and Italy, but no comparable action was taken against people of German or Italian ancestry.

On average, Asian Americans have income above the national median. At the same time, however, the poverty rate in many Asian American communities—including San Francisco's Chinatown—is well above average.

Relocation meant selling homes, furnishings, and businesses on short notice for pennies on the dollar. As a result, almost the entire Japanese American population was economically devastated. In military prisons—surrounded by barbed wire and guarded by armed soldiers—families crowded into single rooms, often in buildings that had previously sheltered livestock. The internment ended in 1944 when the U.S. Supreme Court declared it unconstitutional, although the last camp did not close until 1946 (after the war had ended). In 1988, Congress awarded $20,000 to each of the victims as token compensation for the hardships they endured.

After World War II, Japanese Americans staged a dramatic recovery. Having lost their traditional businesses, many entered new occupations; driven by cultural values stressing the importance of education and hard work, Japanese Americans have enjoyed remarkable success. In 2007, the median income of Japanese American families was more than 40 percent higher than the national average, and the rate of poverty among Japanese Americans was well below the national figure.

Upward social mobility has encouraged cultural assimilation and intermarriage. Younger generations of Japanese Americans rarely live

SEEING SOCIOLOGY in Everyday Life

Do you think Latinos are fairly represented in today's television shows and films? Explain your position.

Table 5 The Social Standing of Hispanic Americans, 2007

	All Hispanics	Mexican Americans	Puerto Ricans	Cuban Americans	Entire U.S. Population
Median family income	$40,566	$40,419	$42,300	$52,113	$61,355
Percentage in poverty	21.5%	22.0%	24.3%	13.8%	12.5%
Completion of four or more years of college (age 25 and over)	12.3%	8.6%	15.5%	25.0%	9.4%

Source: U.S. Census Bureau (2008).

in residential enclaves, as many Chinese Americans do, and most marry non-Japanese partners. In the process, some have abandoned their traditions, including the Japanese language. A high proportion of Japanese Americans, however, belong to ethnic associations as a way of maintaining their ethnic identity. Still, some appear to be caught between two worlds: no longer culturally Japanese yet, because of racial differences, not completely accepted in the larger society.

Recent Asian Immigrants

More recent immigrants from Asia include Filipinos, Indians, Koreans, Vietnamese, Guamanians, and Samoans. The Asian American population increased by 87 percent between 1990 and 2007 and currently accounts for more than one-third of all immigration to the United States (U.S. Department of Homeland Security, 2008b).

The entrepreneurial spirit is strong among Asian immigrants. In part this reflects cultural patterns that stress achievement and self-reliance, but having one's own small business is also a strategy for dealing with societal prejudice and discrimination. Small business success is one reason that Asian American family income is above the national average, but it is also true that in many of these businesses, a number of family members work long hours.

Another factor that raises the family income of Asian Americans is a high level of schooling. As shown in Table 4, for all categories of Asian Americans, the share of adults with a four-year college degree is well above the national average. Among Asian Indian Americans, who have the highest educational achievement of all Asian Americans, more than two-thirds of all men and women over the age of twenty-five have completed college, a proportion that is more than twice the national average. This remarkable educational achievement is one reason that Asian Indian Americans had a median family income of $92,925 in 2007, about 50 percent higher than the national average.

In sum, a survey of Asian Americans presents a complex picture. The Japanese come closest to having achieved social acceptance. But some surveys reveal greater prejudice against Asian Americans than against African Americans (Parrillo & Donahue, 2005). Median income data suggest that many Asian Americans have prospered. But these numbers reflect the fact that many Asian Americans live in Hawaii, California, or New York, where incomes are high but so are living costs. Then, too, many Asian Americans remain poor. One thing is clear—their high immigration rate and their increasing political clout mean that people of Asian ancestry will play a central role in U.S. society in the decades to come (Takaki, 1998; Barbassa, 2009).

Hispanic Americans/Latinos

In 2007, the number of people of Hispanic descent in the United States topped 45 million (15.1 percent of the population), surpassing the number of Asian Americans (13.4 million, or 4.4 percent of the U.S. population) and even African Americans (39 million, or 12.8 percent) and making Hispanics the largest racial or ethnic minority. However, keep in mind that few people who fall into this category describe themselves as "Hispanic" or "Latino." Like Asian Americans, Hispanics are really a cluster of distinct populations, each of which identifies with a particular ancestral nation and particular families may or may not feel a part of a national Hispanic community (Marín & Marín, 1991; Jiménez, 2007). About two out of three Hispanics (some 29 million) are Mexican Americans, or "Chicanos." Puerto Ricans are next in population size (4 million), followed by Cuban Americans (1.6 million). Many other nations of Latin America are represented by smaller numbers.

Although the Hispanic population is increasing all over the country, most Hispanic Americans still live in the Southwest. One of three Californians is Latino (in greater Los Angeles, almost half the people are). National Map 3, shows the distribution of the Hispanic, African American, Asian American, and Arab American populations across the United States.

Median family income for all Hispanics—$40,566 in 2007, as shown in Table 5—is well below the national average.[5] As the following sections explain, however, some categories of Hispanics have fared better than others.

Mexican Americans

Some Mexican Americans are descendants of people who lived in a part of Mexico annexed by the United States after the Mexican

[5]The 2007 median age of the U.S. Hispanic population was 27.6 years, far below the non-Hispanic white median of 40.8 years. This difference accounts for some of the disparity in income and education.

SEEING SOCIOLOGY in Everyday Life

On your campus, do students ever seem to downplay their ethnicity as a way to "fit in"? Explain.

American War (1846–48). Most, however, are more recent immigrants. Indeed, more immigrants now come to the United States from Mexico than from any other country.

Like many other immigrants, many Mexican Americans have worked as low-wage laborers, on farms and in factories. Table 5 shows that the 2007 median family income for Mexican Americans was $40,419, which is two-thirds of the national average. Almost one-fourth of Chicano families are poor—nearly twice the national average. Finally, despite gains since 1980, Mexican Americans still have a high dropout rate and receive much less schooling, on average, than the U.S. population as a whole.

Puerto Ricans

The island of Puerto Rico, like the Philippines, became a U.S. possession when the Spanish-American War ended in 1898. In 1917, Congress passed the Jones Act, which made Puerto Ricans (but not Filipinos) U.S. citizens and made Puerto Rico a territory of the United States.

New York City is home to nearly 1 million Puerto Ricans. However, about one-third of this community is severely disadvantaged. Adjusting to cultural patterns on the mainland—including, for many, learning English—is one major challenge; also, Puerto Ricans with dark skin encounter prejudice and discrimination. As a result, more people return to Puerto Rico each year than arrive. Between 1990 and 2007, the Puerto Rican population of New York actually fell by about 100,000 (Navarro, 2000; U.S. Census Bureau, 2008).

This "revolving door" pattern limits assimilation. About 70 percent of Puerto Rican families in the United States speak Spanish at home. Speaking Spanish keeps ethnic identity strong but limits economic opportunity. Puerto Ricans also have a higher incidence of woman-headed households than most other Hispanics, a pattern that puts families at greater risk of poverty (U.S. Census Bureau, 2007).

Table 5 shows that the 2007 median family income for Puerto Ricans was $42,300, or about 70 percent of the national average. Although long-term mainland residents have made economic gains, more recent immigrants from Puerto Rico continue to struggle to find work. Overall, Puerto Ricans remain the most socially disadvantaged Hispanic minority.

Cuban Americans

Within a decade after the 1959 Marxist revolution led by Fidel Castro, 400,000 Cubans had fled to the United States. Most settled with other Cuban Americans in Miami. Many were highly educated business and professional people who wasted little time becoming as successful in the United States as they had been in their homeland.

Table 5 shows that the 2007 median household income for Cuban Americans was $52,113, above that of other Hispanics but still well below the national average. The 1.6 million Cuban Americans living in the United States today have managed a delicate balancing act, achieving in the larger society while holding on to much of their traditional culture. Of all Hispanics, Cubans are the most likely to speak Spanish in their homes: Eight out of ten families do so. However, cultural distinctiveness and highly visible communities, such as Miami's Little Havana, provoke hostility from some people.

Arab Americans

Arab Americans are another U.S. minority that is increasing in size. Like Hispanic Americans, these are people whose ancestors lived in a variety of countries. What is sometimes called "the Arab world" includes twenty-two nations and stretches across northern Africa, from Mauritania and Morocco on Africa's west coast to Egypt and Sudan on Africa's east coast, and extends into the Middle East (western Asia), including Iraq and Saudi Arabia. Not all the people who live in these nations are Arabs, however; for example, the Berber people in Morocco and the Kurds of Iraq are not Arabs.

Arab cultures differ from society to society, but they share widespread use of the Arabic alphabet and language and have Islam as their dominant religion. But keep in mind that "Arab" (an ethnic

The strength of family bonds and neighborhood ties is evident in Carmen Lomas Garza's painting *Barbacoa para Cumpleaños* (Birthday Party Barbecue).

SEEING SOCIOLOGY in Everyday Life

Look closely at the maps. Can you explain why various categories of people tend to be concentrated in certain regions of the United States?

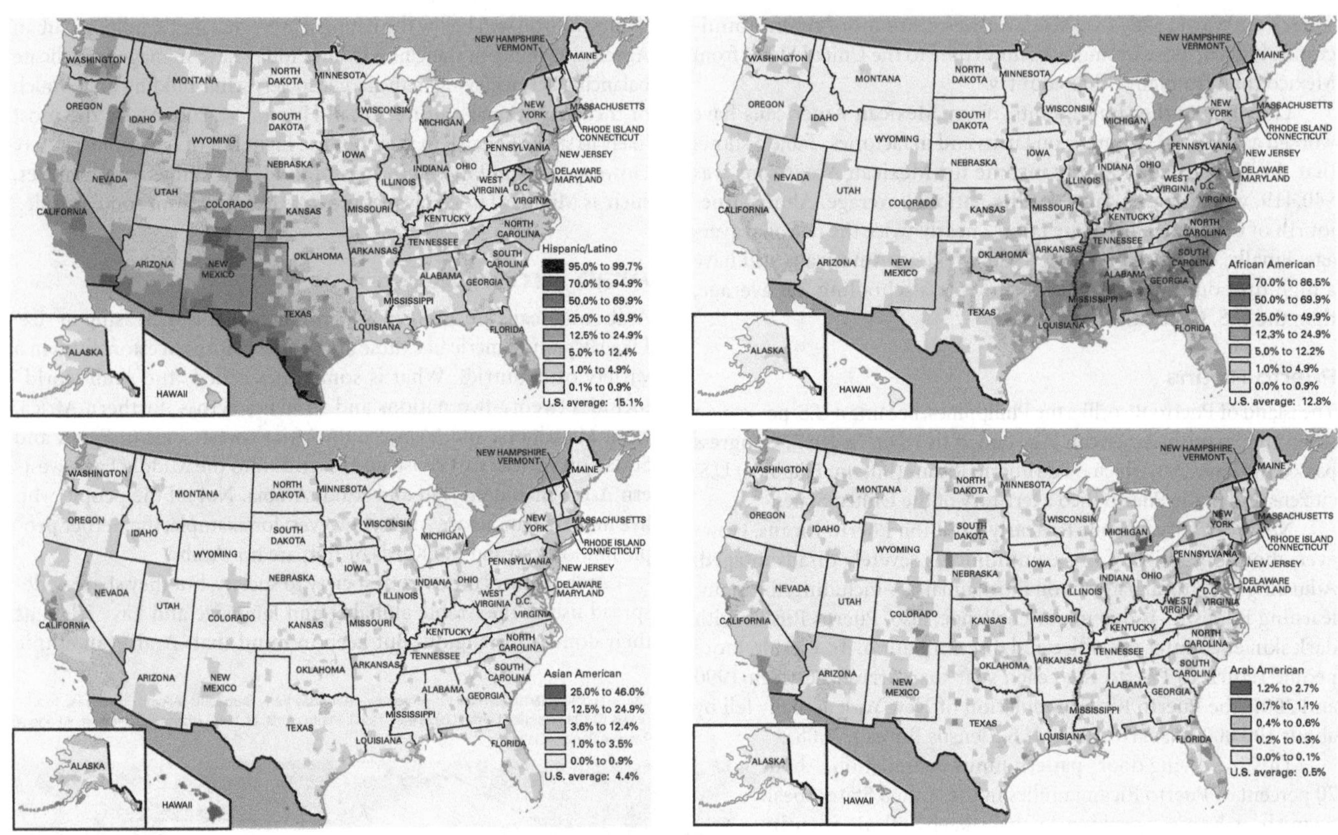

Seeing Ourselves

NATIONAL MAP 3

The Concentration of Hispanics or Latinos, African Americans, Asian Americans, and Arab Americans, by County

In 2007, people of Hispanic or Latino descent represented 15.1 percent of the U.S. population, compared with 12.8 percent African Americans, 4.4 percent Asian Americans, and 0.5 percent Arab Americans. These maps show the geographic distribution of these categories of people in 2000. Comparing them we see that the southern half of the United States is home to far more minorities than the northern half. But do they all concentrate in the same areas? What patterns do the maps reveal?

Source: U.S. Census Bureau (2008).

category) is not the same as "Muslim" (a follower of Islam). A majority of the people living in most Arab countries are Muslims, but some Arabs are Christians or followers of other religions. In addition, most of the world's Muslims do not live in Africa or the Middle East and are not Arabs.

Because many of the world's nations have large Arab populations, immigration to the United States has created a culturally diverse population of Arab Americans. Some Arab Americans are Muslims, and some are not; some speak Arabic, and some do not; some maintain the traditions of their homeland, and some do not. As is the case with Hispanic Americans and Asian Americans, some are recent immigrants, and some have lived in this country for decades or even for generations.

As noted in Table 1, the government gives the official number of Arab Americans as 1.5 million, but because people may not declare their ethnic background, the actual number may be twice as high.[6] The largest populations of Arab Americans have ancestral ties to Lebanon (32 percent of all Arab Americans), Egypt (12 percent), and

SEEING SOCIOLOGY in Everyday Life

Do you know of any highly educated immigrants who worked as professionals in their birth nations and who are now performing working-class jobs here in the United States? Why might immigrants have to do this?

Syria (10 percent). Most Arab Americans (71 percent) report ancestral ties to one nation, but 29 percent report both Arab and non-Arab ancestry (U.S. Census Bureau, 2008). A look at National Map 3 shows the Arab American population is distributed throughout the United States.

Included in the Arab American population are people of all social classes. Some are highly educated professionals who work as physicians, engineers, and professors; others are working-class people who perform various skilled jobs in factories or on construction sites; still others do service work in restaurants, hospitals, or other settings or work in small family businesses. As shown in Table 6, median family income for Arab Americans is slightly above the national average ($65,291 compared to the national median of $61,355 in 2007), but Arab Americans have a much higher than average poverty rate (17.1 percent versus 12.5 percent for the population as a whole) (U.S. Census Bureau, 2008).

There are large, visible Arab American communities in a number of U.S. cities, including New York, Chicago, Los Angeles, Houston, and Dearborn (Michigan). Even so, Arab Americans may choose to downplay their ethnicity as a way to avoid prejudice and discrimination. The fact that many terrorist attacks against the United States and other nations have been carried out by Arabs has fueled a stereotype that links being Arab (or Muslim) with being a terrorist. This stereotype is unfair because it blames an entire category of people for actions by a few individuals. But it is probably the reason that the social distance research discussed earlier in this chapter shows students expressing more negative attitudes toward Arabs than toward any other racial or ethnic category. Its also helps explain why Arab Americans have been targets of an increasing number of hate crimes and why many Arab Americans feel that they are subject to "ethnic profiling" that threatens their privacy and freedom (Ali & Juarez, 2003; Ali, Lipper, & Mack, 2004; Hagopian, 2004).

White Ethnic Americans

The term "white ethnics" recognizes the ethnic heritage and social disadvantages of many white people. White ethnics are non-WASPs whose ancestors lived in Ireland, Poland, Germany, Italy, or other European countries. More than half the U.S. population falls into one or more white ethnic categories.

Table 6 The Social Standing of Arab Americans, 2007

	Arab Americans	Entire U.S. Population
Median family income	$65,291	$61,355
Percentage in poverty	17.1%	12.5%
Completion of four or more years of college (age 25 and over)	44.8%	29.4%

Source: U.S. Census Bureau (2008).

Corbis - NY/Peter Yates

Arab American communities can be found in many large cities on the East and West Coasts of the United States, but the heaviest concentrations are found across the upper Midwest. This mosque rises above the cornfields in a rural area near Toledo, Ohio.

High rates of emigration from Europe during the nineteenth century first brought Germans and Irish and then Italians and Jews to our shores. Despite cultural differences, all shared the hope that the United States would offer greater political freedom and economic opportunity than their homelands. Most did live better in this country, but the belief that "the streets of America were paved with gold" turned out to be a far cry from reality. Most immigrants found only hard labor for low wages.

White ethnics also endured their share of prejudice and discrimination. Many employers shut their doors to immigrants, posting signs that warned "None need apply but Americans" (Handlin, 1941:67). In 1921, Congress enacted a quota system that greatly limited immigration, especially by southern and eastern Europeans, who were likely to have darker skin and different cultural backgrounds than the dominant WASPs. This quota system continued until 1968.

In response to prejudice and discrimination, many white ethnics formed supportive residential enclaves. Some also established footholds in certain businesses and trades: Italian Americans entered the construction industry; the Irish worked in construction and in civil service jobs; Jews predominated in the garment industry; many Greeks (like the Chinese) worked in the retail food business (W. M. Newman, 1973).

[6]The 2007 median age for Arab Americans was 30.8 years, below the national median of 36.6 years.

SEEING SOCIOLOGY in Everyday Life

Do you know your school's policy on affirmative action?

CONTROVERSY & DEBATE

Affirmative Action: Solution or Problem?

STEPHANIE: I think Gruttner got, well, a raw deal. She should have been admitted.

GINA: Perhaps. But diversity is important. I believe in affirmative action.

MARCO: Maybe some people do get into college more easily. But that includes guys like me whose father went here.

Barbara Gruttner, who is white, claimed that she was the victim of racial discrimination. She maintained that the University of Michigan Law School had unfairly denied her application for admission while admitting many less qualified African American applicants. The basis of her claim was the fact that Michigan, a state university, admitted just 9 percent of white students with her grade point average and law school aptitude test scores while admitting 100 percent of African American applicants with comparable scores.

In 2003, the U.S. Supreme Court heard Gruttner's complaint in a review of the admissions policies of both the law school and the undergraduate program at the University of Michigan. In a 6–3 decision, the Court ruled against Gruttner, claiming that the University of Michigan Law School could use a policy of affirmative action that takes account of the race of applicants in the interest of creating a socially diverse student body. At the same time, however, the Court struck down the university's undergraduate admissions policy, which awarded points not only for grades and college board scores but also for being a member of an underrepresented minority. A point system of this kind, the Court ruled, is too close to the rigid quota systems rejected by the Court in the past.

Aurora Photos, Inc./Carl D. Walsh

With this ruling, the Supreme Court continued to oppose quotalike systems while at the same time reaffirming the importance of racial diversity on campus. Thus colleges and universities can take account of race in order to increase the number of traditionally underrepresented students as long as race is treated as just one variable in a process that evaluates each applicant as an individual (Stout, 2003).

How did the controversial policy of affirmative action begin? The answer takes us back to the end of World War II, when the U.S. government funded higher education for veterans of all races. The so-called G.I. Bill held special promise for African Americans, most of whom needed financial assistance to enroll in college. By 1960, government funding helped 350,000 black men and women attend college.

There was just one problem: These individuals were not finding the kinds of jobs for which they were qualified. So the Kennedy administration devised a program of "affirmative action" to provide broader opportunities to qualified minorities. Employers were instructed to monitor hiring, promotion, and admissions policies to eliminate discrimination against minorities, even if unintended.

Defenders of affirmative action see it, first, as a sensible response to our nation's racial and eth-

Many working-class people still live in traditional neighborhoods, although those who prospered have gradually assimilated. Most descendants of immigrants who labored in sweatshops and lived in crowded tenements now lead more comfortable lives. As a result, their ethnic heritage has become a source of pride.

Race and Ethnicity: Looking Ahead

The United States has been and will remain a land of immigrants. Immigration has brought striking cultural diversity and tales of hope, struggle, and success told in hundreds of languages.

Millions of immigrants arrived in a great wave that peaked about 1910. The next two generations saw gradual economic gains and at least some assimilation into the larger society. The government also extended citizenship to Native Americans (1924), foreign-born Filipinos (1942), Chinese Americans (1943), and Japanese Americans (1952).

Another wave of immigration began after World War II and swelled as the government relaxed immigration laws in the 1960s. Today, about 1.5 million people come to the United States each year—about 1 million legally and another 500,000 illegally. Today's immigrants come not from Europe but from Latin America and Asia, with Mexicans, Asian Indians, and Filipinos arriving in the largest numbers.

SEEING SOCIOLOGY in Everyday Life

Can you provide examples of xenophobia in our society today?

nic history, especially for African Americans, who suffered through two centuries of slavery and a century of segregation under Jim Crow laws. Throughout our history, they claim, being white gave people a big advantage. They see minority preference today as a step toward fair compensation for unfair majority preference in the past.

Second, given our racial history, many analysts doubt that the United States will ever become a color-blind society. They claim that because prejudice and discrimination are rooted deep in U.S. culture, simply claiming that we are color-blind does not mean that everyone will be treated fairly.

Third, supporters maintain that affirmative action has worked. Where would minorities be if the government had not enacted this policy in the 1960s? Major employers, such as fire and police departments in large cities, began hiring minorities and women for the first time only because of affirmative action. This program has helped expand the African American middle class and increased racial diversity on college campuses and in the workplace.

About 80 percent of African Americans support affirmative action. But 73 percent of white people and 56 percent of Hispanics *oppose* preferences for African Americans (NORC, 2007). Critics point out, first of all, that affirmative action was intended as a temporary remedy to ensure fair competition but soon became a system of "group preferences" and quotas—in short, a form of "reverse discrimination," favoring people not because of performance but because of race, ethnicity, or sex.

Second, critics say, if racial preferences were wrong in the past, they are wrong now. Why should whites today, many of whom are far from privileged, be penalized for past discrimination that was in no way their fault? Our society has undone most of the institutional prejudice and discrimination of earlier times—doesn't the election of an African American president suggest that? Giving entire categories of people special treatment compromises standards of excellence and calls into question the real accomplishments of minorities.

A third argument against affirmative action is that it benefits those who need it least. Favoring minority-owned corporations or holding places in law school helps already privileged people. Affirmative action has done little for the African American underclass that needs the most help.

There are good arguments for and against affirmative action, and people who want our society to have more racial or ethnic equality fall on both sides of the debate. Voters in a number of states, including California, Washington, Michigan, and Nebraska, have passed ballot initiatives banning the use of affirmative action based on gender or race. In 2008, however, voters in Colorado voted down such a proposal. So the country remains divided on this issue. The disagreement is not whether people of all colors should have equal opportunity but whether the current policy of affirmative action is part of the solution or part of the problem.

WHAT DO YOU THINK?

1. In view of the fact that society has historically favored males over females and whites over people of color, would you agree that white males have received more "affirmative action" than anyone? Why or why not?
2. Should affirmative action include only disadvantaged categories of minorities (say, African Americans and Native Americans) and exclude more affluent categories (such as Japanese Americans)? Why or why not?
3. Do you think the election of Barack Obama as the nation's first African American president suggests that affirmative action is no longer needed? Why or why not?

Sources: Bowen & Bok (1999), Kantrowitz & Wingert (2003), NORC (2007), Flynn (2008), and Leff (2008).

Many new arrivals face the same kind of prejudice and discrimination experienced by those who came before them. In fact, recent years have witnessed rising hostility toward foreigners (an expression of *xenophobia,* from Greek roots meaning "fear of what is strange"). In 1994, California voters passed Proposition 187, which stated that illegal immigrants should be denied health care, social services, and public education; it was later overturned in federal court. More recently, voters there mandated that all children learn English in school. Some landowners in the Southwest have taken up arms to discourage the large number of illegal immigrants crossing the border from Mexico, and our nation is increasing border security as we also wonder how to best deal with the more than 12 million illegal immigrants already here.

Even minorities who have been in the United States for generations feel the sting of prejudice and discrimination. Affirmative action, a policy meant to provide opportunities for members of racial and ethnic minorities, continues to be hotly debated in this country, as the Controversy & Debate box describes.

Like other minorities, today's immigrants hope to gain acceptance and to blend into U.S. society without completely giving up their traditional culture. Some still build racial and ethnic enclaves so that in many cities across the country, the Little Havanas and Koreatowns of today stand alongside the Little Italys and Chinatowns of the past. In addition, new arrivals still carry the traditional hope that their racial and ethnic identities can be a source of pride rather than a badge of inferiority.

Seeing Sociology in Everyday Life

Race And Ethnicity

Is our society becoming more tolerant, more accepting of racially and ethnically mixed couples and friendship groups?

As the social distance research presented in this chapter shows, today's college students express greater acceptance of social diversity. Look at the two corporate advertisements shown here. What evidence of greater acceptance do you see? In your opinion, does this evidence mean that our society has really changed? Why or why not?

Images courtesy of The Advertising Archives

Here's an ad from 1957, when the civil rights movement was just getting under way. Based on what you have read in this chapter, how does this reflect what U.S. society was like fifty years ago in terms of racial segregation?

HINT On the face of it, today's ads suggest far greater racial and ethnic tolerance than was true fifty years ago, when we rarely saw images of people of different categories interacting with one another. The social distance research noted in this chapter also supports the idea that tolerance is increasing. Being more racially inclusive is also a smart business policy because of the increasing economic resources of various minority categories of the U.S. population.

Images courtesy of The Advertising Archives

Especially in the case of advertising aimed at young people, racial and ethnic mixing has become the rule. How accurately does this image reflect everyday life? Do you think young people differ from older people in their degree of social tolerance? Explain.

Applying SOCIOLOGY in Everyday Life

1. Thinking about your own campus, can you point to ways in which race does not matter in students' lives? In what ways does race still matter? On balance, how important is race today?

2. Does your college or university take account of race and ethnicity in its admissions policies? Ask to speak with an admissions officer to see what you can learn about your school's use of race and ethnicity in admissions. Ask whether there is a "legacy" policy that favors children of parents who attended the school.

3. Give several of your friends or family members a quick quiz, asking them what share of the U.S. population is white, Hispanic, African American, and Asian (see Table 1). Why do you think most white people exaggerate the African American population? (C. A. Gallagher, 2003)

MAKING THE GRADE

Race and Ethnicity

The Social Meaning of Race and Ethnicity

RACE refers to socially constructed categories based on biological traits a society defines as important.

- The meaning and importance of race vary from place to place and over time.
- Societies use racial categories to rank people in a hierarchy, giving some people more money, power, and prestige than others.
- In the past, scientists created three broad categories—Caucasoids, Mongoloids, and Negroids—but there are no biologically pure races.

ETHNICITY refers to socially constructed categories based on cultural traits a society defines as important.

- Ethnicity reflects common ancestors, language, and religion.
- The importance of ethnicity varies from place to place and over time.
- People choose to play up or play down their ethnicity.
- Societies may or may not set categories of people apart based on differences in ethnicity.

race a socially constructed category of people who share biologically transmitted traits that members of a society consider important

ethnicity a shared cultural heritage

minority any category of people distinguished by physical or cultural difference that a society sets apart and subordinates

✓ *Minorities are people of various racial and ethnic categories who are visually distinctive and disadvantaged by a society.*

Prejudice and Stereotypes

PREJUDICE is a rigid and unfair generalization about a category of people.

- The social distance scale is one measure of prejudice.
- One type of prejudice is the **STEREOTYPE**, an exaggerated description applied to every person in some category.
- **RACISM**, a very destructive type of prejudice, asserts that one race is innately superior or inferior to another.

There are four **THEORIES OF PREJUDICE**:

- **Scapegoat theory** claims that prejudice results from frustration among people who are disadvantaged.
- **Authoritarian personality theory** (Adorno) claims that prejudice is a personality trait of certain individuals, especially those with little education and those raised by cold and demanding parents.
- **Culture theory** (Bogardus) claims that prejudice is rooted in culture; we learn to feel greater social distance from some categories of people.
- **Conflict theory** claims that prejudice is a tool used by powerful people to divide and control the population.

prejudice a rigid and unfair generalization about an entire category of people

stereotype a simplified description applied to every person in some category

racism the belief that one racial category is innately superior or inferior to another

scapegoat a person or category of people, typically with little power, whom people unfairly blame for their own troubles

Discrimination

DISCRIMINATION refers to actions by which a person treats various categories of people unequally.

- Prejudice refers to *attitudes*; discrimination involves *actions*.
- Institutional prejudice and discrimination are biases built into the operation of society's institutions, including schools, hospitals, the police, and the workplace.
- Prejudice and discrimination perpetuate themselves in a vicious circle, resulting in social disadvantage that fuels additional prejudice and discrimination.

discrimination unequal treatment of various categories of people

institutional prejudice and discrimination bias built into the operation of society's institutions

Majority and Minority: Patterns of Interaction

PLURALISM means that racial and ethnic categories, although distinct, have roughly equal social standing.

- U.S. society is pluralistic in that all people in the United States, regardless of race or ethnicity, have equal standing under the law.
- U.S. society is not pluralistic in that all racial and ethnic categories do not have equal social standing.

ASSIMILATION is a process by which minorities gradually adopt the patterns of the dominant culture.

- Assimilation involves changes in dress, language, religion, values, and friends.
- Assimilation is a strategy to escape prejudice and discrimination and to achieve upward social mobility.
- Some categories of people have assimilated more than others.

pluralism a state in which people of all races and ethnicities are distinct but have equal social standing

assimilation the process by which minorities gradually adopt patterns of the dominant culture

miscegenation biological reproduction by partners of different racial categories

segregation the physical and social separation of categories of people

genocide the systematic killing of one category of people by another

SEGREGATION is the physical and social separation of categories of people.

- Although some segregation is voluntary (as by the Amish), majorities usually segregate minorities by excluding them from neighborhoods, schools, and occupations.
- *De jure* segregation is segregation by law; *de facto* segregation describes settings that contain only people of one category.
- Hypersegregation means having little social contact with people beyond the local community.

GENOCIDE is the systematic killing of one category of people by another.

- Historical examples of genocide include the extermination of Jews by the Nazis and the killing of Western-leaning people in Cambodia by Pol Pot.
- Recent examples of genocide include Hutus killing Tutsis in the African nation of Rwanda, Serbs killing Bosnians in the Balkans of Eastern Europe, and systematic killing in the Darfur region of Sudan.

Race and Ethnicity in the United States

NATIVE AMERICANS, the earliest human inhabitants of the Americas, have endured genocide, segregation, and forced assimilation. Today, the social standing of Native Americans is well below the national average.

WHITE ANGLO-SAXON PROTESTANTS (WASPs) were most of the original European settlers of the United States, and many continue to enjoy high social position today.

AFRICAN AMERICANS experienced more than two centuries of slavery. Emancipation in 1865 gave way to segregation by law (the so-called Jim Crow laws). In the 1950s and 1960s, a national civil rights movement resulted in legislation that outlawed segregated schools and overt discrimination in employment and public accommodations. Today, despite legal equality, African Americans are still disadvantaged.

ASIAN AMERICANS have suffered both racial and ethnic hostility. Although some prejudice and discrimination continue, both Chinese and Japanese Americans now have above-average income and schooling. Asian immigrants—especially Koreans, Indians, and Filipinos—now account for more than one-third of all immigration to the United States.

HISPANIC AMERICANS/LATINOS, the largest U.S. minority, include many ethnicities sharing a Spanish heritage. Mexican Americans, the largest Hispanic minority, are concentrated in the southwest region of the country and are the poorest Hispanic category. Cubans, concentrated in Miami, are the most affluent Hispanic category.

ARAB AMERICANS are a growing U.S. minority. Because they come to the United States from so many different nations, Arab Americans are a culturally diverse population, and they are represented in all social classes. They have been a target of prejudice and hate crimes in recent years as a result of a stereotype that links all Arab Americans with terrorism.

WHITE ETHNIC AMERICANS are non-WASPs whose ancestors emigrated from Europe in the nineteenth and twentieth centuries. In response to prejudice and discrimination, many white ethnics formed supportive residential enclaves.

MAKING THE GRADE

Sample Test Questions

Multiple-Choice Questions

1. *Race* refers to _______ considered important by a society, and *ethnicity* refers to _______.
   a. biological traits; cultural traits
   b. cultural traits; biological traits
   c. differences; what we have in common
   d. what we have in common; differences

2. What share of the U.S. population consists of people of Hispanic ancestry?
   a. 45.1 percent
   b. 35.1 percent
   c. 25.1 percent
   d. 15.1 percent

3. A minority is defined as a category of people who
   a. have physical traits that make them different.
   b. are less than half the society's population.
   c. are defined as both different and disadvantaged.
   d. are below average in terms of income.

4. In this country, four states now have a "minority majority." Which of the following is not one of them?
   a. California
   b. Florida
   c. Hawaii
   d. New Mexico

5. Research using the Bogardus social distance scale shows that U.S. college students
   a. are less prejudiced than students fifty years ago.
   b. believe that Arabs and Muslims should be kept out of the country.
   c. have the strongest prejudice against African Americans.
   d. All of the above are correct.

6. *Prejudice* is a matter of _______, and *discrimination* is a matter of _______.
   a. biology; culture
   b. attitudes; behavior
   c. choice; social structure
   d. what rich people think; what rich people do

7. The United States is not truly pluralistic because
   a. part of our population lives in "ethnic enclaves."
   b. this country has a history of slavery.
   c. different racial and ethnic categories are unequal in social standing.
   d. All of the above are correct.

8. Which term is illustrated by immigrants from Ecuador learning to speak the English language?
   a. genocide
   b. segregation
   c. assimilation
   d. pluralism

9. During the late 1400s, the first Europeans came to the Americas; Native Americans
   a. followed shortly thereafter.
   b. had just migrated from Asia.
   c. came with them from Europe.
   d. had inhabited this land for 30,000 years.

10. Which of the following is the largest category of Asian Americans in the United States?
   a. Chinese Americans
   b. Japanese Americans
   c. Korean Americans
   d. Vietnamese Americans

ANSWERS: 1 (a); 2 (d); 3 (c); 4 (b); 5 (a); 6 (b); 7 (c); 8 (c); 9 (d); 10 (a).

Essay Questions

1. What is the difference between race and ethnicity? What does it mean to say that race and ethnicity are socially constructed?
2. What is a minority? Support the claim that African Americans and Arab Americans are both minorities in the United States, using specific facts from the chapter.

Aging and the Elderly

DanitaDelimont.com/ © Keren Su

Growing older involves changes to our bodies. But societies shape our experiences at every stage of life, defining older people in distinctive ways that involve important disadvantages.

Omni-Photo Communications, Inc./Tony Perrottet

Aging and the Elderly

Michael Newman

Getty Images Inc./Martin Bydalek

CHAPTER OVERVIEW

This chapter explores the process of growing old and explains why aging is a dimension of social stratification. The importance of understanding aging is increasing along with the elderly share of our population.

AP Wide World Photos/Knoxville News Sentinel, Saul Young

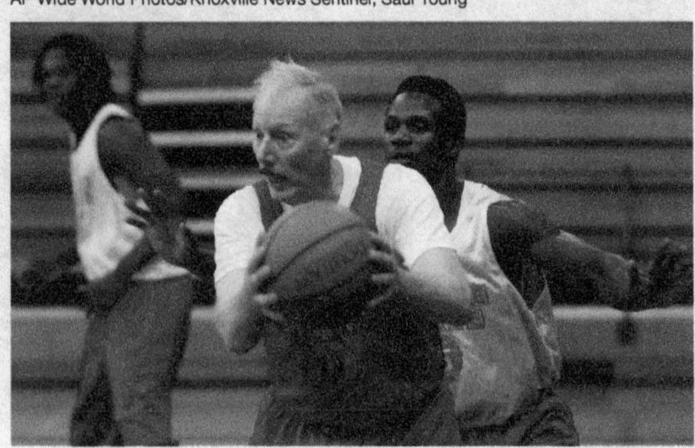

It was a good game for the basketball team at Roane State Community College in Tennessee as hundreds of students cheered as the clock ran out and the team posted a big victory over rival King College. But it was a special night for team member Ken Mink, who late in the game scored two points from the free-throw line. What's so unusual about that? Mink, a full-time student at Roane State, is seventy-three years old. Returning to college for a degree he never completed when he was younger, Mink began practicing with the basketball team and finally got the chance to play his first game in fifty-two years (Associated Press, 2008).

Does it seem odd for someone in his seventies to be playing a sport? Or even being enrolled in college? In our society, it is certainly not the norm. As we age, our lives change, and not simply in ways that reflect our biology. Society, too, is at work. In fact, society organizes our lives in patterned ways that correspond to being a child, an adolescent, an adult, and an older person. As this chapter explains, growing old in the United States brings with it distinctive experiences and also significant disadvantages, including lower income, prejudice, and discrimination in the workplace. For this reason, like class, gender, and race, growing old is a dimension of social stratification. The importance of learning about old age is increasing all the time because the number of older people in the U.S. population is greater than ever and rising rapidly.

The Graying of the United States

A quiet but powerful revolution is reshaping the United States. As shown in Figure 1, in 1900, the United States was a young nation, with half the population under age twenty-three; just 4 percent had reached sixty-five. But the number of elderly people—women and men aged sixty-five or older—increased tenfold during the last century. By 2009, the number of seniors exceeded 38 million and half the population was over thirty-seven. Seniors now outnumber teenagers, and they account for 12.7 percent of the entire population. By 2035, the number of seniors will double again to more than 77 million, and about half the country's people will be over forty (U.S. Census Bureau, 2008).

In nearly all high-income nations, the share of elderly people is increasing rapidly. There are two reasons for this increase: low birth rates (people are having fewer children) and increasing longevity (people are living longer).

In the United States, the ranks of the elderly will swell even more rapidly as the first of the baby boomers—some 78 million strong—reach age sixty-five in 2011. As recent political debate shows, there are serious questions about the ability of the current Social Security system to meet the needs of so many older people.

Birth Rate: Going Down

The U.S. birth rate has been falling for more than a century. This is the usual trend as societies industrialize. Why? Because in industrial societies, children are more likely to survive into adulthood, and so couples have fewer children. In addition, although to farming families children are an economic asset, to families in industrial societies children are an economic liability. In other words, children no longer add to their family's financial income but instead are a major expense.

Finally, as more and more women work outside the home, they choose to have fewer children. This trend reflects both the rising standing of women and advances in birth control technology over the past century.

Life Expectancy: Going Up

Life expectancy in the United States is going up. In 1900, a typical female born here could expect to live just forty-eight years, and a male, forty-six years. By contrast, females born in 2006 can look forward to living 80.7 years, and males can expect to live 75.4 years (Heron et al., 2008).

SEEING SOCIOLOGY in Everyday Life

In what specific ways would you expect campus life to change as more older people return to college for retraining? Do you see these changes as positive or not? Why?

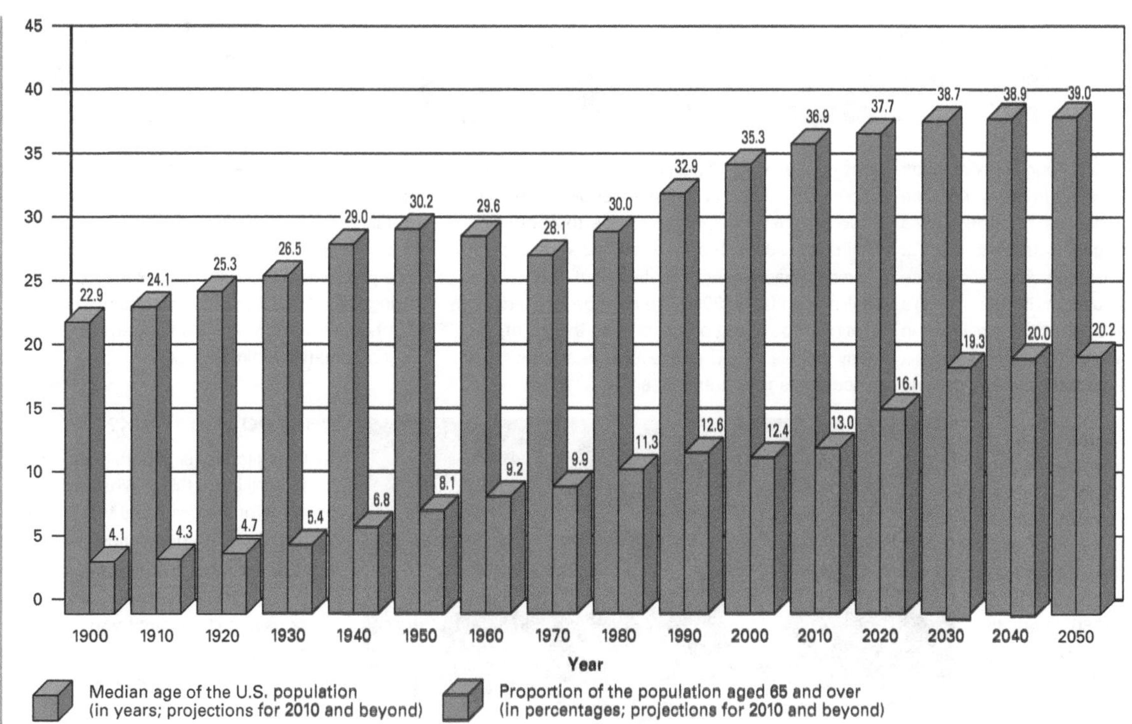

FIGURE 1 **The Graying of U.S. Society**

The proportion of the U.S. population over the age of sixty-five tripled during the last century. The median age of the U.S. population has now passed thirty-five years and will continue to rise.

Source: U.S. Census Bureau (2008).

This longer life span is one result of the Industrial Revolution. Greater material wealth and advances in medicine have raised living standards so that people benefit from better housing and nutrition. In addition, medical advances have almost eliminated infectious diseases—such as smallpox, diphtheria, and measles—that killed many infants and children a century ago. Other medical advances help us fend off cancer and heart disease, which claim most of the U.S. population, but now later in life.

As life becomes longer, the oldest segment of the U.S. population—people over eighty-five—is increasing rapidly and is already forty times greater than in 1900. These men and women now number 5.4 million (about 1.8 percent of the total population). Their numbers will grow to almost 20 million (about 4.3 percent of the total) by the year 2050 (U.S. Census Bureau, 2008).

This major increase in the elderly population will change our society in many ways. As the number of older people retiring from the labor force goes up, the proportion of nonworking adults—already about ten times greater than in 1900—will demand ever more health care and other resources. The ratio of working-age adults to nonworking elderly people, called the *old-age dependency ratio,* will fall from the current level of five to one to about three to one by the year 2030 (U.S. Social Security Administration, 2008). With fewer and fewer workers to support tomorrow's swelling elderly population, what security can today's young people expect in their old age? The Thinking Globally box takes a closer look at a country where the graying of the population is taking place even faster than in the United States: Japan.

An Aging Society: Cultural Change

As the average age of the population rises and the share over age sixty-five climbs ever higher, cultural patterns are likely to change. Through much of the twentieth century, the young rarely mixed with the old, so most people learned little about old age. But as this country's elderly population steadily increases, age segregation will decline. Younger

MAKING THE GRADE

The average age of the U.S. population is about thirty-seven; Japan's average age is forty-four.

gerontology the study of aging and the elderly

THINKING GLOBALLY

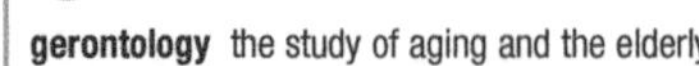

Can Too Many Be Too Old? A Report from Japan

With an average age of forty-four, the population of Japan is among the oldest in the world. One cause of the aging Japanese population is a declining birth rate, which has fallen to just 1.2 children born for every woman. A second cause of Japan's aging population is the nation's increasing life expectancy. Girls born in Japan in 2008 can expect to live, on average, eighty-six years, and boys can expect to live seventy-nine years.

Looking ahead, Japan's future population patterns are setting off alarms. First, the low birth rate is not enough to replace the country's population. This means that the number of Japanese people—now 127 million—will steadily fall to about 94 million by 2050. Second, by 2050, half the Japanese population will be older than fifty-five. This means that the country's labor force will shrink by millions of people, a change that may well reduce economic output and lower living standards. Third, the Japanese worry about how their society will support their increasing population of seniors. In 2008, some 23 percent of Japan's people were sixty-five or older; this share will rise to about one-third by 2030. Today, three workers support every person over sixty-five. But this ratio is falling so that by 2050, the old-age dependency ratio will be about one to one. At this point, elderly people would not receive nearly as much income as they currently enjoy.

The Japanese case is all the more important because it is not unique. Other nations, including Italy and Spain, have populations almost as old as Japan's, and by 2050, they will face the same problems. The United States is among the "youngest" of the high-income countries. But what happens elsewhere will happen here, too. It is just a matter of time.

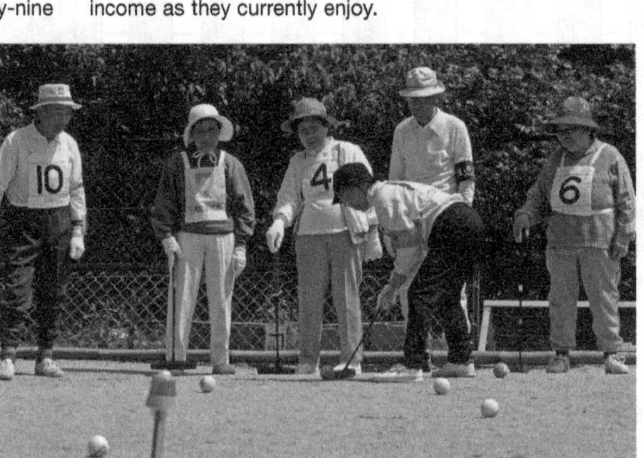

Corbis – NY/Tom Wagner

WHAT DO YOU THINK?

1. Living longer is generally thought to be a good thing. What are some of the problems that come with an aging population?
2. When a nation's average age passes fifty, what changes to popular culture might you expect?
3. How might immigration be a strategy to raise the old-age dependency ratio?

Sources: Porter (2004), Haub (2008), and U.S. Census Bureau (2008).

people will see more seniors on the highways, at shopping malls, and at sporting events. In addition, the design of buildings—including homes, stores, stadiums, and college classrooms—is likely to change to ease access for older shoppers, sports fans, and students.

As the chapter-opening story of Ken Mink suggests, colleges are also opening their doors to more older people, and seniors are becoming a familiar sight on many campuses. As baby boomers (people born between 1946 and 1964) enter old age, many are deciding to put off retirement and complete degrees or train for new careers. Community colleges, which offer extensive programs that prepare people for new types of work, are now offering a wide range of "second career" programs that attract older people (Olson, 2006).

Of course, the extent of contact with older people depends a great deal on where in the country you live. The elderly represent a far greater share of the population in some regions, especially in the midsection, from North Dakota and Minnesota down to Texas, as shown in National Map 1.

When thinking about how an aging population will change our ways of life, keep in mind that seniors are socially diverse. Being "elderly" is a category open to everyone, if we are lucky enough to live that long. Elders in the United States are women and men of all classes, races, and ethnic backgrounds.

The "Young Old" and the "Old Old"

Analysts sometimes distinguish two cohorts of the elderly, roughly equal in size (Himes, 2001). The younger elderly are between sixty-five and seventy-five and typically live independently with good health and financial security; they are likely to be living as couples. The older elderly are past age seventy-five and are more likely to have health and money problems and to be dependent on others. Because of their greater longevity, women outnumber men in the elderly population, an imbalance that grows greater with advancing age. Among the "oldest old," those over age eighty-five, 67 percent are women.

Sheila Markham and her many elderly friends in rural Boyd County, Nebraska, have a hard time finding young people to shovel their winter snow.

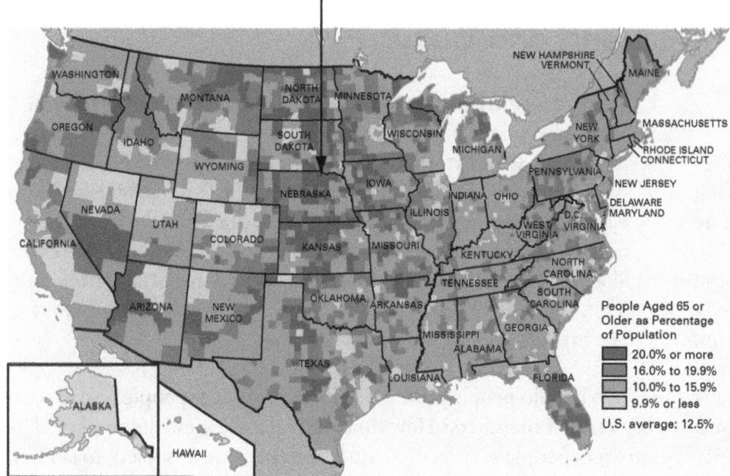

Seeing Ourselves

NATIONAL MAP 1

The Elderly Population across the United States

Common sense suggests that elderly people live in the Sunbelt, enjoying the warmer climate of the South and Southwest. Although it is true that Florida has a disproportionate share of people over age sixty-five, it turns out that most counties with high percentages of older people are in the Midwest. What do you think accounts for this pattern? Hint: Which regions of the United States do younger people leave in search of jobs?

Source: U.S. Census Bureau (2008).

Growing Old: Biology and Culture

Studying the graying of a society's population is the focus of **gerontology** (derived from the Greek word *geron,* meaning "old person"), *the study of aging and the elderly.* Gerontologists—who work in many disciplines, including medicine, psychology, and sociology—investigate not only how people change as they grow old but also the different ways in which societies around the world define old age.

Biological Changes

Aging consists of gradual, ongoing changes in the body. But how we experience life's transitions—whether we welcome our maturity or complain about physical decline—depends largely on how our cultural system defines the various stages of life. In general, U.S. culture takes a positive view of biological changes that occur early in life. Through childhood and adolescence, people look forward to expanding opportunities and responsibilities.

But today's youth-oriented culture takes a dimmer view of the biological changes that happen later on. Few people receive congratulations for getting old, at least not until they reach eighty-five or ninety. Rather, we offer sympathy to friends as they turn forty, fifty, and sixty and make jokes to avoid facing up to the fact that advancing age will put us all on a slippery slope of physical and mental decline. In short, we assume that by age fifty or sixty, people stop growing *up* and begin growing *down.*

Growing old brings on predictable changes: gray hair, wrinkles, height and weight loss, and declining strength and vitality. After age fifty, bones become more brittle, and the older people get, the longer it takes for injuries to heal. In addition, advancing age means that the odds of developing a chronic illness (such as arthritis or diabetes) or a life-threatening condition (like heart disease or cancer) rise. The senses—taste, sight, touch, smell, and especially hearing—become less sharp with advancing age (Treas, 1995; Metz & Miner, 1998).

Though health becomes more fragile as people get older, most elderly men and women are not disabled by their physical condition. Only about one in ten seniors reports trouble walking, and fewer than one in five needs intensive care in a hospital or nursing home. About 11 percent need help with shopping, chores, or other daily activities. Overall, only 31 percent of people over age seventy-five characterize their health as "fair" or "poor"; 69 percent consider their overall condition "good" or "excellent." In fact, the share of seniors reporting good or excellent health is going up (Pleis & Lethbridge-Çejku, 2006; Centers for Disease Control and Prevention, 2007; Adams, Barnes, & Vickerie, 2008).

Of course, some elders have better health than others. Health problems become more common after people reach the age of seventy-five. In addition, because women typically live longer than men, they suffer more from chronic disabilities like arthritis. Well-to-do people also fare better because they live and work in safer and more healthful environments and can afford better medical care. Almost 80 percent of elderly people with annual incomes over $35,000 assess their own health as "excellent" or "good," but that figure drops below half for people with incomes under $20,000. Lower income and stress linked to prejudice and discrimination also explain why only 60 percent of older African Americans assess their health in positive terms, compared to 76 percent of elderly white

MAKING THE GRADE

Carefully read the discussion below explaining two key ways that culture shapes the process of aging.

people (Federal Interagency Forum, 2008; National Center for Health Statistics, 2009).

Psychological Changes

Just as we tend to overstate the physical problems of old age, we sometimes exaggerate the psychological changes that accompany growing old. The common view about intelligence over the life course can be summed up as "What goes up must come down."

If we measure skills such as sensorimotor coordination—the ability to arrange objects to match a drawing—we do find a steady decline after midlife. The ability to learn new material and to think quickly also declines, although not until around age seventy. Even then, only about 9 percent of adults over age seventy suffer symptoms ranging from mild memory loss to more serious mental conditions. For most, the ability to apply familiar ideas holds steady with advancing age, and the capacity for thoughtful reflection and spiritual growth actually increases (Baltes & Schaie, 1974; Metz & Miner, 1998; Cortez, 2008).

We all wonder if we will think or feel differently as we get older. Gerontologists report that for better or worse, the answer is usually no. The most common personality changes with advancing age are becoming less materialistic, more mellow in attitudes, and more thoughtful. Generally, two elderly people who had been childhood friends would recognize in each other the same personality traits that brought them together as youngsters (Neugarten, 1977; Wolfe, 1994).

Aging and Culture

November 1, Kandy, Sri Lanka. *Our little van struggles up the steep mountain incline. Breaks in the lush vegetation offer spectacular views that interrupt our conversation about growing old. "Then there are no old-age homes in your country?" I ask. "In Colombo and other cities, I am sure," our driver responds, "but not many. We are not like you Americans." "And how is that?" I counter, stiffening a bit. His eyes remain fixed on the road: "We would not leave our fathers and mothers to live alone."*

When do people grow old? How do younger people regard society's oldest members? How do elderly people view themselves? The answers people give to these questions vary from society to society, showing that although aging is a biological process, it is also a matter of culture.

How long and how well people live depend, first, on a society's technology and standard of living. Through most of human history, as the English philosopher Thomas Hobbes (1588–1679) famously put it, people's lives were "nasty, brutish, and short" (although Hobbes himself made it to the ripe old age of ninety-one). In his day, most people married and had children as teenagers, became middle-aged in their twenties, and died from various illnesses in their thirties and forties. Many of history's great men and women never reached what we would call old age at all: The English poet Keats died at age twenty-

© Dorling Kindersley

Corbis – NY/© John Garrett/Corbis

The reality of growing old is as much a matter of culture as it is of biology. In the United States, being elderly often means being inactive; yet in many other countries of the world, elders often continue many familiar and productive routines.

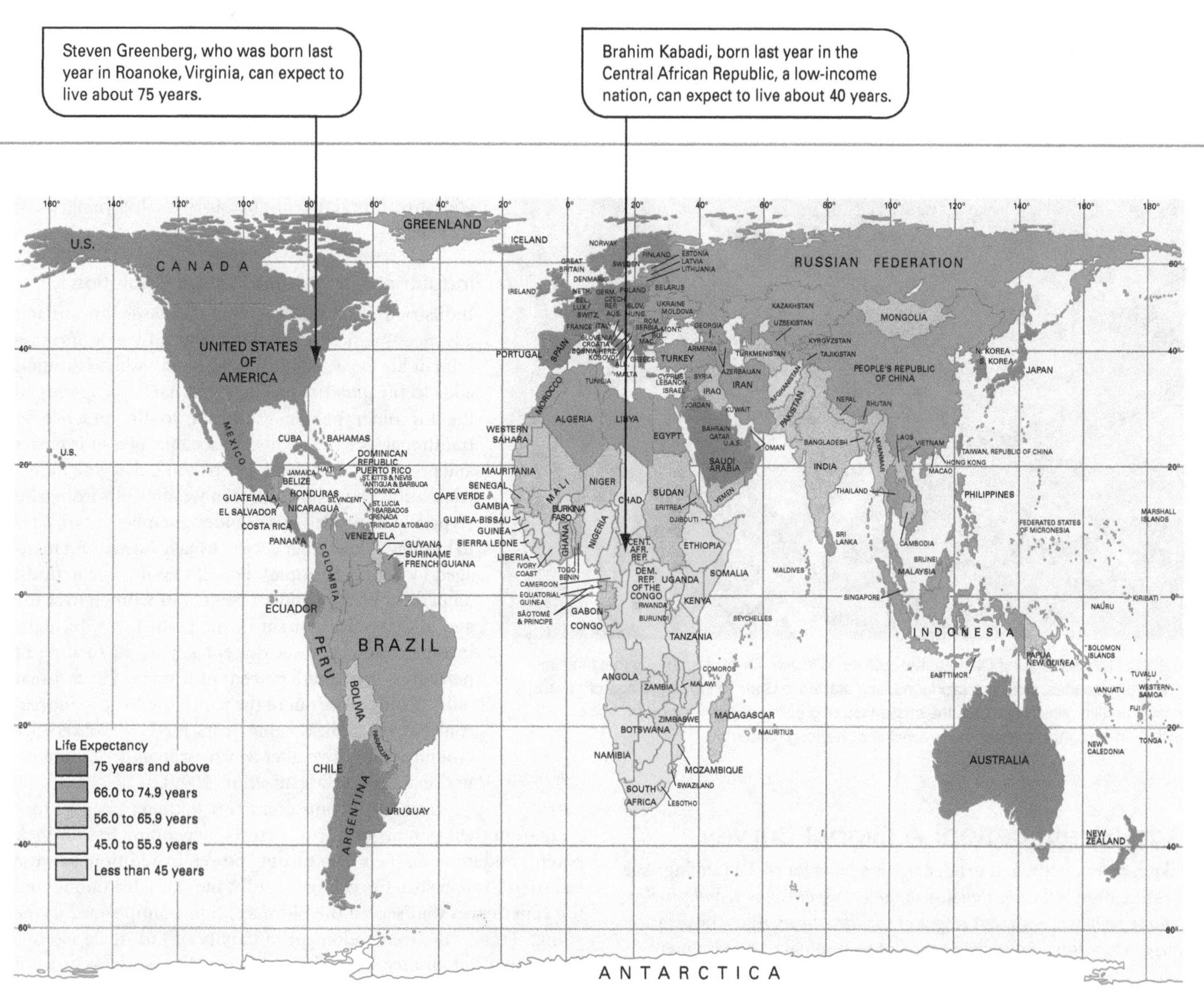

Window on the World

GLOBAL MAP 1 Life Expectancy in Global Perspective

Life expectancy shot up during the twentieth century in high-income countries, including Canada, the United States, Western Europe, Japan, and Australia. A newborn in the United States can now expect to live about seventy-eight years, and our life expectancy would be greater still were it not for the high risk of death among infants born into poverty. Because poverty is the rule in much of the world, lives are correspondingly shorter, especially in parts of Africa, where life expectancy may be less than forty years.

Source: Population Reference Bureau (2008).

six; Mozart, the Austrian composer, at thirty-five. Among famous writers, none of the three Brontë sisters lived to the end of her thirties; Edgar Allan Poe died at forty, Henry David Thoreau at forty-five, Oscar Wilde at forty-six, and William Shakespeare at fifty-two.

By about 1900, however, rising living standards and advancing medical technology in the United States and Western Europe combined to extend longevity to about age fifty. As Global Map 1 shows, this is still the figure in many low-income countries today. In high-income nations, however, increasing affluence has added almost thirty years to the average life span.

Just as important as longevity is the value societies attach to their senior members. All societies distribute basic resources unequally. We now turn to the importance of age in this process.

age stratification the unequal distribution of wealth, power, and privilege among people at different stages of the life course

gerontocracy a form of social organization in which the elderly have the most wealth, power, and prestige

SEEING SOCIOLOGY in Everyday Life

Our society is sometimes described as a "youth culture." Why do people say this? Do you agree? Explain your answer.

Everett Collection/Warner Bros.

In 2008, Hollywood actor Clint Eastwood, who is known for his tough-guy roles in films over past decades, directed, produced, and starred in *Gran Torino* at the age of seventy-eight. The film, which explores the challenges of growing older in a modern society, ended up being the biggest money-maker of his long career.

Age Stratification: A Global Survey

Like race, ethnicity, and gender, age is a basis for social ranking. **Age stratification** is *the unequal distribution of wealth, power, and privilege among people at different stages of the life course*. Age stratification varies according to a society's level of technological development.

Hunting and Gathering Societies

Without the technology to produce a surplus of food, hunters and gatherers must be nomadic. This means that survival depends on physical strength and stamina. As members of these societies grow old (in this case, about age thirty), they become less active and may even be considered an economic burden and, when food is in short supply, abandoned (Sheehan, 1976).

Pastoral, Horticultural, and Agrarian Societies

Once societies develop the technology to raise their own crops and animals, they produce a surplus. In such societies, some individuals build up considerable wealth over a lifetime. Of all age categories, the most privileged are typically the elderly, a pattern called **gerontocracy**, *a form of social organization in which the elderly have the most wealth, power, and prestige*. Old people, particularly men, are honored and sometimes feared by their families, and they remain active leaders of society until they die. This respect for the elderly also explains the widespread practice of ancestor worship in agrarian societies.

Industrial and Postindustrial Societies

Industrialization pushes living standards upward and advances medical technology, both of which increase human life expectancy. But although industrialization adds to the *quantity* of life, it can harm the *quality* of life for older people. Contrary to the practice in traditional societies, industrial societies give little power and prestige to the elderly. The reason is that with industrialization, the prime source of wealth shifts from land (typically controlled by the oldest members of society) to businesses and other goods (usually owned and managed by younger people). For all low-income nations, 35 percent of men and 19 percent of women over the age of sixty-five remain in the labor force. In high-income countries, these percentages are far smaller: 14 percent of men and 8 percent of women. The fact that older people move out of the paid labor force is one reason that the peak earning years for U.S. workers are around age fifty-five, after which earnings decline (International Labour Organization, 2009).

In high-income countries, younger people move away from their parents to pursue careers, depending less on their parents and more on their own earning power. In addition, because industrial, urban societies change rapidly, the skills, traditions, and life experiences that served the old may seem unimportant to the young. Finally, the tremendous productivity of industrial nations means that not all members of a society need to work, so most of the very old and the very young play nonproductive roles.

The long-term effect of all these factors transforms *elders* (a word with positive connotations) into *the elderly* (a term that carries far less prestige). In postindustrial societies such as the United States and Canada, economic and political leaders are usually people between the ages of forty and sixty who combine experience with up-to-date skills. Even as the U.S. population, on average, is getting older, the country's corporate executives are getting younger, declining from an average age of fifty-nine in 1980 to fifty-five today (Herring, 2005).

In rapidly changing sectors of the economy, especially the high-tech fields, many key executives are younger still, sometimes barely out of college. Industrial societies often give older people only marginal participation in the economy because they lack the knowledge and training demanded in a fast-changing marketplace.

Some occupations are dominated by older people. The average farmer is fifty-five; the average age of the entire U.S. labor force is only forty-one. More than one-fourth of today's farmers are over the age of

MAKING THE GRADE

Notice the big differences between women and men in living arrangements.

sixty-five. Older people also predominate in other traditional occupations, working as barbers, tailors, and shop clerks, and in jobs that involve minimal physical activity, such as night security guards (Yudelman & Kealy, 2000; U.S. Department of Agriculture, 2004).

Japan: An Exceptional Case

Throughout the last century, Japan stood out as an exception to the rule that industrialization lowers the social standing of older people. Not only is the share of seniors in Japan increasing as fast as anywhere in the world, but Japan's more traditional culture gives older people great importance. Most elders in Japan live with an adult daughter or son, and they play a significant role in family life. Elderly men in Japan are also more likely than their U.S. counterparts to stay in the labor force, and in many Japanese corporations, the oldest employees enjoy the greatest respect. But Japan is becoming more like other industrial nations, where growing old means giving up some measure of social importance. In addition, a long economic downturn has left Japanese families less able to care for their older members, which may further weaken the traditional importance of elders (Ogawa & Retherford, 1997; Onishi, 2006; Lah, 2008).

Transitions and Challenges of Aging

We confront change at each stage of life. Old age has its rewards, but of all stages of the life course, it presents the greatest challenges.

Physical decline in old age is less serious than most younger people think. But even so, older people endure pain, limit their activities, increase their dependency on others, lose dear friends and relatives, and face up to their own mortality. Because our culture places such a high value on youthfulness, aging in the United States often means added fear and self-doubt. As one retired psychologist quipped about old age, "Don't let the current hype about the joys of retirement fool you. They are not the best of times. It's just that the alternative is even worse" (Rubenstein, 1991).

Finding Meaning

Erik Erikson theorized that elderly people must resolve a tension of "integrity versus despair." No matter how much they still may be learning and achieving, older people recognize that their lives are nearing an end. Thus elderly people spend more time reflecting on their past, remembering disappointments as well as accomplishments. Integrity, to Erikson (1963, orig. 1950; 1980), means assessing your life realistically. Without such honesty, this stage of life may turn into a time of despair—a dead end with little positive meaning.

Table 1 Living Arrangements of the Elderly, 2007

	Men	Women
Living alone	19.0%	38.6%
Living with spouse	72.8	42.2
Living with other relatives or nonrelatives	8.2	19.2

In 2007, some 3.5 percent of elderly people lived in nursing homes. This number includes people from all of these categories.

Source: U.S. Census Bureau (2008).

In a classic study of people in their seventies, Bernice Neugarten (1971) found that some people cope with growing older better than others. Worst off are those who fail to come to terms with aging; they develop *disintegrated and disorganized personalities* marked by despair. Many of these people end up as passive residents of hospitals or nursing homes.

Slightly better off are people with *passive-dependent personalities.* They have little confidence in their abilities to cope with daily events, sometimes seeking help even if they do not really need it. Always in danger of social withdrawal, their life satisfaction level is relatively low.

A third category develops *defended personalities,* living independently but fearful of aging. They try to shield themselves from the reality of old age by fighting to stay youthful and physically fit. Although it is good to be concerned about health, setting unrealistic standards breeds stress and disappointment.

Most of Neugarten's subjects, however, displayed what she termed *integrated personalities,* coping well with the challenges of growing old. As Neugarten sees it, the key to successful aging lies in keeping personal dignity and self-confidence while accepting growing old.

Social Isolation

Being alone can cause anxiety at any age, but isolation is most common among elderly people. Retirement closes off one source of social interaction, physical problems may limit mobility, and negative stereotypes of the elderly as "over the hill" may discourage younger people from close social contact with them.

But the greatest cause of social isolation is the death of significant others, especially the death of a spouse. One study found that almost three-fourths of widows and widowers cited loneliness as their most serious problem (Lund, 1989).

The problem of social isolation falls more heavily on women because they typically outlive their husbands. Table 1 shows that 73 percent of men aged sixty-five and over live with spouses, but only 42 percent of elderly women do. In addition, 39 percent of older

Seeing SOCIOLOGY in the 

Grandparents Raising Grandkids: "Everybody Understands"

BY STACY BYRNE
April 6, 2009

At a brown-bag lunch meeting earlier this year, Elaine Steiger told how her eight-year-old great-grandson Micah has been acting rebellious lately.

"He won't go to church with me," Steiger said. "He's mad at me."

Steiger and her husband, Emil, who recently died, have raised the boy since he was a baby. They eventually adopted him.

"Both of his parents landed in prison," she said. "Since he turned eight it seems like he's having more problems. He's not seeing his mother as much as he'd like to."

Steiger is not able to vent about the daily frustrations of parenthood to her co-workers; she is seventy-two and retired seven years ago from working in the kitchen at Benefis Health System.

So she finds others who are experiencing the same ups and downs that come with parenting grandchildren—people who understand and might have advice or just an open ear and a shoulder to cry on—at the Grandparents Raising Grandchildren Support Group that meets monthly at Westgate Mall.

"I have one of those, too," said Mariellen Ritts, who also is raising an eight-year-old grandson. "His problem is the kids he's hanging out with at school."

As the discussion continued, some of the others—grandparents, great-grandparents and foster grandparents—threw in whatever advice they had to offer. Then Ritts, who acts as the group leader, said she would arrange for a speaker to come in and talk about behavioral issues among elementary school kids.

Another grandparent then brought up the grandparent-rights bills being presented at the Legislature. She explained what the bills were and told when they would be heard.

The group also made plans for a chili feed and talked about some of the speakers and events in the months to come.

"When I first got into that group (about five years ago), I didn't realize there were that many (other grandparents) out there," said Ritts, adding there are more than sixty members, though usually less than half attend the meetings.

Ritts said they discuss problems they or their grandchildren are having, they support each other during court battles, and they lean on each other when they find themselves lacking parental rights.

"It's just a good group because we understand each other," said Steiger, adding it's comforting to hear other people's stories. "We shed many tears, but everybody understands when you break down. We're all in the same boat."

Dr. Sandra Bailey started the Grandparents Raising Grandchildren Project through Montana State University Extension after seeing the need to provide grandparents with resources to help with the challenges associated with raising their grandchildren. . . .

The network of grandparents raising grandchildren support groups popping up around the

women (especially the "older elderly") live alone, compared to 19 percent of older men (U.S. Census Bureau, 2008).

For most older people, family members are the major source of social support. The majority of U.S. seniors have at least one adult child living no more than 10 miles away. About half of these nearby children visit their parents at least once a week, although research confirms that daughters are more likely than sons to visit regularly (Lin & Rogerson, 1994; Rimer, 1998). In addition, older people are playing an increasing role in the lives of not only their children but also their grandchildren. Seeing Sociology in the News takes a closer look.

Retirement

Beyond earnings, work provides us with an important part of our personal identity. Therefore, retirement means not only a reduction in income but also less social prestige and perhaps some loss of purpose in life.

Some organizations help ease this transition. Colleges and universities, for example, confer the title "professor emeritus" (*emeritus* in Latin means "fully earned") on retired faculty members, many of whom are permitted to keep library privileges, a parking space, and an e-mail account. These highly experienced faculty can be a valuable resource not only to students but to younger professors as well (Parini, 2001).

Because seniors are socially diverse, there is no single formula for successful retirement. Part-time work occupies many people entering old age and provides some extra cash as well. Grandparenting is an enormous source of pleasure for many older people. Volunteer work is another path to rewarding activity, especially for those who have saved enough so that they do not have to work—one reason that volunteerism is increasing more among seniors than in any other age category (Gardyn, 2000; Savishinsky, 2000; Shapiro, 2001).

Although retirement is a familiar idea, the concept developed only within the past century or so in high-income countries. High-income societies are so productive that not everyone needs to work; in addition, advanced technology places a premium on up-to-date skills. Therefore, retirement emerged as a strategy to permit younger workers—presumably those with the most current knowledge and training—to have the largest presence in the labor force. Fifty years ago, most companies in the United States even had a mandatory retirement age, typically between sixty-five and seventy, although in the 1970s, Congress enacted laws phasing out such policies so that they apply to only a few occupations today. For example, air traffic controllers hired after 1972 must retire at age fifty-six, commercial airline pilots must retire at age sixty, and most police officers and firefighters must retire between fifty-five and sixty (Gokhale, 2004). In most high-income societies, then, retirement is a personal choice made possible by private and government pension programs. In low-income nations, most people do not have the opportunity to retire from paid work.

Even in high-income nations, of course, people can choose to retire only if they can afford to do so. Generally speaking, when ecostate is an example of how the project is helping. The project, with the help of AARP and several state agencies, also offers parent education classes, coordinates a statewide task force to address grandparents' needs, produces fact sheets and newsletters, and operates a library of reference materials on family and parenting.

Through the project, grandparents can find information about the Women Infant Children (WIC) program, Temporary Assistance for Needy Families (TANF), Children's Health Insurance Plan (CHIP), DPHHS Senior and Long Term Care (SLTC), plus everything from food stamps to Medicaid to finding child care.

Jona McNamee, extension agent at the Cascade County Extension office, said some people make quilts for the grandparents and others donate meals or various services, such as haircuts and manicures. . . .

Marion Mullins was raised by her grandmother, and now she is raising three of her own grandchildren. . . .

Mullins leads the Busy Beavers 4-H Club that meets every other Saturday at the First English Lutheran Church, "unless there's a wedding or something," she said. She's been teaching the kids how to sew, cook, garden and do ceramics and woodworking.

"I'm drawing on what I learned when I was in 4-H," she said. "I had an excellent teacher; I remember everything she taught me."

Most of the kids in the group are being raised by their grandparents, though the group is open to anyone ages 6 to 18 who would like to join. It only costs $5 a year, plus the occasional cost of supplies, to join a 4-H club, where kids can learn skills that will help them throughout their lives.

"They're getting some sort of direction; they're learning new tasks," Mullins said. "My guys, they've learned to do their own laundry; they're learning how to cook. One of my kids is ADHD, and he excels with his cooking. Also I've let him sew a little bit and he excels at that."

Mullins said many of the kids in the Busy Beavers come from families that don't have a lot of money. But people donate to the group ("someone donated the wood for the woodworking"), and she has the molds and is able to fire the ceramics and supply the paint.

"If someone wanted to donate materials for sewing, they could take it to the extension office," she said.

WHAT DO YOU THINK?

1. Do you think that, in general, grandparents should have specific rights with respect to their grandchildren? If so, what rights? Why?
2. Why do you think the number of grandparents raising young children is going up?
3. What benefits do grandparents gain by raising grandchildren?

Adapted from the original article, "Grandparents Raising Grandkids: Everybody Understands," by Stacy Byrne, *Great Falls Tribune*, April 6, 2009, www.greatfallstribune.com.

nomic times are good, people save more and think about retiring early. This was generally the case in the United States during the second half of the twentieth century. By 2005, the median net worth of senior households was about $200,000. Greater wealth permitted more people to retire earlier, and so the median retirement age fell from sixty-eight in 1950 to sixty-three by 2005.

However, the economic downturn that began in 2007 has had the opposite effect, forcing older people to confront the harsh reality that their retirement "nest egg" has been cracked by the sinking stock market and disappearing pensions. With so much wealth suddenly gone, many find that they must continue to work. A recent policy to deal with hard times is "staged retirement," in which people continue working well past the age of sixty-five, reducing their hours at work to a point that allows them to build greater financial security (Kadlec, 2002; McCartney, 2005; Koskela, 2008).

Some retired people, including many whose investments have declined in value or who now face expenses that they cannot afford, are being forced to go back to paid work. The Seeing Sociology in Everyday Life box takes a closer look.

Aging and Poverty

By the time they reach sixty-five, most people have paid off their home mortgages and their children's college expenses. But the costs of medical care, household help, and home utilities (like heat) typically go up. At the same time, retirement often means a significant decline in income. The good news is that over recent decades, seniors have built up more wealth than ever before (as noted, a median net worth of about $200,000 in 2005). However, most of this is tied up in the value of their homes, which has fallen in recent years. And home values do not provide income for everyday expenses. The economic downturn has also hurt many seniors, as employers have cut back retirement pensions and benefits at the same time that investment income has declined. Today's reality, then, is that most people over age sixty-five get most of their income from the government in the form of Social Security. This helps explain why the risk of poverty rises after midlife, as shown in Figure 2.

Looking back in time, the poverty rate among the elderly fell from about 35 percent in 1960 to 9.7 percent in 2007—below the 12.5 percent rate for the entire population. The long-term trend since about 1980 shows that seniors have posted a 35 percent increase in average income (in constant dollars), double the increase in income of people under thirty-five (U.S. Census Bureau, 2008).

Several factors have boosted the financial strength of seniors. Better health now allows people who want to work to stay in the labor force, and more of today's older couples earn two incomes. Government policy, too, has helped older people, because programs benefiting the elderly—including Social Security—now amount to almost half of all government spending, even as spending on children has remained flat. But the recent economic downturn has canceled out many of these advantages as people have lost some of the pension income they were counting on, and as more companies reduce

SEEING SOCIOLOGY in Everyday Life

The argument supporting a mandatory retirement age for airline pilots rests on the fact that the lives of hundreds of people are, literally, in their hands. What about surgeons, who currently are not subject to mandatory retirement? Should there be such a requirement or not? Why?

SEEING SOCIOLOGY in Everyday Life

Do you think that the adult children of elderly people should be expected to help with the financial needs of their parents? Why or why not?

SEEING SOCIOLOGY IN EVERYDAY LIFE

Back to Work! Will We Ever Get to Retire?

Sixty-year-old Martha Perry used to think about old age as the "golden years." Perry had worked hard for decades, and it had paid off. The sale of her small business, added to years of regular savings, netted her a total of about $1 million, which she invested. Based on the projected earnings from her investments, with additional income from Social Security, Perry figured she was set for the rest of her life. She looked forward to playing golf, enjoying an active social life, and traveling.

That was before the stock market tumble that began in 2008. A year later, her accountant gave her some bad news: Her nest egg had lost half its value. With barely half the income she expected—only about $16,000 a year—Perry's travel plans have been put on hold. "I'm going to have to look for part-time work," she says, shaking her head. "But something tells me it's going to end up being full-time work."

The severe recession that began in 2007 has sent stock prices tumbling and caused home values to fall. This economic downturn has hit everyone hard, but older people who rely on investment income have suffered more than most. Many have seen their retirement vanish as quickly as the money in their 401(k) investment portfolios. Still others have lost retirement investments as a result of corporate scandals. That explains why millions of older people who had hoped to retire are still working and millions of retirees who can no longer make ends meet are now reading the want ads and once again looking for work.

This trend helps explain why the share of older people in the labor force is now going up. Certainly, some seniors are happy to continue their careers, and others enjoy working part time. But in the past, many seniors did so by choice, enjoying their jobs while knowing they could retire whenever they wanted to. Now millions of people realize that they no longer have a choice. Worse, they wonder whether they will ever be able to step out of the labor force. For those who do not like the jobs they have, of course, the future will be far less happy. The bottom line: The dream of "early retirement," widespread a decade ago, is all but gone.

Getty Images, Inc. – Liaison/Howell

People used to believe that if they "played by the rules" and worked hard for decades, they could expect a comfortable retirement. What has the recent economic downturn done to this idea?

WHAT DO YOU THINK?

1. What is the relationship between how well the economy is doing and people's retirement plans?
2. Why does "phased retirement" for many older people really mean "delayed retirement"?
3. Do you know anyone who has had a pension reduced or canceled by a corporation? How has that affected the person's financial security?

Sources: Kadlec (2002) and Koskela (2008).

or cancel retirement benefits, workers and retirees are receiving less to fund their future.

As we have seen in earlier chapters, some categories of people face particular challenges. Disadvantages linked to race and ethnicity throughout the life course persist in old age. In 2007, the poverty rate among elderly Hispanics (17.1 percent) and African Americans (23.2 percent) was two to three times higher than the rate for elderly non-Hispanic whites (7.4 percent) (U.S. Census Bureau, 2008).

Gender also shapes the lives of people as they age. Among full-time workers, women over sixty-five had median earnings of $31,517 in 2007, compared to $45,340 for men over sixty-five. A quick calculation shows that these older full-time working women earned just 70 percent as much as comparable men. Thus the income gap linked to gender is greater among older people than among younger people (recall that *all* working women earn 78 percent as much as *all* working men). This is because older women typically have much less schooling than men their age, so they hold lower-paying jobs, which are also less likely to provide pensions later on.

But because most elderly people have retired from the labor force, a more realistic financial picture must take account of all seniors. When we include both those who are working and those who are not, median individual income is far lower: $15,714 for women, which is 57 percent of the $27,454 earned by men (U.S. Census Bureau, 2008). In light of these low averages, it is easy to see why seniors—and especially women, who are less likely to have pensions or income other than Social Security—are concerned about expenses

caregiving information and unpaid care provided to a dependent person by family members, other relatives, or friends

ageism prejudice and discrimination against older people

such as the costs of health care and prescription drugs, both of which are rising fast (Fetto, 2003a; Institute for Women's Policy Research, 2007).

In the United States, today as in decades past, growing old (especially for women and other minorities) increases the risk of poverty. One government study found that elderly households typically spend about 80 percent of their income on housing, food, health care, and other basic necessities. This points to the conclusion that most seniors are just getting by (Federal Interagency Forum, 2008).

Finally, poverty among the elderly is often hidden from view. Because of personal pride and a desire to remain independent, many elderly people hide financial problems, even from their own families. People who have supported their children for years find it difficult to admit that they can no longer provide for themselves.

Diversity Snapshot

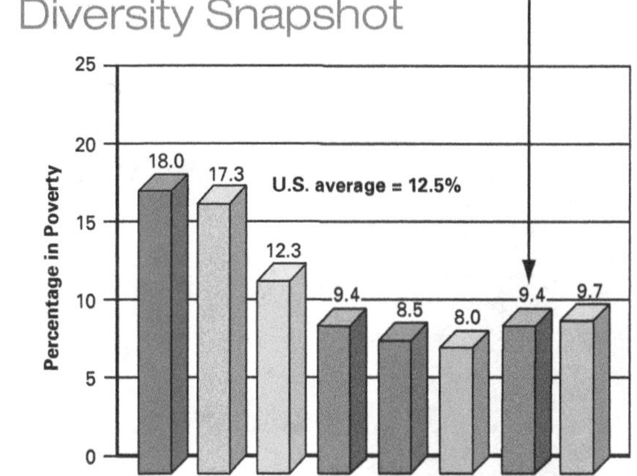

FIGURE 2 **U.S. Poverty Rates, by Age, 2007**

The highest poverty rate is for young people. But among older people, the rate rises once again.

Source: U.S. Census Bureau (2008).

Caregiving

In an aging society, the need for caregiving is bound to increase. **Caregiving** refers to *informal and unpaid care provided to a dependent person by family members, other relatives, or friends.* Although parents provide caregiving to children, the term is more often applied to the needs of elderly men and women. Indeed, today's middle-aged adults are called the "sandwich generation" because many will spend as much time caring for their aging parents as for their own children.[1]

Who Are the Caregivers?

Surveys show that 80 percent of caregiving to elders is provided by family members, in most cases by one person. Most caregivers live close to the older person. In addition, most caregiving is provided by women, most often daughters or wives. This gender norm is so strong that daughters-in-law are more likely than blood-related sons to care for an aging parent (National Alliance for Caregiving and AARP, 2004; U.S. Department of Health and Human Services, 2004).

About two-thirds of caregivers are married, and one-third are also responsible for young children. When we add the fact that half of all caregivers also have a part- or full-time job, it is clear that caregiving is a responsibility over and above what most people already consider a full day's work. Half of all primary caregivers spend more than twenty hours per week providing elder care.

Elder Abuse

Abuse of older people takes many forms, from passive neglect to active torment; it includes verbal, emotional, financial, and physical harm. At least 1 million elderly people (3 percent of the total) suffer serious maltreatment each year, and three times as many (about 10 percent) suffer abuse at some point. Like other forms of family violence, abuse of the elderly often goes unreported because the victims are reluctant to talk about their plight (Holmstrom, 1994; M. Thompson, 1997, 1998; National Center on Elder Abuse, 2005).

Many caregivers experience fatigue, emotional distress, and guilt over not being able to do more. Abuse is most likely to occur if the caregiver not only finds the work difficult but also (1) works full time, (2) cares for young children, (3) is poor, (4) feels little affection for the older person, (5) finds the elderly person very difficult, and (6) gets no support or help from others.

But the relatively small share of cases involving abuse should not overshadow the positive side of caregiving. Helping another person is a selfless act of human kindness that affirms the best in us and provides a source of personal enrichment and satisfaction (Lund, 1993).

Ageism

Ideology—including racism and sexism—serves to justify the social disadvantages of minorities. In the same way, sociologists use the term **ageism** for *prejudice and discrimination against older people.* Elderly people are the primary targets of ageism, although middle-aged

[1]This discussion of caregiving is based on Lund (1993) and additional information provided by Dale Lund.

SEEING SOCIOLOGY in Everyday Life

On your campus, are the most popular faculty members younger instructors or older instructors? Do you think that age plays into a professor's student evaluations? If so, how?

SEEING SOCIOLOGY in Everyday Life

Do you think elderly people should be considered a minority? Explain why or why not.

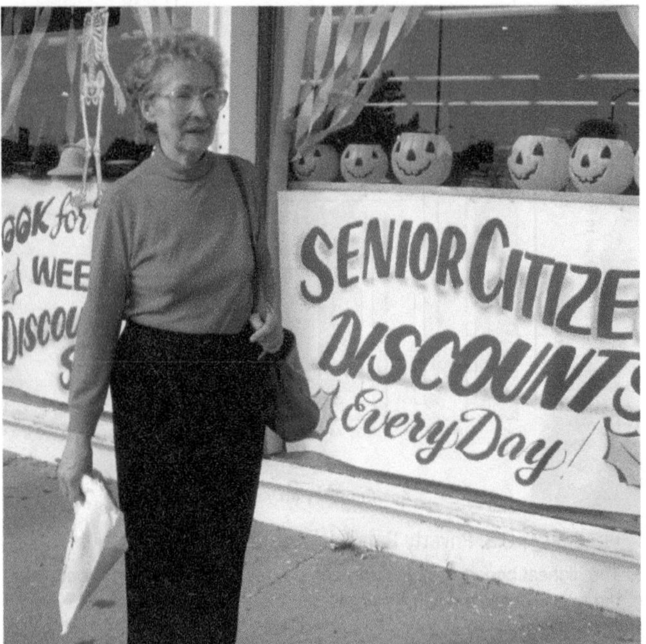

In the United States, it is common for businesses to offer a "senior discount" to people over sixty-five (sometimes even fifty-five). What is the reason for this practice? Would you prefer a policy of offering discounts to single parents with children, a category of people at much higher risk of poverty?

people can suffer as well. Examples of ageism include passing over qualified older job applicants in favor of younger workers or firing older workers first.

Like racism and sexism, ageism can be blatant (as when a company decides not to hire a sixty-year-old applicant because of her age) or subtle (as when a nurse speaks to elderly patients in a condescending tone, as if they were children). Also like racism and sexism, ageism builds physical traits into stereotypes. In the case of the elderly, some people consider gray hair, wrinkled skin, and stooped posture signs of personal incompetence. Negative stereotypes portray the aged as helpless, confused, unable to deal with change, and generally unhappy. Even "positive" images of sweet little old ladies and eccentric old gentlemen are stereotypes that gloss over individuality and ignore years of experience and accomplishment (Butler, 1975; E. Cohen, 2001).

Sometimes ageism reflects a bit of truth. Statistically speaking, older people are more likely than younger people to be mentally and physically impaired. But we slip into ageism when we make unfair generalizations about an entire category of people.

Betty Friedan (1993), a pioneer of the modern feminist movement, believes that ageism is deeply rooted in our culture. She points out that few elderly people appear in the mass media; only a small percentage of television shows, for example, feature main characters over age sixty. More generally, when most of us think about older people, it is often in negative terms: This older man *lacks* a job, that older woman has *lost* her vitality, and seniors *look back* to their youth. In short, says Friedan, we often treat being old as if it were a disease, marked by decline and deterioration, for which there is no cure.

Even so, Friedan believes that older women and men in the United States are discovering that they have more to contribute than others give them credit for. Advising small business owners, designing housing for the poor, teaching children to read—there are countless ways in which older people can help others and at the same time enhance their own lives.

The Elderly: A Minority?

Elderly people in the United States face social disadvantages. Does that mean that the elderly are a minority in the same way as, say, African Americans or women?

The elderly appear to meet the definition of a minority because they have a clear social identity based on their age and they are subject to prejudice and discrimination. But Gordon Streib (1968) counters that we should not think of elderly people as a minority. First, minority status is usually both permanent and exclusive. That is, a person is an African American or a woman *for life* and cannot become part of the dominant category of whites or men. But being elderly is an *open* status because people are elderly for only part of their lives, and everyone who has the good fortune to live long enough grows old.

Second, the seniors at highest risk of being poor or otherwise disadvantaged fall into categories of people—women, African Americans, Hispanics—who are at highest risk of being poor throughout the life course. As Streib sees it, it is not so much that the old grow poor as that the poor grow old.

If so, old people are not a minority in the same sense as other categories. It might be better to say that the elderly are a part of our population that faces special challenges as they age.

Theoretical Analysis of Aging

Let us now apply sociology's theoretical approaches to gain insight into how society shapes the lives of the elderly. We will consider the structural-functional, symbolic-interaction, and social-conflict approaches in turn.

disengagement theory the idea that society functions in an orderly way by removing people from positions of responsibility as they reach old age

activity theory the idea that a high level of activity increases personal satisfation in old age

Structural-Functional Analysis: Aging and Disengagement

Drawing on the ideas of Talcott Parsons—an architect of the structural-functional approach—Elaine Cumming and William Henry (1961) explain that the physical decline and death that accompany aging can disrupt society. In response, society *disengages* the elderly, gradually transferring statuses and roles from the old to the young so that tasks are performed with minimal interruption. **Disengagement theory** is *the idea that society functions in an orderly way by removing people from positions of responsibility as they reach old age.*

Disengagement ensures the orderly operation of society by removing aging people from productive roles before they are no longer able to perform them. Another benefit of disengagement in a rapidly changing society is that it makes room for young workers, who typically have the most up-to-date skills and training. Disengagement provides benefits to aging people as well. Although most sixty-year-olds in the United States wish to keep working, most begin to think about retirement and perhaps cut back a bit on their workload. Exactly when people begin to disengage from their careers, of course, depends on their health, enjoyment of the job, and financial situation.

Retiring does not mean being inactive. Some people start a new career and others pursue hobbies or engage in volunteer work. In general, people in their sixties start to think less about what they *have been doing* and begin to think more about what they *want to do* with the rest of their lives (Palmore, 1979; Schultz & Heckhausen, 1996).

CRITICAL REVIEW Disengagement theory explains why rapidly changing high-income societies tend to define their oldest members as socially marginal. But there are several limitations to this approach.

First, especially in recent years, many workers have found that they cannot disengage from paid work because they need the income. Second, some elderly people, rich or poor, do not want to disengage from work they enjoy. Disengagement may also mean losing friends and social prestige. Third, it is not clear that the societal benefits of disengagement outweigh its social costs, which include the loss of human resources and the need to take care of people who might otherwise be able to support themselves. As the number of elderly people swells, finding ways to help seniors remain independent is a high priority. Fourth, any rigid system of disengagement does not take account of the widely differing abilities of the elderly. This concern leads us to the symbolic-interaction approach.

CHECK YOUR LEARNING State clearly the basic idea behind disengagement theory. How does disengagement benefit the aging individual? How does it benefit society?

Paul Barton

Disengagement theory suggests that society gradually removes responsibilities from people as they grow old. Activity theory counters that like people at any stage of life, elders find life worthwhile to the extent that they stay active. As a result, many older men and women seek out new jobs, hobbies, and social activities.

Symbolic-Interaction Analysis: Aging and Activity

Drawing on the symbolic-interaction approach, **activity theory** is *the idea that a high level of activity increases personal satisfaction in old age.* Because everyone bases social identity on many roles, disengagement is bound to reduce satisfaction and meaning in the lives of older people. What seniors need is not to be pushed out of roles but to have many productive or recreational options. The importance of having choices is especially great for today's sixty-five-year-old, who can look forward to about twenty more years of life (Smart, 2001; M. W. Walsh, 2001).

Activity theory does not reject the idea of job disengagement; it simply says that people need to find new roles to replace those they leave behind. Research confirms that elderly people who maintain a high activity level find the most satisfaction in their lives.

Activity theory also recognizes that the elderly are diverse, with a variety of interests, needs, and physical abilities. For this reason, the activities that people choose and the pace at which they pursue them are always an individual matter (Neugarten, 1977; Moen, Dempster-McClain, & Williams, 1992).

CRITICAL REVIEW Activity theory shifts the focus of analysis from the needs of society (as stated in disengagement theory) to the needs of the elderly themselves. It emphasizes the

MAKING THE GRADE

In one important sense, activity theory, which says that people must be active to find meaning in life, is a direct challenge to disengagement theory.

APPLYING THEORY

Aging and the Elderly

	Structural-Functional Approach	Symbolic-Interaction Approach	Social-Conflict Approach
What is the level of analysis?	Macro-level	Micro-level	Macro-level
How do we understand growing old?	The fact that people grow old and eventually die can disrupt the operation of society. Therefore, societies disengage the elderly from important tasks and other responsibilities as they reach old age.	For elders, like everyone else, being active encourages both health and happiness. Therefore, elders strive to maintain a high activity level, replacing roles they leave with new roles.	Aging is one dimension of social stratification. Generally, middle-aged people have the most wealth and power. Poor people, women, and other minorities face the greatest disadvantages as they grow old.

social diversity of elderly people and highlights the importance of choice in any government policy.

A limitation of this approach is that it assumes that elders are both healthy and competent, which may or may not be the case. Another problem with this approach is that it ignores the fact that many of the problems older people face—such as poverty—have more to do with society than with themselves. We turn now to that point of view: social-conflict theory.

CHECK YOUR LEARNING Explain what activity theory says about aging. How does this approach challenge disengagement theory?

Social-Conflict Analysis: Aging and Inequality

A social-conflict analysis is based on the idea that access to opportunities and social resources differs for people in different age categories. For this reason, age is a dimension of social stratification. In the United States, middle-aged people enjoy the greatest power and the most opportunities and privileges, and the elderly and people under the age of twenty-five have a higher risk of poverty. Employers who replace senior workers with younger men and women in order to keep wages low may not intend to discriminate against older people. However, according to recent court rulings, if such policies have the effect of causing special harm to older people, they amount to discrimination.

The social-conflict approach claims that our industrial-capitalist economy creates an age-based hierarchy. In line with Marxist thought, Steven Spitzer (1980) points out that a profit-oriented society devalues any category of people that is less productive. To the extent that older people do not work, our society labels them as mildly deviant.

Social-conflict analysis also draws attention to various dimensions of social inequality within the elderly population. Differences of class, race, ethnicity, and gender divide older people as they do everyone else. For this reason, some seniors have far greater economic security, access to better medical care, and more options for personal satisfaction in old age than others. Elderly white people typically enjoy advantages denied to older minorities. And women—an increasing majority as people age—suffer the social and economic disadvantages of both sexism and ageism.

CRITICAL REVIEW The social-conflict approach adds to our understanding of the aging process by highlighting age-based inequality and pointing out that capitalism devalues elderly people who are less productive. But critics claim that the real culprit is *industrialization.* As evidence they point to the fact that the elderly are not better off under a socialist system, as a Marxist analysis implies. Furthermore, the idea that either industrialization or capitalism necessarily causes the elderly to suffer is challenged by the long-term rise in income and well-being experienced by seniors in the United States. The Applying Theory table summarizes what we learn from each of the theoretical approaches.

CHECK YOUR LEARNING What does Marxist theory teach us about aging in a capitalist society?

SEEING SOCIOLOGY in Everyday Life

Ask members of your class if they have ever seen a person die. Do the responses support the idea that modern society separates death from life?

Death and Dying

> To every thing there is a season,
> And a time for every matter under heaven:
> A time to be born and a time to die . . .

These lines from the biblical book of Ecclesiastes state two basic truths about human existence: the fact of birth and the inevitability of death. Just as life varies throughout history and around the world, death has many faces. We conclude this chapter with a brief look at the changing character of death, the final stage in the process of growing old.

Historical Patterns of Death

In the past, death was a familiar part of life. Many children died soon after birth, a fact that led many parents to delay naming children until they were one or two years old. For those fortunate enough to survive infancy, illness, accidents, and natural catastrophes made life uncertain at best.

Sometimes food shortages forced societies to protect the majority by sacrificing the least productive members. *Infanticide* is the killing of newborn infants, and *geronticide* is the killing of the elderly.

Because death was commonplace, it was readily accepted. Medieval Christianity assured believers that death fit into the divine plan for human existence. Here is how the historian Philippe Ariès describes Sir Lancelot, one of King Arthur's knights of the Round Table, preparing for death when he thinks he is mortally wounded:

> His gestures were fixed by old customs, ritual gestures which must be carried out when one is about to die. He removed his weapons and lay quietly upon the ground. . . . He spread his arms out, his body forming a cross . . . in such a way that his head faced east toward Jerusalem. (1974:7–8)

As societies gradually learned more about health and medicine, death became less of an everyday experience. Fewer children died at birth, and accidents and disease took a smaller toll among adults. As a result, most people living in high-income societies today view dying as extraordinary, something that happens to the very old or to younger people in rare and tragic cases. Back in 1900, about one-third of all deaths in the United States occurred before the age of five and fully two-thirds before the age of fifty-five. Today, by contrast, 84 percent of people in the United States die *after* reaching the age of fifty-five. Death and old age are closely linked in our culture.

The Modern Separation of Life and Death

Now removed from everyday experience, death seems somehow unnatural. Social conditions prepared our ancestors to accept death, but modern society's youth culture and aggressive medical technology foster a desire for eternal youth and immortality. Death has become separated from life.

Corbis – NY/Chris Rainier

In many traditional societies, people express great respect not only for elders but also for their ancestors. Dani villagers in New Guinea mummified the body of this elder in a sitting position so that they could continue to honor him and feel his presence in their daily lives.

Death is also *physically* removed from everyday activities. The clearest evidence of this is that many of us have never seen a person actually die. Our ancestors typically died at home in the presence of family and friends, but most deaths today occur in impersonal settings such as hospitals and nursing homes. Even in hospitals, dying patients occupy a special part of the building, and hospital morgues are located well out of sight of patients and visitors alike (Ariès, 1974; Lee, 2002).

Ethical Issues: Confronting Death

In a society in which technology gives us the power to prolong life, moral questions about when and how people should die are more pressing than ever. For example, the national debate in 2005 surrounding the death of Terri Schiavo, who was kept alive by mechanical means for fifteen years, was not just about the fate of one woman; many people feel we need a better understanding of what the "right to die" rules should be.

MAKING THE GRADE

Even death is now a cultural factor; in many cases, it results from a decision.

SEEING SOCIOLOGY in Everyday Life

Where do you stand on the right-to-die debate? Why?

THINKING GLOBALLY

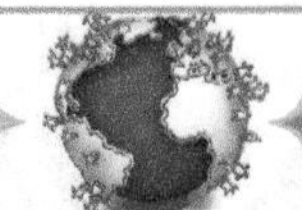

Death on Demand: Euthanasia in the Netherlands

Marcus Erich picked up the telephone and called his brother Arjen. In a quiet voice, thirty-two-year-old Marcus announced, "Friday at five o'clock." When the time came, Arjen was there, having driven to his brother's farmhouse south of Amsterdam. They said their final good-byes. Soon afterward, Marcus's physician arrived. Marcus and the doctor spoke for a few moments, and then the doctor prepared a "cocktail" of barbiturates and other drugs. As Marcus drank the mixture, he made a face, joking, "Can't you make this sweeter?"

As the minutes passed, Marcus lay back and his eyes closed. But after half an hour, he was still breathing. At that point, according to their earlier agreement, the physician administered a lethal injection. Minutes later, Marcus's life came to an end.

Events like this take us to the heart of the belief that people have a "right to die." Marcus Erich was dying of AIDS. For five years, his body had been wasting away, and he was suffering greatly with no hope of recovery. He wanted his doctor to end his life.

The Netherlands, a small nation in northwestern Europe, has gone further than any other in the world in allowing mercy killing, or euthanasia. A 1981 Dutch law allows a physician to assist in a suicide if the following five conditions are met:

1. The patient must make a voluntary, well-considered, and repeated request to a doctor for help in dying.
2. The patient's suffering must be unbearable and without hope of improvement.
3. The doctor and the patient must discuss alternatives.
4. The doctor must consult with at least one colleague who has access to the patient and the patient's medical records.
5. The assisted suicide must be performed in accordance with sound medical practice.

Getty Images Inc. – Hulton Archive Photos/Reuters/Dutch Tv

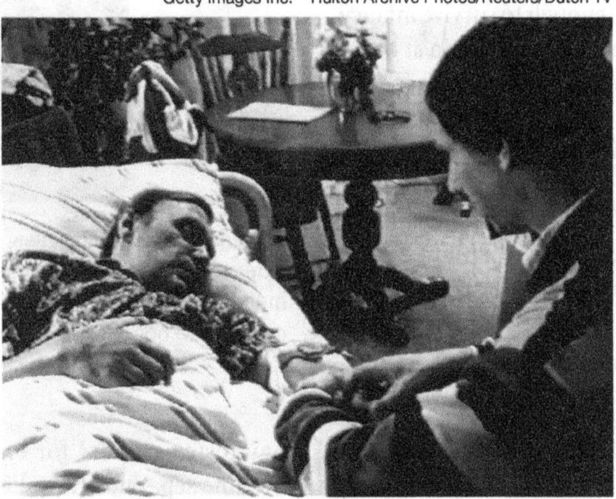

The Netherlands has been at the forefront of the movement to extend active euthanasia. Recently, a doctor administering a fatal injection to a man suffering from Lou Gehrig's disease was shown on Dutch national television. Where do you stand on this issue?

Official records indicate that doctors end about 2,000 lives a year in the Netherlands, and the number has been rising slowly but steadily. But because many cases are never reported, the actual number may be two or three times as high. Critics point to the fact that in recent years, Dutch doctors have brought about the death of people who, due to their illness, were not able to clearly state their desire to die. Although the Dutch policy of euthanasia enjoys widespread popular support in the Netherlands, it remains controversial in the world as a whole.

WHAT DO YOU THINK?

1. What advantages and benefits do you see in the Dutch law permitting physician-assisted suicide?
2. What are the disadvantages or dangers of such a law?
3. What about cases in which a person is very ill and cannot state the desire to die or not to die? Should euthanasia be permitted in such cases? If so, when and why?

Sources: Della Cava (1997), Mauro (1997), and B. Barr (2004).

When Does Death Occur?

Perhaps the most basic question is the most difficult: Exactly how do we define death? Common sense suggests that life ceases when breathing and heartbeat stop. But the ability of medical personnel to resuscitate someone after a heart attack and artificially sustain breathing makes such definitions of death obsolete. Medical and legal experts in the United States continue to debate the meaning of death, but many now consider death an *irreversible* state involving no response to stimulation, no movement or breathing, no reflexes, and no indication of brain activity (Wall, 1980; D. G. Jones, 1998).

The Right-to-Die Debate

Terri Schiavo remained alive without evidence of being conscious or responsive to her surroundings for fifteen years following a heart attack that cut off blood to her brain. Debate surrounding this case, which ended with her death after her feeding tube was removed, shows that many people are less afraid of death than of the prospect of being kept alive at all costs. In other words, medical technology that can sustain life also threatens personal freedom by letting doctors or others rather than the dying person decide when life is to end. In response, people who support a "right to die" seek control over

euthanasia assisting in the death of a person suffering from an incurable disease

their own deaths just as they seek control over their lives (Ogden, 2001).

After thoughtful discussion, patients, families, and physicians may decide not to take "heroic measures" to keep a person alive. Physicians and family members may issue a "do not resuscitate" order, which will allow a patient who stops breathing to die. *Living wills*—documents stating which medical procedures an individual wants and does not want under specific conditions—are now widely used.

A more difficult issue involves mercy killing, or **euthanasia** (also known as "mercy killing")—*assisting in the death of a person suffering from an incurable disease.* Euthanasia (from the Greek, meaning "a good death") poses an ethical dilemma because it involves not just refusing treatment but actively taking steps to end life. Some people see euthanasia as an act of kindness, while others consider it a form of murder.

Is there a right to die? People with incurable diseases can choose not to have treatment that might prolong their lives. But whether a doctor should be allowed to help bring about death is a matter of debate. In 1997, voters in Oregon passed a right-to-die initiative (the Death with Dignity Act). Although this law has been challenged repeatedly ever since, Oregon physicians can legally assist in ending the lives of patients; since then, Oregon physicians have legally assisted in the deaths of about 350 patients (Leff, 2008.) In 1997, the U.S. Supreme Court, in *Vacco* v. *Quill,* declared that the U.S. Constitution recognizes no right to die. This decision discouraged other states from considering laws similar to the one in Oregon; only in neighboring Washington in 2008 did voters pass a ballot initiative permitting physician-assisted suicide (Leff, 2008).

Supporters of the right-to-die movement hold up as a model the Netherlands, which has the most permissive euthanasia law in the world. How does the Dutch system operate? The Thinking Globally box takes a closer look.

Should the United States hold the line on euthanasia or follow the lead of the Dutch? Right-to-die advocates maintain that a person facing extreme suffering should be able to choose to live or die. And if death is the choice, medical assistance can help people toward a "good death." Surveys show that two-thirds of U.S. adults support giving people the option of dying with a doctor's help (NORC, 2007).

On the other side of the debate, opponents fear that laws allowing physician-assisted suicide invite abuse. Pointing to the Netherlands, critics cite surveys indicating that in most cases, the five conditions for physician-assisted suicide are not met. In particular, most physicians do not consult with another doctor or even report the euthanasia to authorities. Of greater concern is the fact that in about one-fifth of all physician-assisted suicides, the patient never explicitly asks to die. This is so even though half of these patients are conscious and capable of making decisions themselves (Gillon, 1999). This fact—and the steadily rising number of physician-assisted suicides in the Netherlands—leads opponents to argue that legalizing physician-assisted suicide puts a nation on a slippery slope toward more and more euthanasia. How can we be sure, they ask, that ill people won't be pushed into accepting death by doctors who consider suicide the right choice for the terminally ill or by family members who are weary of caring for them or want to avoid the expenses of medical treatment?

AP Wide World Photos/Beth A. Keiser

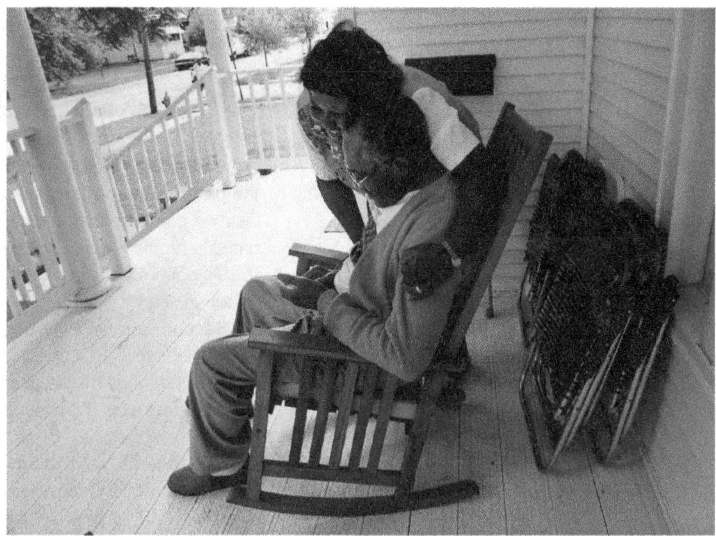

Unlike a hospital, which tries to save and extend life, the hospice movement tries to give dying people greater comfort, including the companionship and support of family members.

Evidence drawn from the United States does not raise fears in the same way. In Oregon, the number of annual cases of physician-assisted suicide has remained low—around thirty a year. No matter how the right-to-die debate eventually turns out, we have entered a new era when it comes to dying. Today, individuals, family members, and medical personnel must face death not as a medical fact but as a negotiated outcome.

Bereavement

Elisabeth Kübler-Ross (1969) found that most people usually confront their own death in stages. Initially, individuals react with *denial,* followed by *anger;* then they try *negotiation,* hoping for divine intervention. Gradually, they fall into *resignation* and finally reach *acceptance.*

SEEING SOCIOLOGY in Everyday Life

How might recent efforts to extend health care to everyone figure into the "limits" debate?

CONTROVERSY & DEBATE

Setting Limits: Must We "Pull the Plug" on Old Age?

SIMONE: I'm almost sixty now. When I'm eighty-five, I want the best medical care I can find. Why shouldn't I get it?

JUAN: I'll tell you why—because our society can't spend more and more money on extending the lives of old people when so many children are at risk.

SERGIO: I guess the answer depends on whether you're young or old.

As the U.S. elderly population soars, as new technology gives us more power to prolong life, and as medical care gets increasingly expensive, many people now wonder just how much old age we can afford. Currently, about half the average person's lifetime spending for medical care occurs during the final years of life, and the share is rising. Against the spiraling costs of prolonging life, we well may ask if what is medically *possible* is morally *desirable*. In the decades to come, warns the gerontologist Daniel Callahan (1987), an elderly population ready and eager to extend their lives will eventually force us either to "pull the plug" on old age or to shortchange everyone else.

Just raising this issue, Callahan admits, seems cold and heartless. But consider that the bill for the elderly's health topped $400 billion in 2007—more than four times what it cost in 1980. This dramatic increase reflects the current policy of directing more and more medical resources to studying and treating the diseases and disabilities of old age.

So Callahan makes the case for limits. First, the more we spend on behalf of the elderly, the less we can provide for others. With poverty a growing problem among children, can we afford to spend more and more on the oldest members of our society?

Second, a *longer* life does not necessarily mean a *better* life. Cost aside, does heart surgery that prolongs the life of an eighty-four-year-old woman a year or two necessarily improve the quality of her life? Cost considered, would those resources yield more "quality of life" if used, say, to give a ten-year-old child a kidney transplant? Or to provide basic care and comfort to hundreds of low-income seniors?

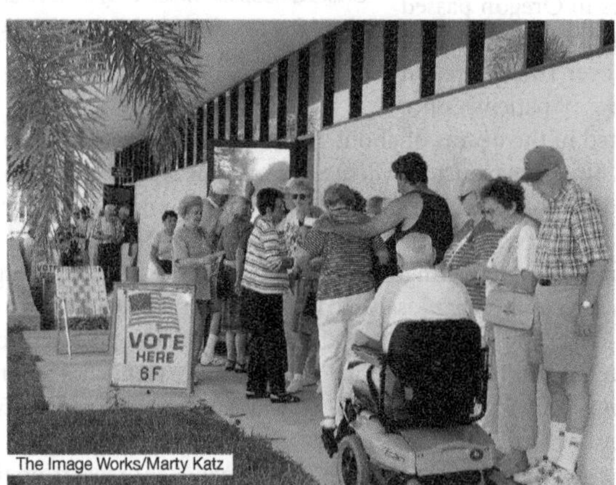

The Image Works/Marty Katz

The share of our population over the age of sixty-five is going up. in addition, older people are very likely to vote. What do these facts lead you to predict about government policy dealing with health care for the elderly?

Third, we need to reconsider our view of death as an enemy to be conquered at all costs. Rather, he suggests, a more realistic position for an aging society is to treat death as a natural end to the life course. If we cannot make peace with death for our own well-being, then in a society with limited resources, we must do it for the benefit of others.

But not everyone agrees. Shouldn't people who have worked all their lives and made our society what it is enjoy our generosity in their final years? Would it be right to deny medical care to aging people who are able and willing to pay for it?

Today, we face questions that few people would have imagined even fifty years ago: Is peak longevity good for everyone? Is it even *possible* for everyone?

WHAT DO YOU THINK?

1. Should doctors and hospitals use a double standard, offering more complete care to the youngest people and limited care to society's oldest members? Why or why not?
2. Do you think that a goal of the medical establishment should be to extend life at all costs? Explain your position.
3. How should society balance the needs of high-income seniors with the needs of those with little or no money to pay for medical care as they age?

Sources: Callahan (1987), and U.S. Census Bureau (2008).

According to some researchers, bereavement follows the same pattern of stages. The people closest to a dying person may initially deny the reality of impending death and then gradually reach a point of acceptance. Other investigators, however, question any linear "stage theory," arguing that bereavement is a very personal and unpredictable process (Lund, Caserta, & Dimond, 1986; Lund, 1989; Cutcliffe, 1998). What experts do agree on, however, is the fact that how family and friends view an impending death has an effect on the person who is dying. By accepting an approaching death, others can help the dying person do the same; denying the death isolates the dying person, who is not able to share feelings and experiences with others.

Everett Collection/Warner Bros.

In the 2007 film *The Bucket List*, two terminally ill men, played by Jack Nicholson (shown above) and Morgan Freeman, set out to experience many grand adventures before they "kick the bucket." Approaching the end of life—if we see it coming—can provide opportunities to resolve many issues that we have carried with us for decades.

Many dying people find support in the *hospice movement.* Unlike a hospital, which is designed to cure disease, a hospice helps people have a good death. These care centers for dying people try to minimize pain and suffering—either at the center or at home—and encourage family members to stay close by. Most hospices also provide social support for family members experiencing bereavement (Foliart & Clausen, 2001).

Under the best of circumstances, bereavement often involves profound grief. Research documents that bereavement is less intense for someone who accepts the death of a loved one and has brought satisfactory closure to the relationship. Such closure also allows family and friends to comfort one another more effectively after a death occurs.

Reaching closure is not possible when a death is unexpected, and survivors' social disorientation may last for years. One study of middle-aged women who had recently experienced the death of their husbands found that many felt they had lost not only a spouse but also their reason for living. Therefore, dealing successfully with bereavement requires the time and social support necessary to form a new sense of self and recognize new life options (Atchley, 1983; Danforth & Glass, 2001). With the number of older people in the United States increasing so fast, understanding death and dying is taking on greater importance.

Aging: Looking Ahead

This chapter has explored the graying of the United States and other high-income nations. By 2050, the number of elderly people in this country will exceed the entire country's population in 1900. In addition, one in four of tomorrow's seniors will be over age eighty-five. In decades to come, then, society's oldest members will gain a far greater voice in everyday life. Younger people will find that careers relating to gerontology—the study of the elderly—are sure to gain in importance.

With more elderly people living longer, will our society have the support services to sustain them? Remember that as the needs of the elderly increase, a smaller share of younger people will be there to respond and pay the bills with their taxes. What about the spiraling medical costs of an aging society? As the baby boomers enter old age, some analysts paint a doomsday picture of the United States, with desperate and dying elderly people everywhere (Longino, 1994). Addressing the need for health care—for old and young alike—is one important task facing the Obama administration.

But there is also good news. For one thing, the health of tomorrow's elderly people—today's middle-aged adults—will be better than ever: Smoking is way down, and more people are becoming aware of the national problem of obesity and are eating more healthfully. Such trends suggest that the elderly may well become more vigorous and independent. Tomorrow's seniors will also enjoy the benefits of steadily advancing medical technology, although, as the Controversy & Debate box explains, how much of the country's medical resources older people can claim is already being hotly debated.

Another positive sign over the past several decades is the growing financial strength of the elderly. The economic downturn after 2000, which intensified in 2008, has been stressful, and many elderly people have lost income, retirement benefits, and equity in their homes. But it is likely that the long-term trend will remain fairly bright for most seniors, and it may turn out that tomorrow's elderly—the baby boomers—will be more affluent than ever. Why? One important fact is that the baby boomers are the first generation of the U.S. population whose women have been in the labor force most of their lives. For this reason, the boomers are likely to have substantial savings and pension income.

At the same time, younger adults will face a mounting responsibility to care for aging parents. A falling birth rate coupled with a growing elderly population will demand that middle-aged people perform an increasing share of caregiving for the very old.

Most of us need to learn more about caring for aging parents, which includes far more than meeting physical needs. More important lessons involve communicating, expressing love, and facing up to eventual death. In caring for our parents, we will also teach important lessons to our children, including the skills they will need, one day, to care for us.

Seeing Sociology in Everyday Life

Aging and the Elderly

How are older adults changing today's society?

A lot has been said about the baby boomers—the women and men born between 1945 and 1964—who were the driving force behind many of the changes that took place in the 1960s and 1970s. Civil rights, women's rights, and gay rights reflect just some of the social movements they invented or carried on. Now, as this cohort begins to enter old age, they are rewriting the rules once again, this time about what it means to be old.

HINT The baby boomers have been a cohort making change, and as they have aged they have redefined every stage of life. As elders, they appear determined to maintain active lives well beyond the traditional time of retirement. The celebrities pictured here also suggest that older people can be sexy—and the generation that brought sex out into the open for young people is defining sex as a part of growing old. The social justice values that defined the boomers as young people seem to still drive them as seniors. Most of all, they appear determined that their political voice will be heard.

Mick Jagger and Keith Richard launched the "Rolling Stones" almost fifty years ago and they continue to perform as they reach their late sixties. What do these stars of popular culture say about older men?

A much younger Paul McCartney wrote the lyrics to "When I'm Sixty-Four," probably never imagining that he would still be still be writing music and performing today—he will reach age seventy in 2012. In what ways is he a role model for elders?

AP Wide World Photos/Ryan Remiorz, CP

Getty Images/James Devaney/WireImage

Judy Collins turned seventy in 2009 and continues a busy career as a folk singer and political activist. In what ways do you expect older people to reshape U.S. politics?

Joan Baez has also been a folk singer and political activist for more than half a century. These women have supported numerous social movements, ranging from opposition to the use of land mines to the antiwar movement. In what ways do you expect older people to reshape U.S. politics?

AP Wide World Photos/Henny Ray Abrams

AP Wide World Photos/Evan Agostini

Applying SOCIOLOGY in Everyday Life

1. Ask several faculty nearing retirement and several who have already retired about the practices and policies of your college or university for helping older faculty when they retire. Based on what you learn, decide whether retiring from an academic career is harder or easier than retiring from other types of work (say, construction work or a job as a corporate manager), and explain why.
2. Look through an issue of a popular magazine, such as *Time, Newsweek,* or *People,* and study the pictures of men and women in news stories and advertising. What share of the pictures show elderly people? In what types of advertising are they featured?
3. Obtain a copy of a living will (do an online search), and try to respond to all the questions it asks. How does filling out this form affect your thinking about death?

MAKING THE GRADE

VISUAL SUMMARY

Aging and the Elderly

The Graying of the United States

The "graying of the United States" means that the average age of the U.S. population is steadily going up.

- In 1900, the median age was 23, and elderly people were 4% of the population.
- By 2030, the median age will be almost 40, and elderly people will be 19% of the population.

In high-income countries like the United States, the share of elderly people has been increasing for two reasons:

- Birth rates have been falling as families choose to have fewer children.
- Life expectancy has been rising as living standards improve and medical advances reduce deaths from infectious diseases.

✓ *As the U.S. population ages, cultural patterns are likely to change, with elderly people becoming more evident in everyday life.*

Growing Old: Biology and Culture

BIOLOGICAL AND PSYCHOLOGICAL CHANGES are associated with aging.

- Although people's health becomes more fragile with advancing age, affluent elderly people experience fewer health problems than poor people, who cannot afford quality medical care.
- Psychological research confirms that growing old does not result in overall loss of intelligence or major changes in personality.

Although aging is a biological process, how elderly people are regarded by society is a matter of **CULTURE**. The age at which people are defined as old varies:

- Until several centuries ago, old age began as early as 30.
- In poor societies today, where life expectancy is low, people become old at 50 or even 40.

gerontology the study of aging and the elderly

age stratification the unequal distribution of wealth, power, and privilege among people at different stages of the life course

gerontocracy a form of social organization in which the elderly have the most wealth, power, and prestige

AGE STRATIFICATION: A GLOBAL SURVEY

In *hunting and gathering societies*, where survival depends on physical stamina, both the very young and the very old contribute less to society.

In *agrarian societies*, elders are typically the most privileged and respected members of society, a pattern known as **gerontocracy**.

In *industrial* and *postindustrial societies*, the social standing of the elderly is low because the fast pace of social change is dominated by the young.

Transitions and Challenges of Aging

PERSONAL CHALLENGES that elderly people face include

- the realization that one's life is nearing an end
- social isolation caused by the death of friends or a spouse, physical disability, or retirement from one's job
- reduced social prestige and a loss of purpose in life due to retirement

A person's risk of **POVERTY** rises after midlife, although since 1960, the poverty rate for the elderly has fallen and is now below the poverty rate for the population as a whole.

- The aged poor include categories of people—such as single women and people of color—who are at high risk of poverty at any age.
- Some retired people have had to return to work in order to make ends meet, a result of the recent economic downturn.

caregiving informal and unpaid care provided to a dependent person by family members, other relatives, or friends

ageism prejudice and discrimination against older people

The need for **CAREGIVING** is increasing in our aging society.

- Most caregiving for the elderly is performed by family members, typically women.
- About 1 to 2 million elderly people are victims of **ELDER ABUSE** each year.

AGEISM—prejudice and discrimination against older people—is used to justify age stratification.

- Like racism and sexism, ageism builds physical traits into stereotypes that make unfair generalizations about all elderly people.

✓ *The fact that the elderly include men and women of all races, ethnicities, and social classes suggests that older people are not a minority.*

Theoretical Analysis of Aging

The **STRUCTURAL-FUNCTIONAL APPROACH** points to the role that aging plays in the orderly operation of society.

- **Disengagement theory** suggests that society helps the elderly disengage from positions of social responsibility before the onset of disability or death.
- The process of disengagement provides for the orderly transfer of statuses and roles from the older to the younger generation.

The **SYMBOLIC-INTERACTION APPROACH** focuses on the meanings that people attach to growing old.

- **Activity theory** claims that a high level of activity increases people's personal satisfaction in old age.
- People must find new roles in old age to replace the ones they left behind.

disengagement theory the idea that society functions in an orderly way by removing people from positions of responsibility as they reach old age

activity theory the idea that a high level of activity increases personal satisfaction in old age

The **SOCIAL-CONFLICT APPROACH** highlights the inequalities in opportunities and social resources available to people in different age categories.

- A capitalist society's emphasis on economic efficiency leads to the devaluation of those who are less productive, including the elderly.
- Some categories of elderly people—namely, women and other minorities—have less economic security, less access to quality medical care, and fewer options for personal satisfaction in old age than others.

See the Applying Theory table.

Death and Dying

HISTORICAL PERSPECTIVE

- In the past, death was a familiar part of everyday life and was accepted as a natural event that might occur at any age.
- Modern society has set death physically apart from everyday activities, and advances in medical technology have resulted in people's inability or unwillingness to accept death.
- This avoidance of death also reflects the fact that most people in high-income societies die in old age.

ETHICAL ISSUES: CONFRONTING DEATH

- Our society's power to prolong life has sparked a debate as to the circumstances under which a dying person should be kept alive by medical means.
- People who support a person's right to die seek control over the process of their own dying.
- **Euthanasia** poses an ethical dilemma because it involves not just refusing treatment but actively taking steps to end a person's life.

euthanasia assisting in the death of a person suffering from an incurable disease; also known as *mercy killing*

BEREAVEMENT

- Some researchers believe that the process of bereavement follows the same pattern of stages as a dying person coming to accept approaching death: denial, anger, negotiation, resignation, and acceptance.
- The **hospice movement** offers support to dying people and their families.

✓ *The fact that more people today are living longer raises questions about society's ability and responsibility to care for them as they age.*

MAKING THE GRADE

Sample Test Questions

Multiple-Choice Questions

1. **Where in the world is the share of the elderly population increasing most quickly?**
   a. low-income nations
   b. all the world's nations
   c. high-income nations
   d. the United States

2. **What is the average (median) age of the U.S. population?**
   a. sixty-seven years
   b. fifty-seven years
   c. forty-seven years
   d. thirty-seven years

3. **As we look at older people in the United States, we find a larger share of**
   a. men.
   b. women.
   c. well-off people.
   d. married people.

4. **What effect does industrialization have on the social standing of the oldest members of a society?**
   a. Social standing goes down.
   b. There is little or no effect.
   c. Social standing goes up.
   d. Social standing goes up for men and down for women.

5. **The term *gerontocracy* refers to a society where**
   a. there is a lot of social inequality.
   b. men dominate women.
   c. religious leaders are in charge.
   d. the oldest people have the most wealth, power, and prestige.

6. **The idea of retirement first appears in which type of society?**
   a. hunting and gathering
   b. pastoral
   c. industrial
   d. postindustrial

7. **In the United States, the poverty rate for people over the age of sixty-five is**
   a. higher than the national average.
   b. the same as the national average.
   c. lower than the national average.
   d. higher than among any other age category.

8. **Which category of people in the United States provides most of the caregiving to elderly people?**
   a. professionals working in the home
   b. nurses
   c. other elderly people
   d. women

9. **The structural-functional approach to aging involves**
   a. disengagement theory.
   b. activity theory.
   c. social inequality.
   d. All of the above are correct.

10. **A document in which a person states which medical procedures he or she wishes to be used or avoided under specific conditions is known as a**
    a. death wish.
    b. living will.
    c. legal trust.
    d. power of attorney.

ANSWERS: 1 (c); 2 (d); 3 (b); 4 (a); 5 (d); 6 (c); 7 (c); 8 (d); 9 (a); 10 (b).

Essay Questions

1. What is the "graying of the United States"? What two factors are causing this trend? What are some of the likely consequences of this trend for our way of life?
2. How is ageism like sexism and racism? How is it different? If older people are disadvantaged, should they be considered a minority? Why or why not?

Families

Keith Brofsky/Brand

Families are an important social institution in every society, guiding the behavior of both young and old as well as playing a part in continuing social inequality. Many debates surround today's families, including exactly what relationships should be considered families.

The Image Works/Richard Lord

Families

Contact Press Images Inc./David Burnett

PhotoEdit Inc./Mark Richards

CHAPTER OVERVIEW

This chapter explores the family, a major social institution. The chapter begins by introducing a number of important concepts that sociologists use to describe and analyze families.

PhotoEdit Inc./Michael Newman

Rosa Yniguez is one of seven children who grew up in Jalisco, Mexico, in a world in which families worked hard, went to church regularly, and were proud of having many children. Rosa remembers visiting the home of friends of her parents who had a clock in their living room with a picture of each of their twelve children where the numbers on the clock face would be.

Now thirty-five years old, Rosa is living in San Francisco and working as a cashier in a department store. In some respects, she has carried on her parents' traditions—but not in every way. Recalling her childhood, she says, "In Mexico, many of the families I knew had six, eight, ten children. Sometimes more. But I came to this country to get ahead. That is simply impossible with too many kids." As a result of her desire to keep her job and make a better life for her family, Yniguez has decided to have no more than the three children she has now.

A tradition of having large families has helped make Hispanics the largest ethnic minority in the United States. But today more and more Latinas are making the same decision as Rosa Yniguez and opting to have fewer children. Studies show that the birth rate for all immigrant women has been dropping during the past decade (Navarro, 2004; U.S. Census Bureau, 2008).

Families have been with us for a very long time. But as this story indicates, U.S. families are changing in response to a number of factors, including the desire of women to have more career options and to provide better lives for their children. In fact, the family is changing faster than any other social institution (Bianchi & Spain, 1996). This chapter explores the changes in family life, as well as the diversity of families both around the world and here in the United States.

Families: Basic Concepts

The **family** is *a social institution found in all societies that unites people in cooperative groups to care for one another, including any children.* Family ties are also called **kinship**, *a social bond based on common ancestry, marriage, or adoption.* All societies contain families, but exactly who people call their kin has varied through history and varies today from one culture to another. From the point of view of any individual, families change as we grow up, leaving the family into which we were born to form a family of our own.

Here as in other countries, families form around **marriage**, *a legal relationship, usually involving economic cooperation, sexual activity, and childbearing.* The traditional belief in the United States is that people should marry before having children; this expectation is found in the word *matrimony,* which in Latin means "the condition of motherhood." Today, 61 percent of children are born to married couples, but 39 percent are born to single women who may or may not live with a partner.

Families, then, have become more diverse. Which relationships are and are not considered a family can have important consequences, because employers typically extend benefits such as health care only to family members. The U.S. Census Bureau, which collects data used by sociologists, counts as families only people living together who are linked by "blood, marriage, or adoption."[1] All Census Bureau data on families in this chapter are based on that definition. However, the trend in the United States is toward a broader definition of families to include both homosexual and heterosexual partners and unmarried as well as married couples who live together. These *families of affinity* are made up of people who think of themselves as a family and wish others to see them that way.

[1]According to the U.S. Census Bureau, there were 116 million U.S. households in 2007. Of these, 78.4 million (68 percent) met the bureau's definition of "family." The remaining living units contained single people or unrelated individuals living together. In 1950, fully 90 percent of all households were families.

family a social institution found in all societies that unites people in cooperative groups to care for one another, including any children

kinship a social bond based on common ancestry, marriage, or adoption

extended family a family composed of parents and children as well as other kin; also known as a *consanguine family*

nuclear family a family composed of one or two parents and their children; also known as a *conjugal family*

marriage a legal relationship, usually involving economic cooperation, sexual activity, and childbearing

endogamy marriage between people of the same social category

exogamy marriage between people of different social categories

monogamy marriage that unites two partners

polygamy marriage that unites a person with two or more spouses

polygyny marriage that unites one man and two or more women

polyandry marriage that unites one woman and two or more men

Families: Global Variations

How closely related do people have to be to consider themselves a "family"? In preindustrial societies, people commonly recognize the **extended family,** *a family consisting of parents and children as well as other kin.* This group is sometimes called the *consanguine family* because it includes everyone with "shared blood." With industrialization, however, increased social mobility and geographic migration give rise to the **nuclear family,** *a family composed of one or two parents and their children.* The nuclear family is also called the *conjugal family* (*conjugal* means "based on marriage"). Although many people in our society think of kinship in terms of extended families, most people carry out their everyday routines within a nuclear family.

The family is changing most quickly in nations that have a large welfare state. In the Thinking Globally box, the sociologist David Popenoe takes a look at Sweden, which, he claims, is home to the weakest families in the world.

Getty Images/Peter Kramer

Getty Images – Entertainment/Junko Kimura

Families in the United States have diverse forms, and celebrity couples represent them all. Although same-sex couples can marry in only six states, they are becoming more common across the country; television personality Rosie O'Donnell lives with her partner, Kelli Carpenter, and their four children. Cohabitation without marriage is also becoming more common in our society; Brad Pitt and Angelina Jolie live together and have three adopted children and three biological children.

Marriage Patterns

Cultural norms, and often laws, identify people as suitable or unsuitable marriage partners. Some marital norms promote **endogamy,** *marriage between people of the same social category.* Endogamy limits potential partners to people of the same age, race, religion, or social class. By contrast, **exogamy** is *marriage between people of different social categories.* In rural areas of India, for example, people are expected to marry someone of the same caste (endogamy) but from a different village (exogamy). The reason for endogamy is that people of similar position pass along their standing to their offspring, maintaining the traditional social hierarchy. Exogamy, on the other hand, links communities and encourages the spread of culture.

In high-income nations, laws permit only **monogamy** (from the Greek, meaning "one union"), *marriage that unites two partners.* Global Map 1 shows that monogamy is the rule throughout North and South America as well as Europe, although many countries in Africa and southern Asia permit **polygamy** (from the Greek, meaning "many unions"), *marriage that unites a person with two or more spouses.* Polygamy has two forms. By far the more common form is **polygyny** (from the Greek, meaning "many women"), *marriage that unites one man and two or more women.* For example, Islamic nations in the Middle East and Africa permit men up to four wives. Even so, most Islamic families are monogamous because few men can afford to support several wives and even more children.

Polyandry (from the Greek, meaning "many men" or "many husbands") is *marriage that unites one woman and two or more men.* This extremely rare pattern exists in Tibet, a mountainous land where agriculture is difficult. There, polyandry discourages the division of land into parcels too small to support a family and divides the hard work of farming among many men.

Most of the world's societies have at some time permitted more than one marital pattern. Even so, most marriages have been monogamous (Murdock, 1965, orig. 1949). This historical preference for monogamy reflects two facts of life: Supporting several spouses is very expensive, and the number of men and women in most societies is roughly equal.

Residential Patterns

Just as societies regulate mate selection, they also designate where a couple lives. In preindustrial societies, most newlyweds live with one set of parents who offer them protection, support, and assistance. Most common is the norm of **patrilocality** (Greek for "place of the father"), *a residential pattern in which a married couple lives with or near the husband's family.* But some societies (such as the North American Iroquois) favor **matrilocality** (meaning "place of

patrilocality a residential pattern in which a married couple lives with or near the husband's family

matrilocality a residential pattern in which a married couple lives with or near the wife's family

neolocality a residential pattern in which a married couple lives apart from both sets of parents

descent the system by which members of a society trace kinship over generations

patrilineal descent a system tracing kinship through men

matrilineal descent a system tracing kinship through women

bilateral descent a system tracing kinship through both men and women

THINKING GLOBALLY

The Weakest Families on Earth? A Report from Sweden

INGE: In Sweden, we have a government that takes care of every person!

SAM: In the United States, we have families to do that. . . .

We in the United States can envy the Swedes for avoiding many of our worst social problems, including violent crime, drug abuse, and savage poverty. Instead, this Scandinavian nation seems to fulfill the promise of the modern welfare state, with a large and professional government bureaucracy that sees to virtually all human needs.

But one drawback of such a large welfare state, according to David Popenoe (1991, 1994), is that Sweden has the weakest families on Earth. Because people look to the government, not spouses, for economic assistance, Swedes are less likely to marry than members of almost all other high-income societies. For the same reason, Sweden also has a high share of adults living alone (42 percent, compared to 27 percent in the United States). In addition, a large proportion of couples live together outside marriage (27 percent, versus 9 percent in the United States), and 55 percent of all Swedish children (compared to 39 percent in the United States) are born to unmarried parents. Average household size in Sweden is almost the smallest in the world (2.1 persons, versus 2.6 in the United States). Finally, Swedish couples, whether married or not, are more likely to break up than partners in the United States or any other high-income nation.

Popenoe claims that a growing culture of individualism and self-fulfillment, along with the declining influence of religion, began eroding Swedish families in the 1960s. The movement of women into the labor force also played a part. Today, Sweden has the lowest proportion of women who are homemakers (10 percent, versus 22 percent in the United States) and the highest percentage of women in the labor force (68 percent, versus 59 percent in the United States).

But most important, according to Popenoe, is the expansion of the welfare state. The Swedish government offers its citizens a lifetime of services. Swedes can count on the government to deliver and school their children, provide comprehensive health care, support them when they are out of work, and pay for their funerals.

Many Swedes supported this welfare state, thinking it would strengthen families. But as Popenoe sees it, government is really *replacing* families. Take the case of child care: The Swedish government operates child care centers that are staffed by professionals and available regardless of parents' income. However, the government gives nothing to parents who wish to care for their children in their own home. In effect, government benefits encourage people to let the state do what family members used to do for themselves.

But if Sweden's system has solved so many social problems, why should anyone care about the family getting weaker? For two reasons, says Popenoe. First, it is very expensive for government to provide many "family" services; this is the main reason that Sweden has one of the highest rates of taxation in the world. Second, at any price, Popenoe says that government employees in large child care centers cannot provide children with the same love and emotional security given by two parents living as a family. When it comes to taking care of people—especially young children—small, intimate groups do the job better than large, impersonal organizations.

Getty Images, Inc. - Taxi/John Terence Turner

WHAT DO YOU THINK?

1. Do you agree with Popenoe that government should not replace families? Explain your answer.
2. In the United States, we have a much smaller welfare state than Sweden has. Should our government do more for its people? Why or why not?
3. With regard to children, list two specific things that government can do better than parents and two things that parents do better than government.

the mother"), *a residential pattern in which a married couple lives with or near the wife's family.* Societies that engage in frequent local warfare tend toward patrilocality, so sons are close to home to offer protection. On the other hand, societies that engage only in distant warfare may be either patrilocal or matrilocal, depending on whether its sons or daughters have greater economic value (Ember & Ember, 1971, 1991).

Industrial societies show yet another pattern. Finances permitting, they favor **neolocality** (from the Greek, meaning "new place"), *a residential pattern in which a married couple lives apart from both sets of parents.*

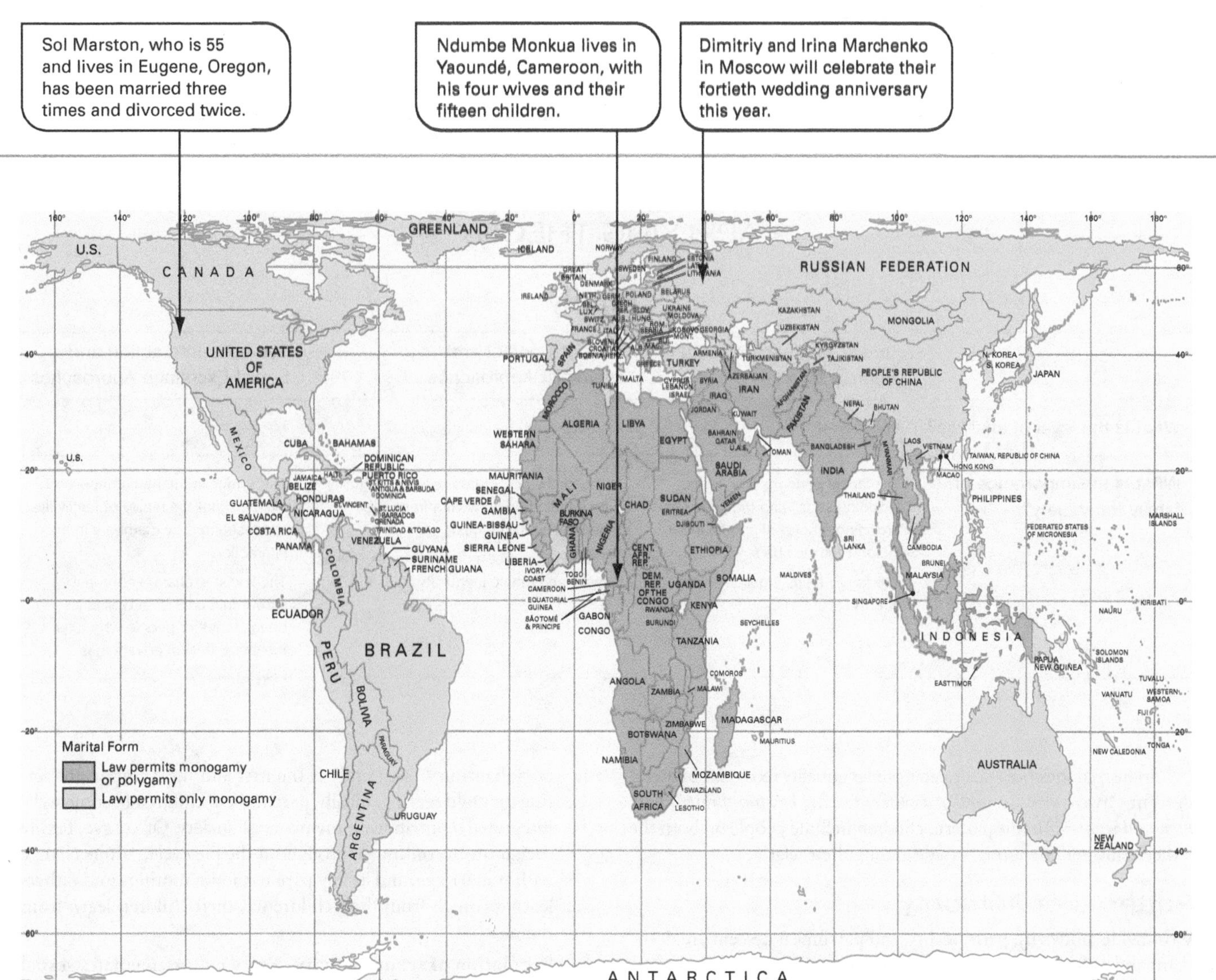

Window on the World

GLOBAL MAP 1 **Marital Form in Global Perspective**

Monogamy is the only legal form of marriage throughout the Western Hemisphere and in much of the rest of the world. In most African nations and in southern Asia, however, polygamy is permitted by law. In many cases, this practice reflects the influence of Islam, a religion that allows a man to have up to four wives. Even so, most marriages in these countries are monogamous, primarily for financial reasons.

Source: *Peters Atlas of the World* (1990) with updates by the author.

Patterns of Descent

Descent refers to *the system by which members of a society trace kinship over generations.* Most preindustrial societies trace kinship through either the father's side or the mother's side of the family. **Patrilineal descent**, the more common pattern, is *a system tracing kinship through men.* In this pattern, children are related to others only through their fathers. Tracing kinship through patrilineal descent ensures that fathers pass property on to their sons. Patrilineal descent characterizes most pastoral and agrarian societies, in which men produce the most valued resources. A less common pattern is **matrilineal descent**, *a system tracing kinship through women.* Matrilineal descent, in which mothers pass property to their daughters, is found more frequently in horticultural societies, where women are the main food producers.

SEEING SOCIOLOGY in Everyday Life

In terms of patterns of descent, how would you describe the common practice in the United States of a woman adopting her husband's last name after marriage?

incest taboo a norm forbidding sexual relations or marriage between certain relatives

APPLYING THEORY

Family

	Structural-Functional Approach	Social-Conflict and Feminist Approaches	Symbolic-Interaction and Social-Exchange Approaches
What is the level of analysis?	Macro-level	Macro-level	Micro-level
What is the importance of family for society?	The family performs vital tasks, including socializing the young and providing emotional and financial support for members. The family helps regulate sexual activity.	The family perpetuates social inequality by handing down wealth from one generation to the next. The family supports patriarchy as well as racial and ethnic inequality.	The symbolic-interaction approach explains that the reality of family life is constructed by members in their interaction. The social-exchange approach shows that courtship typically brings together people who offer the same level of advantages.

Industrial societies with greater gender equality recognize **bilateral descent** ("two-sided descent"), *a system tracing kinship through both men and women.* In this pattern, children include people on both the father's side and the mother's side among their relatives.

Patterns of Authority

Worldwide, polygyny, patrilocality, and patrilineal descent are dominant and reflect the common global pattern of patriarchy. In industrial societies like the United States, men are still typically heads of households, and most U.S. parents give children their father's last name. However, more egalitarian family patterns are evolving, especially as the share of women in the labor force goes up.

Theoretical Analysis of Families

The three major theoretical approaches offer a range of insights about the family. The Applying Theory table summarizes what we can learn from each approach.

Functions of the Family: Structural-Functional Analysis

According to the structural-functional approach, the family performs many vital tasks. For this reason, the family is often called the "backbone of society."

1. **Socialization**. The family is the first and most important setting for child rearing. Ideally, parents help children become well-integrated, contributing members of society. Of course, family socialization continues throughout the life cycle. Adults change within marriage, and as any parent knows, mothers and fathers learn as much from their children as their children learn from them.
2. **Regulation of sexual activity**. Every culture regulates sexual activity in the interest of maintaining kinship organization and property rights. The **incest taboo** is *a norm forbidding sexual relations or marriage between certain relatives.* Although the incest taboo exists in every society, exactly which relatives cannot marry varies from one culture to another. The matrilineal Navajo, for example, forbid marrying any relative of one's mother. Our bilateral society applies the incest taboo to both sides of the family but limits it to close relatives, including parents, grandparents, siblings, aunts, and uncles. But even brother-sister (but not parent-child) marriages existed among the ancient Egyptian, Incan, and Hawaiian nobility (Murdock, 1965, orig. 1949).

Reproduction between close relatives of any species can result in mental and physical damage to offspring. Yet only human beings observe an incest taboo, a fact suggesting that the key reason for controlling incest is social. Why? First, the incest taboo limits sexual competition in families by restricting sex to

SEEING SOCIOLOGY in Everyday Life

Thinking about the "marriage marketplace," why do you think women have traditionally been less willing than men to reveal their age?

spouses. Second, because kinship defines people's rights and obligations toward one another, reproduction among close relatives would hopelessly confuse kinship ties and threaten social order. Third, forcing people to marry outside their immediate families ties together the larger society.

3. **Social placement.** Families are not needed for people to reproduce, but they do help maintain social organization. Parents pass on their own social identity—in terms of race, ethnicity, religion, and social class—to their children at birth.
4. **Material and emotional security.** Many people view the family as a "haven in a heartless world," offering physical protection, emotional support, and financial assistance. Perhaps this is why people living in families tend to be happier, healthier, and wealthier than people living alone (Goldstein & Kenney, 2001; U.S. Census Bureau, 2008).

CRITICAL REVIEW Structural-functional analysis explains why society, at least as we know it, is built on families. But this approach glosses over the diversity of U.S. family life and ignores how other social institutions (such as government) could meet some of the same human needs. Finally, structural-functionalism overlooks negative aspects of family life, including patriarchy and family violence.

CHECK YOUR LEARNING Identify four important functions of the family for society.

Women have long been taught to see marriage as the key to a happy life. Social-conflict theory, however, points to the fact that marriage often means a lifetime sentence of unpaid domestic labor. Susan Pyzow's painting *Bridal Bouquet* makes the point.

Inequality and the Family: Social-Conflict and Feminist Analysis

Like the structural-functional approach, the social-conflict approach, including feminist analysis, considers the family central to our way of life. But rather than focusing on ways that kinship benefits society, this approach points out how the family perpetuates social inequality.

1. **Property and inheritance.** Friedrich Engels (1902, orig. 1884) traced the origin of the family to men's need (especially in the upper classes) to identify heirs so that they could hand down property to their sons. Families thus concentrate wealth and reproduce the class structure in each new generation.
2. **Patriarchy.** Feminists link the family to patriarchy. To know their heirs, men must control the sexuality of women. Families therefore transform women into the sexual and economic property of men. A century ago in the United States, most wives' earnings belonged to their husbands. Today, women still bear most of the responsibility for child rearing and housework (Benokraitis & Feagin, 1995; Stapinski, 1998; England, 2001).
3. **Race and ethnicity.** Racial and ethnic categories persist over generations because most people marry others like themselves. Endogamous marriage supports racial and ethnic hierarchies.

CRITICAL REVIEW Social-conflict and feminist analysis shows another side of family life: its role in social stratification. Engels criticized the family for its support of capitalism. But noncapitalist societies also have families (and family problems). The family may be linked to social inequality, as Engels argued, but the family carries out societal functions not easily accomplished by other means.

CHECK YOUR LEARNING Point to ways in which families support social inequality.

SEEING SOCIOLOGY in Everyday Life

How similar are your parents (or you and your spouse) in terms of age, social class, race, ethnicity, and education?

Corbis RF/PNC

According to social exchange theory, people form relationships based on what each offers to the other. Generally partners see the exchange as fair or "about even." What do you think is the exchange involved in this marriage?

Constructing Family Life: Micro-Level Analysis

Both structural-functional and social-conflict analyses view the family as a structural system. By contrast, micro-level analysis explores how individuals shape and experience family life.

The Symbolic-Interaction Approach

Ideally, family living offers an opportunity for *intimacy*, a word with Latin roots meaning "sharing fear." As family members share many activities over time, they identify with each other and build emotional bonds. Of course, the fact that parents act as authority figures often limits their closeness with younger children. But as children approach adulthood, kinship ties typically open up to include sharing confidences with greater intimacy (Macionis, 1978).

The Social-Exchange Approach

Social-exchange analysis, another micro-level approach, describes courtship and marriage as forms of negotiation (Blau, 1964). Dating allows each person to assess the advantages and disadvantages of a potential spouse. In essence, exchange analysts suggest, people "shop around" for partners to make the best "deal" they can.

In patriarchal societies, gender roles dictate the elements of exchange: Men bring wealth and power to the marriage marketplace, and women bring beauty. The importance of beauty explains women's traditional concern with their appearance. But as women have joined the labor force, they are less dependent on men to support them, and so the terms of exchange are converging for men and women.

CRITICAL REVIEW Micro-level analysis balances structural-functional and social-conflict visions of the family as an institutional system. Both the interaction and exchange viewpoints focus on the individual experience of family life. However, micro-level analysis misses the bigger picture: Family life is similar for people in the same social and economic categories. The Applying Theory table summarizes what we can learn by applying each of the theoretical approaches to family life.

CHECK YOUR LEARNING How does a micro-level approach to understanding family differ from a macro-level approach? State the main ideas of the symbolic-interaction approach and the social-exchange approach.

Stages of Family Life

The family is a dynamic institution, with marked changes across the life course. New families begin with courtship and evolve as the new partners settle into the realities of married life. Next, for most couples at least, come the years spent developing careers and raising children, leading to the later years of marriage, after the children have left home to form families of their own. We will look briefly at each of these four stages.

Courtship

November 2, Kandy, Sri Lanka. Winding through the rain forest of this beautiful island, our van driver, Harry, recounts how he met his wife. Actually, he explains, it was more of an arrangement: The two families were both Buddhist and of the same caste. "We got along well, right from the start," recalls Harry. "We had the same background. I suppose she or I could have said no. But love marriages happen in the city, not in the village where I grew up."

In rural Sri Lanka, as in rural areas of low- and middle-income countries throughout the world, most people consider courtship too important to be left to the young (Stone, 1977). *Arranged marriages* are alliances between extended families of similar social standing and usually involve an exchange not just of children but also of wealth and favors. Romantic love has little to do with marriage, and parents may make such arrangements when their children are very

MAKING THE GRADE

Recall that arranged marriage is a pattern associated with caste systems. A greater emphasis on love and personal choice in mate selection arises in class systems.

homogamy marriage between people with the same social characteristics

infidelity sexual activity outside one's marriage

THINKING GLOBALLY

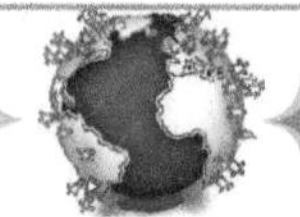

Early to Wed: A Report from Rural India

Sumitra Jogi cries as her wedding is about to begin. Are they tears of joy? Not exactly. This "bride" is an eighteen-month-old squirming in the arms of her mother. The groom? A boy of seven.

In a remote, rural village in India's western state of Rajasthan, two families gather at midnight to celebrate a traditional wedding ritual. It is May 2, in Hindu tradition an especially good day to marry. Sumitra's father smiles as the ceremony begins; her mother cradles the infant, who has fallen asleep. The groom, dressed in a special costume with a red and gold turban on his head, gently reaches up and grasps the baby's hand. Then, as the ceremony reaches its conclusion, the young boy leads the child and mother around the wedding fire three-and-one-half times as the audience beams at the couple's first steps together as husband and wife.

Child weddings are illegal in India, but in the rural regions, traditions are strong and marriage laws are hard to enforce. As a result, thousands of children marry each year. "In rural Rajasthan," explains one social welfare worker, "all the girls are married by age fourteen. These are poor, illiterate families, and they don't want to keep girls past their first menstrual cycle."

For the immediate future, Sumitra Jogi will remain with her parents. But in eight or ten years, a second ceremony will send her to live with her husband's family, and her married life will begin.

AP Wide World Photos

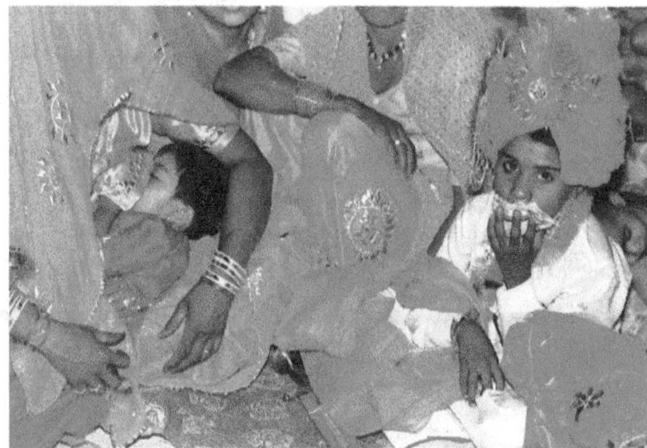

The eighteen-month-old girl on the left is breastfeeding during her wedding ceremony in a small village in the state of Rajasthan, India; her new husband is seven years old. Although outlawed, such arranged marriages involving children are still known to take place in traditional, remote areas of India.

If the responsibilities of marriage lie years in the future, why do families push their children to marry at such an early age? Parents of girls know that the younger the bride, the smaller the dowry offered to the groom's family. Then, too, when girls marry this young, there is no question about their virginity, which raises their value on the marriage market. Arranged marriages are an alliance between families. No one thinks about love or the fact that the children are too young to understand what is taking place (J. W. Anderson, 1995).

WHAT DO YOU THINK?

1. Why are arranged marriages common in very traditional regions?
2. List several advantages and disadvantages of arranged marriages from the point of view of the families involved.
3. Can you point to ways in which mate selection in the United States is "arranged" by society?

young. A century ago in Sri Lanka and India, for example, half of all girls married before reaching age fifteen (Mayo, 1927; Mace & Mace, 1960). As the Thinking Globally box explains, child marriage is still found in some parts of the world today.

Because traditional societies are more culturally homogeneous, almost all young men and women have been well socialized to be good spouses. Therefore, parents can arrange marriages with little thought about whether or not the two individuals involved are *personally* compatible because they know that the partners will be *culturally* compatible.

Industrialization both erodes the importance of extended families and weakens tradition. As young people begin the process of choosing their own mate, dating sharpens courtship skills and allows sexual experimentation. Marriage is delayed until young people complete their schooling, build the financial security needed to live apart from their parents, and gain the experience needed to select a suitable partner.

Romantic Love

Our culture celebrates *romantic love*—affection and sexual passion for another person—as the basis for marriage. We find it hard to imagine marriage without love, and popular culture—from fairy tales like "Cinderella" to today's television sitcoms and dramas—portrays love as the key to a successful marriage.

Our society's emphasis on romance motivates young people to "leave the nest" to form new families of their own, and physical passion can help a new couple through the often difficult adjustments of living together (W. J. Goode, 1959). On the other hand, because feelings change over time, romantic love is a less stable foundation for marriage than social and economic considerations, which is one reason that the divorce rate is much higher in the United States than in nations in which culture is a stronger guide in the choice of a partner.

American Dating—Muslim Style

BY TOM A. PETER
April 28, 2008

It was an all-American college moment on the Michigan State University campus in East Lansing: Tosif Khatri was laughing and chatting with two fellow students—both women—as they walked to a local cafe.

But the buzz of Mr. Khatri's cellphone popped the bubble. It was his cousin calling to invoke a bit of the family's old country Indian-Muslim traditions. "Not that it's any of my business or anything like that," the cousin said, "but are you, like, hanging out with girls right now?"

"I said 'Oh, no . . . it's nothing silly or anything like that, it's just for the sake of a student event," Khatri recalls.

"Okay. I was just checking," signed off the suspicious cousin.

From an Islamic perspective, Khatri hadn't done anything wrong. He was hanging with two female colleagues to discuss organizational matters for the Muslim Student Association (MSA). But the line blurs when Khatri admits that the outing was also an excuse to socialize. Many Muslims would even call such a mixed-sex meeting haram, sinful.

. . . Outings like this happen increasingly among American Muslims as they integrate into the United States. Reactions like Khatri's watchful cousin's illustrate the challenge young Muslim men and women face trying to interact, let alone "date."

The careful rules that dictate male-female interaction and courtship quite simply can't be applied in the United States as they are in predominately Muslim countries. What's more, Islamic teachings lay out few undisputable guidelines when it comes to finding and meeting a mate; every Muslim tradition has its own interpretation. So, what an Indian Muslim might find permissible could be off-limits for an Arab Muslim.

The result: U.S. Muslims are pioneering ways to read Muslim rules in ways that make sense in an American context.

While Muslim courtship rules vary around the globe—from arranged marriages (possibly never seeing your partner's face before the wedding night) to looser versions (spending time with each other in the company of family)—most Muslims would agree that a guy and a girl going out alone doesn't fly. A popular Hadith, or saying of the prophet Muhammad, warns that when an unwed man and woman are left alone, Satan is the third person in the room.

When Sofia Begg-Latif, the daughter of Indian immigrants, first met Farhan Latif, a Pakistani-American, the two were officers of University of Michigan at Dearborn's MSA. Often MSA leaders spent late nights together organizing events, and as will happen, the longer they worked, the less they talked about work. . . .

When it became clear that both wanted more than a working relationship, Latif couldn't respectably just ask Begg-Latif out for dinner and a movie. Instead, he told her that he'd like to speak with her parents for permission to court. She agreed, and they began a traditional courtship in the presence of their families, never spending time alone or kissing until they were married. . . .

But even in our country, sociologists point out, society aims Cupid's arrow more than we like to think. Most people fall in love with others of the same race, of comparable age, and of similar social class. Our society "arranges" marriages by encouraging **homogamy** (literally, "like marrying like"), *marriage between people with the same social characteristics.*

The extent of homogamy is greater for some categories of our population (such as younger people and immigrants from traditional societies) than for others (older people and those who do not live according to strict traditions). Seeing Sociology in the News describes courtship patterns among young Muslims on the campuses of U.S. colleges and universities.

Settling In: Ideal and Real Marriage

Our culture gives the young an idealized, "happily ever after" picture of marriage. Such optimism can lead to disappointment, especially for women, who are taught to view marriage as the key to personal happiness. Also, romantic love involves a good deal of fantasy: We fall in love with others not always as they are but as we want them to be.

Sexuality, too, can be a source of disappointment. In the romantic haze of falling in love, people may see marriage as an endless sexual honeymoon, only to face the sobering realization that sex becomes a less-than-all-consuming passion. Although the frequency of marital sex does decline over time, about two in three married people report that they are satisfied with the sexual dimension of their relationship. In general, couples with the best sexual relationships experience the most satisfaction in their marriages. Sex may not be the key to marital bliss, but more often than not, good sex and good relationships usually go together (Laumann et al., 1994; T. W. Smith, 2006).

Infidelity—*sexual activity outside one's marriage*—is another area where the reality of marriage does not match our cultural ideal. In a recent survey, 91 percent of U.S. adults said sex outside of marriage is "always wrong" or "almost always wrong." Even so, 16 percent of men and 13 percent of women indicated on a private, written questionnaire that they had been sexually unfaithful to their partners at least once (NORC, 2007:298, 1877).

Child Rearing

Despite the demands children make on us, adults in this country overwhelmingly identify raising children as one of life's greatest joys. Today, about half of U.S. adults say that two children is the ideal number, and few people want more than three (NORC, 2007:294, 574). This is a change from two centuries ago, when *eight* children was the average.

Big families pay off in preindustrial societies because children supply needed labor. People therefore regard having children as a wife's duty, and without effective birth control, childbearing is a regular event. Of course, a high death rate in preindustrial societies prevents many children from reaching adulthood; as late as 1900, one-third of children born in the United States died by age ten.

While the romantic attraction that provided the initial sparks may help them blend into the American cultural landscape, there's a negative stigma in the Muslim community that they married for love.

"People always say, 'Was it a love marriage or an arranged marriage?' " says Begg-Latif. . . .

Just as the MSA provided a key social forum for the Latifs to negotiate their love connection, it has proved such a successful Muslim matchmaker that it's been nicknamed the "Matrimonial Student Association." It provides a place for single Muslims to meet without getting too personal and it's always under the safety net of working toward Islamic goals. On many university campuses, MSA members like Khatri ruffle conservatives' feathers by going out for group dinners or social outings after meetings.

While these informal meetings happen, the concept of dating for fun simply does not exist in Islam. Any potential match is judged, pursued, or abandoned based on marriage potential.

In the United States, however, many Muslims—especially Arabs—have re-interpreted parts of the courtship process to allow for something closer to the American way.

"I think it's widely accepted now among Muslims in America that things are not the same as they were in their country of origin, whether it's Sudan, Pakistan, or Egypt," says Imam Mohamed Magid, the executive director of the All Dulles Area Muslim Society in Sterling, Va. . . .

Hanaa Soltan, a newlywed in her late 20s, is grateful for the new dating flexibility. Her family allowed her to take advantage of nikah, an old tradition that allows something close to American dating. Under Islamic law, nikah is a legal marriage that entitles couples to all the privileges of marriage. In practice, most using a nikah remain chaste until their wedding night. If the couple decides to break up during the nikah, there's far less stigma than getting divorced after the marriage ceremony. . . .

For Soltan, a nikah allowed her to spend time alone with her fiancé. . . . They could go out to dinner alone and Soltan could even remove her veil in front of her husband-to-be.

"We have our religious beliefs and we have Arab culture to a certain extent, but at the end of the day we're all born and raised here . . . and you don't have to stick to what your parents did," says Soltan, who's now happily married.

WHAT DO YOU THINK?

1. How does leaving one country to live in another raise problems concerning proper behavior involving dating and other activities?
2. How do campus religious and cultural organizations in the United States help many young people from traditional societies engage in courtship that meets traditional standards?
3. From a sociological point of view, why do traditional societies try to control the dating behavior of young people? Why do less traditional societies (such as the United States) give young people more dating freedom?

By Tom A. Peter. Reproduced with permission from the April 28, 2008, issue of *The Christian Science Monitor* (www.csmonitor.com).

Economically speaking, industrialization transforms children from an asset to a liability. It now costs almost $300,000 to raise one child, including college tuition (Lino, 2008). No wonder the average size of the U.S. family dropped steadily during the twentieth century to one child per family![2]

The trend toward smaller families is most evident in high-income nations. The picture differs in low-income countries in Latin America, Asia, and especially Africa, where many women have few alternatives to bearing children. In such societies, between four and six children is still the norm.

Parenting is a very expensive, lifelong commitment. As our society has given people greater choices about family life, more U.S. adults have decided to delay childbirth or to remain childless. In 1960, almost 90 percent of women between twenty-five and twenty-nine who had ever married had at least one child; today, this proportion is just 69 percent (U.S. Census Bureau, 2008).

No one doubts that almost all parents care deeply about their children, but about two-thirds of parents in the United States say they don't have enough time to spend with their kids (K. Clark, 2002; Cohn, 2007). But unless we accept a lower standard of living, economic realities demand that most parents pursue careers outside the home, even if that means devoting less time to their children. For many families, including the Yniguez family described in the opening to this chapter, having fewer children is an important step toward resolving the tension between work and parenting (Gilbert, 2005).

Children of working parents spend most of the day at school. But after school, some 5.6 million children (14 percent of five- to fourteen-year-olds) are *latchkey kids* who are left to fend for themselves (U. S. Census Bureau, 2008). Traditionalists in the "family values" debate charge that many mothers work at the expense of their children, who receive less parenting. Progressives counter that such criticism targets women for wanting the same opportunities men have long enjoyed.

Congress took a step toward easing the conflict between family and job responsibilities by passing the Family and Medical Leave Act in 1993. This law allows up to ninety days of unpaid leave from work to care for a new child or to deal with a serious family emergency. Still, most adults in this country have to juggle parental and job responsibilities. When parents work, who cares for the kids? The Seeing Sociology in Everyday Life box provides the answer.

The Family in Later Life

Increasing life expectancy in the United States means that couples who remain married will stay together for a long time. By about age

[2]According to the U.S. Census Bureau, the median number of children per family was 0.93 in 2007. Among all families, the medians were 0.80 for whites, 1.22 for African Americans, and 1.40 for Hispanics.

SEEING SOCIOLOGY in Everyday Life

Have other family members paid for any of your schooling?

SEEING SOCIOLOGY in Everyday Life

After the death of a spouse, men are more likely than women to remarry. Can you explain why?

"Son, you're all grown up now. You owe me two hundred and fourteen thousand dollars."

sixty, most have finished the task of raising children. At this point, marriage brings a return to living with only a spouse.

Like the birth of children, their departure—creating an "empty nest"—requires adjustments, although a marriage often becomes closer and more satisfying. Years of living together may have lessened a couple's sexual passion, but understanding and commitment often increase.

Personal contact with children usually continues because most older adults live a short distance from at least one of their children. One-third of all U.S. adults (56 million) are grandparents. Most grandparents help with child care and other responsibilities. Among African Americans, who have a high rate of single parenting, grandmothers have an especially important position in family life (U.S. Census Bureau, 2006; AARP Foundation, 2007).

The other side of the coin is that more adults in midlife now care for aging parents. The empty nest may not be filled by a parent coming to live in the home, but many adults find that caring for parents, who now live to eighty, ninety, and beyond, can be as taxing as raising young children. The oldest of the baby boomers—now past sixty—are called the "sandwich generation" because many (especially women) will spend as many years caring for their aging parents as they did caring for their children (Lund, 1993).

The final and surely the most difficult transition in married life comes with the death of a spouse. Wives typically outlive their husbands because of their greater life expectancy and the fact that women usually marry men several years older than themselves. Wives can thus expect to spend some years as widows. The challenge of living alone following the death of a spouse is especially great for men, who usually have fewer friends than widows and may lack housekeeping skills.

U.S. Families: Class, Race, and Gender

Dimensions of inequality—social class, ethnicity and race, and gender—are powerful forces that shape marriage and family life. This discussion addresses each factor in turn, but bear in mind that they overlap in our lives.

Social Class

Social class determines both a family's financial security and its range of opportunities. Interviewing working-class women, Lillian Rubin (1976) found that wives thought a good husband was one who held a steady job, did not drink too much, and was not violent. Rubin's middle-class respondents, by contrast, never mentioned such things; these women simply *assumed* that a husband would provide a safe and secure home. Their ideal husband was someone they could talk to easily, sharing feelings and experiences.

Clearly, what women (and men) think they can hope for in marriage—and what they end up with—is linked to their social class. Much the same holds for children; boys and girls lucky enough to be born into more affluent families enjoy better mental and physical health, develop more self-confidence, and go on to greater achievement than children born to poor parents (McLeod & Shanahan, 1993; Duncan et al., 1998).

Ethnicity and Race

Ethnicity and race are powerful social forces that can affect family life. Keep in mind, however, that American Indian, Latino, and African American families (like all families) do not fit any single generalization or stereotype (Allen, 1995).

American Indian Families

American Indians display a wide variety of family types. Some patterns emerge, however, among people who migrate from tribal reser-

MAKING THE GRADE

Remember that family patterns for American Indians, Latinos, or any other racial or ethnic category vary by social class and that the experiences of family life may also differ for women and men.

SEEING SOCIOLOGY in Everyday Life

Looking at the figure below, which arrangement for child care do you prefer? Why?

SEEING SOCIOLOGY IN EVERYDAY LIFE

Who's Minding the Kids?

Traditionally, the task of providing daily care for young children fell to stay-at-home mothers. But with a majority of mothers and fathers now in the labor force, finding quality, affordable child care is a high priority for parents.

The figure shows the various arrangements reported by working mothers to care for children under the age of five. Half of these children receive care at home from a parent (23 percent) or a relative (27 percent). Of the remaining half of these children, 25 percent attend preschool or a day care program, 9 percent are cared for in a nonrelative's home, 8 percent are cared for in their own home by a nanny or babysitter, and 8 percent have no regular arrangement (U.S. Census Bureau, 2008).

The use of day care programs has doubled over the past decade because many parents cannot find affordable in-home care for their children. Some day care centers are so big that they amount to "tot lots" where parents "park" their children for the day. The impersonality of such settings and the rapid turnover in staff prevent the warm and consistent nurturing that young children need to develop a sense of trust. But other child care centers offer a secure and healthful environment. Research suggests that *good* care centers are good for children; *bad* facilities are not.

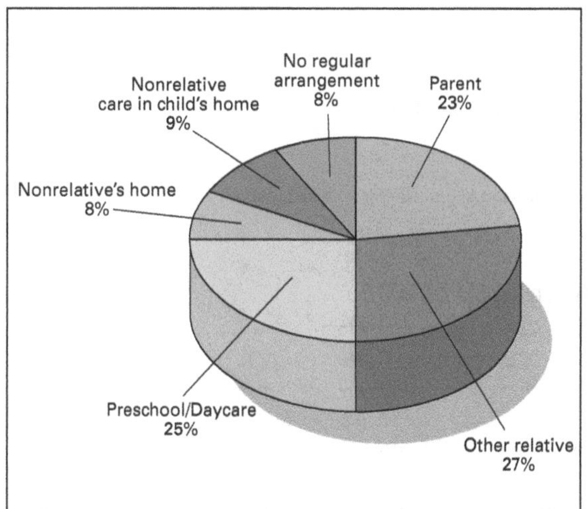

Working mothers report that a majority of their young children receive care in the home.

WHAT DO YOU THINK?

1. Why do so many parents have trouble finding affordable child care? Should employers do more?
2. As parents, would you and your partner be willing to limit your working hours to allow child care at home? Why or why not?
3. How can parents assess the quality of a child care center? What should they look for?

vations to cities. Women and men who arrive in cities often seek out others—especially kin and members of the same tribe—for help getting settled. One study, for example, tells the story of two women migrants to the San Francisco area who met at a meeting of an Indian organization and realized that they were of the same tribe. The women and their children decided to share an apartment, and soon after, the children began to refer to one another as brothers, sisters, and cousins. As the months passed, the two mothers came to think of themselves as sisters (Lobo, 2002).

Migration also creates many "fluid households" with changing membership. In another case from the same research, a large apartment in San Francisco was rented by a woman, her aunt, and their children. Over the course of the next month, however, they welcomed into their home more than thirty other urban migrants, who stayed for a short time until they found housing of their own. Such patterns of mutual assistance, often involving real and fictional kinship, are common among all low-income people.

American Indians who leave tribal reservations for the cities are typically better off than those who stay behind. Because people on reservations have a hard time finding work, they cannot easily form stable marriages, and problems such as alcoholism and drug abuse can shatter the ties between parent and child.

Latino Families

Many Latinos enjoy the loyalty and support of extended families. Traditionally, too, Latino parents exercise considerable control over children's courtship, considering marriage an alliance of families, not just a union based on romantic love. Some Latino families also follow conventional gender roles, encouraging *machismo*—strength, daring, and sexual conquest—among men and treating women with respect but also close supervision.

However, assimilation into the larger society is changing these traditional patterns. As the story opening this chapter explained, many women who come to California from Mexico favor smaller families. Similarly, many Puerto Ricans who migrate to New York do not maintain the strong extended family ties they knew in Puerto Rico. Traditional male authority over women has also lessened, especially among affluent Latino families, whose number has tripled in

SEEING SOCIOLOGY in Everyday Life

Surveys report that most U.S. teens now claim they have dated someone of another race. Do you think the proportion of mixed-race marriages will rise in the next twenty years? Why or why not?

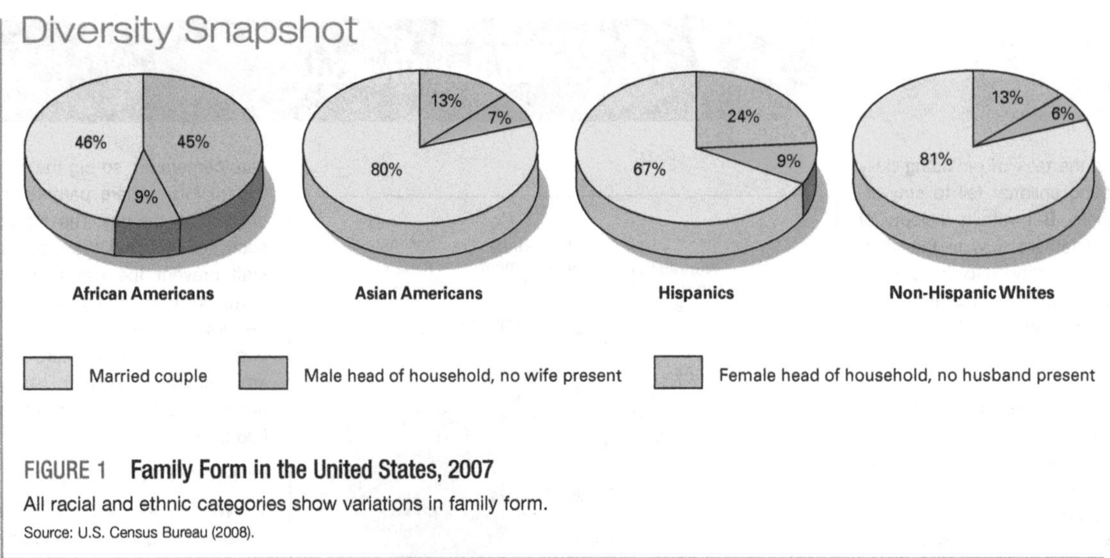

FIGURE 1 Family Form in the United States, 2007
All racial and ethnic categories show variations in family form.
Source: U.S. Census Bureau (2008).

the past twenty years (Lach, 1999; Navarro, 2004; Raley, Durden, & Wildsmith, 2004).

Overall, however, the typical Hispanic family had an income of $40,566 in 2007, or 66 percent of the national average (U.S. Census Bureau, 2008). Many Hispanic families suffer the stress of unemployment and other poverty-related problems.

African American Families

African American families face economic disadvantages: The typical African American family earned $40,143 in 2007, which was 65 percent of the national average. People of African ancestry are three times as likely as non-Hispanic whites to be poor, and poverty means that both parents and children are likely to experience unemployment, substandard housing, and poor health.

Under these circumstances, maintaining a stable marriage is difficult. Consider that 29 percent of African American women in their forties have never married, compared to about 9 percent of white women of the same age. This means that African American women—often with children—are more likely to be single heads of households. Figure 1 shows that women headed 45 percent of all African American families in 2007, compared to 24 percent of Hispanic families, 13 percent of non-Hispanic white families, and 13 percent of Asian or Pacific Islander families (U.S. Census Bureau, 2008).

Regardless of race, single-mother families are always at high risk of poverty. Twenty-one percent of single families headed by non-Hispanic white women are poor. Higher yet, the poverty rate among families headed by African American women (37 percent) and Hispanic women (38 percent) is strong evidence of how the intersection of class, race, and gender can put women at a disadvantage. African American families with both wife and husband in the home, which represent 46 percent of the total, are much stronger economically, earning 80 percent as much as comparable non-Hispanic white families. But 70 percent of African American children are born to single women, and 35 percent of African American boys and girls are growing up poor today, meaning that these families carry much of the burden of child poverty in the United States (U.S. Census Bureau, 2008; Martin et al., 2009).

Ethnically and Racially Mixed Marriages

Most spouses have similar social backgrounds with regard to class and race. But over the course of the twentieth century, when it came to choosing a marriage partner, ethnicity came to matter less and less. In recent decades, for example, a woman of German and French ancestry might readily marry a man of Irish and English background without inviting any particular reaction from their families or from society in general.

Even so, race remains a powerful factor in mate selection. Before a 1967 Supreme Court decision (*Loving* v. *Virginia*), interracial marriage was actually illegal in sixteen states. Today, African, Asian, and Native Americans represent 18 percent of the U.S. population; if people ignored race in choosing spouses, we would expect about the same share of marriages to be mixed. The actual proportion of mixed marriages is 4 percent, showing that race remains important in social relations. But most people claim that race and ethnicity should not matter in choosing a partner. In addition, the age at first marriage has been rising to an average of 27.5 for men and 25.6 for women. Young people who marry when they are older are more likely to make

SEEING SOCIOLOGY in Everyday Life

Given the high level of divorce in the United States, do you think it would be more accurate to call our marriage system "serial monogamy" (one partner after another)? Explain.

choices about partners with less input from parents. One consequence of this increasing freedom of choice is that the share of ethnically and racially mixed marriages is increasing (Rosenfeld & Kim, 2005; U.S. Census Bureau, 2008).

The most common type of "mixed" couple includes one partner who is Hispanic (the largest racial or ethnic minority category) and one who is not, but today's couples include just about every imaginable combination. In about half of all "mixed" marriages, one or both partners claim to have a multiracial or multiethnic identity. Such couples are likely to live in the West; in five states—Hawaii, Alaska, California, Nevada, and Oklahoma—more than 10 percent of all married couples are interracial (Lee & Edmonston, 2005; U.S. Census Bureau, 2008).

Gender

The sociologist Jessie Bernard (1982) claimed that every marriage is actually two different relationships: the woman's marriage and the man's marriage. The reason is that few marriages have two equal partners. Although patriarchy has weakened, most people still expect husbands to be older and taller than their wives and to have more important, better-paid jobs.

Why, then, do many people think that marriage benefits women more than men? The positive stereotype of the carefree bachelor contrasts sharply with the negative image of the lonely spinster, suggesting that women are fulfilled only through being wives and mothers.

However, Bernard claimed, married women actually have poorer mental health, less happiness, and more passive attitudes toward life than single women. Married men, on the other hand, generally live longer, are mentally better off, and report being happier overall than single men. These differences suggest why, after divorce, men are more eager than women to find a new partner.

Bernard concluded that there is no better assurance of long life, health, and happiness for a man than a woman well socialized to devote her life to taking care of him and providing the security of a well-ordered home. She is quick to add that marriage *could* be healthful for women if husbands did not dominate wives and expect them to do almost all the housework. Survey responses confirm that couples rank "sharing household chores" as among the most important factors that contribute to a successful marriage (Pew Research Center, 2007a).

Transitions and Problems in Family Life

The newspaper columnist Ann Landers once remarked that one marriage in twenty is wonderful, five in twenty are good, ten in twenty are tolerable, and the remaining four are "pure hell." Families can be a source of joy, but for some, the reality falls far short of the ideal.

Corbis - NY/Zefa

For most of our nation's history, interracial marriage was illegal. Although the last of these laws was struck down forty years ago, race and ethnicity continue to guide the process of courtship and marriage. Even so, interracial relationships are becoming more and more common.

Divorce

U.S. society strongly supports marriage, and about nine out of ten people at some point "tie the knot." But many of today's marriages unravel. Figure 2 shows the tenfold increase in the U.S. divorce rate over the past century. By 2007, almost four marriages in ten were eventually ending in divorce (for African Americans, the rate was about six in ten). From another angle, of all people over the age of fifteen, 21 percent of men and 23 percent of women have been divorced at some point. Ours is the highest divorce rate in the world; it is more than $1^1/_2$ times as high as in Canada and Japan and more than four times higher than in Italy and Ireland (European Union, 2009).

The high U.S. divorce rate has many causes (Furstenberg & Cherlin, 1991; Etzioni, 1993; Popenoe, 1999; Greenspan, 2001):

1. **Individualism is on the rise.** Today's family members spend less time together. We have become more individualistic and more concerned about personal happiness and earning income than about the well-being of our partners and children.

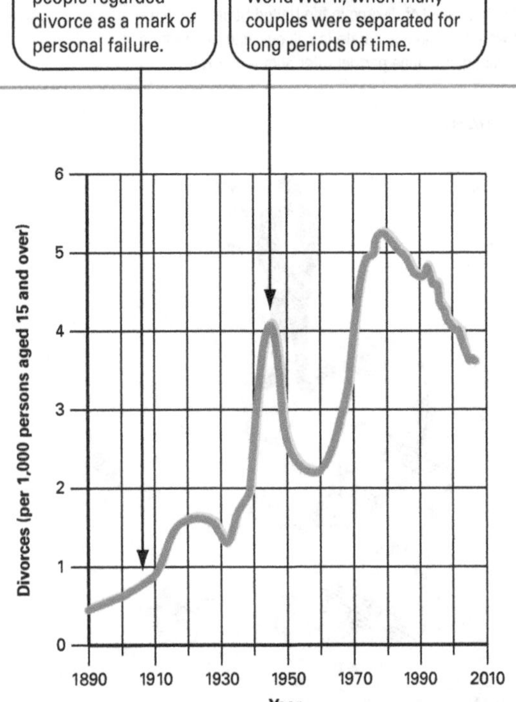

FIGURE 2 **Divorce Rate for the United States, 1890–2007**

Over the long term, the U.S. divorce rate has gone up. Since about 1980, however, the trend has been downward.

Source: U.S. Census Bureau (2009).

2. **Romantic love fades.** Because our culture bases marriage on romantic love, relationships may fail as sexual passion fades. Many people end a marriage in favor of a new relationship that promises renewed excitement and romance.
3. **Women are less dependent on men.** Women's increasing participation in the labor force has reduced wives' financial dependence on husbands. Therefore, women find it easier to leave unhappy marriages.
4. **Many of today's marriages are stressful.** With both partners working outside the home in most cases, jobs leave less time and energy for family life. This makes raising children harder than ever. Children do stabilize some marriages, but divorce is most common during the early years of marriage, when many couples have young children.
5. **Divorce has become socially acceptable.** Divorce no longer carries the powerful stigma it did several generations ago. Family and friends are now less likely to discourage couples in conflict from divorcing.
6. **Legally, a divorce is easier to get.** In the past, courts required divorcing couples to show that one or both were guilty of behavior such as adultery or physical abuse. Today, all states allow divorce if a couple simply declares that the marriage has failed. Concern about easy divorces, shared by more than half of U.S. adults, has led some states to consider rewriting their marriage laws (Phillips, 2001; NORC, 2007).

SEEING SOCIOLOGY in Everyday Life

Reading about "who divorces," point to ways in which society shapes individual choice.

Who Divorces?

At greatest risk of divorce are young spouses—especially those who marry after a brief courtship—who lack money and emotional maturity. The chance of divorce also rises if the couple marries after an unexpected pregnancy or if one or both partners have substance abuse problems. People whose parents divorced also have a higher divorce rate themselves. Researchers suggest that a role-modeling effect is at work: Children who see parents go through divorce are more likely to consider divorce themselves (Amato, 2001). Finally, people who are not religious are more likely to divorce than those who have strong religious beliefs (Amato, 2001; Pew Research Center, 2008).

Divorce is also more common when both partners have successful careers, perhaps because of the strains of a two-career marriage but also because financially secure people do not feel that they have to remain in an unhappy home. Finally, men and women who divorce once are more likely to divorce again, probably because high-risk factors follow them from one marriage to another (Glenn & Shelton, 1985).

Divorce and Children

Because mothers usually gain custody of children but fathers typically earn more income, the well-being of children often depends on fathers' making court-ordered child support payments. As Figure 3 indicates, courts award child support in 57 percent of all divorces involving children. Yet in any given year, almost half the children legally entitled to support receive only partial payments or no payments at all. Some 3.2 million "deadbeat dads" fail to support their youngsters. In response, federal legislation now mandates that employers withhold money from the earnings of fathers or mothers who fail to pay up; it is a serious crime to refuse to make child support payments or to move to another state to avoid making them (U.S. Census Bureau, 2008).

The effects of divorce on children go beyond financial support. Divorce can tear young people from familiar surroundings, entangle them in bitter feuding, and distance them from a parent they love. Most serious of all, many children blame themselves for their parents' breakup. Divorce changes the course of many children's lives, causing emotional and behavioral problems and raising the risk of dropping out of school and getting into trouble with the law. Many experts counter that divorce is better for children than staying in a family torn by tension and violence. In any case, parents should remember that if they consider divorce, more than their own well-being is at stake (Wallerstein & Blakeslee, 1989; Amato & Sobolewski, 2001).

SEEING SOCIOLOGY in Everyday Life

A girl who has been an only child becomes part of a "blended family" and suddenly has two older brothers. What adjustments might she have to make?

family violence emotional, physical, or sexual abuse of one family member by another

Remarriage and Blended Families

Four out of five people who divorce remarry, most within four years. Nationwide, more than one-third of all new marriages are now remarriages for at least one partner. Men, who benefit more from wedlock, are more likely than women to remarry (U.S. Census Bureau, 2008).

Remarriage often creates *blended families,* composed of children and some combination of biological parents and stepparents. With brothers, sisters, half-siblings, a stepparent—not to mention a biological parent who may live elsewhere and be married to someone else with other children—young people in blended families face the challenge of defining many new relationships and deciding just who is part of the nuclear family. Parents often have trouble defining responsibilities for household work among people unsure of their relationships to each other. When the custody of children is an issue, exspouses can be an unwelcome presence for people in a new marriage. Although blended families require that members adjust to their new circumstances, they offer both young and old the chance to relax rigid family roles (Furstenberg & Cherlin, 2001; McLanahan, 2002).

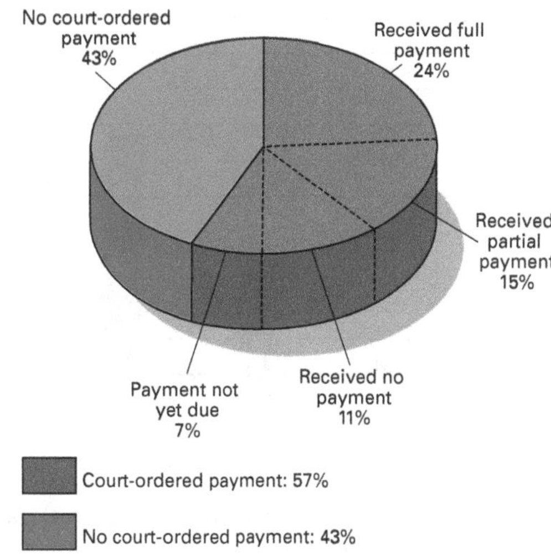

FIGURE 3 **Payment of Child Support after Divorce**
In almost half of all cases of court-ordered child support, the full payment is never received.
Source: U.S. Census Bureau (2008).

Family Violence

The ideal family is a source of pleasure and support. However, the disturbing reality of many homes is **family violence,** *emotional, physical, or sexual abuse of one family member by another.* With the exception of the police and the military, says the sociologist Richard J. Gelles, the family is "the most violent group in society" (quoted in Roesch, 1984:75).

Violence against Women

Family brutality often goes unreported to police. Even so, the U.S. Department of Justice (2008) estimates that about 700,000 adults are victims of domestic violence each year. Of this total, 73 percent of cases involve violence against women, and the remaining 27 percent involve violence against men. Fully 33 percent of women who are victims of homicide (but just 3 percent of men) are killed by spouses, partners, or ex-partners. Nationwide, the death toll from family violence is about 1,400 women each year. Overall, women are more likely to be injured by a family member than to be mugged or raped by a stranger or hurt in an automobile accident (Shupe, Stacey, & Hazlewood, 1987; Blankenhorn, 1995; U.S. Department of Justice, 2008).

Historically, the law defined wives as the property of their husbands, so no man could be charged with raping his wife. Today, however, all states have enacted *marital rape laws.* The law no longer regards domestic violence as a private family matter; it gives victims more options. Now, even without a formal separation or divorce, a woman can obtain court protection from an abusive spouse, and all states have "stalking laws" that forbid one ex-partner from following or otherwise threatening the other. Communities across the United States have established shelters to provide counseling and temporary housing for women and children driven from their homes by domestic violence.

Finally, the harm caused by domestic violence goes beyond the physical injuries. Victims often lose their ability to trust others. One study found that women who had been physically or sexually abused were much less likely than nonvictims to form stable relationships later on (Cherlin et al., 2004).

Violence against Children

Family violence also victimizes children. Each year, there are more than 3 million reports of alleged child abuse or neglect, about 1,500 of them involving a child's death. Child abuse entails more than physical injury; abusive adults misuse power and trust to damage a child's emotional well-being. Child abuse and neglect are most common among the youngest and most vulnerable children (Besharov & Laumann, 1996; U.S. Department of Health and Human Services, 2008).

Although child abusers conform to no simple stereotype, they are more likely to be women (58 percent) than men (42 percent). But almost all abusers share one trait—having been abused themselves as children. Research shows that violent behavior in close relationships is learned; in families, violence begets violence (S. Levine, 2001; U.S. Department of Health and Human Services, 2008).

SEEING SOCIOLOGY in Everyday Life

In what ways do children benefit from growing up in a household with both biological parents?

cohabitation the sharing of a household by an unmarried couple

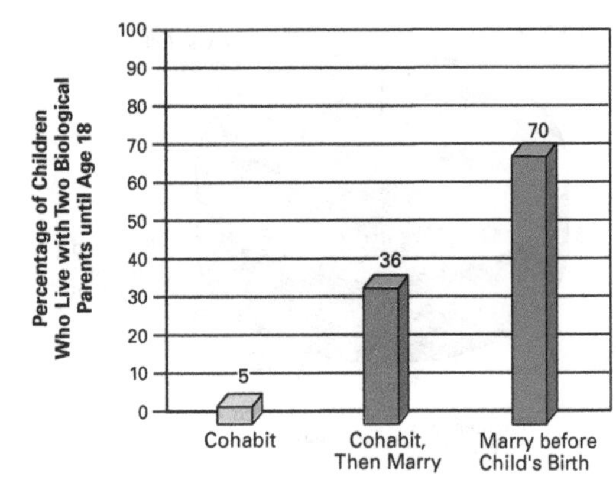

FIGURE 4 **Parental Involvement in Children's Lives: Cohabiting and Married Parents**

Marriage increases the odds that children will remain in the same household with both biological parents as they grow up.

Source: Phillips (2001).

Alternative Family Forms

Most families in the United States are composed of a married couple who raise children. But in recent decades, our society has displayed increasing diversity in family life.

One-Parent Families

Twenty-nine percent of U.S. families with children under eighteen have only one parent in the household, a proportion that more than doubled during the last generation. Put another way, 26 percent of U.S. children now live with only one parent, and almost half will do so before reaching eighteen. One-parent families, 85 percent of which are headed by a single mother, result from divorce, death, or an unmarried woman's decision to have a child (U.S. Census Bureau, 2008).

Single parenthood increases a woman's risk of poverty because it limits her ability to work and to further her education. The opposite is also true: Poverty raises the odds that a young woman will become a single mother. But single parenthood goes well beyond the poor: One-third of women in the United States become pregnant as teenagers, and many decide to raise their children whether they marry or not. Even more important, the number of unmarried women in their twenties, thirties, and forties who decide to have a child is increasing (Pew Research Center, 2007a; Martin et al., 2009).

Looking back at Figure 1, note that 54 percent of African American families are headed by a single parent. Single parenting is less common among Hispanics (33 percent), Asian Americans (20 percent), and non-Hispanic whites (19 percent). In many single-parent families, mothers turn to their own mothers for support. In the United States, then, the rise in single parenting is tied to a declining role for fathers and the growing importance of grandparenting.

Research shows that growing up in a one-parent family usually puts children at a disadvantage. Some studies claim that because a father and a mother each make distinctive contributions to a child's social development, one parent has a hard time doing as good a job alone. But the most serious problem for one-parent families, especially if that parent is a woman, is poverty. On average, children growing up in a single-parent family start out poorer, get less schooling, and end up with lower incomes as adults. Such children are also more likely to be single parents themselves (Blankenhorn, 1995; Kantrowitz & Wingert, 2001; McLanahan, 2002; U.S. Census Bureau, 2008).

Cohabitation

Cohabitation is *the sharing of a household by an unmarried couple.* As a long-term form of family life, with or without children, cohabitation is especially common in the Scandinavian countries and gaining popularity in other European nations. In the United States, the number of cohabiting couples increased from about 500,000 in 1970 to more than 6.2 million today (5.5 million heterosexual couples and 750,000 homosexual couples), or about 6 percent of all households. Almost half of all people between twenty-five and forty-four years of age have cohabited at some point (U.S. Census Bureau, 2008).

Cohabiting tends to appeal to more independent-minded individuals as well as those who favor gender equality (Brines & Joyner, 1999). Most couples cohabit for no more than a few years; at that point, about half decide to marry and half split up. Mounting evidence suggests that living together may actually discourage marriage because partners (especially men) become used to low-commitment relationships. For this reason, cohabiting couples who have children—currently representing about one in eight births in the United States—may not always be long-term parents. Figure 4 shows that just 5 percent of children born to cohabiting couples will live until age eighteen with both biological parents if the parents remain unmarried. The share rises to 36 percent among children whose parents marry at some point, but even this is half of the 70 percent figure among children whose parents married before they were born. When cohabiting couples with children separate, the involvement of both parents, including financial support, is highly uncertain (Popenoe & Whitehead, 1999; Booth & Crouter, 2002; Scommegna, 2002).

Gay and Lesbian Couples

In 1989, Denmark became the first country to permit registered partnerships with the benefits of marriage for same-sex couples. This change

SEEING SOCIOLOGY in Everyday Life

Have you ever lived with a partner? How does cohabitation differ from marriage?

extended social legitimacy to gay and lesbian couples and equalized advantages in inheritance, taxation, and joint property ownership. Since then, Norway (1993), Sweden (1994), Iceland (1996), Finland (2001), the United Kingdom (2004), and Australia (2008) have followed suit. However, only five countries have extended marriage—in name as well as practice—to same-sex couples: the Netherlands (2001), Belgium (2003), Canada (2005), Spain (2005), and South Africa (2006).

In the United States, Massachusetts became the first state to legalize same-sex marriage in 2004. As of 2009, Iowa, Connecticut, Vermont, New Hampshire, and Maine have also changed their laws to allow same-sex marriage. New Jersey, Oregon, and Washington permit same-sex unions with all the rights of marriage.

Back in 1996, the U.S. Congress passed a law defining marriage as joining one man and one woman. Since then, a total of thirty states have amended their constitutions to permit marriage only between one man and one woman. Nonetheless, the trend in public opinion is toward greater acceptance of same-sex marriage. Currently, about one-third of U.S. adults support gay marriage, and half support civil unions providing same-sex couples with the rights enjoyed by married people (Newport, 2005; NORC, 2007:1643; Leff, 2008).

AP WideO World Photos/*The Des Moines Register*, Christopher Gannon

In 2009, Iowa joined the growing number of states that allow same-sex couples to marry. Some people oppose any same-sex relationships; others support civil unions; still others believe that same-sex marriage should be lawful throughout the United States. Where do you stand on this issue? Why?

Most gay couples with children in the United States are raising the offspring of previous heterosexual unions; others have adopted children. But many gay parents are quiet about their sexual orientation, not wishing to draw unwelcome attention to their children or to themselves. In several widely publicized cases, courts have removed children from the custody of homosexual couples, citing a concern for the "best interests" of the children.

Gay parenting challenges many traditional ideas. But it also shows that many gay people value family life as highly as heterosexuals do.

Singlehood

Because nine out of ten people in the United States marry, we tend to view singlehood as a temporary stage of life. However, increasing numbers of people are choosing to live alone. In 1950, only one household in ten contained a single person. By 2007, this share had risen to 27 percent, a total of 31 million single adults (U.S. Census Bureau, 2008).

Most striking is the rising number of single young women. In 1960, 28 percent of U.S. women aged twenty to twenty-four were single; by 2007, the proportion had soared to 76 percent. Underlying this trend is women's greater participation in the labor force. Although most of these women will marry later on, women who are economically secure view a husband as a matter of choice rather than a financial necessity and marry later or, in some cases, not at all (Edwards, 2000).

By midlife, many unmarried women sense a lack of available men. Because we expect a woman to "marry up," the older a woman is, the more education she has, and the better her job, the more difficulty she has finding a suitable husband.

New Reproductive Technologies and Families

Medical advances involving reproductive technologies are also changing families. In 1978, England's Louise Brown became the world's first "test-tube baby"; since then, tens of thousands of children have been conceived outside the womb.

Test-tube babies are the product of *in vitro fertilization*, in which doctors unite a woman's egg and a man's sperm "in glass" (usually not a test tube but a shallow dish) rather than in a woman's body. Doctors then either implant the resulting embryo in the womb of the woman who is to bear the child or freeze it for implantation at a later time.

Modern reproductive technologies allow some couples who cannot conceive by conventional means to have children. These techniques may also eventually help reduce the incidence of birth defects. Genetic screening of sperm and eggs allows medical specialists to increase the odds of having a healthy baby. But new reproductive technologies also raise difficult and troubling questions: When one woman carries an

MAKING THE GRADE

Whatever your view of traditional families, be sure you can point to ways U.S. families have changed since 1960.

CONTROVERSY & DEBATE

Should We Save the Traditional Family?

Aaron: My parents were really goin' at each other last night. Man, I don't know whether they're going to stay together.

Abdul: I hope they do, my friend. Families are what ties society together.

Tawneesha: Listen to you guys! The important thing is for each person to be happy. If being married does it for you, great. But there's lots of different ways for people to find happiness.

What are "traditional families"? Are they vital to our way of life or a barrier to progress? People use the term *traditional family* to mean a married man and woman who at some point in their lives raise children. Statistically speaking, traditional families are less common than they used to be. In 1950, as the figure shows, 90 percent of U.S. households were families—using the Census Bureau's definition of two or more persons related by blood, marriage, or adoption. By 2007, just 68 percent of households were families, due to rising levels of divorce, cohabitation, and singlehood.

"Traditional family" is more than just a handy expression; it is also a moral statement. Belief in the traditional family implies giving high value to becoming and staying married, putting children ahead of careers, and favoring two-parent families over various alternatives.

"Traditional Families Are the Solution"

On one side of the debate, David Popenoe (1993a) has warned of a serious erosion of the traditional family since 1960. At that time, married couples with young children accounted for almost half of all households; today, the figure is 23 percent.

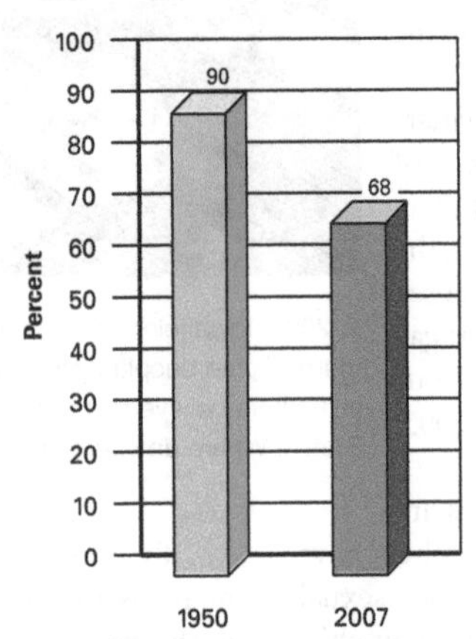

Share of U.S. Households That the Census Bureau Classified as Families, 1950 and 2007

Families were a smaller share of all U.S. households in 2007 compared to 1950.

Singlehood is up, from 10 percent of households in 1960 to 27 percent today. And the divorce rate has risen by 64 percent since 1960, so that nearly four in ten of today's marriages end in permanent separation. Because of both divorce and the increasing number of children born to single women, the share of youngsters who will live with just one parent before age eighteen has almost tripled since 1960 to 26 percent. In other words, just one in four of today's children will grow up with two parents and go on to maintain a stable marriage as an adult (U.S. Census Bureau, 2008).

In light of such data, Popenoe suggests that it may not be an exaggeration to say that the family is falling apart. He sees a fundamental shift from a "culture of marriage" to a "culture of divorce," where traditional vows of marital commitment—"till death do us part"—now amount to little more than "as long as I am happy." The negative consequences of the cultural trend toward weaker families, Popenoe continues, are obvious and can be found everywhere: As we pay less and less attention to children, the crime rate among young people goes up, along with a host of other problem behaviors including underage smoking and drinking, premarital sex, and teen suicide.

As Popenoe sees it, we must work hard and act quickly to reverse current trends. Government cannot be the solution and may even be part of

embryo developed from the egg of another, who is the mother? When a couple divorces, which spouse is entitled to use, or destroy, their frozen embryos? Should parents use genetic screening to select the traits of their child? Such questions remind us that technology changes faster than our ability to understand the consequences of its use (A. Cohen, 1998; Nock, Wright, & Sanchez, 1999).

Families: Looking Ahead

Family life in the United States will continue to change in the years to come, and with change comes controversy. Advocates of "traditional family values" line up against those who support greater personal choice; the Controversy & Debate box outlines some of the issues. Sociologists cannot predict the outcome of this debate, but we can suggest five likely future trends.

First, the divorce rate is likely to remain high, even in the face of evidence that marital breakups harm children. Today's marriages are about as durable as they were a century ago, when many were cut short by death. The difference is that now more couples *choose* to end marriages that fail to live up to their expectations. So even though the divorce rate has declined since 1980, it is unlikely to return to the low rates that marked the early decades of the twentieth century.

Second, family life in the twenty-first century will be more diverse than ever. Cohabiting couples, one-parent families, gay and lesbian families, and blended families are all on the rise. Most families are still based on marriage, and most married couples still have

SEEING SOCIOLOGY in Everyday Life

How important do you think strong families are to the health of our society? What makes a family "strong"?

the problem: Since 1960, as families have weakened, government spending on social programs has soared. To save the traditional family, says Popenoe, we need a cultural turnaround similar to what happened with regard to cigarette smoking. In this case, we must replace our "me first" attitudes with commitment to our spouse and children and publicly endorse the two-parent family as best for the well-being of children.

"Traditional Families Are the Problem" Judith Stacey (1993) provides a feminist viewpoint, saying "good riddance" to the traditional family. In her view, the traditional family is more problem than solution: "The family is not here to stay. Nor should we wish it were. On the contrary, I believe that all democratic people, whatever their kinship preferences, should work to hasten its demise" (Stacey, 1990:269).

The main reason for rejecting the traditional family, Stacey explains, is that it perpetuates social inequality. Families play a key role in maintaining the class hierarchy by transferring wealth as well as "cultural capital" from one generation to another. Feminists criticize the traditional family's patriarchal form, which subjects women to their husbands' authority and gives them most of the responsibility for housework and child care. From a gay rights perspective, she adds, a society that values traditional families also denies homosexual men and women equal participation in social life.

Stacey thus applauds the breakdown of the family as social progress. She does not view the family as a necessary social institution but as a political construction that elevates one category of people—affluent white males—above others, including women, homosexuals, and poor people.

Stacey also claims that the concept of the "traditional family" is increasingly irrelevant in a diverse society in which both men and women work for income. What our society needs, Stacey concludes, is not a return to some golden age of the family but political and economic change, including income parity for women, universal health care and child care, programs to reduce unemployment, and expanded sex education in the schools. Such measures not only help families but also ensure that people in diverse family forms receive the respect and dignity they deserve.

Whether the traditional family is a positive force in U.S. society or a negative one depends on your point of view.

WHAT DO YOU THINK?

1. To strengthen families, David Popenoe suggests that parents put children ahead of their own careers by limiting their joint workweek to sixty hours. Do you agree? Why or why not?
2. Judith Stacey thinks that marriage is weaker today because women are rejecting patriarchal relationships. What do you think about this argument?
3. Do we need to change family patterns for the well-being of our children? As you see it, what specific changes are called for?

children. But the diversity of family forms implies a trend toward more personal choice.

Third, men will play a limited role in child rearing. In the 1950s, a decade that many people view as the "golden age" of families, men began to withdraw from active parenting (Snell, 1990; Stacey, 1990). In recent years, a countertrend has become evident, with some older, highly educated men staying at home with young children, many using computer technology to continue their work. But the stay-at-home dad represents no more than 10 percent of fathers with young children (U.S. Census Bureau, 2008). The bigger picture is that the high U.S. divorce rate and the increase in single motherhood are weakening children's ties to fathers and increasing children's risk of poverty.

Fourth, families will continue to feel the effects of economic changes. In many homes today, both household partners work, reducing marriage and family life to the interaction of weary men and women who must try to fit a little "quality time" with their children into an already full schedule. The long-term effects of the two-career couple on families as we have known them are likely to be mixed.

Fifth and finally, the importance of new reproductive technologies will increase. Ethical concerns about whether what *can* be done *should* be done will slow these developments, but new approaches to reproduction will continue to alter the traditional experience of parenthood.

Despite the changes and controversies that have shaken the family in the United States, most people still report being happy as partners and parents. Marriage and family life are likely to remain foundations of our society for generations to come.

Seeing Sociology in Everyday Life

Families

How do the mass media portray the family?

Everybody is familiar with the traditional families portrayed in popular 1950s television shows such as *Ozzie Harriet* and *Leave It To Beaver*. Both of these shows had a working father, homemaker mother, and two (wonderful) sons. But, as the images below suggest, today's television shows are not as family-centered.

HINT The general pattern found in the mass media today is certainly different from that common in the 1950s, the so-called "golden age of families." Today's television shows emphasize that careers often leave little time for family (*House*) or that, for a variety of reasons, stable marriages are the exception rather than the rule (all the shows illustrated here). Does Hollywood have an anti-family bias? This is hard to answer; perhaps script writers find that nonconventional family forms make for more interesting stories. In any case, most television shows make clear that people of all ages (well, maybe not Gregory House) are capable of finding and maintaining satisfying relationships, whether or not those relationsips conform to a traditional family form.

The most popular television show of 2009 is *House*, which revolves around a brainy but belligerent physician and his colleagues at an upscale New Jersey hospital. None of the main characters in the show is married; none has children; and none gets along well with parents. Why might this be the case?

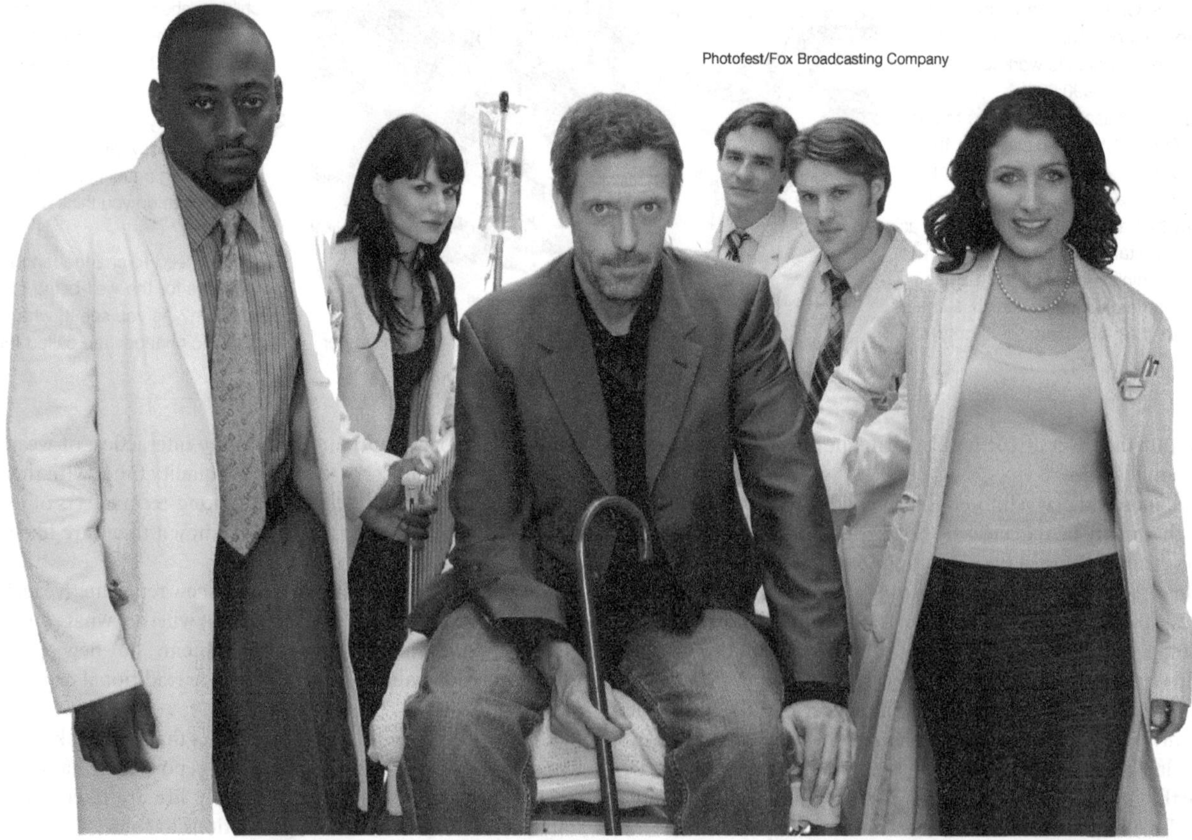

Photofest/Fox Broadcasting Company

Andrew Eccles/© The CW/Courtesy Everett Collection

Another hit television series is *Gossip Girl*, about a group of young people from well-off families in New York. Other than their wealth, what can you say about the families that these young people come from?

Greg Gayne/© CBS/courtesy Everett Collection

Another popular show is *Two and a Half Men*, in which Charlie Sheen plays a young bachelor who is joined by his twice-divorced brother and his brother's young son. What can you say about the way this show presents family life?

Applying SOCIOLOGY in Everyday Life

1. List your favorite television shows and, in each case, describe the importance the show gives to family life. What family forms are presented in the show? Are families a source of happiness to people or not?

2. Relationships with various family members differ. With which family member—mother, father, brother, sister—do you most readily share confidences? Why? Which family member would you turn to first in a crisis, and why? Who in your family would be the last to know?

3. Parents and grandparents can be a wonderful source of information about changes in marriage and the family. Ask them at what ages they married, what their married lives have been like, and what changes in family life today stand out for them. Compare the answers of two or more relatives. Are they very different?

VISUAL SUMMARY

MAKING THE GRADE

Families

Families: Basic Concepts

All societies are built on *kinship*. The **FAMILY** varies across cultures and over time:

- In industrialized societies such as the United States, *marriage* is monogamous.
- Preindustrial societies recognize the *extended family*; industrialization gives rise to the *nuclear family*.
- Many preindustrial societies permit *polygamy*, of which there are two types: *polygyny* and *polyandry*.
- In global perspective, *patrilocality* is most common, but industrial societies favor *neolocality* and a few societies have *matrilocal residence*.
- Industrial societies use *bilateral descent*; preindustrial societies are either *patrilineal* or *matrilineal*.

family a social institution found in all societies that unites people in cooperative groups to care for one another, including any children

kinship a social bond based on common ancestry, marriage, or adoption

marriage a legal relationship, usually involving economic cooperation, sexual activity, and childbearing

extended family a family consisting of parents and children as well as other kin; also known as a *consanguine family*

nuclear family a family composed of one or two parents and their children; also known as a *conjugal family*

endogamy marriage between people of the same social category

exogamy marriage between people of different social categories

monogamy marriage that unites two partners

polygamy marriage that unites a person with two or more spouses

polygyny marriage that unites one man and two or more women

polyandry marriage that unites one woman and two or more men

patrilocality a residential pattern in which a married couple lives with or near the husband's familiy

matrilocality a residential pattern in which a married couple lives with or near the wife's familiy

neolocality a residential pattern in which a married couple lives apart from both sets of parents

descent the system by which members of a society trace kinship over generations

patrilineal descent a system tracing kinship through men

matrilineal descent a system tracing kinship through women

bilateral descent a system tracing kinship through both men and women

Theoretical Analysis of Families

The **STRUCTURAL-FUNCTIONAL APPROACH** identifies major family functions that help society operate smoothly:

- socialization of children to help them become well-integrated members of society
- regulation of sexual activity in order to maintain kinship organization and property rights
- giving children a social identity within society in terms of race, ethnicity, religion, and social class
- providing material and emotional support to family members

The **SOCIAL-CONFLICT APPROACH** and **FEMINIST APPROACH** point to ways in which families perpetuate social inequality

- Families ensure the continuation of the class structure by passing on wealth to their children.
- Families perpetuate gender roles by establishing men as the heads of the household and by assigning the responsibility for child rearing and housework to women.
- The tendency of people to marry others like themselves supports racial and ethnic hierarchies.

The **incest taboo**, which restricts sexual relations between certain relatives, exists in all societies.

incest taboo a norm forbidding sexual relations or marriage between certain relatives

- The **SYMBOLIC-INTERACTION APPROACH** explores how family members build emotional bonds in the course of everyday family life.
- The **SOCIAL-EXCHANGE APPROACH** sees courtship and marriage as a process of negotiation in which each person weighs the advantages and disadvantages of a potential partner.

See the Applying Theory table.

Stages of Family Life

COURTSHIP AND ROMANTIC LOVE

- Arranged marriages are common in preindustrial societies.
- Courtship based on romantic love is central to mate selection in the United States and leads to the formation of new families.
- The contrast between our culture's idealized vision of marriage and the everyday realities of married life can lead to disappointment and failed marriages.

homogamy marriage between people with the same social characteristics

infidelity sexual activity outside one's marriage

CHILD REARING

- Large families are necessary in preindustrial societies because children are a source of needed labor.
- Family size has decreased over time as industrialization increases the costs of raising children.
- As more women choose to go to school or join the labor force, fewer children are born.
- The "family values" debate revolves around who cares for children when both parents work outside the home.

THE FAMILY IN LATER LIFE

- The departure of children, known as the "empty nest," requires adjustments to family life.
- Many middle-aged couples care for aging parents, and many older couples are active grandparents.
- The final transition in marriage begins with the death of a spouse.

U.S. Families: Class, Gender, and Race

SOCIAL CLASS is a powerful force that shapes family life.

- Social class determines a family's financial security and opportunities available to family members.
- Children born into rich families typically have better mental and physical health and go on to achieve more in life than children born into poor families.

GENDER affects family dynamics because husbands dominate in most marriages.

- Research suggests that marriage provides more benefits for men than for women.
- After divorce, men are more likely than women to remarry.

ETHNICITY AND RACE can affect a person's experience of family life, although no single generalization fits all families within a particular category.

- Migration of American Indians from reservations to cities creates many "fluid households" with changing membership.
- The traditional pattern of extended families common to Latinos is changing as Latinos assimilate into the larger U.S. society.
- African American families face severe economic disadvantages, and more than one-third of African American children are growing up poor.

Most married couples have similar social background with regard to class and race, but over the past century, ethnicity has mattered less and less.

Transitions and Problems in Family Life

DIVORCE

The divorce rate is seven times what it was a century ago; four in ten of today's marriages will end in divorce. Researchers point to six causes:

- Individualism is on the rise.
- Romantic love fades.
- Women are less dependent on men.
- Many of today's marriages are stressful.
- Divorce is socially acceptable.
- Legally, a divorce is easier to get.

REMARRIAGE

- Four out of five people who divorce eventually remarry.
- Remarriage creates blended families that include children from previous marriages.

FAMILY VIOLENCE

- Family violence, which victimizes mostly women and children, is far more common than official records indicate.
- Most adults who abuse family members were themselves abused as children.

family violence emotional, physical, or sexual abuse of one family member by another

cohabitation the sharing of a household by an unmarried couple

Alternative Family Forms

ONE-PARENT FAMILIES

- The proportion of one-parent families—now 29% of all families in the United States—more than doubled during the last generation.
- Single parenthood increases a woman's risk of poverty, which puts children at a disadvantage.

COHABITATION

- Almost half of all people 25 to 44 years of age have cohabited at some point.
- Research shows that children born to cohabiting couples are less likely to live with both biological parents until age 18 than children born to married parents.

GAY AND LESBIAN COUPLES

- Although only Massachusetts, Connecticut, Vermont, New Hampshire, Maine, and Iowa allow same-sex marriage, many gay men and lesbians form long-lasting relationships and, increasingly, are becoming parents.

SINGLEHOOD

- One in four households today—up from one in ten in 1950—contains a single person.
- The number of young women who are single is rising dramatically, a result of women's greater participation in the workforce and lessened dependence on men for material supoort.

New Reproductive Technologies

- Although ethically controversial, new reproductive technologies are changing conventional ideas of parenthood.

MAKING THE GRADE

Sample Test Questions

Multiple-Choice Questions

1. **The family is a social institution that is found in**
   a. most but not all societies.
   b. low-income nations but typically not in high-income nations.
   c. high-income nations but typically not in low-income nations.
   d. every society.

2. **What is the term sociologists use for a family containing parents, children, and other kin?**
   a. a nuclear family
   b. an extended family
   c. a family of affinity
   d. a conjugal family

3. **A system of marriage that unites one woman with two or more men is called**
   a. polygamy.
   b. polygyny.
   c. polyandry.
   d. bilateral marriage.

4. **Sociologists claim that marriage in the United States follows the principle of homogamy, which means that partners are**
   a. people of the same sex.
   b. people who are socially alike in terms of class, age, and race.
   c. people who marry due to social pressure.
   d. selected based on love rather than by parents.

5. **Which of the following are included among the functions of the family?**
   a. socialization of children
   b. regulation of sexual activity
   c. social placement of children
   d. All of the above are correct.

6. **Which theoretical approach states that people select partners who have about the same to offer as they do?**
   a. the structural-functional approach
   b. the social-exchange approach
   c. the social-conflict approach
   d. the feminist approach

7. **Which of the following transitions in married life is usually the hardest for people?**
   a. birth of the second child
   b. last child leaving home
   c. death of a spouse
   d. retiring from the labor force

8. **In the United States, many Latino families are characterized by**
   a. strong extended kinship.
   b. parents exerting a great deal of control over their children's courtship.
   c. traditional gender roles.
   d. All of the above are correct.

9. **For which category of the U.S. population is the highest proportion of children born to single women?**
   a. African Americans
   b. Asian Americans
   c. Hispanic Americans
   d. non-Hispanic white Americans

10. **Which category of people in the United States is at the highest risk of divorce?**
    a. gay and lesbian couples
    b. young people who marry after a short courtship
    c. a couple whose parents never experienced divorce
    d. a couple facing a wanted and expected pregnancy

ANSWERS: 1 (d); 2 (b); 3 (c); 4 (b); 5 (d); 6 (b); 7 (c); 8 (d); 9 (a); 10 (b).

Essay Questions

1. Sociologists point to ways in which family life reflects not just individual choices but the structure of society as well. Provide three examples of how society shapes family life.
2. Overall, do you think families in the United States are becoming weaker or simply more diverse? Support your position.

Education

Redux Pictures/Vanessa Vick/*The New York Times*

In the modern world, education emerges as a new social institution as societies develop schooling to prepare people for future work. Earning a college degree has a powerful and positive effect on future earnings.

AP Wide World Photos

Education

CHAPTER OVERVIEW

This chapter explains the operation of education, a major social institution. The chapter begins with a global survey of schooling and then focuses on education in the United States.

When Lisa Addison was growing up in Baltimore, her teachers always said she was smart and should go to college. "I liked hearing that," she recalls. "But I didn't know what to do about it. No one in my family had ever gone to college. I didn't know what courses to take in high school. I had no idea of how to apply to a college. How would I pay for it? What would it be like if I got there?"

Discouraged and uncertain, Addison found herself "kind of goofing off in school." After finishing high school, she spent the next fifteen years working as a waitress in a restaurant and then as a kitchen helper in a catering company. Now, at the age of thirty-eight, Addison has decided to go back to school. "I don't want to do this kind of work for the rest of my life. I *am* smart. I can do better. At this point, I *am* ready for college."

Addison took a giant step through the door of the Community College of Baltimore County, speaking to counselors and setting her sights on an associate's degree in business. When she finishes the two-year program, she plans to transfer to a four-year university to complete a bachelor's degree. Then she hopes to go back into the food service industry—but this time as manager at higher pay (Toppo & DeBarros, 2005).

Higher education is part of the American dream for almost all young people in the United States. But many face the types of challenges that delayed Lisa Addison in her journey toward a college degree. Especially for people growing up in low-income families, often with parents who are not college graduates, the odds of getting to college can be small.

Who goes to college in the United States? What difference does higher education make in the type of job you get or the money you make? This chapter answers these questions by focusing on **education**, *the social institution through which society provides its members with important knowledge, including basic facts, job skills, and cultural norms and values.* In high-income nations such as the United States, education is largely a matter of **schooling**, *formal instruction under the direction of specially trained teachers.*

Education: A Global Survey

In the United States, young people expect to spend most of their first eighteen years in school. This was not the case a century ago, when just a small elite had the privilege of attending school. Even today, most young people in poor countries receive only a few years of formal schooling.

Schooling and Economic Development

The extent of schooling in any society is tied to its level of economic development. In low- and middle-income countries, which are home to most of the world's people, families and communities teach young people important knowledge and skills. Formal schooling, especially learning that is not directly connected to survival, is available mainly to wealthy people who may not need to work and who can pursue personal enrichment. The word *school* is from a Greek root that means "leisure." In ancient Greece, famous teachers such as Socrates, Plato, and Aristotle taught aristocratic, upper-class men who had plenty of spare time. The same was true in ancient China, where the famous philosopher K'ung Fu-tzu (Confucius) shared his wisdom with a privileged few.

December 30, the Cuzco region, Peru. High in the Andes Mountains of Peru, families send their children to the local school. But "local" can mean 3 miles away or more, and there are no buses, so these children, almost all from poor families, walk at least an hour each way. Schooling is required by law, but in the rural highlands, some parents prefer to keep their children at home where they can help with the farming and livestock.

education the social institution through which society provides its members with important knowledge, including basic facts, job skills, and cultural norms and values

schooling formal instruction under the direction of specially trained teachers

Today, the limited schooling that takes place in lower-income countries reflects the national culture. In Iran, for example, schooling is closely tied to Islam. Similarly, schooling in Bangladesh (Asia), Zimbabwe (Africa), and Nicaragua (Latin America) has been shaped by the distinctive cultural traditions of these nations.

All lower-income countries have one trait in common when it comes to schooling: There is not much of it. In the world's poorest nations (including several in Central Africa), more than one-fourth of all children never get to school (World Bank, 2009). Worldwide, more than one-third of all children never reach the secondary grades (what we call *high school*). As a result, about one-fifth of the world's people cannot read or write. Global Map 1 shows the extent of illiteracy around the world, and the following national comparisons illustrate the link between the extent of schooling and economic development.

SEEING SOCIOLOGY in Everyday Life

The extent of schooling is one good measure of economic development.

Landov Media/Antony Njuguna/ Reuters

In many low-income nations, children are as likely to work as they are to attend school, and girls receive less schooling than boys. But the doors to schooling are now opening to more girls and women. These young women are studying nursing at Somalia University in downtown Mogadishu.

Schooling in India

India has recently become a middle-income country, but people there still earn only about 6 percent of U.S. average income, and most poor families depend on the earnings of children. Even though India has outlawed child labor, many children continue to work in factories—weaving rugs or making handicrafts—up to sixty hours per week, which greatly limits their opportunities for schooling.

Today, almost 90 percent of children in India complete primary school, typically in crowded schoolrooms where one teacher may face as many as sixty children, twice as many as in the average U.S. public school classroom. Barely half of Indian children go on to secondary school, and very few enter college. As a result, 34 percent of India's people are not able to read and write (UNESCO, 2009).

Patriarchy also shapes Indian education. Indian parents are joyful at the birth of a boy because he and his future wife will both contribute income to the family. But there are economic costs to raising a girl: Parents must provide a dowry (a gift of wealth to the groom's family), and after her marriage, a daughter's work benefits her husband's family. Therefore, many Indians see less reason to invest in the schooling of girls, so only 49 percent of girls (compared to 59 percent of boys) reach the secondary grades. What do the girls do while the boys are in school? Most of the children working in Indian factories are girls—a family's way of benefiting from their daughters while they can (UNESCO, 2008).

Schooling in Japan

Schooling has not always been part of the Japanese way of life. Before industrialization brought mandatory education in 1872, only a privileged few attended school. Today, Japan's educational system is widely praised for producing some of the world's highest achievers.

The early grades concentrate on transmitting Japanese traditions, especially a sense of obligation to family. Starting in their early teens, students take a series of difficult and highly competitive examinations. Their scores on these written tests, which are like the Scholastic Assessment Test (SAT) in the United States, decide the future of all Japanese students.

More men and women graduate from high school in Japan (93 percent) than in the United States (87 percent). But competitive examinations allow just half of high school graduates—compared to 66 percent in the United States—to enter college. Understandably, Japanese students (and their parents) take entrance examinations very seriously. About half attend "cram schools" to prepare for the exams, which means very late nights completing homework. Such hard work is one reason that Japanese students often nap in class—seen by teachers as the mark of a serious student (Steger, 2006; UNESCO, 2008).

Japanese schooling produces impressive results. In a number of fields, notably mathematics and science, Japanese students outperform students in almost every other high-income nation, including the United States (OECD, 2009).

Schooling in Great Britain

During the Middle Ages, schooling was a privilege of the British nobility, who studied classical subjects, having little concern for the practical skills needed to earn a living. But as the Industrial Revolution

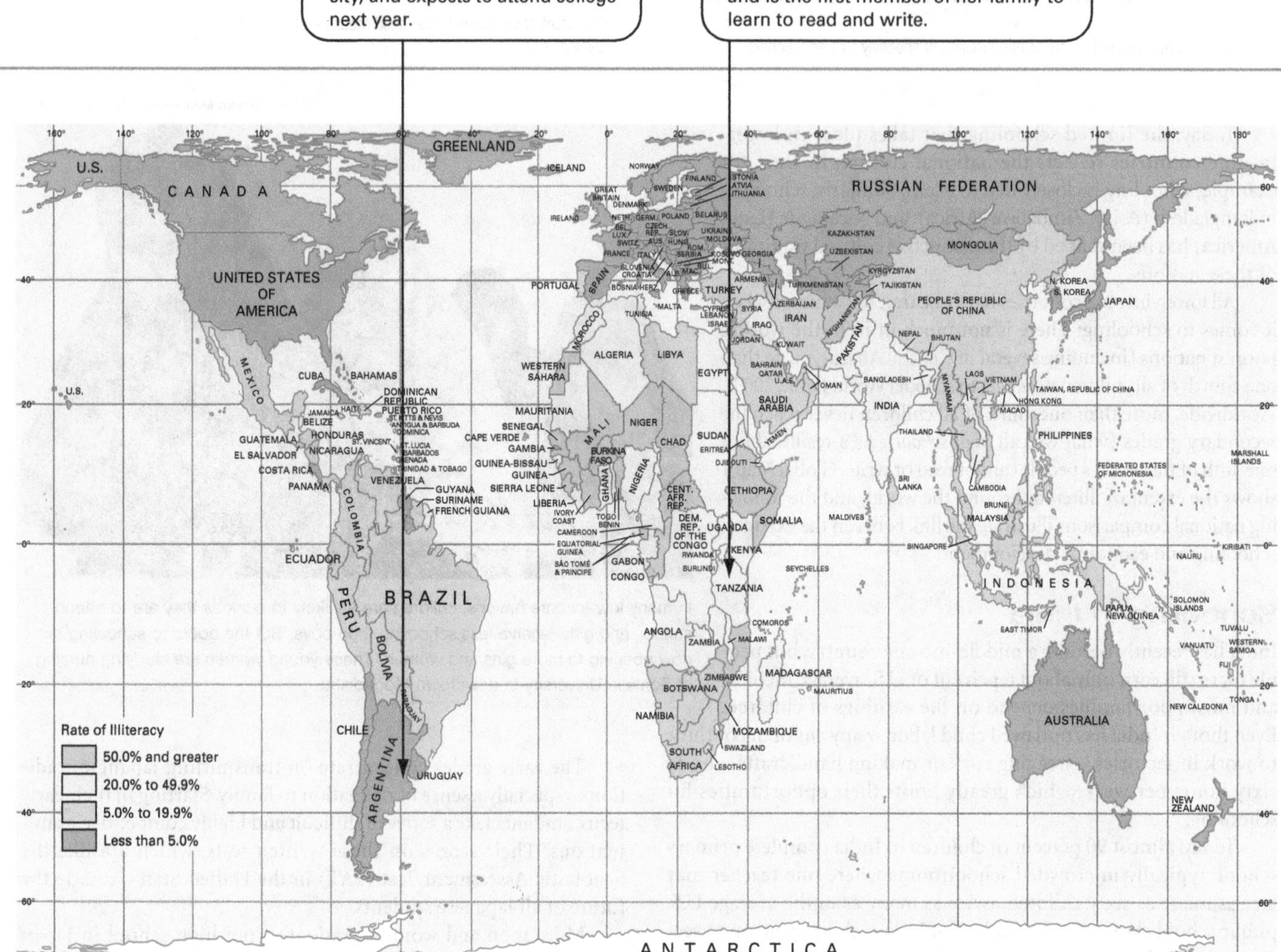

Window on the World

GLOBAL MAP 1 Illiteracy in Global Perspective

Reading and writing skills are widespread in high-income countries, where illiteracy rates generally are below 5 percent. In much of Latin America, however, illiteracy is more common, one consequence of limited economic development. In fifteen nations—fourteen of them in Africa—illiteracy is the rule rather than the exception; there people rely on the oral tradition of face-to-face communication rather than the written word.

Source: UNESCO (2009).

created a need for an educated labor force, and as working-class people demanded access to schools, a rising share of the population entered the classroom. British law now requires every child to attend school until age sixteen.

Traditional class differences still affect British schooling. Most wealthy families send their children to what the British call *public schools,* which we would refer to as private boarding schools. These elite schools enroll about 7 percent of British students and teach not only academic subjects but also the special patterns of speech, mannerisms, and social graces of the British upper class. Because these academies are very expensive, most British students attend state-supported day schools (Department for Children, Schools, and Families, 2008).

The British have tried to reduce the importance of social background in schooling by expanding their university system and linking

MAKING THE GRADE

Our country's expansion of schooling has been not only to prepare people for jobs, but in pursuit of the goal of equal opportunity.

SEEING SOCIOLOGY in Everyday Life

What is your career goal? Are the courses you are taking geared to helping you realize this goal?

admission to competitive entrance examinations. For the students who score the highest, the government pays most of the college costs. But many well-to-do children who do not score very well still manage to get into Oxford or Cambridge, the most prestigious British universities, on a par with our own Yale, Harvard, and Princeton. Many "Oxbridge" graduates go on to positions at the top of the British power elite: Most of the highest-ranking members of the British government have "Oxbridge" degrees.

These brief sketches of schooling in India, Japan, and Great Britain show the crucial importance of economic development. In poor countries, many children—especially girls—work rather than go to school. Rich nations enact mandatory education laws to prepare an industrial workforce as well as to satisfy demands for greater equality. But a nation's history and culture still matter, as we see in the intense competition of Japanese schools, the traditional social stratification that shapes schools in Great Britain, and, in the next section, the practical emphasis found in the schools of the United States.

Table 1 Educational Achievement in the United States, 1910–2008

Year	High School Graduates	College Graduates	Median Years of Schooling
1910	13.5%	2.7%	8.1
1920	16.4	3.3	8.2
1930	19.1	3.9	8.4
1940	24.1	4.6	8.6
1950	33.4	6.0	9.3
1960	41.1	7.7	10.5
1970	55.2	11.0	12.2
1980	68.7	17.0	12.5
1990	77.6	21.3	12.4
2000	84.1	25.6	12.7
2008	86.6	29.4	N.A.

Notes: Figures are for people 25 years of age and over. Percentage of high school graduates includes those who go on to college. Percentage of high school dropouts can be calculated by subtracting the percentage of high school graduates from 100 percent. N.A. = not available.

Source: U.S. Census Bureau (2009).

Schooling in the United States

The United States was among the first countries to set a goal of mass education. By 1850, about half the young people between the ages of five and nineteen were enrolled in school. By 1918, all states had passed a *mandatory education law* requiring children to attend school until the age of sixteen or completion of the eighth grade. Table 1 shows that a milestone was reached in the mid-1960s when for the first time a majority of U.S. adults had a high school diploma. Today, 86.6 percent have completed high school, and 29.4 percent have a four-year college degree (U.S. Census Bureau, 2009).

The U.S. educational system is shaped by both our high standard of living (which means that young people typically do not have to work) and our democratic principles (the idea that schooling should be provided to everyone). Thomas Jefferson thought the new nation could become democratic only if people learned to read. Today, the United States has an outstanding record of higher education for its people: No other country has as large a share of adults with university degrees (U.S. Census Bureau, 2008).

Schooling in the United States also tries to promote *equal opportunity.* National surveys show that most people think schooling is crucial to personal success, and a majority also believe that everyone has the chance to get an education consistent with personal ability and talent (NORC, 2007). However, this opinion expresses our cultural ideals rather than reality. A century ago, for example, few women had the chance to go to college, and even today, most men and women who attend college come from families with above-average incomes.

In the United States, the educational system stresses the value of *practical* learning, knowledge that prepares people for future jobs. This emphasis is in line with what the educational philosopher John Dewey (1859–1952) called *progressive education,* having the schools make learning relevant to people's lives. Similarly, students seek out subjects of study that they feel will give them an advantage when they are ready to compete in the job market. For example, as concerns about international terrorism have risen in recent years, so have the numbers of students choosing to study geography, international conflict, and Middle Eastern history and culture (M. Lord, 2001).

The Functions of Schooling

Structural-functional analysis looks at ways in which formal education supports the operation and stability of society. We look briefly at five ways in which this happens.

Socialization

Technologically simple societies look to families to teach skills and values and thus transmit a way of life from one generation to the next. As societies gain more complex technology, they turn to trained teachers to develop and pass on the more specialized knowledge that adults will need to take their place in the workforce.

In primary school, children learn language and basic mathematical skills. Secondary school builds on this foundation, and for many students, college allows further specialization. In addition, all schooling teaches cultural values and norms. For example, civics classes instruct students in our political way of life, and rituals such as saluting the flag foster patriotism. Likewise, activities such as spelling bees develop competitive individualism and a sense of fair play.

MAKING THE GRADE

Manifest functions refer to consequences that are widely understood; *latent functions* refer to those less commonly recognized.

Bob Daemmrich Photography, Inc.

Graduation from college is an important event in the lives of an ever-increasing number of people in the United States. Look over the discussion of the functions of schooling. How many of these functions do you think people in college are aware of? Can you think of other social consequences of going to college?

Cultural Innovation

Faculty at colleges and universities create culture as well as pass it on to students. Research in the sciences, the social sciences, the humanities, and the fine arts leads to discovery and changes in our way of life. For example, medical research at major universities has helped increase life expectancy, just as research by sociologists and psychologists helps us learn how to enjoy life more so that we can take advantage of our longevity.

Social Integration

Schooling molds a diverse population into one society sharing norms and values. This is one reason that states enacted mandatory education laws a century ago at a time when immigration was very high. In light of the ethnic diversity of many urban areas today, schooling continues to serve this purpose.

Social Placement

Schools identify talent and match instruction to ability. Schooling increases meritocracy by rewarding talent and hard work regardless of social background and provides a path to upward social mobility.

Latent Functions of Schooling

Schooling also serves several less widely recognized functions. It provides child care for the growing number of one-parent and two-career families. In addition, schooling occupies thousands of young people in their teens and twenties who would otherwise be competing for limited opportunities in the job market. High schools, colleges, and universities also bring together people of marriageable age. Finally, schools establish networks that serve as a valuable career resource throughout life.

CRITICAL REVIEW Structural-functional analysis stresses ways in which formal education supports the operation of a modern society. However, this approach overlooks how the classroom behavior of teachers and students can vary from one setting to another, a focus of the symbolic-interaction approach discussed next. In addition, structural-functional analysis says little about many problems of our educational system and how schooling helps reproduce the class structure in each generation, which is the focus of social-conflict analysis found in the final theoretical section of the chapter.

CHECK YOUR LEARNING Identify the five functions of schooling for the operation of society.

Schooling and Social Interaction

The basic idea of the symbolic-interaction approach is that people create the reality they experience in their day-to-day interaction. We use this approach to explain how stereotypes can shape what goes on in the classroom.

The Self-Fulfilling Prophecy

The Thomas theorem states that situations that people define as real become real in their consequences. Put another way, people who expect others to act in certain ways often encourage that very behavior. Doing so, people set up a *self-fulfilling prophecy.*

Jane Elliott, an elementary school teacher in the all-white community of Riceville, Iowa, carried out a simple experiment that showed how a self-fulfilling prophecy can take place in the classroom. In 1968, Elliot was teaching a fourth-grade class when Dr. Martin Luther King Jr. was assassinated. Her students were puzzled and asked why a national hero had been brutally shot. Elliott responded by asking her white students what they thought about people of color, and she was stunned to find out that they held many powerful negative stereotypes.

Everett Collection/MGM

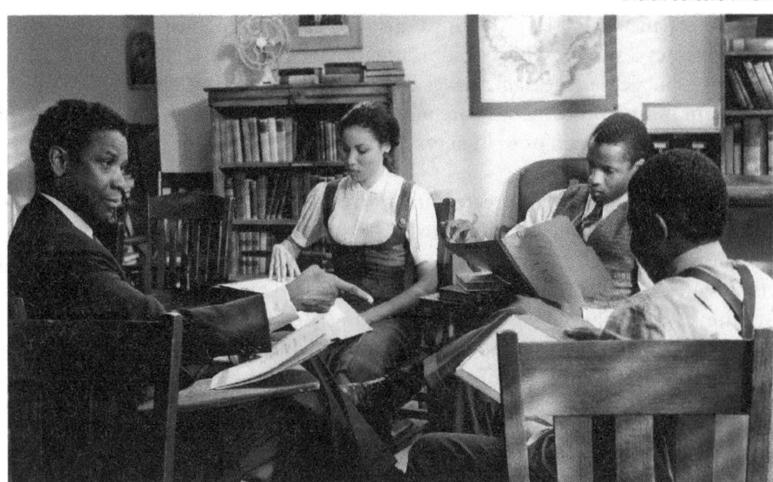

How well young people perform in school depends a lot on what people expect of them. The 2007 film *The Great Debaters* is based on the true story of a coach at an all-black college in Texas during the 1930s. Believing in the abilities of his students, he guides them to become one of the best debate teams in the country.

To show the class the harmful effects of such stereotypes, Elliott performed a classroom experiment. She found that almost all of the children in her class had either blue eyes or brown eyes. She told the class that children with brown eyes were smarter and worked harder than children with blue eyes. To be sure everyone could easily tell which category a child fell into, pieces of brown or blue colored cloth were pinned to every student's collar.

Elliott recalls the effect of this "lesson" on the way students behaved: "It was just horrifying how quickly they became what I told them they were." Within half an hour, Elliot continued, a blue-eyed girl named Carol had changed from a "brilliant, carefree, excited little girl to a frightened, timid, uncertain, almost-person." Not surprisingly, in the hours that followed, the brown-eyed students came to life, speaking up more and performing better than they had done before. The prophecy had been fulfilled: Because the brown-eyed children thought they were superior, they became superior in their classroom performance—as well as "arrogant, ugly, and domineering" toward the blue-eyed children. For their part, the blue-eyed children began underperforming, becoming the inferior people they believed themselves to be.

At the end of the day, Elliott took time to explain to everyone what they had experienced. She applied the lesson to race, pointing out that if white children thought they were superior to black children, they would expect to do better in school, just as many children of color who live in the shadow of the same stereotypes would underperform in school. The children also realized that the society that teaches these stereotypes, as well as the hate that often goes with them, encourages the kind of violence that ended the life of Dr. King (Kral, 2000).

CRITICAL REVIEW The symbolic-interaction approach explains how we all build reality in our everyday interactions with others. When school officials define some students as "gifted," for example, we can expect teachers to treat them differently and the students themselves to behave differently as a result of having been labeled in this way. If students and teachers come to believe that one race is academically superior to another, the behavior that follows may be a self-fulfilling prophecy.

One limitation of this approach is that people do not just make up such beliefs about superiority and inferiority. Rather, these beliefs are built into a society's system of social inequality, which brings us to the social-conflict approach.

CHECK YOUR LEARNING How can the labels that schools place on some students affect the students' actual performance and the reactions of others?

Schooling and Social Inequality

Social-conflict analysis explains how schooling both causes and perpetuates social inequality. In this way, it can explain how stereotypes of "good" and "bad" students described in the symbolic-interaction discussion arise in the first place. In addition, a social-conflict approach challenges the structural-functional idea that schooling develops everybody's talents and abilities by claiming that schooling plays a part in social stratification.

Social Control

Schooling is a way of controlling people, reinforcing acceptance of the status quo. Samuel Bowles and Herbert Gintis (1976) claim that the rise of public education in the late nineteenth century came at exactly the same time that factory owners needed an obedient and disciplined workforce. Once in school, immigrants learned not only the English language but also the importance of following orders.

Standardized Testing

Here is a question of the kind historically used to measure the academic ability of school-age children in the United States:

Painter is to *painting* as _____ is to *sonnet.*
(a) driver (b) poet (c) priest (d) carpenter

tracking assigning students to different types of educational programs

The correct answer is "(b) poet": A painter creates a painting just as a poet creates a sonnet. This question supposedly measures logical reasoning, but getting the right answer also depends on knowing what each term means. Students who are unfamiliar with the sonnet as a Western European form of written verse are not likely to answer the question correctly.

The organizations that create standardized tests claim that this type of bias has been all but eliminated because they carefully study response patterns and drop any question that favors one racial or ethnic category. But critics insist that some bias based on class, race, or ethnicity will always exist in formal testing. Because test questions will always reflect our society's dominant culture, minority students are placed at a disadvantage (Crouse & Trusheim, 1988; Putka, 1990).

School Tracking

Despite controversy over standardized tests, most schools in the United States use them for **tracking**, *assigning students to different types of educational programs*, such as college preparatory classes, general education, and vocational and technical training.

Tracking supposedly helps teachers meet each student's individual needs and abilities. However, one education critic, Jonathan Kozol (1992), considers tracking an example of "savage inequalities" in our school system. Most students from privileged backgrounds do well on standardized tests and get into higher tracks, where they receive the best the school can offer. Students from disadvantaged backgrounds typically do less well on these tests and end up in lower tracks, where teachers stress memorization and put little focus on creativity.

Based on these concerns, schools across the United States are cautious about making tracking assignments and give students the chance to move from one track to another. Some schools have even dropped tracking entirely. Tracking can help match instruction with students' abilities, but rigid tracking can have a powerful impact on students' learning and self-concept. Young people who spend years in higher tracks tend to see themselves as bright and able; students in lower tracks end up with less ambition and low self-esteem (Bowles & Gintis, 1976; Oakes, 1985; Kilgore, 1991; Kozol, 1992).

Inequality among Schools

Just as students are treated differently within schools, schools themselves differ in important ways. The biggest difference is between public and private schools.

Public and Private Schools

Across the United States, about 90 percent of the 56 million primary and secondary school children attend state-funded public schools. The rest go to private schools.

Bob Daemmrich Photography, Inc.

Corbis – NY/Jim Cummins

Sociological research has documented the fact that young children living in low-income communities typically learn in classrooms like the one on the left, with large class sizes and low budgets that do not provide for high technology and other instructional materials. Children from high-income communities typically enjoy classroom experiences such as the one shown on the right, with small classes and the latest learning technology.

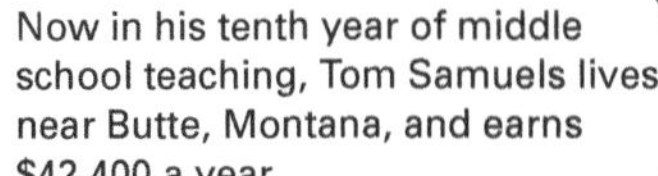

Fresh out of college, J. P. Saunders just landed a teaching job in Albany, New York, with a starting salary of $42,000 a year.

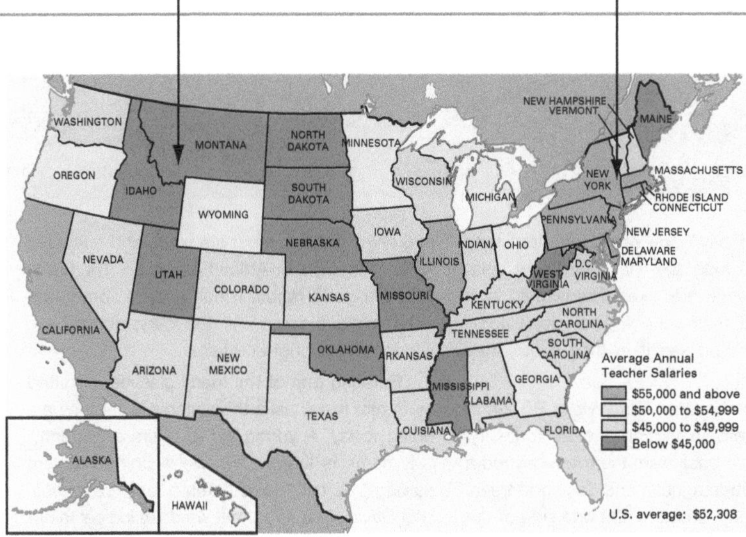

Seeing Ourselves

NATIONAL MAP 1

Teachers' Salaries across the United States

In 2008, the average public school teacher in the United States earned $52,308. The map shows the average teacher salary for all the states; they range from a low of $36,674 in South Dakota to a high of $64,424 in California. Looking at the map, what pattern do you see? What do high-salary (and low-salary) states have in common?

Source: National Education Association, ***Rankings and Estimates: Rankings of the States, 2007, and Estimates of School Statistics, 2008.*** Washington, D.C.: National Education Association, 2008.

Most private school students attend one of the 7,500 *parochial schools* (*parochial* is from Latin, meaning "of the parish") operated by the Roman Catholic Church. The Catholic school system grew rapidly a century ago as cities swelled with immigrants. Enrolling their children in Catholic schools helped the new arrivals hold onto their religious heritage in a new and mostly Protestant society. Today, after decades of flight from the inner city by white people, many parochial schools enroll non-Catholics, including a growing number of African Americans whose families seek an alternative to the neighborhood public school.

Protestants also have private schools, often known as Christian academies. These schools are favored by parents who want religious instruction for their children as well as higher academic and disciplinary standards.

There are also about 6,800 nonreligious private schools in the United States that enroll mostly young people from well-to-do families. These are typically prestigious and expensive preparatory ("prep") schools, modeled on British boarding schools, that not only provide strong academic programs but also convey the values and teach the way of life of the upper class. Many "preppies" maintain lifelong school-based social networks that provide numerous social advantages.

Are private schools qualitatively better than public schools? Research shows that holding family social background constant, students in private schools do outperform those in public schools on standard measures of academic success. The advantages of private schools include smaller classes, more demanding coursework, and greater discipline (Coleman & Hoffer, 1987; Peterson & Llaudet, 2006).

Inequality in Public Schooling

But even public schools are not all the same. Differences in funding result in unequal resources; consequently, children in more affluent areas receive a better education than children living in poor communities. National Map 1 shows one key way in which resources differ: Average yearly teacher salaries vary by as much as $25,000 in state-by-state comparisons.

At the local level, differences in school funding can be dramatic. Winnetka, Illinois, one of the richest suburbs in the United States, spends more than $13,000 a year on each of its students, compared to less than $8,000 in poor areas like Laredo, Texas, and in recent years, these differences have grown (Winter, 2004). The Thinking About Diversity box shows the effects of funding differences in the everyday lives of students.

Because schools are typically funded through local property taxes, schools in more affluent areas will offer a better education than schools in poor communities. This difference also benefits whites over minorities, which is why some districts enacted a policy of *busing*, transporting students to achieve racial balance and equal opportunity in schools. Although only 5 percent of U.S. schoolchildren are bused to schools outside their neighborhoods, this policy is controversial. Supporters claim that given the reality of racial segregation, the only way government will adequately fund schools in poor, minority neighborhoods is if white children from richer areas attend. Critics respond that busing is expensive and undermines the concept of neighborhood schools. But almost everyone agreed on one thing: Given the racial imbalance of most urban areas, an effective busing scheme would have to join inner cities and suburbs, a plan that has never been politically possible.

SEEING SOCIOLOGY in Everyday Life

Do you think all children in the community in which you grew up received equal schooling? Explain.

THINKING ABOUT DIVERSITY: RACE, CLASS, & GENDER

Schooling in the United States: Savage Inequality

"Public School 261? Head down Jerome Avenue and look for the mortician's office." Off for a day studying the New York City schools, Jonathan Kozol parks his car and walks toward PS 261. Finding PS 261 is not easy because the school has no sign. In fact, the building is a former roller rink and doesn't look much like a school at all.

The principal explains that this is in a minority area of the North Bronx, so the population of PS 261 is 90 percent African American and Hispanic. Officially, the school should serve 900 students, but it actually enrolls 1,300. The rules say class size should not exceed thirty-two, but Kozol observes that it sometimes approaches forty. Because the school has just one small cafeteria, the children must eat in three shifts. After lunch, with no place to play, students squirm in their seats until told to return to their classrooms. Only one classroom in the entire school has a window to the world outside.

Toward the end of the day, Kozol remarks to a teacher about the overcrowding and the poor condition of the building. She sums up her thoughts: "I had an awful room last year. In the winter, it was 56 degrees. In the summer, it was up to 90."

"Do the children ever comment on the building?" Kozol asks.

"They don't say," she responds, "but they know. All these kids see TV. They know what suburban schools are like. Then they look around them at their school. They don't comment on it, but you see it in their eyes. They understand."

Several months later, Kozol visits PS 24, in the affluent Riverdale section of New York City. This school is set back from the road, beyond a lawn planted with magnolia and dogwood trees, which are now in full bloom. On one side of the building is a playground for the youngest children; behind the school are playing fields for the older kids. Many people pay the high price of a house in Riverdale because the local schools have such an excellent reputation. There are 825 children here; most are white and a few are Asian, Hispanic, or African American. The building is in good repair. It has a large library and even a planetarium. All the classrooms have windows with bright curtains.

Entering one of the many classes for gifted students, Kozol asks the children what they are doing today. A young girl answers confidently, "My name is Laurie, and we're doing problem solving." A tall, good-natured boy continues, "I'm David. One thing that we do is logical thinking. Some problems, we find, have more than one good answer." Kozol asks if such reasoning is innate or if it is something a child learns. Susan, whose smile reveals her braces, responds, "You know some things to start with when you enter school. But we learn some things that other children don't. We learn certain things that other children don't know because we're *taught* them."

Joel Gordon Photography/Susan Lerner

Across the United States, many inner-city schools lack the facilities to provide a good education.

WHAT DO YOU THINK?

1. Are there differences between schools in your city or town? Explain.
2. Why do you think there is little public concern about schooling inequality?
3. What changes would our society have to make to eliminate schooling inequality?

Source: Adapted from Kozol (1992:85–88, 92–96).

Since the 1990s, busing students to achieve racial balance in schools has sharply declined. Although there was some modest decline in racial segregation in U.S. public schools between 1970 and 1990, there has been little change since then (Logan, Oakley, & Stowell, 2008).

But other policies to address unequal schools have emerged. One plan is to provide money equally across a state. This is the approach taken by Vermont, which passed a law that distributes per-student tax money equally to all communities.

But not everyone thinks that money is the key to good schooling. A classic report by a research team headed by James Coleman (1966) confirmed that students in mostly minority schools suffer from larger class size, insufficient libraries, and fewer science labs. But the Coleman report cautioned that more money by itself would

MAKING THE GRADE

Kozol's account in the box is a "reproduction theory" stating that schooling transmits advantage or disadvantage from parents to children. Downey's research confirms that schooling cannot overcome differences in family resources but it does reduce the gap between rich and poor.

not magically improve schooling. More important are the cooperative efforts and enthusiasm of teachers, parents, and the students themselves. In other words, even if school funding were exactly the same everywhere (as in Vermont), students who benefit from more *cultural capital*—that is, those whose parents value schooling, read to their children, and encourage the development of imagination—would still perform better. In short, we should not expect schools alone to overcome marked social inequality in the United States (Schneider et al., 1998; Israel, Beaulieu, & Hartless, 2001).

Further research confirms the difference that home environment makes in a student's school performance. A research team studied the rate at which school-age children gain skills in reading and mathematics (Downey, von Hippel, & Broh, 2004). Because U.S. children go to school six to seven hours a day, five days a week, and do not attend school during summer months, the researchers calculate that children spend only about 13 percent of their waking hours in school. During the school year, high-income children learn somewhat more quickly than low-income children, but the learning gap is far greater during the summer season when children are not in school. The researchers conclude that when it comes to student performance, schools matter, but the home and local neighborhood matter more. Put another way, schools close some of the learning gap that is created by differences in family resources, but they do not "level the playing field" between rich and poor children the way we like to think they do.

Access to Higher Education

Schooling is the main path to good jobs. But only 67 percent of U.S. high school graduates enroll in college immediately after graduation. Among young people eighteen to twenty-four years old, about 39 percent are enrolled in college (National Center for Education Statistics, 2009).

A crucial factor affecting access to U.S. higher education is family income. College is expensive: Even at state-supported institutions, annual tuition averages about $6,600, and admission to the most exclusive private colleges and universities exceeds $45,000 a year. As shown in Figure 1, nearly two-thirds of children from families with incomes above $75,000 annually (roughly the richest 30 percent, who fall within the upper-middle class and upper class) attend college, but only 25 percent of young people from families earning less than $20,000 go on to higher education (U.S. Census Bureau, 2008).

These economic differences are one reason that the education gap between whites and minorities widens at the college level. As Figure 2 shows, African Americans are not quite as likely as non-Hispanic whites to graduate from high school and are much less likely to complete four or more years of college. Hispanics, many of whom speak Spanish as their first language, have a lower rate of high school graduation, and again, the gap is much greater when it comes to college degrees. Schooling is an important path to social mobility in our society, but the promise of schooling has not overcome the racial inequality that exists in the United States.

Completing college brings many rewards, including higher earnings. In the past forty years, as our economy has shifted to work that requires processing information, the gap in average income between people who complete only high school and those who earn a four-year college degree has more than doubled. In fact, today, a college degree adds as much as $1 million to a person's lifetime income. In simple terms, higher education is a good investment.

Table 2 gives details. In 2007, men who were high school graduates averaged $37,855, and college graduates averaged $62,087. The ratios in parentheses show that a man with a bachelor's degree earns 2.7 times as much in annual income as a man with eight or fewer years of schooling. Across the board, women earn less than men,

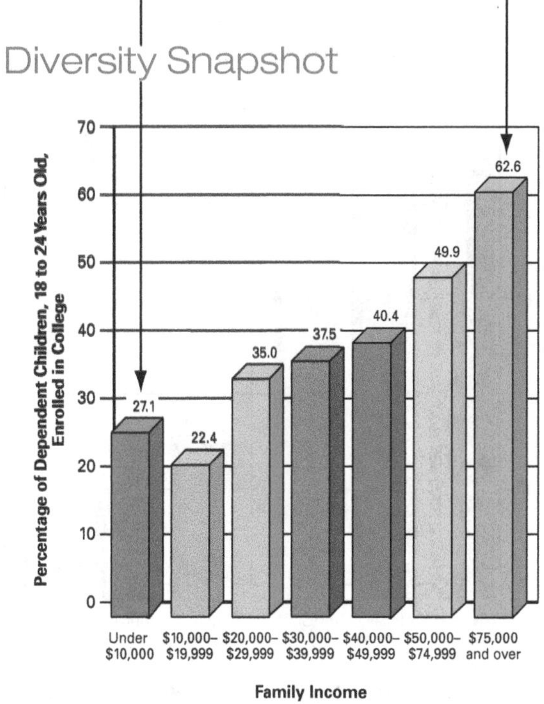

FIGURE 1 **College Attendance and Family Income, 2005**

The higher a family's income, the more likely it is that children will attend college.

Source: U.S. Census Bureau (2006).

SEEING SOCIOLOGY in Everyday Life

Are there specific things parents can do to improve their children's learning? How did your parents affect your learning?

SEEING SOCIOLOGY in Everyday Life

In Table 2, compare the earnings of college graduates with high school graduates to see the value of a college degree.

Diversity Snapshot

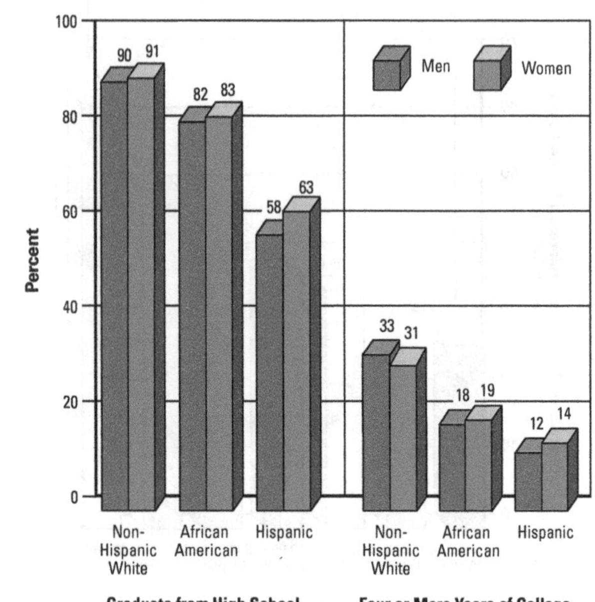

FIGURE 2 **Educational Achievement for Various Categories of People, Aged 25 Years and Over, 2007**

U.S. society still provides less education to minorities.

Source: U.S. Census Bureau (2007).

although as with men, added years of schooling boosts their income, although not quite as much. Keep in mind that for both men and women, some of the greater earnings have to do with social background, because those with the most schooling are likely to come from relatively well-off families to begin with.

Greater Opportunity: Expanding Higher Education

With some 18.2 million people enrolled in colleges and universities, the United States is the world leader in providing a college education to its people. This country also enrolls more students from abroad than any other.

One reason for this achievement is that there are 4,314 colleges and universities in the United States. This number includes 2,629 four-year institutions (which award bachelor's degrees) as well as 1,685 two-year colleges (which award associate's degrees). Some two-year colleges are private, but most are publicly funded community colleges that serve a local area (usually a city or a county) and charge a low tuition (National Center for Education Statistics, 2008).

Because higher education is a key path to better jobs and higher income, the government makes money available to help certain categories of people pay the costs of college. After World War II, the GI Bill provided college funds to veterans, with the result that tens of thousands of men and women were able to attend college. Some branches of the military continue to offer college money to enlistees; in addition, veterans continue to benefit from a number of government grants and scholarships.

Community Colleges

Since the 1960s, the expansion of state-funded community colleges has further increased access to higher education. According to the National Center for Education Statistics (2008), the 1,685 two-year colleges across the United States now enroll 37 percent of all college undergraduates.

Community colleges provide a number of specific benefits. First, their relatively low tuition cost places college courses and degrees within the reach of millions of families that could not otherwise afford them. Many students at community colleges today are the first in their families to pursue a college degree. The lower cost of community colleges is especially important during periods of economic recession. When the economy slumps and people lose their jobs, college enrollments soar, especially at community colleges.

Second, community colleges have special importance for minorities. Currently, almost half of all African American and Hispanic undergraduates in the United States attend community colleges.

Table 2 Median Income by Sex and Educational Attainment, 2007

Education	Men	Women
Professional degree	$100,000 (4.3)	$71,098 (3.9)
Doctorate	92,089 (3.9)	68,989 (3.8)
Master's degree	76,284 (3.3)	55,426 (3.0)
Bachelor's degree	62,087 (2.7)	45,773 (2.5)
1–3 years of college	44,899 (1.9)	32,837 (1.8)
4 years of high school	37,855 (1.6)	27,240 (1.5)
9–11 years of school	29,317 (1.3)	20,398 (1.1)
0–8 years of school	23,375 (1.0)	18,261 (1.0)

Notes: Figures are for persons aged 25 years and over working full time. The earnings ratio, in parentheses, indicates what multiple of the lowest income level a person with the indicated amount of additional schooling earns.

Source: U.S. Census Bureau (2008).

MAKING THE GRADE

The social-conflict approach claims that schooling transforms family privilege into personal merit. This means that, although we understand that earning a college degree is a personal achievement, family privilege plays a major part in getting people to college in the first place.

SEEING SOCIOLOGY in Everyday Life

Are you the first in your family to attend college? If not, for how many generations before you have family members attended college?

APPLYING THEORY

Education

	Structural-Functional Approach	Symbolic-Interaction Approach	Social-Conflict Approach
What is the level of analysis?	Macro-level	Micro-level	Macro-level
What is the importance of education for society?	Schooling performs many vital tasks for the operation of society, including socializing the young and encouraging discovery and invention to improve our lives. Schooling helps unite a diverse society by teaching shared norms and values.	How teachers define their students—as well as how students think of themselves—can become real to everyone and affect students' educational performance.	Schooling maintains social inequality through unequal schooling for rich and poor. Within individual schools, tracking provides privileged children with a better education than poor children.

Third, although it is true that community colleges serve local populations, two-year colleges also attract students from around the world. Many community colleges recruit students from abroad, and about 20 percent of all foreign students enrolled on a U.S. campus are studying at community colleges (National Center for Education Statistics, 2008).

Fourth, the top priority of faculty who work at large universities is typically research, but the most important job for community college faculty is teaching. Thus although teaching loads are high (typically four or five classes each semester), community colleges appeal to faculty who find their greatest pleasure in the classroom. Community college students often get more attention from faculty than students at large universities (Jacobson, 2003).

Finally, community colleges teach the knowledge and career skills that countless people depend on to find the jobs they want. Seeing Sociology in the News takes a closer look.

Privilege and Personal Merit

If attending college is a rite of passage for rich men and women, as social-conflict analysis suggests, then *schooling transforms social privilege into personal merit.* Given our cultural emphasis on individualism, we tend to see credentials as badges of ability rather than as symbols of family affluence (Sennett & Cobb, 1973).

When we congratulate the new graduate, we rarely recognize the resources—in terms of both money and cultural capital—that made this achievement possible. Yet young people from families with incomes exceeding $200,000 a year average more than 350 points higher on the SAT college entrance examination than young people from families with less than $20,000 in annual income (College Board, 2009). The richer students are more likely to get into college; once there, they are also more likely to complete their studies and get a degree. In a *credential society*—one that evaluates people on the basis of their schooling—companies hire job applicants with the best education. This process ends up helping people with advantages to begin with and harming those who are already disadvantaged (Collins, 1979).

CRITICAL REVIEW Social-conflict analysis links formal education to social inequality to show how schooling transforms privilege into personal worthiness and social disadvantage into personal deficiency. However, the social-conflict approach overlooks the extent to which finishing a degree reflects plenty of hard work and the extent to which schooling provides upward social mobility for talented women and men from all backgrounds. In addition, despite the claims that schooling supports the status quo, today's college curricula challenge social inequality on many fronts.

CHECK YOUR LEARNING Explain several ways in which education is linked to social inequality.

The Applying Theory table sums up what the theoretical approaches show us about education.

Seeing SOCIOLOGY in the 

The New York Times

Community College: Dream Catchers

By JOHN MERROW
April 22, 2007

Matters were simpler 100 years ago, when junior colleges were created to prepare deserving students for the final two years of a university. In fact, the very first public junior college, in Joliet, Ill., was set up in a high school, as the equivalent of grades 13 and 14.

Community colleges today do far more than offer a ladder to the final years. They train the people who repair your furnace, install your plumbing, take your pulse. They prepare retiring baby boomers for second or third careers, and provide opportunities for a growing number of college-age students turning away from the high cost and competition at universities. And charged with doing the heavy remedial lifting, community colleges are now as much 10th and 11th grade as 13th and 14th.

It's a long to-do list on a tightening public purse. Two-year colleges receive less than 30 percent of state and local financing for higher education, according to the American Association of Community Colleges. Yet they are growing much faster than four-year colleges and universities, enrolling nearly half of all undergraduates. That's 6.6 million students. Add those taking just a course or two, and the total reaches some 12 million.

Kay M. McClenney, director of the annual Community College Survey of Student Engagement, calls America's two-year colleges "today's Ellis Island," because they serve a disproportionate number of immigrants, first-generation citizens and minorities. . . .

Midlife, Starting Over

. . . At 51, [Brian Bullas] is determined to redefine himself. With his wife working days, bartending seemed a logical career choice when his son was small. Today, he has a different view. . . . "Bartending has been a pretty stagnant job," he said. "I think I can give more to myself and to my family and to society by trying a new career that I think I'm going to be good at."

After graduating from San Diego City College next month and passing the licensing exam, Mr. Bullas will be a registered nurse. He will be in great demand, because the country desperately needs nurses. The national shortfall, of about 6 percent, is particularly acute in California. A 2006 report by the Hospital Association of Southern California estimates that the state currently needs 22,500 registered nurses and predicted a shortage of 116,000 by 2020. Two-year institutions train some 60 percent of the nation's new nurses.

Mr. Bullas says he "won the lottery" when he was able to start classes. He did get lucky: three of four applicants to City's nursing program are accepted but are immediately placed on a waiting list. There just isn't enough room.

"They're qualified, we tell them they're qualified, but then they have to go off and flip burgers or tend bar or do whatever, until their number comes up," says Terrence Burgess, the college president.

Problems in the Schools

An intense debate revolves around the quality of schooling in the United States. Perhaps because we expect our schools to do so much—teach, equalize opportunity, instill discipline, and fire our children's imagination—people are divided on whether public schools are doing their job. Although almost half of adults give schools in their local community a performance grade of A or B, just about the same number give a grade of C or below (Bushaw & Gallup, 2008).

Discipline and Violence

When many of today's older teachers think back to their own student days, school "problems" consisted of talking out of turn, chewing gum, breaking the dress code, or cutting class. Today, schools are grappling with serious issues such as drug and alcohol abuse, teenage pregnancy, and outright violence. Although almost everyone agrees that schools should teach personal discipline, many think the job is no longer being done.

Schools do not create violence; in most cases, violence spills into the schools from the surrounding society. In the wake of a number of school shootings in recent years, many school districts have adopted zero-tolerance policies that require suspension or expulsion for serious misbehavior or bringing weapons on campus.

Deadly school shootings—including the deaths of thirty-three students at Virginia Tech University in 2007 and the deaths of eight students at Northern Illinois University in 2008—have shocked the nation. Such tragic incidents also raise serious questions about balancing students' right to privacy (typically, laws forbid colleges from informing parents of a student's grades or mental health issues) and the need to ensure the safety of the campus population. In the Virginia Tech case, had the university been able to bring the young man's mental health problems to the attention of the police or his family, the tragedy might have been prevented (Gibbs, 2007; Shedden, 2008).

Student Passivity

If some schools are plagued by violence, many more are filled with students who are bored. Some of the blame for passivity can be placed on the fact that electronic devices, from television to iPods, now consume more of young people's time than school, parents, and community activities. But schools must share the blame because the educational system itself encourages student passivity (Coleman, Hoffer, & Kilgore, 1981).

Bureaucracy

The small, personal schools that served countless local communities a century ago have evolved into huge educational factories. In a study

"It's not uncommon up and down the state to have wait lists that go two and three years out." . . .

Mr. Bullas chose this route because City's nursing classes are scheduled for the convenience of working adults and because the cost is low.

Community colleges attract a lot of men and women like Brian Bullas. In a study conducted by ACT Inc. and the American Association of Community Colleges, more than 35 percent of students indicated that changing careers was the major reason they were taking classes.

Mr. Bullas already has a degree in sociology from the University of San Diego, where he played varsity baseball. He was drafted by the Oakland A's but played only in the minors and Canada, he says, before turning to restaurant work and bartending. The road to where he is today has been a triathlon of classwork and clinical and personal responsibilities—eight hours two days a week at the hospital and two in the classroom; four or five nights, eight hours a night, at the Marine Room. "I have a couple of days where I carpool kids to school, do the shopping, and help out with homework when I can with my son," he said.

The stress, just getting through it, shows in his face. It helps that his wife ("a saint") has a good job managing a health club. "I do keep in contact with her to let her know where I am and what I'm doing," he said, laughing.

Mr. Bullas has studied in a parking lot, waiting for his son at baseball or basketball or water polo; he does schoolwork behind the bar when it's slow. "They let you know that you should have a book in your car at all times," he said.

He is a focused learner who furiously takes notes during a demonstration of an IV pole. Afterward, he goes up to the teacher to ask questions.

He thinks about that day when he will enter a patient's room for the first time on his own. "I know I'm going to have support," he said. "But I also know that the patient's life is in my hands, and I want to be sure I've done my homework."

WHAT DO YOU THINK?

1. In your opinion, what are the most important contributions of community colleges to our society?
2. Why do some people describe community colleges as "today's Ellis Island," referring to the place where tens of millions of immigrants got their start in the United States?
3. Have you or someone you know attended a community college? If so, does the story of Brian Bullas ring true?

Adapted from the original article, "Community College; Dream Catchers" by John Merrow, published in *The New York Times* on April 22, 2007.

of high schools across the United States, Theodore Sizer (1984:207–9) identified five ways in which large, bureaucratic schools undermine education:

1. **Rigid uniformity.** Bureaucratic schools run by outside specialists (such as state education officials) generally ignore the cultural character of local communities and the personal needs of their children.
2. **Numerical ratings.** School officials define success in terms of numerical attendance records and dropout rates and "teach to the tests," hoping to raise achievement test scores. In the process, they overlook dimensions of schooling that are difficult to quantify, such as creativity and enthusiasm.
3. **Rigid expectations.** Officials expect fifteen-year-olds to be in the tenth grade and eleventh-graders to score at a certain level on a standardized verbal achievement test. Rarely are exceptionally bright and motivated students permitted to advance more quickly or graduate early. Similarly, poor performers are pushed from grade to grade, doomed to fail year after year.
4. **Specialization.** Students in middle school and high school learn Spanish from one teacher, receive guidance from another, and are coached in sports by still others. Students shuffle between fifty-minute periods throughout the school day. As a result, no school official comes to know the child well.
5. **Little individual responsibility.** Highly bureaucratic schools do not empower students to learn on their own. Similarly, teachers have little say in what they teach in their classes and how they do it; any change in the pace of learning risks disrupting the system.

Of course, with 56 million schoolchildren in the United States, schools must be bureaucratic to get the job done. But Sizer recommends that we "humanize" schools by reducing rigid scheduling, cutting class size, and training teachers more broadly so that they become more involved in the lives of their students. Overall, as James Coleman (1993) has suggested, schools need to be less "administratively driven" and more "output-driven." Perhaps this transformation could begin by ensuring that graduation from high school depends on what students have learned rather than simply on the number of years they have spent in the building.

College: The Silent Classroom

Passivity is also common among college and university students. Sociologists rarely study the college classroom—a curious fact, considering how much time they spend there. One exception was a study at a coeducational university where David Karp and William Yoels (1976) found that even in small classes, only a few students spoke up. Passivity seems to be a classroom norm, and students may even become irritated if one of their number is especially talkative.

SEEING SOCIOLOGY in Everyday Life

How many of your classes encourage active student discussion? Is participation more common in some disciplines than in others? Why?

Lawrence Migdale/Pix/Lawrence Migdale

For all categories of people in the United States, dropping out of school greatly reduces the chances of getting a good job and earning a secure income. Why is the dropout rate particularly high among Hispanic Americans?

According to Karp and Yoels, most students think classroom passivity is their own fault. Yet as anyone who observes young people outside the classroom knows, they are usually active and vocal. It is clearly the schools that teach students to be passive and to view instructors as experts who serve up "knowledge" and "truth." Most college students find little value in classroom discussion and see their proper role as listening quietly and taking notes. As a result, the researchers estimate, just 10 percent of college class time is used for discussion.

Faculty can bring students to life in their classrooms by making use of four teaching strategies: (1) calling on students by name when they volunteer, (2) positively reinforcing student participation, (3) asking analytical rather than factual questions and giving students time to answer, and (4) asking for student opinions even when no one volunteers a response (Auster & MacRone, 1994).

Dropping Out

If many students are passive in class, others are not there at all. The problem of *dropping out*—quitting school before earning a high school diploma—leaves young people (many of whom are disadvantaged to begin with) unprepared for the world of work and at high risk of poverty. For example, school dropouts account for more than 50 percent of all people receiving welfare assistance and more than 80 percent of the prison population (Christle, Jolivette, & Nelson, 2007).

Although the dropout rate has declined slightly in recent decades, a sad fact is that today's children are actually less likely to complete high school than their parents were (Ripley, 2008). Currently, 8.7 percent of people between the ages of sixteen and twenty-four have dropped out of school, a total of some 3.5 million young women and men. Dropping out is least pronounced among non-Hispanic whites (5.3 percent), higher among non-Hispanic African Americans (8.4 percent), and highest of all among Hispanics (21.4 percent) (National Center for Education Statistics, 2009). These are the official statistics, which include young people who are known to have left school. But a number of researchers estimate that the actual dropout rates are probably at least twice the government's numbers (Thornburgh, 2006).

Some students drop out because of problems with the English language, others because of pregnancy, and some because they must work to help support their family. For children growing up in families with income in the bottom 25 percent, the dropout rate is more than five times higher than for children living in high-income families (National Center for Education Statistics, 2009). These data suggest that many dropouts are young people whose parents also have little schooling, revealing a multigenerational cycle of disadvantage.

Academic Standards

Perhaps the most serious educational issue confronting our society is the quality of schooling. In 1983, a comprehensive report on the quality of U.S. schools, titled *A Nation at Risk,* was issued by the National Commission on Excellence in Education (NCEE). It begins with this alarming statement:

> If an unfriendly foreign power had attempted to impose on America the mediocre educational performance that exists today, we might well have viewed it as an act of war. As it stands, we have allowed this to happen to ourselves. (1983:5)

Supporting this claim, the report notes that "nearly 40 percent of seventeen-year-olds cannot draw inferences from written material; only one-fifth can write a persuasive essay; and only one-third can solve mathematical problems requiring several steps" (NCEE, 1983:9). Furthermore, scores on the SAT have shown little improvement over time. In 1967, mean scores for students were 516 on the mathematical test and 543 on the verbal test; by 2008, the average in mathematics had dropped 1 point to 515, and the verbal average had plunged to just 502. Nationwide, one-third of high school students—and more

functional illiteracy a lack of the reading and writing skills needed for everyday living.

than half in urban schools—fail to master even the basics in reading, math, and science on the National Assessment of Educational Progress examination (Barnes, 2002a; National Assessment of Education Progress, 2007; College Board, 2009).

For many people, even basic literacy is at issue. **Functional illiteracy**, *a lack of the reading and writing skills needed for everyday living*, is a problem for one in four U.S. children. For older people, about 30 million U.S. adults (about 14 percent of the total) lack basic skills in reading and writing.

A Nation at Risk recommended drastic reform. First, it called for schools to require *all* students to complete several years of English, mathematics, social studies, general science, and computer science. Second, schools should not promote students until they meet achievement standards. Third, teacher training must improve, and teachers' salaries must be raised to draw talent into the profession. The report concluded that schools must meet public expectations and that citizens must be prepared to pay for a job well done.

What has happened in the years since this report was issued? In some respects, schools have improved. A report by the National Center for Education Statistics (2008) noted some decline in the dropout rate, a trend toward schools' offering more challenging courses, and a larger share of high school graduates going to college. At the same time, the evidence suggests that a majority of elementary school students are falling below standards in reading; in many cases, they can't read at all. In short, although some improvement is evident, much remains to be done.

The United States spends more on schooling its children than almost any other nation—half again more than in Japan and double the average in Europe. Even so, a recent government report comparing the academic performance of fifteen-year-olds in fifty-seven countries found that the United States placed twenty-ninth in science and thirty-fifth in mathematics. Such statistics fuel fears that our country is losing its leadership in science to other nations, including China, India, and South Korea (OECD, 2007b).

Cultural values also play a part in how hard students work at their schooling. For example, U.S. students are generally less motivated and do less homework than students in Japan. Japanese young people also spend sixty more days in school each year than U.S students. Perhaps one approach to improving academic performance is simply to have students spend more time in school.

Grade Inflation

Academic standards depend on using grades that have clear meaning and are awarded for work of appropriate quality. Yet recent decades have seen substantial *grade inflation*, the awarding of ever-higher grades for average work. Though not necessarily found in every school, the trend toward grade inflation is evident across the country in both high schools and colleges.

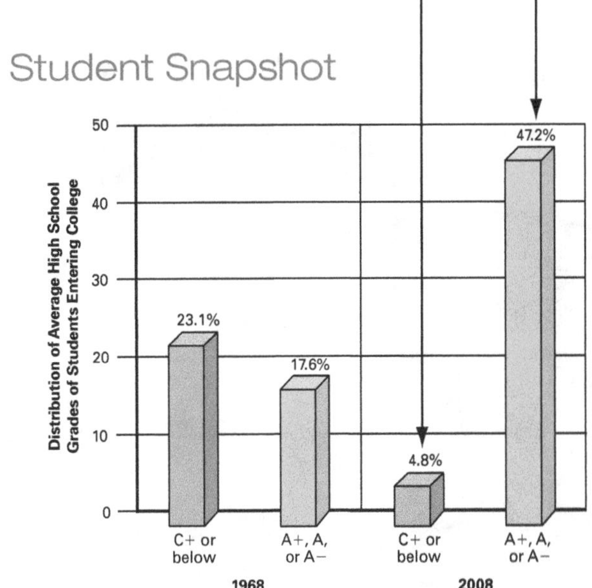

FIGURE 3 **Grade Inflation in U.S. High Schools**

In recent decades, teachers have given higher and higher grades to students.

Sources: Astin et al. (2002) and Pryor et al. (2008).

One study of high school grades revealed a dramatic change in grades between 1968 and 2008. In 1968, as shown in Figure 3, the high school records of students who had just entered college included more grades of C+ and below than grades of A−, A, and A+. By 2008, however, these A grades outnumbered grades of C+ and below by almost ten to one (Pryor et al., 2008).

A few colleges and universities have enacted policies that limit the share of A's (generally to one-third of all grades). But there is little evidence that grade inflation will slow down anytime soon. As a result, the C grade (which used to mean "average") may all but disappear, making just about every student "above average."

What accounts for grade inflation? In part, today's teachers are concerned about the morale and self-esteem of their students and perhaps their own popularity. In any case, teachers clearly are not as "tough" as they used to be. At the same time, the ever more competitive process of getting into college and graduate school puts increasing pressure on high schools and colleges to award high grades (Astin et al., 2002).

SEEING SOCIOLOGY in Everyday Life

Recall that U.S. students spend only about 13 percent of their waking hours in school. Do you think they should spend more time in school? Explain your answer.

AP Wide World Photos/Pat Sullivan

Charter schools, one part of the school choice movement, encourage personal discipline and academic excellence. Do you support school choice? Why or why not?

Current Issues in U.S. Education

Our society's schools continuously confront new challenges. This section explores several recent and important educational issues.

School Choice

Some analysts claim that our public schools teach poorly because they have no competition. Giving parents options for schooling their children might force all schools to do a better job. This is the essence of a policy called *school choice.*

The goal of school choice is to create a market for schooling so that parents and students can shop for the best value. According to one proposal, the government would give vouchers to families with school-age children and allow them to spend that money at public, private, or parochial schools. In recent years, major cities, including Indianapolis, Minneapolis, Milwaukee, Cleveland, Chicago, and Washington, D.C., as well as the states of Florida and Illinois, have experimented with choice plans aimed at making public schools perform better to win the confidence of families.

Supporters claim that giving parents a choice about where to enroll their children is the only sure way to improve all schools. But critics (including teachers' unions) charge that school choice amounts to giving up on our nation's commitment to public education and that it will do little to improve schools in central cities, where the need is greatest (A. Cohen, 1999; Morse, 2002).

In 2002, President George W. Bush signed a new education bill that downplayed vouchers in favor of another approach to greater choice. Starting in the 2005–06 school year, all public schools began testing every child in reading, mathematics, and science in grades three through eight. Although the federal government will provide more aid to schools where students do not perform well, if those schools do not show improvements in test scores over a period of time, their students will have the choice of either special tutoring or transportation to another school. This program, called "No Child Left Behind," has succeeded in showing which schools are not doing a good job educating children and has raised some measures of student performance. At the same time, however, there has been little change in many of the worst-performing schools (Lindlaw, 2002; Wallis & Steptoe, 2007).

A more modest type of school choice involves *magnet schools,* almost 2,700 of which now exist across the country. Magnet schools offer special facilities and programs that promote educational excellence in a particular field, such as computer science, foreign languages, science and mathematics, or the arts. In school districts with magnet schools, parents can choose the school best suited to their child's particular talents and interests.

Another school choice strategy involves *charter schools,* public schools that are given more freedom to try out new policies and programs. There are more than 4,000 such schools in forty-one states, Washington, D.C., and Puerto Rico; they enroll 1.2 million students, 60 percent of whom are minorities. In many of these schools, students have demonstrated high academic achievement—a requirement for renewal of the charter (U.S. Charter Schools, 2008).

A final development in the school choice movement is *schooling for profit.* Advocates of this plan say that school systems can be operated by private profit-making companies more efficiently than by local governments. Private schooling is nothing new, of course; more than 28,000 schools in the United States are currently run by private organizations and religious groups. What is new is that hundreds of public schools, enrolling hundreds of thousands of students, are now run by private businesses for profit.

Research confirms that many public school systems suffer from bureaucratic bloat, spending too much and teaching too little. And our society has long looked to competition to improve quality. Evidence suggests that for-profit schools have greatly reduced

SEEING SOCIOLOGY in Everyday Life

Have you ever attended a magnet school, charter school, or for-profit school? If so, was it a good experience?

mainstreaming integrating students with disabilities or special needs into the overall educational program.

administrative costs, but the educational results appear mixed. Although several companies claim to have improved student learning, some cities have cut back on business-run schools. In recent years, school boards in Baltimore, Miami, Hartford, and Boston have canceled the contracts of for-profit schooling corporations. But other cities are deciding to give for-profit schooling a try. For example, after Philadelphia's public school system failed to graduate one-third of its students, the state of Pennsylvania took over that city's schools and turned over most of them to for-profit companies, and student test scores have gone up. In light of conflicting evidence about the performance of for-profit schools, emotions among both supporters and critics of this policy continue to run high, with each side claiming to speak for the well-being of the schoolchildren caught in the middle (Sizer, 2003; Garland, 2007; Richburg, 2008).

Home Schooling

Home schooling is gaining popularity across the United States. About 1.5 million children (almost 3 percent of all school-age children) receive their formal schooling at home.

Why do parents undertake the enormous challenge of schooling their own children? Some twenty years ago, most of the parents who pioneered home schooling (which is now legal in every state) wanted to give their children a strongly religious upbringing. Today, however, many are mothers and fathers who simply do not believe that public schools are doing a good job, and they think they can do better. To benefit their children, they are willing to alter work schedules and relearn algebra or other necessary subjects. Many belong to groups in which parents pool their efforts, specializing in what each knows best.

Advocates of home schooling point out that given the poor performance of many public schools, no one should be surprised that a growing number of parents are stepping up to teach their own children. In addition, this system works—on average, students who learn at home outperform those who learn in school. Critics argue that home schooling reduces the amount of funding going to local public schools, which ends up hurting the majority of students. In addition, as one critic point out, home schooling "takes some of the most affluent and articulate parents out of the system. These are the parents who know how to get things done with administrators" (Chris Lubienski, quoted in Cloud & Morse, 2001:48).

Schooling People with Disabilities

Many of the 6.7 million children with disabilities in the United States face special challenges getting to and from school; once there, many with crutches or wheelchairs cannot negotiate stairs and other obstacles inside school buildings. Other children with developmental disabilities such as mental retardation require extensive personal attention from specially trained teachers. Because of these challenges, many children with mental and physical disabilities have received a public education only after persistent efforts by parents and other concerned citizens (Horn & Tynan, 2001; U.S. Department of Education, 2008).

Bob Daemmrich Photography, Inc.

Educators have long debated the best way to teach children with disabilities. On one hand, such children may benefit from separate facilities staffed by specially trained teachers. On the other hand, children are less likely to be stigmatized as "different" if they are included in regular classrooms. One way to "mainstream" children with special needs is to provide them with teaching assistants who offer the help they need throughout the day.

About half of all children with disabilities are schooled in special facilities; the rest attend public schools, many in regular classes. Most schools avoid expensive "special education" in favor of **mainstreaming**, *integrating students with disabilities or special needs into the overall educational program.* Mainstreaming is a form of *inclusive education* that works best for physically impaired students who have no difficulty keeping up academically with the rest of the class. A benefit of putting children with and without disabilities in the same classroom is allowing everyone to learn to interact with people who are different from themselves.

SEEING SOCIOLOGY in Everyday Life

Have you considered a career in teaching? If so, why? If not, what changes might make the field more appealing to you?

SEEING SOCIOLOGY IN EVERYDAY LIFE

The Twenty-First-Century Campus: Where Are the Men?

MEG: I mean, what's with this campus not having enough men?
TRICIA: It's no big deal. I'd rather focus on my work.
MARK: I think it's, like, really cool for us guys.

A century ago, the campuses of colleges and universities across the United States might as well have hung out a sign that read "Men Only." Almost all of the students and faculty were male. There were a small number of women's colleges, but many more schools—including some of the best-known U.S. universities such as Yale, Harvard, and Princeton—barred women outright.

Since then, women have won greater social equality. By 1980, the number of women enrolled at U.S. colleges finally matched the number of men.

In a surprising trend, however, the share of women on campus has continued to increase. As a result, in 2005, men accounted for only 43 percent of all U.S. undergraduates. Meg DeLong noticed the gender imbalance right away when she moved into her dorm at the University of Georgia at Athens; she soon learned that just 39 percent of her first-year classmates were men. In some classes, there were few men, and women usually dominated discussions. Out of class, DeLong and many other women soon complained that having so few men on campus hurt their social life. Not surprisingly, most of the men felt otherwise (Fonda, 2000).

What accounts for the shifting gender balance on U.S. campuses? One theory is that young men are drawn away from college by the lure of jobs, especially in high technology. This pattern is sometimes termed the "Bill Gates syndrome," after the man who dropped out of college and soon became the world's richest person by helping to found Microsoft. In addition, analysts point to an anti-intellectual male culture. Young women are drawn to learning and seek to do well in school, but young men attach less importance to studying. Rightly or wrongly, more men seem to think they can get a good job without investing years of their lives and a considerable amount of money in getting a college degree.

The gender gap is evident in all racial and ethnic categories and at all class levels. Among African Americans on campus, only 33 percent are men. The lower the income level, the greater the gender gap in college attendance.

Many college officials are concerned about the lack of men on campus. In an effort to attract more balanced enrollments, some colleges are adopting what amounts to affirmative action programs for males. But courts in several states have already ruled such policies illegal. Many colleges, therefore, are turning to more active recruitment; admissions officers are paying special attention to male applicants and stressing a college's strength in mathematics and science—areas traditionally popular with men. In the same way that colleges across the country are striving to increase their share of minority students, the hope is that they can also succeed in attracting a larger share of men.

Kevin Virobik-Adams, Progressive Photo

WHAT DO YOU THINK?

1. Among high school students, are men less concerned than women about academic achievement? Why or why not?
2. Is there a gender imbalance on your campus? Does it create problems? What problems? For whom?
3. What programs or policies do you think might increase the number of men going to college?

Adult Education

In 2005, more than 94 million U.S. adults over twenty-five were enrolled in some type of schooling. These older students range in age from the mid-twenties to the seventies and beyond and make up 39 percent of students in degree-granting programs. Adults in school are more likely to be women than men, and most have above-average incomes.

Why do adults return to the classroom? The most obvious reasons given are to advance a career or train for a new job, but many are in class simply for personal enrichment (U.S. Census Bureau, 2006).

The Teacher Shortage

A major challenge for U.S. schools is hiring enough teachers to fill the classrooms. A number of factors—including low salaries, frustration, and retirement, as well as rising enrollment and reductions in class size—have combined to create more than 300,000 teaching vacancies in the United States each year.

How will these slots be filled? About the same number of people graduate with education degrees each year. Most of them do not have a degree in a specific field, such as mathematics, biology, or

AP Wide World Photos/Douglas C. Pizac

Because our public schools face many challenges, controversy over education policy is likely to continue in the years to come. What recent issues have been debated in your state?

English, and many have trouble passing state certification tests in the subject they want to teach. As a result, many schools, especially in low-income neighborhoods, are taught by teachers who may be just one chapter ahead of their students (Quaid, 2008).

This means that the teacher shortage is really a shortage of *good* teachers. For our nation's public schools to improve, two things must happen: First, teachers who do not teach well must receive additional training or lose their jobs, and second, well-qualified people need to be attracted into the classroom (Ripley, 2008).

Getting rid of bad teachers (and perhaps bad principals, too) means changing rules that make it difficult or impossible to fire someone after a few years on the job. Gaining well-qualified teachers depends on adopting various recruitment strategies. Some schools offer incentives such as higher salaries (the average salary for a thirty-year-old teacher in public schools is only about $37,000 a year) to draw into teaching people who already have had successful careers. Some schools provide signing bonuses (especially for hard-to-fill positions in mathematics and chemistry) or give housing allowances (in cities such as New York, where the cost of housing is often out of the reach of teachers). President Obama (2007) has written that he believes that school districts should pay highly qualified and effective teachers as much as $100,000 a year—but, he adds, they must also be able to dismiss unqualified and ineffective teachers.

Other policy ideas include having community colleges play a larger role in teacher education and having government and school boards make it easier for well-trained people to get the certification they need to enter the classroom. Finally, many school districts are going global, actively recruiting in countries such as Spain, India, and the Philippines to bring talented women and men from around the world to teach in U.S. classrooms (Philadelphia, 2001; Evelyn, 2002; Ripley, 2008; Wallis, 2008).

Debate about education in the United States extends beyond the issues noted here. The Seeing Sociology in Everyday Life box highlights the declining share of college students who are men.

Schooling: Looking Ahead

Although the United States still leads the world in sending people to college, the public school system continues to struggle with serious problems. In terms of quality of schooling, this country has fallen behind many other high-income nations, a fact that calls into question the future strength of the United States on the world stage.

Many of the problems of schooling discussed in this chapter have their roots in the larger society. We cannot expect schools *by themselves* to provide high-quality education. Schools will improve only to the extent that students, teachers, parents, and local communities commit themselves to educational excellence. In short, educational problems are *social* problems for which there is no quick fix.

For much of the twentieth century, there were just two models for education in the United States: public schools run by the government and private schools operated by nongovernmental organizations. In recent decades, however, many new ideas about schooling have emerged, including schooling for profit and a wide range of school choice programs. In the decades ahead, we are likely to see some significant changes in mass education, guided in part by social science research into the outcomes of different strategies.

Another factor that will continue to reshape schools is new information technology. Today, all but the poorest primary and secondary schools use computers for instruction. Computers encourage students to be more active and allow them to progress at their own pace. Even so, computers will never bring to the educational process the personal insights and imagination of a motivated human teacher.

Nor will technology ever solve all the problems that plague our schools, including violence and rigid bureaucracy. What we need is a broad plan for social change that renews this country's early ambition to provide universal schooling of high quality—a goal that we have yet to achieve.

Seeing Sociology in Everyday Life

Education

How big is our society's inequality in schooling?

All schools, of course, differ in many ways. But there are several tiers of schooling in the United States, and these reflect the social class standing of the students they enroll. The images below provide a closer look at this educational hierarchy.

At the top of the schooling hierarchy are private boarding schools. The best of these schools, such as Lawrenceville School in New Jersey, have large endowments, small classes with extremely well-trained and very dedicated teachers, and magnificent campuses with facilities that rival those of the nation's top colleges. What do you estimate is the annual cost to attend such a school?

HINT Private boarding schools provide an outstanding education, and the independent living experience also helps students prepare for success in a good college or university. Although schools like Lawrenceville provide financial aid to many students, the cost of a single year at such a school for most students is about $50,000, which is just about as much as the average family earns in a year. Suburban high schools are supported through tax money; yet the cost of homes in these affluent communities is typically hundreds of thousands of dollars, putting this level of schooling out of reach for a large share of U.S. families. Public schools in the inner city enroll students from families with below-average incomes, which means these schools have the highest percentage of minority students. Liberal Democrats such as the Obamas strongly support public education, but they, like most other residents of the White House (Amy Carter went to public school), have chosen private schooling for their children, whether for educational or security reasons.

Michael Branscomb/The Lawrenceville School

In the middle of the educational hierarchy are the best public high schools, most of which are found in suburban communities. This classroom in Briarcliff High School in Briarcliff Manor, New York, has small classes with good teachers and offers many extra-curricular activities. What level of income do you think is typical of the families who are able to send their children to schools such as this?

Redux Pictures/ Suzanne DeChillo/ *The New York Times*

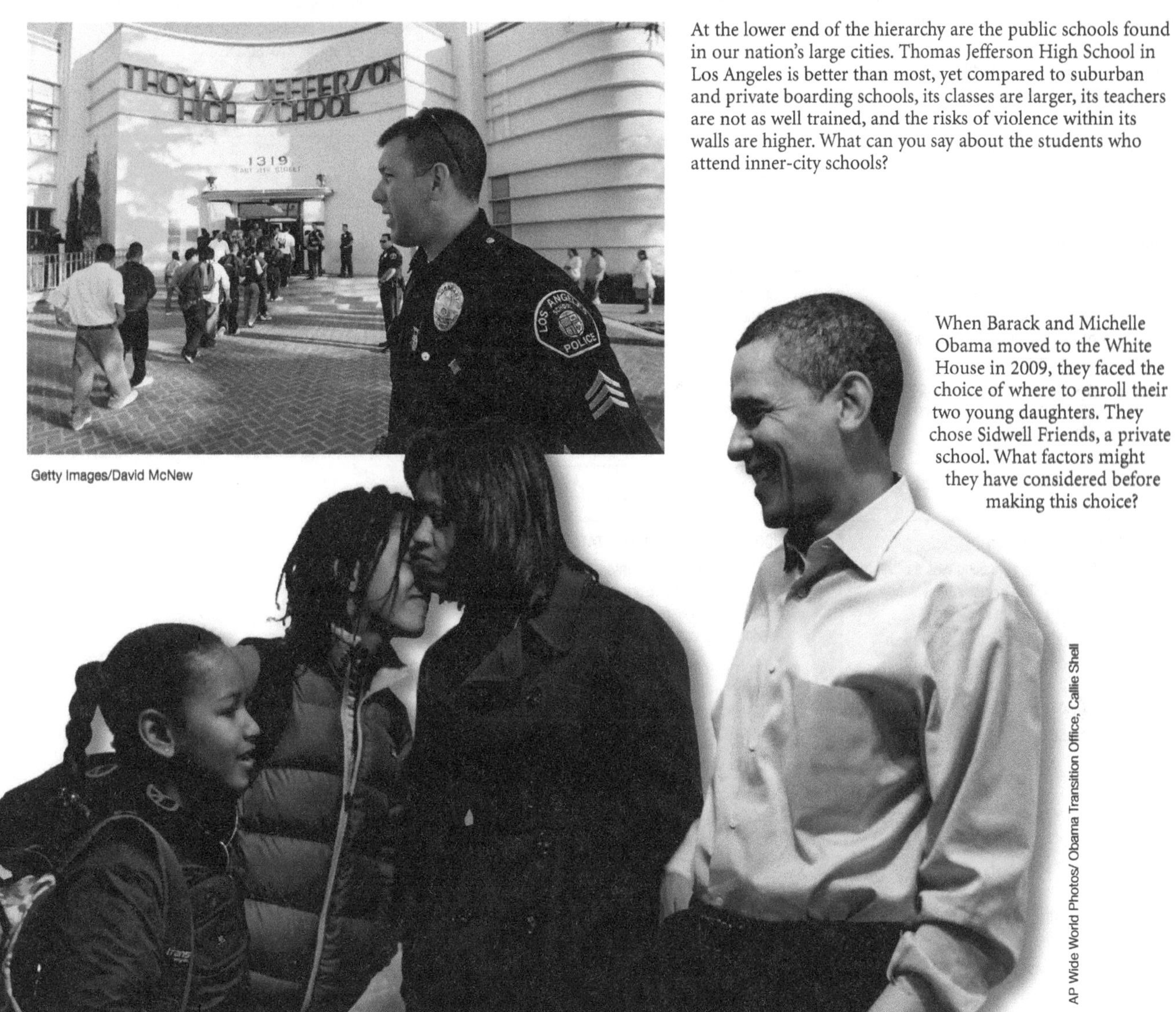

Getty Images/David McNew

At the lower end of the hierarchy are the public schools found in our nation's large cities. Thomas Jefferson High School in Los Angeles is better than most, yet compared to suburban and private boarding schools, its classes are larger, its teachers are not as well trained, and the risks of violence within its walls are higher. What can you say about the students who attend inner-city schools?

When Barack and Michelle Obama moved to the White House in 2009, they faced the choice of where to enroll their two young daughters. They chose Sidwell Friends, a private school. What factors might they have considered before making this choice?

AP Wide World Photos/ Obama Transition Office, Callie Shell

Applying SOCIOLOGY in Everyday Life

1. Make a visit to a public or private secondary school near your college or home. What is the typical social background of students enrolled there? Does the school have a tracking policy? If so, find out how it works. How much importance does a student's social background have in making a tracking assignment?

2. Most people agree that teaching our children is important work. Yet teachers earn relatively low salaries. See what you can learn about the average salary of teachers in your community, and compare it to the pay of other workers. Do you think teachers are paid enough?

3. Since the passage of the Americans with Disabilities Act of 1990, schools have tried to "accommodate" students with a broader range of physical and mental disabilities. Talk to officials on your campus about policies at your school and how laws of this kind are changing education.

MAKING THE GRADE

Education

Education: A Global Survey

EDUCATION is the social institution for transmitting knowledge and skills, as well as teaching cultural norms and values.

- In preindustrial societies, education occurs informally within the family.
- Industrial societies develop formal systems of schooling to educate their children.
- Differences in schooling in societies around the world today reflect both cultural values and each country's level of economic development.

education the social institution through which society provides its members with important knowledge, including basic facts, job skills, and cultural norms and values

schooling formal instruction under the direction of specially trained teachers

SCHOOLING IN INDIA

- Despite the fact that India is now a middle-income country, patriarchy continues to shape education in India. Many more boys attend school than girls, who are often expected to work in factories at young ages.
- Today, almost 90% of children in India complete primary school, but barely half of them go on to secondary school.

SCHOOLING IN JAPAN

- The earliest years of schooling in Japan concentrate on transmitting Japanese cultural traditions.
- More men and women graduate from high school in Japan (93%) than in the United States (87%), but only half of high school graduates gain college admission, which is determined by highly competitive examinations.

SCHOOLING IN GREAT BRITAIN

- During the Middle Ages, schooling was a privilege of the British nobility. The Industrial Revolution created a need for a literate workforce.
- Traditional class differences still affect British schooling; elite schools, which enroll 7% of British students, provide a path for admission to the most prestigious universities.

SCHOOLING IN THE UNITED STATES

- The United States was among the first countries to undertake compulsory mass education, reflecting both democratic political ideals and the needs of the industrial-capitalist economy.
- Schooling in the United States claims to promote equal opportunity, but the opportunity to go to college is closely tied to family income.
- The U.S. educational system stresses the value of practical learning that prepares young people for their place in the workforce.

The Functions of Schooling

The **STRUCTURAL-FUNCTIONAL APPROACH** focuses on the ways in which schooling contributes to the orderly operation of society. Key functions of schooling include:

- *Socialization*—teaching the skills that young people need to succeed in life, as well as cultural values and norms
- *Cultural innovation*—providing the opportunity for academic research that leads to important discoveries
- *Social integration*—molding a diverse population into one society by teaching cultural norms and values
- *Social placement*—reinforcing meritocracy and providing a path for upward social mobility
- *Latent functions*—providing child care and the opportunity for building social networks

Schooling and Social Interaction

The **SYMBOLIC-INTERACTION APPROACH** looks at how we build reality in our day-to-day interactions.

- The "self-fulfilling prophecy" describes how self-image can have important consequences for how students perform in school. If students think they are academically superior, they are likely to perform better; students who think they are inferior are likely to perform less well.

Schooling and Social Inequality

The **SOCIAL-CONFLICT APPROACH** links schooling to inequality involving class, race, and gender.

- Formal education serves as a means of generating conformity to produce obedient adult workers.
- Standardized tests have been criticized as culturally biased tools that may lead to labeling less privileged students as personally deficient.
- **Tracking** has been challenged by critics as a program that gives a better education to privileged youngsters.
- The majority of young people in the United States attend state-funded public schools. A small proportion of students—usually the most well-to-do—attend elite private college preparatory schools.
- Differences in school funding affect the quality of education: Public schools in more affluent areas offer a better education than schools in poor areas.
- Largely due to the high cost of college, only 66% of U.S. students enroll in college directly after high school graduation; the higher a family's income, the more likely it is that children will attend college.
- Earning a college degree today adds as much as $1 million to a person's lifetime income.

tracking assigning students to different types of educational programs

See the Applying Theory table.

Problems in the Schools

VIOLENCE permeates many schools, especially in poor neighborhoods.

- Critics charge that schools today fall short in their attempts to teach personal discipline.

The bureaucratic character of schools fosters **STUDENT PASSIVITY**. Schools have evolved into huge educational factories that

- demand rigid uniformity
- define success in terms of numerical ratings
- hold rigid expectations of students
- require too much specialization
- instill little individual responsibility in students

The high school **DROPOUT RATE**—currently 8.7% of young people—leaves many young people unprepared for the world of work and at high risk of poverty.

- The dropout rate for children in families with income in the bottom 25% is more than four times higher than for children living in high-income families.

DECLINING ACADEMIC STANDARDS are reflected in

- today's lower average scores on achievement tests
- the functional illiteracy of a significant proportion of high school graduates
- grade inflation

functional illiteracy a lack of the reading and writing skills needed for everyday living

Current Issues in U.S. Education

The **SCHOOL CHOICE MOVEMENT** seeks to make schools more accountable to the public. Innovative school choice options include

- magnet schools
- schooling for profit
- charter schools

HOME SCHOOLING

- The original pioneers of home schooling did not believe in public education because they wanted to give their children a strongly religious upbringing.
- Home schooling advocates today point to the poor performance of public schools.

SCHOOLING PEOPLE WITH DISABILITIES

- In the past, children with mental or physical disabilities were schooled in special classes.
- **Mainstreaming** affords them broader opportunities and exposes all children to a more diverse student population.

ADULT EDUCATION

- Adults represent a growing proportion of students in the United States.
- Most older learners are women who are engaged in job-related study.

THE TEACHER SHORTAGE

- More than 300,000 teaching positions go unfilled in the United States each year due to low salaries, frustration, retirement, rising enrollments, and reduced class size.
- To address this shortage, many school districts are recruiting teachers from abroad.

mainstreaming integrating students with disabilities or special needs into the overall educational program

✓ *Because the problems of our schools have their roots in the larger society, improvement will require a national commitment.*

✓ *The widespread use of computers in schools today is evidence that the Information Revolution is changing the way we learn.*

MAKING THE GRADE

Sample Test Questions

Multiple-Choice Questions

1. **In the United States and other countries, laws requiring all children to attend school were enacted following**
   a. national independence.
   b. the Industrial Revolution.
   c. World War II.
   d. the computer age.

2. **Japan differs from the United States in that getting into college depends more on**
   a. athletic ability.
   b. race and ethnicity.
   c. family money.
   d. scores on achievement tests.

3. **What share of the U.S. adult population has completed high school?**
   a. 45.3 percent
   b. 65.5 percent
   c. 85.7 percent
   d. 99.9 percent

4. **Using a structural-functional approach, schooling carries out the task of**
   a. tying together a diverse population.
   b. creating new culture.
   c. socializing young people.
   d. All of the above are correct.

5. **A social-conflict approach highlights how education**
   a. reflects and reinforces social inequality.
   b. helps prepare students for their future careers.
   c. has both latent and manifest functions.
   d. All of the above are correct.

6. **The importance of community colleges to U.S. higher education is reflected in the fact that they**
   a. greatly expand the opportunity to attend college.
   b. enroll almost 40 percent of all U.S. college students.
   c. enroll half of all African American and Hispanic college students.
   d. All of the above are correct.

7. **What share of people in the United States between the ages of sixteen and twenty-four drop out before completing high school?**
   a. 1.3 percent
   b. 9.3 percent
   c. 29.3 percent
   d. 39.3 percent

8. **Support for the school choice movement is based on the claim that U.S. public schools perform poorly because**
   a. they have no competition.
   b. many schools lack enough funding.
   c. the national poverty rate is high.
   d. too many parents are not involved in the schools.

9. **This chapter provides lots of evidence to support the claim that**
   a. U.S. schools are better than those in other high-income nations.
   b. most public schools perform well and most private schools do not.
   c. without involving the entire society, schools cannot improve the quality of education.
   d. All of the above are correct.

10. **About what share of all U.S. college students today are men?**
   a. 63 percent
   b. 53 percent
   c. 43 percent
   d. 33 percent

ANSWERS: 1 (b); 2 (d); 3 (c); 4 (d); 5 (a); 6 (d); 7 (b); 8 (a); 9 (c); 10 (c).

Essay Questions

1. Why does industrialization lead societies to expand their systems of schooling? In what ways has schooling in the United States been shaped by our economic, political, and cultural systems?
2. From a structural-functional perspective, why is schooling important to the operation of society? From a social-conflict point of view, how does schooling reproduce social inequality in each generation?

Population, Urbanization, and Environment

Shutterstock/Tony Campbell

An increasing share of our planet's population lives in cities. Researchers study the differences between rural and urban life, and they also track global population increase and the ways in which human societies are altering the natural environment.

Peter Arnold, Inc./Mark Edwards

Population, Urbanization, and Environment

The Image Works/James Marshall

Stock Connection/Joe Sohm/Chromosohm

CHAPTER OVERVIEW

This chapter explores three related dimensions of social change: population dynamics, urbanization, and increasing threats to the natural environment.

Getty Images/Nina Raingold

Looking for a new place to live after you finish college? Crosby, North Dakota, would really like you to call it home. The town's officials will do more than welcome you—they will give you a free piece of land on which to build a house. As a bonus, they will throw in a free membership in the local country club.

Ellsworth, Kansas, also wants you. The town leaders will match Crosby's offer of free land and go one better, paying you $1,000 cash to get you started on building your new home.

Perhaps the best deal of all is found in Plainville, Kansas. In addition to free land, you can forget about property taxes for the next ten years!

Why are these towns so eager to attract new residents? The answer is that they are all in the Great Plains, the central region of the United States extending from North Dakota all the way down to Texas that has lost much of its population in recent decades. The town leaders of Crosby (current population 1,100), Ellsworth (2,500), and Plainville (2,000) are offering these fantastic deals because they are worried that unless there is a turnaround, their towns may disappear, as hundreds of nearby communities already have (Greene, 2005).

All across the Great Plains, towns are hanging on by a thread. This chapter investigates population patterns, explaining why people move from place to place, why some cities get so large, and why small towns sometimes die. It also looks at the effects on the physical environment of population change and our entire way of life.

Demography: The Study of Population

When humans first began to cultivate plants some 12,000 years ago, Earth's entire *Homo sapiens* population was around 5 million, about the number living in Minnesota today. Very slow growth pushed the global total in 1 C.E. to perhaps 300 million, or about the population of the United States today.

Starting around 1750, world population began to spike upward. We now add more than 80 million people to the planet each year; today, the world holds 6.7 billion people (Population Reference Bureau, 2008).

The causes and consequences of this drama are the basis of **demography,** *the study of human population.* Demography (from Greek, meaning "description of people") is a cousin of sociology that analyzes the size and composition of a population and studies how and why people move from place to place. Demographers not only collect statistics but also raise important questions about the effects of population growth and suggest how it might be controlled. The following sections present basic demographic concepts.

Fertility

The study of human population begins with how many people are born. **Fertility** is *the incidence of childbearing in a country's population.* During her childbearing years, from the onset of menstruation (typically in the early teens) to menopause (usually in the late forties), a woman is capable of bearing more than twenty children. But *fecundity,* or maximum possible childbearing, is sharply reduced by cultural norms, finances, and personal choice.

Demographers describe fertility using the **crude birth rate,** *the number of live births in a given year for every 1,000 people in a population.* To calculate a crude birth rate, divide the number of live births in a year by the society's total population, and multiply the result by 1,000. In the United States in 2007, there were 4.3 million live births in a population of 301 million, yielding a crude birth rate of 14.3 (Tejada-Vera & Sutton, 2008).

January 18, Coshocton County, Ohio. Having just finished the mountains of meat and potatoes that make up a typical Amish meal, we have gathered in the living room of Jacob Raber, a member of this rural Amish community. Mrs. Raber, a mother of four, is telling us about Amish life. "Most of the women I know have five or six children," she says with a smile, "but certainly not everybody—some have eleven or twelve!"

A country's birth rate is described as "crude" because it is based on the entire population, not just women in their childbearing years.

SEEING SOCIOLOGY in Everyday Life

How do you think low-fertility societies differ from high-fertility societies with respect to (1) age at first marriage, (2) opportunities available to women, and (3) attitudes toward homosexuality? Explain your responses.

demography the study of human population

fertility the incidence of childbearing in a country's population

crude birth rate the number of live births in a given year for every 1,000 people in a population

mortality the incidence of death in a country's population

crude death rate the number of deaths in a given year for every 1,000 people in a population

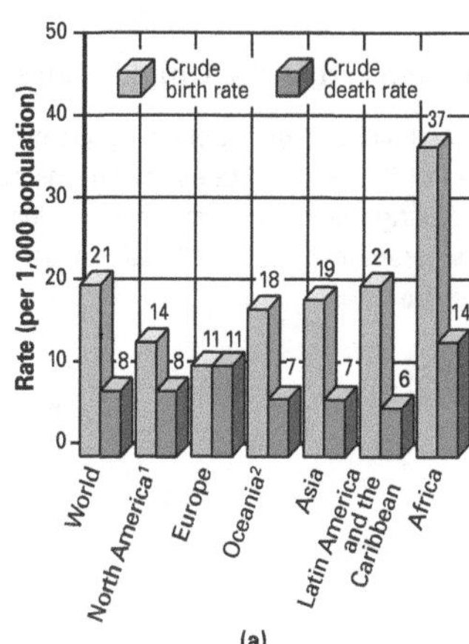

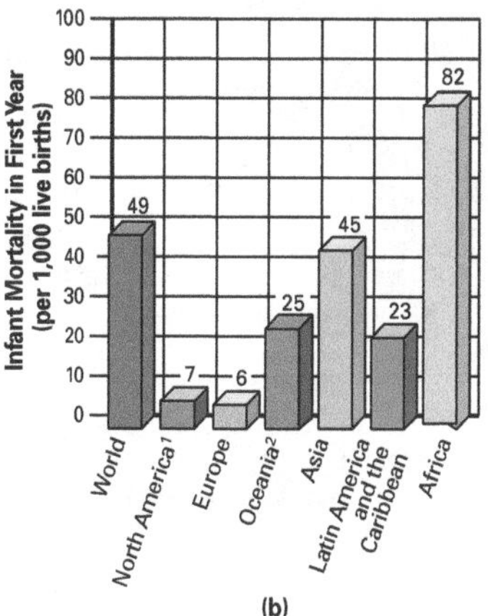

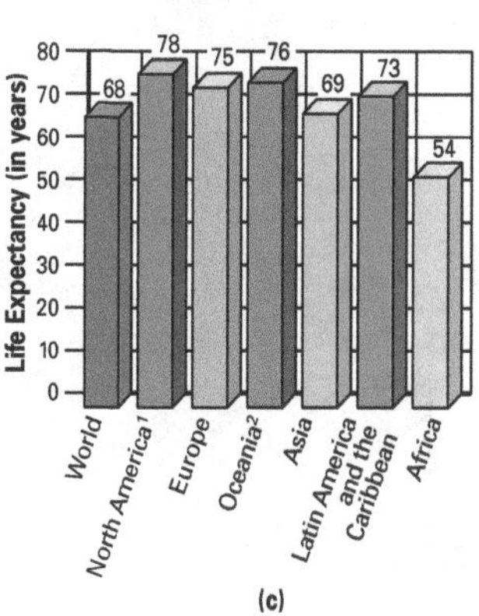

FIGURE 1 **(a) Crude Birth Rates and Crude Death Rates, (b) Infant Mortality Rates, and (c) Life Expectancy around the World, 2008**

By world standards, North America has a low birth rate, an average death rate, a very low infant mortality rate, and high life expectancy.

[1] United States and Canada.

[2] Australia, New Zealand, and South Pacific Islands.

Source: Population Reference Bureau (2009).

In addition, this measure ignores differences between various categories of the population: Fertility among the Amish, for example, is quite high, and fertility among Asian Americans is low. But the crude measure is easy to calculate and allows rough comparisons of the fertility of one country or region in relation to others. Part (a) of Figure 1 shows that on a global scale, the crude birth rate of North America is low.

Mortality

Population size also reflects **mortality,** *the incidence of death in a country's population.* To measure mortality, demographers use the **crude death rate,** *the number of deaths in a given year for every 1,000 people in a population.* This time, we take the number of deaths in a year, divide by the total population, and multiply the result by 1,000. In 2007, there were 2.4 million deaths in the U.S. population of 301 million, yielding a crude death rate of 8.0 (Tejada-Vera & Sutton, 2008). Part (a) of Figure 1 shows that this rate is about average.

A third useful demographic measure is the **infant mortality rate,** *the number of deaths among infants under one year of age for each 1,000 live births in a given year.* To compute infant mortality, divide the number of deaths of children under one year of age by the number of live births during the same year, and multiply the result by 1,000. In 2007, there were 28,600 infant deaths and 4.3 million live births in the United States. Dividing the first number by the second and multiplying the result by 1,000 yields an infant mortality rate of 6.6. Part (b) of Figure 1 indicates that by world standards, North American infant mortality is very low.

But remember that differences exist among various categories of people. For example, African Americans, with nearly three times the burden of poverty as whites, have an infant mortality rate of 13.3—more than twice the white rate of 5.6.

Low infant mortality greatly raises **life expectancy,** *the average life span of a country's population.* U.S. males born in 2006 can expect to live 75.4 years, and females can look forward to 80.7 years. As part (c) of Figure 1 shows, life expectancy in North America is twenty-four years greater than is typical of low-income countries of Africa.

Migration

Population size is also affected by **migration,** *the movement of people into and out of a specified territory.* Movement into a territory, or *immigration,* is measured as an *in-migration rate,* calculated as the number of people entering an area for every 1,000 people in the

Cheryl Richardson, age 36, has just moved to Las Vegas to work in the expanding tourism industry, which has boosted the region's population.

Tom and Ellen Posten, in their sixties, live in Wichita County, Kansas; like many other families in the area, their children have all moved out of the county in search of better jobs.

infant mortality rate the number of deaths among infants under one year of age for each 1,000 live births in a given year

life expectancy the average life span of a country's population

migration the movement of people into and out of a specified territory

sex ratio the number of males for every 100 females in a nation's population

age-sex pyramid a graphic representation of the age and sex of a population

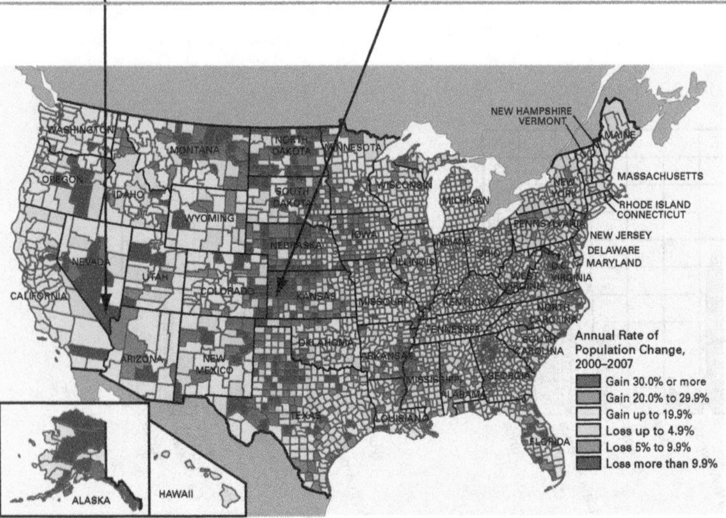

Seeing Ourselves

NATIONAL MAP 1

Population Change across the United States

This map shows that since 2000, population has been moving from the heartland of the United States toward the coasts. What do you think is causing this internal migration? What types of people do you think remain in counties that are losing population?

Source: U.S. Census Bureau (2009).

population. Movement out of a territory, or *emigration,* is measured in terms of an *out-migration rate,* the number leaving for every 1,000 people. Both types of migration usually occur at the same time; the difference between them is the *net migration rate.*

All nations experience internal migration, that is, movement within their borders from one region to another. National Map 1 shows where the U.S. population is moving and the places left behind (as suggested by the chapter opening, notice the heavy losses in the Plains States in the middle of the country).

Migration is sometimes voluntary, as when people leave a small town and move to a larger city. In such cases, "push-pull" factors are typically at work; a lack of jobs "pushes" people to move, and more opportunity elsewhere "pulls" them to a larger city. Migration can also be involuntary, as during the forced transport of 10 million Africans to the Western Hemisphere as slaves or when Hurricane Katrina forced tens of thousands of people to flee New Orleans.

Population Growth

Fertility, mortality, and migration all affect the size of a society's population. In general, rich nations (such as the United States) grow as much from immigration as from natural increase; poorer nations (such as Pakistan) grow almost entirely from natural increase.

To calculate a population's natural growth rate, demographers subtract the crude death rate from the crude birth rate. The natural growth rate of the U.S. population in 2007 was 6.3 per 1,000 (the crude birth rate of 14.3 minus the crude death rate of 8.0), or about 0.6 percent annual growth.

Global Map 1 shows that population growth in the United States and other high-income nations is well below the world average of 1.2 percent. Earth's low-growth continents are Europe (currently posting a slight decline, expressed as a *negative* 0.1 percent annual rate), North America (0.6 percent), and Oceania (1.1 percent). Close to the global average are Asia (1.2 percent) and Latin America (1.5 percent). The highest growth region in the world is Africa (2.4 percent).

A handy rule of thumb for estimating a nation or region's growth is to divide the number 70 by the population growth rate; this yields the *doubling time* in years. Thus an annual growth rate of 2 percent (found in parts of Latin America) doubles a population in thirty-five years, and a 3 percent growth rate (found in some countries in Africa) drops the doubling time to just twenty-three years. The rapid population growth of the poorest countries is deeply troubling because these countries can barely support the populations they have now.

Population Composition

Demographers also study the makeup of a society's population at a given point in time. One variable is the **sex ratio,** *the number of males for every 100 females in a nation's population.* In 2007, the sex ratio in the United States was 97 (97 males for every 100 females). Sex ratios are usually below 100 because, on average, women outlive men. Because Plainville, Kansas, has an aging population, its sex ratio is 89, or 89 males for every 100 females. In India, however, the sex ratio is 106 because many parents value sons more than daughters and may either abort a female fetus or, after birth, give more care to their male children, raising the odds that a female child will die.

A more complex measure is the **age-sex pyramid,** *a graphic representation of the age and sex of a population.* Figure 2 presents the age-sex pyramids for the populations of the United States and Mexico. Higher mortality with advancing age gives these figures

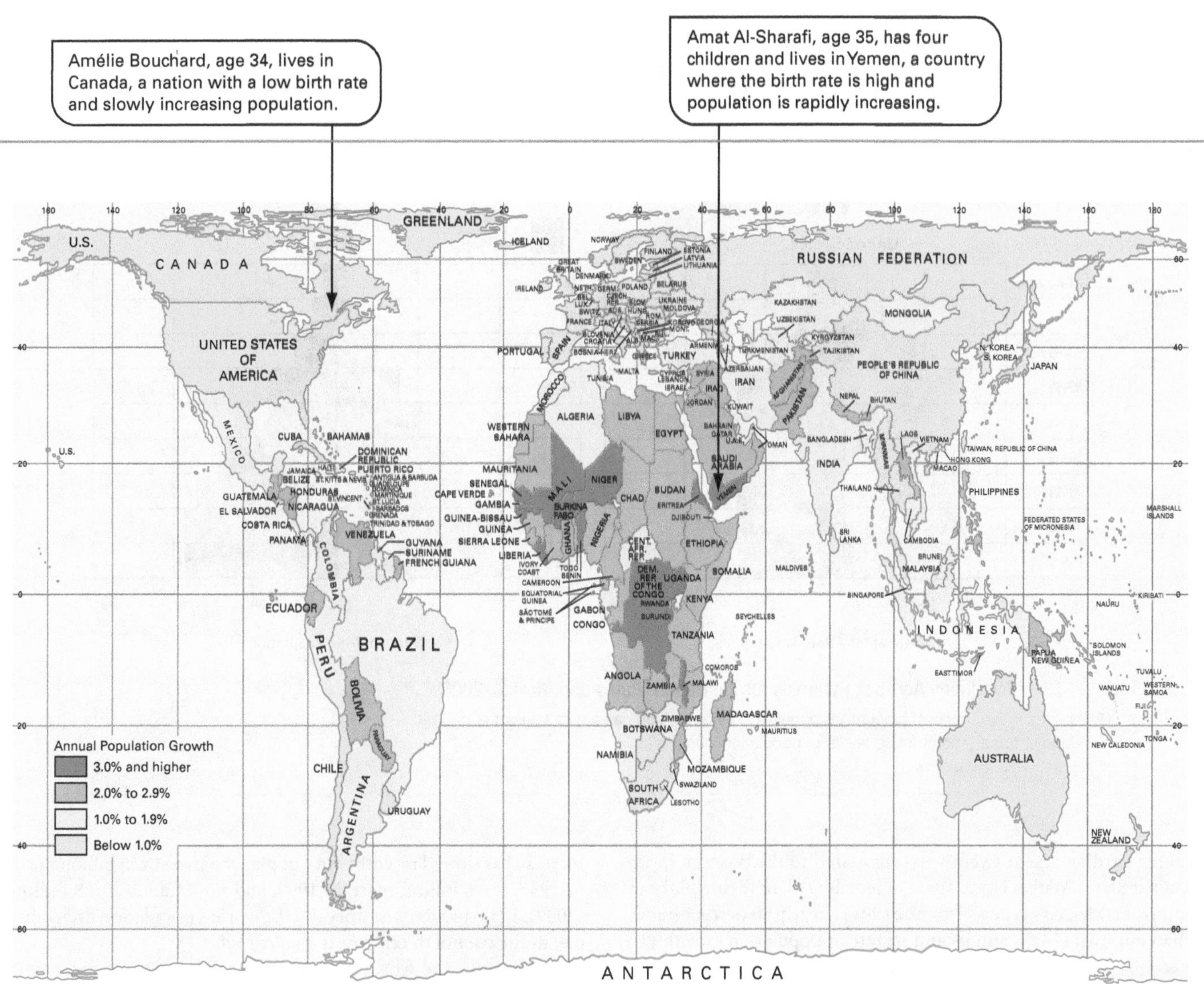

Window on the World

GLOBAL MAP 1 **Population Growth in Global Perspective**

The richest countries of the world—including the United States, Canada, and the nations of Europe—have growth rates below 1 percent. The nations of Latin America and Asia typically have growth rates around 1.5 percent, a rate that doubles a population in forty-seven years. Africa has an overall growth rate of 2.4 percent (despite only small increases in countries with a high rate of AIDS), which cuts the doubling time to twenty-nine years. In global perspective, we see that a society's standard of living is closely related to its rate of population growth: Population is rising fastest in the world regions that can least afford to support more people.

Source: Population Reference Bureau (2009).

a rough pyramid shape. In the U.S. pyramid, the bulge in the middle reflects high birth rates during the *baby boom* from the mid-1940s to the mid-1960s. The contraction for people in their twenties and thirties reflects the subsequent *baby bust.* The birth rate of 14.3 in 2007 is still well below the high of 25.3 in 1957.

Comparing the U.S. and Mexican age-sex pyramids reveals different demographic trends. The pyramid for Mexico, like that of other lower-income nations, is wide at the bottom (reflecting higher birth rates) and narrows quickly by what we would term middle age (due to higher mortality). In short, Mexico is a much younger society,

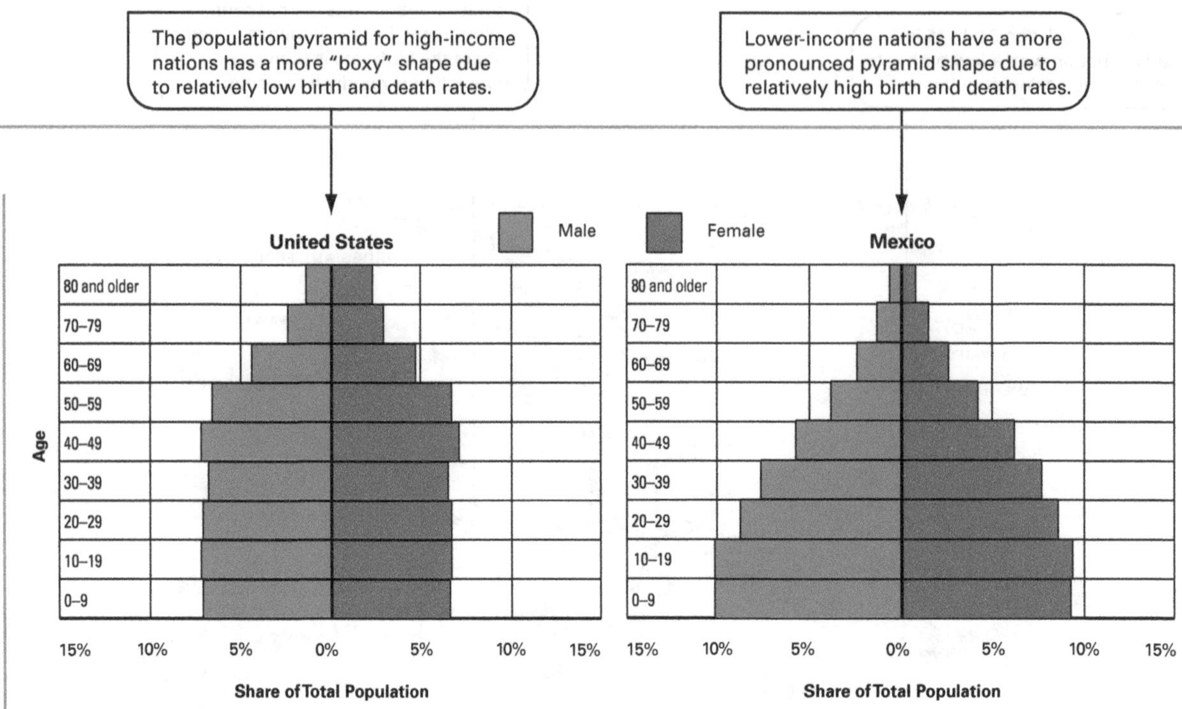

FIGURE 2 **Population Age-Sex Pyramids for the United States and Mexico, 2008**

By looking at the shape of a country's population pyramid, you can tell its level of economic development and predict future levels of population increase.

Source: U.S. Census Bureau (2009).

with a median age of twenty-six, compared to thirty-seven in the United States. With a larger share of females still in their childbearing years, Mexico's crude birth rate (20) is nearly 50 percent higher than our own (14.3), and its annual rate of population growth (1.1 percent) is almost twice the U.S. rate (0.6 percent).

History and Theory of Population Growth

In the past, people wanted large families because human labor was the key to productivity. In addition, until rubber condoms were invented in the mid-1800s, prevention of pregnancy was uncertain at best. But high death rates from infectious diseases put a constant brake on population growth.

A major demographic shift began about 1750 as the world's population turned upward, reaching the 1 billion mark by 1800. This milestone (which took all of human history to reach) was repeated barely a century later in 1930, when a second billion people were added to the planet. In other words, not only was population increasing, but the *rate* of growth was accelerating. Global population reached 3 billion by 1962 (just thirty-two years later) and 4 billion by 1974 (only twelve years after that). The rate of world population increase has slowed recently, but our planet passed the 5 billion mark in 1987, the 6 billion mark in 1999, and now stands at 6.8 billion (2009). In no previous century did the world's population even double; in the twentieth century, it *quadrupled.*

Currently, the world is gaining 80 million people each year; 97 percent of this increase is in poor countries. Experts predict that Earth's population will reach 7 billion very soon and will climb more slowly to about 9 billion by 2050 (United Nations Population Reference Division, 2009). Given the world's troubles feeding the present population, such an increase is a matter of urgent concern.

Malthusian Theory

The sudden population spurt 250 years ago sparked the development of demography. Thomas Robert Malthus (1766–1834), an English economist and clergyman, warned that population increase would soon lead to social chaos. Malthus (1926, orig. 1798) calculated that population would increase in what mathematicians call a *geometric progression,* illustrated by the series of numbers 2, 4, 8, 16, 32, and so on. At such a rate, Malthus concluded, world population would soon soar out of control.

Food production would also increase, Malthus explained, but only in *arithmetic progression* (as in the series 2, 3, 4, 5, 6, and so on)

SEEING SOCIOLOGY in Everyday Life

Using the age-sex pyramid for the United States shown in Figure 2, why do you think many people are concerned that there will not be enough workers to pay for the retirement of the baby boom generation? How does the pyramid shape change as more and more baby boomers enter retirement?

demographic transition theory a thesis that links population patterns to a society's level of technological development

because even with new agricultural technology, farmland is limited. Thus Malthus presented a distressing vision of the future: people reproducing beyond what the planet could feed, leading ultimately to widespread starvation and war over what resources were left.

Malthus recognized that artificial birth control or abstinence might change his prediction. But he considered one morally wrong and the other impractical. Famine and war therefore stalked humanity in Malthus's mind, and he was justly known as "the dismal parson."

CRITICAL REVIEW Fortunately, Malthus's prediction was flawed. First, by 1850, the European birth rate began to drop, partly because children were becoming an economic liability rather than an asset and partly because people began using artificial birth control. Second, Malthus underestimated human ingenuity: Modern irrigation techniques, fertilizers, and pesticides increased farm production far more than he could have imagined.

Some people criticized Malthus for ignoring the role of social inequality in world abundance and famine. For example, Karl Marx (1967, orig. 1867) objected to viewing suffering as a "law of nature" rather than the curse of capitalism. More recently, "critical demographers" have claimed that saying poverty is caused by high birth rates in low-income countries amounts to blaming the victims. On the contrary, they see global inequality as the real issue (Horton, 1999; Kuumba, 1999).

Still, Malthus offers an important lesson. Habitable land, clean water, and fresh air are limited resources, and greater economic productivity has taken a heavy toll on the natural environment. In addition, medical advances have lowered death rates, pushing up world population. Common sense tells us that no level of population growth can go on forever. People everywhere must become aware of the dangers of population increase.

CHECK YOUR LEARNING What did Malthus predict about human population increase? About food production? What was his overall conclusion?

AP Wide World Photos

This street scene in Kolkata (Calcutta), India, conveys the vision of the future found in the work of Thomas Robert Malthus, who feared that population increase would overwhelm the world's resources. Can you explain why Malthus had such a serious concern about population? How is demographic transition theory a more hopeful analysis?

Demographic Transition Theory

A more complex analysis of population change is **demographic transition theory,** *a thesis that links population patterns to a society's level of technological development.* Figure 3 shows the demographic consequences at four levels of technological development.

Preindustrial, agrarian societies (Stage 1) have high birth rates because of the economic value of children and the absence of birth control. Death rates are also high because of low living standards and limited medical technology. Deaths from outbreaks of disease cancel out births, so population rises and falls only slightly over time. This was the case for thousands of years in Europe before the Industrial Revolution.

Stage 2, the onset of industrialization, brings a demographic transition as death rates fall due to greater food supplies and scientific medicine. But birth rates remain high, resulting in rapid population growth. It was during Europe's Stage 2 that Malthus formulated his ideas, which accounts for his pessimistic view of the future. The world's poorest countries today are in this high-growth stage.

In Stage 3, a mature industrial economy, the birth rate drops, curbing population growth once again. Fertility falls because most children survive to adulthood and because high living standards make raising children expensive. In short, affluence transforms children from economic assets into economic liabilities. Smaller families, made possible by effective birth control, are also favored by women working outside the home. As birth rates follow death rates downward, population growth slows further.

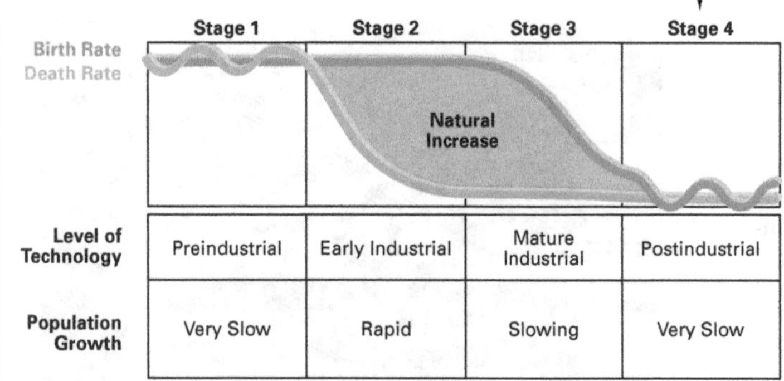

FIGURE 3 **Demographic Transition Theory**

Demographic transition theory links population change to a society's level of technological development.

Stage 4 corresponds to a postindustrial economy in which the demographic transition is complete. The birth rate keeps falling, partly because dual-income couples gradually become the norm and partly because the cost of raising children continues to increase. This trend, linked to steady death rates, means that population grows only very slowly or even decreases. This is the case today in Japan, Europe, and the United States.

CRITICAL REVIEW Demographic transition theory suggests that the key to population control lies in technology. Instead of the runaway population increase feared by Malthus, this theory sees technology slowing growth and spreading material plenty.

Demographic transition theory is linked to modernization theory. Modernization theorists are optimistic that poor countries will solve their population problems as they industrialize. But critics, notably dependency theorists, strongly disagree. Unless there is a redistribution of global resources, they maintain, our planet will become increasingly divided into industrialized "haves," enjoying low population growth, and nonindustrialized "have-nots," struggling in vain to feed more and more people.

CHECK YOUR LEARNING Explain the four stages of demographic transition theory.

Global Population Today: A Brief Survey

What can we say about population in today's world? Drawing on the discussion so far, we can identify important patterns and reach several conclusions.

MAKING THE GRADE

Demographic transition theory is linked to modernization theory.

The Low-Growth North

When the Industrial Revolution began in the Northern Hemisphere, the population increase in Western Europe and North America was a high 3 percent annually. But in the centuries since, the growth rate has steadily declined, and in 1970, it fell below 1 percent. As our postindustrial society settles into Stage 4, the U.S. birth rate is at about the replacement level of 2.1 children per woman, a point demographers term **zero population growth,** *the rate of reproduction that maintains population at a steady level.* More than eighty nations, almost all of them rich, are at or below the point of zero population growth.

Among the factors that serve to hold down population in these postindustrial societies include a high proportion of men and women in the labor force, rising costs of raising children, trends toward later marriage and singlehood, and widespread use of contraceptives and abortion.

In high-income nations, then, population increase is not the pressing problem that it is in poor countries. On the contrary, many governments in high-income countries, including Italy and Japan, are concerned about a future problem of *underpopulation* because declining population size may be difficult to reverse and because the swelling ranks of the elderly can look to fewer and fewer young people for support (Kent & Mather, 2002; Population Reference Bureau, 2009).

The High-Growth South

Population is a critical problem in poor nations of the Southern Hemisphere. No nation of the world lacks industrial technology entirely; demographic transition theory's Stage 1 applies today to remote rural areas of low-income nations. But much of Latin America, Africa, and Asia is at Stage 2, with a mix of agrarian and industrial economies. Advanced medical technology, supplied by rich countries, has sharply reduced death rates, but birth rates remain high. This is why poor countries now account for two-thirds of Earth's people and 97 percent of global population increase.

In some of the world poorest countries, such as the Democratic Republic of the Congo in Africa, women still have, on average, more than six children during their lifetimes. But in most poor countries, birth rates have fallen from about six children per woman (typical in 1950) to about three. But this level of fertility is still high enough to make global poverty much worse. This is why leaders in the battle against global poverty point to the importance of reducing fertility rates in low-income nations.

Notice, too, that a key element in controlling world population growth is improving the status of women. Why? Because of this simple truth: Give women more life choices and they will have fewer children. History has shown that women who are free to decide when

SEEING SOCIOLOGY in Everyday Life

Typically, immigrants are younger than most people in their new country. What is the likely effect of high immigration on a country's ability to support more and more older people?

zero population growth the rate of reproduction that maintains population at a steady level

urbanization the concentration of population into cities

and where to marry, bear children as a matter of choice, and have access to education and to good jobs will limit their own fertility (Axinn & Barber, 2001; Roudi-Fahimi & Kent, 2007).

The Demographic Divide

High- and low-income nations display very different population dynamics, a gap that is sometimes called the *demographic divide.* In Italy, a high-income nation with very low growth, women average just over one child in their lifetimes. Such a low birthrate means that the number of annual births is less than the number of deaths. This means that at the moment, Italy is actually *losing* population. Looking ahead to 2050, and even assuming some gains from immigration, Italy's population is projected to be about the same as it is today. But the share of elderly people in Italy—now 20 percent—will only increase as time goes on.

How different the patterns are in a low-income nation such as the Democratic Republic of the Congo. There, women still average six to seven children, so even with a high mortality rate, this nation's population will triple by 2050. The share of elderly people is extremely low—about 3 percent—and half that country's people are below the age of fifteen. With such a high growth rate, it is no surprise that the problem of poverty is bad and getting worse: About three-fourths of the people are undernourished (Population Reference Bureau, 2009).

In sum, a demographic divide now separates rich countries with low birth rates and aging populations from poor countries with high birth rates and very young population. Just as humanity has devised ways to reduce deaths around the world, it must now bring down population growth, especially in poor countries where projections suggest a future as bleak as that imagined by Thomas Malthus centuries ago.

China stands out as a nation that that has taken a strong stand on reducing population increase. That country's one-child policy, enacted back in the 1970s, has reduced China's population by about 250 million. Yet as the Thinking About Diversity box explains, this policy has been controversial.

Fertility in the United States has fallen during the past century and is now quite low. But some categories of the U.S. population have much higher fertility rates. One example is the Amish, a religious society living in rural areas of Ohio, Pennsylvania, and other states. It is common for Amish couples to have five, six, or more children. Why do you think the Amish favor large families?

Urbanization: The Growth of Cities

October 8, Hong Kong. The cable train grinds to the top of Victoria Peak, where we behold one of the world's most spectacular vistas: the city of Hong Kong at night! A million bright, colorful lights ring the harbor as ships, ferries, and traditional Chinese junks slowly slip by. Day or night, few places match Hong Kong for sheer energy: This small city is as economically productive as the state of Wisconsin or the nation of Finland. We could sit here for hours entranced by the spectacle of Hong Kong.

Throughout most of human history, the sights and sounds of great cities such as Hong Kong, Paris, and New York were simply unimaginable. Our distant ancestors lived in small, nomadic groups, moving as they depleted vegetation or hunted migratory game. The tiny settlements that marked the emergence of civilization in the Middle East some 12,000 years ago held only a small fraction of Earth's people. Today, the largest three or four cities of the world hold as many people as the entire planet did back then.

Urbanization is *the concentration of population into cities.* Urbanization redistributes population within a society and transforms many patterns of social life. We will trace these changes in terms of three urban revolutions: the emergence of cities 10,000 years ago, the development of industrial cities after 1750, and the explosive growth of cities in poor countries today.

The Evolution of Cities

Cities are a relatively new development in human history. Only about 12,000 years ago did our ancestors begin living in permanent settlements, which set the stage for the *first urban revolution.*

SEEING SOCIOLOGY in Everyday Life

With global population increasing, would you support expanding the one-child policy to other countries? Why or why not?

THINKING ABOUT DIVERSITY: RACE, CLASS, & GENDER

Where Are the Girls? China's One-Child Policy

The parents had argued for hours. But Yang, the father, was determined, and Jianying, the mother, was exhausted. Finally, Yang wrested the baby from Jianying's arms. The decision was made; the girl had to go. Yang put several extra layers of clothing on his daughter and lay the newborn in a cardboard box lined with blankets. Next to her, he placed a small bottle of milk. Then Yang lifted the box and carried it off into the dark night toward the distant village, leaving behind his wife sobbing, "Yang, I beg you, bring back my baby!"

Yet in her heart, she too knew that this must be done. Half an hour later, Yang arrived in the village and found his way to the local school. He kissed his daughter goodbye and set her makeshift crib on the steps of the school, knowing that when dawn broke she would be found by school officials and cared for. With tears in his eyes, Yang said a quick prayer to his ancestors to keep the baby safe from harm. Then he turned and again disappeared into the night, knowing that he would never see or hear from her again.

This story may be heartbreaking, but it is one that has occurred tens of thousands of times in China. What would prompt parents to give up a child? Why would a father abandon his daughter in a public place? The answer lies in China's population control policy and the nation's cultural traditions.

Back in the 1970s, the high Chinese birth rate was fueling a rapid population increase. Government leaders could see that the country's economic development depended on controlling population growth. As a result, they passed a law stating that a family can have only one child. Couples who follow the one-child policy can expect rewards such as a better job, a higher salary, and maybe even a larger apartment. On the other hand, parents who violate the law by having a second child face a stiff fine, and their second child may not be eligible for educational and health care benefits.

The government actively promotes the one-child message in the mass media, in popular songs, and in the schools. But education is not the government's only tactic; enforcement officials can be found in most neighborhoods and workplaces. Most Chinese willingly comply with the policy, praising it as good for the country. Those who do not must face the consequences.

Modern China is determined to control population increase. But China is also a country steeped in a tradition of male dominance. If government rules permit only one child, most families would prefer a boy. Why? Parents see boys as a better investment because sons will carry on the family name and will honor the obligation to care for their aging parents. On the other hand, girls will end up caring for their *husbands'* parents, leading most Chinese to see raising daughters as a waste of precious resources. The Chinese government has expanded women's rights and opportunities, but patriarchal traditions are deeply rooted in the country's history, and attitudes change slowly.

Around the world, the one-child policy has attracted both praise and condemnation. On the positive side, analysts agree that it has succeeded in its goal of reducing the rate of population increase. This trend, in turn, has helped raise living standards and lifted China to the ranks of middle-income nations. Many one-child families are happy with the added income from women who now work outside the home, and parents now have more to spend on a child's schooling.

But the one-child policy also has a dark side, which is shown in the story that began this box. Since the law was passed, as many as 1 million girls have "disappeared." In some cases, parents who learn the woman is carrying a female fetus may choose abortion so they can "try again." In other cases, family members decide to kill a female infant soon after birth. In still other cases, girls survive but are never recorded in the birth statistics, so that parents can try again to have a son. Such girls grow up as "noncitizens" who can never go to school or receive treatment at a local health clinic. Finally, some parents, like those described earlier, give up or abandon their daughter in the hope that the child may find a home elsewhere.

China's one-child policy has certainly held population increase in check. But it has had a dramatic toll on the female population of China. In one recent year, the nation's birth records showed almost 1 million fewer girls than boys. The Chinese population is now about 250 million lower than it would have been without the one-child policy, but the country's population is also steadily becoming more and more male.

China's one-child policy is advertised on billboards throughout the country.

WHAT DO YOU THINK?

1. Point to the reasons China's one-child policy has attracted praise and also blame. On balance, do you think this is a good policy? Can you think of a better way to control population? Explain.
2. What about cases where parents think they can afford additional children? Should family size be a couple's decision? Or does government have a responsibility to look out for the entire country's well-being?
3. Do you now understand why almost all of the babies U.S. parents adopt from China are girls?

Sources: Hesketh, Lu, & Xing (2005), Baochang et al. (2007), and Yardley (2008).

SEEING SOCIOLOGY in Everyday Life

As the sections describing preindustrial and industrial cities explain, the size and shape of a city provide clues to a society's technology and culture.

The First Cities

Hunting and gathering forced people to move all the time; however, once our ancestors discovered how to domesticate animals and cultivate crops, they were able to stay in one place. Raising their own food also created a material surplus, which freed some people from food production and allowed them to build shelters, make tools, weave cloth, and take part in religious rituals. The emergence of cities led to both higher living standards and job specialization.

The first city that we know of was Jericho, which lies to the north of the Dead Sea in what is now the West Bank. When first settled some 10,000 years ago, it was home to only 600 people. But as the centuries passed, cities grew to tens of thousands of people and became the centers of vast empires. By 3000 B.C.E., Egyptian cities flourished, as did cities in China about 2000 B.C.E. and in Central and South America about 1500 B.C.E. In North America, however, only a few Native American societies formed settlements; widespread urbanization had to await the arrival of European settlers in the seventeenth century.

Preindustrial European Cities

European cities date back some 5,000 years to the Greeks and later the Romans, both of whom created great empires and founded cities across Europe, including Vienna, Paris, and London. With the fall of the Roman Empire, the so-called Dark Ages began as people withdrew into defensive walled settlements and warlords battled for territory. Only in the eleventh century did Europe become more peaceful; trade flourished once again, allowing cities to grow.

Medieval cities were quite different from those familiar to us today. Beneath towering cathedrals, the narrow and winding streets of London, Brussels, and Florence teemed with merchants, artisans, priests, peddlers, jugglers, nobles, and servants. Occupational groups such as bakers, carpenters, and metalworkers clustered together in distinct sections or "quarters." Ethnicity also defined communities as residents tried to keep out people who differed from themselves. The term "ghetto" (from the Italian *borghetto,* meaning "outside the city walls") was first used to describe the neighborhood in which the Jews of Venice were segregated.

Industrial European Cities

As the Middle Ages came to a close, steadily increasing commerce enriched a new urban middle class, or *bourgeoisie* (French, meaning "townspeople"). With more and more money, the bourgeoisie soon rivaled the hereditary aristocracy.

By about 1750, the Industrial Revolution triggered a *second urban revolution,* first in Europe and then in North America. Factories unleashed tremendous productive power, causing cities to grow bigger than ever before. London, the largest European city, reached 550,000 people by 1700 and exploded to 6.5 million by 1900 (A. F. Weber, 1963, orig. 1899; Chandler & Fox, 1974).

Cities not only grew but changed shape as well. Older winding streets gave way to broad, straight boulevards to handle the increasing flow of commercial traffic. Steam and electric trolleys soon crisscrossed the expanding cities. Because land was now a commodity to be bought and sold, developers divided cities into regular-sized lots (Mumford, 1961). The center of the city was no longer the cathedral but a bustling central business district filled with banks, retail stores, and tall office buildings.

With a new focus on business, cities became more crowded and impersonal. Crime rates rose. Especially at the outset, a few industrialists lived in grand style, but most men, women, and children barely survived by working in factories.

Organized efforts by workers to improve their lives eventually brought changes to the workplace, better housing, and the right to vote. Public services such as water, sewer systems, and electricity further improved urban living. Today, some urbanites still live in poverty, but a rising standard of living has partly fulfilled the city's historical promise of a better life.

The Growth of U.S. Cities

Most of the Native Americans who inhabited North America for thousands of years before the arrival of Europeans were migratory people who formed few permanent settlements. The spread of villages and towns came after European colonization.

Colonial Settlement, 1565–1800

In 1565, the Spanish built a settlement at Saint Augustine, Florida, and in 1607, the English founded Jamestown, Virginia. The first lasting settlement came in 1624, when the Dutch established New Amsterdam, later renamed New York.

New York and Boston (founded by the English in 1630) started out as tiny villages in a vast wilderness. They resembled medieval towns in Europe, with narrow, winding streets that still curve through lower Manhattan and downtown Boston. When the first census was completed in 1790, as Table 1 shows, just 5 percent of the nation's people lived in cities.

Urban Expansion, 1800–1860

Early in the nineteenth century, as cities along the East Coast grew bigger, towns sprang up along the transportation routes that opened the American West. By 1860, Buffalo, Cleveland, Detroit, and Chicago were changing the face of the Midwest, and about one-fifth of the U.S. population lived in cities.

Urban expansion was greatest in the northern states; New York City, for example, had ten times the population of Charleston, South

metropolis a large city that socially and economically dominates an urban area

suburbs urban areas beyond the political boundaries of a city

megalopolis a vast urban region containing a number of cities and their surrounding suburbs

SEEING SOCIOLOGY in Everyday Life

Is there a class difference in people's use of the streets as a place to meet and greet others? For example, do you think working-class people are more likely to use the streets in this way than middle-class suburbanites?

Table 1 Urban Population of the United States, 1790–2000

Year	Population (in millions)	Percentage Living in Cities
1790	3.9	5.1%
1800	5.3	6.1
1820	9.6	7.3
1840	17.1	10.5
1860	31.4	19.7
1880	50.2	28.1
1900	76.0	39.7
1920	105.7	51.3
1940	131.7	56.5
1960	179.3	69.9
1980	226.5	73.7
2000	281.4	79.0

Source: U.S. Census Bureau (2009).

Carolina. The division of the United States into the industrial-urban North and the agrarian-rural South was one major cause of the Civil War (Schlesinger, 1969).

The Metropolitan Era, 1860–1950

The Civil War (1861–65) gave an enormous boost to urbanization as factories strained to produce weapons. Waves of people deserted the countryside for cities in hopes of finding better jobs. Joining them were tens of millions of immigrants, mostly from Europe, forming a culturally diverse urban mix.

In 1900, New York's population soared past the 4 million mark, and Chicago, a city of only 100,000 people in 1860, was closing in on 2 million. Such growth marked the era of the **metropolis** (from the Greek, meaning "mother city"), *a large city that socially and economically dominates an urban area.* Metropolises became the economic centers of the United States. By 1920, urban areas were home to a majority of the U.S. population.

Industrial technology pushed the urban skyline ever higher. In the 1880s, steel girders and mechanical elevators permitted buildings to rise more than ten stories high. In 1930, New York's Empire State Building was hailed as an urban wonder, reaching 102 stories into the clouds.

Urban Decentralization, 1950–Present

The industrial metropolis reached its peak about 1950. Since then, something of a turnaround—termed *urban decentralization*—has occurred as people have left downtown areas for outlying **suburbs,** *urban areas beyond the political boundaries of a city.* The old industrial cities of the Northeast and Midwest stopped growing, and some lost considerable population in the decades after 1950. At the same time, suburban populations increased rapidly. The urban landscape of densely packed central cities evolved into sprawling suburban regions.

Suburbs and Urban Decline

Imitating the European aristocracy, some of the rich had town houses in the city as well as large country homes beyond the city limits. But not until after World War II did ordinary people find a suburban home within their reach. With more and more cars in circulation, new four-lane highways, government-backed mortgages, and inexpensive tract homes, the suburbs grew rapidly. By 1999, most of the U.S. population lived in the suburbs and shopped at nearby malls rather than in the older and more distant downtown shopping districts (Pederson, Smith, & Adler, 1999; Macionis & Parrillo, 2010).

As many older cities of the Snowbelt—the Northeast and Midwest—lost higher-income taxpayers to the suburbs, they struggled to pay for expensive social programs for the poor who remained. Many cities fell into financial crisis, and urban decay became severe. Soon the inner city came to be synonymous with slums, crime, drugs, unemployment, poverty, and minorities.

The urban critic Paul Goldberger (2002) points out that the decline of central cities has also led to a decline in the importance of public space. Historically, the heart of city life was played out on the streets. The French word for a sophisticated person is *boulevardier,* which literally means "street person"—a term that has a negative meaning in the United States today. The active life that once took place on public streets and in public squares now takes place in shopping malls, the lobbies of cineplex theaters, and gated residential communities—all privately owned spaces. Further reducing the vitality of today's urban places is the spread of television, the Internet, and other media that people use without leaving home.

Postindustrial Sunbelt Cities

As older Snowbelt cities fell into decline, Sunbelt cities in the South and the West began to grow rapidly. The soaring populations of cities such as Los Angeles and Houston reflect a population shift to the Sunbelt, where 60 percent of U.S. people now live. In addition, most of today's immigrants enter the country in the Sunbelt region. In 1950, nine of the ten biggest U.S. cities were in the Snowbelt; in 2007, seven of the top ten were in the Sunbelt (U.S. Census Bureau, 2008).

Unlike their colder counterparts, Sunbelt cities came of age after urban decentralization began. So although cities like Chicago have long been enclosed by a ring of politically independent suburbs, cities like Houston have pushed their boundaries outward to include suburban communities. Chicago covers 227 square miles; Houston is more than twice that size, and the greater Houston urban area covers almost 9,000 square miles—an area the size of the state of New Jersey.

MAKING THE GRADE

The megalopolis, edge cities, and the "rural rebound" are all aspects of population decentralization as cities spread outward after 1950.

The great sprawl of Sunbelt cities has drawbacks. Many people in cities such as Atlanta, Dallas, Phoenix, and Los Angeles complain that unplanned growth results in traffic-clogged roads, poorly planned housing developments, and schools that cannot keep up with the inflow of children. Not surprisingly, voters in many communities across the United States have passed ballot initiatives seeking to limit urban sprawl (Lacayo, 1999; Romero & Liserio, 2002; W. Sullivan, 2007).

Bloomberg News/Jamie Rector/Bloomberg News

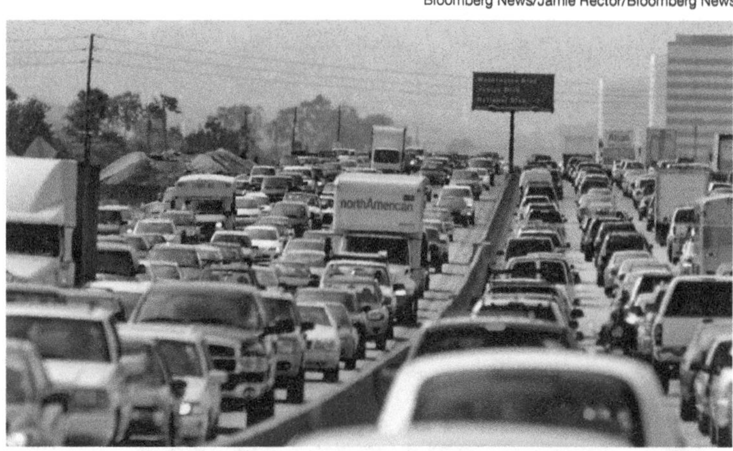

In recent decades, many U.S. cities in the Sunbelt have spread outward in a process called urban sprawl. Los Angeles, for example, now covers about 500 square miles, and even with a vast system of freeways, people moving around the city often find themselves stuck in slow-moving traffic. What are other disadvantages of urban sprawl?

Megalopolis: The Regional City

Another result of urban decentralization is urban regions or regional cities. The U.S. Census Bureau (2009) recognizes 374 *metropolitan statistical areas* (MSAs). Each includes at least one city with 50,000 or more people. The bureau also recognizes 579 *micropolitan statistical areas,* urban areas with at least one city of 10,000 to 50,000 people. *Core-based statistical areas* (CBSAs) include both metropolitan and micropolitan statistical areas.

The biggest CBSAs contain millions of people and cover large areas that extend into several states. In 2008, the largest MSA was New York and its adjacent urban areas in Long Island, western Connecticut, northern New Jersey, and eastern Pennsylvania, with a total population of 22 million. Next in size is the CBSA in southern California that includes Los Angeles, Riverside, and Long Beach, with a population of almost 18 million.

As regional cities grow, they begin to overlap. In the early 1960s, the French geographer Jean Gottmann (1961) coined the term **megalopolis** to designate *a vast urban region containing a number of cities and their surrounding suburbs.* Along the East Coast, a 400-mile megalopolis stretches all the way from New England to Virginia. Other supercities cover the eastern coast of Florida and stretch from Cleveland west to Chicago.

Edge Cities

Urban decentralization has also created *edge cities,* business centers some distance from the old downtowns. Edge cities—a mix of corporate office buildings, shopping malls, hotels, and entertainment complexes—differ from suburbs, which contain mostly homes. The population of suburbs peaks at night, but the population of edge cities peaks during the workday.

As part of expanding urban regions, most edge cities have no clear physical boundaries. Some do have names, including Las Colinas (near the Dallas–Fort Worth airport), Tyson's Corner (in Virginia, near Washington, D.C.), and King of Prussia (northwest of Philadelphia). Other edge cities are known only by the major highways that flow through them, including Route 1 in Princeton, New Jersey, and Route 128 near Boston (Garreau, 1991; Macionis & Parrillo, 2010).

The Rural Rebound

Over the course of U.S. history, as shown by the data in Table 1, the urban population of the nation has increased steadily. Immigration has played a part in this increase because most newcomers settle in cities. At the same time, there has been considerable migration from rural areas to urban places, typically by people seeking greater social, educational, and economic opportunity.

However, since about 1990, three-fourths of the rural counties across the United States gained population, a trend analysts have called the "rural rebound." Most of this gain resulted from the migration of people from urban areas. This trend has not affected all rural places: As the opening to this chapter explains, many small towns in rural areas (especially in the Plains States) are struggling to stay alive. But even there, losses slowed during the 1990s.

The greatest gains have come to rural communities that offer scenic and recreational attractions, such as lakes, mountains, and ski areas. People are drawn to rural communities not only by their natural beauty but also by their slower pace of life: less traffic, less crime, and cleaner air. A number of companies have relocated to rural counties, which has increased economic opportunity for the rural population (K. M. Johnson, 1999; Johnson & Fuguitt, 2000; D. Johnson, 2001).

Gemeinschaft a type of social organization in which people are closely tied by kinship and tradition

Gesellschaft a type of social organization in which people come together only on the basis of individual self-interest

SEEING SOCIOLOGY in Everyday Life

How might Tönnies explain social patterns such as our high rate of divorce, widespread fear of crime, and incidents of "road rage" on the highways?

Getty Images/Michael Smith

The rural rebound has been most pronounced in towns that offer spectacular natural beauty. There are times when people living in the scenic town of Park City, Utah, cannot even find a parking space.

Urbanism as a Way of Life

Early sociologists in Europe and the United States focused their attention on the rise of cities and how urban life differed from rural life. We briefly examine their accounts of urbanism as a way of life.

Ferdinand Tönnies: *Gemeinschaft* and *Gesellschaft*

In the late nineteenth century, the German sociologist Ferdinand Tönnies (1855–1937) studied how life in the new industrial metropolis differed from life in rural villages. From this contrast, he developed two concepts that have become a lasting part of sociology's terminology.

Tönnies (1963, orig. 1887) used the German word ***Gemeinschaft*** ("community") to refer to *a type of social organization in which people are closely tied by kinship and tradition.* The *Gemeinschaft* of the rural village joins people in what amounts to a single primary group.

By and large, argued Tönnies, *Gemeinschaft* is absent in the modern city. On the contrary, urbanization creates ***Gesellschaft*** ("association"), *a type of social organization in which people come together only on the basis of individual self-interest.* In the *Gesellschaft* way of life, individuals are motivated by their own needs rather than by a desire to help improve the well-being of everyone. By and large, city dwellers have little sense of community or common identity and look to others mainly when they need something. Tönnies saw in urbanization a weakening of close, long-lasting social relations in favor of the brief and impersonal ties or secondary relationships typical of business.

Emile Durkheim: Mechanical and Organic Solidarity

The French sociologist Emile Durkheim agreed with much of Tönnies's thinking about cities. However, Durkheim countered that urbanites do not lack social bonds; they simply organize social life differently than rural people.

Durkheim described traditional, rural life as *mechanical solidarity,* social bonds based on common sentiments and shared moral values. With its emphasis on tradition, Durkheim's concept of mechanical solidarity bears a striking similarity to Tönnies's *Gemeinschaft.* Urbanization erodes mechanical solidarity, Durkheim explained, but it also generates a new type of bonding, which he called *organic solidarity,* social bonds based on specialization and interdependence. This concept, which parallels Tönnies's *Gesellschaft,* reveals an important difference between the two thinkers. Both thought the growth of industrial cities weakened tradition, but Durkheim optimistically pointed to a new kind of solidarity. Where societies had been built on *likeness* (mechanical solidarity), Durkheim now saw social life based on *difference* (organic solidarity).

For Durkheim, urban society offered more individual choice, moral tolerance, and personal privacy than people find in rural villages. In sum, Durkheim thought that something is lost in the process of urbanization, but much is gained.

Georg Simmel: The Blasé Urbanite

The German sociologist Georg Simmel (1858–1918) offered a microanalysis of cities, studying how urban life shapes the everyday experience of individuals. According to Simmel, individuals perceive the city as a crush of people, objects, and events. To prevent being overwhelmed by all this stimulation, urbanites develop a *blasé attitude,* tuning out

SEEING SOCIOLOGY in Everyday Life

How would Simmel explain cases of people turning away from others in need on the grounds that they simply "don't want to get involved"?

MAKING THE GRADE

Tönnies's concept of *Gemeinschaft* corresponds to Durkheim's mechanical solidarity; *Gesellschaft* corresponds to organic solidarity.

Pieter Breughel the Elder (c. 1525/30-1569), *Peasant Dance*, c. 1565, Kunsthistorisches Museum, Vienna/Superstock, Inc.

Peasant Dance (left, c. 1565), by Pieter Breughel the Elder, conveys the essential unity of rural life forged by generations of kinship and neighborhood. By contrast, Lily Furedi's *Subway (right)* communicates the impersonality common to urban areas. Taken together, these paintings capture Tönnies's distinction between *Gemeinschaft* and *Gesellschaft*.

Pieter Breughel the Elder (c. 1525/30-1569), *Peasant Dance*, c. 1565, Kunsthistorisches Museum, Vienna/Superstock. Lily Furedi, American. *Subway*. Oil on canvas, 99 x 123 cm. National Collection of Fine Arts, Washington, D.C./Smithsonian Institute.

Lily Furedi (1896–1969) American, *Subway*, ca. 1934. Oil on canvas, 39 in. x 48 1/4 in. (99.1 x 122.6 cm). Transfer from the U.S. Department of the Interior, National Park Service. Smithsonian American Art Museum, Washington, DC, USA, Art Resource, NY

much of what goes on around them. Such detachment does not mean that city dwellers lack compassion for others; they simply keep their distance as a survival strategy so that they can focus their time and energy on the people and things that really matter to them.

The Chicago School: Robert Park and Louis Wirth

Sociologists in the United States soon joined the study of rapidly growing cities. Robert Park, a leader of the first U.S. sociology program at the University of Chicago, sought to add a street-level perspective by getting out and studying real cities. As he said of himself, "I suspect that I have actually covered more ground, tramping about in cities in different parts of the world, than any other living man" (1950:viii). Walking the streets, Park found the city to be an organized mosaic of distinctive ethnic communities, commercial centers, and industrial districts. Over time, he observed, these "natural areas" develop and change in relation to one another. To Park, the city was a living organism—a human kaleidoscope.

Another major figure in the Chicago School of urban sociology was Louis Wirth (1897–1952). Wirth (1938) is best known for blending the ideas of Tönnies, Durkheim, Simmel, and Park into a comprehensive theory of urban life.

Wirth began by defining the city as a setting with a large, dense, and socially diverse population. These traits result in an impersonal, superficial, and transitory way of life. Living among millions of others, urbanites come into contact with many more people than residents of rural areas. So when city people notice others at all, they usually know them not in terms of *who they are* but *what they do*—as, for instance, the bus driver, the florist, or the grocery store clerk. Specialized urban relationships are pleasant for all concerned, but self-interest rather than friendship is usually the main reason behind the interaction.

The impersonal nature of urban relationships, together with the great social diversity found in cities today, makes city dwellers more tolerant than rural villagers. Rural communities often jealously enforce their narrow traditions, but the heterogeneous population of a city rarely shares any single code of moral conduct (T. C. Wilson, 1985, 1995).

CRITICAL REVIEW In both Europe and the United States, early sociologists presented a mixed view of urban living. Rapid urbanization troubled Tönnies, and Wirth saw personal ties and traditional morality lost in the anonymous rush of the city. Durkheim and Park emphasized urbanism's positive face, pointing to more personal freedom and greater personal choice.

One problem with all these views is that they paint urbanism in broad strokes that overlook the effects of class, race, and gender. There are many kinds of urbanites—rich and poor, black and white, Anglo and Latino, women and men—all leading distinctive lives (Gans, 1968). As the Thinking About Diversity box explains, the share of minorities in the largest U.S. cities

urban ecology the study of the link between the physical and social dimensions of cities

THINKING ABOUT DIVERSITY: RACE, CLASS, & GENDER

Minorities Now a Majority in the Largest U.S. Cities

According to the results of the 2000 census, minorities—Hispanics, African Americans, and Asians—are now a majority of the population in 48 of the 100 largest U.S. cities, up from 30 in 1990.

What accounts for the change? One reason is that large cities have been losing their non-Hispanic white population. Santa Ana, California, for example, lost 38 percent of its 1990 white population; the drop was 40 percent in Birmingham, Alabama, and a whopping 53 percent in Detroit, Michigan. The white share of the population of all 100 of the largest cities fell from 52.1 percent in 1990 to 43.8 percent in 2000, as the figure shows.

But an even bigger reason for the minority-majority trend is the increase in immigration. Immigration, coupled with higher birth rates among new immigrants, resulted in a 43 percent gain in the Hispanic population (almost 4 million people) of the largest 100 cities between 1990 and 2000. The Asian population also surged by 40 percent (more than 1.1 million people). The African American population was steady over the course of the 1990s. Political officials and other policymakers have been watching these figures closely, for the future vitality of the largest U.S. cities depends on meeting the needs and welcoming the contributions of the swelling minority populations.

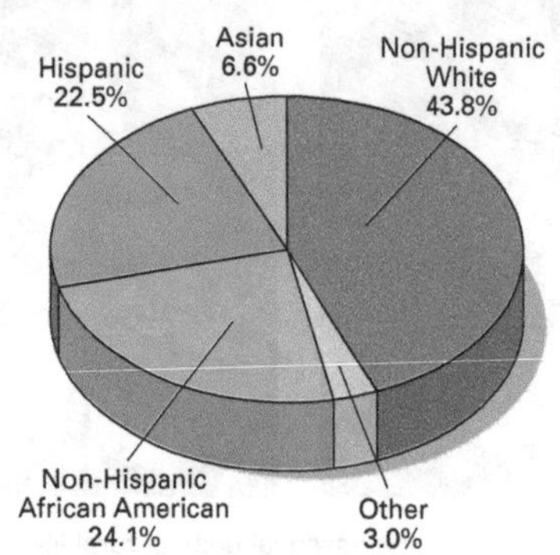

Population Profile for the 100 Largest U.S. Cities, 2000

Racial and ethnic minorities make up a majority of the population of this country's 100 largest cities.

Source: U.S. Census Bureau (2001).

WHAT DO YOU THINK?

1. Why are the minority populations of large U.S. cities increasing?
2. What positive changes and what challenges does a minority majority bring to a city?
3. Before Hurricane Katrina, African Americans represented 60 percent of the population of New Orleans; afterward, the share was about 40 percent. What difference might this change make in the city's immediate future?

Sources: Schmitt (2001) and U.S. Census Bureau (2008).

increased sharply during the 1990s. We see social diversity most clearly in cities, where various categories of people are large enough to form distinct, visible communities (Macionis & Parrillo, 2010).

CHECK YOUR LEARNING Of these urban sociologists—Tönnies, Durkheim, Park, and Wirth—which were more positive about urban life? Which were more negative? In each case, explain why.

Urban Ecology

Sociologists (especially members of the Chicago School) developed **urban ecology,** *the study of the link between the physical and social dimensions of cities.* One issue of interest to urban ecologists is why cities are located where they are. Broadly speaking, the first cities emerged in fertile regions where the ecology favored raising crops. In addition, preindustrial people were concerned with defense, so they built their cities on mountains (ancient Athens was perched on an outcropping of rock) or surrounded by water (Paris and Mexico City were founded on islands). With the coming of the Industrial Revolution, economic considerations gained importance, which explains why all the major U.S. cities were situated near rivers or natural harbors that facilitated trade.

Urban ecologists also study the physical design of cities. In 1925, Ernest W. Burgess, a student and colleague of Robert Park's, described land use in Chicago in terms of *concentric zones.* City centers, Burgess observed, are business districts bordered by a ring of factories, followed by residential rings with housing that becomes more expensive the farther it is from the noise and pollution of the city's center.

Homer Hoyt (1939) refined Burgess's observations, noting that distinctive districts sometimes form *wedge-shaped sectors.* For example, one fashionable area may develop next to another, or an industrial district may extend outward from a city's center along a train or trolley line.

Chauncy Harris and Edward Ullman (1945) added yet another insight: As cities decentralize, they lose their single-center form in favor of a *multicentered model.* As cities grow, residential areas, indus-

SEEING SOCIOLOGY in Everyday Life

The decline of industrial production is evident in the decline of industrial cities, such as Detroit.

trial parks, and shopping districts typically push away from one another. Few people wish to live close to industrial areas, for example, so the city becomes a mosaic of distinct districts.

Social area analysis investigates what people in particular neighborhoods have in common. Three factors seem to explain most of the variation: family patterns, social class, and race and ethnicity (Shevky & Bell, 1955; Johnston, 1976). Families with children look for areas with single-family homes or large apartments and good schools. The rich seek high-prestige neighborhoods, often in the central city near cultural attractions. People with a common race or ethnic heritage tend to cluster in distinctive communities.

Brian Berry and Philip Rees (1969) tie together many of these insights. They explain that distinct family types tend to settle in the concentric zones described by Burgess. Specifically, households with many children tend to live in the outer areas of a city, while "young singles" cluster toward the city's center. Social class differences are primarily responsible for the sector-shaped districts described by Hoyt—for instance, the rich occupy one "side of the tracks" and the poor the other. And racial and ethnic neighborhoods are found at various points throughout the city, consistent with Harris and Ullman's multicentered model.

AP Wide World Photos/Paul Sancya

The industrial revolution created great cities across the United States. In recent decades, however, the movement of industry abroad has brought decline to Detroit and other older cities in the "rustbelt." From this abandoned warehouse, we see the headquarters of General Motors, which, in 2009, declared bankruptcy. What do you see as the future of such cities?

Urban Political Economy

In the late 1960s, many large U.S. cities were rocked by riots. In the wake of this unrest, some analysts turned away from the ecological approach to a social-conflict understanding of city life. The *urban political economy* model applies Karl Marx's analysis of conflict in the workplace to conflict in the city (Lindstrom, 1995).

Political economists reject the ecological approach's view of the city as a natural organism with particular districts and neighborhoods developing according to an internal logic. They claim that city life is defined by larger institutional structures, especially the economy. Capitalism, which transforms the city into real estate traded for profit and concentrates wealth and power in the hands of the few, is the key to understanding city life. From this point of view, for example, the decline in industrial Snowbelt cities after 1950 was the result of deliberate decisions by the corporate elite to move their production facilities to the Sunbelt (where labor is cheaper and less likely to be unionized) or to move them out of the country entirely to low-income nations (Molotch, 1976; Castells, 1977, 1983; Lefebvre, 1991; Jones & Wilson, 1999).

CRITICAL REVIEW The fact that many U.S. cities are in crisis, with widespread poverty, high crime, and barely functioning schools, seems to favor the political economy model over the urban ecology approach. But one criticism applies to both: They focus on U.S. cities during a limited period of history. Much of what we know about industrial cities does not apply to preindustrial U.S. towns in our own past or to the rapidly growing cities in many poor nations today. It is unlikely that any single model of cities can account for the full range of urban diversity.

CHECK YOUR LEARNING In your own words, explain what the urban ecology theories and the urban political economy theory teach us about cities.

Urbanization in Poor Nations

November 16, Cairo, Egypt. People call the vast Muslim cemetery in Old Cairo the "City of the Dead". In truth, it is very much alive: Tens of thousands of squatters have moved into the mausoleums, making this place an eerie mix of life and death. Children run across the stone floors, clotheslines stretch between the monuments, and an occasional television antenna protrudes from a tomb roof. With Cairo's population increasing at the rate of 1,000 people a day, families live where they can.

MAKING THE GRADE

Be sure you understand when and where the three urban revolutions occurred.

ecology the study of the interaction of living organisms and the natural environment

natural environment Earth's surface and atmosphere, including living organisms, air, water, soil, and other resources necessary to sustain life

ecosystem a system composed of the interaction of all living organisms and their natural environment

environmental deficit profound long-term harm to the natural environment caused by humanity's focus on short-term material affluence

As noted earlier, twice in its history, the world has experienced a revolutionary expansion of cities. The first urban revolution began about 8000 B.C.E. with the first urban settlements and continued until permanent settlements were in place on several continents. About 1750, the second urban revolution took off; it lasted for two centuries as the Industrial Revolution spurred rapid growth of cities in Europe and North America.

A third urban revolution is now under way. Today, approximately 75 percent of people in industrial societies are already city dwellers. But extreme urban growth is occurring in low-income nations. In 1950, about 25 percent of the people in poor countries lived in cities. In 2008, the world became mostly urban for the first time in history with more than half of humanity living in cities (Population Reference Bureau, 2009).

Not only are more people urban; cities are also getting bigger. In 1950, only seven cities in the world had populations over 5 million, and only two of these were in low-income countries. By 2008, forty-nine cities had passed this mark, and thirty-two of them were in less developed nations (Brockerhoff, 2000; United Nations, 2008).

This third urban revolution is taking place because many poor nations have entered the high-growth Stage 2 of the demographic transition. Falling death rates have fueled population increases in Latin America, Asia, and especially Africa. For urban areas, the rate of increase is *twice* as high because in addition to natural increase, millions of people leave the countryside each year in search of jobs, health care, education, and conveniences such as running water and electricity.

Cities do offer more opportunities than rural areas, but they provide no quick fix for the massive problems of escalating population and grinding poverty. Many cities in less economically developed nations—including Mexico City, Egypt's Cairo, India's Kolkata (formerly Calcutta), and Manila in the Philippines—are simply unable to meet the basic needs of much of their populations. All these cities are surrounded by wretched shantytowns—settlements of makeshift homes built from discarded materials. Even city dumps are home to thousands of poor people, who pick through the piles of waste hoping to find enough to eat or sell to make it through another day.

Environment and Society

The human species has prospered, rapidly expanding over the entire planet. An increasing share of the global population now lives in cities, complex settlements that offer the promise of a better life than that found in rural villages.

But these advances have come at a high price. Never before in history have human beings placed such demands on the planet. This disturbing development brings us to the final section of this chapter: the interplay between the natural environment and society. Like demography, **ecology** is another cousin of sociology, formally defined as *the study of the interaction of living organisms and the natural environment.* Ecology rests on the research of natural scientists as well as social scientists. This text focuses on the aspects of ecology that involve familiar sociological concepts and issues.

The **natural environment** is *Earth's surface and atmosphere, including living organisms, air, water, soil, and other resources necessary to sustain life.* Like every other species, humans depend on the natural environment to survive. Yet with our capacity for culture, humans stand apart from other species; we alone take deliberate action to remake the world according to our own interests and desires, for better and for worse.

Why is the environment of interest to sociologists? Simply because environmental problems, from pollution to acid rain to global warming, do not arise from the natural world operating on its own. Such problems result from the specific actions of human beings, which means they are *social* problems.

The Global Dimension

The study of the natural environment requires a global perspective. The reason is simple: Regardless of political divisions among nations, the planet is a single **ecosystem,** *a system composed of the interaction of all living organisms and their natural environment.*

The Greek meaning of *eco* is "house," reminding us that this planet is our home and that all living things and their natural environment are interrelated. A change in any part of the natural environment ripples throughout the entire global ecosystem.

Consider, from an ecological point of view, our national love of hamburgers. People in North America (and, increasingly, around the world) have created a huge demand for beef, which has greatly expanded the ranching industry in Brazil, Costa Rica, and other Latin American nations. To produce the lean meat sought by fast-food corporations, cattle in Latin America feed on grass, which uses a great deal of land. Latin American ranchers get the land for grazing by clearing thousands of square miles of forests each year. These tropical forests are vital to maintaining Earth's atmosphere. Deforestation ends up threatening everyone, including people in the United States enjoying their hamburgers (N. Myers, 1984a).

Technology and the Environmental Deficit

Sociologists point to a simple formula: $I = PAT$, where environmental impact (I) reflects a society's population (P), its level of affluence (A), and its level of technology (T). Members of societies with simple technology—hunters and gatherers—hardly affect the

MAKING THE GRADE

I = PAT is an important environmental idea; be sure you understand its meaning.

SEEING SOCIOLOGY in Everyday Life

Can you identify ways in which the mass media and our popular culture (music, films, and television) encourage people to support the logic of growth?

environment because they are few in number, are poor, and have only simple technology. On the contrary, nature affects their lives as they follow the migration of game, watch the rhythm of the seasons, and suffer from natural catastrophes such as fires, floods, droughts, and storms.

Societies at intermediate stages of technological development have a somewhat greater capacity to affect the environment. Such societies are both larger and richer. But the environmental impact of horticulture (small-scale farming), pastoralism (the herding of animals), and even agriculture (the use of animal-drawn plows) is limited because people still rely on muscle power for producing food and other goods.

Humans' ability to control the natural environment increased dramatically with the Industrial Revolution. Muscle power gave way to engines that burn fossil fuels: coal at first and then oil. Such machinery affects the environment in two ways: We consume more natural resources, and we release more pollutants into the atmosphere. Even more important, armed with industrial technology, we are able to bend nature to our will, tunneling through mountains, damming rivers, irrigating deserts, and drilling for oil in the arctic wilderness and on the ocean floor. This explains why people in rich nations, who represent just 22 percent of humanity, account for half of the world's energy use (World Bank, 2008).

Not only do high-income societies use more energy, but they produce 100 times more goods than people in agrarian societies do. Higher living standards in turn increase the problem of solid waste (because people ultimately throw away most of what they produce) and pollution (industrial production generates smoke and other toxic substances).

From the start, people recognized the material benefits of industrial technology. But only a century later did they begin to see the long-term effects on the natural environment. Today, we realize that the technological power to make our lives better can also put the lives of future generations at risk, and there is a national debate about how to address this issue. Seeing Sociology in the News describes one high school's efforts to address environmental issues.

Evidence is mounting that we are running up an **environmental deficit,** *profound long-term harm to the natural environment caused by humanity's focus on short-term material affluence* (Bormann, 1990). The concept of environmental deficit is important for three reasons. First, it reminds us that environmental concerns are *sociological,* reflecting societies' priorities about how people should live. Second, it suggests that much environmental damage—to the air, land, and water—is *unintended.* By focusing on the short-term benefits of, say, cutting down forests, strip mining, or using throwaway packaging, we fail to see their long-term environmental effects. Third, in some respects, the environmental deficit is *reversible.* Societies have created environmental problems but can also undo many of them.

Corbis - NY//Wilfried Krecichwost/Zefa

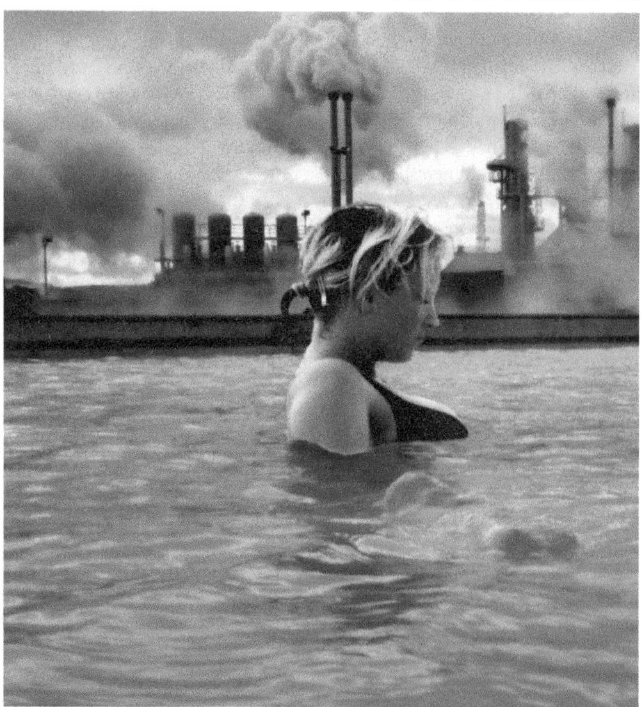

The most important insight sociology offers about our physical world is that environmental problems do not simply "happen." Rather, the state of the natural environment reflects the ways in which social life is organized—how people live and what they think is important. The greater the technological power of a society, the greater that society's ability to threaten the natural environment.

Culture: Growth and Limits

Whether we recognize environmental dangers and decide to do something about them is a cultural matter. Thus along with technology, culture has powerful environmental consequences.

The Logic of Growth

When you turn on the television news, you might hear a story like this: "The government reported bad economic news today, with the economy growing by only half a percent during the first quarter of the year." If you stop to think about it, our culture defines an economy that isn't growing as "stagnant" (which is bad) and an economy that is getting smaller as a "recession" or a "depression" (which is *very* bad). What is "good" is *growth*—the economy getting bigger and bigger. More cars, bigger homes, more income, more spending—the idea of *more* is at the heart of our cultural definition of living well (McKibben, 2007).

Seeing SOCIOLOGY in the 

Rolling Stone

Boyz Under the Hood

By DAVID KUSHNER
December 18, 2008

Even among the roughest schools in the country, West Philadelphia High School stands out. Situated among boarded-up abandoned buildings and graffiti-covered crack houses, the school has had dozens of arson fires. A Spanish teacher was beaten bloody with a fire extinguisher. A music instructor got a broken jaw after being slugged by a pupil for trying to take away a cell phone. One 15-year-old girl was left for dead after having her face slashed while waiting for her school bus. She survived, but needed 114 stitches.

But in the automotive shop class in a garage next door, a group of African American students and their scrappy white teacher are making their school famous for something else: building the world's greenest car. Kids in baggy jeans and sideways hats mill around a sleek purple car they built that runs on biodiesel. Sparks fly from a chainsaw as one boy cuts through an aluminum plate, his long afro held back by the strap of his scuffed goggles.

Behind a windowed wall, half a dozen girls are busy at their iMacs. Samantha Wright . . . boots up a solar charging station she designed using an image of a rundown Philadelphia parking lot from Google Earth, and augmented it with green roofs and cars. "The photoactive panels convert the sunlight into direct energy," she explains, pointing to a carport onscreen. "We're changing the world, man. I never expected to be doing that."

Like the other kids in the shop, Wright, the daughter of a phone sex worker and absentee dad, overcame incredible odds to find a haven here at the Electric Vehicle X Club, an after-school program that has been turning these cars and kids around, and that's not all. While Washington and Detroit hit the skids on delivering alternative fuel cars for the masses, these inner-city teens are churning out some of the most badass and competitive eco-wheels on the planet for as little as $15,000. As the blog Treehugger puts it, they're "sending a message to the major U.S. auto manufacturers: if we can do it, why can't you?"

In addition to clocking their suburban opponents at state science fairs, the EVX Club has crushed colleges and high-financed corporate start-ups with back-to-back titles in the coveted Northeast Sustainable Energy Association's Tour De Sol, a prestigious eco-car challenge. They modified a Saturn to run on soybean fuel, and transformed a Slovakian kit car into a wildly sporty hybrid called the Hybrid X. "Hybrids don't have to be slow and ugly like a Prius," says 18-year-old EV member, Lawrence Jones-Mahoney. "They can be efficient and cool."

Now the team is racing to prove their cars—and themselves—to the world. They're the dark horse entrants in the Progressive Automotive X-Prize: a worldwide contest to build a car, suitable for mass production, that gets 100 miles per gallon. The contest runs through summer 2010, and the winner gets $10 million. . . .

Simon Hauger, the 38-year-old neighborhood hero who runs the West Philly High auto school, is working overtime with his students to win. But the checkered flag is theirs. "The fact that

One of the reasons we define growth in positive terms is that we value *material comfort,* believing that money and the things it buys improve our lives. We also believe in the idea of *progress,* thinking the future will be better than the present. In addition, we look to *science* to make our lives easier and more rewarding. In simple terms, "having things is good," "life gets better," and "people are clever." Taken together, such cultural values form the *logic of growth.*

An optimistic view of the world, the logic of growth holds that more powerful technology has improved our lives and that new discoveries will continue to do so in the future. Throughout the history of the United States and other high-income nations, the logic of growth has been the driving force behind settling the wilderness, building towns and roads, and pursuing material affluence.

However, "progress" can lead to unexpected problems, including strain on the environment. The logic of growth responds by arguing that people (especially scientists and other technology experts) will find a way out of any problem that growth places in our path. For example, before the world runs short of oil, we will come up with hydrogen, solar, or nuclear engines or some other as yet unknown technology to meet the world's energy needs.

Environmentalists counter that the logic of growth is flawed because it assumes that natural resources such as oil, clean air, fresh water, and topsoil will always be plentiful. We can and will exhaust these *finite* resources if we continue to pursue growth at any cost. Echoing Malthus, environmentalists warn that if we call on Earth to support increasing numbers of people, we will surely deplete finite resources, destroying the environment—and ourselves—in the process.

The Limits to Growth

If we cannot invent our way out of the problems created by the logic of growth, perhaps we need another way of thinking about the world. Environmentalists therefore counter that growth must have limits. Stated simply, the *limits-to-growth thesis* is that humanity must put in place policies to control the growth of population, production, and use of resources in order to avoid environmental collapse.

In *The Limits to Growth,* a controversial book that was influential in launching the environmental movement, Donella Meadows and her colleagues (1972) used a computer model to calculate the planet's available resources, rates of population growth, amount of land available for cultivation, levels of industrial and food production, and amount of pollutants released into the atmosphere. The authors concede that any long-range predictions are speculative, and some critics think they are plain wrong (Simon, 1981). But right or wrong, the conclusions of the study call for serious consideration. First, the authors claim that we are quickly we've come this far," Hauger says, looking around the room, "we've already won." . . .

When a go-kart was donated to the school, Hauger decided to start an after-school science group that would work on building an electric motor for the kart. He called it the Electric Vehicle Club. One by one, kids trickled in after school—gang members, drug dealers. One kid had a 150 IQ, but a mom on crack and a dad dying of AIDS. The kid was bouncing between foster homes and stealing credit cards on the side. But when Hauger slapped a wrench in the kid's hand, he was transformed. "When he would work on a project, he would block out all the crap in his life," Hauger recalls, "and he became a mad scientist. Working on this made all the math and science hands on." . . .

As word of Hauger's club spread, kids got turned on not only by getting under the hood, but by making cars that can better the planet—and busting labels along the way. "There's a stereotype that urban kids are just violent and don't care about anything," says Wright, "but we know the environment is important, and we can do something about it."

For the EV club's next project, they modified a silver Jeep Wrangler to go electric. Clueless how to proceed, they hit the Net—downloading instructions from an obscure eco-geek magazine called *Mother Earth*. With Hauger guiding them and improvising plenty, they ripped out the gas engine and stored 217 lead acid batteries in a custom aluminum casing. When they drove their electric hot rod Jeep into the city's science fair of microscopes and Bunsen burners, jaws dropped. "The judges didn't know what to do with it," Hauger recalls. Then they gave West Philly High the top prize. . . .

As the current 15 kids on the EVX team mill around the garage, talk turns to the plans for the Auto X prize. "As crazy as it sounds, I think we have a shot at winning," Hauger says. While the competition is focusing on high-priced cars that look like the Jetsons, the EVX team is taking a decidedly more accessible—and they hope—winning approach. . . .

. . . The EVX team's legacy is already spreading among those in the eco-car pursuit. "It's inspiring that a contest can inspire a group like that to compete," says Darryl Siry, spokesperson for Tesla, "it says something about who they are. I recommend they not listen to people who tell them this is how it's done. Innovation comes from figuring out solutions and answers to problems in new ways."

WHAT DO YOU THINK?

1. Do you think that many people think of environmental issues as the concerns mainly of more well-off people? Explain.
2. Would you make environmental study part of the curriculum of every school in the country? Why or why not?
3. What specific strategies or policies would you suggest to encourage greater environmental understanding on the part of this country's young people?

consuming Earth's finite resources. Supplies of oil, natural gas, and other energy sources are declining, and will continue to drop, a little faster or slower depending on the conservation policies of rich nations and the speed with which other nations such as India and China continue to industrialize. Within the next 100 years, resources will run out, crippling industrial output and causing a decline in food production.

This limits-to-growth theory shares Malthus's pessimism about the future. People who accept it doubt that current patterns of life are sustainable for even another century. Perhaps we all can learn to live with less. This may not be as hard as you might think: Research shows, for example, that as material consumption has gone up in recent decades, there has been no increase in levels of personal happiness (D. G. Myers, 2000). In the end, environmentalists warn, either make fundamental changes in how we live, placing less strain on the natural environment, or widespread hunger and conflict will force change on us.

Solid Waste: The Disposable Society

Across the United States, people generate a massive amount of solid waste—about 1.4 billion pounds *every day*. Figure 4 shows the average composition of a typical community's trash.

As a rich nation of people who value convenience, the United States has become a *disposable society*. We consume more products than virtually any other nation, and many of these products have throwaway packaging. For example, fast food is served with cardboard, plastic, and Styrofoam containers that we throw away within minutes. Countless other products, from film to fishhooks, are elaborately packaged to make the products more attractive to the customer and to discourage tampering and theft.

Manufacturers market soft drinks, beer, and fruit juices in aluminum cans, glass jars, and plastic containers, which not only consume finite resources but also generate mountains of solid waste. Then there are countless items intentionally designed to be disposable: pens, razors, flashlights, batteries, even cameras. Other products, from light bulbs to automobiles, are designed to have a limited useful life and then become unwanted junk. As Paul Connett (1991) points out, even the words we use to describe what we throw away—*waste, litter, trash, refuse, garbage, rubbish*—show how little we value what we cannot immediately use. But this was not always the case, as the Seeing Sociology in Everyday Life box later in this chapter explains.

Living in a rich society, the average person in the United States consumes hundreds of times more energy, plastics, lumber, water, and other resources than someone living in a low-income country such as Bangladesh or Tanzania and nearly twice as much as people

SEEING SOCIOLOGY in Everyday Life

Do you think that having more, in a materialistic sense, is the path to personal happiness? Why or why not?

SEEING SOCIOLOGY in Everyday Life

Think about how specific ways we live put more or less strain on the natural environment.

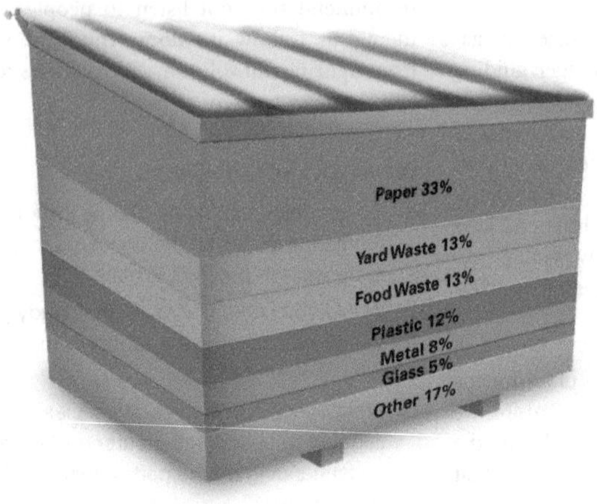

FIGURE 4 **Composition of Community Trash**

We throw away a wide range of material, with paper the single largest part of our trash.

Source: U.S. Environmental Protection Agency (2008).

in some other high-income countries such as Sweden and Japan. This high level of consumption means not only that we in the United States use a disproportionate share of the planet's natural resources but also that we generate most of the world's refuse.

We like to say that we throw things "away." But most of our solid waste never goes away. Rather, it ends up in landfills, which are, literally, filling up. Material in landfills can pollute underground water supplies. Although in most places, laws now regulate what can be discarded in a landfill, the Environmental Protection Agency has identified 1,331 dump sites across the United States containing hazardous materials that are polluting water both above and below the ground. In addition, what goes into landfills all too often stays there, sometimes for centuries. Tens of millions of tires, diapers, and other items we bury in landfills each year do not decompose but will remain as an unwelcome legacy for future generations.

Environmentalists argue that we should address the problem of solid waste by doing what many of our grandparents did: Use less and turn "waste" into a resource. Part of the solution is *recycling,* reusing resources we would otherwise discard. Recycling is an accepted practice in Japan and many other nations, and it is becoming more common in the United States, where we now reuse about one-third of waste materials (U.S. Environmental Protection Agency, 2008). The share is increasing as laws require the recovery and reuse of certain materials such as glass bottles and aluminum cans and as the business of recycling becomes more profitable.

Water and Air

Oceans, lakes, and streams are the lifeblood of the global ecosystem. Humans depend on water for drinking, bathing, cooking, cleaning, recreation, and a host of other activities.

According to what scientists call the *hydrologic cycle,* Earth naturally recycles water and refreshes the land. The process begins as heat from the sun causes Earth's water, 97 percent of which is in the oceans, to evaporate and form clouds. Because water evaporates at lower temperatures than most pollutants, the water vapor that rises from the seas is relatively pure, leaving various contaminants behind. Water then falls to the Earth as rain, which drains into streams and rivers and finally returns to the sea. Two major concerns about water, then, are supply and pollution.

Water Supply

Less than 1 percent of Earth's water is suitable for drinking. It is not surprising, then, that for thousands of years, water rights have figured prominently in laws around the world. Today, some regions of the world, especially the tropics, enjoy plentiful fresh water, using a small share of the available supply. However, high demand, coupled with modest reserves, makes water supply a matter of concern in much of North America and Asia, where people look to rivers rather than rainfall for their water. In China, aquifers are dropping rapidly. In the Middle East, water supply is reaching a critical level. Iran is rationing water in its capital city. In Egypt, the Nile River provides just one-sixth as much water per person as it did in 1900. Across northern Africa and the Middle East, as many as 1 billion people may lack the water they need for irrigation and drinking by 2025 (United Nations Environmental Programme, 2008).

Rising population and the development of more complex technology have greatly increased the world's appetite for water. The global consumption of water (now estimated at 150 billion cubic feet per year) has tripled since 1950 and is rising steadily. As a result, even in parts of the world that receive plenty of rainfall, people are using groundwater faster than it can be replenished naturally. In the Tamil Nadu region of southern India, for example, so much groundwater is being used that the water table has fallen 100 feet over the last several decades. Mexico City—which has sprawled to some 1,400 square miles—has pumped so much water from its underground aquifer that the city has sunk 30 feet during the past century and continues to drop about 2 inches per year. Farther north in the United States, the Ogallala aquifer, which lies below seven states from South Dakota to Texas, is now being pumped so rapidly that some experts fear it could run dry in just a few decades.

In light of such developments, we must face the reality that water is a valuable and finite resource. Greater conservation of water by individuals (the average person consumes 359,000 gallons in a

SEEING SOCIOLOGY in Everyday Life

Las Vegas is one of the fastest-growing U.S. cities—and it is built in a desert. Do you think the future water needs of this city's people (and those of the entire Southwest) are ensured? What will we do if the answer turns out to be no?

SEEING SOCIOLOGY IN EVERYDAY LIFE

Why Grandma Macionis Had No Trash

Grandma Macionis, we always used to say, never threw anything away. She was born and raised in Lithuania—the "old country"—where life in a poor village shaped her in ways that never changed, even after she came to the United States as a young woman and settled in Philadelphia.

In her later years, when I knew her, I can remember the family traveling together to her house to celebrate her birthday. We never knew what to get Grandma, because she never seemed to need anything. She lived a simple life and had simple clothes and showed little interest in "fancy things." She used everything until it wore out. Her kitchen knives, for example, were worn narrow from decades of sharpening. And she hardly ever threw anything away—she recycled all her garbage as compost for her vegetable garden.

After opening a birthday present, she would carefully save the box, wrapping paper, and ribbon, which meant as much to her as whatever gift they surrounded. We all expected her to save every bit of whatever she was given, smiling to each other as we watched her put everything away, knowing she would find a way to use it all again and again.

As strange as Grandma sometimes seemed to her grandchildren, she was a product of her culture. A century ago, in fact, there was little "trash." If socks wore thin, people mended them, probably more than once. When they were beyond repair, they were used as rags for cleaning or sewn with bits of other old clothing into a quilt. Everything had value—if not in one way, then in another.

Culver Pictures, Inc.

During the twentieth century, as women joined men in working outside the home, income went up, and families began buying more and more "time-saving" products. Before long, few people cared about the kind of recycling that Grandma practiced. Soon cities sent crews from block to block to pick up truckloads of discarded material. The era of "trash" had begun.

WHAT DO YOU THINK?

1. Just as Grandma Macionis was a product of her culture, so are we. Do you know people who have plenty but never seem to think they have enough?
2. What cultural values make people today demand time-saving products and "convenience" packaging?
3. In what ways does this box show that the state of the natural environment is a social issue?

lifetime) is part of the answer. However, households around the world account for just 5 percent of water use. It is even more crucial that we curb water consumption by industry, which uses 20 percent of the global total, and farming, which consumes 75 percent of the total for irrigation.

Perhaps new irrigation technology will reduce the future demand for water. But here again, we see how population increase, as well as economic growth, strains our ecosystem (Population Action International, 2000; United Nations Environmental Programme, 2008).

Water Pollution

In large cities from Mexico City to Cairo to Shanghai, many people have no choice but to drink contaminated water. Infectious diseases such as typhoid, cholera, and dysentery, all caused by waterborne microorganisms, spread rapidly through these populations. Besides ensuring ample *supplies* of water, then, we must also protect the *quality* of water.

Water quality in the United States is generally good by global standards. However, even here the problem of water pollution is steadily growing. According to the Sierra Club (2009), an environmental activist organization, U.S. society produces some 500 million pounds of toxic waste each year, and much of it ends up in our rivers and streams. This pollution results not just from intentional dumping but also from the runoff of agricultural fertilizers and lawn chemicals.

A special problem is *acid rain*—precipitation made acidic by air pollution—which destroys plant and animal life. Acid rain begins with power plants burning fossil fuels (oil and coal) to generate electricity; this burning releases sulfuric and nitrous oxides into the air. As the wind sweeps these gases into the atmosphere, they react with the air to form sulfuric and nitric acids, which turns atmospheric moisture acidic.

This is a clear case of one type of pollution causing another: Air pollution (from smokestacks) ends up contaminating water (in lakes and streams that collect acid rain). Acid rain is truly a global phenomenon because the regions that suffer the harmful effects may be

SEEING SOCIOLOGY in Everyday Life

Have you experienced changes in your own world resulting from global warming or other issues discussed here?

rain forests regions of dense forestation, most of which circle the globe close to the equator

global warming a rise in Earth's average temperature due to an increasing concentration of carbon dioxide in the atmosphere

Landov Media/Dave Amit/Reuters

Water is vital to life, and it is also in short supply. The state of Gujarat, in western India, has experienced a long drought. In the village of Natwarghad, people crowd together, lowering pots into the local well, taking what little water is left.

thousands of miles from the source of the original pollution. For instance, British power plants have caused acid rain that has devastated forests and fish in Norway and Sweden, up to 1,000 miles to the northeast. In the United States, we see a similar pattern as midwestern smokestacks have harmed the natural environment of upstate New York and New England.

Air Pollution

Because we are surrounded by air, most people in the United States are more aware of air pollution than contaminated water. One of the unexpected consequences of industrial technology, especially the factory and the motor vehicle, has been a decline in air quality. In London in the mid-twentieth century, factory smokestacks, automobiles, and coal fires used to heat homes all added up to what was probably the worst urban air quality the world has ever known. The fog that some British jokingly called "pea soup" was in reality a deadly mix of pollutants: In 1952, an especially thick haze that hung over London for five days killed 4,000 people.

Air quality improved in the final decades of the twentieth century. Rich nations passed laws that banned high-pollution heating, including the coal fires that choked London. In addition, scientists devised ways to make factories and motor vehicles operate much more cleanly. In fact, today's vehicles produce only a fraction of the pollution that spewed from models of the 1950s and 1960s. And cleaner air has improved human health: Experts estimate that improvement in U.S. air quality over the past several decades has added almost half a year to the average life span (Chang, 2009).

If high-income countries can breathe a bit more easily than they once did, the problem of air pollution in poor societies is becoming more serious. One reason is that people in low-income countries still rely on wood, coal, peat, and other "dirty" fuels to cook their food and heat their homes. In addition, nations eager to encourage short-term industrial development may pay little attention to the longer-term dangers of air pollution. As a result, many cities in Latin America, Eastern Europe, and Asia are plagued by air pollution as bad as London's "pea soup" back in the 1950s.

The Rain Forests

Rain forests are *regions of dense forestation, most of which circle the globe close to the equator.* The largest tropical rain forests are in South America (notably Brazil), west-central Africa, and Southeast Asia. In all, the world's rain forests cover some 1.5 billion acres, or 4.5 percent of Earth's total land surface.

Like other global resources, rain forests are falling victim to the needs and appetites of the surging world population. As noted earlier, to meet the demand for beef, ranchers in Latin America burn forested areas to increase their supply of grazing land. We are also losing rain forests to the hardwood trade. People in rich nations pay high prices for mahogany and other woods because, as the environmentalist Norman Myers (1984b:88) puts it, they have "a penchant for parquet floors, fine furniture, fancy paneling, weekend yachts, and high-grade coffins." Under such economic pressure, the world's rain forests are now just half their original size, and they continue to shrink by at least 1 percent (58,000 square miles) annually, which amounts to about an acre every second. Unless we stop this loss, the rain forests will vanish before the end of this century, and with them will go protection for Earth's biodiversity and climate (Rainforest Foundation, 2009).

Global Warming

Why are rain forests so important? One reason is that they cleanse the atmosphere of carbon dioxide (CO_2). Since the beginning of the Industrial Revolution, the amount of carbon dioxide produced by humans, mostly from factories and automobiles, has risen sharply. Much of this carbon dioxide is absorbed by the oceans. But plants also take in carbon dioxide and expel oxygen. This is why rain forests are vital to maintaining the chemical balance of the atmosphere.

The problem is that production of carbon dioxide is rising while the amount of plant life on Earth is shrinking. To make matters worse,

SEEING SOCIOLOGY in Everyday Life

Do you worry much about global warming? Why or why not?
Do you think global warming could affect you personally? How?

environmental racism patterns of development that expose poor people, especially minorities, to environmental hazards

rain forests are being destroyed mostly by burning, which releases even more carbon dioxide into the atmosphere. Experts estimate that the atmospheric concentration of carbon dioxide is now 40 percent higher than it was 150 years ago and rising rapidly (Gore, 2006; Adam, 2008).

High above Earth, carbon dioxide acts like the glass roof of a greenhouse, letting heat from the sun pass through to the surface while preventing much of it from radiating away from the planet. The result of this *greenhouse effect,* say ecologists, is **global warming,** *a rise in Earth's average temperature due to an increasing concentration of carbon dioxide in the atmosphere.* Over the past century, the global temperature has risen about 1.3° Fahrenheit (to an average of 58° F). Scientists warn that it could rise by 5° to 10° F during this century. Already, the polar ice caps are melting, and scientists predict that increasing average temperatures could melt so much ice that the sea level would rise enough to cover low-lying land all around the world: Water would cover all of Bangladesh, for example, and much of the coastal United States, including Washington, D.C., right up to the steps of the White House. On the other hand, the U.S. Midwest, currently one of the most productive agricultural regions in the world, would probably become more arid.

Some scientists point out that we cannot be sure of the consequences of global warming. Others point to the fact that global temperature changes have been taking place throughout history, apparently having little or nothing to do with rain forests or human activity. A few are optimistic, suggesting that higher concentrations of carbon dioxide in the atmosphere might speed up plant growth (since plants thrive on this gas), and this increase would correct the imbalance and push Earth's temperature downward once again. But the consensus of scientists is now clear: Global warming is a serious problem that threatens the future of all of us (Kerr, 2005; Gore, 2006; International Panel on Climate Change, 2007; Singer, 2007).

Declining Biodiversity

Our planet is home to as many as 30 million species of animals, plants, and microorganisms. As rain forests are cleared and humans extend their control over nature, several dozen unique species of plants and animals cease to exist each day, reducing the planet's *biodiversity.*

But given the vast number of living species, why should we be concerned by the loss of a few? Environmentalists give four reasons. First, our planet's biodiversity provides a varied source of human food. Using agricultural high technology, scientists can "splice" familiar crops with more exotic plant life, making food more bountiful as well as more resistant to insects and disease. Thus biodiversity helps feed our planet's rapidly increasing population.

Second, Earth's biodiversity is a vital genetic resource used by medical and pharmaceutical researchers to produce hundreds of new compounds each year that cure disease and improve our lives. For example, children in the United States now have a good chance of surviving leukemia, a disease that was almost a sure killer two generations ago, because of a compound derived from a tropical flower called the rosy periwinkle. The oral birth control pill, used by tens of millions of women in this country, is another product of plant research involving the Mexican forest yam.

Third, with the loss of any species of life—whether it is the magnificent California condor, the famed Chinese panda, the spotted owl, or even a single species of ant—the beauty and complexity of our natural environment are diminished. And there are clear warning signs of such loss: Three-fourths of the world's 10,000 species of birds are declining in number.

Finally, unlike pollution, the extinction of any species is irreversible and final. An important ethical question, then, is whether we who live today have the right to impoverish the world for those who live tomorrow (E. O. Wilson, 1991; Brown et al., 1993).

Environmental Racism

Conflict theory has given rise to the concept of **environmental racism,** *patterns of development that expose poor people, especially minorities, to environmental hazards.* Historically, factories that spew pollution have stood near neighborhoods of the poor and people of color. Why? In part, the poor themselves were drawn to factories in

Members of small, simple societies, such as the Mentawi in Indonesia, live in harmony with nature; they do not have the technological means to greatly affect the natural world. Although we in complex societies like to think of ourselves as superior to such people, the truth is that there is much we can—indeed, must—learn from them.

MAKING THE GRADE

With its focus on inequality, environmental racism is linked to the social-conflict approach.

ecologically sustainable culture a way of life that meets the needs of the present generation without threatening the environmental legacy of future generations

search of work, and their low incomes often meant they could afford housing only in undesirable neighborhoods. Sometimes the only housing that fit their budgets stood in the very shadow of the plants and mills where they worked.

Nobody wants a factory or dump nearby, but the poor have little power to resist. Through the years, the most serious environmental hazards have been located near Newark, New Jersey (not in upscale Bergen County), in southside Chicago (not wealthy Lake Forest), or on Native American reservations in the West (not in affluent suburbs of Denver or Phoenix) (Commission for Racial Justice, 1994; Bohon & Humphrey, 2000).

Looking Ahead: Toward a Sustainable Society and World

The demographic analysis presented in this chapter reveals some disturbing trends. We see, first, that Earth's population has reached record levels because birth rates remain high in poor nations and death rates have fallen just about everywhere. Reducing fertility will remain a pressing need throughout this century. Even with some recent decline in the rate of population increase, the nightmare Thomas Malthus described is still a real possibility, as the Controversy & Debate box explains.

Getty Images, Inc. - Agence France Presse/Valery Hache

If human ingenuity created the threats to our environment we now face, can humans also solve these problems? In recent years, a number of designs for small, environmentally friendly cars show the promise of new technology. But do such innovations go far enough? Will we have to make more basic changes to our way of life to ensure human survival in the centuries to come?

Further, population growth remains greatest in the poorest countries of the world, which cannot meet the needs of their present populations, much less future ones. Supporting 80 million additional people on our planet each year, 78 million of them in low-income countries, will require a global commitment to provide not just food but housing, schools, and employment as well. The well-being of the entire world may ultimately depend on resolving the economic and social problems of poor, overly populated countries and bridging the widening gulf between "have" and "have-not" nations.

Urbanization is continuing, especially in poor countries. For thousands of years, people have sought out cities in the hope of finding a better life. But the sheer numbers of people who live in today's supercities—including Mexico City, São Paulo (Brazil), Kinshasa (Democratic Republic of the Congo), Mumbai (India), and Manila (Philippines)—have created urban problems on a massive scale.

Around the world, humanity is facing a serious environmental challenge. Part of this problem is population increase, which is greatest in poor countries. But part of the problem is the high levels of consumption in rich nations such as our own. By increasing the planet's environmental deficit, our present way of life is borrowing against the well-being of our children and their children. Globally, members of rich societies, who currently consume so much of Earth's resources, are mortgaging the future security of the poor countries of the world.

The answer, in principle, is to create an **ecologically sustainable culture,** *a way of life that meets the needs of the present generation without threatening the environmental legacy of future generations.* Sustainable living depends on three strategies.

First, the world needs to *bring population growth under control.* The current population of 6.7 billion is already straining the natural environment. Clearly, the higher the world's population climbs, the more difficult environmental problems will become. Even if the recent slowing of population growth continues, the world will have about 9 billion people by 2050. Few analysts think that the planet can support this many people; most argue that we must hold the line at about 7 billion, and some argue that we must *decrease* population in the coming decades (Smail, 2007).

A second strategy is to *conserve finite resources.* This means meeting our needs with a responsible eye toward the future by using resources efficiently, seeking alternative sources of energy, and in some cases, learning to live with less.

A third strategy is to *reduce waste.* Whenever possible, simply using less is the best solution. Learning to live with less is not likely to come easily, but keep in mind the research that suggests that as our society has consumed more and more, people have not become any happier (D. G. Myers, 2000). Recycling programs, too, are part of

SEEING SOCIOLOGY in Everyday Life

What share of the world's people do you think are concerned about global population increase?

CONTROVERSY & DEBATE

Apocalypse: Will People Overwhelm the Planet?

NUSHAWN: I'm telling you, there are too many people already! Where is everyone going to live?

TABITHA: Have you ever been to Kansas? Or Wyoming? There's plenty of empty space out there.

MARCO: Maybe now. But I'm not so sure about our children—or their children. . . .

Are you worried about the world's increasing population? Think about this: By the time you finish reading this box, more than 1,000 people will have been added to our planet. By this time tomorrow, global population will have risen by nearly 220,000. Currently, as the table shows, there are more than four births for every two deaths on the planet, pushing the world's population upward by 80 million annually. Put another way, global population growth amounts to adding another Ethiopia to the world each year.

It is no wonder that many demographers and environmentalists are deeply concerned about the future. Earth has an unprecedented population: The 2.7 billion people we have added since 1974 alone exceed the planet's total in 1900. Might Thomas Robert Malthus, who predicted that overpopulation would push the world into war and suffering, be right after all? Lester Brown and other *neo-Malthusians* predict a coming apocalypse if we do not change our ways. Brown admits that Malthus failed to imagine how much technology (especially fertilizers and altering plant genetics) could boost the planet's agricultural output. But he maintains that Earth's rising population is rapidly outstripping its finite resources. Families in many poor countries can find little firewood, members of rich countries are depleting the oil reserves, and everyone is draining our supply of clean water and poisoning the planet with waste. Some analysts argue that we have already passed Earth's "carrying capacity" for population and we need to hold the line or even reduce global population to ensure our long-term survival.

But other analysts, the *anti-Malthusians,* sharply disagree. Julian Simon points out that two centuries after Malthus predicted catastrophe, Earth supports almost six times as many people who, on average, live longer, healthier lives than ever before. With more advanced technology, people have devised ways to increase productivity and limit population increase. As Simon sees it, this is cause for celebration. Human ingenuity has consistently proved the doomsayers wrong, and Simon is betting it will continue to do so.

Global Population Increase, 2009

	Births	Deaths	Net Increase
Per year	135,474,672	55,644,164	79,810,508
Per month	11,289,556	4,638,680	6,650,876
Per day	371,163	152,505	218,659
Per hour	15,465	6,354	9,111
Per minute	258	106	152
Per second	4.3	1.8	2.5

WHAT DO YOU THINK?

1. Where do you place your bet? Do you think Earth can support 8 or 10 billion people? Explain your reasoning.
2. Fully 97% percent of current population growth is in poor countries. What does this mean for the future of rich nations? For the future of poor ones?
3. What should people in rich countries do to ensure the future of children everywhere?

Sources: Brown (1995), Simon (1995), Scanlon (2001), Smail (2007), and U.S. Census Bureau (2009).

the answer, and recycling can make everyone part of the solution to our environmental problems.

In the end, making all these strategies work depends on a basic change in the way we think about ourselves and our world. Our *egocentric* outlook sets our own interests as standards for how to live, but a sustainable environment demands an *ecocentric* outlook that helps us see how the present is tied to the future and why everyone must work together. Most nations in the southern half of the world are *underdeveloped,* unable to meet the basic needs of their people. At the same time, most countries in the northern half of the world are *overdeveloped,* using more resources than the planet can sustain over time. The changes needed to create a sustainable ecosystem will not come easily, and they will be costly. But the price of not responding to the growing environmental deficit will certainly be greater (Kellert & Bormann, 1991; Brown et al., 1993; Population Action International, 2000; Gore, 2006).

Finally, consider that the great dinosaurs dominated this planet for some 160 million years and then perished forever. Humanity is far younger, having existed for a mere 250,000 years. Compared to the rather dimwitted dinosaurs, our species has the gift of great intelligence. But how will we use this ability? What are the chances that our species will continue to flourish 160 million years—or even 160 years—from now? The answer depends on the choices that will be made by one of the 30 million species living on Earth: human beings.

Seeing Sociology in Everyday Life

Population, Urbanization, and Environment

Why is the environment a social issue?

As this chapter explains, the state of the natural environment depends on how society is organized, especially the importance a culture attaches to consumption and economic growth.

HINT If expansion is "good times," then contraction is a "recession" or perhaps even a "depression." Such a worldview means that it is normal—or even desirable—to live in a way that increases stress on the natural environment. Sustainability, an idea that is especially important as world population increases, depends on learning to live with what we have or maybe even learning to live with less. Although many people seem to think so, it really doesn't require a 6,000-pound SUV to move around urban areas. Actually, it might not require a car at all. This new way of thinking requires that we do not define social standing and personal success in terms of what we own and what we consume. Can you imagine a society like that? What would it be like?

Newscom/Richard B. Levine

We learn to see economic expansion as natural and good. When the economy stays the same for a number of months, we say we are experiencing "stagnation." How do we define a period when the economy gets smaller, as happened during the fall of 2008?

What would it take to convince members of our society that smaller (rather than bigger) might be better? Why do we seem to prefer not just bigger cars but bigger homes and more and more material possessions?

Applying SOCIOLOGY in Everyday Life

1. Here is an illustration of the problem of runaway growth (Milbrath, 1989:10): "A pond has a single water lily growing on it. The lily doubles in size each day. In thirty days, it covers the entire pond. On which day does it cover half the pond?" When you realize the answer, discuss the implications of this example for population increase.
2. Draw a mental map of a city familiar to you with as much detail of specific places, districts, roads, and transportation facilities as you can. Compare your map to a real one or, better yet, a map drawn by someone else. Try to account for the differences.
3. As an interesting exercise, carry a trash bag around for a single day, and collect everything you throw away. Most people are surprised to find that the average person in the United States discards close to 5 pounds of paper, metal, plastic, and other materials daily (over a lifetime, that's about 50 tons).

Population, Urbanization, and Environment

Demography: The Study of Population

✓ *Demography analyzes the size and composition of a population and how and why people move from place to place. Demographers collect data and study several factors that affect population.*

FERTILITY
- Fertility is the incidence of childbearing in a country's population.
- Demographers describe fertility using the **crude birth rate**.

MORTALITY
- Mortality is the incidence of death in a country's population.
- Demographers measure mortality using both the **crude death rate** and the **infant mortality rate.**

MIGRATION
The **net migration rate** is the difference between the in-migration rate and the out-migration rate.

POPULATION GROWTH
In general, rich nations grow almost as much from immigration as from natural increase; poorer nations grow almost entirely from natural increase.

POPULATION COMPOSITION
Demographers use **age-sex pyramids** to show the composition of a population graphically and to project population trends.

demography the study of human population

fertility the incidence of childbearing in a country's population

crude birth rate the number of live births in a given year for every 1,000 people in a population

mortality the incidence of death in a country's population

crude death rate the number of deaths in a given year for every 1,000 people in a population

infant mortality rate the number of deaths among infants under one year of age for each 1,000 live births in a given year

life expectancy the average life span of a country's population

migration the movement of people into and out of a specified territory

sex ratio the number of males for every 100 females in a nation's population

age-sex pyramid a graphic representation of the age and sex of a population

History and Theory of Population Growth

- Historically, world population grew slowly because high birth rates were offset by high death rates.
- About 1750, a demographic transition began as world population rose sharply, mostly due to falling death rates.
- In the late 1700s, Thomas Robert Malthus warned that population growth would outpace food production, resulting in social calamity.
- **Demographic transition theory** contends that technological advances gradually slow population increase.
- World population is expected to reach between 8 billion and 9 billion by 2050.

✓ *Currently, the world is gaining 80 million people each year, with 97% of this increase taking place in poor countries.*

demographic transition theory a thesis that links population patterns to a society's level of technological development

zero population growth the rate of reproduction that maintains population at a steady level

Urbanization: The Growth of Cities

The **FIRST URBAN REVOLUTION** began with the appearance of cities about 10,000 years ago.
- By about 2,000 years ago, cities had emerged in most regions of the world except North America and Antarctica.
- Preindustrial cities have low-rise buildings; narrow, winding streets; and personal social ties.

A **SECOND URBAN REVOLUTION** began about 1750 as the Industrial Revolution propelled rapid urban growth in Europe.
- The physical form of cities changed as planners created wide, regular streets to facilitate commerce.
- The emphasis on business, as well as the increasing size of cities, made urban life more impersonal.

urbanization the concentration of population into cities

metropolis a large city that socially and economically dominates an urban area

suburbs urban areas beyond the political boundaries of a city

megalopolis a vast urban region containing a number of cities and their surrounding suburbs

IN THE UNITED STATES, urbanization has been going on for more than 400 years and continues today.
- Urbanization came to North America with European colonists.
- By 1850, hundreds of new cities had been founded from coast to coast.
- By 1920, a majority of the U.S. population lived in urban areas.
- Since 1950, the decentralization of cities has resulted in the growth of suburbs and edge cities and a "rebound" in rural population.
- Nationally, Sunbelt cities—but not the older Snowbelt cities—are increasing in size and population.

Urbanism as a Way of Life

✓ *Rapid urbanization during the nineteenth century led early sociologists to study the differences between rural and urban life. These early sociologists included, in Europe, Tönnies, Durkheim, and Simmel, and in the United States, Park and Wirth.*

FERDINAND TÖNNIES built his analysis on the concepts of ***Gemeinschaft*** and ***Gesellschaft***.

- *Gemeinschaft*, typical of the rural village, joins people in what amounts to a single primary group.
- *Gesellschaft*, typical of the modern city, describes individuals motivated by their own needs rather than by a desire to help improve the well-being of the community.

EMILE DURKHEIM agreed with much of Tönnies's thinking but claimed that urbanites do not lack social bonds; the basis of social solidarity simply differs in the two settings. He described

- **mechanical solidarity**—social bonds based on common sentiments and shared moral values. This type of social solidarity is typical of traditional, rural life.
- **organic solidarity**—social bonds based on specialization and interdependence. This type of social solidarity is typical of modern, urban life.

Gemeinschaft a type of social organization in which people are closely tied by kinship and tradition

Gesellschaft a type of social organization in which people come together only on the basis of individual self-interest

urban ecology the study of the link between the physical and social dimensions of cities

GEORG SIMMEL claimed that the overstimulation of city life produced a blasé attitude in urbanites.

ROBERT PARK, at the University of Chicago, claimed that cities permit greater social freedom.

LOUIS WIRTH saw large, dense, heterogeneous populations creating an impersonal and self-interested, though tolerant, way of life.

Urbanization in Poor Nations

- The world's first urban revolution took place about 8000 B.C.E. with the first urban settlements.
- The second urban revolution took place after 1750 in Europe and North America with the Industrial Revolution.
- A third urban revolution is now occurring in poor countries. Today, most of the world's largest cities are found in less developed nations.

Environment and Society

The state of the **ENVIRONMENT** is a social issue because it reflects how human beings organize social life.

- Societies increase the **environmental deficit** by focusing on short-term benefits and ignoring the long-term consequences brought on by their way of life.
- The more complex a society's technology, the greater its capacity to alter the natural environment.

- The *logic-of-growth thesis* supports economic development, claiming that people can solve environmental problems as they arise.
- The *limits-to-growth thesis* states that societies must curb development to prevent eventual environmental collapse.

ENVIRONMENTAL ISSUES include

- **Disposing of solid waste**—54% of what we throw away ends up in landfills, which are filling up and can pollute groundwater.
- **Protecting the quality of water and air**—The supply of clean water is already low in some parts of the world. Industrial technology has caused a decline in air quality.
- **Protecting the rain forests**—Rain forests help remove carbon dioxide from the atmosphere and are home to a large share of this planet's living species. Under pressure from development, the world's rain forests are now half their original size and are shrinking by about 1% annually.
- **Environmental racism**—Conflict theory has drawn attention to the pattern by which the poor, especially minorities, suffer most from environmental hazards.

ecology the study of the interaction of living organisms and the natural environment

natural environment Earth's surface and atmosphere, including living organisms, air, water, soil, and other resources necessary to sustain life

ecosystem a system composed of the interaction of all living organisms and their natural environment

environmental deficit profound long-term harm to the natural environment caused by humanity's focus on short-term material affluence

rain forests regions of dense forestation, most of which circle the globe close to the equator

global warming a rise in Earth's average temperature due to an increasing concentration of carbon dioxide in the atmosphere

environmental racism patterns of development that expose poor people, especially minorities, to environmental hazards

ecologically sustainable culture a way of life that meets the needs of the present generation without threatening the environmental legacy of future generations

MAKING THE GRADE

Sample Test Questions

Multiple-Choice Questions

1. ***Demography* is defined as the study of**
   a. democratic political systems.
   b. human culture.
   c. human population.
   d. the natural environment.

2. **Which region of the world has *both* the lowest birth rate and the lowest infant mortality rate?**
   a. Latin America
   b. Europe
   c. Africa
   d. Asia

3. **Typically, high-income nations grow mostly from _____, and low-income nations grow from _____.**
   a. immigration; natural increase
   b. emigration; natural increase
   c. natural increase; immigration
   d. internal migration; natural increase

4. **In general, the higher the average income of a country,**
   a. the faster the population increases.
   b. the slower the population increases.
   c. the lower the level of immigration.
   d. the lower the level of urbanization.

5. **In the United States, urban decentralization has caused**
   a. the expansion of suburbs.
   b. the development of vast urban regions.
   c. the growth of edge cities.
   d. All of the above are correct.

6. **Which term was used by Ferdinand Tönnies to refer to a type of social organization in which people come together on the basis of individual self-interest?**
   a. mechanical solidarity
   b. organic solidarity
   c. *Gesellschaft*
   d. *Gemeinschaft*

7. **The world's third urban revolution is now taking place in**
   a. the United States.
   b. Europe and Japan.
   c. middle-income nations.
   d. low-income nations.

8. **The *environmental deficit* refers to**
   a. long-term harm to the environment caused by a shortsighted focus on material affluence.
   b. the public's lack of interest in the natural environment.
   c. the fact that natural scientists ignore the social dimensions of environmental problems.
   d. the lack of funding for important environmental programs.

9. **Which of the following statements reflects the "limits to growth" thesis?**
   a. People are rapidly consuming Earth's finite resources.
   b. Whatever problems technology creates, technology can solve.
   c. The quality of life on Earth is getting better.
   d. Higher living standards today will benefit future generations.

10. ***Environmental racism* is the idea that**
    a. few minorities are found within the environmental movement.
    b. prejudice is the major cause of pollution and other environmental problems.
    c. environmental dangers are greatest for the poor and minorities.
    d. All of the above are correct.

ANSWERS: 1 (c); 2 (b); 3 (a); 4 (b); 5 (d); 6 (c); 7 (d); 8 (a); 9 (a); 10 (c).

Essay Questions

1. According to demographic transition theory, how does economic development affect population patterns?
2. According to Ferdinand Tönnies, Emile Durkheim, Georg Simmel, and Louis Wirth, what characterizes urbanism as a way of life? Note several differences in the ideas of these thinkers.

Social Change: Traditional, Modern, and Postmodern Societies

Social Change: Traditional, Modern, and Postmodern Societies

PhotoEdit Inc./Bill Bachmann

Social change often brings together traditional and moden ways of life. Sociologists study the process of social change, pointing to its causes and to the fact that the consequences of change are both expected and unexpected as well as both helpful and harmful.

PhotoEdit Inc./Jeff Greenberg

Social Change: Traditional, Modern, and Postmodern Societies

Shutterstock/Mircea Bezergheanu

iStockphoto International/ Royalty Free/Dmitriy Shironosov/Courtesy of www.istockphoto.com

CHAPTER OVERVIEW

This chapter explores social change, explaining how modern societies differ from earlier, traditional societies. It begins by describing the process of social change and some of its causes.

Culver Pictures, Inc.

The five-story, red brick apartment building at 253 East Tenth Street in New York City has been standing for more than a century. In 1900, one of the twenty small apartments in the building was occupied by thirty-nine-year-old Julius Streicher; Christine Streicher, age thirty-three; and their four young children. The Streichers were immigrants, having come in 1885 from their native Germany to New York, where they met and married.

The Streichers probably considered themselves successful. Julius operated a small clothing shop a few blocks from his apartment; Christine stayed at home, raised the children, and did the housework. Like most people in the country at that time, neither Julius nor Christine had graduated from high school, and they worked ten to twelve hours a day, six days a week. Their income—which was average for that time—was about $35 a month, or roughly $425 a year. (In today's dollars, that would be slightly more than $11,000, which would put the family well below the poverty line.) They spent almost half of their income for food; most of the rest went for rent.

Today, Dorothy Sabo resides at 253 East Tenth Street, living alone in the same apartment where the Streichers spent much of their lives. Now eighty-seven, she is retired from a career teaching art at a nearby museum. In many respects, Sabo's life has been far easier than the life the Streichers knew. For one thing, when the Streichers lived there, the building had no electricity (people used kerosene lamps and candles) and no running water (Christine Streicher spent most of every Monday doing laundry, using water she carried from a public fountain at the end of the block). There were no telephones, no television, and of course no computers. Today, Dorothy Sabo takes all these conveniences for granted. Although she is hardly rich, her pension and Social Security amount to several times as much (in constant dollars) as the Streichers earned.

But Sabo has her own worries. She is concerned about the environment and often speaks out about global warming. A century ago, if the Streichers and their neighbors were concerned about "the environment," they probably would have meant the smell coming up from the street. At a time when motor vehicles were just beginning to appear in New York City, carriages, trucks, and trolleys were all pulled by horses—thousands of them. These animals dumped 60,000 gallons of urine and 2.5 million pounds of manure on the streets each and every day (Simon & Cannon, 2001).

It is difficult for most people today to imagine how different life was a century ago. Not only was life much harder back then, but it was also much shorter. Statistical records show that a century ago, life expectancy was just forty-six years for men and forty-eight years for women, compared to about seventy-five and eighty-one years today (Heron et al., 2008).

Over the past 100 years, much has changed for the better. Yet as this chapter explains, social change is not all positive. Even changes for the better can have negative consequences, creating unexpected new problems. As you will see, early sociologists were mixed in their assessment of *modernity,* changes brought about by the Industrial Revolution. Likewise, today's sociologists point to both good and bad aspects of *postmodernity,* the recent transformations of society caused by the Information Revolution and the postindustrial economy. One thing is clear: For better and worse, the rate of change has never been faster than it is now.

social change the transformation of culture and social institutions over time

SEEING SOCIOLOGY in Everyday Life

What would you say have been the two or three most important changes that have occurred during your lifetime? Explain your answer.

What Is Social Change?

In earlier chapters, we examined relatively fixed or *static* social patterns, including status and role, social stratification, and social institutions. We also looked at the *dynamic* forces that have shaped our way of life, ranging from innovations in technology to the growth of bureaucracy and the expansion of cities. These are all dimensions of **social change**, *the transformation of culture and social institutions over time.* The process of social change has four major characteristics:

1. **Social change happens all the time.** "Nothing is constant except death and taxes" goes the old saying. Yet even our thoughts about death have changed dramatically as life expectancy in the United States has doubled over the past 100 or so years. And back in the Streichers' day, people in the United States paid no taxes on their earnings; taxation increased dramatically over the course of the twentieth century, along with the size and scope of government. In short, even the things that seem constant are subject to the twists and turns of change.

    Still, some societies change faster than others. Hunting and gathering societies change quite slowly; members of today's high-income societies, by contrast, experience significant change within a single lifetime.

    It is also true that in a given society, some cultural elements change faster than others. William Ogburn's theory of *cultural lag* (1964) states that material culture (that is, things) usually changes faster than nonmaterial culture (ideas and attitudes). For example, the genetic technology that allows scientists to alter and perhaps even create life has developed more rapidly than our ethical standards for deciding when and how to use it.

2. **Social change is sometimes intentional but often it is unplanned.** Industrial societies actively promote many kinds of change. For example, scientists seek more efficient forms of energy, and advertisers try to convince us that life is incomplete without an iPod or some other gadget. Yet rarely can anyone envision all the consequences of the changes that are set in motion.

    Back in 1900, when the country still relied on horses for transportation, many people looked ahead to motorized vehicles that would carry them in a single day distances that used to take weeks or months. But no one could see how much the mobility provided by automobiles would alter everyday life in the United States, scattering family members, threatening the environment, and reshaping cities and suburbs. Nor could automotive pioneers have predicted the more than 41,000 deaths that occur in car accidents each year in the United States alone (National Highway Traffic Safety Administration, 2008).

3. **Social change is controversial.** The history of the automobile shows that social change brings both good and bad consequences. Capitalists welcomed the Industrial Revolution because new technology increased productivity and swelled profits. However, workers feared that machines would make their skills obsolete and resisted the push toward "progress."

    Today, as in the past, changing patterns of social interaction between black people and white people, women and men, and gays and heterosexuals are welcomed by some people and opposed by others.

4. **Some changes matter more than others.** Some changes (such as clothing fads) have only passing significance; others (like the invention of computers) may change the world. Will the Information Revolution turn out to be as important as the Industrial Revolution? Like the automobile and television, the computer has both positive and negative effects, providing new kinds of jobs while eliminating old ones, isolating people in offices while linking people in global electronic networks, offering vast amounts of information while threatening personal privacy.

Paul Gauguin, French, (1848-1903), *Nave Nave Moe (Sacred Spring)*, 1894. Hermitage, St. Petersburg, Russia. Oil on canvas, 73 x 98 cm. © The Bridgeman Art Library International Ltd.

In response to the accelerating pace of change in the nineteenth century, Paul Gauguin left his native France for the South Pacific, where he was captivated by a simpler and seemingly timeless way of life. He romanticized this environment in many paintings, including *Nave Nave Moe (Sacred Spring)*.

Paul Gauguin, French (1848–1903), *Nave Nave Moe (Sacred Spring)*, 1894. Hermitage, Saint Petersburg, Russia. Oil on canvas, 73 × 98 cm. © The Bridgeman Art Library International Ltd.

SEEING SOCIOLOGY in Everyday Life

Look at the various changes in the United States over the past century. In each case, think about how the change affected everyday social life.

modernity social patterns resulting from industrialization

modernization the process of social change begun by industrialization

Getty Images, Inc. AFP/Mike Clarke/AFP

These young men are performing in a hip-hop dance marathon in Hong Kong. Hip-hop music, dress style, and dancing have become popular in Asia, a clear case of cultural diffusion. Social change occurs as cultural patterns move from place to place, but people in different societies don't always have the same understanding of what these patterns mean. How might Chinese youth understand hip-hop differently from the young African Americans in the United States who originated it?

Causes of Social Change

Social change has many causes. In a world linked by sophisticated communication and transportation technology, change in one place often sets off change elsewhere.

Culture and Change

Consider three important sources of cultural change. First, *invention* produces new objects, ideas, and social patterns. Rocket propulsion research, which began in the 1940s, has produced spacecraft that reach toward the stars. Today we take such technology for granted; during this century, a significant number of people may well travel in space.

Second, *discovery* occurs when people take note of existing elements of the world. For example, medical advances offer a growing understanding of the human body. Beyond the direct effects on human health, medical discoveries have stretched life expectancy, setting in motion the "graying" of U.S. society.

Third, *diffusion* creates change as products, people, and information spread from one society to another. Ralph Linton (1937a) recognized that many familiar elements of our culture came from other lands. For example, the cloth used to make our clothing was developed in Asia, the clocks we see all around us were invented in Europe, and the coins we carry in our pockets were devised in what is now Turkey.

In general, material things change more quickly than cultural ideas. That is, breakthroughs such as the science of cloning occur faster than our understanding of when—and even whether—they are morally desirable.

Conflict and Change

Inequality and conflict in a society also produce change. Karl Marx saw class conflict as the engine that drives societies from one historical era to another. In industrial-capitalist societies, he maintained, the struggle between capitalists and workers pushes society toward a socialist system of production.

In the more than 125 years since Marx's death, this model has proved simplistic. Yet Marx correctly foresaw that social conflict arising from inequality (involving not just class but also race and gender) would force changes in every society, including our own, to improve the lives of working people.

Ideas and Change

Max Weber also contributed to our understanding of social change. Although Weber agreed that conflict could bring about change, he traced the roots of most social change to ideas. For example, people with charisma (Martin Luther King Jr. was one example) can carry a message that changes the world.

Weber also highlighted the importance of ideas by showing how the religious beliefs of early Protestants set the stage for the spread of industrial capitalism. The fact that industrial capitalism developed primarily in areas of Western Europe where the Protestant work ethic was strong proved to Weber (1958, orig. 1904–05) the power of ideas to bring about change.

Ideas also direct social movements. Change occurs when people join together in the pursuit of a common goal, such as cleaning up the environment or improving the lives of oppressed people.

Demographic Change

Population patterns also play a part in social change. A century ago, as the chapter opening suggested, the typical household (4.8 people) was almost twice as large as it is today (2.6 people). Women are

Martina Serfass, age 54, is a nurse who lives near Decorah, Iowa; most of the people in her community have lived there all their lives.

Serge Smith-Heiser, age 27, lives in an apartment complex in Fort Lauderdale, Florida, and thinks of his city as a place where people come and go. He arrived two years ago in search of a new job.

MAKING THE GRADE

Be sure you understand the four traits of modernization identified by Peter Berger.

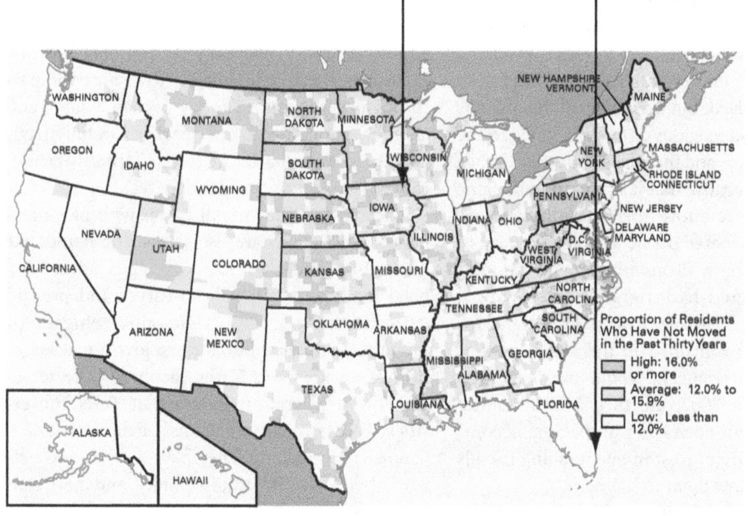

Seeing Ourselves

NATIONAL MAP 1

Who Stays Put? Residential Stability across the United States

Overall, only about 9 percent of U.S. residents have not moved during the past thirty years. Counties with a higher proportion of "long-termers" typically have experienced less change over recent decades: Many neighborhoods have been in place since before World War II, and many of the same families live in them. As you look at the map, what can you say about these stable areas? What accounts for the fact that most of these counties are rural and at some distance from the coasts?

Source: U.S. Census Bureau (1996).

having fewer children, and more people are living alone. In addition, change is taking place as our population grows older. Percent of the U.S. population was over age sixty-five in 2008, three times the proportion in 1900. By the year 2030, seniors will account for 20 percent of the total (U.S. Census Bureau, 2008). Medical research and health care services already focus extensively on the elderly, and life will change in countless additional ways as homes and household products are redesigned to meet the needs of older consumers.

Migration within and among societies is another demographic factor that promotes change. Between 1870 and 1930, tens of millions of immigrants entered the industrial cities in the United States. Millions more from rural areas joined the rush. As a result, farm communities declined, cities expanded, and for the first time, the United States became a mostly urban nation. Similar changes are taking place today as people move from the Snowbelt to the Sunbelt and mix with new immigrants from Latin America and Asia.

Where in the United States have demographic changes been greatest, and which areas have been least affected? National Map 1 provides one answer, showing counties where the largest share of people have lived in their present homes for thirty years or more.

One community that has recently experienced striking demographic change is the small city of Lewiston, Maine. Seeing Sociology in the News explains what is happening there.

Modernity

A central concept in the study of social change is **modernity,** *social patterns resulting from industrialization.* In everyday usage, *modernity* (its Latin root means "lately") refers to the present in relation to the past. Sociologists include in this catchall concept all of the social patterns that were set in motion by the Industrial Revolution, which began in Western Europe in the 1750s. **Modernization,** then, is *the process of social change begun by industrialization.* The timeline inside the back cover of this text highlights important events that mark the emergence of modernity. Table 1 provides a snapshot of some of the changes that took place during the twentieth century.

Four Dimensions of Modernization

Peter Berger (1977) identified four major characteristics of modernization:

1. **The decline of small, traditional communities.** Modernity involves "the progressive weakening, if not destruction, of the . . . relatively cohesive communities in which human beings have found solidarity and meaning throughout most of history" (1977:72). For thousands of years, in the camps of hunters and gatherers and in the rural villages of Europe and North America, people lived in small communities where social life revolved around family and neighborhood. Such traditional worlds gave each person a well-defined place that, although limiting the range of choice, offered a strong sense of identity, belonging, and purpose.

   Small, isolated communities still exist in remote corners of the United States, of course, but they are home to only a small percentage of our nation's people. These days, their isolation is only geographic: Cars, telephones, television, and the Internet give rural families the pulse of the larger society and connect them to the entire world.

Seeing SOCIOLOGY in the 

Newsweek

The Refugees Who Saved Lewiston

By JESSE ELLISON
January 26, 2009

Barely a decade ago, Lewiston, Maine, was dying. The once bustling mill town's population had been shrinking since the 1970s; most jobs had vanished long before, and residents (those who hadn't already fled) called the decaying center of town "the combat zone." That was before a family of Somali refugees discovered Lewiston in 2001 and began spreading the word to immigrant friends and relatives that housing was cheap and it looked like a good place to build new lives and raise children in peace. Since then, the place has been transformed. Per capita income has soared, and crime rates have dropped. In 2004, *Inc.* magazine named Lewiston one of the best places to do business in America, and in 2007, it was named an "All-America City" by the National Civic League, the first time any town in Maine had received that honor in roughly 40 years. . . .

Immigrants from Somalia may sound like improbable rescuers for a place like Lewiston. Maine is one of the whitest states in the country, second only to Vermont, and its old families have a reputation for distinct chilliness toward "outsiders." And many of the immigrants spoke no English at all when they arrived. But even beyond the obvious racial, cultural and religious differences between the Muslim newcomers and the locals, the town's image had become so negative that it was hard to imagine people choosing to move there. "Nothing could have rightfully prepared them," says Paul Badeau of the Lewiston-Auburn Economic Growth Council. "And nothing could have rightfully prepared us, either." It wasn't easy at first. Townspeople feared for the few jobs that remained in the area, and they warned that the strangers would overload local social services. In 2002, the then Mayor Laurier Raymond wrote an open letter to the Somali community begging them to stop encouraging friends and family to follow them to Maine.

But the Somalis kept coming, followed by Sudanese, Congolese and other Africans. By some estimates, 4,000 new immigrants have moved to Lewiston since 2001, and dozens are still arriving every month. Eight years ago, the town's adult-education center had only 76 students learning English as a second language. Now some 950 pass through every year. . . . Today, Somali women and children in donated winter parkas carefully navigate the snowbanks in the town's formerly crime-ridden low-income residential area.

The center of town still has pawnbrokers and bars, but now there are also shops with names like Mogadishu and Baracka, with signs advertising halal foods and selling headscarves and prepaid African phone cards. "Generally, refugees or migrants that come into a town give a new injection of energy," says Karen Jacobsen, director of the Forced Migration Program at Tufts University's Feinstein International Famine Center. "Somalis particularly. They have a very good network [with strong] trading links, and new economic activities they bring with them." Retailers sell clothes and spices imported from Africa; other entrepreneurs have launched restaurants and

---

2. **The expansion of personal choice**. Members of traditional, preindustrial societies view their lives as shaped by forces beyond human control—gods, spirits, fate. As the power of tradition weakens, people come to see their lives as an unending series of options, a process Berger calls *individualization.* Many people in the United States, for example, choose a "lifestyle" (sometimes adopting one after another), showing an openness to change. Indeed, a common belief in our modern culture is that people *should* take control of their lives.
3. **Increasing social diversity**. In preindustrial societies, strong family ties and powerful religious beliefs enforce conformity and discourage diversity and change. Modernization promotes a more rational, scientific worldview as tradition loses its hold and people gain more and more individual choice. The growth of cities, the expansion of impersonal bureaucracy, and the social mix of people from various backgrounds combine to encourage diverse beliefs and behavior.
4. **Orientation toward the future and a growing awareness of time**. Premodern people model their lives on the past, but people in modern societies think more about the future. Modern people are not only forward-looking but also optimistic that new inventions and discoveries will improve their lives.

   Modern people organize their daily routines down to the very minute. With the introduction of clocks in the late Middle Ages, Europeans began to think not in terms of sunlight and seasons but in terms of hours and minutes. Preoccupied with efficiency and personal gain, modern people demand precise measurement of time and are likely to agree that "time is money." Berger points out that one good indicator of a society's degree of modernization is the share of people wearing wristwatches.

Finally, recall that modernization touched off the development of sociology itself. The discipline originated in the wake of the Industrial Revolution in Western Europe, where social change was proceeding most rapidly. Early European and U.S. sociologists tried to analyze the rise of modern society and its consequences, both good and bad, for human beings.

Ferdinand Tönnies: The Loss of Community

The German sociologist Ferdinand Tönnies (1855–1937) produced a lasting account of modernization in his theory of *Gemeinschaft* and *Gesellschaft.* Like Peter Berger, whose work he influenced, Tönnies (1963, orig. 1887) viewed modernization as the progressive loss of *Gemeinschaft,* or human community. As Tönnies saw it, the Industrial Revolution weakened the social fabric of family and tradition by small businesses providing translation services, in-home care for the elderly and other social services. There's even a business consultant. "Increasingly, there's an acceptance that immigration is associated with good economic growth," says urban-studies specialist Richard Florida, director of the University of Toronto's Martin Prosperity Institute. "How is Maine going to grow? It's a big state with a sparse population. One of the ways to grow quickly is import people."

Commerce isn't all the Somalis are reshaping. Maine has America's highest median age and the lowest percentage of residents under 18. Throughout the 1990s, the state's population of 20- to 30-year-olds fell an average of 3,000 a year. Demographers predict that by 2030, the state will have only two workers for each retiree. "In many small Maine towns they're looking at having to close schools for lack of schoolchildren," says State Economist Catherine Reilly. "It will snowball.... In ten or fifteen years that's going to be the difficulty of businesses finding workers." The same ominous trend is seen in other states with similarly homogenous demographics and low numbers of foreign-born residents—states like Montana, North Dakota and West Virginia. Reilly adds: "If you told a demographer just our racial composition, they would be able to guess that we're an old state with a low birthrate."

Lewiston's sudden jolt is reflected even in enrollment at local universities. Although University of Maine enrollment has dropped systemwide since 2002, the student population at its Lewiston campus jumped 16 percent between 2002 and 2007. And Andover College, which opened a campus in Lewiston in 2004, had to start expanding almost immediately to accommodate a boom in applications. Enrollment doubled in two years. The reason? "Young people didn't want to go to a place that's all white," says Morrison. Practically everyone in Lewiston credits the Somalis' discovery of their town with much of its newfound success. "It's been an absolute blessing in many ways," says Badeau. "Just to have an infusion of diversity, an infusion of culture and of youth. Cultural diversity was the missing piece." The question is whether the rest of Maine—and other states like it—can find their own missing pieces.

WHAT DO YOU THINK?

1. What was the initial reaction of the people of Lewiston, Maine, to the prospect of thousands of immigrants settling in their town? What actually happened?
2. What are some of the changes that immigration brought to this city and state?
3. Do you think young people are more attracted to towns that are more racially and ethnically diverse? Explain.

Adapted from the original article, "The Refugees Who Saved Lewiston" by Jesse Ellison, from *Newsweek*, January 26, 2009.

introducing a businesslike emphasis on facts, efficiency, and money. European and North American societies gradually became rootless and impersonal as people came to associate mostly on the basis of self-interest—the state Tönnies termed *Gesellschaft.*

Early in the twentieth century, at least some parts of the United States could be described using Tönnies's concept of *Gemeinschaft.* Families that had lived for generations in small villages and towns were bound together in a hardworking, slow-moving way of life. Telephones (invented in 1876) were rare; not until 1915 could a person place a coast-to-coast call. Living without television (introduced commercially in the 1920s and not widespread until after 1950), families entertained themselves, often gathering with friends in the evening to share stories, sorrows, or song. Lacking rapid transportation (Henry Ford's assembly line began in 1908, but cars became common only after World War II), many people knew little of the world beyond their hometown.

Inevitable tensions and conflicts divided these communities of the past. But according to Tönnies, because of the traditional spirit of *Gemeinschaft,* people were "essentially united in spite of all separating factors" (1963:65, orig. 1887).

Modernity turns societies inside out so that, as Tönnies put it, people are "essentially separated in spite of uniting factors" (1963:65, orig. 1887). This is the world of *Gesellschaft,* where, especially in large cities, most people live among strangers and ignore the people they pass on the street. Trust is hard to come by in a mobile and anonymous society where people tend to put their personal needs ahead of group loyalty and an increasing majority of adults believe "you can't be too careful" in dealing with people (NORC, 2007:1743). No wonder researchers conclude that even as we become more affluent, the social health of modern societies has declined (D. G. Myers, 2000).

CRITICAL REVIEW Tönnies's theory of *Gemeinschaft* and *Gesellschaft* is the most widely cited model of modernization. The theory's strength lies in combining various dimensions of change: growing population, the rise of cities, and increasing impersonality in social interaction. But modern life, though often impersonal, still has some degree of *Gemeinschaft*. Even in a world of strangers, modern friendships can be strong and lasting. Some analysts also think that Tönnies favored—perhaps even romanticized—traditional societies while overlooking bonds of family, neighborhood, and friendship that continue to flourish in modern societies.

CHECK YOUR LEARNING As types of social organization, how do *Gemeinschaft* and *Gesellschaft* differ?

Emile Durkheim: The Division of Labor

The French sociologist Emile Durkheim shared Tönnies's interest in the profound social changes that resulted from the Industrial Revolution. For Durkheim (1964a, orig. 1893), modernization is defined

division of labor specialized economic activity

anomie a condition in which society provides little moral guidance to individuals

MAKING THE GRADE

Durkheim's concepts match up with those of Tönnies, but be sure to get it right: Mechanical solidarity corresponds to *Gemeinschaft,* and organic solidarity is the same as *Gesellschaft.*

Table 1 The United States: A Century of Change

	1900	2000
National population	76 million	281 million
Share living in cities	40%	80%
Life expectancy	46 years (men), 48 years (women)	74 years (men), 79 years (women)
Median age	22.9 years	35.3 years
Average household income	$8,000 (in 2000 dollars)	$40,000 (in 2000 dollars)
Share of income spent on food	43%	15%
Share of homes with flush toilets	10%	98%
Average number of cars	1 car for every 2,000 households	1.3 cars for every household
Divorce rate	about 1 in 20 marriages	about 8 in 20 marriages
Average gallons of petroleum products consumed	34 per person per year	1,100 per person per year

by an increasing **division of labor,** or *specialized economic activity.* Every member of a traditional society performs more or less the same daily round of activities; modern societies function by having people perform highly specific roles.

Durkheim explained that preindustrial societies are held together by *mechanical solidarity,* or shared moral sentiments. In other words, members of preindustrial societies view everyone as basically alike, doing the same kind of work and belonging together. Durkheim's concept of mechanical solidarity is virtually the same as Tönnies's *Gemeinschaft.*

With modernization, the division of labor becomes more and more pronounced. To Durkheim, this change means less mechanical solidarity but more of another kind of tie: *organic solidarity,* or mutual dependency between people engaged in specialized work. Put simply, modern societies are held together not by likeness but by difference: All of us must depend on others to meet most of our needs. Organic solidarity corresponds to Tönnies's concept of *Gesellschaft.*

Despite obvious similarities in their thinking, Durkheim and Tönnies viewed modernity somewhat differently. To Tönnies, modern *Gesellschaft* amounts to the loss of social solidarity, because modern people lose the "natural" and "organic" bonds of the rural village, leaving only the "artificial" and "mechanical" ties of the big, industrial city. Durkheim had a different view of modernity, even reversing Tönnies's language to bring home the point. Durkheim labeled modern society "organic," arguing that modern society is no less natural than any other, and he described traditional societies as "mechanical" because they are so regimented. Durkheim viewed modernization not as the loss of community but as a change from community based on bonds of likeness (kinship and neighborhood) to community based on economic interdependence (the division of labor). Durkheim's view of modernity is thus both more complex and more positive than Tönnies's view.

CRITICAL REVIEW Durkheim's work, which resembles that of Tönnies, is a highly influential analysis of modernity. Of the two, Durkheim was more optimistic; still, he feared that modern societies might become so diverse that they would collapse into **anomie,** *a condition in which society provides little moral guidance to individuals.* Living with weak moral norms and values, modern people can become egocentric, placing their own needs above those of others and finding little purpose in life.

The suicide rate—which Durkheim considered a good index of anomie—did in fact increase in the United States over the course of the twentieth century, and the vast majority of U.S. adults report that they see moral questions not in clear terms of right and wrong but in confusing "shades of gray" (NORC, 2007:447). Yet shared norms and values still seem strong enough to give most individuals some sense of meaning and purpose. Whatever the hazards of anomie, most people seem to value the personal freedom modern society gives us.

CHECK YOUR LEARNING Define mechanical solidarity and organic solidarity. In his view of the modern world, what makes Durkheim more optimistic than Tönnies?

Max Weber: Rationalization

For Max Weber, modernity meant replacing a traditional worldview with a rational way of thinking. In preindustrial societies, tradition acts as a constant brake on change. To traditional people, "truth" is roughly the same as "what has always been" (1978:36, orig. 1921). To modern people, however, "truth" is the

MAKING THE GRADE

Be sure you see what, from Max Weber's point of view, the scientist, the capitalist, and the bureaucrat have in common.

Pearson Education/PH College

Max Weber maintained that the distinctive character of modern society was its rational worldview. Virtually all of Weber's work on modernity centered on types of people he considered typical of their age: the scientist, the capitalist, and the bureaucrat. Each is rational to the core: The scientist is committed to the orderly discovery of truth, the capitalist to the orderly pursuit of profit, and the bureaucrat to orderly conformity to a system of rules.

result of rational calculation. Because they value efficiency and have little reverence for the past, modern people adopt whatever social patterns allow them to achieve their goals.

Echoing Tönnies and Durkheim, who held that industrialization weakens tradition, Weber declared modern society to be "disenchanted." The unquestioned truths of an earlier time had been challenged by rational thinking. In short, modern society turns away from the gods. Throughout his life, Weber studied various modern "types"—the capitalist, the scientist, the bureaucrat—all of whom share the detached worldview that Weber believed was coming to dominate humanity.

CRITICAL REVIEW Compared with Tönnies and especially Durkheim, Weber was very critical of modern society. He knew that science could produce technological and organizational wonders but worried that science was turning us away from more basic questions about the meaning and purpose of human existence. Weber feared that rationalization, especially in bureaucracies, would erode the human spirit with endless rules and regulations.

CHECK YOUR LEARNING How did Weber understand modernity? What does it mean to say that modern society (think of the scientists, capitalists, and bureaucrats) is "disenchanted"?

Some of Weber's critics think that the alienation he attributed to bureaucracy actually stemmed from social inequality. That criticism leads us to the ideas of Karl Marx.

Karl Marx: Capitalism

For Karl Marx, modern society was synonymous with capitalism; he saw the Industrial Revolution as primarily a *capitalist revolution.* Marx traced the emergence of the bourgeoisie in medieval Europe to the expansion of commerce. The bourgeoisie gradually displaced the feudal aristocracy as the Industrial Revolution gave it a powerful new productive system.

Marx agreed that modernity weakened small communities (as described by Tönnies), sharpened the division of labor (as noted by Durkheim), and encouraged a rational worldview (as Weber claimed). But he saw these simply as conditions necessary for capitalism to flourish. Capitalism, according to Marx, draws population from farms and small towns into an ever-expanding market system centered in cities; specialization is needed for efficient factories; and rationality is exemplified by the capitalists' endless pursuit of profit.

Earlier chapters have painted Marx as a spirited critic of capitalist society, but his vision of modernity also includes a good bit of optimism. Unlike Weber, who viewed modern society as an "iron cage" of bureaucracy, Marx believed that social conflict in capitalist societies would sow seeds of revolutionary change, leading to an

MAKING THE GRADE

This table is a good summary of trends that define our modern society. It also reviews much of what you have studied in earlier chapters.

SUMMING UP

Traditional and Modern Societies: The Big Picture

Elements of Society	Traditional Societies	Modern Societies
Cultural Patterns		
Values	Homogeneous; sacred character; few subcultures and countercultures	Heterogeneous; secular character; many subcultures and countercultures
Norms	Great moral significance; little tolerance of diversity	Variable moral significance; high tolerance of diversity
Time orientation	Present linked to past	Present linked to future
Technology	Preindustrial; human and animal energy	Industrial; advanced energy sources
Social Structure		
Status and role	Few statuses, most ascribed; few specialized roles	Many statuses, some ascribed and some achieved; many specialized roles
Relationships	Typically primary; little anonymity or privacy	Typically secondary; much anonymity and privacy
Communication	Face to face	Face-to-face communication supplemented by mass media
Social control	Informal gossip	Formal police and legal system
Social stratification	Rigid patterns of social inequality; little mobility	Fluid patterns of social inequality; high mobility
Gender patterns	Pronounced patriarchy; women's lives centered on the home	Declining patriarchy; increasing number of women in the paid labor force
Settlement patterns	Small-scale; population typically small and widely dispersed in rural villages and small towns	Large-scale; population typically large and concentrated in cities
Social Institutions		
Economy	Based on agriculture; much manufacturing in the home; little white-collar work	Based on industrial mass production; factories become centers of production; increasing white-collar work
State	Small-scale government; little state intervention in society	Large-scale government; much state intervention in society
Family	Extended family as the primary means of socialization and economic production	Nuclear family retains some socialization functions but is more a unit of consumption than of production
Religion	Religion guides worldview; little religious pluralism	Religion weakens with the rise of science; extensive religious pluralism
Education	Formal schooling limited to elites	Basic schooling becomes universal, with growing proportion receiving advanced education
Health	High birth and death rates; short life expectancy because of low standard of living and simple medical technology	Low birth and death rates; longer life expectancy because of higher standard of living and sophisticated medical technology
Social Change	Slow; change evident over many generations	Rapid; change evident within a single generation

egalitarian socialism. Such a society, as he saw it, would harness the wonders of industrial technology to enrich people's lives and also rid the world of social classes, the source of social conflict and suffering. Although Marx's evaluation of modern, capitalist society was negative, he imagined a future of human freedom, creativity, and community.

CRITICAL REVIEW Marx's theory of modernization is a complex theory of capitalism. But he underestimated the dominance of bureaucracy in modern societies. In socialist societies in particular, the stifling effects of bureaucracy turned out to be as bad as, or even worse than, the dehumanizing aspects of capitalism. The upheavals in Eastern Europe and the former Soviet

mass society a society in which prosperity and bureaucracy have weakened traditional social ties

class society a capitalist society with pronounced social stratification

SEEING SOCIOLOGY in Everyday Life

Identify five examples of "mass culture" that are the same throughout the United States. Name five more that differ from region to region.

Union in the late 1980s and early 1990s reveal the depth of popular opposition to oppressive state bureaucracies.

CHECK YOUR LEARNING How did Marx understand modern society? Of the four theorists just discussed—Tönnies, Durkheim, Weber, and Marx—who was the most optimistic about modern society? Who was the most pessimistic? Explain your responses.

Photograph courtesy of The Whitney Museum of American Art

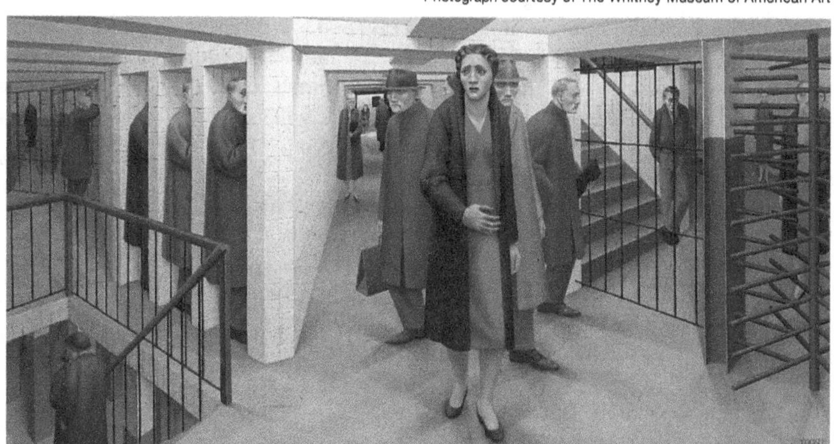

George Tooker's 1950 painting *The Subway* depicts a common problem of modern life: Weakening social ties and eroding traditions create a generic humanity in which everyone is alike yet each person is an anxious stranger in the midst of others.

Source: George Tooker, *The Subway*, 1950, egg tempera on gesso panel, 18 1/8 × 36 1/8 inches, Whitney Museum of American Art, New York. Purchased with funds from the Juliana Force Purchase Award, 50.23. Photograph © Whitney Museum of American Art

Theoretical Analysis of Modernity

The rise of modernity is a complex process involving many dimensions of change, as summarized in the Summing Up table. How can we make sense of so many changes going on all at once? Sociologists have developed two broad explanations of modern society, one guided by the structural-functional approach and the other based on social-conflict theory.

Structural-Functional Theory: Modernity as Mass Society

One broad approach—drawing on the ideas of Ferdinand Tönnies, Emile Durkheim, and Max Weber—understands modernization as the emergence of *mass society* (Kornhauser, 1959; Nisbet, 1966; Berger, Berger, & Kellner, 1974; Pearson, 1993). A **mass society** is *a society in which prosperity and bureaucracy have weakened traditional social ties.* A mass society is highly productive; on average, people have more income than ever. At the same time, it is marked by weak kinship and impersonal neighborhoods, leaving individuals to feel socially isolated. Although many people have material plenty, they are spiritually weak and often experience moral uncertainty about how to live.

The Mass Scale of Modern Life

November 11, on Interstate 275. From the car window, we see BP and Sunoco gas stations, a Kmart and a Wal-Mart, an AmeriSuites hotel, a Bob Evans, a Chi-Chi's Mexican restaurant, and a McDonald's. This road happens to circle Cincinnati, Ohio. But it could be in Boston, Saint Louis, Denver, San Diego, or almost anywhere else in the United States.

Mass-society theory argues, first, that the scale of modern life has greatly increased. Before the Industrial Revolution, Europe and North America formed a mosaic of rural villages and small towns. In these local communities, which inspired Tönnies's concept of *Gemeinschaft,* people lived out their lives surrounded by kin and guided by a shared heritage. Gossip was an informal yet highly effective way of ensuring conformity to community standards. These small communities, with their strong moral values and their low tolerance of social diversity, exemplified the state of mechanical solidarity described by Durkheim.

For example, before 1690, English law demanded that everyone participate regularly in the Christian ritual of Holy Communion (Laslett, 1984). On the North American continent, only Rhode Island among the New England colonies tolerated religious dissent. Because social differences were repressed in favor of conformity to established norms, subcultures and countercultures were few, and change proceeded slowly.

Increasing population, the growth of cities, and specialized economic activity driven by the Industrial Revolution gradually altered this pattern. People came to know one another by their jobs (for example, as "the doctor" or "the bank clerk") rather than by their kinship group or hometown. People looked on most others as strangers. The face-to-face communication of the village was eventually replaced by the impersonal mass media: newspapers, radio, television, and computer networks. Large organizations steadily

MAKING THE GRADE

Mass-society theory is critical of the expansion of the modern state, claiming that large bureaucracies encourage dehumanization. Class-society theory takes a more positive view of the expanding state, claiming that it helps reduce social inequality.

assumed more and more responsibility for seeing to the daily tasks that had once been carried out by family, friends, and neighbors; public education drew more and more people to schools; police, lawyers, and courts supervised a formal criminal justice system. Even charity became the work of faceless bureaucrats working for various social welfare agencies.

Geographic mobility and exposure to diverse ways of life all weaken traditional values. People become more tolerant of social diversity, defending individual rights and freedom of choice. Treating people differently because of their race, sex, or religion comes to be defined as backward and unjust. In the process, minorities at the margins of society gain greater power and broader participation in public life. The election of Barack Obama—an African American—to the highest office in the United States is surely one indicator that ours is now a modern society (West, 2008).

The mass media give rise to a national culture that washes over traditional differences that used to set off one region from another. As one analyst put it, "Even in Baton Rouge, La., the local kids don't say 'y'all' anymore; they say 'you guys' just like on TV" (Gibbs, 2000:42). In this way, mass-society theorists fear, transforming people of various backgrounds into a generic mass may end up dehumanizing everyone.

The Ever-Expanding State

In the small-scale preindustrial societies of Europe, government amounted to little more than a local noble. A royal family formally reigned over an entire nation, but without efficient transportation and efficient communication, even absolute monarchs had far less power than today's political leaders.

As technological innovation allowed government to expand, the centralized state grew in size and importance. At the time the United States gained independence from Great Britain, the federal government was a tiny organization with the main purpose of providing national defense. Since then, government has assumed responsibility for more and more areas of social life: schooling the population, regulating wages and working conditions, establishing standards for products of all sorts, offering financial assistance to the ill and the unemployed, providing loans to students, and recently, bailing out corporations facing economic ruin. To pay for such programs, taxes have soared: Today's average worker labors about four months each year to pay for the broad array of services that government provides.

In a mass society, power resides in large bureaucracies, leaving people in local communities with little control over their lives. For example, state officials mandate that local schools must have a standardized educational program, local products must be government-certified, and every citizen must maintain extensive tax records. Although such regulations may protect people and advance social equality, they also force us to deal more and more with nameless officials in distant and often unresponsive bureaucracies, and they undermine the autonomy of families and local communities.

CRITICAL REVIEW The growing scale of modern life certainly has positive aspects, but only at the price of losing some of our cultural heritage. Modern societies increase individual rights, tolerate greater social differences, and raise standards of living (Inglehart & Baker, 2000). But they are prone to what Weber feared most—excessive bureaucracy—as well as Tönnies's self-centeredness and Durkheim's anomie. Modern society's size, complexity, and tolerance of diversity all but doom traditional values and family patterns, leaving individuals isolated, powerless, and materialistic. Voter apathy is a serious problem in the United States. But should we be surprised that individuals in vast, impersonal societies think no one person can make much of a difference?

Critics sometimes say that mass-society theory romanticizes the past. They remind us that many people in small towns were actually eager to set out for a better standard of living in cities. This approach also ignores problems of social inequality. Critics say this theory attracts conservatives who defend conventional morality and overlook the historical inequality of women and other minorities.

CHECK YOUR LEARNING In your own words, state the mass-society theory of modernity. What are two criticisms of it?

Social-Conflict Theory: Modernity as Class Society

The second interpretation of modernity derives largely from the ideas of Karl Marx. From a social-conflict perspective, modernity takes the form of a **class society**, *a capitalist society with pronounced social stratification.* That is, although agreeing that modern societies have expanded to a mass scale, this approach views the heart of modernization as an expanding capitalist economy, marked with inequality (Habermas, 1970; Harrington, 1984; Buechler, 2000).

Capitalism

Class-society theory follows Marx in claiming that the increasing scale of social life in modern society results from the growth and greed unleashed by capitalism. Because a capitalist economy pursues ever-greater profits, both production and consumption steadily increase.

According to Marx, capitalism rests on "naked self-interest" (Marx & Engels, 1972:337, orig. 1848). This self-centeredness weakens the social ties that once united small communities. Capitalism

MAKING THE GRADE

Both mass- and class-society theories are critical of modernity: the first because of what is lost (traditional social ties), the second because of what remains (persistent social inequality).

also treats people as commodities: a source of labor and a market for capitalist products.

Capitalism supports science, not just as the key to greater productivity but as an ideology that justifies the status quo. That is, modern societies encourage people to view human well-being as a technical puzzle to be solved by engineers and other experts rather than through the pursuit of social justice. For example, a capitalist culture seeks to improve health through scientific medicine rather than by eliminating poverty, which is a core cause of poor health.

Business also raises the banner of scientific logic, trying to increase profits through greater efficiency. Today's capitalist corporations have reached enormous size and control unimaginable wealth as a result of globalization. From the class-society point of view, the expanding scale of life is less a function of *Gesellschaft* than the inevitable and destructive consequence of capitalism.

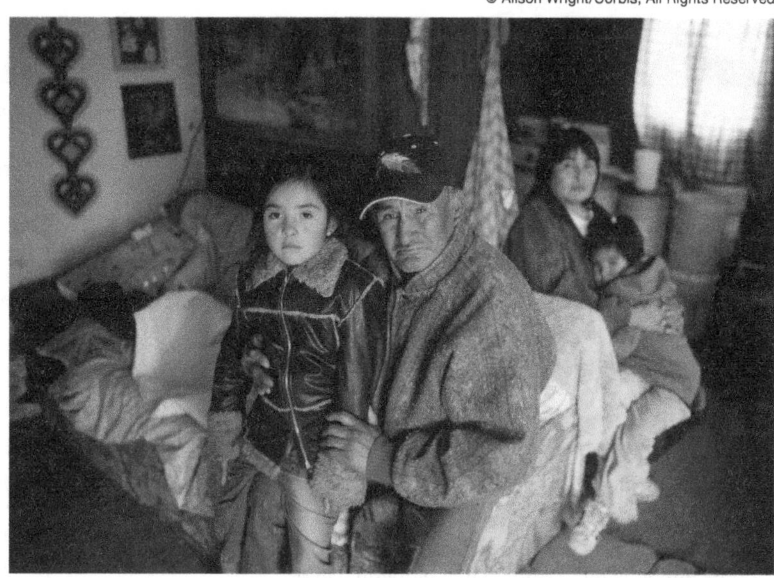

Social-conflict theory sees modernity not as an impersonal mass society but as an unequal class society in which some categories of people are second-class citizens. This Arizona family, like many Native Americans, lives on a reservation, where poverty is widespread and many trailer homes do not have electricity or running water.

Persistent Inequality

Modernity has gradually worn away the rigid categories that set nobles apart from commoners in preindustrial societies. But class-society theory points out that elites are still with us, in the form of capitalist millionaires rather than the nobles of an earlier era. In short, a few people are still born to wealth and power. The United States may have no hereditary monarchy, but the richest 5 percent of the population controls about 60 percent of all privately held property.

What of the state? Mass-society theorists argue that the state works to increase equality and fight social problems. Marx disagreed; he doubted that the state could accomplish more than minor reforms because as he saw it, the real power lies in the hands of capitalists, who control the economy. Other class-society theorists add that to the extent that working people and minorities do enjoy greater political rights and a higher standard of living today, these changes were the result of political struggle, not government goodwill. In short, they conclude, despite our pretensions of democracy, our political economy leaves most people powerless in the face of wealthy elites.

CRITICAL REVIEW Class-society theory dismisses Durkheim's argument that people in modern societies suffer from anomie, claiming instead that they suffer from alienation and powerlessness. Not surprisingly, then, the class-society interpretation of modernity enjoys widespread support among liberals and radicals who favor greater equality and call for extensive regulation (or abolition) of the capitalist marketplace.

A basic criticism of class-society theory is that it overlooks the long-term increasing prosperity of modern societies and the fact that discrimination based on race, ethnicity, and gender is now illegal and is widely regarded as a social problem. In addition, most people in the United States do not want an egalitarian society; they prefer a system of unequal rewards that reflects personal differences in talent and effort.

Based on socialism's failure to generate a high standard of living, few observers think that a centralized economy would cure the ills of modernity. The United States may face a number of social problems—from unemployment to hunger and industrial pollution to war—but these problems are also found in socialist nations.

CHECK YOUR LEARNING In your own words, state the class-society theory of modernity. What are several criticisms of it?

The Summing Up table contrasts the two interpretations of modernity. Mass-society theory focuses on the increasing scale of life and the growth of government; class-society theory stresses the expansion of capitalism and the persistence of inequality.

social character personality patterns common to members of a particular society

tradition-directedness rigid conformity to time-honored ways of living

other-directedness openness to the latest trends and fashions, often expressed by imitating others

MAKING THE GRADE

Riesman's tradition-directedness corresponds to Tönnies's *Gemeinschaft* and Durkheim's mechanical solidarity. Other-directedness is linked to *Gesellschaft* and organic solidarity.

SUMMING UP

Two Interpretations of Modernity

	Mass Society	Class Society
Process of modernization	Industrialization; growth of bureaucracy	Rise of capitalism
Effects of modernization	Increasing scale of life; rise of the state and other formal organizations	Expansion of the capitalist economy; persistence of social inequality

Modernity and the Individual

Both mass- and class-society theories look at the broad societal changes that have taken place since the Industrial Revolution. But from these macro-level approaches we can also draw micro-level insights into how modernity shapes individual lives.

Mass Society: Problems of Identity

Modernity freed individuals from the small, tightly knit communities of the past. Most people in modern societies have the privacy and freedom to express their individuality. However, mass-society theory suggests that so much social diversity, widespread isolation, and rapid social change make it difficult for many people to establish any coherent identity at all (Wheelis, 1958; Berger, Berger, & Kellner, 1974).

People's personalities are largely a product of their social experiences. The small, homogeneous, and slowly changing societies of the past provided a firm, if narrow, foundation for building a personal identity. Even today, the Amish communities that flourish in the United States and Canada teach young men and women "correct" ways to think and behave. Not everyone born into an Amish community can tolerate strict demands for conformity, but most members establish a well-integrated and satisfying personal identity (Kraybill & Olshan, 1994; Kraybill & Hurd, 2006).

Mass societies are quite another story. Socially diverse and rapidly changing, they offer only shifting sands on which to build a personal identity. Left to make many life decisions on their own, many people—especially those with greater wealth—face a bewildering array of options. The freedom to choose has little value without standards to help us make good choices, and in a tolerant mass society, people may find little reason to choose one path over another. As a result, many people shuttle from one identity to another, changing their lifestyles, relationships, and even religions in search of an elusive "true self." Given the widespread "relativism" of modern societies, people without a moral compass lack the security and certainty once provided by tradition.

To David Riesman (1970, orig. 1950), modernization brings changes in **social character**, *personality patterns common to members of a particular society*. Preindustrial societies promote what Riesman calls **tradition-directedness**, *rigid conformity to time-honored ways of living*. Members of traditional societies model their lives on those of their ancestors, so that "living a good life" amounts to "doing what our people have always done."

Tradition-directedness corresponds to Tönnies's *Gemeinschaft* and Durkheim's mechanical solidarity. Culturally conservative, tradition-directed people think and act alike. Unlike the conformity sometimes found in modern societies, the uniformity of tradition-directedness is not an effort to imitate a popular celebrity or follow the latest fashions. Instead, people are alike because they all draw on the same solid cultural foundation. Amish women and men exemplify tradition-directedness; in Amish culture, tradition ties everyone to ancestors and descendants in an unbroken chain of righteous living.

Members of diverse and rapidly changing societies consider a tradition-directed personality deviant because it seems so rigid. Modern people, by and large, prize personal flexibility, the capacity to adapt, and sensitivity to others. Riesman calls this type of social character **other-directedness**, *openness to the latest trends and fashions, often expressed by imitating others*. Because their socialization occurs in societies that are continuously in flux, other-directed people develop fluid identities marked by superficiality, inconsistency, and change. They try on different "selves" almost like new clothing, seek out role models, and engage in varied performances as they move from setting to setting (Goffman, 1959). In a traditional society, such "shiftiness" makes a person untrustworthy, but in a changing, modern society, the chameleonlike ability to fit in virtually anywhere is very useful.

SEEING SOCIOLOGY in Everyday Life

Have you ever felt difficulty deciding "who you are"? Do you try to be a different person in different settings?

MAKING THE GRADE

In a sense, mass-society theory claims that modern people have too much freedom and choice; class-society theory claims that we have too little.

Getty Images Inc. – Stone Allstock/Ed Pritchard

AP Wide World Photos/Wally Santana

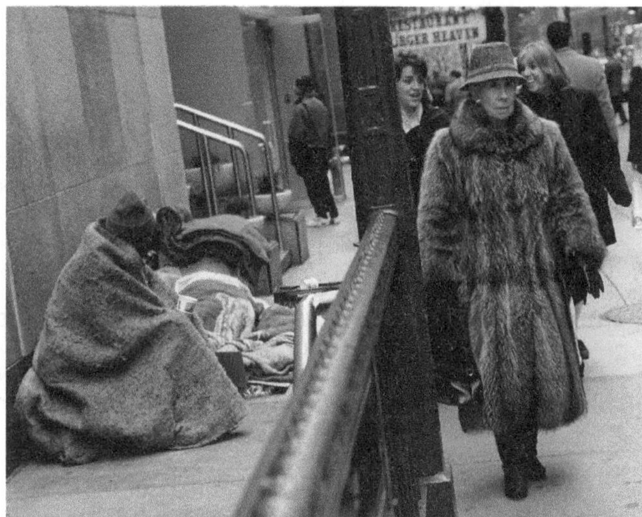

Mass-society theory relates feelings of anxiety and lack of meaning in the modern world to rapid social change that washes away tradition. This notion of modern emptiness is captured in the photo at the left. Class-society theory, by contrast, ties such feelings to social inequality, by which some categories of people are made into second-class citizens (or not made citizens at all), an idea expressed in the photo at the right.

In societies that value the up-to-date rather than the traditional, people look to others for approval, using members of their own generation rather than elders as role models. Peer pressure can be irresistible to people without strong standards to guide them. Our society urges individuals to be true to themselves. But when social surroundings change so rapidly, how can people develop the self to which they should be true? This problem lies at the root of the identity crisis so widespread in industrial societies today. "Who am I?" is a nagging question that many of us struggle to answer. In truth, this problem is not so much us as the inherently unstable mass society in which we live.

Class Society: Problems of Powerlessness

Class-society theory paints a different picture of modernity's effects on individuals. This approach maintains that persistent social inequality undermines modern society's promise of individual freedom. For some people, modernity serves up great privilege, but for many, everyday life means coping with economic uncertainty and a growing sense of powerlessness (K. S. Newman, 1993; Ehrenreich, 2001).

For racial and ethnic minorities, the problem of relative disadvantage looms even larger. Similarly, although women participate more broadly in modern societies, they continue to run up against traditional barriers of sexism. This approach rejects mass-society theory's claim that people suffer from too much freedom. According to class-society theory, our society still denies a majority of people full participation in social life.

The expanding scope of world capitalism has placed more of Earth's population under the influence of multinational corporations. As a result, more than three-fourths of the world's income is concentrated in the high-income nations, where just 22 percent of its people live. Is it any wonder, class-society theorists ask, that people in poor nations seek greater power to shape their own lives?

The problem of widespread powerlessness led Herbert Marcuse (1964) to challenge Max Weber's statement that modern society is rational. Marcuse condemned modern society as irrational for failing to meet the needs of so many people. Although modern capitalist societies produce unparalleled wealth, poverty remains the daily plight of more than 1 billion people. Marcuse adds that technological advances further reduce people's control over their own lives. High technology gives a great deal of power to a small core of specialists—not the majority of people—who now dominate the discussion of when to go to war, what our energy policy should be, and how people should pay for health care. Countering the common view that technology *solves* the world's problems, Marcuse believed that science *causes* them. In sum, class-society theory asserts that people suffer because modern societies concentrate knowledge, wealth, and power in the hands of a privileged few.

SEEING SOCIOLOGY in Everyday Life

In 1970, Alvin Toffler coined the phrase "future shock" to describe the effect of social change that comes so rapidly that it overwhelms us. Do you think the pace of change has become overwhelming? Does our world need more change, or do we have too much already? Explain your answers.

THINKING GLOBALLY

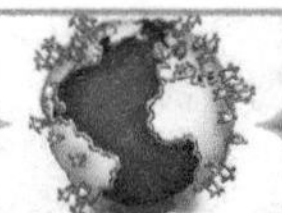

Does "Modernity" Mean "Progress"? The Kaiapo of the Amazon and the Gullah of Georgia

The firelight flickers in the gathering darkness. Chief Kanhonk sits, as he has done at the end of the day for many years, ready to begin an evening of animated storytelling (Simons, 2007). This is the hour when the Kaiapo, a small society in Brazil's lush Amazon region, celebrate their heritage. Because the Kaiapo are a traditional people with no written language, the elders rely on evenings by the fire to pass along their culture to their children and grandchildren. In the past, evenings like this have been filled with tales of brave Kaiapo warriors fighting off Portuguese traders who were in pursuit of slaves and gold.

But as the minutes pass, only a few older villagers assemble for the evening ritual. "It is the Big Ghost," one man grumbles, explaining the poor turnout. The "Big Ghost" has indeed descended on them; its bluish glow spills from windows throughout the village. The Kaiapo children—and many adults as well—are watching sitcoms on television. The installation of a satellite dish in the village several years ago has had consequences far greater than anyone imagined. In the end, what their enemies failed to do with guns, the Kaiapo may well do to themselves with prime-time programming.

The Kaiapo are among the 230,000 native peoples who inhabit Brazil. They stand out because of their striking body paint and ornate ceremonial dress. During the 1980s, they became rich from gold mining and harvesting mahogany trees. Now they must decide whether their newfound fortune is a blessing or a curse.

Mauri Rautkari

To some, affluence means the opportunity to learn about the outside world through travel and television. Others, like Chief Kanhonk, are not so sure. Sitting by the fire, he thinks aloud: "I have been saying that people must buy useful things like knives and fishing hooks. Television does not fill the stomach. It only shows our children and grandchildren white people's things." Bebtopup, the oldest priest, nods in agreement: "The night is the time the old people teach the young people. Television has stolen the night" (Simons, 2007:522).

Far to the north, in the United States, half an hour by ferry from the coast of Georgia, lies the swampy island community of Hog Hammock. The seventy African American residents of the island today trace their ancestry back to the first slaves who settled there in 1802.

Walking past the colorful houses nestled among pine trees draped with Spanish moss, visitors feel transported back in time. The local people, known as Gullahs (or in some places, Geechees)

Modernity and Progress

In modern societies, most people expect, and applaud, social change. We link modernity to the idea of *progress* (from the Latin, meaning "moving forward"), a state of continual improvement. We see stability as stagnation.

Given our bias in favor of change, our society tends to regard traditional cultures as backward. But change, particularly toward material affluence, is a mixed blessing. As the Thinking Globally box shows, social change is too complex simply to equate with progress.

Even getting rich has both advantages and disadvantages, as the cases of the Kaiapo and the Gullah show. Historically, among people in the United States, a rising standard of living has made lives longer and materially more comfortable. At the same time, many people wonder if today's routines are too stressful, with families often having little time to relax or simply be together. Perhaps this is why, in the United States, even as material prosperity has increased, measures of happiness have declined (D. G. Myers, 2000; Inglehart, Welzel, & Foa, 2009).

Science, too, has its pluses and minuses. People in the United States are more confident than people in other nations that science improves our lives (Inglehart et al., 2000). But surveys also show that many adults in the United States feel that science "makes our way of life change too fast" (NORC, 2007).

New technology has always sparked controversy. A century ago, the introduction of automobiles and telephones allowed more rapid transportation and more efficient communication. But at the same time, such technology weakened traditional attachments to hometowns and even to families. Today, people might well wonder whether computer technology will do the same thing, giving us access to people around the world but shielding us from the community right outside our doors; providing more information than ever before but in the process threatening personal privacy. In short,

MAKING THE GRADE

The importance of a global perspective is seeing that "tradition" and "modernity" are not simply opposites but are often found in unexpected combinations in societies around the world.

speak a mixture of English and West African languages. They fish, living much as they have for hundreds of years.

But the future of this way of life is now in doubt. Few young people who are raised in Hog Hammock can find work beyond fishing and making traditional crafts. "We have been here nine generations and we are still here," says one local. Then, referring to the island's nineteen children, she adds, "It's not that they don't want to be here, it's that there's nothing here for them—they need to have jobs" (Curry, 2001:41).

Just as important, with people on the mainland looking for waterside homes for vacations or year-round living, the island has become prime real estate. Not long ago, one of the larger houses went up for sale, and the community was shocked to learn that its asking price was more than $1 million. The locals know only too well that higher property values will mean high taxes that few can afford to pay. In short, Hog Hammock is likely to become another Hilton Head, once a Gullah community on the South Carolina coast that is now home to well-to-do people from the mainland.

The odds are that the people of Hog Hammock will be selling their homes and moving inland. But few people are happy at the thought of selling out, even for a good price. After all, moving away will mean the end of their cultural heritage.

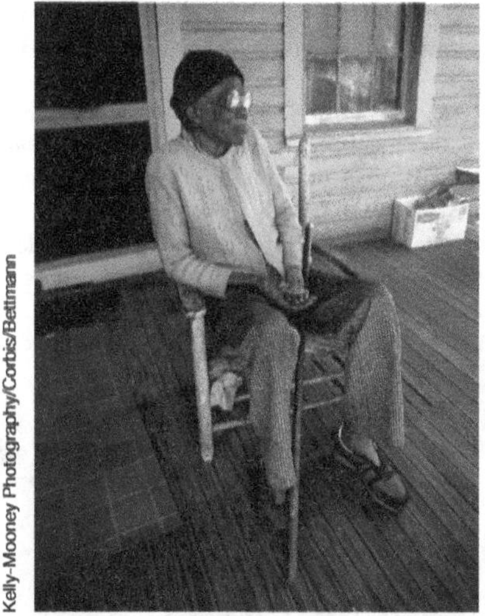

Kelly-Mooney Photography/Corbis/Bettmann

The stories of both the Kaiapo and the people of Hog Hammock show us that change is not a simple path toward "progress." These people may be moving toward modernity, but this process will have both positive and negative consequences. In the end, both groups of people may enjoy a higher standard of living with better homes, more schooling, and new technology. But their new affluence will come at the price of their traditions. The drama of these people is now being played out around the world as more and more traditional cultures are being lured away from their heritage by the affluence and materialism of rich societies.

WHAT DO YOU THINK?

1. Why is social change both a winning and a losing proposition for traditional peoples?
2. Do the changes described here improve the lives of the Kaiapo? What about the Gullah community?
3. Do traditional people have any choice about becoming modern? Explain your answer.

we all realize that social change comes faster all the time, but we may disagree about whether a particular change is good or bad for society.

Modernity: Global Variation

__October 1, Kobe, Japan.__ Riding the computer-controlled monorail high above the streets of Kobe or the 200-mile-per-hour bullet train to Tokyo, we see Japan as the society of the future; its people are in love with high technology. But in other ways, the Japanese remain strikingly traditional: Few corporate executives and almost no senior politicians are women, young people still show seniors great respect, and public orderliness contrasts with the relative chaos of many U.S. cities.

Japan is a nation at once traditional and modern. This contradiction reminds us that although it is useful to contrast traditional and modern societies, the old and the new often coexist in unexpected ways. In the People's Republic of China, ancient Confucian principles are mixed with contemporary socialist thinking. In Saudi Arabia and Qatar, the embrace of modern technology is mixed with respect for the ancient principles of Islam. Likewise, in Mexico and much of Latin America, people observe centuries-old Christian rituals even as they struggle to move ahead economically. In short, combinations of traditional and modern are far from unusual; rather, they are found throughout the world.

postmodernity social patterns characteristic of postindustrial societies

SEEING SOCIOLOGY IN EVERYDAY LIFE

Tracking Change: Is Life in the United States Getting Better or Worse?

FLORENCE: I think life is great! Don't you?

SAMANTHA: I guess it depends on what you mean by "life."

FLORENCE: Hey, I'm feeling good, and you want to make everything complicated!

SAMANTHA: Well, sorry to sound like a sociology major, but it is. In some ways life is getting better; in other ways, it's not. . . .

We began this chapter with a look at what life was like in a large U.S. city in 1900, more than a century ago. It is easy to see that in many ways, life is far better for us today than it was for our grandparents and great-grandparents. In recent decades, however, not all indicators have been good. Here is a look at some trends shaping the United States since 1970 (Miringoff & Miringoff, 1999; D. G. Myers, 2000).

First, the good news: By some measures, life in this country is clearly improving. Infant mortality has been falling steadily, meaning that fewer and fewer children die soon after birth. In addition, an increasing share of people are reaching old age, and after reaching sixty-five, they are living longer than ever. More good news: The poverty rate among the elderly is well below what it was in 1970. Schooling is another area of improvement: The share of people dropping out of high school is down, and the share completing a college education is up. Even alcohol-related traffic deaths on the highways are down.

Next, a number of indicators show that life is about the same as it was in the 1970s. For example, teenage drug use is about the same now as it was a generation earlier. Unemployment has been way up in the past year or two, but over the past three decades the overall level has stayed about the same. Finally, there is about the same amount of affordable housing in the United States now as there was back in 1970.

Then there is the bad news. By some measures, several having to do with children, the quality of life in the United States has actually fallen. The official rate of child abuse is up, as is the rate of suicide among young people. Although the level of violent crime has fallen over the past fifteen years, it remains above the 1970 level. Average hourly wages, one measure of economic security, show a downward trend, meaning that more families today have to rely on two or more earners to maintain family income. As far as jobs and income are concerned, people's confidence in the future is not as great as it used to be. The number of people without health insurance is also on the rise. And economic inequality in this country—the gap between the rich and the poor—has been increasing.

Overall, the evidence does not support any simple ideas about "progress over time." Social change has been and will continue to be a complex process that reflects the kinds of priorities we set for this nation as well as our will to achieve them.

Getty Images, Inc.- Photodisc./Royalty Free/Buccina Studios

Research shows that people in the United States today are better off economically than were past generations. At the same time, measures of personal happiness appear to be going down. How can you explain this contradiction?

WHAT DO YOU THINK?

1. Some analysts claim that U.S. society embodies a paradox: Over the past three decades, we see increasing economic health but declining social health. Based on the data presented here, do you agree or disagree? Explain your answer.
2. Which of the trends noted in this box do you find most important? Why?
3. Overall, do you think the quality of life in the United States is improving or not? Explain.

Source: U.S. Census Bureau (2008).

Postmodernity

If modernity was the product of the Industrial Revolution, is the Information Revolution creating a postmodern era? A number of scholars think so, and they use the term **postmodernity** to refer to *social patterns characteristic of postindustrial societies.*

The term *postmodernism* has been used for decades in literary, philosophical, and even architectural circles. It moved into sociology on a wave of social criticism that has been building since the spread of left-leaning politics in the 1960s. Although there are many variants of postmodern thinking, all share the following five themes (Hall & Neitz, 1993; Inglehart, 1997; Rudel & Gerson, 1999):

MAKING THE GRADE

Just as the Industrial Revolution marks the onset of modernity, the new postindustrial economy (or Information Revolution) marks the onset of postmodernity.

MAKING THE GRADE

An important sociological insight is that social change always has both positive and negative consequences, so it is simplistic to equate change with "progress."

1. **In important respects, modernity has failed.** The promise of modernity was a life free from want. As postmodernist critics see it, however, the twentieth century was unsuccessful in solving social problems like poverty. This fact is evident in today's high poverty rates, as well as the spreading sense of financial insecurity.
2. **The bright light of "progress" is fading.** Modern people look to the future, expecting that their lives will improve in significant ways. Members (and even leaders) of postmodern societies, however, are less confident about what the future holds. The strong optimism that carried society into the modern era more than a century ago has given way to widespread pessimism; even before the recent economic downturn, most U.S. adults believed that life was getting worse (NORC, 2007:259).
3. **Science no longer holds the answers.** The defining trait of the modern era was a scientific outlook and a confident belief that technology would make life better. But postmodern critics argue that science has not solved many old problems (such as poor health) and has even created new problems (such as pollution and global warming).

   Postmodernist thinkers discredit science, claiming that it implies a singular truth. On the contrary, they maintain, there is no one truth. This means that objective reality does not exist; rather, many realities can result from how we socially construct the world.
4. **Cultural debates are intensifying.** Now that more people have all the material things they really need, ideas are taking on more importance. In this sense, postmodernity is also a postmaterialist era, in which more careers involve working with symbols and in which issues such as social justice, the state of the natural environment, and animal rights command more and more public attention.
5. **Social institutions are changing.** Just as industrialization brought a sweeping transformation to social institutions, the rise of a postindustrial society is remaking society again. For example, the postmodern family no longer conforms to any single pattern; on the contrary, individuals are choosing among many new family forms.

CRITICAL REVIEW Analysts who claim that the United States and other high-income societies are entering a postmodern era criticize modernity for failing to meet human needs. In defense of modernity, there have been marked increases in longevity and living standards over the course of the past century.

Getty Images Inc. - Stone Allstock/Brad Rickerby

Based on everything you have read in this chapter, do you think that, on balance, our society is changing for better or worse? Why?

Even if we accept postmodernist views that science is bankrupt and progress is a sham, what are the alternatives?

CHECK YOUR LEARNING In your own words, state the characteristics of a postmodern society.

Is society getting better or not? The Seeing Sociology in Everyday Life box offers evidence suggesting that life in the United States is getting better in some ways but not in others.

Looking Ahead: Modernization and Our Global Future

Imagine the entire world reduced to a village of 1,000 people. About 200 residents of this "global village" would come from high-income countries. Another 200 people would be so poor that their lives are at risk.

The tragic plight of the world's poor shows that the planet is in desperate need of change. Consider two competing views of why more than 1 billion people around the world are so poor. *Modernization theory* claims that in the past, the entire world was poor and that technological change, especially the Industrial Revolution, enhanced human productivity and raised living standards in many nations.

SEEING SOCIOLOGY in Everyday Life

Do you think there is too much of a "me first" attitude in today's world? Explain your view.

CONTROVERSY & DEBATE

Personal Freedom and Social Responsibility: Can We Have It Both Ways?

SAMUEL: I feel that being free is the most important thing. Let me do what I want!

SANJI: But if everyone felt that way, what would the world be like?

DOREEN: Isn't there a way to be true to ourselves and also take account of other people?

One issue we all have to work out is making decisions that take account of other people. But what, exactly, do we owe others? To see the problem, consider an event that took place in New York City in 1964.

Shortly after midnight on a crisp March evening, Kitty Genovese drove into the parking lot of her apartment complex. She turned off the engine, locked the doors of her vehicle, and headed across the blacktop toward the entrance to her building. Out of nowhere, a man holding a knife lunged at her, and as she screamed in terror and pain, he stabbed her repeatedly. Windows opened above as curious neighbors looked down to see what was going on. But the attack continued for more than thirty minutes until Genovese lay dead in the doorway. The police never identified her killer, and their investigation revealed a stunning fact: *Not one* of the dozens of neighbors who witnessed the attack on Kitty Genovese went to her aid or even called the police.

Alamy Images/Jim West

In today's world, people can find new ways to express age-old virtues such as extending a helping hand to their neighbors in need. In the wake of Hurricane Katrina, thousands of college students from across the country converged on New Orleans to help repair the damage to the stricken city. Are there opportunities for you to get involved in your own community?

Decades after this tragic event, we still confront the question of what we owe others. We prize our individual rights and personal privacy, but sometimes we turn a cold shoulder to people in need. When a cry for help is met with indifference, have we pushed our modern idea of personal freedom too far? In a society of expanding individual rights, can we keep a sense of human community?

These questions highlight the tension between traditional and modern social systems, which we can see in the writings of all the sociologists discussed in this chapter. Tönnies, Durkheim, and others concluded that in some respects, traditional community and modern individualism don't mix. That is, society can unite its members in a moral community only by limiting their

From this point of view, the solution to global poverty is to promote technological development and market economies around the world.

For reasons suggested earlier, however, global modernization may be difficult. Recall that David Riesman portrayed preindustrial people as *tradition-directed* and likely to resist change. So modernization theorists advocate that the world's rich societies help poor countries grow economically. Industrial nations can speed development by exporting technology to poor regions, welcoming students from these countries, and providing foreign aid to stimulate economic growth.

A review of modernization theory points to some success with policies in Latin America and to greater success in the small Asian countries of Taiwan, South Korea, Singapore, and Hong Kong (since 1997 part of the People's Republic of China). But jump-starting development in the poorest countries of the world poses greater challenges. And even where dramatic change has occurred, modernization involves a trade-off. Traditional people, such as Brazil's Kaiapo, may gain wealth through economic development, but they lose their cultural identity and values as they are drawn into a global "McCulture" based on Western materialism, pop music, trendy clothes, and fast food. One Brazilian anthropologist expressed hope about the future of the Kaiapo: "At least they quickly understood the consequences of watching television. . . . Now [they] can make a choice" (Simons, 2007:523).

But not everyone thinks that modernization is really an option. According to a second approach to global stratification, *dependency theory,* today's poor societies have little ability to modernize, even if they want to. From this point of view, the major barrier to economic development is not traditionalism but global domination by rich capitalist societies.

SEEING SOCIOLOGY in Everyday Life

Does the balance between individual freedom and personal responsibility differ for men and women? If so, how, and why?

range of personal choices about how to live. In short, although we value both community and freedom, we can't have it both ways.

The sociologist Amitai Etzioni (1993, 1996, 2003) has tried to strike a middle ground. The *communitarian movement* rests on the simple idea that with rights must come responsibilities. Put another way, our pursuit of self-interest must be balanced by a commitment to the larger community.

Etzioni claims that modern people have become too concerned about individual rights. We expect the system to work for us, but we are reluctant to support the system. For example, we believe that people accused of a crime have the right to their day in court, but fewer and fewer of us are willing to perform jury duty; similarly, we are quick to accept government services but resent having to support these services with our taxes.

The communitarians advance four proposals to balance individual rights and public responsibilities. First, our society should halt the expanding "culture of rights" by which we put our own interests ahead of social responsibility. The U.S. Constitution, which is quoted so often when discussing individual rights, does not guarantee us the right to do whatever we want. Second, we must remember that all rights involve responsibilities; for society to work, we must all play a part. Third, the well-being of everyone may require limiting our individual rights; for example, pilots and bus drivers who are responsible for public safety may be asked to take drug tests. Fourth, no one can ignore key responsibilities such as upholding the law and responding to a cry for help from someone like Kitty Genovese.

The communitarian movement appeals to many people who believe in both personal freedom and social responsibility. But Etzioni's proposals have drawn criticism from both sides of the political spectrum. To those on the left, serious problems ranging from voter apathy and street crime to disappearing pensions and millions of workers without medical care cannot be solved with some vague notion of "social responsibility." As they see it, what we need is expanded government programs to protect people and lessen inequality.

Conservatives, on the political right, see different problems in Etzioni's proposals (Pearson, 1995). As they see it, the communitarian movement favors liberal goals, such as confronting prejudice and protecting the environment, but ignores conservative goals such as strengthening religious belief and supporting traditional families.

Etzioni responds that the criticism coming from both sides suggests that he has found a moderate, sensible answer to a serious problem. But the debate may also indicate that in a society as diverse as the United States, people who are so quick to assert their rights are not so quick to agree on their responsibilities.

WHAT DO YOU THINK?

1. Have you ever failed to come to the aid of someone in need or danger? Why?
2. Half a century ago, President John F. Kennedy stated, "Ask not what your country can do for you; ask what you can do for your country." Do you think that people today support this idea? Why or why not?
3. Are you willing to serve on a jury? Do you mind paying your fair share of taxes? Would you be willing to perform a year of national service after you graduate from college? Explain your answers.

Dependency theory asserts that rich nations achieved modernization at the expense of poor ones, by taking poor nations' natural resources and exploiting their human labor. Even today, the world's poorest countries remain locked in a disadvantageous economic relationship with rich nations, dependent on wealthy countries to buy their raw materials and in return provide them with whatever manufactured products they can afford. According to this view, continuing ties with rich societies only perpetuates current patterns of global inequality.

Whichever approach you find more convincing, keep in mind that change in the United States is no longer separate from change in the rest of the world. At the beginning of the twentieth century, most people in today's high-income countries lived in relatively small settlements with limited awareness of the larger world. Today, the world has become one huge village because the lives of all people are increasingly interconnected.

The twentieth century witnessed unprecedented human achievement. Yet solutions to many problems of human existence—including finding meaning in life, resolving conflicts between nations, and eliminating poverty—have eluded us. The Controversy & Debate box examines one dilemma: balancing individual freedom and personal responsibility. To this list of pressing matters have been added new concerns, such as controlling population growth and establishing an environmentally sustainable society. In the coming years, we must be prepared to tackle such problems with imagination, compassion, and determination. Our growing understanding of human society gives us reason to be hopeful that we can get the job done.

Seeing Sociology in Everyday Life

Social Change: Traditional, Modern, and Postmodern Societies

Is tradition the opposite of modernity?

Conceptually, this may be true. But as this chapter explains, traditional and modern social patterns combine in all sorts of interesting ways in our everyday lives. Look at the photographs below, and identify elements of tradition and modernity. Do they seem to go together, or are they in conflict? Why?

HINT Although sociologists analyze tradition and modernity as conceptual opposites, every society combines these elements in various ways. People may debate the virtues of traditional and modern life, but the two patterns are found almost everywhere. Technological change always has social consequences—for example, the use of cell phones changes people's social networks and economic opportunities; similarly, the spread of McDonald's changes not only what people eat but where and with whom they share meals.

Alamy Images/Paul Prescott

These young girls live in the city of Istanbul in Turkey, a country that has long debated the merits of traditional and modern life. What sets off traditional and modern ways of dressing? Do you think such differences are likely to affect patterns of friendship? Would the same be true in the United States?

AP Wide World Photos/Efrem Lukatsky

When the first McDonald's restaurant opened in the city of Kiev in Ukraine, many people stopped by to taste a hamburger and see what "fast food" was all about. As large corporations expand their operations around the world, do they tip the balance away from tradition in favor of modernity? How?

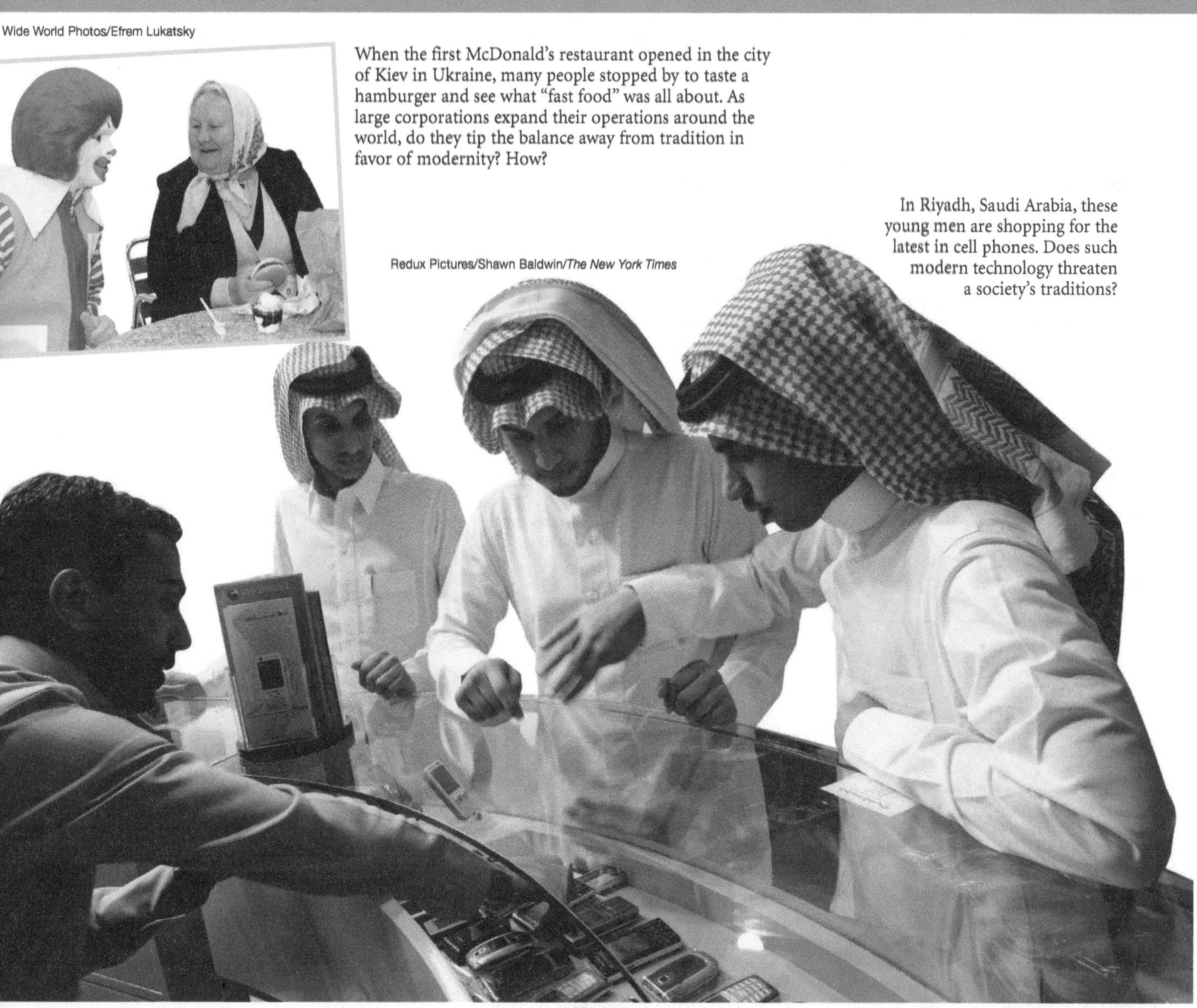

Redux Pictures/Shawn Baldwin/*The New York Times*

In Riyadh, Saudi Arabia, these young men are shopping for the latest in cell phones. Does such modern technology threaten a society's traditions?

Applying SOCIOLOGY in Everyday Life

1. How do tradition and modernity combine in your life? Point to several ways in which you are traditional and several ways in which you are thoroughly modern.
2. Ask people in your class or friendship group to make five predictions about U.S. society in the year 2050, when today's twenty-year-olds will be senior citizens. Compare notes. On what issues is there agreement?
3. Do you think the rate of social change has been increasing? Do some research about modes of travel—including walking, riding animals, bicycles, trains, cars, airplanes, and rockets. At what point in history did each of these ways of moving come into being? What pattern do you see?

MAKING THE GRADE

Social Change: Traditional, Modern, and Postmodern Societies

What Is Social Change?

SOCIAL CHANGE is the transformation of culture and social institutions over time. Every society changes all the time, sometimes faster, sometimes more slowly. Social change often generates controversy.

social change the transformation of culture and social institutions over time

Causes of Social Change

CULTURE

- *Invention* produces new objects, ideas, and social patterns.
- *Discovery* occurs when people take notice of existing elements of the world.
- *Diffusion* creates change as products, people, and information spread from one society to another.

SOCIAL CONFLICT

- Karl Marx claimed that class conflict between capitalists and workers pushes society toward a socialist system of production.
- Social conflict arising from class, race, and gender inequality has resulted in social changes that have improved the lives of working people.

IDEAS
Max Weber traced the roots of most social changes to ideas:

- The fact that industrial capitalism developed first in areas of Western Europe where the Protestant work ethic was strong demonstrates the power of ideas to bring about change.

DEMOGRAPHIC FACTORS
Population patterns play a part in social change:

- The aging of U.S. society has resulted in changes to family life and the development of consumer products to meet the needs of the elderly.
- Migration within and between societies promotes change.

Modernity

MODERNITY refers to the social consequences of industrialization, which include

- the decline of traditional communities
- the expansion of personal choice
- increasing social diversity
- focus on the future

modernity social patterns resulting from industrialization

modernization the process of social change begun by industrialization

division of labor specialized economic activity

anomie Durkheim's term for a condition in which society provides little moral guidance to individuals

FERDINAND TÖNNIES described modernization as the transition from *Gemeinschaft* to *Gesellschaft*, a process characterized by the loss of traditional community and the rise of individualism.

EMILE DURKHEIM saw modernization as a society's expanding division of labor. *Mechanical solidarity*, based on shared activities and beliefs, is gradually replaced by *organic solidarity*, in which specialization makes people interdependent.

MAX WEBER saw modernity as the decline of a traditional worldview and the rise of rationality. Weber feared the dehumanizing effects of modern rational organization.

KARL MARX saw modernity as the triumph of capitalism over feudalism. Capitalism creates social conflict, which Marx claimed would bring about revolutionary change leading to an egalitarian socialist society.

Analysis of Modernity

STRUCTURAL-FUNCTIONAL THEORY: MODERNITY AS MASS SOCIETY

- According to **mass-society theory**, modernity increases the scale of life, enlarging the role of government and other formal organizations in carrying out tasks previously performed by families in local communities.
- Cultural diversity and rapid social change make it difficult for people in modern societies to develop stable identities and to find meaning in their lives.

SOCIAL-CONFLICT THEORY: MODERNITY AS CLASS SOCIETY

- According to **class-society theory**, modernity involves the rise of capitalism into a global economic system resulting in persistent social inequality.
- By concentrating wealth in the hands of a few, modern capitalist societies generate widespread feelings of alienation and powerlessness.

mass society a society in which prosperity and bureaucracy have weakened traditional social ties

class society a capitalist society with pronounced social stratification

social character personality patterns common to members of a particular society

tradition-directedness rigid conformity to time-honored ways of living

other-directedness openness to the latest trends and fashions, often expressed by imitating others

See the Summing Up tables.

Modernity and the Individual

Both mass-society theory and class-society theory are macro-level approaches; from them, however, we can also draw micro-level insights into how modernity shapes individual lives.

MASS SOCIETY: PROBLEMS OF IDENTITY

- Mass-society theory suggests that the great social diversity, widespread isolation, and rapid social change of modern societies make it difficult for individuals to establish a stable social identity.

David Riesman described the changes in social character that modernity causes:

- Preindustrial societies exhibit **tradition-directedness**: Everyone in society draws on the same solid cultural foundation, and people model their lives on those of their ancestors.
- Modern societies exhibit **other-directedness**: Because their socialization occurs in societies that are continuously in flux, other-directed people develop fluid identities marked by superficiality, inconsistency, and change.

CLASS SOCIETY: PROBLEMS OF POWERLESSNESS

- Class-society theory claims that the problem facing most people today is economic uncertainty and powerlessness.
- Herbert Marcuse claimed that modern society is irrational because it fails to meet the needs of so many people.
- Marcuse also believed that technological advances further reduce people's control over their own lives.
- People suffer because modern societies have concentrated both wealth and power in the hands of a privileged few.

Modernity and Progress

Social change is too complex and controversial simply to be equated with progress:

- A rising standard of living has made lives longer and materially more comfortable; at the same time, many people are stressed and have little time to relax with their families; measures of happiness have declined over recent decades.
- Science and technology have brought many conveniences to our everyday lives, yet many people are concerned that life is changing too fast; the introduction of automobiles and advanced communications technology has weakened traditional attachments to hometowns and even to families.

✓ *Although we often think of tradition and modernity as opposites, traditional and modern elements coexist in most societies.*

Looking Ahead: Modernization and Our Global Future

Modernization theory links global poverty to the power of tradition. Rich nations can help poor countries develop their economies.

Dependency theory explains global poverty as the product of the world economic system. The operation of multinational corporations makes poor nations economically dependent on rich nations.

Postmodernity

POSTMODERNITY refers to the cultural traits of postindustrial societies. Postmodern criticism of society centers on the failure of modernity, and specifically science, to fulfill its promise of prosperity and well-being.

postmodernity social patterns characteristic of postindustrial societies

MAKING THE GRADE

Sample Test Questions

Multiple-Choice Questions

1. **Sociologists use the term "modernity" to refer to social patterns that emerged**
   a. with the first human civilizations.
   b. after the fall of Rome.
   c. after the Industrial Revolution.
   d. along with the Information Revolution.

2. **Which of the following are common causes of social change?**
   a. invention of new ideas and things
   b. diffusion from one cultural system to another
   c. discovery of existing things
   d. All of the above are correct.

3. **Karl Marx highlighted the importance of which of the following in the process of social change?**
   a. immigration and demographic factors
   b. ideas
   c. social conflict
   d. cultural diffusion

4. **Max Weber's analysis of how Calvinism helped create the spirit of capitalism highlighted the importance of which of the following in the process of social change?**
   a. invention
   b. ideas
   c. social conflict
   d. cultural diffusion

5. **Which term was used by Ferdinand Tönnies to describe a traditional society?**
   a. *Gemeinschaft*
   b. *Gesellschaft*
   c. mechanical solidarity
   d. organic solidarity

6. **According to Emile Durkheim, modern societies have**
   a. respect for established tradition.
   b. widespread alienation.
   c. common values and beliefs.
   d. an increasing division of labor.

7. **For Max Weber, modernity meant the rise of _____; for Karl Marx, modernity meant _____.**
   a. capitalism, anomie
   b. rationality, capitalism
   c. tradition, self-interest
   d. specialization, *Gesellschaft*

8. **Which of the following statements about modernity as a mass society is *not* correct?**
   a. There is more poverty today than in past centuries.
   b. Kinship ties have become weaker.
   c. Bureaucracy, including government, has increased in size.
   d. People experience moral uncertainty about how to live.

9. **Sociologists who describe modernity in terms of class society focus on which of the following?**
   a. rationality as a way of thinking about the world
   b. mutual dependency
   c. the rise of capitalism
   d. the high risk of anomie

10. **David Riesman described the other-directed social character typical of modern people as**
    a. rigid conformity to tradition.
    b. eagerness to follow the latest fashions and fads.
    c. strong individualism.
    d. All of the above are correct.

ANSWERS: 1 (c); 2 (d); 3 (c); 4 (b); 5 (a); 6 (d); 7 (b); 8 (a); 9 (c); 10 (b).

Essay Questions

1. Discuss how Tönnies, Durkheim, Weber, and Marx described modern society. What are the similarities and differences in their understandings of modernity?
2. What traits lead some analysts to call the United States a "mass society"? Why do other analysts describe the United States as a "class society"?

INDEX

H

N